Human Resource Management

Human Resource Management

THIRTEENTH EDITION

ROBERT L. MATHIS
University of Nebraska at Omaha

JOHN H. JACKSON
University of Wyoming

SOUTH-WESTERN
CENGAGE Learning

Australia • Brazil • Japan • Korea • Mexico • Singapore • Spain • United Kingdom • United States

Human Resource Management,
13th Edition
Robert L. Mathis
John H. Jackson

Vice President of Editorial, Business:
Jack W. Calhoun

Publisher: Joseph Sabatino

Sr. Acquisitions Editor: Michele Rhoades

Sr. Developmental Editor: Susanna C. Smart

Sr. Editorial Assistant: Ruth Belanger

Marketing Manager: Clint Kernen

Content Project Manager: Corey Geissler

Media Editor: Rob Ellington

Sr. Frontlist Buyer, Manufacturing:
Kevin Kluck

Production Service: Integra

Sr. Art Director: Tippy McIntosh

Internal and Cover Designer: c miller design

Cover Image: © John Foxx, Stockbyte,
Getty Images

Sr. Rights Acquisitions Specialist, Images:
Deanna Ettinger

Rights Acquisitions Specialist, Text: Mardell
Glinski Schultz

For product information and technology assistance, contact us at
Cengage Learning Customer & Sales Support, 1-800-354-9706

For permission to use material from this text or product,
submit all requests online at **www.cengage.com/permissions**
Further permissions questions can be emailed to
permissionrequest@cengage.com

Library of Congress Control Number: 2010930409

Student Edition ISBN-13: 978-0-538-45315-8
Student Edition ISBN-10: 0-538-45315-X

South-Western Cengage Learning
5191 Natorp Boulevard
Mason, OH 45040
USA

For your course and learning solutions, visit **www.cengage.com**

Purchase any of our products at your local college store or at our preferred online store **www.cengagebrain.com**

Printed in the United States of America
1 2 3 4 5 6 7 14 13 12 11 10

Dedications

TO

Jo Ann Mathis
for managing efforts on this book, and
Julie Foster and Lee Skoda as key supporters.

R. D. and M. M. Jackson,
who were successful managers of people for many years

Contents in Brief

Contents

SECTION 2

Jobs and Labor 107

SECTION 3
Training and Development 247

SECTION 4

Compensation 357

SECTION 5

Employee Relations 465

Preface

To reach a thirteenth edition is an honor for a textbook and its authors. The authors of *Human Resource Management* are gratified that it has become the leader in both the academic market for human resource texts and in the market for human resource professionals.

For academics, the book is a standard in HR classes. It is also used to provide HR knowledge as part of professional degree programs. For HR professionals, the book is extensively used in the pursuit of HR professional education and certifications, specifically the PHR and SPHR from the Human Resource Certification Institute (HRCI).

In preparing the thirteenth edition of the book, we have extensively reviewed the academic, governmental, and practitioner literature published since the last revision. Further, we have asked academics and practitioners, both those who use this book and those who do not, to provide input on the previous edition and what coverage should be added, deleted, or changed. We have always been receptive to input from our adopters and reviewers and have made extensive use of their observations and ideas. Consequently, we have reorganized some chapters, incorporated relevant new topics, and updated references so that readers can be certain that they are getting the most current HR content possible.

THE THIRTEENTH EDITION

GLOBAL

Human resource management and the organizations in which it takes place are facing challenges from a changing environment. The thirteenth edition reflects those challenges and as always suggests ways to deal with them. For example, consider the following:

U.S. and Global Economics

During the past few years, both in the United States and worldwide, economic shifts have created major organizational impacts. Some em-ployers have closed operations or reduced their workforces, while others have increased theirs. Many employers are expanding throughout the world and, as they do, different cultural considerations affect HR management. Rather than having a separate chapter on global HR management, the coverage of global issues has been integrated throughout the chapters and is indicated by a global icon.

Strategic HR Management

HR management in more and more companies is becoming a part of organizational strategy decisions. To address strategic HR management, Chapter 2 has been significantly revised and expanded to show why HR management is an important strategic contributor to the success of the organization.

In most chapters the topical connection to strategy also is discussed. For example, the strategic natures of recruiting (Chapter 6), talent management (Chapter 9), compensation (Chapter 11), and benefits (Chapter 13) all consider the implications for strategy of decisions made in these areas.

Measuring HR Effectiveness through Metrics

MEASURE

Closely related to strategic HR management is the need to measure the value of HR management activities. The output of HR must be justified to executives in organizations by using financial and other data. The value of HR management activities is measured by cost–benefit analysis, profit per employee, new hire success, and similar metrics. Thus, HR efforts can be justified financially and the value that HR management brings to the company's goals can be documented.

The thirteenth edition includes sections in most chapters called "HR Metrics" that identify how different activities can be measured. A special metrics icon is used to identify this content.

Workforce Changes

The demographics of workers in the United States and globally are shifting. Diversity of employees based on ethnicity, aging, gender, and other factors is changing legal requirements and HR efforts needed. Beginning in Chapter 1, workforce changes are identified as well as why they must be managed effectively. In Chapters 4 and 5, workforce composition differences and their HR implications are identified. Throughout other chapters workforce composition issues are discussed as part of the context for the relevant HR topics.

Attracting, Retaining, and Managing Talent

A key part of managing the workforce is having the right people with the right capabilities in the right jobs—and being able to retain them. These HR concerns exist in most organizations and are emphasized in information on recruiting, selection, job design, training, retention, talent management, and compensation. These topics emphasize HR's role in ensuring that organizations have sufficient and productive workforces, both currently and in the future.

HR, Technology, and the Internet

The use of technology in HR has expanded dramatically and is continuing to change HR management activities with executives, managers, and employees. The Internet, Web-based resources, social media, and blogs all affect HR management. Throughout the chapters of this edition is a feature titled "HR Online" that highlights how technology is being used in HR. Also, many chapters cover HR technology topics in the specific content areas.

The Internet continues to be a valuable tool for HR professionals and affects a number of HR activities. To provide immediate links for readers, numerous "Logging On" features have been incorporated throughout the text. This feature identifies websites that contain useful sources of HR information about topics being discussed and contains specific Web address links. Also, references from Web addresses are cited in the chapter notes as appropriate.

ORGANIZATION OF THE THIRTEENTH EDITION

The thirteenth edition reflects both the continuity and changes occurring in HR management. The following highlights some of the significant content throughout the book section by section.

Section I: Environment of Human Resource Management

The first three chapters of the book examine factors in the changing environment in which the HR function operates. The first chapter looks at human capital, HR as a core competency, HR ethics, and HR challenges. The necessary competencies for HR careers are also discussed. Chapter 2 addresses strategic HR management, environmental analyses, global competitiveness, HR technology, and metrics to evaluate the effectiveness of HR management.

Equal employment opportunity (EEO) is a key HR concern, both legally and operationally. Chapter 3 addresses the laws, regulations, and court decisions that determine the legal framework of EEO. Furthermore, the chapter looks at implementing equal employment and dealing with affirmative action, sexual harassment, age discrimination, and other issues.

Section 2: Jobs and Labor

Chapter 4 discusses workforce composition and describes workflow, scheduling, and other job design issues that have an impact on organizations and the people working in them. The chapter concludes with coverage of job analysis and the approaches to job analysis. Chapter 5 contains content on HR planning, job satisfaction, and employee turnover and retention.

Chapter 6 focuses on recruiting in different labor markets. It discusses the difficulties of recruiting employees with special skills—and new methods to attract those individuals. The chapter contains significant content on Internet recruiting and the evaluation of recruiting efforts. An expansion of the coverage on selection in Chapter 7 encompasses the selection strategy choices that management must make. The discussion of testing, interviewing approaches, and other selection techniques reflects the current research and practices in HR management.

Section 3: Training and Development

Because talent management is a growing concern for many employers, major content additions in this section have been made to emphasize the nature and importance of talent management. Chapter 8 discusses the strategic role training plays in organizations and how training can be linked to business strategies and organizational competitiveness. Specific content on adult learning and new training design and means of delivery is provided. As the text addresses the growing use of *e-learning,* it discusses both the contributions and problems associated with Web-based training. Chapter 9 on talent management and development looks at the methods organizations use to expand the capabilities of their human resources, the nature of talent management, and succession planning.

Chapter 10 emphasizes performance management and the role of the performance appraisal process in enhancing the development of human resources in organizations. The chapter expands the material on identifying and measuring employee performance, including additional information on the numerous approaches used.

Section 4: Compensation

Compensation is viewed broadly as total rewards that include base pay, variable pay, and benefits. Employers are facing great pressure to control those expenditures while also being competitive to attract and retain employees. Chapter 11 discusses the strategic nature of total rewards and then looks at compensation. The coverage of legal requirements, base compensation, pay for performance, and variable pay programs has been revised and updated.

Chapter 12 discusses variable pay, which can include incentives such as those for sales employees. It concludes with an overview of executive compensation and issues of current concern in that area. Chapter 13 highlights the growing changes and increasing costs of benefits that are facing HR professionals and their organizations. Specific expanded content discusses health care costs and issues, as well as retirement and other forms of benefits.

Section 5: Employee Relations

Employee relations include several evolving areas. One such area is risk management, which incorporates health, safety, and security. The coverage in Chapter 14 identifies the nature of risk management, current health and safety issues, OSHA compliance requirements, health promotion, prevention of workplace violence, and the importance of workplace security. Revised content identifies the need for HR to develop disaster and recovery plans for such situations as natural disasters, terrorist threats, or pandemics.

The various issues associated with employee rights and discipline—such as employment-at-will, privacy rights, and substance abuse—have been highlighted in Chapter 15. The chapter also looks at such emerging issues as electronic monitoring, privacy, e-mail, and other employee rights affected by technology. It concludes with a discussion on employee terminations.

The changing role of unions in the U.S. economy and the reasons for the decline in the percentage of workers in unions are discussed in Chapter 16. In addition to covering the basic laws and regulations governing union/management relations in the United States, the chapter includes coverage of collective bargaining and grievance management as key components of union/management relations.

CHANGES TO THIS EDITION

- **NEW:** Each chapter contains a new end-of-chapter exercise, called HR Experiential Problem Solving, which provides a problem, asks one to three brief questions about it, and suggests resources to resolve it.
- **NEW:** All end-of-chapter Cases are new.
- **NEW:** End-of-chapter Supplemental Cases have been increased from one to two per chapter.
- **NEW:** An expanded appendix section provides additional information on a variety of topics.
- **NEW:** Material on HR as an organizational contributor from Chapter 2 is now combined with new Chapter 1.
- **NEW:** Previous edition Chapters 4 and 5 are combined into a new Chapter 3 to put EEO laws and their management in one chapter.
- **NEW:** Chapter 4 on jobs and job analysis was formerly Chapter 6 and is significantly changed to reflect how HR addresses workers, and the contributions of various types of diverse workers.
- Chapter 5 on HR planning and retention has major changes, with material combined from several other chapters. Sections revised include HR planning components, individual workers in organizations, and turnover.

- Chapter 6 on recruiting and labor markets (formerly Chapter 7) has revised coverage of strategic recruiting as tied to HR planning, labor market components, and strategic decisions, as well as additional content on Internet recruiting methods.
- Chapter 7 (formerly Chapter 8) expands the topic of placement to include common mismatch situations between people and jobs, immigration status verification to include E-Verify, and controversies in selection testing
- Chapter 8 (formerly Chapter 9) expands strategy and training, planning for training and orientation, evaluation of orientation, and instructional strategies, and includes new research on the assessment of e-learning use in training.
- Each chapter has been brought up-to-date on any changes in HR research or the laws that have transpired since the twelfth edition.

CHAPTER FEATURES

Each chapter begins with specific learning objectives. Next, the "HR Headline" feature contains a concise example of a contemporary HR problem, situation, or practice to illustrate topics covered. Throughout the text, most chapters also include an "HR Best Practices" feature that highlights effective HR management in real-world companies. Additionally, chapters contain "HR On-the-Job," a feature that presents suggestions on how to handle specific HR issues or situations. The "Logging On" feature provides links to additional materials beyond the text content. To highlight how information technology affects HR management, some chapters contain "HR Online" and "HR Perspective" features that address specific HR issues, ethical concerns, technology, or interesting employer HR efforts.

Each chapter concludes with a point-by-point "Summary" and a "Critical Thinking Activities" section that provides critical thinking queries. At the end of every chapter is an

"HR Experiential Problem Solving" exercise, and a "Case" that presents a real-life HR problem or situation using real organizations as examples. Further, two additional "Supplemental Cases" are available in each chapter on the text website. They briefly describe typical HR problems faced in organizations. Finally, reference "Notes" cite sources used in the chapter, with particular attention given to the inclusion of the most current references and research. More than 80% of the references are new or updated from the previous edition.

SUPPLEMENTS

Instructor's Manual with Video Guide

The instructor's manual, revised by Dr. Fraya Wagner-Marsh, Eastern Michigan University, represents one of the most exciting and useful instructor's aids available. Comprehensive teaching materials are provided for each chapter—including overviews, outlines, instructor's notes, suggested answers to end-of-chapter Review and Application Questions, suggested questions for the "HR Headline," "HR Online," "HR Best Practices," and "HR On-the-Job" features, suggested answers to the end-of-chapter case questions, and suggested questions and comments on the supplemental cases for each chapter. In addition, a video guide section describes the video segments that are available on an Instructor's DVD to help integrate chapter content through current, interesting examples.

Test Bank

The test bank is significantly revised and upgraded from previous editions, and contains more than 1,800 test questions prepared by Janelle Dozier. Multiple-choice, true/false, and essay questions are provided for every chapter. Answers are cross-referenced to pages within the text so that it is easy to pinpoint where relevant material is found. Questions are identified by type—definition, application, and analytical—and also include

AACSB tags for general (NATIONAL) and topic-specific (LOCAL) designations.

ExamView

ExamView contains all of the questions in the printed test bank. Instructors can add or edit questions, instructions, and answers. Questions may be selected by previewing them on screen, selecting them randomly, or selecting them by number. Instructors can also create quizzes online whether over the Internet, a local area network, or a wide area network.

PowerPoint Slide Presentation

Instructor PowerPoint slides, prepared by Charlie Cook of the University of West Alabama, are available on both the Instructor's Resource CD and on the password-protected Instructor's Resources Website. Approximately 400 slides are included.

Handbook for Human Resource Faculty

New to this edition, the Handbook for Human Resource Faculty, originally created by Corinne Livesay of Bryan College, has been revised by Laura L. Wolfe of Louisiana State University to provide additional teaching aids such as Generating Interest discussion topics, Dealing with Trouble Spots features that provide resources to address challenges, and Involving Students sections that suggest activities and resources.

Instructor's Resource CD

The Instructor's Resource CD includes the instructor's manual, test bank, ExamView, the Handbook for Human Resource Faculty, the Video Guide, and PowerPoint presentation slides for instructor convenience.

On-The-Job Video Package

A majority of the book's video collection is new and features companies with innovative

HR practices, many of which have been recognized for their excellence in HR practices. Both small and large companies are featured in the videos, and all video content is closely tied to concepts within the text. These include interviews with Metropolitan Bakery, Yale Repertory Theater, Zappos, The Fruit Guys, and many others. The videos are available on DVD for the instructor.

The HRCI 2009 Outline

The HRCI 2009 outline is featured in this edition to effectively prepare students with the latest body of knowledge of human resource management from which the certification exams are taken.

Student Resource Guide

Designed from a student's perspective by Tonya Elliott, a certified HR professional, this useful study guide provides aids that students can use to maximize results in the classroom and on exams and, ultimately, in the practice of HR. Chapter objectives and chapter outlines aid students in reviewing for exams. Study questions include matching, true/false, idea completion, multiple-choice, and essay questions. Answer keys are provided for immediate feedback to reinforce learning.

Product Support Website

Please visit our product support website, *http://www.cengage.com/management/mathis*, which offers additional instructional and learning tools to complement our text.

- **NEW:** The new CourseMate online learning system helps students manage their homework, make the most of every study minute, and immediately view their progress. Interactive study tools, homework assignments, and self-testing opportunities help students earn the grade they want within the course and assist as them in effectively preparing for professional examinations.

CengageNOW

This powerful and fully integrated online teaching and learning system provides instructors with flexibility and control, saves valuable time, and improves outcomes. Students benefit by having choices in the way they learn through a unique personalized learning path made possible by CengageNOW.

- Homework, assignable and automatically graded
- Integrated e-book
- Personalized learning paths
- Interactive course assignments
- Assessment options, including AACSB learning standards achievement reporting
- Test delivery
- Course management tools, including Grade Book
- WebCT and Blackboard integration

Speak with your South-Western sales representative about integrating CengageNOW into your courses. Visit *www.cengage.com/now* today to learn more!

WebTutor™ for Blackboard® or WebCT®

This dynamic learning and instructional resource harnesses the power of the Internet to deliver innovative learning aids that actively engage students. Multimedia resources include animated tutorials, quizzes with immediate feedback, online exercises to reinforce principles learned, and online discussion to encourage continuing communication between students and instructors.

ACKNOWLEDGMENTS

The success of each edition of *Human Resource Management* can largely be attributed to our reviewers, who have generously offered both suggestions for improvements and new ideas for the text. We sincerely thank the following reviewers:

Collette M. Arens Bates	*Western Illinois University*	Linsey C. Willis	*Florida Atlantic University*
Callie Burnley	*California State University, Fullerton*	Ryan D. Zimmerman	*Texas A&M*
Cathy Dubois	*Kent State University*		
Andrea D. Ellinger	*University of Illinois at Champaign-Urbana*		
Yezdi Godiwalla	*University of Wisconsin, Whitewater*		
Mark A. Johnson	*Idaho State University*		
Carlos Jon	*Keller Graduate School*		
Thomas Kanick	*Southern New Hampshire University*		
Stan Malos	*San Jose State University*		
Patrick McHugh	*George Washington University*		
Bob Meier	*Robert Morris College*		
David Nye	*Athens University*		
Kristin D. Scott	*Clemson University*		
Larry Siefert	*Webster University*		
Romilia Singh	*University of Wisconsin, Milwaukee*		
Susan Stewart	*Western Illinois University*		
K. J. Tullis	*University of Central Oklahoma*		
Fraya Wagner-Marsh	*Eastern Michigan University*		

Finally, some leading HR professionals provided ideas and assistance. Appreciation is specifically expressed to Sean Valentine, Patti Meglich, Sandra Washa, Steve Williams, Kathy McKee, and Frank Giancola. Those who assisted with many critical details of manuscript preparation include Jo Ann Mathis, Carolyn Foster, and our copyeditor, Linda Ireland.

The authors thank Joe Sabatino, Publisher, Michele Rhoades, Senior Acquisitions Editor, and Susan Smart, Senior Developmental Editor, for their guidance and involvement. We also appreciate the support of our Content Project Manager, Corey Geissler, whose efforts contributed significantly to making the final product appealing. Thanks go also to our Media Editor, Rob Ellington, for pulling together the text website, and to our Marketing Manager, Clint Kernen, for getting the word out about the new edition.

The authors feel confident that this edition will continue as the standard for the HR field. We believe it offers a relevant and current look at HR management, and we are optimistic that those who use the book will agree.

Robert L. Mathis, SPHR   John H. Jackson
Omaha, Nebraska   Laramie, Wyoming

Environment of Human Resource Management

1

Human Resource Management in Organizations

After you have read this chapter, you should be able to:

- Define human capital and identify the seven categories of HR activities.
- Discuss how organizational culture and HR are related and identify four areas that are part of these relationships.
- Explain how organizational ethical issues affect HR management.
- Provide an overview of six challenges facing HR today.
- Describe how the major roles of HR management are being transformed.
- Explain the key competencies needed by HR professionals and why certification is important.

The Challenges and Crises Facing HR Management

(PhotoLink/Photodisc/Getty Image)

During the past few years, economic downturns, industry crises, bank failures, closings of plants and stores, changes in global operations, and other factors have significantly affected organizations, managers, and Human Resource (HR) management professionals. For HR and other executives, these changes have led to decisions about layoffs, reductions in work hours, and cuts or elimination of some employee benefits. HR is facing a different world because of these problems.

Other issues have created different workforce strategies as well. A recent survey found that the highest-demand jobs include jobs like registered nurse, elementary and secondary school teacher, accountant and auditor, general and operations manager, network software engineer, and jobs that contain significant professional responsibilities. The increased demand for these jobs has been caused by economic shifts in staffing that have affected manufacturing, retail, and other industries.

These examples illustrate why HR must change. Organizational and HR executives, managers, and employees are dealing in various ways with major issues. According to surveys, some of the biggest problems include:

- Adjusting benefits programs due to increasing costs
- Attracting and retaining key employees
- Planning for replacement of "baby boomers" when they retire
- Using talent management to train and develop capabilities of employees for future job needs

- Dealing with the expanded personal and organizational use of HR technology through blogs, wikis, twitters, text-messaging, and other formats
- Complying with revised and changing federal, state, and local legal requirements affecting discrimination, treatment errors, unionization, and other issues

The manner in which all these conflicting issues are managed can influence how HR plans and contributes to organizational culture and performance.[1]

As the HR Headline indicates, managing people in changing organizations is part of what is currently being done by supervisors, managers, and executives. People as *human assets* are the "glue" that holds all the other assets, such as financial and physical ones, together and guides their use to better achieve results. Certainly, the cashiers, supervisors, and other employees at Wal-Mart or Walgreen's or the doctors, nurses, receptionists, technical professionals, and other employees at a hospital allow all the other assets of their organization to be used to provide customer or patient services. How effectively people at all levels contribute to organizational results is part of the challenge. Managing people as human resources is essential in organizations of all sizes and types.

As a field, human resource management is undergoing significant transformation. **Human resource (HR) management** is designing management systems to ensure that human talent is used effectively and efficiently to accomplish organizational goals. Whether employees are in a big company with thousands of jobs or a small nonprofit agency, managing people in an organization is about more than simply administering a pay program, designing training, or avoiding lawsuits. If human resources are to be an important part of successfully competing in the marketplace, a different level of thinking about HR management is necessary. Productive, creative people working in flexible, effective organizations that provide rewarding work for individuals is important for all managers, not just those in HR departments. People in organizations can be a core competency.

Human resource (HR) management Designing management systems to ensure that human talent is used effectively and efficiently to accomplish organizational goals.

HUMAN RESOURCES AS ORGANIZATIONAL CORE COMPETENCY

The development and implementation of specific organizational strategies must be based on the areas of strength in an organization. Referred to as *core competencies*, those strengths are the foundation for creating a competitive advantage for an organization. A **core competency** is a unique capability that creates high value and differentiates an organization from its competition.

Core competency A unique capability that creates high value and differentiates an organization from its competition.

Figure 1-1 shows some possible areas where human resources may become part of core competencies. Certainly, many organizations have identified that having their human resources as core competencies differentiates them from their competitors and is a key determinant of competitive advantages.[2]

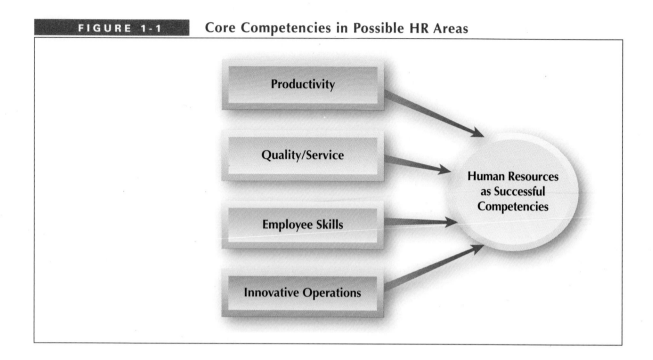

FIGURE 1-1   Core Competencies in Possible HR Areas

Human Capital and HR

Human capital is not solely the people in organizations—it is what those people bring and contribute to organizational success. **Human capital** is the collective value of the capabilities, knowledge, skills, life experiences, and motivation of an organizational workforce.

Sometimes human capital is called *intellectual capital* to reflect the thinking, knowledge, creativity, and decision making that people in organizations contribute. For example, firms with high intellectual capital may have technical and research employees who create new biomedical devices, formulate products that can be patented, or develop new software for specialized uses. All these organizational contributions illustrate the potential value of human capital. A few years ago, a Nobel prize-winning economist, Gary Becker, expanded the view of human capital by emphasizing that countries managing human capital better are more likely to have better economic results.[3]

The importance of human capital in organizations can be seen in various ways. One is sheer costs. In some industries, such as the restaurant industry, employee-related expenditures may exceed 60% of total operating costs. With such significant levels comes an increasing need to measure the value of human capital and how it is changing through HR metrics, discussed in Chapter 2.

HR Functions

Human capital The collective value of the capabilities, knowledge, skills, life experiences, and motivation of an organizational workforce.

HR management can be thought of as seven interlinked functions taking place within organizations, as depicted in Figure 1-2. Additionally, external forces—legal, economic, technological, global, environmental, cultural/geographic, political, and social—significantly affect how HR functions are designed, managed, and changed. The functions can be grouped as follows:

- **Strategic HR Management:** As part of maintaining organizational competitiveness, *strategic planning* for *HR effectiveness* can be increased

FIGURE 1-2   HR Management Functions

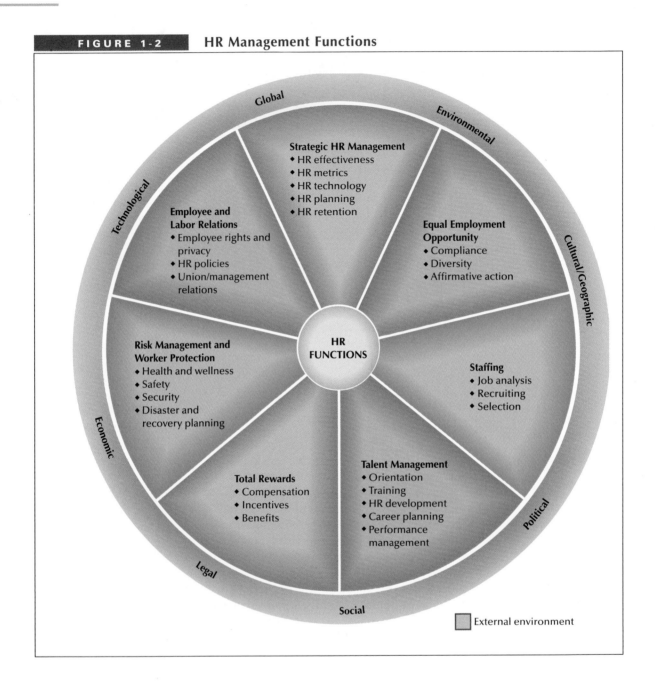

through the use of *HR metrics* and *HR technology*. These topics are covered in Chapter 2.

- **Equal Employment Opportunity:** *Compliance* with equal employment opportunity (EEO) laws and regulations affects all other HR activities. The nature of EEO is discussed in Chapter 3.
- **Staffing:** The aim of staffing is to provide a sufficient supply of qualified individuals to fill jobs in an organization. *Workers, job design,* and *job analysis* lay the foundation for staffing by identifying what *diverse people* do in their jobs and how they are affected by them. Through *HR planning,* managers anticipate the future supply of and demand for employees and the nature of workforce issues, including the *retention* of employees. These factors are used when *recruiting* applicants for job openings. The *selection*

process is concerned with choosing qualified individuals to fill those jobs. These staffing activities are discussed in Chapters 4, 5, 6, and 7.

- **Talent Management and Development:** Beginning with the *orientation* of new employees, talent management and development includes different types of *training.* Also, *HR development* and *succession* planning of employees and managers is necessary to prepare for future challenges. *Career planning* identifies paths and activities for individual employees as they move within the organization. Assessing how well employees perform their jobs is the focus of *performance management.* Activities associated with talent management are examined in Chapters 8, 9, and 10.

- **Total Rewards:** *Compensation* in the form of *pay, incentives,* and *benefits* rewards people for performing organizational work. To be competitive, employers develop and refine their basic *compensation* systems and may use *variable pay programs* such as incentive rewards. The rapid increase in the cost of *benefits,* especially health care benefits, will continue to be a major issue for most employers. Compensation, variable pay, and benefits activities are discussed in Chapters 11, 12, and 13.

- **Risk Management and Worker Protection:** Employers must address various workplace risks to ensure protection of workers by meeting legal requirements and being more responsive to concerns for workplace *health* and *safety.* Also, workplace *security* has grown in importance along with *disaster and recovery planning,* and these activities are examined in Chapter 14.

LOGGING ON

International Association for Human Resource Information Management (IHRIM)
The International Association for Human Resource Information Management (IHRIM) is the world's leading clearinghouse for the HRMS industry for information management, systems issues, trends, and technology. Visit its website at www.ihrim.org.

- **Employee and Labor Relations:** The relationship between managers and their employees must be handled legally and effectively. *Employer and employee rights* must be addressed. It is important to develop, communicate, and update *HR policies and procedures* so that managers and employees alike know what is expected. In some organizations, *union/management relations* must be addressed as well. Activities associated with employee rights and labor/management relations are discussed in Chapters 15 and 16.

HR MANAGEMENT'S CONTRIBUTING ROLE

Human Resources can create value and impact organizational results more in some organizations than others. Being the core competency mentioned earlier, HR may aid organizations in a number of ways. Given the changes in economic situations, workers, workforce challenges, and other factors, employers can face significant reputation problems. One survey of global senior managers in 20 countries found that more than 60% indicated they had less trust in their corporations than a year before.[4] This study illustrates why HR must be at the heart of enhancing organizational culture.

Organizational Culture and HR

Organizational culture
The shared values and beliefs in an organization.

The ability of an organization to use its human capital as a core competency depends in part on the organizational culture that is operating. **Organizational culture** consists of the shared values and beliefs that give members of an organization meaning and provide them with rules for behavior. The culture of an organization is seen in the norms of expected behaviors, values, philosophies, rituals, and symbols used by its employees, and it evolves over a period of time. Only if an organization has a history in which people have shared experiences for years does a culture stabilize. A relatively new firm, such as a business existing for less than 2 years, may not have developed a stabilized culture.

HR Values and Organizational Cultures Central to organizational culture are *values* that are inherent in the ways organizations and their members treat people both inside and outside the organization. Similar values are likely to exist with some executives, managers, and HR professionals, as well, which can affect the nature of the organizational culture.

Values may be used to define opportunities, plan strategies, and view operational concerns, as highlighted in Chapter 2. Values in an organizational culture can become relatively constant and enduring over time. Newcomers learn the values and culture from the senior employees; hence, the rules of behavior are perpetuated. These rules may or may not be beneficial, so the values and culture can either facilitate or limit performance. They also affect employee morale and how conflicts are resolved.[5]

Competitive Advantage of Organizational Culture Organizational culture should be seen as the "climate" of the organization that employees, managers, customers, and others experience. This culture affects service and quality, organizational productivity, and financial results. One facet of the culture of the organization, as viewed by the people in it, is that culture may affect the attraction and retention of competent employees.[6]

Alignment of the organizational culture and HR helps organizational performance. One competitive aspect of an organizational culture is creativity and innovation. Efforts in this area can enhance the organizational culture by developing or revising current and new products and services, acquiring new businesses, and performing other activities with competitive advantages.[7]

GLOBAL

Global Cultural Factors Cultural forces represent an important concern affecting international HR management. One only has to look at the conflicts caused by politics, religion, and ethnicity in Africa, the Middle East, and other parts of the world to see the importance of culture in international organizations. Convincing individuals from different religious, ethnic, or tribal backgrounds to work together in a global firm may be difficult in some areas.

One widely used way to classify and compare cultures was developed by Geert Hofstede, a Dutch scholar and researcher. Hofstede conducted research on more than 100,000 IBM employees in 53 countries, and he defined five dimensions useful in identifying and comparing cultures:[8]

- Inequality in power
- Individualism/group orientation
- Masculinity/femininity
- Uncertainty avoidance
- Long-term/short-term orientation

Differences in many other facets of culture could be discussed, but it is enough to note that international HR managers and professionals must recognize that cultural dimensions differ from country to country and even within countries. Therefore, the HR activities appropriate in one culture or country may have to be altered to fit appropriately into another culture, country, or geographic area.

Organizational Productivity

HR management can play a significant role in organizations by helping to create a culture that emphasizes effectiveness and productivity. In its most basic sense, **productivity** is a measure of the quantity and quality of work done, considering the cost of the resources used. Productivity can be a competitive advantage because when the costs to produce goods and services are lowered by effective processes, lower prices can be charged or more revenue made. Better productivity does not necessarily mean more output; perhaps fewer people (or less money or time) are used to produce the same amount.

One useful way of measuring the productivity of human resources is to consider **unit labor cost**, which is computed by dividing the average cost of workers by their average levels of output. Using unit labor costs, one can see that paying relatively high wages still can result in a firm being economically competitive if high productivity levels are achieved. Low unit labor costs can be a basis for a strategy focusing on human resources. Productivity and unit labor costs can be evaluated at the global, country, organizational, departmental, or individual level as part of various HR measurement metrics.

Productivity Measure of the quantity and quality of work done, considering the cost of the resources used.

Unit labor cost Computed by dividing the average cost of workers by their average levels of output.

Improving Organizational Productivity Productivity at the organizational level ultimately affects profitability and competitiveness in a for-profit organization and total costs in a not-for-profit organization. Perhaps of all the resources used for productivity in organizations, the ones often most closely scrutinized are the human resources. Examples as indicated in Figure 1-3 of

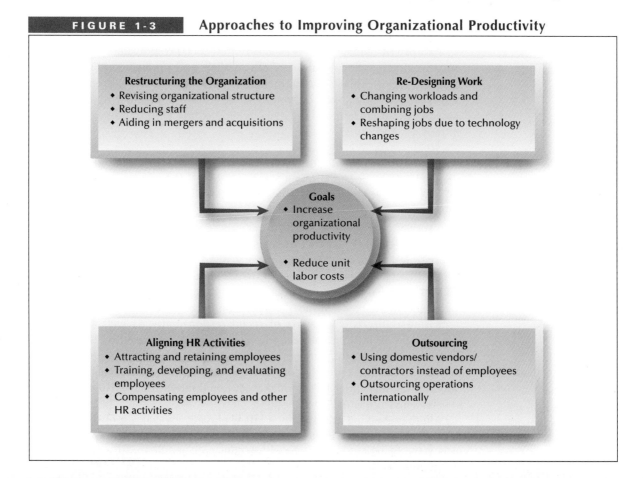

FIGURE 1-3   **Approaches to Improving Organizational Productivity**

Restructuring the Organization
• Revising organizational structure
• Reducing staff
• Aiding in mergers and acquisitions

Re-Designing Work
• Changing workloads and combining jobs
• Reshaping jobs due to technology changes

Goals
• Increase organizational productivity
• Reduce unit labor costs

Aligning HR Activities
• Attracting and retaining employees
• Training, developing, and evaluating employees
• Compensating employees and other HR activities

Outsourcing
• Using domestic vendors/ contractors instead of employees
• Outsourcing operations internationally

HR management efforts designed to enhance organizational productivity are as follows:

- *Organizational restructuring* involves eliminating layers of management and changing reporting relationships, as well as cutting staff through downsizing, layoffs, and early retirement buyout programs. That has become a concern in a number of industries as economic factors have changed.[9]
- *Redesigning work* often involves having fewer employees who work longer hours and perform multiple job tasks. It may also involve replacing workers with capital equipment or making them more efficient by use of technology or new processes.
- *Aligning HR activities* means making HR efforts consistent with organizational efforts to improve productivity. This alignment includes ensuring that HR functions are not working against productivity.
- *Outsourcing analyses* involve HR in conducting cost-benefit analyses to justify outsourcing. Additional factors may include negotiating with outsourcing vendors, ensuring that contractors domestically and internationally are operating legally and appropriately, and linking organizational employees to the employees of the outsourcing firm. Outsourcing is discussed further in Chapter 2.

Social Responsibilities and HR

Organizational influences have changed as individuals, employers, governmental agencies, and other entities have evolved. Social responsibility and networking have become more prevalent as organizational culture issues.

Part of HR management is to ensure that social responsibility is integrated into the organizational culture. Both explicit and implicit requirements are needed.[10] The explicit requirements include specific regulations, policies, and training. The implicit ones aid the organizational culture in encouraging appropriate organizational behavior when dealing with customers, suppliers, employees, and others.

HR Advantages and Social Responsibilities Corporate social responsibility by HR has numerous advantages. One of the most important is the ability to attract and retain employees.[11] Socially responsible jobs are increasingly popular, especially with college students, who will be future workers. One survey by Panetta Institute for Public Policy found that almost half of the college students had their greatest interest in working for a more socially responsible corporation, while others wanted to work for governmental or nonprofit organizations.[12] These statistics indicate how attracting individuals with social responsibilities before hiring may lead to lower turnover and higher productivity when they become employees.

Sustainability is a key part of social responsibility, as well as playing a key HR role in dealing with economic challenges. **Sustainability** is being able to continue to operate, survive, and adjust to significant changes. Balancing business needs and social factors, such as layoffs, job losses, business reputations, ethics, and other factors makes sustainability a part of HR in changing business environments.[13]

Another evolving area in which HR is playing a social responsibility role is in creating a "green" culture. Although that may seem unusual, participating in environmental improvement efforts can enhance employees' views of the

Sustainabilty Being able to continue to operate, survive, and adjust to significant changes.

"Growing Green" in HR

Getting employees involved in green efforts is growing. Such efforts may affect the organizational corporate image with customers, employees, and throughout the business community in the area. Also, these programs can result in reduced operational costs linked to HR policies on recycling, creating less waste and pollution, reducing lighting and power usage, and many other means. According to a survey of 2,500 hiring managers, green programs also may create more jobs for employee environmental specialists.

Firms that have emphasized green have found that the effects on attracting, retaining, and motivating workers of all types can be positive. For instance, General Electric highlights its "Ecomagination" on its recruiting website. In Chicago a number of firms in different industries offer green-job training programs for environmental specialists, as well as other participants.

A broader value of playing a key green role is that it can result in more organizational strategic emphasis. Organizations such as Mitsubishi International, Google, Emory University, and others have established sustainability officers to lead environmental efforts. For instance, Google switched a California facility to more solar power, guided by those officers.

HR has a key role in green efforts. The need to communicate, train, and enforce the relevant green requirements with employees and managers throughout the organization is important. Also, safety and health issues may be affected by these efforts. In summary, HR management will have an increasingly green role in both large and small companies.[14]

social responsibility of a firm. Participation in different types of these efforts also can aid in recruiting employees, especially those who have higher views of such firms.[15] As the HR Perspective discusses, the role of HR in green efforts is growing in importance.

GLOBAL

Global Social Responsibility and HR As organizations have more and more workers and businesses in various countries, social responsibility globally is becoming more of an HR issue. Global practices of social responsibility are often conducted through HR and may include collecting/donating money for local charities or national disasters and numerous other activities. Doing these activities results in higher organizational images globally, better employee morale and loyalty, and more competitive advantages with consumers.[16]

Customer Service and Quality Linked to HR

Linking HR to social responsibility, customer service, and quality significantly affects organizational effectiveness. Having managers and employees focus on customers contributes significantly to achieving organizational goals and maintaining competitive advantages. In most organizations, service quality is greatly influenced by individual employees who interact with customers. Employee job satisfaction also can be influenced by positive customer satisfaction.[17] Customers often consider continuity of customer service representatives as important when making marketing and sales decisions.

Unfortunately, overall customer satisfaction with sales quality has declined in the United States and other countries. For example, the decline in customer satisfaction has affected many of the U.S. airlines. Even though some airlines have made efforts to improve services, customers continue to be rather skeptical of the improvements in the industry.[18]

Employee Engagement and HR Culture

What is evident from the previous discussions is that the engagement of employees is a crucial goal and link to an effective organizational culture and HR's role in it. **Employee engagement** is the extent to which individuals feel linked to organizational success and how the organization performs positively. Numerous studies have shown that engaged employees are less likely to quit, more likely to encourage other persons to become employees, and more likely to commit to activities positively outside of their organizations. One study found that highly engaged employees are almost 80% more likely to be top performers and miss fewer work days.[19] The unfortunate lack of a positive culture can lead to more employee dissatisfaction, turnover, poor service, and other undesirable outcomes and behaviors. That is why employee engagement is such a crucial part of effective HR management and is linked to social networking.

Social Networking and Engagement An integral part of employee engagement is social networking. This networking involves communicating to other employees, nonwork friends, community contacts, and others. Previously, social networking primarily was done through personal contacts as well as oral communications. However, networking has become a massive issue for employees and employers as technology has expanded through e-mailing, text-messaging, twitters, blogs, and many other formats.

Some employees, especially younger ones, use such technology to communicate almost constantly with others. This expansive use of technological methods may create both good and bad images for employees and employers, as well as work-related legal issues. One survey by Deloitte found that 60% of executives believe they should know how workers use network profiles. Also, 75% of employers indicated that using social networks online makes creating a negative company image easier.[20]

However, some organizations have found that using social networks online can aid in recruiting new employees. Use of various types of technology can lead to recruiting more people, as well as reducing recruiting costs.[21] The use of these technologies and issues in this area are discussed more in other chapters on specific HR resources and issues.

ORGANIZATIONAL ETHICS AND HR MANAGEMENT

Employee engagement
The extent to which individuals feel linked to organizational success and how the organization performs positively.

Closely linked with the strategic role of HR is the way managers and HR professionals influence the ethics of people in organizations. How those ethics affect work and lives for individuals may aid in producing more positive work outcomes.[22] As Figure 1-4 indicates, establishing HR ethical areas can lead to organizational and individual consequences.[23]

The need for great attention to ethics has grown in the past few years, as evidenced by the corporate scandals at numerous financial and investment firms in the United States and globally. These scandals illustrate that ethical lapses are not just symbolic; they affect numerous firms and employees. The

| FIGURE 1-4 | Business Ethics and HR Management Consequences |

BUSINESS ETHICS

HR Management Ethical Areas

- Staffing
- Training
- Labor relations
- Legal compliance

- Compensation
- Development
- Performance management
- HR policies

Consequences

- Job satisfaction
- Reduced turnover
- Decreased absenteeism

- Organizational commitment
- Higher job performance
- Ethical decision making

LOGGING ON

Ethics & Policy Integration Centre

The Ethics & Policy Integration Centre is an online resource for ethical and policy issues. Visit the website at www.ethicaledge.com.

expansion of the Internet has led to more publicity about ethical issues, including ethics electronic job boards and postings.[24] An increase in ethics issues has been identified by the Ethics Resource Center. One survey of 3,000 U.S. workers found that within a year, 52% had seen one incident of misconduct and 36% had observed two or more ethical violations. The survey also reported that almost 70% of their employers had done ethics training.[25]

Ethical Behavior and Organizational Culture

Numerous writers on business ethics consistently stress that the primary determinant of ethical behavior is organizational culture, which is the shared values and beliefs in an organization mentioned earlier. Every organization has a culture, and that culture influences how executives, managers, and employees act in making organizational decisions. For example, if meeting objectives and financial targets is stressed, then it should not be a surprise when executives and managers fudge numbers or falsify cost records. However, a positive ethical culture exists in many organizations. When the following four elements of ethics programs exist, ethical behavior is more likely to occur:

- A written code of ethics and standards of conduct
- Training on ethical behavior for all executives, managers, and employees
- Advice to employees on ethical situations they face, often made by HR
- Systems for confidential reporting of ethical misconduct or questionable behavior

Cisco Makes Global Ethics Important and Fun

Cisco Systems, a technology firm with more than 60,000 employees worldwide, has emphasized ethics in interesting ways. Until a few years ago, Cisco did ethics training and enforcement like many other firms by using organization-required sessions and procedures. However, Cisco now uses a constantly available ethics program through its firm communications, Internet, and even television programs similar to *American Idol*.

To conduct its ethics awareness, Cisco enables employees worldwide to view the *Ethics Idol* via television on its intranet. Cartoon individuals present different ethical situations and then have "judges" give decisions. Employees vote on the best answer to each situation. More than 10,000 Cisco employees participate voluntarily in these network analyses. Many employees look at the *Ethics Idol* after work rather than during business hours. After the employees vote, Cisco's ethics office professionals then give the best answer

linked to Cisco company standards and compliance requirements.

Using these creative and entertaining means has enhanced awareness of ethical issues throughout the firm. A new ethics document has been updated regularly, and more than 90% of Cisco employees have become certified in reviewing the code of the firm. Merging ethics issues, technology, and regular interactive training has led to ethical understanding and behavior by Cisco employees. Other firms have similar programs, but Cisco's efforts are a model of ethical training and engagement.

This creative ethics program is an expansion of Cisco's corporate responsibility efforts. For years Cisco has been a leader in the "Corporate Citizens" listing on business ethics, and one of only three firms that have been recognized every year. Although other firms have ethics programs, Cisco's broad efforts illustrate how expanding ethical training and engagement of employees can be effective.[26]

An ethical business culture is based first on organizational mission and values. Other related factors can include shareholders, long-term perspectives, process integrity, and leadership effectiveness.[27] The roles of boards, CEOs, other executives, and HR leaders are vital in setting the culture for ethics globally as well as locally. Training of employees is crucial, and how they respond to situations may be linked to their expectations, motivations, and other factors.[28] As the HR Best Practices indicates, Cisco has emphasized ethics using creative and effective means throughout its global business world.

Ethics and Global Differences

GLOBAL

Differences in legal, political, and cultural values and practices in different countries often raise ethical issues for global employers who must comply with both their home-country laws and the laws of other countries. With the changes in the global economy in the past few years, a France-based entity, the Organization for Economic Cooperation (OECD), has emphasized the effects of ethics. The OECD has recommended that global multinational firms establish and implement stricter ethical standards to aid business development.[29]

The different legal, political, and cultural factors in other countries can lead to ethical and legal conflicts for global managers. Some global firms have established guidelines and policies to reduce the payments of bribes, but even those efforts do not provide detailed guidance on handling the situations that can arise.

HR's Role in Organizational Ethics

Organizations that are seen as ethical in the way they operate have longer-term success. Because people in organizations are making ethical decisions on a daily basis, HR management plays a key role as the "keeper and voice" of organizational ethics. All managers, including HR managers, must deal with ethical issues and be sensitive to how they interplay with HR activities. Instead of relying just on HR policies or laws, people must be guided by values and personal behavior "codes," including these two questions:

- Does the behavior or result meet all applicable *laws, regulations,* and *government codes*?
- Does the behavior or result meet both *organizational standards* and *professional standards* of ethical behavior?

There are a number of different views about the importance of HR in ensuring that ethical practices, justice, and fairness are present throughout HR practices. Figure 1-5 identifies some of the most frequent areas of ethical misconduct involving HR activities.

Ethical issues pose fundamental questions about fairness, justice, truthfulness, and social responsibility. Just complying with a wider range of requirements, laws, and regulations cannot cover every ethical situation that executives, managers, HR professionals, and employees will face. Yet, having all the elements of an ethics program may not prevent individual managers or executives from engaging in or failing to report unethical behavior. Even HR staff members may be reluctant to report ethics concerns, primarily because of fears that doing so may affect their current and future employment.

Critical for guiding ethical decisions and behavior is training. Firms such as Best Buy, Caterpillar, and others have training for all employees via the Internet or in person. How to address difficult and conflicting situations is part

| FIGURE 1-5 | Examples of HR-Related Ethical Misconduct Activities |

Compensation	Employee Relations	Staffing and Equal Employment
• Misrepresenting hours and time worked • Falsifying work expense reports • Personal bias in performance appraisals and pay increases • Deliberate inappropriate overtime classifications • Accepting personal gains/gifts from vendors	• Employees lying to supervisors and coworkers • Executives/managers e-mailing false public information to customers and vendors • Misusing/stealing organizational assets and supplies • Intentionally violating safety/health regulations	• Discriminatory favoritism in hiring and promotion • Sexual harassment of other employees • EEO discrimination in recruiting and interviewing • Conducting inappropriate background investigations

of effective HR management training efforts.[30] To help HR professionals deal with ethical issues, the Society for Human Resource Management has developed a code of ethics for its members and provides information on handling ethical issues and policies.[31]

HR Ethics and Sarbanes-Oxley The Sarbanes-Oxley Act (SOX) was passed by Congress to make certain that publicly traded companies follow accounting controls that could reduce the likelihood of illegal and unethical behaviors. A number of HR facets must be managed in line with SOX. The biggest issues are linked to executive compensation and benefits, but SOX sections 404, 406, 802, and 806 require companies to establish ethics codes, develop employee complaint systems, and have antiretaliation policies for employees who act as whistle blowers to identify wrongful actions. HR has been involved in routing people through the massive compliance verification effort that has occurred.

Numerous other local, state, and federal laws may relate to organizational and employee ethical issues. Some additional federal laws include the False Claims Act, Foreign Corrupt Practices Act, and others. Given all these laws, regulations, and issues, a broad study of ethics is philosophical, complex, and beyond the scope of this book. The intent here is to concisely identify ethical aspects of HR management. Various ethical issues in HR management are also highlighted throughout the text as appropriate.

CURRENT AND FUTURE HR MANAGEMENT CHALLENGES

As the way HR is managed in organizations changes, some challenges are affecting all employers. Responding effectively requires a competent HR presence to deal with the challenges. A wide range of factors are putting more planning, administrative, and cost pressures on organizations both in the United States and globally. Some of these new challenges and increased pressures are discussed next.

Organizational Cost Pressures and Restructuring

An overriding theme facing managers and organizations is to operate in a "cost-less" mode, which means continually looking for ways to reduce costs of all types—financial, operations, equipment, and labor. Pressures from global competitors have forced many U.S. firms to close facilities, use international outsourcing, adapt their management practices, increase productivity, and decrease labor costs in order to become more competitive. The growth of information technology, particularly that linked to the Internet, has influenced HR management as it handles the number, location, and required activities of employees.

These shifts have caused some organizations to reduce the number of employees, while at the same time scrambling to attract and retain employees with different capabilities than were previously needed. Responding to organizational cost pressures and restructurings, as well as the other HR challenges, has resulted in the transformation of HR management in organizations.

Economics and Job Changes

The shifts in the U.S. and global economy in the past years have changed the number and types of jobs present in the United States. The recession in

2007–2009 affected many industries such as automotive and financial firms. In general, the United States has continued to have private- and public-sector jobs that are service economy in nature, and many of the additional jobs to be filled in the next several years will be in the service industry rather than manufacturing firms.

Occupational Shifts Projections of growth in some jobs and decline in others illustrate the shifts occurring in the U.S. economy. Figure 1-6 lists occupations that are expected to experience the greatest growth in percentage and numbers for the period ending in 2016. Most of the fastest-growing occupations percentage-wise are related to information technology and health care. However, when the growth in the number of jobs is compared to the percentage growth, an interesting factor is evident. The highest growth of jobs by percentage is in occupations that generally require more education and expertise training, whereas the numerical growth of several jobs is in occupations requiring less education and jobs that are lower-skilled.

Another aspect of the shifting economy is revealed in the types of jobs that have the greatest decline in numbers. They include stock clerks, cashiers, packers, file clerks, and farmers/ranchers.[32] These declines reflect shifts in economic factors and how those jobs are being combined with others or eliminated due to business changes.

Workforce Availability and Quality Concerns Various parts of the United States face significant workforce shortages that exist due to an inadequate supply of workers with the skills needed to perform the jobs being added. It may not be that there are too few people—only that there are too few with many

| FIGURE 1-6 | Fastest Growth in Job Changes to 2016 |

Percentage Increase in Jobs		Increase in Job Numbers	
Network systems/data communications analysts	53%	Registered nurses	587,000
Personal/home care aides	51%	Retail salespersons	557,000
Home health aides	49%	Customer service reps	545,000
Computer software engineers	44%	Food preparations workers	452,000
Veterinary technologists	41%	Office clerks	404,000
Personal financial advisors	41%	Personal/home care aides	389,000
Makeup artists	40%	Home health aides	384,000
Medical assistants	35%	Postsecondary teachers	382,000

Source: U.S. Bureau of Labor Statistics, www.bls.gov.

of the skills being demanded. For instance, one survey of more than 2,000 employers found that the hardest jobs to fill are engineers, nurses, technicians, teachers, and sales representatives.[33]

Even though many Americans are graduating from high school and college, employers are concerned about the preparation and specific skills of new graduates. Comparisons of international test results show that students in the United States perform slightly above average in math and science, but *well below* students in some other directly competitive nations. Also, graduates with degrees in computers, engineering, and the health sciences remain in short supply relative to the demand for them. That is another reason why international outsourcing has grown. Unless major improvements are made to U.S. educational systems, U.S. employers will be unable to find enough qualified workers for the growing number of skilled jobs of all types. That is why talent management and development has become one of the most important issues emphasized by HR management.

Talent Management and Development A broad focus of HR professionals is on talent management and development to address the workforce and job changes. Despite the economic pressures, the emphasis on talent management has appeared on the HR scene in organizations of all sizes and in all industries. Some forces behind the emphasis on talent management have included:

- The impending retirement of baby boomers worldwide
- Shortages of skilled workers of certain types and at certain levels
- Increasing global competition for human resource talent
- Growth in technology capable of automating talent management processes

These and other factors have forced organizations to develop a more strategic, integrated, and automated approach to talent management.

Whether it involves attracting, recruiting, and hiring qualified talented individuals, or training and developing employees for current and future jobs, talent management is crucial. A survey by McKinsey and Company of 200 companies found that better-performing firms hired more qualified people, established more specific performance expectations, and worked to link employees to corporate culture and strategies.[34] Further discussion of talent management occurs in later chapters.

Growth in Contingent Workforce *Contingent workers* (temporary workers, independent contractors, leased employees, and part-timers) represent about one-fourth of the U.S. workforce. Many employers operate with a core group of regular employees who have critical skills, and then expand and shrink the workforce by using contingent workers.

The number of contingent workers has grown for many reasons. One reason is the economic factor. Temporary workers are used to replace full-time employees, and many contingent workers are paid less and/or receive fewer benefits than regular employees. For instance, omitting contingent workers from health care benefits saves some firms 20% to 40% in labor costs.

Another reason for the increased use of contingent workers is that it may reduce legal liability for some employers. As more and more employment-related lawsuits have been filed, employers have become more wary about adding regular full-time employees. By using contract workers, including those in other countries, employers may

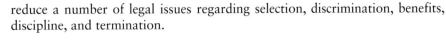

reduce a number of legal issues regarding selection, discrimination, benefits, discipline, and termination.

Globalization of Organizations and HR

GLOBAL

The internationalization of business has proceeded at a rapid pace. Many U.S. firms, both large and small, receive a substantial portion of their profits and sales from other countries. Firms such as Coca-Cola, Exxon, Mobil, Microsoft, and General Electric derive half or more of total sales and profits from outside the United States. The reverse is also true. For example, Toyota, based in Japan, has grown its market share and its number of jobs in the United States and North America. Also, Toyota, Honda, Nissan, and other Japanese automobile manufacturers, electronics firms, and suppliers have maintained operations in the United States, whereas Chrysler and General Motors have had to reduce major operations.

The globalization of business has shifted from trade and investment to the integration of global operations, management, and strategic alliances, which has significantly affected the management of human resources. Individuals from other countries are employees. There are three types of global workers: expatriate, host-country national, and third-country national.

An **expatriate** is a citizen of one country who is working in a second country and employed by an organization headquartered in the first country. Experienced expatriates can provide a pool of talent that can be tapped as the organization expands its operations more broadly into even more countries.

A **host-country national** is a citizen of one country who is working in that country and employed by an organization headquartered in a second country. Host-country nationals often know the culture, politics, laws, and business customs better than an outsider would.

A **third-country national** is a citizen of one country who is working in a second country and employed by an organization headquartered in a third country. For example, a U.S. citizen working for a British oil company as a manager in Norway is a third-county national. Staffing with third-country nationals shows a truly global approach.

Attracting global talent has created political issues. For instance, U.S. employers are having a difficult time hiring enough engineers and educated tech workers, but U.S. federal legislation restricts the quota for high-skilled workers to be admitted from other countries in light of the large amount of illegal immigration and high numbers of unemployed U.S. workers that are occurring.

Global Economic Factors Economic factors are linked to different political, legal, cultural, and economic systems. In many developed countries, especially in Europe, employment restrictions and wage levels are high. When labor costs in the United States are compared with those in Germany and Korea, the differences are significant, as Figure 1-7 shows. As a result of these differences, many U.S. and European firms are moving jobs to lower-wage countries and other continental locations.

Critics of globalization cite the extremely low wage rates paid by the international firms and the substandard working conditions that exist in some underdeveloped countries. Various advocacy groups have accused global firms of being "sweatshop employers." Thus, some global employers have made efforts to ensure that foreign factories adhere to more appropriate HR standards, while others have not. Global employers counter that even though the

Expatriate A citizen of one country who is working in a second country and employed by an organization headquartered in the first country.

Host-country national A citizen of one country who is working in that country and employed by an organization headquartered in a second country.

Third-country national A citizen of one country who is working in a second country and employed by an organization headquartered in a third country.

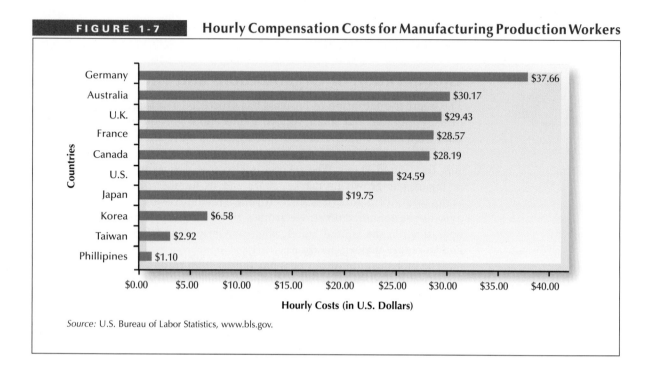

FIGURE 1-7   **Hourly Compensation Costs for Manufacturing Production Workers**

Source: U.S. Bureau of Labor Statistics, www.bls.gov.

wage rates in some countries are low, their employees often receive the highest wages and experience the best working conditions that exist in those local countries. Also, they argue, more people have jobs in the host countries, which allows them to improve their living standards.

Global Legal and Political Factors Firms in the United States, Europe, and elsewhere are accustomed to relatively stable political and legal systems. However, many nations function under turbulent and varied legal and political systems. International firms in many industries have dramatically increased security for both operations and employees. Terrorist threats and incidents have significantly affected airlines, travel companies, construction firms, and even retailers such as McDonald's. HR management must respond to such concerns as part of transnational operations and risk management efforts.

Therefore, HR-related efforts vary in character and stability. Compliance with laws and company actions on wages, benefits, union relations, worker privacy, workplace safety, and other issues illustrate the importance of HR management when operating transnationally. As a result, it is crucial for HR professionals to conduct a comprehensive review of the political environment and employment laws before beginning operations in a country. The role and nature of labor unions should be a part of that review.

Workforce Demographics and Diversity

The U.S. workforce has been changing dramatically. It is more diverse racially and ethnically, more women are in it than ever before, and the average age of its members is increasing. As a result of these demographic shifts, HR management in organizations has had to adapt to a more varied labor force both externally and internally. In addition to the issues discussed in the following sections, this growing diversity and aging of the workforce has raised employer concerns and means that HR is having to devote more time and effort to ensuring that nondiscriminatory policies and practices are followed. The effective management of diversity issues in organizations is getting more attention, as will be highlighted in later chapters.

Racial/Ethnic Diversity Racial and ethnic minorities account for a growing percentage of the overall labor force, with the percentage of Hispanics equal to or greater than the percentage of African Americans. Immigrants will continue to expand that growth. An increasing number of individuals characterize themselves as *multiracial,* suggesting that the American "melting pot" is blurring racial and ethnic identities.

Racial/ethnic differences have also created greater cultural diversity because of the accompanying differences in traditions, languages, religious practices, and so on. For example, global events have increased employers' attention to individuals who are Muslim, and more awareness and accommodation for Islamic religious beliefs and practices have become a common concern. Workforce diversity is further discussed in Chapter 4.

Women in the Workforce Women constitute about 50% of the U.S. workforce, but may be a majority in certain occupations. For instance, the membership of HR professionals in the Society for Human Resource Management (SHRM) is more than 75% female.[35] Additionally, numerous women workers are single, separated, divorced, or widowed, and therefore are "primary" income earners. A growing number of U.S. households include "domestic partners," who are committed to each other though not married and who may be of the same or the opposite sex. Many of the women in these partnerships, as well as many who are married, have partners or spouses who also are employed.

For many workers in the United States, balancing the demands of family and work is a significant challenge. Although that balancing has always been a concern, the increased number of working women and dual-career couples has resulted in greater tensions for many workers, both male and female. Employers have had to respond to work/family concerns in order to retain employees. Responses have included greater use of job sharing, the establishment of child-care services, increased flexibility in hours, and varied work-life programs.

Aging Workforce In many economically developed countries, the population is aging, resulting in a significantly aging workforce. In the United States, during the second decade of the twenty-first century, a significant number of experienced employees will be retiring, changing to part-time, or otherwise shifting their employment. Replacing the experience and talents of longer-service workers is a growing challenge facing employers in all industries.

This loss of longer-service workers is frequently referred to as a "brain drain," due to the capabilities and experience of these workers, and employers are having to develop programs to retain them, have them mentor and transfer knowledge to younger employees, and find ways for them to continue contributing by limited means. One study found that 65% of baby boomers want to continue working part-time and avoid full-time employment.[36]

HR Technology

Greater use of technology has led to organizational use of a *human resource management system (HRMS),* which is an integrated system providing information used by HR management in decision making. This terminology emphasizes that making HR decisions, not just building databases and using technology, is the primary reason for compiling data in an information system.

Purposes for Expanding HR Technology The rapid expansion of HR technology serves two major purposes in organizations. One relates to administrative and operational efficiency, and the other to effectiveness. The first purpose is to improve the efficiency with which data on employees and HR activities are compiled. The most basic example is the automation of payroll and benefits activities. Another common use of technology is tracking EEO/affirmative action activities. Beyond those basic applications, the use of Web-based information systems has allowed the HR unit in organizations to become more administratively efficient and communicate more quickly to employees.

The second purpose of the use of HR technology is related to strategic HR planning. Having accessible data enables HR planning and managerial decision making to be based to a greater degree on information rather than relying on managerial perceptions and intuition.

Greater Uses of HR Technology The greater uses of technologies are affecting how HR activities are performed in many ways. To illustrate, numerous

Wikis, Blogs, Twitters, and HR

HR *online*

The explosive growth of the Internet has resulted in many employees and managers participating in wikis, blogs, twitters, text-messaging, and other techniques. Some of the HR aspects of the Internet are highlighted here.

In a wiki, which is a widely available website for individuals to make comments, employees can communicate both positive and negative messages on many topics. Employers have used wikis, such as Wikipedia and other sources, to increase the exchange of ideas and information among a wide range of individuals. Wikis are one example of *collaborative HR*. This process of collaboration can lead to HR professionals from several different organizations jointly working to address shared business problems and interacting regularly with other professionals.

Blogs are Web logs kept by individuals or groups to post and exchange information on a range of topics. People create and use more than one million blogs daily. The subjects of blogs vary. An example of company use would be CEOs or HR executives exchanging information with employees immediately on operational or other important occurrences. Many bloggers are young and college-educated. Often, HR

professionals are not as involved in blogs as some other employees, but they are having to ramp up their awareness and usage of this format.

An even newer technology tool is twitter, which is a microblog that allows people to send and receive tweets. Basically, a tweet is a quick message of less than 140 characters through which individuals quickly send information to others. Whether such information is valid, positive or negative, or useful is a topic of continuing controversy. Some firms use twitters to send out policy changes, competitive services details, and many other organizational messages, but individuals can use twitters inappropriately and send critical, obscene, or even harassing details to other employees.

These technology tools and others create significant HR issues, including ethical and disciplinary actions. Firms must establish policies and regulations on how all of this technology can and should be used. For example, IBM has established guidelines directing that the use of twitters must be responsible, protect privacy, and correct mistakes made by individual tweets. Throughout this text, the various HR technology means will be discussed as they apply to specific HR activities.[37]

firms provide a Web-based employee self-service program to their worldwide staffs. Employees can go online to access and change their personal data, enroll in or change benefits programs, and prepare for performance reviews. As discussed in the HR Online box, the explosive use of wikis, blogs, twitters, and other technology is affecting HR significantly. Additional examples of how various HR activities are being transformed by technology will be presented throughout the chapters of this text.

Measuring HR Impact through Metrics

Traditionally, much of HR has focused on administrative activities, and on counting them, such as the number of people hired, total benefits costs, and so on. However, as HR has grown in importance and changed, it has had to develop measurements of its results, including financial, in order to justify its activities. Whether it is measuring the cost of hiring someone, calculating the turnover costs when persons leave the firm, or doing a return-on-investment analysis of training results and expenses, HR has had to become more analytical and develop *metrics* that measure the HR efforts, much like financial officers measure their responsibilities. HR metrics are discussed as part of Chapter 2, as well as throughout the text.

MANAGING HR IN ORGANIZATIONS

In a real sense, *every* manager in an organization is an HR manager. Sales managers, head nurses, drafting supervisors, college deans, and accounting supervisors all engage in HR management, and their effectiveness depends in part on the success of organizational HR systems. However, it is unrealistic to expect a nursing supervisor or an engineering manager to know about the nuances of equal employment regulations or how to design and administer a compensation and benefits system. For that reason, many organizations have people in an HR department who specialize in these activities, but HR in smaller organizations may be somewhat different.

Smaller Organizations and HR Management

In the United States and worldwide, small businesses employ more than 50% of all private-sector employees and generate new jobs each year.[38] In surveys over several years by the U.S. Small Business Association (SBA), the issues identified as significant concerns in small organizations were consistent: having sufficient numbers of qualified workers, the rapidly increasing costs of benefits, rising taxes, and compliance with government regulations. Notice these concerns have an HR focus, especially when governmental compliance with wage/hour, safety, equal employment, and other regulations are considered. HR efforts through recruiting, employee empowerment, and training have been found to contribute positively to sales growth in various small service industry firms.[39] As a result, for many smaller organizations, HR issues are often significant.

However, not every small organization is able to maintain an HR department. In a company with an owner and only three employees, the owner usually takes care of HR issues. As an organization grows, often a clerical employee is added to handle payroll, benefits, and required HR recordkeeping.

If new employees are hired, supervisors and managers usually do the recruiting, selecting, and training. These HR activities reduce the time that supervisors and managers have to focus on operations, sales and marketing, accounting, and other business areas. Thus, for both small and large employers, numerous HR activities are being outsourced to specialized vendors. Typically, at 80 to 100 employees, an organization will need to designate a person to specialize in HR management. Other HR jobs are added as the company gets larger and as HR technology increasingly becomes available for small- and medium-sized organizations.

HR Cooperation with Operating and Line Managers

In departments such as accounting, network technology, operations, customer service, and others, cooperation between line and operating managers, supervisors, executives, and HR staff is necessary for HR efforts to succeed. In many cases, the HR professionals and staff members design processes and systems that the operating managers must help implement. The exact division of labor between HR and other departments varies from organization to organization.

Throughout this book, figures labeled "Typical Division of HR Responsibilities" illustrate how HR responsibilities in various areas may be divided in organizations having specialized HR departments. The first such example, Figure 1-8, shows how the responsibilities for a familiar activity—recruiting planning—might be divided between the HR department and the operating managers in an organization.

How HR Is Seen in Organizations

For a number of years, HR departments and individuals have been viewed in different ways, both positive and negative. HR management is necessary, especially due to the huge number of government regulations enacted over the past decades. However, the role of protecting corporate assets against the many legal issues often puts HR management in an enforcement role that may be seen as restrictive and administratively focused.

FIGURE 1-8   **Typical Division of HR Responsibilities: Recruiting**

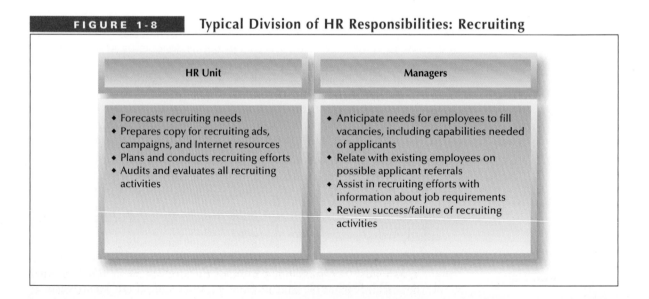

HR Unit	Managers
• Forecasts recruiting needs • Prepares copy for recruiting ads, campaigns, and Internet resources • Plans and conducts recruiting efforts • Audits and evaluates all recruiting activities	• Anticipate needs for employees to fill vacancies, including capabilities needed of applicants • Relate with existing employees on possible applicant referrals • Assist in recruiting efforts with information about job requirements • Review success/failure of recruiting activities

Negative Views of HR The legal compliance role and other administrative aspects of HR staff can create conflicting views. The negative perception by some employees, managers, and executives is that HR departments and personnel are too bureaucratic, too administratively focused, too detail-oriented, too costly, and not effective change agents.[40] Various authors have referred to HR departments as "dinosaurs" or "gatekeepers" who build silos and resist changes. These critics do not see HR as making significant organizational contributions.

Unfortunately, these views are accurate in some HR departments. Those HR departments concern themselves with the "administrivia" of personnel policies and practices—which companies are increasingly outsourcing to contractors who can do these tasks more cheaply and efficiently. Frequently, HR managers are seen as being more concerned about *activities* than *results*, and HR efforts as too seldom linking to employee, managerial, and business performance organizational metrics. As would be expected, numerous HR professionals have criticized these views as being too negative and not what HR is actually doing in many organizations.

Positive, Contributing Views of HR Despite many criticisms, HR *can be* respected if done well and truly brought into the realm of business strategy. HR can and should be a special part of any organization, which means viewing the people and their talents as an opportunity for creating greater organizational competitive advantages. That is why HR in many organizations has recognized the need to change even more to overcome the negative images. As previously indicated, economic, global, workforce, and other aspects are increasingly creating challenging practices for HR professionals.[41]

Key for a more positive view is for HR to expand as a business contributor, as will be highlighted in the following sections. One leader in creating this view, among others, has been Dave Ulrich. He and other advocates have emphasized that HR needs to become more of a change agent and shift positively how HR impacts organizatons.[42] The different roles of HR and how they need to be changing and expanding are discussed next.

HR MANAGEMENT ROLES

Several roles can be fulfilled by HR management. The nature and extent of these roles depend on both what upper management wants HR management to do and what competencies the HR staff have demonstrated. Three roles are typically identified for HR. The focus of each of them, as shown in Figure 1-9, is as follows:

- *Administrative:* Focusing on clerical administration and recordkeeping, including essential legal paperwork and policy implementation.
- *Operational and employee advocate:* Managing most HR activities in line with the strategies and operations that have been identified by management and serving as employee "champion" for employee issues and concerns.
- *Strategic:* Helping to define the strategy relative to human capital and its contribution to organizational results.

The administrative role traditionally has been the dominant role for HR. However, as Figure 1-9 indicates, a broader transformation in HR is needed so that significantly less HR time and fewer HR staff are used just for clerical

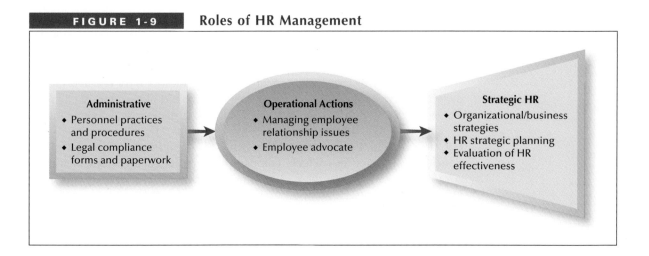

FIGURE 1-9   Roles of HR Management

Administrative
- Personnel practices and procedures
- Legal compliance forms and paperwork

Operational Actions
- Managing employee relationship issues
- Employee advocate

Strategic HR
- Organizational/business strategies
- HR strategic planning
- Evaluation of HR effectiveness

administration. The emphasis on the operational and employee advocate role is growing in most organizations. The greatest challenge is for more strategic HR management. The biggest barriers to HR becoming more strategic, according to one study, are transaction of administrative tasks (42%), lack of strategic HR involvement (31%), and insufficient HR budgets (22%).[43] A closer look at each of the HR roles and how these roles are being transformed follows.

Administrative Role of HR

The administrative role of HR management has been heavily oriented to processing and recordkeeping. This role has given HR management in some organizations the reputation of being staffed by paper shufflers who primarily tell managers and employees what cannot be done. If limited to the administrative role, HR staff are seen primarily as clerical and lower-level administrative aides to the organization. Two major shifts driving the transformation of the administrative role are greater use of technology and outsourcing.

Technology Transforming HR To improve the administrative efficiency of HR and the responsiveness of HR to employees and managers, more HR functions are becoming available electronically or are being done on the Internet using Web-based technology. Technology is being used in most HR activities, from employment applications and employee benefits enrollments to e-learning using Internet-based resources.

Outsourcing of HR Increasingly, many HR administrative functions are being outsourced to vendors. This outsourcing of HR administrative activities has grown dramatically in HR areas such as employee assistance (counseling), retirement planning, benefits administration, payroll services, and outplacement services.

The primary reasons why HR functions are outsourced are to save money on HR staffing, to take advantage of specialized vendor expertise and technology, and to be able to focus on more strategic HR activities. These activities are being outsourced to firms both in the United States and worldwide. Such contracting for HR services is an evolving practice that continues to change the administrative HR functions for many employers, as discussed further in Chapter 2.

Operational and Employee Advocate Role for HR

HR often has been viewed as the "employee advocate" in organizations. As the voice for employee concerns, HR professionals traditionally may serve as "company morale officers," but they spend considerable time on HR "crisis management," dealing with employee problems that are both work-related and not work-related. Employee advocacy helps ensure fair and equitable treatment for employees regardless of personal background or circumstances. Sometimes the HR advocate role may create conflict with operating managers. However, without the HR advocate role, employers could face even more lawsuits and regulatory complaints than they do now.

The operational role requires HR professionals to cooperate with various departmental and operating managers and supervisors, to identify and implement needed programs and policies in the organization. Operational activities are tactical in nature. Compliance with equal employment opportunity and other laws is ensured, employment applications are processed, current openings are filled through interviews, supervisors are trained, safety problems are resolved, and wage and benefit questions are answered. These efforts require matching HR activities with the strategies of the organization.

Strategic Role for HR

Differences between the operational and strategic roles exist in a number of HR areas. The strategic HR role means that HR professionals are proactive in addressing business realities and focusing on future business needs, such as strategic planning, compensation strategies, the performance of HR, and measuring its results. However, HR often does not help formulate strategies for the organization as a whole; instead it merely carries them out through HR activities.

Many executives, managers, and HR professionals are increasingly seeing the need for HR management to become a greater strategic contributor to the "business" success of organizations. Even not-for-profit organizations, such as governmental and social service entities, must manage their human resources in a business-oriented manner. In fact, it has been suggested that the HR function should be managed as its own business. Therefore, a large number of senior HR executives are selected from outside HR experience. Doing this means that these individuals have a business focus, not just HR experience.[44]

HR should be responsible for knowing what the true cost of human capital is for an employer. For example, it may cost two times key employees' annual salaries to replace them if they leave. Turnover is something HR can help control, and if it is successful in saving the company money with good retention and talent management strategies, those may be important contributions to the bottom line of organizational performance.

"Contributing at the Table" The role of HR as a *strategic business partner* is often described as "having a seat at the table," and contributing to the strategic directions and success of the organization. That means HR is involved in *devising* strategy in addition to *implementing* strategy. Part of HR's contribution is to have financial expertise and to produce financial results, not just employee morale or administrative efficiencies. Therefore, a significant concern for chief financial officers (CFOs) is whether HR executives are equipped to help plan and meet financial requirements.[45]

However, even though this strategic role of HR is recognized, many organizations still need to make significant progress toward fulfilling it. Some examples of areas where strategic contributions can be made by HR are:

- Evaluating mergers and acquisitions for organizational "compatibility," structural changes, and staffing needs
- Conducting workforce planning to anticipate the retirement of employees at all levels and identify workforce expansion in organizational strategic plans
- Leading site selection efforts for new facilities or transferring operations to international outsourcing locations based on workforce needs
- Instituting HR management systems to reduce administrative time, equipment, and staff by using HR technology
- Working with executives to develop a revised sales compensation and incentives plan as new products or services are rolled out to customers

LOGGING ON

HRN Management Group

Information on strategic issues for HR, including news and success stories for key HR decision makers, is available by linking to the HRN Management Group website at www.hronline.com.

HR MANAGEMENT COMPETENCIES AND CAREERS

As HR management becomes more complex, greater demands are placed on individuals who make HR their career specialty. Despite the HR criticism and concerns mentioned earlier, a significant number of individuals have made HR their career field. Even readers of this book who do not become HR managers and professionals will find it useful to know about the competencies required for effective HR management.

HR Competencies

The transformation of HR toward being more strategic has implications for the competencies needed by HR professionals. Views of HR have changed over the years as the needed competencies and the results have differed. Research has indicated that HR professionals at all levels need the following: [46]

- Strategic knowledge and impact means
- Legal, administrative, and operational capabilities
- Technology knowledge and usage abilities

Senior HR leaders may need additional capabilities and competencies. According to an overview from a SHRM study, senior HR leaders also need: (a) more business, strategic, HR, and organizational knowledge; (b) ability to lead changes due to credibility; and (c) ethical behavior and results orientation/performance. [47]

For individuals with HR as their career, these competencies help establish their value as professional resources. The changes in organizations and the workforce mean that HR as a career field is being altered and will continue to require more efforts by HR professionals at all levels.

HR Management as a Career Field

A variety of jobs exists within the HR career field, ranging from executive to clerical. As an employer grows large enough to need someone to focus primarily on HR activities, the role of the **HR generalist** emerges—that is, a person who has responsibility for performing a variety of HR activities. Further growth leads to the addition of **HR specialists,** or individuals who have in-depth knowledge and expertise in limited areas of HR. The most common areas of HR specialty, in order of frequency, are benefits, employment and recruitment, and compensation.[48]Appendix F contains examples of HR-related job descriptions of both a generalist and a specialist.

HR jobs can be found in corporate headquarters as well as in field and subsidiary operations. A compensation analyst or HR director might be found at a corporate headquarters. An employment manager for a manufacturing plant and a European HR manager for a global food company are examples of field and subsidiary HR professionals. The two types of jobs have different career appeals and challenges, which may affect the recruiting, selection, promotions, and development of individuals.

LOGGING ON

HR Certification Institute
For information on the HRCI certification process, go to www.hrci.org.

HR Professionalism and Certification

Depending on the job, HR professionals may need considerable knowledge about employment regulations, finance, tax law, statistics, and information systems. In most cases, they also need extensive knowledge about specific HR activities. The broad range of issues faced by HR professionals has made involvement in professional associations and organizations important. For HR generalists, the largest organization is the Society for Human Resource Management (SHRM). Public-sector HR professionals tend to be concentrated in the International Personnel Management Association (IPMA). Two other prominent specialized HR organizations are the WorldatWork Association and the American Society for Training and Development (ASTD).

One characteristic of a professional field is having a means to certify that members have the knowledge and competence needed in the profession. The CPA for accountants and the CLU for life insurance underwriters are examples. Certification can be valuable to individuals and useful to employers as they select and promote certified individuals.[49] The most well-known certification programs for HR generalists are administered by the Human Resource Certification Institute (HRCI), which is affiliated with SHRM. More than 100,000 professionals have an HRCI certification.

HRCI Certification The most widely known HR certifications are the Professional in Human Resources (PHR) and the Senior Professional in Human Resources (SPHR), both sponsored by HRCI. Annually, thousands of individuals take the certification exams. HRCI also sponsors a Global Professional in Human Resources (GPHR) certification. Eligibility requirements for PHR, SPHR, and GPHR certifications have been updated. These requirements, effective 2011, are shown in Figure 1-10.

Additionally, eligible individuals must pass the appropriate exam. Appendix A identifies test specifications and knowledge area covered by the PHR and SPHR. Readers of this book can identify specific competencies for the HRCI outline to aid them in getting a PHR or SPHR. Certification from HRCI also exists for global HR professionals in the GPHR. Global certification recognizes the growth in HR responsibilities in organizations throughout the world and covers appropriate global HR subject areas noted through SHRM.

HR generalist A person who has responsibility for performing a variety of HR activities.

HR specialist A person who has in-depth knowledge and expertise in a limited area of HR.

FIGURE 1-10   HR Certifications at a Glance

The certification exams test on experience-based knowledge; therefore, you must possess a **minimum of two years of professional (exempt-level) HR experience**.

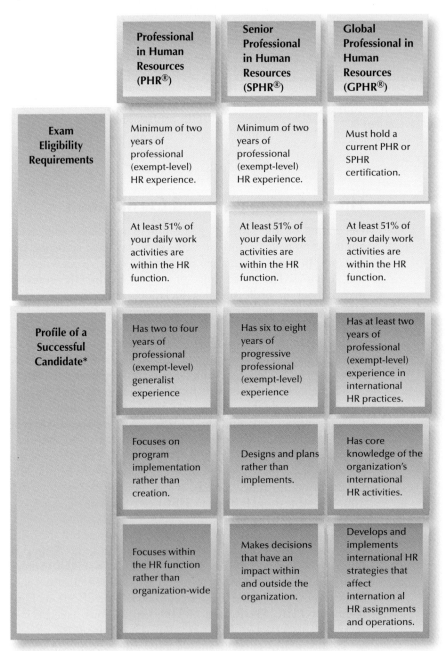

	Professional in Human Resources (PHR®)	Senior Professional in Human Resources (SPHR®)	Global Professional in Human Resources (GPHR®)
Exam Eligibility Requirements	Minimum of two years of professional (exempt-level) HR experience.	Minimum of two years of professional (exempt-level) HR experience.	Must hold a current PHR or SPHR certification.
	At least 51% of your daily work activities are within the HR function.	At least 51% of your daily work activities are within the HR function.	At least 51% of your daily work activities are within the HR function.
Profile of a Successful Candidate*	Has two to four years of professional (exempt-level) generalist experience	Has six to eight years of progressive professional (exempt-level) experience	Has at least two years of professional (exempt-level) experience in international HR practices.
	Focuses on program implementation rather than creation.	Designs and plans rather than implements.	Has core knowledge of the organization's international HR activities.
	Focuses within the HR function rather than organization-wide	Makes decisions that have an impact within and outside the organization.	Develops and implements international HR strategies that affect internation al HR assignments and operations.

*In addition to meeting the exam eligibility requirements, successful exam candidates usually have the above work experience.

WorldatWork Certifications The WorldatWork Association has certifications emphasizing compensation and benefits. The four certifications are as follows:

- Certified Compensation Professional (CCP)
- Certified Benefits Professional (CBP)
- Certified Work-Life Professional (CWLP)
- Certified Global Remuneration (CGR)

Other HR Certifications Increasingly, employers hiring or promoting HR professionals are requesting certifications as a "plus." HR professionals feel that various HR certifications give them more credibility with corporate peers and senior managers. Additional certification programs for HR specialists and generalists are sponsored by various organizations, and the number of certifications is being expanded.[50] For specialists, some well-known programs include the following:

- Certified Recognition Professional (CRP) sponsored by the Recognition Professionals International
- Certified Employee Benefits sponsored by the International Foundation of Employee Benefits Plans
- Certified Professional in Learning and Performance sponsored by the American Society for Training and Development
- Certified Safety Professional (CSP) and Occupational Health and Safety Technologist (OHST) sponsored by the American Society of Safety Engineers
- Certified Professional Outsourcing (CSO) provided by the Human Resource Outsourcing Association
- Certified Graphics Communications Manager (CGCM) and Certified Mail Manager (CMM) sponsored by the International Personnel Management Association

Most individuals who want to succeed in the field must update their knowledge continually. One way of staying current on HR is to tap information in current HR literature and relevant associations, as listed in Appendix B of this book. Overall, certifying knowledge is a trend in numerous professions, and HR illustrates the importance of certification by making many different types available. Given that many people may enter HR jobs with limited formal HR training, certifications help both individuals and their employers to make HR management a better performing part of their organizations.

SUMMARY

- HR management ensures that human talent is used effectively and efficiently to accomplish organizational goals.
- As an organization core competency, human resources has a unique capability that creates high value and differentiates an organization from competitors in areas such as productivity, quality/service, employee skills, and innovative changes.
- Human capital is the collective value of the capabilities, knowledge, skills, life experiences, and motivation of an organizational workforce.

- HR management activities can be grouped as follows: strategic HR management; equal employment opportunity; staffing; talent management; compensation and benefits; health, safety, and security; and employee and labor relations.
- As part of organizational culture, HR plays a significant role through affecting human values, competitive advantages, and global cultures.
- Contributions by HR can include productivity improvement, meeting social responsibilities,

enhancing customer service and quality, and expanding employee engagement.

- Ethical behavior is crucial in HR management, and HR professionals regularly face a number of ethical issues and consequences both domestically and globally.
- Numerous HR challenges exist currently, including organizational cost pressures, economics and job changes, talent management and development, technology expansion, and measuring HR.
- All organizations need HR management, but larger ones are more likely to have a specialized HR function.

- HR management must fulfill three roles: (1) administrative, (2) operational and employee advocate, and (3) strategic.
- All levels of HR professionals need competencies in strategic knowledge and impacts; capabilities in legal, administrative, and operational areas; and technology knowledge abilities. Senior HR leaders need these areas plus others to be effective.
- Current knowledge about HR management is required for professionals in the HR career field, and professional certification has grown in importance for HR generalists and specialists.

CRITICAL THINKING ACTIVITIES

1. Discuss several areas in which HR can affect organizational culture positively or negatively.

2. Give some examples of ethical issues that you have experienced in jobs, and explain how HR did or did not help resolve them.

3. Why is it important for HR management to transform from being primarily administrative and operational to becoming a more strategic contributor?

4. Assume you are an HR director with a staff of seven people. A departmental objective is for all staff members to become professionally certified within a year. Using Internet resources of HR associations such as www.shrm.org and www.WorldatWork.org, develop a table that identifies four to six certifications that could be obtained by your staff members, and show the important details for each certification.

HR EXPERIENTIAL PROBLEM SOLVING

Your company, a growing firm in the financial services industry, is extremely sensitive to the issues surrounding business ethics. The company wants to be proactive in developing a business ethics training program for all employees both to ensure the company's reputation as an ethical company in the community and to help maintain the industry's high standards. As the HR Director and someone who values the importance of having all employees trained in the area of business ethics, you are in charge of developing the ethics training program.

It needs to be a basic program that can be presented to all employees in the company. Resources for business ethics information can be found at www.business-ethics.org/primer1.html.

1. What legislative act prompted many U.S. companies to develop internal ethical policies and procedures?

2. What are key concepts related to business ethics that should be considered in the development of the ethics training program?

CASE

HR, Culture, and Business Results Success at Google, Scripps, and UPS

Firms in a variety of industries have been recognized as being among the Most Admired Companies by *Fortune* magazine. Others have been highlighted as being the Best Companies to Work For by *Fortune* or as Optimas Award winners by *Workforce Management*. These recognitions contain some common elements because of how HR management has contributed to organizational success and is being positively viewed by employees. Three examples are highlighted here.

One recognized firm is Google, which is well known by many individuals because of its Internet components. Google has an HR image as a creative contributor to business objectives through its work environment guided by HR. According to the head of HR at Google, Lazio Bock, the overriding key of HR at Google is its emphasis on organizational culture and business objectives. The focus of Google HR is on giving its employees flexibility to produce results, not just following core job requirements. Consequently, HR at Google has established innovative efforts for its people and has made the administrative part of HR efficient. Minimizing numerous HR administrative forms, data, and reports by using technology has occurred, which would be expected in a prominent technology firm.

At Google, HR communicates to its employees extensively about business objectives, organizational results, and relevant current information. Because many of the Google employees are stock shareholders also, they have a personal interest in Google being a successful business. Thus they continuously want to know the operational results by seeing current reports, data, and information. Overall, Google's HR approach is unique in comparison to the approaches at other companies recognized by *Fortune*, but its success illustrates that how HR is established and operates can be a key to organizational success.

A different firm with a variety of organizations and a strong HR culture is Scripps Network, a prominent television and communications corporation. At Scripps, HR plays a core role in establishing strategic goals and efforts. Even when Scripps has merged separate media firms, HR has focused on getting the cultures of the two entities to integrate effectively.

Several HR functions are used to support the culture and core values at Scripps. One is an active pay-for-performance system to reward employees at higher job levels with base pay increases, annual incentives, and long-term incentives. Another key part of HR efforts at Scripps is that HR emphasizes leadership development throughout the firm. Additionally, the firm has widely used work variability efforts such as work-life balance, telecommuting, and worker flexible schedules. These are done as part of a core value at Scripps of "compassion/support."

A different firm with an extended history of effectively integrating corporate culture and HR is UPS, the transportation and logistics delivery firm that operates worldwide. Its culture is different from the cultures of Google and Scripps; however, for more than a decade, UPS has been recognized for its corporate integrity, culture, and HR inclusion with employees.

UPS has emphasized linking HR with business objectives and uses communication and intranet programs to ensure that employees are kept constantly informed on business objectives and workforce challenges. One well-recognized component at UPS is the established codes of conduct that are consistently reviewed with all employees. These reviews include specific examples of ethical situations that employees may face and how to respond to them. Annually, managers complete a "conduct code" report that asks specific questions about ethical problems that have arisen during the year.

These three firms are in different industries, have different cultures, and use a variety of HR efforts. However, each of them has been recognized for implementing HR as core to their organizational cultures and successful business results.[51]

QUESTIONS

1. How does the integration of HR with the organizational culture contribute to the success of Google, Scripps, and UPS? To find ideas, go to the corporate website for each of these companies and search for additional insights.

2. Discuss how some of the cultural facets mentioned compare to those among employers you have worked for, and explain the difference in the views of these various employers.

SUPPLEMENTAL CASES

Phillips Furniture

This case describes a small company that has grown large enough to need a full-time HR person. You have been selected to be the HR manager, and you have to decide what HR activities are needed and the role HR is to play. (For the case, go to www.cengage.com/management/mathis.)

Sysco

As a large food services and distribution firm, Sysco had to revise its HR management. Review this case and identify how the Sysco changes modified HR's importance. (For the case, go to www.cengage.com/management/mathis.)

NOTES

1. Based on "Where the Jobs Are," *HR Magazine*, March 2009, 18; Peter Coy, Help Wanted," *Business Week*, May 11, 2009, 40–45; "HR's Insight into the Economy," *SHRM Workplace Visions*, No. 4 (2008), www.shrm.org/research.

2. Alan Clardy, "Human Resource Development and the Resource-Based Model of Core Competencies," *Human Resource Development Review*, 7 (2008), 387–407.

3. "What Is Human Capital?" *SHRM Knowledge Center*, August 22, 2008, www.shrm.org/TemplatesTools.

4. Sheila Bonini, et al., "Rebuilding Corporate Reputations," *The McKinsey Quarterly*, June 2009, www.mckinseyquarterly.com.

5. Scott Flander, "The HR Personality," *Human Resource Executive*, February 2008, 1, 20–32.

6. Charles Rothrock and David Gregory, "How Corporate Culture Affects Organizational Value," *SHRM White Paper*, April 1, 2006, www.shrm.org.

7. "Creativity and Innovation," *SHRM Workplace Visions*, No. 1 (2007), 1–8.

8. Geert Hofstede, *Culture's Consequences: Comparing Values, Behaviors, Institutions, and Organizations Across Cultures*, 2nd ed. (Thousand Oaks, CA: Sage, 2001); John W. Bing, "Hofstede's Consequences: The Impact of His Work on Consulting and Business Practices," *Academy of Management Executive*, February 2004, 80–87.

9. Michael Mandel, "Productivity's Up and That's a Worry," *Business Week*, May 25, 2009, 22–23.

10. Dirk Matten and Jeremy Moon, "'Implicit and Explicit' CSR: A Conceptual Framework for a Comparative Understanding of Corporate Social Responsibility," *Academy of Management Review*, 33 (2008), 404–424.

11. Adrienne Fox, "Corporate Social Responsibility Pays Off," *HR Magazine*, August 2007, 43–47.

12. "Socially Responsible Jobs Most Popular," *USA Today*, May 14, 2009, 6D.

13. "Can Sustainability Initiatives Survive in a Tough Economy?" *SHRM Workplace Visions*, No. 2 (2009), 1–6.

14. Based on "Green Jobs and Programs on the Rise," *Worldat Work Newsline*, April 22, 2009; Don Sanford and Sara Duffy, "Going Green: A Means to Attract and Retain," *WorkSpan*, May 2009, 100–106; Nancy H. Woodword, "New Breed of Human Resource Leader: Going Green . . .," *HR Magazine*, June 2008, 52–61.

15. Kjell A. Brekke and Karine Nyborg, "Attracting Responsible Employees: Green Productions as Labor Market Screening," *Resource & Energy Economics*, 30 (2008), 509–526.

16. "Social Responsibility and HR Strategy," *SHRM Workplace Visions*, No. 2 (2007), 1–8.

17. Rebecca M.J. Wells, "Outstanding Customer Satisfaction: The Key to a Talented Workforce?" *Academy of Management Perspectives*, August 2007, 87–89.

18. Jenna McGregor, "When Service Means Survival," *Business Week*, March 2, 2009, 26–33.

19. "Highly Engaged Workers More Productive, Less likely to Quit," *Worldat Work Newsline*, April 2, 2009.

20. Lydell C. Bridgeford, "Employers, Workers Clash over Social Networks," *Employee Benefit News*, June 9, 2009, http:ebn-benefitsnews .com.

21. Lauren Leader-Chivee and Ellen Cowan, "Networking the Way to Success: On-line Social Networks for Workplace and Competitive Advantage," *People and Strategy*, 30 (2008), 40–46.

22. K. Koonmee, et al., "Ethics Institutionalized, Quality of Work Life, and Employee Related Outcomes," *Journal of Business Research*, 63 (2010), 20–26.

23. Sean Valentine, "Human Resource Management, Ethical Context, and Personnel Consequences," forthcoming *Journal of Business Research Online*, 62 (2009).

24. Theresa Minton Eversole, "Job-Board Industry Addresses Ethical Concerns," *2008 HR Trendbook*, 30.

25. Ethics Resource Center, www.ethics .org.

26. Based on Michael O'Brien, "'Idol'-izing Ethics," *Human Resource Executive Online*, May 16, 2009.

27. Alexandria Ardichvilli, et al., "Characteristics of Ethical Business Cultures," *Journal of Business Ethics*, 85 (2009), 445–451.

28. Scott Sonenshein, "The Role of Construction, Intuition, and Justification in Responding to Ethical Issues at Work," *Academy of Management Review*, 32 (2007), 1022–1040.

29. Frank Kilmo, "Stricter Ethical Standards Called Key to Global Recovery," February 18, 2009, *HR News*, www.shrm.org.

30. Jean Thilmany, "Supporting Ethical Employees," *HR Magazine*, September 2007, 105–112.

31. To view the code of ethics and its development, go to www.shrm.org.

32. "Occupational Employment Projections to 2016," *Monthly Labor Review*, November 2007, www.bls.gov.

33. "The Hardest Jobs to Fill in America," *Forbes*, June 4, 2009, www.Forbes.com.

34. Mary Siegfried, "Skilled Talent, Not Technology, Drives Value," *Inside Supply Management*, May 2009, 26–27; McKinsey and Company, *The Talent Factor in Purchasing,* 2007, www.McKinsey.com.

35. For composition of HR membership in SHRM, go to www.shrm.org.

36. Karen Colligan, "Is Your Company Ready for the Brain Drain?" *Workspan*, October 2008, 97–99.

37. Based on a variety of publications, including www.wikipedia.com; Frank Giancola, "Getting Up to Speed on the HR Blogosphere," *WorldatWork*, March 31, 2009, www.worldatwork.org; and "Managing the Tweets," *BusinessWeek*, June 1, 2009, 20–21.

38. *Small Business by the Numbers* and other reports from the U.S. Small Business Administration, www.sba.gov.

39. Levent Altinay, et al., "Exploring the Relationship Between the Human Resource Practices and Growth in Small Service Firms," *Service Industries Journal*, 28 (2008), 919–937.

40. For example, see John Sullivan, "HR's Dinosaurs," *Workforce Management*, March 26, 2007, 58ff.; Keith Hammond, "Why We Hate HR," *Fast Company*, August 2005, 40.

41. Leon Rubis, "HR Is Easier Said than Done, Says Jack Welch," May 5, 2009, *HR News*, www.shrm.org.

42. Dave Ulrich, "Are You a Change Agent?" *Workforce Management*, June 9, 2008, 22–23.

43. "Examining Strategic Versus Transitional Approaches to HR," *Proven Results: Research Meets Real World* (Norcross, GA: EmployEase, 2009), www.employease.com.

44. Jessica Marquez, "Not the Usual Suspects," *Workforce Management*, November 5, 2007, 23–30.

45. David McCann, "Memo to CFOs: Don't Trust HR," March 10, 2009, www.CFO.com.

46. Dave Ulrich, et al., *HR Competencies* (Alexandria, VA: SHRM, 2008).

47. Amanda Benedict, et al., "Leading Now, Leading the Future: What Senior HR Leaders Need to Know," *SHRM Executive Summary*, February 2009, 1–23.

48. *HR Department Benchmarks and Analysis* (Washington, DC: Bureau of National Affairs). For more details, go to www.bna.com.

49. Kris Dunn, "What Are HR Certifications Worth?" *Workforce Management Online*, December 2007, www.workforce.com.

50. "A New Seat at the Table," *Employee Benefit News*, September 1, 2008, 28–32.

51. Fay Hansen, "Special Report: The HR Profession—HR at America's Most Admired Companies," *Workforce Management*, June 23, 2008, 1, 24–32; Bob King, "Packard: Creating a Great Culture Makes for Great TV," *Workspan*, October 2008, 23–28; Richard Stolz, "What HR Will Stand For," *Human Resource Executive*, January 2003, 20–28.

2

Strategic HR Management and Planning

After you have read this chapter, you should be able to:

- Summarize the strategic planning process and how it drives the organizational activities.

- Outline how strategic HR management is linked to the organizational strategies.

- Discuss how internal and external environmental factors affect HR strategies.

- List HR strategic challenges faced by modern organizations.

- Explain how technology is affecting HR management practices and employees.

- Identify how organizations can measure and assess the effectiveness of HR management practices.

Strategic Utilization of Talent Benefits Health Care Organization

Courtesy of Lee Memorial Health System.

Lee Memorial Health System tapped its workers' heads and hearts to resuscitate the organization. In 2008, economic conditions put Ft. Myers's largest employer on life support, and this key provider of health care turned to its employees to reduce costs and prevent layoffs.

Because front-line workers are closer to the action than supervisors, they can more easily spot inefficiencies and waste. Lee Memorial's HR staff encouraged middle managers to hold honest, frank discussions with their staff to explain the urgency of the situation. Getting the attention of employees was not especially difficult because many of them had been personally touched by the national economic crisis. Helping employees make the connection between organizational health and their job security led to outstanding results for both the hospital and its staff.

Employees and physicians involved in a lean/Six Sigma project identified areas for cost reduction. Improved patient flow saved the hospital $5 million. Modifying the employee Paid Time Off (PTO) program to be consistent with other local employers saved $4 million. In total, Lee Memorial Health System reduced costs by $45 million and increased revenues by $25 million. A major success was that Lee Memorial saved 200 positions that had been slated for layoffs.

The approach of Lee Memorial's managers in actively soliciting and engaging employees demonstrates the value of sharing information about organizational business conditions with employees and giving them a stake in the outcomes. Putting the survival of the organization on every employee's radar allowed Lee Memorial to gain a competitive advantage through effective utilization of its human resources.[1]

The **strategy** an organization follows is its proposition for how to compete successfully and thereby survive and grow. Several different approaches to strategy formation exist. Most organizations have a relatively formal process for developing a written strategy encompassing a 5-year period with objectives and goals for each unit.

Strategic decisions relate to using resources in such a way that the organization can outperform its competitors. Organizations seek to achieve and maintain a competitive advantage in the marketplace by delivering high-quality products and services to their customers in a way that competitors cannot duplicate. Strategies might include revising existing products, acquiring new businesses, or developing new products or services using existing capabilities. Other strategic approaches might be to maintain a secure position with a single stable product (like WD-40) or to emphasize a constant stream of new products (like Apple). These are all viable strategies for different businesses, but the strategies chosen will determine the number, nature, and capabilities of people needed in the organization. Further, the people already in the organization may limit the strategies that might be successful.[2]

Regardless of which specific strategies are adopted for guiding an organization, having the right people in the right place at the right time will be critical to make the overall strategies work. If a strategy requires worker skills that are currently not available in the company, it will require time to find and hire people with those skills. Strategic HR management entails providing input into organizational strategic planning and developing specific HR initiatives to help achieve the organizational goals. While it seems important to consider HR in the overall organizational strategy, estimates are that only 30% of HR professionals are full strategic partners. Their primary role remains that of providing input to top management.[3]

Although HR administrative and legally mandated tasks are important, strategic HR means adding value by improving the performance of the business. Some businesses are highly dependent on human capital for a competitive advantage; others are less so. For example, the productivity of a steel mill depends more on the efficiency of furnaces and quality of raw materials than on human resources. However, every business strategy must be carried out by people, and therefore human capital is a vital element to business success. An important aspect of strategic HR management covered in this chapter is the measurement and determination of the value of human capital and HR practices.[4]

Strategy An organization's proposition for how to compete successfully and thereby survive and grow.

LOGGING ON

People Trak — Strategic HR Software
This firm provides strategic human resources management and planning software for organizations. Visit their website at www.people-trak.com/strategic_hr.asp.

STRATEGIC PLANNING

Strategic planning
The process of defining organizational strategy and allocating resources toward its achievement.

Strategic planning is the process of defining an organizational strategy, or direction, and making decisions on allocating the resources of the organization (capital and people) to pursue this strategy. Successful organizations engage in this core business process on an ongoing basis. The plan serves as the roadmap that gives the organization direction and aligns resources. The process involves several sequential steps that focus on the future of the organization.[5]

FIGURE 2-1	Strategic Planning Process

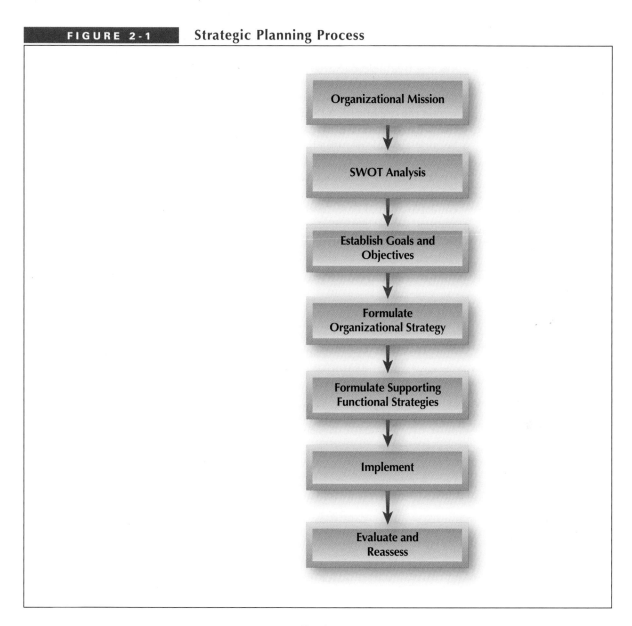

Strategy Formulation

The strategic planning cycle typically covers a 5-year time frame, and management considers both internal and external forces when formulating the strategic plan. Figure 2-1 shows the strategic planning process for the organization.[6]

The guiding force behind the strategic planning process is the **organizational mission**, which is the core reason for the existence of the organization and what makes it unique. The mission statement is usually determined by the organizational founders or leaders and sets the general direction for the organization.

The planning process begins with an assessment of the current state of the business and the environmental forces that may be important during the planning cycle. Analysis of the strengths, weaknesses, opportunities, and threats (SWOT) is a typical starting point because it allows managers to consider both internal and external conditions, which are discussed in more detail later in the chapter. The analysis helps managers to formulate a strategic plan

Organizational mission
The core reason for the existence of the organization and what makes it unique.

that considers the organizational ability to deal with the situation at hand.[7] The planning process is an ongoing cycle with managers continuously monitoring and responding to changes in the environment and competitive conditions.

Managers then determine the objectives for the planning cycle and formulate organization-level strategies to accomplish those objectives. Each function within the organization then formulates strategies that will link to and support the organization-level strategies. The strategic plan is evaluated periodically because conditions may change and managers must react to the ever-changing environment.

Strategic HR management refers to the use of human resource management (HRM) practices to gain or keep a competitive advantage. Talent acquisition, talent deployment, talent development, and rewarding talent are all strategic HRM approaches that can impact the organizational ability to achieve its strategic objectives.[8] The focus of HR initiatives is evolving from a traditional emphasis to a strategic emphasis, as detailed in Figure 2-2. Because business strategies affect HR

Strategic HR management
Refers to the use of employees to gain or maintain a competitive advantage.

FIGURE 2-2   **Traditional HR versus Strategic HR**

FOCUS	TRADITIONAL HR	STRATEGIC HR
View of organization	• Micro • Narrow skill application	• Macro • Broad skill application
Critical skills	• Organization • Administration • Compliance • Transactional • Tactical	• Strategic • Planning • Diagnostic • Analytical (metrics) • Consultative
View of employees	• Head count • Cost-based • Exploitable resource	• Contributors • Asset-based • Critical resource
Planning outlook	• Short-term • Low-risk • Traditional: utilizes tried-and-true approaches	• Long-term • High-risk • Experimental: tries novel approaches
HR systems and practices	• Routine, traditional • Reactive • Responds to stated needs	• Adaptive, innovative • Anticipatory, proactive • Recognizes unstated needs
Education and training	• Traditional HRM generalists and specialists • Other specialties	• Business acumen • Comprehensive HRM body of knowledge • Organizational development

plans and policies, consideration of human resource issues should be part of the strategy formulation process. Strategic HR deals with the contributions that HR strategies make to achieving organizational effectiveness and competitive advantage and how these HR contributions are accomplished. Therefore, HR should be involved in implementing strategies that affect and are influenced by people.[9]

An important element of strategic HRM is to develop processes in the organization that help align individual employee performance with the organizational strategic objectives. When employees understand the organizational priorities, they can better contribute by applying their skills to advance the organizational strategic goals. Employees who understand the "big picture" can make decisions that will contribute to the objectives of the firm. HRM practices that facilitate this include talent development and reward systems that channel employee efforts toward the organizational bottom line.[10]

Strategic Competencies for HR Professionals The HR professional wears many hats and must possess a wide variety of skills to successfully contribute at the strategic planning table. The following six primary strategic competencies are critical for HR professionals:[11]

- *Credible Activist:* challenges assumptions and offers a point of view
- *Culture and Change Steward:* shapes the organizational culture, makes changes happen
- *Talent Manager/Organization Designer:* acquires and deploys talent, embeds capabilities into the organizational structure
- *Strategy Architect:* recognizes business trends, forecasts potential obstacles to business success, and builds overall strategy
- *Operational Executor:* efficiently and effectively carries out tactical HR activities
- *Business Ally:* understands the business value chain, and establishes internal partnerships with line managers

Operationalizing HR Management Strategies Specific HR management strategies depend on the strategies and plans of the organization. Figure 2-3 highlights some common areas where HR should develop and implement appropriate strategies.[12] To contribute in a meaningful way in the strategic planning process, HR professionals provide the perspective and expertise to managers by performing the following functions:

- *Understand the business:* Knowing the financials and key drivers of business success are important to understanding the need for certain strategies.
- *Focus on the key business goals:* Programs that have the greatest relevance to business objectives should get priority.
- *Know what to measure:* Metrics are a vital part of assessing success, which means picking those measures that directly relate to the business goals.
- *Prepare for the future:* Strategic thinking requires preparing for the future, not focusing on the past—except as a predictor of the future.

HR AS ORGANIZATIONAL CONTRIBUTOR

In organizations where there are identifiable core competencies related to people, HR practices play a significant strategic role in enhancing organizational effectiveness. Effective management of talent provides managers with

---

FIGURE 2-3　**Strategic Human Resource Management**

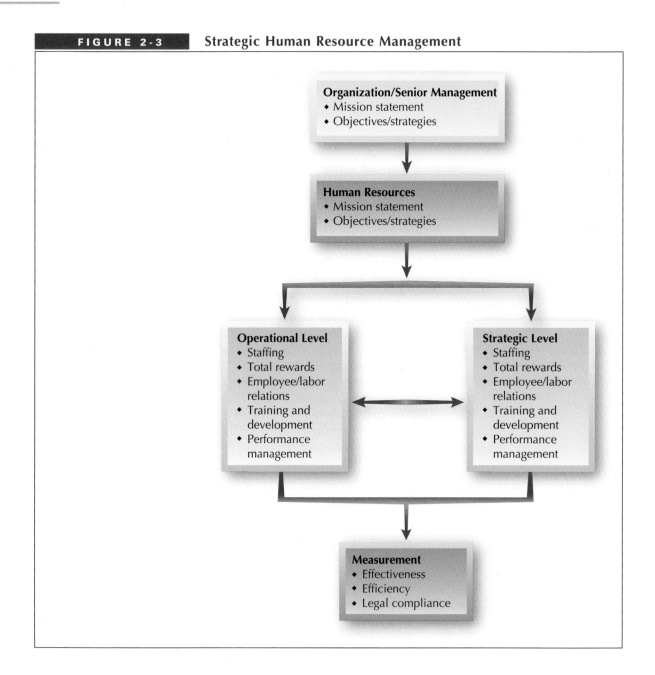

high-quality human resources to carry out the organizational strategies. As discussed in Chapter 1, strategic HR management plays a significant role in the following strategies:

- Organizational productivity
- Customer service and quality
- Financial contributions.

High-Performance Work Practices

A wide array of data from both academics and consulting firms shows that HR practices really do make a significant difference to business outcomes. Many HR "Best Practices" are identified in chapters throughout this book.

The examples will illustrate how HR strategies that foster these practices pay off for both employers and employees. Some recognized HR best practices include:[13]

- *Incentive compensation:* Pay-for-performance systems that tie employee rewards directly to successful performance of job responsibilities
- *Training:* Talent development programs to ensure that all employees have the proper knowledge, skills, and abilities to perform their jobs and to grow with the organization
- *Employee participation:* Soliciting and using employee ideas and suggestions to give employees a sense of importance and value to the organization
- *Selectivity:* Setting stringent hiring standards to maintain a high level of quality when bringing employees into the organization
- *Flexible work arrangements:* Providing alternative work schedules to help employees balance their personal and professional lives

Organizations that implement such practices have increased return on assets by 5% and reduced employment turnover by 20%. Research has also shown that market value, return on equity, and other operational performance measures are better in organizations that adopt high-performance work practices.[14]

HR Effectiveness and Financial Performance

Effectiveness for organizations is a measure of the ability of a program, project, or task to produce a specific desired effect or result that can be measured. **Efficiency** is the degree to which operations are done in an economical manner. Efficiency can also be thought of as a short-term measure that compares inputs and costs directly against outputs and benefits. HR management and financial executives work together to make certain that HR practices contribute financially to organizational effectiveness.

There are many different ways of measuring the financial contributions of HR and many challenges associated with doing so. Return on investment (ROI) is a common measure used by financial professionals to assess the value of an investment. For example, if a firm invests $20,000 for a supervisory training program, what does it gain in lower worker compensation costs, lower legal costs, higher employee productivity, and lower employee turnover? The benefits of HR programs are not always immediately visible which is what makes measuring HR's impact such a challenge. However, efforts should be made to financially assess HR practices.[15] Later in this chapter the discussion of HR metrics will highlight some specific HR measurement approaches. The HR Perspective discusses an interesting approach at IBM to harness the power of numbers in managing human resources.

Effectiveness The ability to produce a specific desired effect or result that can be measured.

Efficiency The degree to which operations are done in an economical manner.

ENVIRONMENTAL ANALYSIS

Environmental scanning The assessment of internal and external environmental conditions that affect the organization.

Before the managers in an organization begin strategic planning, they study and assess the dynamics of the environment in which they operate to better understand how these conditions might affect their plans. The process of **environmental scanning** helps to pinpoint strengths, weaknesses, opportunities, and threats that the organization will face during the planning horizon.

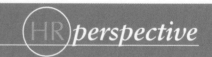

Numbers Add Up for IBM

Turning workers into numbers sounds not only difficult but also somewhat insensitive and heartless. However, mathematical models are helping IBM to harness human resources and allow its employees to thrive. IBM has long relied on detailed data and sophisticated algorithms to manage its supply chain and manufacturing processes, but the business has changed. IBM has shifted to a focus on services rather than building computer hardware. This increases the need to optimize the workforce so that the right individuals are available when customers need specific talents.

Building a profile for each employee involves determining the specific knowledge and strengths of each worker. Résumés and project records are used to identify skills and experiences. Online calendars, cell phones, and PDAs show how employees use their time and who they interact with. Call records and emails define the social network each employee has developed. This inventory of talent can be used by managers to better schedule work and create project teams.

Think of the manager who needs to deploy a team to work on assignment for a particular client. She could sit down and put the dates and skills needed into the talent inventory system. The results would come back telling her which workers are available with the right skill set, whether several proposed team members have worked together in the past, and how much they are paid. She would then be able to configure the ideal team within the budget limits.

Talent development could be enhanced by reviewing the combination of skills and experiences that high performers possess. To build the strength of the talent pipeline, employees could be "cloned" to duplicate successful employees based upon their profiles. The social networks of employees could be tapped to identify prospective employees or customers. Scheduling of workers would be aided by defining their skills and matching them to the thousands of small tasks that need to be accomplished on each project.

Although IBM has just begun mining the data and building the mathematical models to utilize human resources, the future will be based less on guesswork and more on proven formulas for success.[16]

The internal environment includes the quality and quantity of talent, the organizational culture, and the talent pipeline and leadership bench strength. The external environment includes many economic, political, and competitive forces that will shape the future. Figure 2-4 shows the HR elements of a SWOT analysis.[17]

Internal Environmental Analysis

The strengths and weaknesses of the organization represent factors within the organization that either create or destroy value. When assessing the internal environment, managers evaluate the quantity and quality of human resources, HR practices, and the organizational culture. The organizational culture is discussed at greater length in Chapter 1.

The strength of the talent pipeline is particularly important as the organization plans its future. Fulfilling strategic objectives is impossible without sufficient skills and talent. Leadership development and succession planning programs ensure that high-quality talent will be available to carry out the strategy. Effective development programs can reduce the high failure rate of people in leadership positions. Selecting individuals with the right talents

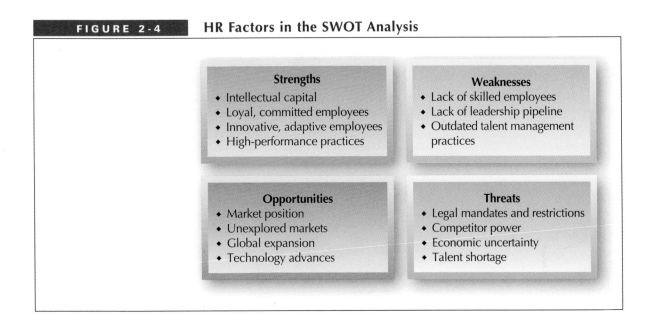

FIGURE 2-4   **HR Factors in the SWOT Analysis**

Strengths
- Intellectual capital
- Loyal, committed employees
- Innovative, adaptive employees
- High-performance practices

Weaknesses
- Lack of skilled employees
- Lack of leadership pipeline
- Outdated talent management practices

Opportunities
- Market position
- Unexplored markets
- Global expansion
- Technology advances

Threats
- Legal mandates and restrictions
- Competitor power
- Economic uncertainty
- Talent shortage

and teaching them leadership skills can improve the quality of leaders and promote strategic success. **Succession planning** is the process of identifying a plan for the orderly replacement of key employees. The succession plan is the blueprint for managing the internal talent pipeline. Managers identify individuals who can fulfill new roles in the future and include them in the succession plan. This internal pool of talent is the reserve needed to meet the objectives in the strategic plan.[18] Succession planning is explained in greater detail in Chapter 9.

External Environmental Analysis

Opportunities and threats emerge from the external environment and can impact the outcomes for the organization. Many of these forces are not within the organizational control, but must be considered in the scanning process. Dealing with uncertainty in the external environment is becoming a critical skill for planners.[19] The external environmental scan includes an assessment of economic conditions, legislative/political influences, demographic changes, and geographic and competitive issues, as shown in Figure 2-5.

Economic Conditions The prevailing business climate will affect strategic planning because the future is shaped by current conditions. Productivity levels, interest rates, economic growth, consumer prices, inflation, and unemployment rates affect the business outlook. Access to credit, capital, and labor affect the organizational ability to grow and to provide desired rewards to employees. During times of high economic growth, labor and material shortages are more likely. During economic downturns, resources are underutilized and organizations seek to increase productivity and to lower costs. When facing difficult economic conditions, firms may react by implementing severe workforce reductions, compensation cuts, and other drastic measures to remain viable.[20] These actions have strategic implications for the organization because they may leave the organization vulnerable when the economy improves.

Succession planning The process of identifying a plan for the orderly replacement of key employees.

| FIGURE 2-5 | Areas of External Environmental Scan |

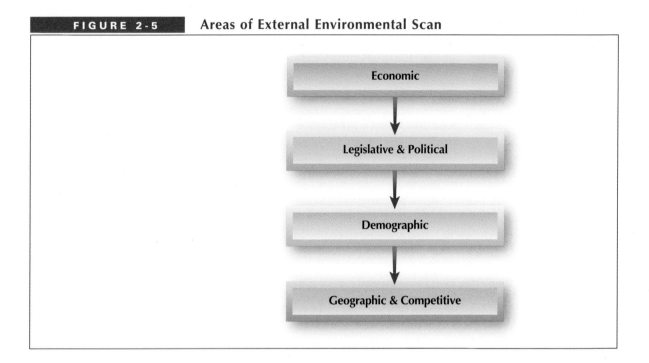

Inflation rates can influence the revenue stream for the organization as well as employee expectations regarding compensation. As the unemployment rate rises, the number of qualified people looking for work increases. This poses challenges for the organizations because the sheer volume of applicants can overwhelm the selection process.

Legislative/Political Influences An expanding and often bewildering collection of government regulations affects the labor market and organization practices. Consideration of current and pending legislation should be a part of the assessment process because new mandates might impact how the organization operates during the planning horizon.

Legislation regarding taxes, labor unions, compensation, benefits, employment, and safety and health affect the HR practices in all organizations. Many aspects of the employment relationship are regulated, and strategic planning must be done with these restrictions in mind. The social and regulatory priorities of political parties also influence how business operates, with particular programs gaining or losing support. In summary, an organization considers a complex variety of government policies, regulations, and laws during the strategic planning process.

Demographic Changes Significant demographic changes are occurring that will impact the composition of the future workforce. The U.S. Census Bureau projects that by 2042 non-Hispanic whites will no longer comprise the majority of the U.S. population.[21] These population shifts and demographic changes can affect the organizational strategy in several ways. Consumer demographics influence the demand for products and services. For example, as the population ages, demand for medical services and assistive devices will increase. Workforce demographics will also affect the quality and quantity of labor available to the organization.

NASA Launches Workforce Realignment

In 2010 the space shuttle program will be discontinued and thousands of NASA engineers and scientists will be affected. The Constellation program, which will succeed the space shuttle program, will not launch for 5 years. If the skilled shuttle staffers decide to retire rather than wait for the replacement program, NASA will face a serious knowledge gap.

NASA administrators must determine what people and skills will be needed to develop the Constellation program. Employees who do not have the critical skills may be allowed to leave or laid off. However, a congressional ban prohibits massive layoffs at the space agency. Also, a government panel is studying manned spaceflight programs to determine if the shuttle should truly be taken out of service.

All of the uncertainty facing NASA and its employees creates a major challenge of keeping employees engaged and committed. Leaders have been making themselves more visible, holding "all-hands" meetings,

and communicating more frequently. Websites provide news on the transition and help employees to find new jobs. HR staff is working with managers to map the skills for the next program and comparing them to the skills of the current workers. They have found that systems engineering and project management skills are lacking, and they are developing training to fill the skill shortages. Fortunately, training for the transition has not disrupted current operations. The remainder of transition period will be devoted to transferring those skills to the retained employees.

In addition to the tangible transition issues, there are intangible issues such as dealing with fear of the unknown, breaking up of teams that have worked together for years, and grief for the end of a program that many individuals worked on their entire careers. Dealing with the stress and honoring the value of the shuttle program are helping employees to maintain morale and optimism while facing a new frontier.[22]

Among the factors influencing workforce diversity are age, gender, generational differences, race, and ethnicity. Managers assess changes in the workforce composition because the diverse needs and expectations of a heterogenous workforce require creative and flexible solutions. A one-size-fits-all approach to recruitment, compensation, training, and performance management will no longer be effective. The anticipated retirement of baby boomers in the near future will leave many organizations without sufficient skilled talent. NASA faces a serious workforce issue, and the HR Best Practices box describes their strategy for dealing with it.

LOGGING ON

Society for Human Resource Management
The Society for Human Resource Management is the largest association devoted to Human Resource Management. Some of the most essential and comprehensive resources available for Human Resource professionals are contained within the SHRM website at www.shrm.org.

Geographic and Competitive Concerns The local industrial base and economic conditions affect the strategic planning process. Where an organization locates its operations plays a role in how well it will perform. Being located in an industry hub (like Silicon Valley for IT firms) provides the infrastructure and supply base the organization needs to succeed. The local industry is centered on the particular industry, and resources, including skilled talent, are more readily available. If operations are located in a sparsely populated area, the organization will face staffing challenges if the strategy involves substantial growth. An understanding of geographic advantages and disadvantages can help managers develop appropriate plans.

Competitors exist in both the product and labor markets. Competition in the product market determines the potential for the organization. If the organization is in a highly competitive industry (such as consumer electronics), strategies for growth rely heavily on innovation and driving down product costs. Competition in the labor market establishes the pricing for high-quality talent and determines the availability of workers. A detailed competitive analysis in both product and labor markets provides important information to managers regarding the possibility of meeting strategic objectives.

GLOBAL COMPETITIVENESS AND STRATEGIC HR

GLOBAL

The globalization of business has meant that more organizations now operate across borders with ties to foreign operations, international suppliers, vendors, employees, and other business partners. A global presence can range from importing and exporting to operating as a **multinational corporation (MNC)**. An MNC, sometimes called a "transnational corporation," is a corporation that has facilities and other assets in at least one country other than its home country. Because human resources are considered assets, the definition of MNC covers a large number of companies.

Global Framework

Mastering the global complexities of managing human resources is important not only for HR results, but also for the overall success of the organization. Companies operating globally must deliver basic HR services while also overcoming various operational, cultural, and organizational obstacles.[23] Even organizations that operate primarily in the domestic market face pressure from foreign competitors. The supply chain is increasingly internationally dispersed, and foreign business practices influence operations in the United States. Technology advances have eliminated many barriers to operating on a global scale. In addition, workers from numerous countries may seek employment in the United States, and managers and HR professionals must be prepared to deal with the needs of this labor force.[24]

Having a global HR mind-set means looking at HR issues from an international perspective, using ideas and resources throughout the world, and ensuring openness to other cultures and ideas. To effectively compete on an international scale, the organization needs expertise to administer all HR activities in a wide range of nations. Policies and practices should be established to address the unique demands for operating in a global context. Managers determine which policies should be standardized and which should be tailored for each locale.[25] For example, the organization may decide to standardize talent development and succession planning but permit local managers to establish compensation and labor relations policies. An ideal international approach strikes a balance between home-country and host-country policies that utilizes the best practices within the organization.

The following sections address specific issues that should be considered when formulating international strategies.

Multinational corporation (MNC) A corporation that has facilities and other assets in at least one country other than its home country.

Global Legal and Regulatory Factors

Globally-operating organizations must be aware of widely varying legal and regulatory systems due to politics, economic differences, and other factors. Emerging economies, in particular, pose major challenges to smooth operations and reliable conditions.[26] Having to know about and comply with laws on many HR-related issues is crucial. Therefore, senior executives and HR professional must review each country's legal and regulatory factors, both before and during ongoing operations. Also they must be trained in how to deal with the nuances of the requirements in each country.

Offshoring

Competitive pressure to lower costs has resulted in many jobs being moved overseas in recent years. **Offshoring** is the relocation by a company of a business process or operation from one country to another. Firms offshore the production of goods as well as the delivery of services to lower-wage countries. Call centers in India are an example of business service offshoring to countries with well-educated, English-speaking workers. Product and software development projects are increasingly being offshored due to the loss of science and engineering talent in the United States. Predictions are that offshoring will increase in the future, and few firms have plans to return offshored jobs to the home country.[27]

Decisions to offshore operations are made as part of a broader strategic assessment. Economic conditions in both the domestic and global marketplace, the loss of intellectual talent and institutional knowledge, and the potential for lower quality are all issues that managers face. To maximize the success of offshoring, organizations should utilize the following approaches:[28]

- Design work processes to allow workers to hand off the project from one to the next.
- Open the channels of communication by investing in technologies to support real-time interaction.
- Build common ground by sharing knowledge across locations.

Global Staffing

Staffing for global operations includes a wide variety of alternatives. The optimal solution is to combine the expertise of local employees with the organization-specific knowledge of employees from the home country (headquarters). Some countries require that the organization employ a certain percentage of workers from the host country. Figure 2-6 shows four strategic approaches to international staffing. Each organization will use a staffing model that best fits its culture and strategic goals.

An expatriate is an employee living and working in a different country from where he or she is a citizen. Moving an employee to an overseas assignment for an extended period requires careful selection, training, and planning to make the experience a success.[29] The return of an expatriate (called repatriation) must be well planned and executed for the organization to gain the benefits of the overseas assignment.

Leadership development is especially important for MNCs. It is becoming more important for individuals in top management positions to have international experience so that they understand the worldwide marketplace. Effective selection and development processes are needed to ensure that the right individuals are chosen for these roles. Leading across cultures requires specific skills, and organizations should provide formal training along with expatriate assignments to develop leaders who can achieve results in this demanding environment.[30]

Offshoring The relocation by a company of a business process or operation from one country to another.

| FIGURE 2-6 | Strategic Approaches to International Staffing |

Ethnocentric Policy
- *Managers from headquaters staff key positions*
- Ensures control over subsidiary location operations
- Eases transfer of policies from headquarters to subsidiary

Polycentric Policy
- *Host-country nationals staff key positions*
- Reduces cultural mishaps and misunderstanding
- Coordination with headquarters may be problematic

Geocentric Policy
- *An international cadre of skilled managers are assigned to global subsidiaries regardless of nationality*
- Leverages technical and managerial expertise

Regiocentric Policy
- *Key positions are filled by individuals in the region of the subsidary (i.e., European Union countries)*
- Capitalizes on cultural and language similiarities within the region

HR PLANNING IN MERGERS AND ACQUISITIONS

The overall purpose of a merger or acquisition is to generate shareholder value by creating a more competitive, cost-efficient company by combining two existing companies. Strategic HRM can contribute to the success of mergers and acquisitions (M&As). Research has clearly shown that the majority of M&As fail to deliver on the expected financial, marketing, or product gains, with only about one-third of companies reporting that they achieved their goals.[31] A significant number of failed ventures can trace their roots to HR issues that were not properly addressed such as loss of key staff, culture clashes, and poor communication. To maximize the chances of a successful integration, HR should be involved before, during, and after the deal is completed. Figure 2-7 shows the HR activities and focus during each stage of the merger process.

Before the Deal

To determine whether or not the two organizations should combine, a rigorous process of due diligence is conducted. **Due diligence** is a comprehensive assessment of all aspects of the business being acquired. Financial, sales and marketing, operations, and human resource staffs are all involved before the final decision is made to merge or acquire the company. Each function determines the assets and liabilities of the target company to ascertain whether there are serious risks to the buyer. HR professionals review issues related to legal compliance, compensation and benefits programs, quality of talent, and labor contract obligations. Early identification of potential problems such as underfunded

Due diligence A comprehensive assessment of all aspects of the business being acquired.

| FIGURE 2-7 | HR Activities during M&A |

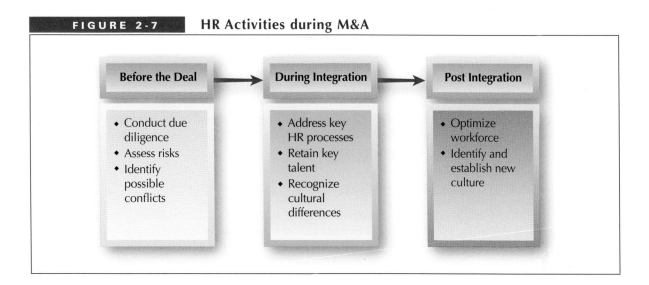

Before the Deal	During Integration	Post Integration
• Conduct due diligence • Assess risks • Identify possible conflicts	• Address key HR processes • Retain key talent • Recognize cultural differences	• Optimize workforce • Identify and establish new culture

pension liabilities or incompatible labor agreements helps management plan for an orderly transition. Due diligence is even more complex when the M&A involves companies in different countries. A thorough, objective analysis of the HR-related issues is critical to make good business decisions.[32]

During Integration

After the deal has been closed, the focus of HR activity switches to the orderly transition of basic HR processes such as payroll and benefits migration. During the first 60 days after the acquisition, HR must deliver high-quality administrative and operational support to employees and managers. The immediate concerns are often about basic services needed to run the operations. Frequent communication, employee hotlines, and guidance for managers all contribute to employee retention and loyalty during the chaotic early days of the transition. Early in the transition, managers focus on identifying key talent and establishing initiatives to retain these critical employees. Retention bonuses, special assignments, and enhanced severance can be used to keep key talent in place during the integration stage.[33]

Integrating HR information systems is important to provide managers with information about employee capabilities, performance, and potential. The acquiring organization cannot make optimum human resource assessments without access to historical information on all employees. An inventory of knowledge, skills, and expertise along with performance information provide the data for making suitable assignments for employees from both organizations. Gathering all relevant HR information in a single database helps managers to analyze and compare employee skills and to make informed decisions about which employees should be retained.

As the businesses are merged, culture conflicts will emerge. For example, when HP and Compaq merged in 2001, cultural differences were recognized and addressed. HP had a culture that fostered innovation by giving employees autonomy and opportunities for professional development. Compaq, on the other hand, was a fast-paced company that made decisions quickly. The merger has been successful because of the blending of the best parts of the culture in each company.[34] Changing the organizational culture depends upon changing behavior in the organization. Four important factors in changing culture are:[35]

- *Define the desired behaviors:* Provide behavioral examples of how people are expected to act and tie these behaviors to the performance management system.
- *Deploy role models:* Select leaders that exemplify the desired behaviors and make them visible throughout the organization.
- *Provide meaningful incentives:* Reward the role models with recognition to reinforce their behavior and to signal the rest of the organization.
- *Provide clear and consistent messages:* Align what you say with what you do and reward.

Post Integration

To realize the expected benefits of a merger, the months following the initial integration are critical. Culture changes started in the early days must be maintained. Practical issues regarding talent management and development along with combining compensation systems will solidify the new, united organization. Failure to effectively blend the workforces and move beyond the "us-and-them" mentality can lead to inferior business results, a loss of shareholder value, and the failure of the merger. Continued change efforts are needed to bring all employees to the "one organization" mentality. Breaking down the barriers between the previous practices at each organization and implementing the best from both organizations will give employees a sense of value and importance. Ultimately, the outcomes of the deal result from how HR issues are addressed.[36] The HR Perspective details the strategies that Dow uses to ensure that acquisitions deliver as promised.

Dow's Formula for Successful Acquisitions

HR *perspective*

Dow is a diversified chemical company with $49 billion in annual revenues and 43,000 employees worldwide. Since its founding in 1897, much of the company growth has come through mergers and acquisitions. Because Dow's acquisition activities are central to its organizational growth strategy, top leaders formulated an approach to ensure success. Although significant emphasis was placed on pre-deal activities, little was done to ensure the post-deal success. Various employees in operating units might work on the acquisition as a temporary assignment, but would return to their regular jobs after the deal was done. The implementation of the M&A Technology Center provided a systematic approach to handle the complicated process of acquiring and integrating new companies into the Dow corporate structure.

The M&A Technology Center is staffed with a full-time group of experts in the M&A process. Members of the Center document the processes used, gather data to assess results, capture and share "lessons learned," and create templates and tools for future use. The Center oversees all acquisition activity at Dow by drawing on the experience and skills of its staff. Due to the success of the Center, Dow leaders took the idea one step further and instituted the HR Center for Mergers and Acquisitions to address the unique HR tasks associated with integrating acquired companies. Staffed with seasoned professionals who can assess and make recommendations on issues related to labor relations, compensation and benefits, training, change management, and other HR disciplines, the HR Center is involved from the very beginning of each potential acquisition through final integration.

The HR Center surveys Dow business leaders each year to assess the effectiveness of the process. Results have been very positive and indicate that HR has added high value to the M&A process at Dow.[37]

STRATEGIC CHALLENGES

Because the objective of strategic planning is to anticipate future events and conditions, managers should evaluate and revise the plan on a periodic basis. Some have called into question the value of strategic planning in light of the economic volatility in the recent past.[38] However, organizations would fare much worse with no plan in place. Recent events highlight the impact of environmental forces on organizations and emphasize the need to remain watchful and attentive to changing conditions.

Attracting and retaining the right talent is an ongoing challenge as the needs of the business change over time. The United States has continued to move from a manufacturing economy to a service economy. This shifting economic base leads to structural mismatches between workers and jobs. Workers with outdated skills are unable to fill the technical and health service jobs employers need. Ongoing retraining can help overcome these problems if strategic planning has identified them.[39] Organizations need to plan for both the quantity and quality of the workforce over the planning horizon. Having sufficient workers with the right qualifications is essential to achieve the strategic plan. If the firm employs too many people for its needs, a talent surplus exists; if too few, a talent shortage. Because of the rapidly changing conditions, the organization may face a surplus in some parts of the business while facing a shortage in others. Figure 2-8 shows the tactics organizations might use to deal with talent supply imbalances.

FIGURE 2-8   **Managing Talent Supply Imbalances**

MANAGING A TALENT SURPLUS	MANAGING A TALENT SHORTAGE
Reduce employee work hours or compensation	Increase employee work hours through overtime
Attrition	Outsource to a third party
Freeze hiring	Implement alternative work arrangements
Voluntary separation programs	Use contingent workers (temporaries, independent contractors)
Downsizing/reduction in force (RIF)	Reduce employee turnover

Managing a Talent Surplus

A talent surplus can be managed within a strategic HR plan in a number of ways. The reasons for the surplus will guide the ultimate steps taken by the organization. If the workforce has the right qualifications but the sales revenue has fallen, the primary strategies would involve retaining workers while cutting costs. However, if the workforce is not appropriately trained for the jobs needed, the organization may lay off those employees who cannot perform the work. Managers may use various strategies in a progressive fashion to defer workforce reductions until absolutely necessary.[40]

Reduction in Work Hours or Compensation In order to retain qualified employees, managers may institute reduced work hours on a temporary basis. Selected groups of employees may have their workweek reduced or all employees can be asked to take a day or week off without pay. For example, Zurn Plumbing Service, a small family-owned company, asked its 15 full-time workers to take a day off without pay each week in order to keep all of them on the payroll and avoid layoffs.[41] When the economy improves, these skilled employees will be available to handle the increased workload.

Across-the-board pay cuts can reduce labor costs while retaining skilled employees. It is important that pay cuts start at the very top of the organization so that employees do not bear all of the hardship. Uniform pay cuts can be felt as a shared sacrifice for the survival of the firm. Organizations may also reduce employee benefits, such as eliminating matching 401K contributions or raising employee health insurance premiums. HR should closely monitor the situation and reinstate pay and benefits levels when the economic outlook improves to maintain employee loyalty and a sense of fairness.

Attrition and Hiring Freezes Attrition occurs when individuals quit, die, or retire and are not replaced. By use of attrition, no one is cut out of a job, but those who remain must handle the same workload with fewer people. Unless turnover is high, attrition will eliminate only a relatively small number of employees in the short run, but it can be a viable alternative over a longer period of time. Therefore, employers may combine attrition with a freeze on hiring. Employees usually understand this approach better than they do other downsizing methods.

Voluntary Separation Programs Organizations can reduce the workforce while also minimizing legal risks if employees volunteer to leave. Often firms entice employees to volunteer by offering them additional severance, training, and benefits payments. Early retirement buyouts are widely used to encourage more senior workers to leave organizations early. As an incentive, employers may offer expanded health coverage and additional buyout payments to employees so that they will not be penalized economically until their pensions and Social Security benefits take effect. These programs are viewed as a way to accomplish workforce reductions without resorting to layoffs.

Voluntary separation programs appeal to employers because they can reduce payroll costs significantly over time. Although the organization faces some up-front costs, it does not incur as many continuing payroll costs. Using such programs is also viewed as a more humane way to reduce staff than terminating long-service, loyal employees. In addition, as long as buyouts are truly voluntary, the organization offering them is less exposed to age discrimination suits. One drawback is that some employees the company would like to retain might take advantage of a buyout.

Workforce Downsizing It has been given many names, including downsizing, rightsizing, and reduction in force (RIF), but it almost always means cutting employees.[42] Layoffs on a broad scale have occurred with frightening regularity in recent years. Trimming underperforming units or employees as part of a plan that is based on sound organizational strategies may make sense. After a decade of many examples and studies, it is clear that downsizing has worked for some firms. However, it does not increase revenues; it is a short-term cost-cutting measure that can result in a long-term lack of talent. When companies cannibalize the human resources needed to change, restructure, or innovate, disruption follows for some time. Also, downsizing can hurt productivity by leaving "surviving" employees overburdened and demoralized.

Best practices for companies carrying out layoffs include:[43]

- Identify the work that is core to sustaining a profitable business.
- Identify the knowledge, skills, and competencies needed to execute the business strategy.
- Protect the bottom line and the corporate brand.
- Constantly communicate with employees.
- Pay attention to the survivors.

A common myth is that those who are still around after downsizing are so grateful to have a job that they pose no problems to the organization. However, some observers draw an analogy between those who survive downsizing and those who survive wartime battles. Bitterness, anger, disbelief, and shock all are common reactions. For those who survive workforce cuts, the culture and image of the firm as a "lifetime" employer often are gone forever.[44]

Severance benefits and outplacement services may be offered by companies to cushion the shock of layoffs and protect the company from litigation. **Severance benefits** are temporary payments made to laid-off employees to ease the financial burden of unemployment. One common strategy is to offer laid-off employees severance benefits that require employees to release the organization from legal claims. Severance benefits are typically based upon length of service with the company, often one or two weeks' pay per year of service. Outplacement services are provided to give displaced employees support and assistance. Outplacement typically includes personal career counseling, résumé preparation services, interviewing workshops, and referral assistance. Such services are generally provided by outside firms that specialize in outplacement assistance and whose fees usually are paid by the employer. Assisting laid-off workers with gaining new employment can help to alleviate the financial burden on employees and preserve the company image.[45]

Legal Considerations for Workforce Reductions

HR must be involved during workforce adjustments to ensure that the organization does not violate any of the nondiscrimination or other laws governing workforce reductions. Selection criteria for determining which employees will be laid off must comply with Title VII of the Civil Rights Act as well as the Age Discrimination in Employment Act and the Americans with

Severance benefits
Temporary payments made to laid-off employees to ease the financial burden of unemployment.

Disabilities Act. A careful analysis and disparate impact review should be conducted before final decisions are made.[46]

There is no legal requirement to provide severance benefits, and loss of medical benefits is a major problem for laid-off employees. However, under the federal Consolidated Omnibus Budget Reconciliation Act (COBRA), displaced workers can retain their group medical coverage for up to 18 months for themselves, and for up to 36 months for their dependents, if they pay the premiums themselves. Federal stimulus programs in 2009 included enhanced COBRA coverage for displaced workers.

Employers must also comply with the Older Workers Benefit Protection Act (OWBPA) when implementing RIFs. The OWBPA requires employers to disclose the ages of both terminated and retained employees in layoff situations, and a waiver of rights to sue for age discrimination must meet certain requirements. The worker must be given something of value ("consideration") in exchange for the waiver of right to sue, typically severance benefits. When laying off a group of employees, workers over age 40 who are being laid off must be granted 45 days in which to consider accepting severance benefits and waiving their right to sue.

To provide employees with adequate notice of plant closings or mass layoffs, a federal law was passed, the Worker Adjustment and Retraining Notification (WARN) Act. This law requires private or commercial organizations that employ 100 or more full-time workers who have worked more than 6 months in the previous year to give a 60-day notice before implementing a layoff or facility closing that involves more than 50 people. However, workers who have been employed less than 6 months in the prior year, as well as part-time staff members working fewer than 20 hours per week, are not counted toward the total of 50 employees. Despite not being formally counted to determine implementation of the law, these individuals should still be given some form of notice.[47] The WARN Act imposes heavy fines on employers who do not follow the required process and give proper notice.

Managing a Talent Shortage

Managing a shortage of employees seems simple enough—simply hire more people. However, as mentioned earlier, there can be mismatches between the qualifications needed by employers and the skills possessed by workers. Manpower's list of the 10 hardest jobs to fill in the United States includes engineers, nurses, teachers, IT staff, and skilled trades.[48] For these jobs, there may not always be sufficient qualified workers to hire. Companies can use a number of alternative tactics to manage a talent shortage:

- Use overtime
- Outsource work
- Implement alternate work arrangements
- Bring back recent retirees
- Use contingent workers
- Reduce turnover

The existing workers can work overtime to produce goods or services. This strategy can work on a short-term basis but is not a solution for a longer-term talent shortage. Workers may appreciate the extra hours and pay for awhile, but eventually fatigue sets in and productivity and quality may drop and injuries and absenteeism may increase. Reducing turnover of qualified employees should be an ongoing effort to maintain a talented workforce.

Special attention may be required in times of talent shortages to hold on to skilled employees.

Alternate work arrangements, nontraditional schedules that provide flexibility to employees, include job sharing and telecommuting. These are creative solutions to attract and retain skilled employees who want flexibility. Employees are given more freedom in determining when and how they will perform their jobs. These arrangements are not costly to the organization but do require management support and planning to be effective.[49] Retirees may be rehired on a part-time or temporary basis to fill talent gaps. The advantage is that these individuals are already trained and can be productive immediately. Care must be taken not to interfere with pension payments or other benefits tied to retirement.

The use of contingent employees, which are noncore employees who work at an organization on a temporary or as-needed basis, can provide short-term help. Professional employer organizations can lease employees to the firm, which is often a good solution for technical talent. Independent contractors can be hired on an as-needed basis to fill talent shortages. The use of independent contractors must be managed closely to ensure compliance with wage and hour, safety, and employee benefit statutes. When using contingent workers, special efforts are needed to assimilate them into the workforce and avoid an "us-and-them" mentality. Contingent workers fill an important need and managers can maximize their contributions through good employee relations practices.

Outsourcing involves transferring the management and/or routine performance of a business function to an external service provider. Organizations in the United States outsource a wide variety of noncore functions in order to reduce costs or to obtain skills and expertise not available in the organization. A common HR function that is outsourced is payroll. The organization pays an outside firm to administer its payroll and does not incur the fixed cost of a payroll department. Highly skilled and complex tasks may be outsourced to a firm with greater know-how and economies of scale.[50] Planning and executing outsourced tasks should include HR to ensure legal compliance and appropriate employee integration.

LOGGING ON

U.S. Department of Labor, Bureau of Labor Statistics
This website contains data on workforce composition and trends from the U.S. Department of Labor, Bureau of Labor Statistics. Visit the site at www.stats .bls.gov.

TECHNOLOGY CHALLENGES

Technological advances have a major impact on organizations. New methods for communicating, processing information, and manufacturing have led to economic development around the globe. Evolving technologies using math, science, and the arts can improve life and living conditions. However, the improvements created by technology often mean that people and organizations must change in order to fully benefit from these advances. Evolutions in technology will continue to present exciting, but difficult challenges to managers.

Effects on Work and Organizations

Jobs have undergone major changes as a result of technology advances. In many cases, monotonous, repetitive operations have evolved into complex knowledge work that requires a new skill set. Work that previously was

Alternate work arrangements Nontraditional schedules that provide flexibility to employees.

Outsourcing Transferring the management and performance of a business function to an external service provider.

done by hand has been replaced by robotics and automation. Tool and die makers, once prized for their intricate, precision hand work, are now utilizing computer-aided design (CAD) and computer numerically controlled (CNC) software to complete their tasks. Rather than having workers standing on the assembly line alone performing small specialized tasks, today's workplaces utilize teams of workers collaborating and sharing a wide variety of tasks. The skills needed in this work setting are very different from those of the past; communication, collaboration, technical ability, and adaptability are necessary for success in the future.[51]

The introduction of computers made redundant not only typewriters but also the job of secretary and the lengthy process of creating, editing, and producing written correspondence. Digital imaging has changed the way medical diagnostic tests are taken, read, and stored. A radiologist working remotely can interpret images, and patients can be treated faster than ever before.[52] Continuous improvement is an essential strategy for all organizations in the production of goods or the delivery of services. Customer demands for new product features, customized services, higher quality, and greater value mean that employees must continually acquire knowledge and skills in a dynamic environment.

Continuous improvement in an organization typically involves ongoing efforts to develop and implement better methods. Recall the HR Headline and Lee Memorial Health System's use of continuous improvement processes to enhance patient flow and reduce costs. Technology is enabling organizations to improve work flow and process. Business process reengineering (BPR) is a fundamental rethinking and radical redesign of business processes to achieve dramatic improvements in cost, quality, speed, and service.[53]

Scheduling work, tracking time and attendance, and monitoring employee productivity are all easier with the aid of technology. Workforce management software systems create and balance workloads that can save organizations significant labor costs by matching staffing levels to peak and nonpeak service demands. This can lead to employee discontent because of the inconvenience of shortened workdays or nontraditional schedules for employees. Daycare arrangements may be disrupted, and employees may compete for prime work schedules. HR and operations staff must work cooperatively to ensure that steps taken to improve efficiency do not create employee relations issues.[54]

Effects on Communication

Technology has increased employee expectations regarding the speed and frequency of communication from managers. Employees are no longer content to wait for the monthly company newsletter or find out the latest news through formal channels. Company intranet portals can be a prime source of information for employees and should be used to inform employees about important events within the organization and the industry. The HR Perspective discusses how Verizon Wireless uses its HR portal to enhance employee communication.

Facebook, LinkedIn, and other social networking sites allow employees to remain in constant contact with people inside and outside of the organization. Instant messages and cell-phone texting allow for real-time communication. The line between employees' personal and professional lives becomes blurred as these virtual communities are frequently accessed from the worksite. Potential litigation and damage to the organizational reputation and brand pose risks to the organization if access and content are not properly monitored.[55]

Verizon Engages Employees via Web Portal

Employee engagement, that is, employees' involvement with, commitment to, and satisfaction with work, has been tied to retention, productivity, profits, and sustainability. Engaged workers are willing to perform at levels beyond their stated job requirements, are more customer-focused, and produce higher-quality and long-term financial results for the organization. Therefore, organizations seeking to maximize employee engagement must identify specific actions that can lead to engagement.

An integral component in driving employee engagement is effective communication. Particularly in harsh economic times, employees need to understand the challenges faced by the organization so that they can accept changes in compensation, work hours, and performance expectations. Messages must be honest, direct, and consistently address critical employee concerns. The range of communications channels provides multiple avenues for connecting with employees and providing vital information that will foster engagement.

Verizon Wireless, widely known for its engaged workforce, has embraced the HR portal as a main vehicle for communicating with its employees. The company developed an online HR portal called "About You." Accessible through the intranet, About You allows employees to make crucial connections between their daily work performance and their Total Rewards package. Real-time details about short-term incentive payouts, wellness initiatives, development programs, and other resources are available at their fingertips. The HR portal is tied to Verizon's HRIS which delivers personalized employee information on demand. Self-service tools like "To Do" lists that outline key tasks, approving expense reports, and tracking time and attendance simplify the employee's life and cement connections between the employee and the company. The user interface mimics the online experience outside the workplace for a seamless, familiar feel.

Verizon's high level of employee engagement results from utilizing technology to deliver its employee-centered, honest communication messages.[56]

The explosive growth of Twitter in a relatively short period of time shows how quickly new communication channels emerge. Organizations must continually monitor and adapt to these new communication technologies to connect with customers and employees.

Effects on Work Processes

Monitoring employee actions and performance is much easier and less expensive due to technological advances. Transponders in semitrailer trucks can record speed, mileage, and other operating data to evaluate driver performance. Video surveillance to reduce employee misconduct such as theft or cheating, or to track productivity is simple to implement. Computer use is routinely monitored, and the Society for Human Resource Management (SHRM) found that more than one-third of organizations have either disciplined or terminated employees for improper use of company computers or Internet access.[57]

The majority of organizations have e-mail use policies in place and monitor employee e-mail use. In general, the courts have supported employer monitoring, and there are few legal restrictions on employer action. Organizations typically address two issues—managing employee performance and creating a positive work environment. Concerns about productivity and employee

FIGURE 2-9   **Factors Involved in Proper Monitoring of Employee E-Mail**

REASONS TO MONITOR	POTENTIAL PROBLEMS
The organization is legally responsible for its employees' conduct and must limit exposure to liability (sexual harassment, etc.)	Poorly implemented or excessive monitoring can reduce trust and openness
Protect intellectual property and ensure that proprietary information is not disclosed to outside parties	Employer should not monitor employees' external e-mail accounts, only those hosted by the organization
Ensure that employees are productive and using computer and Internet access to perform their jobs	The blurring of personal and professional time leads to employees working on "their" time, and they expect to have some personal time during the workday
U.S. laws may require monitoring for financial reporting and compliance with Sarbanes-Oxley	Legal standards vary around the world, and global companies must comply with numerous requirements

performance must be balanced with concerns for privacy and positive employee relations. Monitoring can lead to a lack of trust and may discourage creativity and the free exchange of ideas between employees. Figure 2-9 shows some of the important factors involved in proper monitoring of employee e-mail.[58]

Effects on HR Activities

Electronic human resource management systems (e-HRM) is the planning, implementation, and application of information technology to perform HR activities. Sometimes called virtual HRM or business-to-employee (B2E) systems, using technology to support HR activities increases the efficiency of the administrative HR function and reduces costs. Managers benefit from the availability of relevant information about employees. Properly designed e-HRM systems provide historical information on performance, pay, training, career progress, and disciplinary actions. Organizations can make better HR-related decisions as a result. To maximize the value of technology, e-HRM systems should be integrated into the overall IT plan and enterprise software of the organization.[59]

Electronic human resource management systems (e-HRM) The planning, implementation, and application of information technology to perform HR activities.

Technology can be used to support every function within human resource management. Recruiting and selection processes have changed dramatically with Web-based job boards, online applications, and even online interviewing. Training is now conducted with the aid of videos, podcasts, Web-enabled training programs, and virtual classrooms. Employee self-service has simplified benefit enrollment and administration by allowing employees to find health care providers and file claims online. Succession planning and career development are enhanced with real-time information on all employees and their potential career progression. One of the most important ways in which technology can contribute to organizational performance is through the collection and analysis of HR-related data. Identifying trends and modeling future conditions help managers to plan and optimize human resources.

LOGGING ON

Social Media Governance
This is an online database of social media policies from companies, governments, and nonprofit entities. Visit the website at www.socialmediagovernance.com/policies.php.

MEASURING EFFECTIVENESS OF HR INITIATIVES

A long-standing myth perpetuates the notion that one cannot really measure the value of HR practices. That myth has hurt HR's credibility because it suggests that either HR efforts do not add value or they are too far removed from business results to matter. That notion is, of course, untrue. HR, like all other functions, must be evaluated by considering the results of its actions and the value it adds to the organization. Unfortunately, the perceptions of managers and employees in many organizations are mixed because HR has not always measured and documented its contributions or communicated those results to executives, managers, and employees. Further, accounting practices treat expenditures on human capital and talent development as expenses rather than capital investments. This encourages a consumption attitude rather than a long-term investment strategy.[60]

People-related costs are typically the largest controllable expense in organizations. Effective management of these costs can make the difference in the survival of the organization. Collecting and analyzing HR information can pinpoint waste and improper allocation of human resources. It is important that managers understand financial and operational measures that drive the business and relate HR decisions to key performance indicators (KPIs). Metrics, benchmarking, balanced scorecards, and audits can help the organization track HR performance and measure the value of HR practices.[61]

HR Metrics

HR metrics are specific measures tied to HR performance indicators. Metrics are typically used to assess the HR function and results within the organization over time. A metric can be developed using costs, quantity, quality, timeliness, and other designated goals. Metrics can be developed to track both HR's efficiency and effectiveness. A pioneer in developing HR measurements, Jac Fitz-Enz, has identified a wide range of HR metrics. A number of key HR metrics are shown in Figure 2-10.[62]

HR and line managers collect and share the data needed to track performance. Data to track these measures come from several sources within the organization. Financial data are needed to determine costs for various HR activities. Performance and turnover data can be found in HR and operations records. The real value in using metrics is not in the collection and reporting of

HR metrics Specific measures tied to HR performance indicators.

FIGURE 2-10   **Key HR Metrics**

HR Staff and Expenses	Staffing
• HR-to-employee ratio • Total HR staff • HR expenses per FTE	• Number of positions filled • Time to fill • Cost per hire • Annual turnover rate
Compensation	**Training**
• Annual wage and salary increases • Payroll as a percentage of operating expenses • Benefit costs as a percentage of payroll	• Hours of training per employee • Total costs for training • Percentage of employees participating in tuition reimbursement program
Retention and Quality	**Development**
• Average tenure of employees • Percentage of new hires retained for 90 days • Performance quality of employees in first year	• Positions filled internally • Percentage of employees with career plan

the results. It is the analysis and the interpretation of the data that can lead to improvements in human capital utilization.[63] Information and historical data are reviewed and studied to determine the reasons for current performance levels and to learn how to improve in the future. HR can help line managers to understand and interpret the results of these measures and translate these findings into effective steps toward improvement.

Unlike financial reporting, there is no standard for the implementation and reporting of HR measures. Managers choose what and how to report to employees, investors, and other interested parties. This lack of consistency in HR reporting makes it difficult to evaluate an organization and to compare HR practices across organizations.[64] The following characteristics should be considered when developing HR metrics:

- Accurate data can be collected.
- Measures are linked to strategic and operational objectives.
- Calculations can be clearly understood.
- Measures provide information valued by executives.
- Results can be compared both externally and internally.
- Measurement data drive HR management efforts.

HR and Benchmarking

Benchmarking is the process of comparing the business processes and outcomes to an industry standard or best practice. In other words, the organization compares itself to "best-in-class" organizations that demonstrate excellence for a specific process. Benchmarking is focused on external practices that the organization can use to improve its own processes and practices. When implementing benchmarking, managers should be careful to find organizations with similar contexts, cultures, operations, and size. Practices that would work effectively in an organization of 500 employees might not transfer very well to an organization with 5,000 employees. The organization should study and choose benchmarks that will have the greatest impact on the organizational performance.[65]

About half of HR professionals report that their organizations collect benchmark data on a planned, periodic basis while the rest collect it as needed. Major obstacles to collecting benchmarks are uncertainty about how to collect the information and what information to collect.[66] Using benchmarking, HR effectiveness is best determined by comparing ratios and measures from year to year. In that way, the organization can track improvements and results from implementing specific HR practices. While benchmarking helps the organization compare its results to other organizations, it does not provide the cause or reason for the relative standing of the organization. So, it is a starting point, not the end point, for improving the organizational HR function.

HR and the Balanced Scorecard

One effective approach to the measurement of the strategic performance of organizations, including their HR departments, is the balanced scorecard. The **balanced scorecard** is a framework organizations use to report on a diverse set of performance measures. Organizations that use a balanced scorecard recognize that focusing strictly on financial measures can limit their view. The balanced scorecard balances financial and nonfinancial measures so that managers focus on long-term drivers of performance and organizational sustainability. As shown in Figure 2-11, the balanced scorecard measures performance in four areas:

- *Financial measures:* Traditional financial measures such as profit and loss, operating margins, utilization of capital, return on investment, and return on assets are needed to ensure that the organization manages its bottom line effectively.
- *Internal business processes:* Product and service quality, efficiency and productivity, conformance with standards, and cycle times can be measured to ensure that the operation runs smoothly and efficiently.
- *Customer relations:* Customer satisfaction, loyalty, and retention are important to ensure that the organization is meeting customer expectations and can depend on repeat business from its customers.
- *Learning and growth activities:* Employee training and development, mentoring programs, succession planning, and knowledge creation and sharing provide the necessary talent and human capital pool to ensure the future of the organization.

Benchmarking Comparing the business results to industry standards.

Balanced scorecard A framework used to report a diverse set of performance measures.

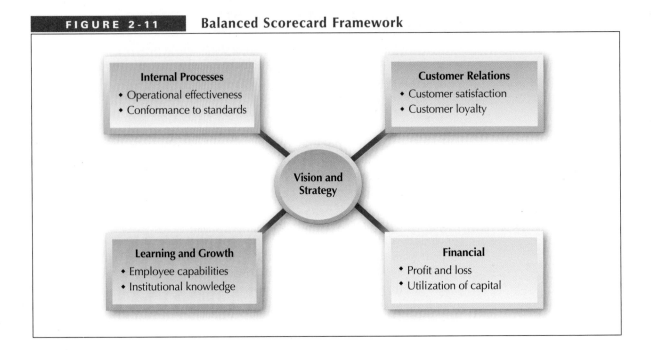

FIGURE 2-11 **Balanced Scorecard Framework**

Organizational results in each of these areas determine if the organization is progressing toward its strategic objectives. For example, some firms have noticed that when survey results show a decline in employee satisfaction, several months later there is a decline in customer loyalty and repeat customer sales. Or expenditures in employee leadership development training can be linked to lower employee turnover and reduced time to hire managers from outside the organization.

More than 60% of organizations claim to use a balanced scorecard approach. Firms as diverse as Blue Cross, Verizon, and the Mayo Clinic have used this approach to align performance measures with their organizational strategy.[67] Using the balanced scorecard requires spending considerable time and effort to identify the appropriate HR measures in each of the four areas and how they tie to strategic organizational success. The balanced scorecard should align with company goals and focus on results. To be effective, the HR scorecard should address three elements—accountability, validity, and actionable results.[68] However, regardless of the time and effort spent trying to develop and use objective measures in the balanced scorecard, subjectivity in what is selected and how the measures are interpreted can still occur.

Human Capital Effectiveness Measures

To fulfill its role as a strategic business partner, HR must quantify things that traditional accounting does not account for. Human resources often provide for both the biggest value and the biggest cost to organizations. Many of the metrics previously discussed reflect people-related costs. Measuring the value is more challenging but equally important.[69] Assessing the value of human resources demonstrates the importance of implementing effective HR practices to maintain a high-quality, engaged workforce.

Human capital refers to the collective value of the intellectual capital (competencies, knowledge, and skills) of the employees in the organization. This capital is the constantly renewable source of creativity and innovativeness in the organization but is not reflected in its financial statements.

Revenue per employee is a basic measure of human capital effectiveness. The formula is Revenue/Head Count (full-time employee equivalents). It is a measure of employee productivity and shows the sales revenue generated by each full-time employee. This measure is commonly used in government reporting (see Bureau of Labor Statistics, BLS) as well as by organizations to track productivity over time. If revenues increase but employee head count remains constant, productivity would increase.

A widely used financial measure that can be applied to measure the contribution and cost of HR activities is **return on investment (ROI)**, which is a calculation showing the value of investments in human resources. It can also be used to show how long it will take for the activities to pay for themselves. The following formula can be used to calculate the potential ROI for a new HR activity:

$$ROI = \frac{C}{A + B}$$

where:

A = Operating costs for a new or enhanced system for the time period
B = One-time cost of acquisition and implementation
C = Value of gains from productivity improvements for the time period

ROI is stressed because it is used in most other functions in an organization and is the "language" used by financial staff and top management. It allows managers to choose among various investment opportunities to determine the best use of funds.

Human capital value added (HCVA) is an adjusted operating profitability figure calculated by subtracting all operating expenses *except* for labor expenses from revenue and dividing by the total full-time head count. It shows the operating profit per full-time employee. Because labor is required to generate revenues, employment costs are added back into operating expense. The formula for HCVA is:

Return on investment (ROI) Calculation showing the value of an investment.

$$\frac{\text{Revenue} - (\text{Operating Expense} - (\text{Compensation} + \text{Benefit Costs}))}{\text{Full-Time Head Count}}$$

Human capital value added (HCVA) Calculated by subtracting all operating expenses *except* for labor expenses from revenue and dividing by the total full-time head count.

Human capital return on investment (HCROI) directly shows the amount of profit derived from investments in labor, the leverage on labor cost. The formula for HCROI uses the same adjusted operating profitability figure as for HCVA, but it is divided by the human capital cost:

$$\frac{\text{Revenue} - (\text{Operating Expense} - (\text{Compensation} + \text{Benefit Costs}))}{(\text{Compensation} + \text{Benefits Costs})}$$

Human capital return on investment (HCROI) Directly shows the operating profit derived from investments in human capital.

Human economic value added (HEVA) shows the wealth created per employee. It shows how much more valuable the organization has become due to the investment in human capital. Wealth is the net operating profit of a firm after the cost of capital is deducted. Cost of capital is the minimum rate of return demanded by shareholders. When a company is making more than the cost of capital, it is creating wealth for shareholders. An HEVA approach requires that all policies, procedures, measures, and methods use cost of

Human economic value added (HEVA) Wealth created per employee.

capital as a benchmark against which their return is judged. Human resource decisions can be subjected to the same analysis. The formula for HEVA is:

$$\frac{\text{Net Profit after Taxes} - \text{Cost of Capital}}{\text{Full-Time Head Count}}$$

Many financial measures can be tracked and reported to show the contribution human resources make to organizational results. Without such measures, it would be difficult to know what is going on in the organization, identify performance gaps, and provide feedback. Managers should require the same level of rigor in measuring HR practices as they do for other functions in the organization.[70]

Regardless of the time and effort placed on HR measurement and HR metrics, the most important consideration is that HR effectiveness and efficiency must be measured regularly for managers to know how HR is contributing to organizational success.

HR Audit

One general means for assessing HR is through an HR audit, which is similar to a financial audit. An **HR audit** is a formal research effort to assess the current state of HR practices in an organization. This audit is used to evaluate how well activities in each of the HR areas (staffing, compensation, health and safety, etc.) have been performed, so that management can identify areas for improvement. An HR audit often helps smaller organizations without a formal HR professional to identify issues associated with legal compliance, administrative processes and recordkeeping, employee retention, and other areas.

HR audit A formal research effort to assess the current state of HR practices.

SUMMARY

- The strategy an organization follows is its proposition for how to compete successfully and thereby survive and grow.
- HR should be involved in the development and implementation of strategic decisions throughout the organization.
- Strategic planning is a core business process that results in a road map of organizational direction.
- Strategic HR management (HRM) refers to the use of HRM practices to gain or keep a competitive advantage by aligning individual employee performance with the organizational strategic objectives.
- Environmental scanning helps to pinpoint strengths, weaknesses, opportunities, and threats that the organization will face during the planning horizon.

- During an external environmental scan, HR managers identify the effects of economic conditions, legislative/political influences, demographic changes, and geographic and competitive issues.
- Mastering the global complexities of managing human resources is important for both HR results and the overall success of the organization.
- HR plays a crucial role in mergers and acquisitions, particularly in dealing with integration and organizational culture issues.
- Managing a talent surplus may require reducing work hours, downsizing through use of attrition and hiring freezes, voluntary separation programs, and workforce downsizing.
- Managing a talent shortage may be addressed through overtime, reducing turnover, using contingent workers, and outsourcing.

- Advances in technology have affected job design, communication, work processes, and HR activities.
- HR effectiveness must be measured using HR metrics that consider both strategic and operational effectiveness.
- Benchmarking allows an organization to compare its practices against "best practices" in different organizations, and HR audits can be used to get a comprehensive overview of HR activities.
- The balanced scorecard can be a useful framework to measure and report on diverse organizational performance measures.

CRITICAL THINKING ACTIVITIES

1. Discuss how technology has changed jobs in an organization where you have worked. What are some HR responses to those changes?

2. What steps can HR professionals take to ensure that mergers and acquisitions are successful? How can HR help during the integration process?

3. How can an organization maintain its image while dealing with a talent surplus? If layoffs are necessary, what would you recommend managers do to ensure that survivors remain committed and productive?

4. As the HR manager for a multinational corporation, you want to identify HR competencies that are critical for global companies. Visit the website for the World Federation of People Management Association (www.wfpma.com) to research the topic and to identify differences in the body of knowledge in different parts of the world.

HR EXPERIENTIAL PROBLEM SOLVING

As the HR Director of a U.S.-based company that is looking at global opportunities in China, you have been asked by the company president to prepare an outline for an HR strategic plan as part of the company's expansion process. You need to develop an HR strategic plan that will integrate the goals, objectives, and strategies of the HR Department with those of the company. The plan also needs to support the objectives of other departments within the company. To get ideas on how to develop an HR strategic plan, go to www.workinfo.com.

1. What is the process to use for identifying the components of the HR strategic planning process?

2. What other company strategic objectives must the HR strategic plan integrate and support?

CASE

Pioneers in HR Analytics

The power of HR metrics and analytics is an untapped resource for many organizations. Human resource information systems (HRIS) are commonly used to capture and store gigabytes of data about employees, but few organizations have mined their data to improve human capital decisions. Most business leaders and HR executives do not make people decisions with the same level of rigor and rationale as they do other business decisions, relying more on intuition and gut feelings. This propagates the myth that the impact of human resources on organizations is either not measurable or not significant. Financial, operational, and marketing decisions all depend heavily on detailed analysis and cost justification. The use of analytics in human resource management can enhance the strategic contribution of HR executives and lead to better decisions and organizational outcomes.

At Superior Energy Services in New Orleans, careful analysis of turnover data shattered previous beliefs about which employees were most likely to quit. The organization was losing skilled oilfield operators and supervisors faster than semiskilled blue-collar workers. This discovery led to implementation of training and coaching programs for supervisory employees, which resulted in a 15% drop in turnover and improved the bottom line of the company. Without this analytic approach to turnover, attention would have been focused on retaining blue-collar workers, which would not have delivered such impressive results.

Thrivent Financial for Lutherans in Minneapolis believed that turnover during the first year of new hires' careers was related to the previous experience they had in their disciplines. The thinking was that if a customer service employee had previously worked in customer service, she was less likely to leave Thrivent in the first year. Analytics dispelled that theory and Thrivent found that the exact opposite was true. Employees with previous experience in the discipline were leaving at a faster rate than those without such experience. Although they have not determined the causes, this data will help Thrivent's leaders to address the real issues. One answer will lead to additional questions and lines of inquiry.

The food service and convenience company Wawa, Inc., assumed that turnover among store clerks was tied to their hourly wage rate. However, the number of hours worked in a week was a much more significant factor in turnover. Employees liked working part-time, and when their work hours exceeded 30 hours per week, they were more likely to quit. Wawa reduced in-store turnover by 60% by scheduling employees for less than 30 hours.

Concerns about an aging workforce and a presumption that a high percentage of employees would retire in the near term led the University of Southern California to carefully analyze employee demographic data. To their surprise, HR found that the nontenured staff employees were, on average, too young to begin retiring en masse. Tenured faculty, while much older, are far more likely to work past the age of 70. The anticipated retirements are still a fact for USC to address. However, managers can plan for this and develop a longer-term transition plan because they are not facing massive retirements in the near future.

The HR executives at Superior Energy Services, Thrivent, Wawa, and USC are harnessing the power of HR data and statistical models to better understand the challenges facing their organizations. Long-held beliefs about the patterns of employee actions and decisions can be analyzed and either supported or debunked. Either way, the organization can address the true issues only if HR looks beyond the surface and digs deeper into the sea of data. Overcoming the fear of number-crunching and developing expertise with metrics and analytics can separate winning organizations from those that get left behind. HR professionals who learn to interpret bits and bytes of employee data will help their organizations succeed well into the future.[71]

QUESTIONS

1. What are some reasons that more organizations do not implement HR analytics? How would you make the case for adopting HR analytics?

2. How can HR professionals develop the needed skills to analyze and interpret metrics? What resources could an HR professional consult to begin building expertise in this area?

SUPPLEMENTAL CASES

Where Do You Find the Bodies?

This case identifies problems associated with HR planning and recruiting in a tight labor market. (For the case, go to www.cengage.com/management/mathis.)

Xerox

This case highlights the challenges of employee retention during stressful and unpredictable times when Xerox was undergoing a significant shift in its strategic focus. (For the case, go to www.cengage.com/management/mathis.)

NOTES

1. Julie C. Ramirez, "Survival of the Fittest," *Human Resource Executive*, April 2009, 30–35.
2. ". . . and HR Planning Is Less Formal," *Personnel Today*, February 27, 2007, 1–3; Sumita Ketkar and P. K. Sett, "HR Flexibility and Firm Performance: Analysis of a Multi-Level Causal Model," *International Journal of Human Resource Management*, 20 (2009), 1009–1038.
3. Edward E. Lawler and John W. Boudreau, "What Makes HR a Strategic Partner?" *People & Strategy*, 32 (2009), 14–22.
4. Beth Tootell, Meredith Blackler, et al., "Metrics: HRM's Holy Grail? A New Zealand Case Study," *Human Resource Management Journal*, 19 (2009), 375–392.
5. Erich Brockmann and Clifford Koen, "Strategic Planning: A Guide for Supervisors," *Supervision*, August 2008, 3–9.
6. NetMBA, "The Strategic Planning Process," www.netmba.com.
7. Thomas Chermack and Bernadette Kasshann, "The Use and Misuse of SWOT Analysis and Implications for HRD Professionals," *Human Resource Development International*, 10 (2007), 383–399.
8. Juan Pablo Gonzalez and Garrett Sheridan, "Get Off the Talent Treadmill: Hardwiring Talent Strategy to Business Strategy," *Workspan*, August 2008, 36–40; Milton Perkins, "Aligning Workforce Strategies with Business Objectives" *SHRM.org Research Articles*, December 7, 2009.
9. Bret J. Becton and Mike Schraeder, "Strategic Human Resources Management—Are We There Yet?" *Journal for Quality and Participation*, January 2009, 11–18.
10. Wendy Boswell, "Aligning Employees with the Organization's Strategic Objectives: Out of Line of Sight, Out of Mind," *International Journal of Human Resource Management*, 17 (2006), 1489–1511.
11. David Ulrich, Wayne Brockbank, et al., *HR Competencies: Mastery of the Intersection of People and Business* (Alexandria, VA: SHRM, 2008).
12. Steve Williams, "A Working Model of Strategic Human Resource Management," 2009, Unpublished manuscript, Alliant International University, San Diego, CA.
13. James Combs, Yongmei Liu, et al., "How Much Do High Performance Work Practices Matter? A Meta-Analysis of Their Effects on Organizational Performance," *Personnel Psychology*, 59 (2006), 501–528; Jason Shaw, Brian Dineen, et al., "Employee-Organization Exchange Relationships, HRM Practices, and Quit Rates of Good and Poor Performers," *Academy of Management Journal*, 52 (2009), 1016–1033.
14. Patrick Wright and Rebecca Kehoe, "Human Resource Practices and Organizational Commitment: A Deeper Examination," *Cornell University CAHRS Working Paper Series*, December 2007.
15. David McCann, "Memo to CFOs: Don't Trust HR," March 10, 2009, CFO.com.
16. Stephen Baker, "Management by the Numbers," *BusinessWeek*, September 8, 2008, 32–38.
17. "Strategic Management—SWOT Analysis" QuickMBA, 2007, www.quickmba.com.
18. Fay Hansen, "Chief Concern: Leaders," *Workforce Management*, July 20, 2009, 17–20; Robert Barnett and Sandra Davis, "Creating Greater Success in Succession Planning," *Advances in Developing Human Resources*, 10 (2008), 721–739; Kris Jensen, "Making Succession Plans Work for Your Company," *Workspan*, May 2009, 57–62.
19. Fay Hansen, "Strategic Workforce Planning in an Uncertain World," *Workforce Management Online*, July 2009, www.workforce.com.
20. Adrienne Fox, "Avoiding Furlough Fallout," *HRMagazine*, September 2009, 36–40.
21. U.S. Census Bureau, Population Division, "U.S. Population Projections," www.census.gov.
22. Bridget Mintz Testa, "New Orbit," *Workforce Management*, August 17, 2009, 16–20.
23. Tom Starner, "Thinking Globally," *Human Resource Executive*, January 2009, 40–42.
24. Marshall Goldsmith, "Human Resources: The Big Issues," *BusinessWeek*, July 8, 2008.
25. SHRM Global Special Expertise Panel, "Things to Think About in International HR Management," 2006–2007.
26. Damien DeLuca and Han Hu, "Evaluate Workforces in Emerging Economies," *HRMagazine*, September 2008, 65–70.
27. Conference Board, "Offshoring Reaches the C-Suite," *2007–2008 ORN Survey Report*; Stephan Manning, Silvia Massini, and Arie

Lewin, "A Dynamic Perspective on Next-Generation Offshoring: The Global Sourcing of Science and Engineering Talent," *Academy of Management Perspectives,* August 2008, 35–54.

28. Kannan Srikanth and Phanish Puranam, "Advice for Outsourcers: Think Bigger," *The Wall Street Journal,* January 25, 2010, R7.

29. Susan Allerow and Rebecca Rosenzwaig, "Effective International HR Management," *Workspan,* December 2008, 85–92; G. A. Gelade, P. Dobson, and K. Auer, "Individualism, Masculinity, and the Sources of Organizational Commitment," *Journal of Cross-Cultural Psychology,* 39, No. 5 (2008), 599–617.

30. Paula Caligiuri and Ibraiz Tarique, "Predicting Effectiveness in Global Leadership Activities," *Journal of World Business,* 44 (2009), 336–346; David Robinson and Michael Harvey, "Global Leadership in a Culturally Diverse World," *Management Decision,* 46 (2008), 466–480.

31. David Wentworth, "M&A Bounces Back: What Have We Learned?" *Institute for Corporate Productivity (i4cp) TrendWatcher,* No. 478, October 2, 2009; Harry Barkema and Mario Schijven, "Toward Unlocking the Full Potential of Acquisitions: The Role of Organizational Restructuring," *Academy of Management Journal,* 51 (2008), 696–722.

32. Jim Candler, "The Critical HR Role in M&A . . . Made Easier," *Workspan,* August 2008, 43–45; John Nigh and Marco Boschetti, "M&A Due Diligence: The 360-Degree View," *Towers Perrin Emphasis,* 2006.

33. Christopher Kummer, "Motivation and Retention of Key People in Mergers and Acquisitions," *Strategic HR Review,* No. 6, 2008, 5–10.

34. Agata Stachowicz-Stanusch, "Culture Due Diligence Based on HP/Compaq Merger Case Study," *Journal of Intercultural Management,* April 2009, 64–81.

35. Aaron Falcione, "Post-Merger Integration: Dealing with Culture," *Workspan,* September 2007, 75–79.

36. Bob Bundy, "The Culture of Combination: Changing Behaviors and Deal Success in Mergers and Acquisitions," *WorldatWork Journal,* Second Quarter, 2007, 35–47.

37. Randolph Croyle and Ava Johnsey, "Dow's Novel Approach to Managing the Human Element of Mergers and Acquisitions," *Global Business and Organizational Excellence,* May/June 2007, 18–26.

38. Joann Lublin and Dana Mattioli, "Strategic Plans Lose Favor," *The Wall Street Journal,* January 25, 2010, B7.

39. Peter Coy, "Help Wanted," *BusinessWeek,* May 11, 2009, 40–45; Judy Keen, "After Layoffs Many Workers Go Back to School for a Fresh Start," *USAToday,* April 8, 2009, 1A.

40. Edward Lawler, "Reducing Labor Costs: Choosing the Right Cost-Cutting Solution for Your Talent Management Strategy," *Workspan,* June 2009, 20–25.

41. Raymund Flandez, "Small Businesses Work Hard to Prevent Layoffs," *The Wall Street Journal,* March 5, 2009, B5.

42. Deborah Stead, "BTW: 'You're Fired,'" *BusinessWeek,* December 22, 2008, 15–16; Michael O'Brien, "Determining Departures," *Human Resource Executive,* April 2009, 44–45; Geoffrey Love and Matthew Kraatz, "Character, Conformity, or the Bottom Line? How and Why Downsizing Affected Corporate Reputation," *Academy of Management Journal,* 52 (2009), 314–335.

43. Taleo/Human Capital Institute, "Recessionary Management: The Top Dos and DON'Ts for Managing Talent in the Current Downturn," January 2009.

44. Susan Wells, "Layoff Aftermath," *HR Magazine,* November 2008, 37–41.

45. "Hewitt Survey Finds U.S. Employers Still Offering Generous Employee Severance Packages Despite Economic Conditions," March 19, 2009, www.hewittassociates.com.

46. Karyn Model, Elaine Reardon, and Christopher Haan, "Navigating a Reduction in Force: Understanding the Economist's Perspective," *Employee Relations Law Journal,* Winter 2008, 16–26.

47. "The Worker Adjustment and Retraining Notification Act: A Guide to Advance Notice of Closings and Layoffs," U.S. Department of Labor Employment and Training Administration Fact Sheet, www.doleta.gov.

48. Manpower, "2009 Talent Shortage Survey Results," www.manpower.com.

49. Mark Schoeff, "Study: Flexibility Programs Gain Ground in Hard Times," *Workforce Management,* July 23, 2009.

50. Sandra Fisher, Michael Wasserman, et al., "Human Resource Issues in Outsourcing: Integrating Research and Practice," *Human Resource Management,* 47 (2008), 501–523.

51. Margaret Hilton, "Skills for Work in the 21st Century: What Does the Research Tell Us?" *Academy of Management Perspectives,* November 2008, 63–78; The Manufacturing Institute, "People and Profitability: A Time for Change," 2009.

52. Brian Mahony, "Healthcare Thought Leaders Predict the Impact of Technology," November 29, 2009, www.trenderresearch.com.

53. David Savino, "The Role of Technology as an Enabler in Job Redesign," *Journal of Technology Management and Innovation,* 4 (2009), 14–23.

54. Vanessa O'Connell, "Retailers Reprogram Workers in Efficiency Push," *The Wall Street Journal,* September 10, 2008, A1; Adrienne Hedger, "The Best Use of Time," *Workforce Management,* May 18, 2009, 44–47.

55. Andrew McIlvaine, "The Generational Techno-Divide," *Human Resource Executive Online,* July 1, 2009, www.hreonline.com; Judy Payne, "Using Wikis and Blogs to Improve Collaboration and Knowledge Sharing," *Strategic HR Review,* No. 3, 2008, 5–12.

56. Antonio Poglianich and Matt Antonek, "Rules of Engagement in Turbulent Times: How Verizon Wireless Uses a Robust HR Portal for Employee Communication," *Global Business and Organizational Excellence,* May/June 2009, 29–35.

57. SHRM Poll, "Has Your Organization Disciplined Employees for Improper Use of Technology?" *Society for Human Resource Management,* June 6, 2007.

58. William Smith and Filiz Tabak, "Monitoring Employee Emails: Is There Any Room for Privacy?" *Academy of Management Perspectives,* November 2009, 33–48.

59. Lexy Martin and Lia Goudy, "Time-Honored Truths," *Human Resource Executive,* June 16, 2009, 30–32.

60. Edward Gordon, "Accounting Change Needed to Address Talent Shortfalls," *Employee Benefits News*, January 2010, 12–13.

61. Bruce Ellig, "Speak the Language of the CFO," *Workspan*, July 2008, 57–62; Kate Feather, "Helping HR to Measure Up: Arming the Soft Function with Hard Metrics," *Strategic HR Review*, No. 1, 2008, 28–33.

62. SHRM, "Human Capital Benchmarking Study: 2009," Society for Human Resource Management, www.shrm.org.

63. Wayne Cascio and John Boudreau, *Investing in People: Financial Impact of Human Resource Initiatives* (Upper Saddle River, NJ: FT Press, 2008).

64. John Dooney, "SHRM Symposium on Human Capital Analytics," Society for Human Resource Management, 2007, www.shrm.org.

65. Robert Greene, "Human Resource Management Strategies: Can We Discover What Will Work Through Benchmarking?" *WorldatWork Journal*, Second Quarter, 2008, 6–15; Dilys Robinson, "Human Capital Measurement: An Approach That Works," *Strategic HR Review*, No. 6, 2009, 5–11.

66. SHRM Poll, "How Often Does Your Organization Collect HR Benchmarks/Metrics?" *Society for Human Resource Management*, February 13, 2008.

67. Nancy Lockwood, "The Balanced Scorecard: An Overview," *SHRM Research Briefly Stated*, June 2006.

68. Margaret Fiester, "Balanced Scorecards, Unclaimed Wages, Data," *HRMagazine*, December 2008, 24.

69. Debbie Whitaker and Laura Wilson, "Human Capital Measurement: From Insight to Action," *Organization Development Journal*, Fall 2007, 59–64.

70. "Human Capital Strategy: Human Capital Measurement," November 30, 2007, www.humancapital strategy.blogspot.com.

71. Based on: Bill Roberts, "Analyze This!" *HR Magazine*, October 2009, 34–41.

3

Equal Employment Opportunity

After you have read this chapter, you should be able to:

- Describe key provisions in Title VII of the Civil Rights Acts of 1964 and 1991.

- Show how women are affected by pay, job assignment, and career issues in organizations.

- Define the two types of sexual harassment and how employers should respond to sexual harassment complaints.

- Identify two means that organizations are using to deal with the aging of their workforces.

- Discuss how reasonable accommodation is made when managing individuals with disabilities and differing religious beliefs.

- Evaluate several arguments supporting and opposing affirmative action.

- Discuss why diversity training is important.

Sexual Harassment at the United Nations

(DANIEL GARCIA/AFP/Getty Images)

The United Nations (U.N.) is struggling with a series of sexual harassment complaints as it strives to protect human rights globally. The U.N.'s global staff includes around 60,000 people stationed around the world. These employees come from many different cultures and backgrounds. The U.N. handles sexual harassment problems differently from other large organizations. Many U.N. managers have diplomatic immunity that protects them from criminal prosecution and from civil lawsuits as well; therefore, the internal justice system of the organization is the only one employees can use. This system dates back to 1946 and employs a "bewildering array" of channels and processes. The net effect has been many harassment cases that have not been settled to anyone's satisfaction.

For example, a female Syrian employee filed a complaint against her boss in the Kuwait office alleging he had made sexual advances, grabbing and kissing her. He then refused to renew her contract when she did not respond. Ten days after a report found evidence of her accusations, the supervisor resigned and could not be disciplined. In another case, a French woman who was in Gaza for the U.N. complained she was harassed by her director. She said he used binoculars to spy on her in her apartment, made sexually explicit comments, and groped her. The Director was cleared at first after an investigation by a "colleague." Another investigation was stymied when the director reached mandatory retirement age. His accuser's employment contract ran out and was not renewed and the case ended. In a final case to illustrate the problem, a translator for the U.N. in Lebanon accused a U.N. security officer of rape, but her employment contract expired before her appeal was heard; that was the end of the case.

Employees at the U.N. in the United States who have been harassed have found that filing a suit in U.S. courts will not work because of the diplomatic immunity.[1] Sexual harassment is an international problem in employment, but the U.N., regardless of whether it has a bigger problem than other international organizations, has some unique difficulties in dealing with it.

In the United States, using race, gender, disability, age, religion, and certain other characteristics as the basis for choosing among people at work is generally illegal. Doing so can also be quite expensive, as fines and back wages can be awarded as well as sizable law suit settlements. Inequality in the treatment of people with different backgrounds has been an issue for many years, but it was the Civil Rights Act of 1964 that started a legislative movement toward leveling the playing field in employment. Initially focus was on race, gender, and religion, but these characteristics were soon followed by age, pregnancy, and individuals with disabilities. Since then numerous Executive Orders, regulations, and interpretations by courts have affected the employer/employee relationship. Perhaps nothing has had the impact of Equal Employment Opportunity (EEO) on HR during the same period of time. See Appendix C for a listing of the relevant federal laws.

Employers have paid (and continue to pay) large amounts for violating EEO laws. Familiarity with EEO requirements and ways to successfully manage workforce diversity are the goals and focus of this chapter.[2]

NATURE OF EQUAL EMPLOYMENT OPPORTUNITY (EEO)

At the core of equal employment is the concept of discrimination. The word *discrimination* simply means "recognizing differences among items or people." For example, employers must discriminate (choose) among applicants for a job on the basis of job requirements and candidates' qualifications. However, when discrimination is based on race, gender, or some other factors, it is illegal and employers face problems. The following bases for protection have been identified by various federal, state, and/or local laws:

- Race, ethnic origin, color (including multiracial/ethnic backgrounds)
- Sex/gender (including pregnant women and also men in certain situations)
- Age (individuals over age 40)
- Individuals with disabilities (physical or mental)
- Military experience (military status employees and Vietnam-era veterans)
- Religion (special beliefs and practices)
- Marital status (some states)
- Sexual orientation (some states and cities)

These categories are composed of individuals who are members of a **protected category** under EEO laws and regulations.

Discrimination remains a concern as the U.S. workforce becomes more diverse. As Figure 3-1 indicates, there are two types of illegal employment discrimination: disparate treatment and disparate impact.

Protected category A group identified for protection under EEO laws and regulations.

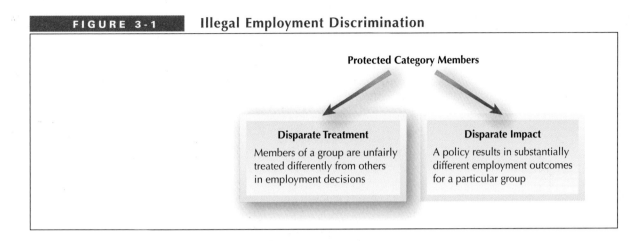

FIGURE 3-1   **Illegal Employment Discrimination**

Protected Category Members

Disparate Treatment
Members of a group are unfairly treated differently from others in employment decisions

Disparate Impact
A policy results in substantially different employment outcomes for a particular group

Disparate Treatment

The first type of illegal discrimination occurs with employment-related situations in which either: (1) different standards are used to judge individuals, or (2) the same standard is used, but it is not related to the individuals' jobs. **Disparate treatment** occurs when members of one group are treated differently from others. For example, if female applicants must take a special skills test not given to male applicants, then disparate treatment may be occurring.[3]

Often disparate treatment cases are based on evidence that an employer's actions were intentionally discriminatory. For example, a manufacturing firm in Cleveland, Ohio, paid almost $1 million to settle an EEO lawsuit involving 20 people, charging that S&Z Tool & Die Company intentionally refused to hire African Americans and women except in clerical jobs.[4]

Disparate treatment
Occurs when members of a group are treated differently from others.

Disparate Impact

Disparate impact occurs when members of a protected category are substantially underrepresented as a result of employment decisions that work to their disadvantage. The landmark case that established the importance of disparate impact as a legal foundation of EEO law is *Griggs v. Duke Power*, 1401 U.S. 424 (1971). The decision by the U.S. Supreme Court established two major points:

Disparate impact
Occurs when members of a protected category are substantially underrepresented as a result of employment decisions that work to their disadvantage.

1. It is not enough to show a lack of discriminatory intent if the employment tool results in a disparate impact that discriminates against one group more than another or continues a past pattern of discrimination.

2. The employer has the burden of proving that an employment requirement is directly job related as a "business necessity." Consequently, the intelligence test and high school diploma requirements of Duke Power were ruled not to be related to the job.

This and a number of other decisions make it clear that employers must be able to document through statistical analyses[5] that disparate treatment and disparate impact have not occurred.[6] Knowing how to perform these analyses is important in order for employers to follow appropriate equal employment guidelines. See Appendix E for information relating to these issues.

LOGGING ON

Equal Employment Opportunity Commission
This website provides information on the EEOC. It includes details on employment discrimination facts, enforcement statistics, and technical assistance programs. Visit the site at www.eeoc.gov.

FIGURE 3-2   **EEO Concepts**

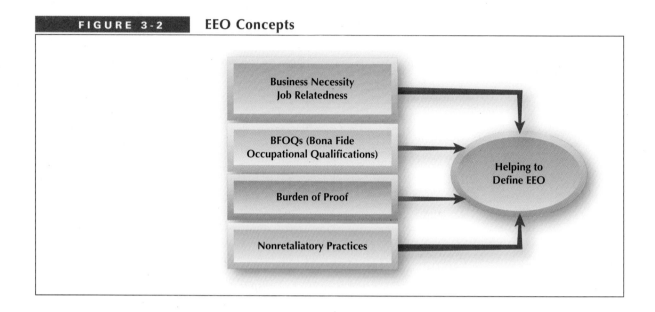

Equal Employment Opportunity Concepts

Several basic EEO concepts have resulted from court decisions, laws, and regulatory actions. The four key areas discussed next (see Figure 3-2) help clarify key EEO ideas.

Business Necessity and Job Relatedness A **business necessity** is a practice necessary for safe and efficient organizational operations. Business necessity has been the subject of numerous court decisions. Educational requirements often are based on business necessity. However, an employer who requires a minimum level of education, such as a high school diploma, must be able to defend the requirement as essential to the performance of the job (job related), which may be difficult. For instance, equating a degree or diploma with the possession of math or reading abilities is considered questionable.

Further, employers are expected to use job-related employment practices. The *Washington v. Davis* case involved the hiring of police officers in Washington, DC. The issue was a reading comprehension and aptitude test given to all applicants for police officer positions. The test contained actual material that the applicants would have to learn during a training program. The city could show a relationship between success in the training program and success as a police officer, although a much higher percentage of women and blacks than white men failed this aptitude test.

The Supreme Court ruled that the City of Washington, DC, did not discriminate unfairly because the test was definitely job related. If a test is clearly related to the job and tasks performed, it is *not illegal* simply because a greater percentage of minorities or women do not pass it. The crucial outcome is that the test must be specifically job related and cannot be judged solely on its disparate impact.[7]

Business necessity
A practice necessary for safe and efficient organizational operations.

Bona Fide Occupational Qualification (BFOQ) Employers may discriminate on the basis of sex, religion, or national origin if the characteristic can be justified as a "bona fide occupational qualification reasonably necessary to the normal operation of the particular business or enterprise." Thus, a **bona fide occupational qualification (BFOQ)** is a characteristic providing a legitimate reason why an employer can exclude persons on otherwise illegal bases of consideration.

What constitutes a BFOQ has been subject to different interpretations in various courts. Legal uses of BFOQs have been found for hiring Asians to wait on customers in a Chinese restaurant or Catholics to serve in certain religious-based positions in Catholic churches.

Burden of Proof Another legal issue that arises when discrimination is alleged is the determination of who has the **burden of proof.** Burden of proof must be established to file suit against employers and establish that illegal discrimination has occurred.

Based on the evolution of court decisions, current laws, and regulations the plaintiff charging discrimination must:

- be *a protected-category member*, and
- prove that *disparate impact* or *disparate treatment* existed.

Once a court rules that a preliminary case has been made, the burden of proof shifts to the employer. The employer then must show that the bases for making employment-related decisions were specifically job related and consistent with considerations of business necessity.

Nonretaliation Employers are prohibited from retaliating against individuals who file discrimination charges. **Retaliation** occurs when employers take punitive actions against individuals who exercise their legal rights. For example, an employee who had reported harassment by a supervisor was fired, but the Supreme Court found that it is unlawful to discriminate against someone who has "made a charge, testified, assisted, or participated in any manner in an investigation, proceeding, or hearing."[8]

To avoid charges of retaliation, the following actions are recommended for employers:

- Train supervisors on what retaliation is and what is not appropriate.
- Conduct a thorough internal investigation of any claims and document the results.
- Take appropriate action when any retaliation occurs.

Progressing Toward Equal Employment Opportunity

After almost 50 years, equal employment continues to be a significant focus of HR management. Discrimination, harassment, and retaliation lawsuits are the legal actions most likely to affect employers. (See HR Perspective: "Officer Dirt.") The number of EEO complaints continues to rise, indicating that more progress is needed to reduce employment discrimination.[9]

Not everyone agrees on the best way to achieve equal employment opportunity. There seems to be little disagreement that the goal is **equal employment,** or employment that is not affected by illegal discrimination. However, the way to achieve that goal is open to debate.[10] One way is to use the "**blind to differences**" approach, which argues that differences among people should be ignored and everyone should be treated equally. The second common approach is **affirmative action,** through which employers are urged to employ people based on their race, age, gender, or national origin. The idea is to make

---

Bona fide occupational qualification (BFOQ) Characteristic providing a legitimate reason why an employer can exclude persons on otherwise illegal bases of consideration.

Burden of proof What individuals who file suit against employers must prove in order to establish that illegal discrimination has occurred.

Retaliation Punitive actions taken by employers against individuals who exercise their legal rights.

Equal employment Employment that is not affected by illegal discrimination.

Blind to differences Differences among people should be ignored and everyone should be treated equally.

Affirmative action Employers are urged to employ people based on their race, age, gender, or national origin to make up for historical discrimination.

"Officer Dirt"

When a former police officer suggested age discrimination was involved in his dismissal, the Kansas City Police Department investigated and decided to fight the case. They might have done a more thorough job, as later was shown.

Anthony Hogan had been a police officer for 24 years. With the jury in state court listening, he countered his supervisor's denials with tape recordings he had made during three meetings in which the supervisor said Officer Hogan was "burned out," "dragging his feet," and "no longer a fireball." Another police official called him "Officer Dirt" because he was "Older than Dirt."

The jury ruled 10–2 in favor of the former officer and awarded him $700,000 in actual damages and $2 million in punitive damages. He settled for $1.95 million during an appeal.

EEOC officials expect an increase in discrimination filings as legislation (e.g., the Lilly Ledbetter Fair Pay Act), economic pressures, and baby boomers reaching retirement age change the landscape for such suits. The case of "Officer Dirt" can provide some useful lessons in dealing with similar claims:

- *Be thorough in the investigation*: Check performance evaluations for the past few years, resist the temptation to talk to only one or two people, and keep a record of interviews.
- *Do not demonize the claimant*: Rather than giving in to the tendency to view someone negatively just because the person has brought a claim, ask what the work record says. Managers get emotional when accused of discrimination, but the result of actions that are not thought out can be a retaliation claim.

One manager notes that "workers are watching and waiting to see how we handle the claim . . . we want others to believe we did the right thing."[11]

---

up for historical discrimination by giving groups who have been affected enhanced opportunities for employment.

RACE/ETHNIC/NATIONAL ORIGIN

The focus now shifts to equal employment laws and necessary considerations for managing HR in light of these laws.

Civil Rights Act of 1964, Title VII

Although the very first civil rights act was passed in 1866, it was not until passage of the Civil Rights Act of 1964 that the keystone of antidiscrimination employment legislation was put into place. The Equal Employment Opportunity Commission (EEOC) was established to enforce the provisions of Title VII, the portion of the act that deals with employment.

Title VII of the Civil Rights Act states that it is illegal for an employer to:

1. *fail or refuse to hire or discharge any individual, or otherwise discriminate against any individual with respect to his compensation, terms, conditions, or privileges of employment because of such individual's race, color, religion, sex, or national origin, or*
2. *limit, segregate, or classify his employees or applicants for employment in any way that would deprive or tend to deprive any individual of employment*

opportunities or otherwise adversely affect his status as an employee because of such individual's race, color, religion, sex, or national origin.

Title VII Coverage Title VII, as amended by the Equal Employment Opportunity Act of 1972, covers most employers in the United States. Any organization meeting one of the criteria in the following list is subject to rules and regulations that specific government agencies have established to administer the act:

- All private employers of 15 or more persons who are employed 20 or more weeks a year
- All educational institutions, public and private
- State and local governments
- Public and private employment agencies
- Labor unions with 15 or more members
- Joint labor/management committees for apprenticeships and training

Title VII has been the basis for several extensions of EEO law. For example, in 1980, the EEOC interpreted the law to include sexual harassment. Further, a number of concepts identified in Title VII are the foundation for court decisions, regulations, and other laws discussed later in the chapter. See Appendix E for information on EEO enforcement.

Executive Orders 11246, 11375, and 11478

Numerous executive orders require that employers holding federal government contracts not discriminate on the basis of race, color, religion, national origin, or sex. An *Executive Order* is issued by the president of the United States to provide direction to government departments on a specific area. The Office of Federal Contract Compliance Programs (OFCCP) in the U.S. Department of Labor has responsibility for enforcing nondiscrimination in government contracts.

Executive Orders 11246, 11375, and 11478 are major federal EEO efforts for government contractors; many states have similar requirements for firms with state government contracts.

Civil Rights Act of 1991

The Civil Rights Act of 1991 requires employers to show that an employment practice is *job related for the position* and is consistent with *business necessity*. The act clarifies that the plaintiffs bringing the discrimination charges must identify the particular employer practice being challenged and must show only that protected-class status played *some role in their treatment*. For employers, this requirement means that an individual's race, color, religion, sex, or national origin *must play no role* in their employment practices. This act allows people who have been targets of intentional discrimination based on sex, religion, or disability to receive both compensatory and punitive damages. One key provision of the 1991 act relates to how U.S. laws on EEO are applied globally.

Managing Racial and National Origin Issues

The original purpose of the Civil Rights Act of 1964 was to address race and national origin discrimination. This concern continues to be important today, and employers must be aware of potential HR issues that are based on race, national origin, and citizenship in order to take appropriate actions.

Employment discrimination can occur in numerous ways, from refusal to hire someone because of the person's race/ethnicity to the questions asked in a selection interview. See Appendix D for examples of legal and illegal question areas. For example, a trucking company settled a discrimination lawsuit by African American employees who were denied job assignments and promotions because of racial bias. In addition to paying a fine, the firm must report to the EEOC on promotions from part-time to full-time for dock worker jobs.

Sometimes racial discriminations can be more subtle. For example, some firms have tapped professional and social networking sites to fill open positions. However, networking sites exclude many people. According to one study, only 5% of LinkedIn users are black and 2% are Hispanic. This lack of access to these sites can easily be viewed as racial discrimination.[12]

Under federal law, discriminating against people because of skin color is just as illegal as discriminating because of race. For example, one might be guilty of color discrimination but not racial discrimination if one hired light-skinned African Americans over dark-skinned people.

Racial/Ethnic Harassment The area of racial/ethnic harassment is such a concern that the EEOC has issued guidelines on it. It is recommended that employers adopt policies against harassment of any type, including ethnic jokes, vulgar epithets, racial slurs, and physical actions. The consequences of not enforcing these policies are seen in a case involving a small business employer that subjected Latinos to physical and verbal abuse. Hispanic males at the firm were subjected to derogatory jokes, verbal abuse, physical harm, and other humiliating experiences. Settling the case was expensive for the employer.

Contrast that case with another that shows the advantage of taking quick remedial action. An employee filed a lawsuit against an airline because coworkers told racist jokes and hung nooses in his workplace. The airline was able to show that each time any employee, including the plaintiff, reported problems, management conducted an investigation and took action against the offending employees. The court ruled for the employer in this case because the situation was managed properly.

Affirmative Action

Through **affirmative action**, employers are urged to hire groups of people based on their race, age, gender, or national origin to make up for historical discrimination. It is a requirement for federal government contractors to document the inclusion of women and racial minorities in the workforce. As part of those government regulations, covered employers must submit plans describing their attempts to narrow the gaps between the composition of their workforces and the composition of labor markets where they obtain employees. However, affirmative action has been the subject of numerous court cases and an ongoing political and social debate both in the United States and globally.[13]

For example, a recent Supreme Court ruling held that race should *not* be used to the detriment of individuals who passed an examination and were qualified for promotions. In this case, the city of New Haven, Connecticut, threw out the results of a test for promotion where more white firefighters passed than blacks or Hispanics. The City claimed it had to junk the tests because they would lead to an avalanche of lawsuits by black candidates who

Affirmative Action
The hiring of groups of people based on their race, age, gender or national origin.

had not passed. The court said fear of litigation was no reason to rely on race to throw out the results.[14]

Supporters offer many reasons why affirmative action is important, while opponents argue firmly against it. Individuals can examine the points of both sides in the debate and compare them with their personal views of affirmative action. The authors of this text believe that whether one supports or opposes affirmative action, it is important to understand why its supporters believe that it is needed and why its opponents believe it should be discontinued. The reasons given most frequently by both sides are highlighted in Figure 3-3.

Managing Affirmative Action Requirements

Affirmative action plan (AAP) A document reporting on the composition of an employer's workforce, required for federal contractors.

Federal, state, and local regulations require many government contractors to compile affirmative action plans to report on the composition of their workforces. An **affirmative action plan (AAP)** is a formal document that an employer compiles annually for submission to enforcement agencies. Generally, contractors with at least 50 employees and $50,000 in government contracts annually must submit these plans. Courts have noted that any employer *may* have a *voluntary* AAP, although employers *must* have such a plan if they are government contractors. Some courts have ordered employers that are not government

---

FIGURE 3-3   **The Debate about Affirmative Action**

Arguments: Why Affirmative Action Is Needed

- Affirmative action is needed to overcome past injustices or eliminate the effects of those injustices.
- Affirmative action creates more equality for all persons, even if temporary injustice to some individuals may result.
- Raising the employment level of protected-class members will benefit U.S. society in the long run.
- Properly used, affirmative action does not discriminate against males or whites.
- Goals indicate progress is needed, not quotas.

Arguments: Why Affirmative Action Is Not Needed

- Affirmative action penalizes individuals (males and whites) even though they have not been guilty of practicing discrimination.
- It is no longer needed as an African American has been elected President.
- Affirmative action results in greater polarization and separatism along gender and racial lines.
- Affirmative action stigmatizes those it is designed to help.
- Goals become quotas and force employers to "play by the numbers."

contractors to submit required AAPs because of past discriminatory practices and violations of laws.

The contents of an AAP and the policies flowing from it must be available for review by managers and supervisors within the organization. Plans vary in length; some are long and require extensive staff time to prepare.

MEASURE

Affirmative Action Plan Metrics A crucial but time-consuming part of an AAP is the analyses. The **availability analysis** identifies the number of protected-class members available to work in the appropriate labor markets for given jobs. This analysis can be developed with data from a state labor department, the U.S. Census Bureau, and other sources. The **utilization analysis** identifies the number of protected-class members employed in the organization and the types of jobs they hold.

Once all the data have been analyzed and compared, then *underutilization* statistics must be calculated by comparing the availability analysis with the utilization analysis. It is useful to think of this stage as a comparison of whether the internal workforce is a "representative sampling" of the available external labor force from which employees are hired.

Using the underutilization data, *goals* and *timetables* for reducing underutilization of protected-class individuals must then be identified. Actions that will be taken to recruit, hire, promote, and train more protected-class individuals are described. The AAP must be updated and reviewed each year to reflect changes in the utilization and availability of protected-category members. If the AAP is audited, the employer must be prepared to provide additional details and documentation. Appendix F provides information about EEO enforcement.

LOGGING ON

The Affirmative Action and Diversity Project
A resource for opinions surrounding the issues of affirmative action and its cultural and economic aspects can be found at http://aad.english.ucsb.edu.

SEX/GENDER DISCRIMINATION LAWS AND REGULATIONS

A number of laws and regulations address discrimination based on sex or gender. Historically, women experienced employment discrimination in a variety of ways. The inclusion of sex as a basis for protected-class status in Title VII of the 1964 Civil Rights Act has led to various areas of legal protection for women.

Pregnancy Discrimination

Availability analysis
Identifies the number of protected-class members available to work in the appropriate labor markets for given jobs.

Utilization analysis
Identifies the number of protected-class members employed in the organization and the types of jobs they hold.

The Pregnancy Discrimination Act (PDA) of 1978 requires that any employer with 15 or more employees treat maternity leave the same as other personal or medical leaves. Closely related to the PDA is the Family and Medical Leave Act (FMLA) of 1993, which requires that individuals be given up to 12 weeks of family leave without pay and also requires that those taking family leave be allowed to return to jobs (see Chapter 13 for details). The FMLA applies to both men and women.

Courts have generally ruled that the PDA requires employers to treat pregnant employees the same as nonpregnant employees with similar abilities or inabilities. Employers have been found to have acted properly when terminating a pregnant employee for excessive absenteeism due to pregnancy-related illnesses, because the employee was not treated differently from other employees with absenteeism problems.

Equal Pay and Pay Equity

The Equal Pay Act of 1963 requires employers to pay similar wage rates for similar work without regard to gender. A *common core of tasks* must be similar, but tasks performed only intermittently or infrequently do not make jobs different enough to justify significantly different wages. Differences in pay between men and women in the same jobs may be allowed because of:

1. Differences in seniority
2. Differences in performance
3. Differences in quality and/or quantity of production
4. Factors other than sex, such as skill, effort, and working conditions

For example, a university was found to have violated the Equal Pay Act by paying a female professor a starting salary lower than salaries paid to male professors with similar responsibilities. In fact, the court found that the woman professor taught larger classes and had more total students than some of the male faculty members.[15]

Ledbetter v. Goodyear Tire & Rubber Co. was a significant U.S. Supreme Court decision on pay discrimination. Ledbetter, a female manager with Goodyear in Alabama, claimed that she was subjected to pay discrimination because she received lower pay during her career back to 1979, even though she did not file suit until 1998.[16] The decision examined this view and stated that the rights of workers to sue for previous years of paid discrimination are limited. However, in 2009 Congress passed the Lilly Ledbetter Fair Pay Act that canceled the Supreme Court ruling. The new law effectively eliminates the statute of limitations for employees to file pay discrimination claims.[17]

Pay equity is the idea that pay for jobs requiring comparable levels of knowledge, skill, and ability should be similar, even if actual duties differ significantly. This theory has also been called *comparable worth* in earlier cases. Some state laws have mandated pay equity for public-sector employees. However, U.S. federal courts generally have ruled that the existence of pay differences between the different jobs held by women and men is not sufficient to prove that illegal discrimination has occurred.

A major reason for the development of the pay equity idea is the continuing gap between the earnings of women and men. For instance, in 1980, the average annual pay of full-time female workers was 60% of that of full-time male workers. By 2008, the reported rate of about 80% showed some progress but a continuing disparity.[18] See Figure 3-4.

Pay equity The idea that pay for jobs requiring comparable levels of knowledge, skill, and ability should be similar, even if actual duties differ significantly.

Sexual Harassment

The Equal Employment Opportunity Commission has issued guidelines designed to curtail sexual harassment. **Sexual harassment** refers to actions that are sexually directed, are unwanted, and subject the worker to adverse employment conditions or create a hostile work environment. Sexual harassment can occur between a boss and a subordinate, among coworkers, and when nonemployees have business contacts with employees.

Most of the sexual harassment charges filed involve harassment of women by men. However, some sexual harassment cases have been filed by men

Sexual harassment Actions that are sexually directed, are unwanted, and subject the worker to adverse employment conditions or create a hostile work environment.

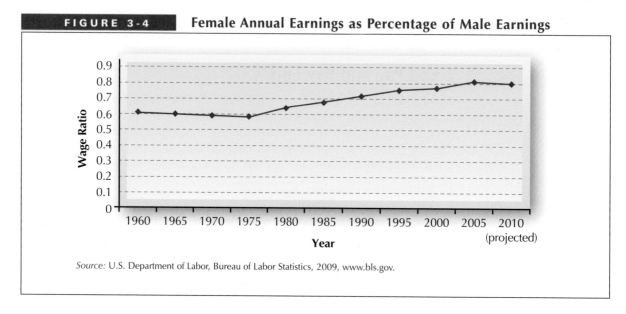

FIGURE 3-4   **Female Annual Earnings as Percentage of Male Earnings**

Source: U.S. Department of Labor, Bureau of Labor Statistics, 2009, www.bls.gov.

against women managers and supervisors, and some have been filed by both men and women for same-sex harassment.

Managing Sex/Gender Issues

The influx of women into the workforce has had major social, economic, and organizational consequences. The percentage of women in the total U.S. civilian workforce has increased dramatically since 1950, to almost 50% today.

This growth in the number of women in the workforce has led to more sex/gender issues related to jobs and careers. A significant issue is related to biology (women bear children) and to tradition (women have a primary role in raising children). A major result of the increasing share of women in the workforce is that more women with children are working. According to the U.S. Bureau of Labor Statistics, about three-fourths of women aged 25–54 are in the workforce. Further, about half of all women currently working are single, separated, divorced, widowed, or otherwise single heads of households. Consequently, they are "primary" income earners, not co-income providers, and must balance family and work responsibilities. This responsibility may affect managers' perceptions of family/work conflict that may lead to promotability issues for women.[19]

To guard against pay inequities that are considered illegal under the Equal Pay Act, employers should follow these guidelines:

- Include all benefits and other items that are part of remuneration to calculate total compensation for the most accurate overall picture.
- Make sure people know how the pay practices work.
- Base pay on the value of jobs and performance.
- Benchmark against local and national markets so that pay structures are competitive.
- Conduct frequent audits to ensure there are no gender-based inequities and that pay is fair internally.

Nontraditional Jobs The right to reassign women from hazardous jobs to ones that may be lower paying but less hazardous because of health-related concerns is another gender-related issue encountered by employers. Fears about

FIGURE 3-5	Women as Percentage of Total Employees by Selected Industries

Higher Percentages		Lower Percentages	
Child day care	95.3 %	Taxi/limousine services	11.6%
Home health care	89.1%	Automotive repair	10.6%
Veterinary services	81.7%	Construction	9.7%
Hospitals	76.7%	Landscaping services	8.6%
Elementary and secondary schools	75.6%	Coal mining	7.2%
Pharmacies and drug stores	64.8%	Rail transportation	5.9%
Travel/reservation services	61.6%	Logging	4.4%

Source: U.S. Department of Labor, Bureau of Labor Statistics, 2008, www.bls.gov.

higher health insurance costs and possible lawsuits involving such problems as birth defects caused by damage sustained during pregnancy have led some employers to institute reproductive and fetal protection policies. However, the U.S. Supreme Court has ruled that such policies are illegal. Also, having different job conditions for men and women is usually held to be discriminatory. Figure 3-5 shows some of the occupations in which women constitute high percentages and low percentages of those employed.

Jobs that pay well but are nontraditional jobs for women include: architects, computer programmers, software engineers, detectives, chefs, engineers, computer repair, construction, building inspectors, machinists, aircraft pilots, and firefighters.[20]

Glass Ceiling For years, women's groups have alleged that women in workplaces encounter a **glass ceiling**, which refers to discriminatory practices that have prevented women and other protected-class members from advancing to executive-level jobs. Women in the United States are making some progress in getting senior-level, managerial, and professional jobs. Nevertheless, women hold only a small percentage of the highest-ranking executive management jobs in big companies. By comparison, women hold a considerably lower percentage of the same kinds of jobs in France, Germany, Brazil, and many other countries.

A related problem is that women have tended to advance to senior management in a limited number of support or staff areas, such as HR and corporate communications. Because executive jobs in these "supporting" areas tend to pay less than jobs in sales, marketing, operations, or finance, the overall impact is to reduce women's career progression and income. Limits that keep women from progressing only in certain fields have been referred to as "glass walls" or "glass elevators." These limitations are seen as being tied to organizational, cultural, and leadership issues.[21]

Glass ceiling Discriminatory practices that have prevented women and other protected-class members from advancing to executive-level jobs.

"Breaking the Glass" A number of employers have recognized that "breaking the glass," whether ceilings, walls, or elevators, is good business for both women and racial minorities. Some of the most common means used to "break the glass" are as follows:

- Establish formal mentoring programs for women and members of racial/ethnic minorities.
- Provide opportunities for career rotation into operations, marketing, and sales for individuals who have shown talent in accounting, HR, and other areas.
- Increase the memberships of top management and boards of directors to include women and individuals of color.
- Establish clear goals for retention and progression of protected-category individuals and hold managers accountable for achieving these goals.
- Allow for alternative work arrangements for employees, particularly those balancing work/family responsibilities.

Individuals with Differing Sexual Orientations

As if demographic diversity did not place enough pressure on managers and organizations, individuals in the workforce today have widely varying life-styles that can have work-related consequences. Legislative efforts have been made to protect individuals with differing lifestyles or sexual orientations from employment discrimination, though at present only a few cities and states have passed such laws.

One visible issue that some employers have had to address is that of individuals who have had or are undergoing sex-change surgery and therapy. Federal court cases and the EEOC have ruled that sex discrimination under Title VII applies to a person's gender at birth. Thus, it does not apply to the new gender of those who have had gender-altering operations. Sexual orientation or sex-change issues that arise at work include the reactions of coworkers and managers and ensuring that such individuals are evaluated fairly and not discriminated against in work assignments, raises, training, or promotions.

Nepotism

Many employers have policies that restrict or prohibit **nepotism**, the practice of allowing relatives to work for the same employer. Other firms require only that relatives not work directly for or with each other or not be placed in positions where collusion or conflict could occur. The policies most frequently cover spouses, brothers, sisters, mothers, fathers, sons, and daughters. Generally, employer antinepotism policies have been upheld by courts, in spite of the concern that they tend to discriminate against women more than men (because women tend to be denied employment or to leave employers more often as a result of marriage to other employees).[22]

Consensual Relationships and Romance at Work

When work-based friendships lead to romance and off-the-job sexual relationships, managers and employers face a dilemma: Should they "monitor" these relationships to protect the firm from potential legal complaints, thereby "meddling" in employees' private, off-the-job lives? Or do they simply ignore these relationships and the potential problems they present? These concerns

Nepotism Practice of allowing relatives to work for the same employer.

are significant, given a survey that found that about 40% of workers have dated coworkers.[23]

Most executives and HR professionals (as well as employees) agree that workplace romances are risky because they have great potential for causing conflict. They strongly agree that romance must not take place between a supervisor and a subordinate. Some employers have addressed the issue of workplace romances by establishing policies dealing with them.[24]

Different actions may be appropriate if a relationship is clearly consensual than if it is forced by a supervisor–subordinate relationship. One consideration is the observation that consensual workplace romances can create hostile work environments for others in organizations.

Dealing with Sexual Harassment

Sexual harassment is a significant concern in many organizations and can occur in a variety of workplace relationships. As shown in Figure 3-6, individuals in many different roles can be sexual harassers. For example, third parties who are neither employers nor employees have been found to be harassers. Both customer service representatives and food servers have won sexual harassment complaints because their employers refused to protect them from regular sexual harassment by aggressive customers.

Most frequently, sexual harassment occurs when a male in a supervisory or managerial position harasses women within his "power structure." However, as noted earlier, women managers have been found guilty of sexually harassing male employees, and same-sex harassment also has occurred. Court decisions have held that a person's sexual orientation neither provides nor precludes a claim of sexual harassment under Title VII. It is enough that the harasser engaged in pervasive and unwelcome conduct of a sexual nature.

FIGURE 3-6   **Potential Sexual Harassers**

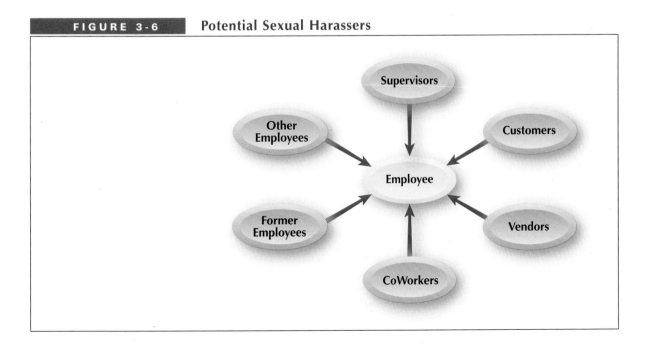

Types of Sexual Harassment

Two basic types of sexual harassment have been defined by EEOC regulations and a large number of court cases. The two types are different in nature and defined as follows:

1. **Quid pro quo** is harassment in which employment outcomes are linked to the individual granting sexual favors.
2. **Hostile environment** harassment exists when an individual's work performance or psychological well-being is unreasonably affected by intimidating or offensive working conditions.

In quid pro quo harassment, an employee may be promised a promotion, a special raise, or a desirable work assignment, but only if the employee grants some sexual favors to the supervisor. The second type, hostile environment harassment, may include actions such as commenting on appearance or attire, telling jokes that are suggestive or sexual in nature, allowing revealing photos and posters to be on display, or making continual requests to get together after work that can lead to the creation of a hostile work environment. Rude and discourteous behavior often is linked to sexual harassment.

As computer and Internet technology has spread, the number of electronic sexual harassment cases has grown.[25] Sexual harassment is increasingly occurring via e-mails and Internet access systems. Cyber sexual harassment may occur when an employee forwards an e-mail joke with sexual content or accesses pornographic websites at work and then shares content with other employees. Cyber stalking, in which a person continually e-mails an employee requesting dates and sending personal messages, is growing as instant messaging expands.

Many employers have policies addressing the inappropriate use of e-mail, company computer systems, and electronic technology usage. Serious situations have led to employee terminations. Once a company disciplined more than 200 employees and fired 50 of them for having e-mailed pornographic images and other inappropriate materials using the company information system.

Many employers have equipped their computer systems with scanners that screen for inappropriate words and images. Offending employees receive warnings and/or disciplinary actions associated with "flagged" items.

Employer Responses to Sexual Harassment

Employers must be proactive to prevent sexual and other types of harassment. If the workplace culture fosters harassment, and if policies and practices do not inhibit harassment, an employer is wise to reevaluate and solve the problem before lawsuits follow.

Only if the employer can produce evidence of taking reasonable care to prohibit sexual harassment does the employer have the possibility of avoiding liability through an affirmative defense.[26] Critical components of ensuring such reasonable care include the following:

- Establish a sexual harassment policy.
- Communicate the policy regularly.
- Train employees and managers on avoiding sexual harassment.
- Investigate and take action when complaints are voiced.

As Figure 3-7 indicates, if an employee has suffered any tangible employment action (such as being denied raises, being terminated, or being refused access to

Quid pro quo Sexual harassment in which employment outcomes are linked to the individual granting sexual favors.

Hostile environment Sexual harassment in which an individual's work performance or psychological well-being is unreasonably affected by intimidating or offensive working conditions.

| FIGURE 3-7 | Sexual Harassment Liability Determination |

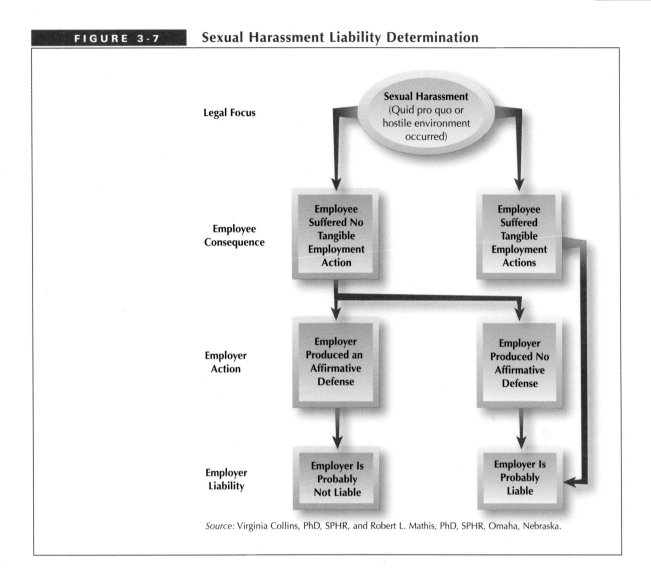

Source: Virginia Collins, PhD, SPHR, and Robert L. Mathis, PhD, SPHR, Omaha, Nebraska.

training) because of sexual harassment, then the employer is liable. Even if the employee has suffered no tangible employment action, if the employer has not produced an affirmative defense, then employer liability still exists.

Harassment Likelihood

GLOBAL

Research suggests that some people are more likely to be sexually harassed than others. For example, one study found that supervisors or women with more workplace authority are more likely to be harassed.[27] Further research suggests that the likelihood of men to sexually harass, and the tolerance for sexual harassment by women vary across countries. Fundamental differences regarding power between men and women and a cultural support of sexual harassment lead to very different sexual harassment situations from country to country. According to this research, Canada, Denmark, Germany, The Netherlands, Sweden, and the United States are likely to have relatively *less* sexual harassment than countries like East Africa, Hong Kong, Indonesia, Malaysia, Mexico, Turkey, and Yugoslavia.[28]

INDIVIDUALS WITH DISABILITIES

The passage of the Americans with Disabilities Act (ADA) in 1990 began the laws and regulations on discrimination against individuals with disabilities. These laws and regulations affect employment matters as well as public accessibility for individuals with disabilities.

Americans with Disabilities Act (ADA)

Organizations with 15 or more employees are covered by the provisions of the ADA, which are enforced by the EEOC. The act applies to private employers, employment agencies, and labor unions.[29] State government employees are not covered by the ADA, which means that they cannot sue in federal courts for redress and damages. However, they may still bring suits under state laws in state courts.

ADA and Job Requirements Discrimination is prohibited against individuals with disabilities who can perform the **essential job functions**—the fundamental job duties—of the employment positions that those individuals hold or desire. These functions do not include marginal functions of the position.

For a qualified person with a disability, an employer must make a **reasonable accommodation**, which is a modification to a job or work environment that gives that individual an equal employment opportunity to perform. EEOC guidelines encourage employers and individuals to work together to determine what are appropriate reasonable accommodations, rather than employers alone making those judgments.

Reasonable accommodation is restricted to actions that do not place an undue hardship on an employer. An **undue hardship** is a significant difficulty or expense imposed on an employer in making an accommodation for individuals with disabilities. The ADA offers only general guidelines in determining when an accommodation becomes unreasonable and will place undue hardship on an employer.

ADA Restrictions and Medical Information The ADA contains restrictions on obtaining and retaining medically related information on applicants and employees. Restrictions include prohibiting employers from rejecting individuals because of a disability and from asking job applicants any question about current or past medical history until a conditional job offer is made. Also, the ADA prohibits the use of preemployment medical exams, except for drug tests, until a job has been conditionally offered.

Who Is Disabled?

As defined by the ADA, a **disabled person** is someone who has a physical or mental impairment that substantially limits that person in some major life activities, who has a record of such an impairment, or who is regarded as having such an impairment. Figure 3-8 shows the most frequent disabilities identified in ADA charges.

However, it is not always concluded that people have disabilities when they feel they are disabled. For example, in a case involving United Parcel Service, the Court ruled that an employee who had high blood pressure but was on blood pressure medications was not disabled under the ADA.[30] Another U.S. Supreme Court case found that an employee who had been fired for drug

Essential job functions
Fundamental job duties.

Reasonable accommodation
A modification to a job or work environment that gives a qualified individual an equal employment opportunity to perform.

Undue hardship Significant difficulty or expense imposed on an employer in making an accommodation for individuals with disabilities.

Disabled person Someone who has a physical or mental impairment that substantially limits life activities, who has a record of such an impairment, or who is regarded as having such an impairment.

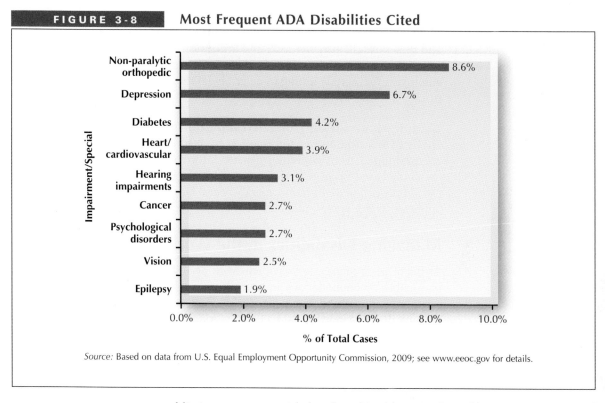

FIGURE 3-8   Most Frequent ADA Disabilities Cited

Source: Based on data from U.S. Equal Employment Opportunity Commission, 2009; see www.eeoc.gov for details.

addiction was not entitled to be rehired because his addiction was not a disability. The ADA does not protect current users of illegal drugs and substances, but it does protect those who are recovering addicts.

Mental Disabilities A growing area of concern to employers under the ADA is individuals with mental disabilities. A mental illness is often more difficult to diagnose than a physical disability. Employers must be careful when considering "emotional" or "mental health" factors such as depression in employment-related decisions. They must not stereotype individuals with mental impairments or disabilities but must instead base their evaluations on sound medical information.

Amendments to ADA (ADAAA) Congress passed amendments to the ADA, effective in 2009, that overruled several key cases and regulations. The effect was to *expand* the definition of disabled individuals to include anyone with a physical or mental impairment that substantially limits one or more major life activities without regard for the ameliorative effects of mitigating measures such as medication, prosthetics, hearing aids, and so on. Major life activities include, among others, walking, seeing, breathing, working, sleeping, concentrating, thinking, and communicating.[31]

Genetic Bias Regulations

Related to medical disabilities is the emerging area of workplace genetic bias. As medical research has revealed the human genome, medical tests have been developed that can identify an individual's genetic markers for various diseases. Whether these tests should be used and how they are used can raise ethical issues.

Employers that use genetic screening tests do so for two primary reasons. Some use genetic testing to make workers aware of genetic problems that may exist so that medical treatments can begin. Others use genetic testing to terminate employees who may make extensive use of health insurance benefits and thus raise the benefits costs and utilization rates of the employer. A major railroad company, Burlington Northern Santa Fe, had to publicly apologize to employees for secretly testing to determine if they were genetically predisposed to carpal tunnel syndrome.

Genetic Information Nondiscrimination Act (GINA) Congress passed GINA to limit the use of information by health insurance plans. Employers are prohibited from collecting genetic information or making employment decisions based on genetic decisions. "Genetic information" includes genetic tests of the employee or family members and family medical history. It does not apply to "water cooler talk," or the inadvertent acquisition of information.[32]

Managing Disabilities in the Workforce

At the heart of managing individuals with disabilities is for employers to make reasonable accommodations in several areas. Common means of reasonable accommodation are shown in Figure 3-9. First, architectural barriers should not prohibit disabled individuals' access to work areas or restrooms. Second, appropriate work tasks must be assigned. Satisfying this requirement may mean modifying jobs, work area layouts, or work schedules or providing special equipment.

Key to making reasonable accommodations is identifying the essential job functions and then determining which accommodations are reasonable so that the individual can perform the core job duties. Fortunately for employers, most accommodations needed are relatively inexpensive.[33]

Recruiting and Selecting Individuals with Disabilities Numerous employers have specifically targeted the recruitment and selection of individuals with disabilities. However, as the HR On-the-Job indicates, questions asked in the employment process should be job related.

FIGURE 3-9	Common Means of Reasonable Accommodation

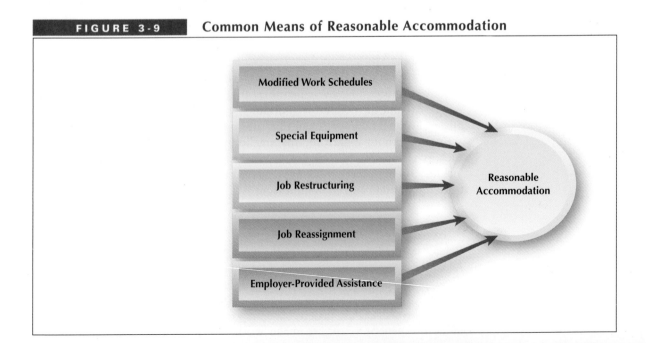

ADA and Employment Questions

The Americans with Disabilities Act prohibits asking job applicants questions about past or current health history until a conditional job offer is made. The offer often is based on passing a physical exam or a medical background check. Any physical or medical requirements must be related to the specific job for which the applicant is being considered.

Two HR areas that are affected are employment applications and interviews. In these areas, a general question such as the following is often used:

> *Can you perform the essential functions of the job for which you are applying with or without accommodation?*

Several examples of specific questions concerning disabilities that should and should not be asked in employment interviews are shown in the following chart. As is evident, the questions that should be asked are specifically related to the job and address essential job functions.

✗ DO NOT ASK
- Do you have any physical or mental disabilities?
- Why are you using crutches, and how did you become injured?
- How many times were you absent due to illness in the past two years?
- Have you been treated for any of the following medical conditions?
- Have you ever filed for or collected workers' compensation?

✓ DO ASK
- How would you perform the essential tasks of the job for which you have applied?
- If hired, which tasks outlined in the job description that you reviewed would be more enjoyable and which ones most difficult?
- Describe your attendance record on your last job.
- Describe any problems you would have reaching the top of a six-foot filing cabinet.
- What did your prior job duties consist of, and which ones were the most challenging?

One common selection test is a physical abilities test, which can be challenged as discriminatory based on the ADA. Such physical tests must be specifically job related, and not general. For example, having all applicants lift 50-pound weights, even though only some warehouse workers will have to lift that much, could be illegal. Also, rather than testing with barbells or other artificial weights, the employer should use the actual 50-pound boxes lifted in performing the specific jobs.

Employees Who Develop Disabilities For many employers, the impact of the ADA has been the greatest when handling employees who develop disabilities, not dealing with applicants who already have disabilities. As the workforce ages, it is likely that more employees will develop disabilities. For instance, a warehouse worker who suffers a serious leg injury while motorcycling away from work may request reasonable accommodation.

Employers must develop responses for handling accommodation requests from individuals who have been satisfactory employees without disabilities, but who now must be considered for accommodations if they are to be able to continue working. Handled inappropriately, these individuals are likely to file either ADA complaints with the EEOC or private lawsuits.

Employees sometimes can be shifted to other jobs where their disabilities do not affect them as much. For instance, the warehouse firm might be able to move the injured repair worker to a purchasing inventory job inside so that climbing and lifting are unnecessary. But the problem for employers is what to do with the next worker who develops problems if an alternative job is not available. Even if the accommodations are just for one employee, the reactions of coworkers must be considered.

Individuals with Mental Disabilities More ADA complaints are being filed by individuals who have or claim to have mental disabilities. The cases that have been filed have ranged from individuals with a medical history of paranoid schizophrenia or clinical depression to individuals who claim that job stress has affected their marriage or sex life. Regardless of the type of employees' claims, it is important that employers respond properly by obtaining medical verifications for claims of mental illnesses and considering accommodation requests for mental disabilities in the same manner as accommodation requests for physical disabilities.

Individuals with Life-Threatening Illnesses The U.S. Supreme Court has determined that individuals with life-threatening illnesses are covered by the ADA. Individuals with leukemia, cancer, or AIDS are all considered as having disabilities, and employers must respond to them appropriately or face charges of discrimination. Numerous individuals with life-threatening illnesses may intend to continue working, particularly if their illness is forecast to be multiyear in nature.

An additional requirement of the ADA is that all medical information be maintained in files separated from the general personnel files. The medical files must have identified security procedures, and limited access procedures must be identified.

Management Focus on ADAAA Adaptation After the changes made by ADAAA, less effort should be placed on determining whether an individual is indeed disabled—the individual probably is disabled. Rather, management should:

- Define essential functions in advance.
- Handle all requests for accommodation properly.
- Interact with the employee with good faith and documentation.
- Know and follow the reasonable accommodation rules.

AGE AND EQUAL EMPLOYMENT OPPORTUNITY

The populations of most developed countries—including Australia, Japan, most European countries, and the United States—are aging. These changes mean that as older workers with a lifetime of experiences and skills retire, HR faces significant challenges in replacing them with workers having the capabilities and work ethic that characterize many mature workers in the United States. Employment discrimination against individuals age 40 and older is prohibited by the Age Discrimination in Employment Act (ADEA).

Age Discrimination in Employment Act (ADEA)

The Age Discrimination in Employment Act (ADEA) of 1967, amended in 1978 and 1986, prohibits discrimination in terms, conditions, or privileges of employment against all individuals age 40 years or older working for employers having 20 or more workers. However, the U.S. Supreme Court has ruled that state employees may not sue state government employers in federal courts because the ADEA is a federal law. The impact of the ADEA is increasing as the U.S. workforce has been aging.[34] Consequently, the number of age discrimination cases has been increasing, according to EEOC reports.

A number of countries have passed age discrimination laws. For example, age discrimination regulations in Great Britain focus on preventing age discrimination in recruitment, promotion, training, and retirement-related actions.[35]

As with most EEO issues, age discrimination details are continuing to be defined by the various courts, with the Supreme Court having decided employers are *not* liable if the disparate age impact is due to "reasonable factors other than age" (RFOA). The specific cases decided recently suggest that the employee retains the heavier burden for proving that the adverse employment action was taken because of the employee's age.[36] However, employers that focus on recruiting or providing "preferential treatment" of older workers do not violate the ADEA.

Older Workers Benefit Protection Act (OWBPA)

This law is an amendment to the ADEA and is aimed at protecting employees when they sign liability waivers for age discrimination in exchange for severance packages. To comply with the act, employees must be given complete accurate information on the available benefits. For example, an early retirement package that includes a waiver stating the employee will not sue for age discrimination if the employee takes the money for early retirement must include a written, clearly understood agreement to that effect.

The impact of the OWBPA is becoming more evident. Industries such as manufacturing and others offer early retirement buyouts to cut their workforces. For instance, Ford and General Motors have offered large buyouts of which thousands of workers have taken advantage.

LOGGING ON

Administration on Aging
This government website provides information on aging and age discrimination from government agencies, associations, and organizations. Visit the site at www.aoa.gov.

Managing Age Discrimination

One issue that has led to age discrimination charges is labeling older workers as "overqualified" for jobs or promotions. In a number of cases, courts have ruled that the term *overqualified* may have been used as a code word for workers being too old, thus causing them not to be considered for employment. Also, selection and promotion practices must be "age neutral." Older workers face substantial barriers to entry in a number of occupations, especially those requiring significant amounts of training or ones where new technology has been recently developed. In some cases involving older employees, age-related comments such as "That's just old Fred" or "We need younger blood" in conversations were used as evidence of age discrimination.

To counter significant staffing difficulties, some employers recruit older people to return to the workforce through the use of part-time and other scheduling options. During the past decade, the number of older workers holding part-time jobs has increased. It is likely that the number of older workers interested in working part-time will continue to grow.

A strategy used by employers to retain the talents of older workers is **phased retirement**, whereby employees gradually reduce their workloads and pay levels. This option is growing in use as a way to allow older workers with significant knowledge and experience to have more personal flexibility, while the organizations retain them for their valuable capabilities. Some firms also rehire their retirees as part-time workers, independent contractors, or consultants.[37] Some provisions in the Pension Protection Act of 2006 allow pension distributions for employees who are reducing their work hours.

RELIGION AND SPIRITUALITY IN THE WORKPLACE

Title VII of the Civil Rights Act identifies discrimination on the basis of religion as illegal. The increasing religious diversity in the workforce has put greater emphasis on religious considerations in workplaces. However, religious schools and institutions can use religion as a bona fide occupational qualification for employment practices on a limited scale. Also, employers must make *reasonable accommodation* efforts regarding an employee's religious beliefs according to the U.S. Supreme Court.

Since the terrorist attacks in New York and Washington, DC, increased discrimination complaints have been filed by Muslims because of treatment or insults made by coworkers and managers.[38] Religious cases also have addressed the issues of beards, mustaches, and hair length and style. African American men, who are more likely than white men to suffer from a skin disease that is worsened by shaving, have filed suits challenging policies prohibiting beards or long sideburns. Generally, courts have ruled for employers in such cases, except where certain religious standards expect men to have facial hair. The legal requirement to reasonably accommodate religious practices and beliefs leads to different types of religious expression in the workplace and different limits to accommodation.[39]

Managing Religious Diversity

Employers increasingly are having to balance the rights of employees with differing religious beliefs. One way to do that is to make reasonable accommodation for employees' religious beliefs when assigning and scheduling work, because many religions have differing days of worship and holidays. For example, some firms have established "holiday swapping pools," whereby Christian employees can work during Passover or Ramadan or Chinese New Year, and employees from other religions can work on Christmas. Other firms allow employees a set number of days off for holidays, without specifying the holidays in company personnel policies. Figure 3-10 indicates common areas for accommodating religious diversity.

One potential area for conflict between employer policies and employee religious practices is dress and appearance. Some religions have standards about appropriate attire for women. Also, some religions expect men to have beards and facial hair, which may violate company appearance policies.[40]

Phased retirement
Approach in which employees gradually reduce their workloads and pay levels.

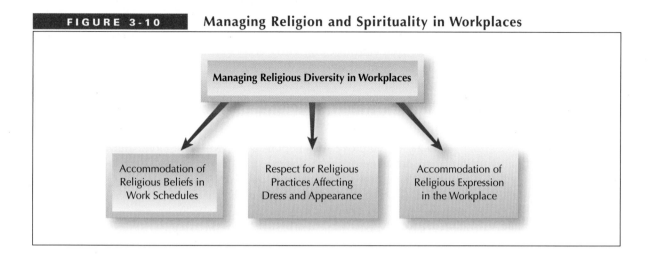

FIGURE 3-10 Managing Religion and Spirituality in Workplaces

Managing Religious Diversity in Workplaces

Accommodation of Religious Beliefs in Work Schedules

Respect for Religious Practices Affecting Dress and Appearance

Accommodation of Religious Expression in the Workplace

Another issue concerns religious expression. In the last several years, employees in several cases have sued employers for prohibiting them from expressing their religious beliefs at work. In other cases, employers have had to take action because of the complaints by workers that employees were aggressively "pushing" their religious views at work, thus creating a "hostile environment." Executives and owners of some firms have strong evangelical Christian beliefs that are carried over into their companies. Some display crosses, have Bible study groups for employees before work, sponsor Christian prayer groups, and support other efforts. But such actions can lead to non-Christians feeling discriminated against, thus creating a "hostile environment." Other areas that may need to be considered when dealing with religion at work are food, on-site religion-based groups, office decorations, and religious practices at work.[41]

MANAGING OTHER DISCRIMINATION ISSUES

Several different employment circumstances have resulted in a number of other key areas of potential discrimination. Some of the key issues are immigration, language, military status, sexual orientation, and appearance and weight.

Immigration Reform and Control Acts (IRCA)

The United States has always had a significant number of immigrants who come to work in this country. The increasing number of immigrants who have entered illegally has led to extensive political, social, and employment-related debates. The existence of more foreign-born workers means that employers must comply with the provisions of the Immigration Reform and Control Acts (IRCA). Employers are required to obtain and inspect I-9 forms, and verify documents such as birth certificates, passports, visas, and work permits. They can be fined if they knowingly hire illegal aliens. E-verify is a federal government source that can be used for this verification.[42] Federal contractors must use it to verify employees legal status.

Visas and Documentation Requirements Various revisions to the IRCA changed some of the restrictions on the entry of immigrants to work in U.S.

organizations, particularly organizations with high-technology and other "scarce skill" areas. More immigrants with specific skills have been allowed legal entry, and categories for entry visas were revised.

Visas are granted by U.S. consular offices (there are more than 200 such offices throughout the world). Many different types of visas exist. Among those most commonly encountered by employers are the B1 for business visitors, H-1B for professional or specialized workers, and L-1 for intracompany transfers.

Usually an employer must sponsor the workers. Companies are not supposed to hire employees to displace U.S. workers, and they must file documents with the Labor Department and pay prevailing U.S. wages to the visa holders. Despite these regulations, a number of unions and other entities view such programs as being used to circumvent the limits put on hiring foreign workers to displace U.S. workers. Given the volatile nature of this area, changes in federal, state, and local laws are likely to continue to be discussed, implemented, and reviewed in court decisions.[43]

Language Issues

As the diversity of the workforce increases, more employees have language skills beyond English. Interestingly, some employers have attempted to restrict the use of foreign languages, while other employers have recognized that bilingual employees have valuable skills

A number of employers have policies requiring that employees speak only English at work. These employers contend that the policies are necessary for valid business purposes. For instance, a manufacturer requires that employees working with dangerous chemicals use English to communicate hazardous situations to other workers and to read chemical labels.

The EEOC has issued guidelines clearly stating that employers may require workers to speak only English at certain times or in certain situations, but the business necessity of the requirements must be justified. Teaching, customer service, and telemarketing are examples of positions that may require English skills and voice clarity.

Some employers have found it beneficial to have bilingual employees so that foreign-language customers can contact someone who speaks their language. Some employers do not pay bilingual employees extra, believing that paying for the jobs being done is more appropriate than paying for language skills that are used infrequently on those jobs. Other employers pay "language premiums" if employees must speak to customers in another language. For instance, one employer pays workers in some locations a bonus if they are required to use a foreign language a majority of the time with customers. Bilingual employees are especially needed among police officers, airline flight personnel, hospital interpreters, international sales reps, and travel guides.

Military Status and USERRA

The employment rights of military veterans and reservists have been addressed in several laws. The two most important laws are the Vietnam Era Veterans Readjustment Assistance Act of 1974 and the Uniformed Services Employment and Reemployment Rights Act (USERRA) of 1994. Under the latter, employees are required to notify their employers of military service obligations. Employers must give employees serving in the military leaves of absence protections under the USERRA, as Figure 3-11 highlights.

FIGURE 3-11   **Uniformed Services Employment and Reemployment Rights Act (USERRA) Provisions**

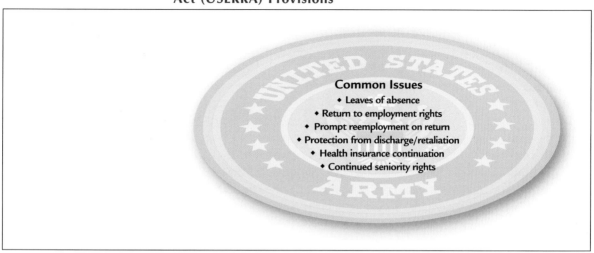

Common Issues
- ◆ Leaves of absence
- ◆ Return to employment rights
- ◆ Prompt reemployment on return
- ◆ Protection from discharge/retaliation
- ◆ Health insurance continuation
- ◆ Continued seniority rights

LOGGING ON

Uniformed Services Employment and Reemployment Rights Act (USERRA)

For information on the U.S. Department of Labor's Uniformed Services Employment and Reemployment Rights Act (USERRA), visit www.dol.gov/vets/programs/userra.

With the use of reserves and National Guard troops abroad, the provisions of USERRA have had more impact on employers. This act does not require employers to pay employees while they are on military leave, but many firms provide some compensation, often a differential. Many requirements regarding benefits, disabilities, and reemployment are covered in the act as well.[44]

Sexual Orientation

Recent battles in a number of states and communities illustrate the depth of emotions that accompany discussions of "gay rights."[45] Some states and cities have passed laws prohibiting discrimination based on sexual orientation or lifestyle. Even the issue of benefits coverage for "domestic partners," whether heterosexual or homosexual, has been the subject of state and city legislation. No federal laws of a similar nature have been passed. Whether gays and lesbians have any special rights under the equal protection amendment to the U.S. Constitution has not been decided by the U.S. Supreme Court.

A related issue is dealing with transgender individuals who have had sex-change surgery. Court cases and the EEOC have ruled that sex discrimination under Title VII applies to a person's gender at birth. Thus, it does not apply to the new gender of those who have had gender-altering operations. Transvestites and individuals with sexual behavior disorders are specifically excluded from being considered as disabled under the Americans with Disabilities Act of 1990. However, some states and several cities have laws prohibiting bias against transgender persons.[46]

Appearance and Weight Discrimination

Several EEO cases have been filed concerning the physical appearance of employees. Court decisions consistently have allowed employers to set dress codes as long as they are applied uniformly. For example, establishing a dress code for women but not for men has been ruled discriminatory. Also, employers should

Discrimination against "Caregivers"

The federal government is receiving increasing complaints that new mothers are being discriminated against on the job, but it is not just new mothers who are complaining. Men also are complaining that if they must care for an aging parent, they are no longer considered on a "fast track" for promotion. The complaints have been numerous enough that the EEOC has issued guidance for employers on the issue (available at the EEOC website under unlawful disparate treatment of workers with caregiving responsibilities). The phenomenon has even received its own label: FRD, or family responsibility discrimination.

Cases under FRD usually involve an employee who must care for a disabled spouse, aging parent, or child. Classic complaints may include retaliation and not being hired or promoted because of caregiving responsibilities. The FRD issue arises as the "sandwich generation," employees with both children and aging relatives, is appearing. Caregivers do not all file suits; some try to hide the fact they are caring for someone in hope of avoiding discrimination.

Family responsibility discrimination charges come in many forms, but the allegations are usually that a person has been disadvantaged in promotion, pay, or work. The lawsuits are usually filed under Title VII or the Family Medical Leave Act, but suits have been filed under the ADA as well. The Supreme Court in 1971 held that women with school-aged children could not be barred from applying for jobs held by fathers of school-aged children. Then the Civil Rights Act of 1991 gave employees claiming sex discrimination the right to a jury trial and damages for emotional suffering and punitive damages.

However, the issue of disparate treatment is not always clear. For example, is a failure to promote a young mother the result of her work history before her current job, current job performance, caregiving, or failure to apply for a specific job opening? This is the type of debate going on in courtrooms regarding FRD.[48]

be cautious when enforcing dress standards for women employees who are members of certain religions that prescribe appropriate and inappropriate dress and appearance standards. Some individuals have brought cases of employment discrimination based on height or weight. The crucial factor that employers must consider is that any weight or height requirements must be related to the job, such as when excess weight would hamper an individual's job performance.[47]

Family Responsibility Discrimination (FRD)

The HR Perspective shows the emergence of a recently identified and labeled discrimination based on complaints "caregivers" have about the way they are treated at work. The EEOC has issued guidelines for employers. The phenomenon has been labeled *family responsibility discrimination* (FRD).

DIVERSITY TRAINING

Traditional diversity training has a number of different goals. One prevalent goal is to minimize discrimination and harassment lawsuits. Other goals focus on improving acceptance and understanding of people with different backgrounds, experiences, capabilities, and lifestyles.

Components of Traditional Diversity Training

Approaches to diversity training vary, but often include at least three components. *Legal awareness* is the first and most common component. Here, the training focuses on the legal implications of discrimination. A limited approach to diversity training stops with these legal "do's and don'ts."

By introducing *cultural awareness*, trainers hope to build greater understanding of the differences among people. Cultural awareness training helps all participants to see and accept the differences in people with widely varying cultural backgrounds.

The third component of diversity training—*sensitivity training*—is more difficult. The aim here is to "sensitize" people to the differences among them and how their words and behaviors are seen by others. Some diversity training includes exercises containing examples of harassment and other behaviors.

Mixed Results for Diversity Training

The effects of diversity training are viewed as mixed by both organizations and participants. A limited number of studies have been done on the effectiveness of diversity training.[49] There is some concern that the programs may be interesting or entertaining, but may not produce longer-term changes in people's attitudes and behaviors toward others with characteristics different from their own.

Some argue that traditional diversity training more often than not has failed, pointing out that it does not reduce discrimination and harassment complaints. Rather than reducing conflict, in a number of situations diversity training has heightened hostility and conflicts. In some firms, it has produced divisive effects, and has not taught the behaviors needed for employees to work well together in a diverse workplace.[50]

This last point, focusing on behaviors, seems to hold the most promise for making diversity training more effective. For instance, dealing with cultural diversity as part of training efforts for sales representatives and managers has produced positive results. Teaching appropriate behaviors and skills in relationships with others is more likely to produce satisfactory results than focusing just on attitudes and beliefs among diverse employees.

Backlash against Diversity Training Efforts

The negative consequences of diversity training may manifest themselves broadly in a backlash against all diversity efforts. This backlash takes two main forms. First, and somewhat surprisingly, the individuals in protected groups, such as women and members of racial minorities, sometimes see the diversity efforts as inadequate and nothing but "corporate public relations." Thus, it appears that by establishing diversity programs, employers are raising the expectation levels of protected-group individuals, but the programs are not meeting the expectations.

On the other side, a number of individuals who are not in protected groups, primarily white males, believe that the emphasis on diversity sets them up as scapegoats for societal problems. Sometimes white males show hostility and anger at diversity efforts. Diversity programs are widely perceived as benefiting only women and racial minorities and taking away opportunities for men and nonminorities. This resentment and hostility is usually directed at affirmative action programs that employers have instituted.[51]

Trainers emphasize that the key to avoiding backlash in diversity efforts is to stress that people can believe whatever they wish, but at work their values are less important than their *behaviors*. Dealing with diversity is not about what people can and cannot *say*; it is about being *respectful* to others.

SUMMARY

- Equal employment is an attempt to level the field of opportunity for all people at work.
- Disparate treatment occurs when members of a protected category are treated differently from others.
- Disparate impact occurs when employment decisions work to the disadvantage of members of protected categories.
- Employers may be able to defend their management practices using business necessity, job relatedness, and bona fide occupational qualifications (BFOQ).
- Title VII of the 1964 Civil Rights Act was the first significant equal employment law. The Civil Rights Act of 1991 both altered and expanded on the 1964 provisions.
- Affirmative action has been intensely litigated, and the debate continues today.
- Several laws on sex/gender discrimination have addressed issues regarding pregnancy discrimination, unequal pay for similar jobs, and sexual harassment.
- It is vital that employers train all employees on what constitutes sexual harassment, promptly investigate complaints, and take action when sexual harassment is found to have occurred.

- As more women have entered the workforce, sex/gender issues in equal employment have included both discrimination through pay inequity and discrimination in jobs and careers.
- The Americans with Disabilities Act (ADA) requires that most employers identify the essential functions of jobs and that they make reasonable accommodations for individuals with disabilities unless doing so would result in undue hardship.
- Age discrimination against persons older than age 40 is illegal, according to the Age Discrimination in Employment Act (ADEA).
- The Immigration Reform and Control Acts (IRCA) identify employment regulations affecting workers from other countries.
- A number of other concerns have been addressed by laws, including discrimination based on religion, military status, and other factors.
- Individuals with disabilities represent a significant number of current and potential employees.
- Employers must make reasonable accommodations for individuals with disabilities, including those with mental or life-threatening illnesses.
- Diversity training has had limited success, possibly because it too often has focused on beliefs rather than behaviors.

CRITICAL THINKING ACTIVITIES

1. If your employer asked you to review the decision *not to hire* an African American applicant for a job, what would you need to consider?

2. Explain why you agree or disagree with affirmative action and how affirmative action may be affected by growing workforce diversity.

3. From your own experience or that of someone you know, give examples of the two types of sexual harassment.

4. Use this text and the U.S. Department of Justice website (www.usdoj.gov/crt/ada/) to identify what is reasonable accommodation and how it is determined.

HR EXPERIENTIAL PROBLEM SOLVING

The leadership in your company has changed as the result of a merger of your company with another company. The other company provides services similar to those provided by your company; however, the workforce demographic varies from that of your existing employees. For instance, the other company in the merger has a culture that recognizes and supports domestic partners. You have received a request to prepare a Diversity Initiative Plan. As HR Manager, you are aware that your existing employees will have issues and concerns and that you will need to institute some new policies, practices, and procedures. A resource for information on developing a Diversity Initiative Plan and diversity training is www.diversitycentral.com.

1. What should the plan include?
2. What diversity training programs should be offered to assist the employees of both companies in merging the two companies together?

CASE

Religious Accommodation?

As immigrants continue to come to the United States from many different cultures and religions, differences will cause some challenges and problems. One area where this has occurred is with Islamic culture and religion in the meat processing industry.

A plant (a fresh chicken facility) belonging to Tyson Foods, Inc., in Shelbyville, Tennessee, is one example. The company hired about 250 people from Somalia. A long-running civil war in their country has forced many Somalis to settle in the United States as refugees, and many Somalis are Muslim.

The union at the plant requested replacing the paid holiday Labor Day with Eid ul-Fitr, a religious holiday marking the end of the Muslim holy month of Ramadan. The request was brought up as part of negotiations for a new labor contract, and was part of the overall contract proposal approved by union members. The plant is often open on Labor Day anyway to meet consumer demand during the barbeque season. Along with holiday pay, the workers also received time and a half for hours worked on Labor Day.

The EEOC says employers may not treat people more or less favorably because of their religion. However, religious accommodation may be warranted unless it would impose an undue hardship on the employer. Flexible scheduling, voluntary time swaps, transfers, and reassignments are possible means of accommodation, along with other policies and practices.

Tyson's consideration of exchanging Labor Day for Eid ul-Fitr brought strong reactions from non-Muslim workers and the general public. The union voted again on the issue and overwhelmingly voted to reinstate Labor Day as a paid holiday. The company's solution was to have eight paid holidays, including a "personal holiday" that could be either the employee's birthday, Eid ul-Fitr, or another day approved by the employee's supervisor. That compromise was acceptable to the workers.

Another company that faced similar issues is JBS-SWIFT, a meat packer with plants in Grand Island, Nebraska, and Greeley, Colorado. That company also hired many Somali Muslims. The issue there was prayer time. In Greeley, the Muslim workers demanded time to pray at sundown—a requirement during Ramadan. The plant works three shifts. More than 300 workers walked out when they were told they could not have the time to pray. More than 100 were fired later, not for walking out but for not returning to work. The walkout touched off protests from workers of different faiths who thought the request for religious accommodation was too much.

The EEOC ruled that JBS-SWIFT had violated the civil rights of the employees it had fired. The company was found to have denied religious accommodation and retaliated against workers who complained. JBS-SWIFT has since set up special prayer rooms at its plants and allows Muslim workers to meet their religious obligations, which include prayers five times daily.[52]

QUESTIONS

1. What is the legal basis for the EEOC to hold that JBS-SWIFT had violated the employees' civil rights?

2. Contrast the solutions to the Tyson situation and the JBS-SWIFT situation. Which is likely to have the greatest positive impact on the company and why?

SUPPLEMENTAL CASES

Keep on Trucking

This case illustrates the problems that can be associated with the use of employment tests that have not been validated. (For the case, http://www.cengage.com/management/mathis.)

Mitsubishi Believes in EEO—Now

This case shows the problems Mitsubishi had with sexual harassment in the United States. (For the case, http://www.cengage.com/management/mathis.)

NOTES

1. Steve Stecklow, "Sexual Harassment Cases Plague the U.N.," *The Wall Street Journal*, May 21, 2009, A1.

2. Scott E. Page, "Making the Difference: Applying a Logic of Diversity," *Academy of Management Perspectives*, November 2009, 6–20.

3. Margaret M. Pinkham, "Employers Should Take Care When Making Decisions about Caregivers," *Employee Relations Law Journal*, Summer 2008, 35–40.

4. Mike Tobin, "S&Z Settles 2003 Bias Case," *The Cleveland Plain Dealer*, August 26, 2006, C1.

5. Mary Birk, "RIFS: Use Statistical Analysis to Avoid Disparate Impact Based on Age," *Legal Report Society for Human Resources Management*, April 2008, 5–8.

6. Anne Lindberg, "Disparate Impact or Disparate Treatment: Either Way Leads to Court," *Trend Watcher*, July 10, 2009, 1–5.

7. *Washington, Mayor of Washington, DC v. Davis*, 74 U.S. 1492 (1976).

8. Cynthia Marcotte Stamer, "Supreme Court Decision May Open Doors to More Retaliation Claims," *Employee Benefit News Legal Alert*, July 31, 2009, 1–5.

9. "Discrimination Charges on the Rise," *Benefit News.com Employee Benefit News*, September 15, 2007, 82; Sam Hananei, "Federal Job Discrimination Complaints Hit Record," *Yahoo! News*, March 11, 2009, 1–2.

10. Lilia M. Corting, "Unseen Injustice: Incivility as Modern Discrimination in Organizations," *Academy of Management Review*, January 2008, 55–75.

11. Robert J. Grossman, "Defusing Discrimination Claims," *HR Magazine*, May 2009, 47–51.

12. Fay Hansen, "Discriminatory Twist in Networking Sites Puts Recruiters in Peril," *Work Force Management*, September 2009, 1–5.

13. Gail Heriot, "Affirmative Action Backfires," *The Wall Street Journal*, August 24, 2007, A15; Jonathan Kaufman, "Fair Enough?" *The Wall Street Journal*, June 14–15, 2008, A1.

14. C. Tuna, N. Koppel, and M. Sanserino, "Job-Test Ruling Cheers Employers," *The Wall Street Journal*, July 1, 2009, B1; Adam Liptak, "Justices Find Bias Against Whites," *The Denver Post*, June 30, 2009, 1A.

15. *EEOC v. Eastern Michigan University*, No. 98-71806 (E.D. Mich., September 3, 1999).

16. Allen Smith, "Pay Bias Figures Prominently in New Supreme Court Forum," *HR News*, September 26, 2009, www.shrm.org/hrnews.

17. "New Law Makes Companies More Vulnerable to Complaints of Pay Discrimination," March 2009, www.towerswatson.com, 1–4.

18. "Lilly Ledbetter Fair Pay Act Signed into Law 1/29/2009," www.compensationresources.com, 1;

Jonathan A. Segal, "I Did It, But . . . ," *HR Magazine*, March 2008, 91–95.

19. J. Hoobler, S. Wayne, and G. Lemmon, "Bosses' Perceptions of Family/Work Conflict and Women's Promotability: Glass Ceiling Effects," *Academy of Management Journal*, October 2009, 939–957.

20. "Nontraditional Occupations for Women 2008," *Ceridian Abstracts*, April 2009, www.hrcompliance.ceridian.com, 1–5.

21. Eddy S. W. Ng, "Why Organizations Choose to Manage Diversity: Toward a Leadership-Based Theoretical Framework," *Human Resource Development Review*, March 2008, 58–78; S. Pichler, P. Simpson, and L. Stroh, "The Glass Ceiling in Human Resources: Exploring the Link Between Women's Representation in Management and the Practices of Strategic HRM and Employee Involvement," *Human Resource Management*, Fall 2008, 463–479.

22. L. Grensing-Pophal, "All in the Family," *HR Magazine*, September 2007, 66–70.

23. "Nearly 40% of Workers Have Had Workplace Romance," *Newsline*, January 31, 2007, www.spherion.com.

24. P. Dvorak, B. Davis, and L. Radnofsky, "Firms Confront Boss-Subordinate Love Affairs," *The Wall Street Journal*, October 27, 2008, B5.

25. Jennifer Thiel, "Harassment Claim Advances," *HR Magazine*, October 2008, 99.

26. "Model Discrimination and Harassment Policy," *Ceridian Abstracts*, www.hrcompliance.ceridian.com, 1–3.

27. Allen Smith, "Study: Women Supervisors Are More Likely to Be Harassed," www.shrm.org, 1.

28. Harsh Luther and Uipan Luther, "A Theoretical Framework Explaining Cross-Cultural Sexual Harassment: Integrating Hofsteds and Schwartz," *Journal of Labor Research*, Winter 2007, 169–188.

29. Stephanie Overman, "EEOC Opinion: Mandated Health Assessments Violate ADA," *Employee Benefit News*, July 2009, 1 and 48.

30. *Murphy v. United Parcel Service*, 527 U.S. 516 (1999).

31. Andrew Slobodien and Katie O'Brien, "The ADA Amendments Act of 2008 and How It Will Change the Workplace," *Employee Relations Law Journal*, Winter 2008, 32–39.

32. Bill Leonard, "The Stealth Statute," *HR Magazine*, December 2008, 47–51; Ann Murrary and Leah Singleton, "Employers Beware: New Antidiscrimination Legislation Has Been Passed," *Employee Relations Law Journal*, Winter 2008, 27–31; Cynthia Stamer, "Group Health Plans Will Face Challenges with GINA," *Employee Benefit News Legal Alert*, May 8, 2009, 1–4.

33. Kelly M. Butler, "10 Million Ways to Fill the Talent Gap," *Employee Benefit News*, March 2007, 22; Laurence P. Postol, "ADAAA Will Result in Renewed Emphasis on Reasonable Accommodations," *SHRM Legal Report*, January 2009, 1–6.

34. Jennifer Levitz, "More Workers Cite Age Bias After Layoffs," *The Wall Street Journal*, March 11, 2009, D1.

35. Rosemary Lucas and Shobana Keegan, "Probing the Basis for Differential Pay Practices of Younger Workers in Low Paying Hospitality Firms," *Human Resource Management Journal*, 18, (2008), 386–404.

36. Heidi Gattau-Fox, "U.S. Supreme Court's Age Discrimination Decision Is Good News for Employers," *Blair D Holm Labor and Employment Law Update*, August 2009, 2–3; Cara Woodson Welch, "The Supreme Court Weighs in on Total Rewards," *Workspan*, July 2008, 20–23.

37. G. Wood, A. Wilkerson, and M. Harcourt, "Age Discrimination and Working Life: Perspectives and Contestations—A Review of the Contemporary Literature," *International Journal of Management Reviews*, Volume 10, 2008, 425–442.

38. David Migoya, "EEOC: Swift Acted with Bias," *The Denver Post*, September 1, 2009, 7B.

39. Eileen Kelly, "Accommodating Religious Expression in the Workplace," *Employer Responsibility and Rights Journal*, 20 (2008), 45–56.

40. Mark Downey, "Keeping the Faith," *HR Magazine*, January 2008, 85–88.

41. Robert Grossman, "Religion at Work," *HR Magazine*, December 2008, 27–33.

42. Bruce Finley, "Immigration Checks Rise," *The Denver Post*, June 1, 2009, 1; Anna Gorman, "Businesses Flock to E-Verify," *Casper Star-Tribune*, May 17, 2009, C2.

43. "Jobs and Immigrants," *The Wall Street Journal*, April 4, 2007, A14; Pia Orrenius and Madeline Zavondny, "Does Immigration Affect Wages?" *Labour Economics*, 14, (2007), 757–773; Scott Wright, "Worksite Enforcement of US Immigration Law," *Employee Relations Law Journal*, Autumn 2008, 66–102.

44. Thomas McKinney, "The USERRA Minefield," *Human Resource Executive*, October 2, 2008, 8.

45. Diane Cadrain, "Sexual Equity in the Workplace," *HR Magazine*, September 2008, 44–48; Bill Leonard, "Workplace Diversity Library—Sexual Orientation," *SHRM Knowledge Center*, April 19, 2007, www.shrm.org.

46. Nancy Day and Patricia Greene, "A Case for Sexual Orientation Diversity Management in Small and Large Organizations," *Human Resource Management*, Fall 2008, 637–654.

47. Catherine Arnst, "Bias of the Bulge," *BusinessWeek*, April 28, 2008, 22; Lisa Finkelstein, et al., "Bias Against Overweight Job Applicants," *Human Resource Management*, Summer 2007, 203–222; Mark Roehling, Richard Posthuma, and James Dulebohn, "Obesity Related 'Perceived Disability' Claims," *Employee Relations Law Journal*, Spring 2007, 30–51.

48. Stephanie Armour, "More Employers Face Caregiver Related Suits," *USA Today*, October 25, 2007, 3B; Stephan Barlas, "Caregivers Unite," *Human Resource Executive*, June 16, 2008, 53–55; C. W. VonBerger, W. T. Marver, and R. Howard, "Family Responsibilities Discrimination: The EEOC Guidance," *Employee Relations Law Journal*, Summer 2008, 14–34.

49. Rohini Anand and Mary-Francis Winters, "A Retrospective of Corporate Diversity Training from 1964 to the Present," *Academy of Management Learning and Education*, September 2008, 356–373.

50. Susan Awbrey, "The Dynamics of Vertical and Horizontal Diversity in Organization and Society," *Human Resource Development Review*, 6 (2007), 7–32.

51. Carol Kulik, et al., "The Rich Get Richer: Predicting Participation in Voluntary Diversity Training," *Journal of Organizational Behavior*, Volume 28 (2007), 753–769.

52. Tom Wray, "Learning to Adapt: Companies Acclimate to a Changing Workforce," *The National Provisioner*, November 1, 2008, 1–2; David Migoya, "EEOC: SWIFT Acted with Bias," *The Denver Post*, September 1, 2009, 7B.

Jobs and Labor

4

Workers, Jobs, and Job Analysis

After you have read this chapter, you should be able to:

- Explain how the diversity of the workforce affects HR management functions.
- Identify components of work flow analysis that must be considered.
- Define *job design* and identify common approaches to varying job design.
- Describe different types of work teams and HR facets that must be considered.
- Discuss how telework and work flexibility are linked to work-life balancing efforts.
- Describe job analysis and the stages and methods used in the process.
- List the components of job descriptions.

Work-Life Balancing

J obs must be balanced with work-life issues. Workforce demographics of employees by racial/ethnic background, age, and gender, indicate that organizations must adjust to the fact that employees want to increase flexibility in their work schedules to accommodate the life outside the job.

A comprehensive study of more than 500 organizations and their employees by the Institute for Corporate Productivity identified two reasons employees want flexible work: (1) much of their work does not require being in the office all of the time, or (2) they have long commutes. Using occupational groups, the study identified that approximately three-fourths of professional employees and half of administrative employees wanted flexible schedules. Women were another group that wanted more flexibility.

A change that has affected work is the growth in telecommuting. Through greater use of technology, more employees are working outside of the workplace. For instance, managers and other employees may work from home, an elder parent's apartment, a client's facility, an airport conference room, a work suite in a hotel resort, or even a vacation location. Thus, balancing workers and jobs with technology and flexibility in work schedules and location is likely to increase in importance, affecting both organizational and individual performance.[1]

(© Getty Images/Jupiter Image)

Throughout organizations of all types, the composition of workers and jobs is shifting in nature. As the HR Headline shows, these shifts are likely to continue growing in the next years, requiring changes in the way some HR functions are done. Relevant changes in the workforce follow.

WORKFORCE COMPOSITION

The existing U.S. workforce is changing, and projections indicate that more shifting will occur in the next few years.[2] To analyze the composition of workers and jobs in the United States, the U.S. Bureau of Labor Statistics (BLS) undertakes studies to identify current and future projected compositions. Because of economic shifts and their effects in different industries, some types of workers are scarce but in high demand, while others are available in excessive numbers.

According to studies by the BLS and various industry groups, health care and health-related jobs are increasing, in part because of the aging U.S. population. The rapid growth in technology is creating a need for more workers with special technical capabilities. However, many manufacturing industries, such as automobile and airline firms, have had significant decline in numbers of jobs and workers. These and other factors make it likely that the workforce composition will continue to change.

Another worker-related shift results from the U.S. workforce becoming more diverse. As organizations develop or increase global operations, diversity in the workforce is becoming more prominent. **Diversity** reflects the differences in human characteristics and composition in an organization. The tangible indicators of diversity that employers must consider include the following:

- Race/ethnicity
- National origin/immigration
- Age/generational differences
- Gender—men and women
- Marital and family status
- Sexual orientation
- Disabilities
- Religion

In addition, individuals can be *multicultural* and be included in several groups.

Business Contribution of Diverse Workers

Different organizations approach the management of diversity from several perspectives.[3] As Figure 4-1 shows, the continuum can run from resistance to creation of an inclusive diversity culture.

For diversity to succeed, the most crucial component is seeing it as a commitment throughout the organization, beginning with top management.[4] Diversity results must be measured, and management accountability for achieving results must be emphasized and rewarded. For instance, PepsiCo, a large food and beverage company, has developed and implemented a Diversity and Inclusion Council so that diversity considerations are part of all strategic efforts. PepsiCo also has regular diversity celebrations, newsletters, and other events. This inclusion of diversity issues throughout the company contributes to PepsiCo's success with employees, managers, and customers.[5]

One survey found that more than 60% of firms were committed to diversity and almost 50% of senior managers recognized the business case for diversity.[6]

Diversity Differences in human characteristics and composition in an organization.

FIGURE 4-1	Various Approaches to Diversity and Their Results

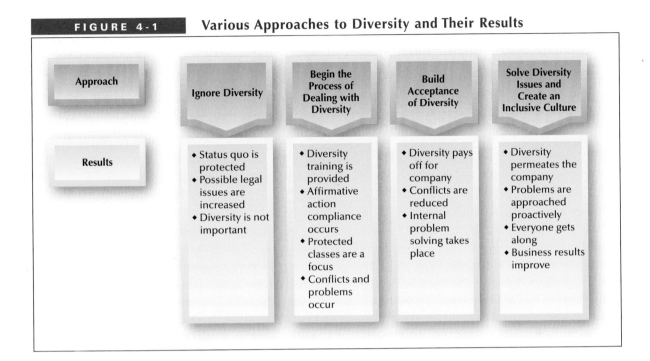

Approach	Ignore Diversity	Begin the Process of Dealing with Diversity	Build Acceptance of Diversity	Solve Diversity Issues and Create an Inclusive Culture
Results	• Status quo is protected • Possible legal issues are increased • Diversity is not important	• Diversity training is provided • Affirmative action compliance occurs • Protected classes are a focus • Conflicts and problems occur	• Diversity pays off for company • Conflicts are reduced • Internal problem solving takes place	• Diversity permeates the company • Problems are approached proactively • Everyone gets along • Business results improve

However, the "business case" for diversity must be linked to key business goals and strategies and organizational results.[7] The business case for diversity includes the following:

- Diversity allows new talent and ideas from employees of different backgrounds, which can enhance organizational performance.
- Diversity helps recruiting and retention because protected-class individuals often prefer to work in organizations with coworkers of various demographics.
- Diversity allows for an increase of market share because customers can be attracted to purchase products and services with varied demographic marketing activities.
- Diversity can lead to lower costs because there may be fewer discrimination lawsuits.

The results of increased diversity for organizations, work groups, individuals, and society/community must be considered. An example of an organization that has utilized diversity is NASA/Goddard Space Flight Center. Diversity at Goddard is a core value and part of its business objectives.[8] Goddard has engaged in recruiting diverse individuals and integrating them through training and other HR actions, which include establishing communications and bulletin board systems that enhance diversity efforts.

One concern with diversity programs is that they may be perceived as benefiting only certain groups of persons and not others. Diversity actions must be well thought out and address both the positive and negative aspects of such programs, given the workforce composition of many organizations.[9]

Race and Ethnicity

Significant race and ethnic shifts in the U.S. population will occur in the next several decades. By the year 2050, racial/ethnic groups currently in the minority

Resolving Language Barriers Pays Off

A firm that has been recognized by a national competitive workforce award is Nebraska Furniture Mart (NFM). Selling furniture, appliances, and many home items, NFM needs numerous individuals to work a wide range of hours every week. Owned primarily by the well-known investor Warren Buffet, NFM has been operating in Nebraska, Iowa, and Kansas.

When NFM expanded from Omaha to Kansas City, it encountered a major turnover of Hispanic employees in its Kansas City operation. As turnover increased, reductions in work quality and productivity resulted. Management recognized that the concerns of both Hispanic customers and employees needed to be better addressed.

Executives, managers, and HR professionals at NFM recognized that they needed to do a better job of attracting, retaining, and training Hispanic workers. They created a three-part effort called "Bienvenido a la Familia de NFM" (Welcome to Our NFM Family). They also expanded recruiting efforts, using Hispanic newspapers. In addition, NFM hired a bilingual interpreter as part of HR, and then offered employees free basic English classes.

The results of these efforts over several years have been very positive, resulting in more recruiting and less turnover of Hispanic workers. Work-related quality and productivity also have increased, particularly in the warehouse where many Hispanic people work. Responding to racial/ethnic diversity in terms of a specific group enhanced HR and organizational performance in NFM.[10]

will likely make up more than 50% of the U.S. population. The Census Bureau says whites represent 67% of the population currently, but will be at approximately 48% in 2050. The Hispanic population will increase dramatically, to about 39% of the overall population, and will exceed the African American population. The Asian population will triple to about 9% by 2050.[11]

These statistics indicate that accommodating racial/ethnic differences are a part of everyday life, and such efforts do bring results. For example, a Michigan manufacturing firm dealt with racial tensions between whites and workers of other ethnic/racial backgrounds. Initially, few nonwhites attended company social events, and if they did, they sat apart from the white population. However, after five years of diversity training and other HR efforts, people of all races and ethnic groups were interacting more frequently and working together more effectively. This example illustrates why efforts to integrate people of different types must be made.[12] Integrated work groups, social events, electronic communications, and other approaches can be used to help with conflict. The HR Best Practices illustrates how Nebraska Furniture Mart has successfully worked with its Hispanic/Latino employees.

Immigrant Workers Another racial/ethnic factor is the growth in the number of immigrants to the United States and other developed countries. The United States has always had a significant number of immigrants who have come to work in this country. The increasing number of immigrants entering illegally has led to extensive political, social, and employment-related issues. In the United States, one concern is the large number of illegal immigrants hired to fill certain jobs at low cost, despite availability of unemployed U.S. workers. With the growth in racial/ethnic immigrants projected to increase and with the likelihood of more changes in immigration laws, HR professionals will have to monitor and manage the immigrant issue as it applies to both company and industry.

Generational Differences

Much has been written about the expectations of individuals in different age groups and generations. For employers, these varied expectations present challenges, especially given economic, global, technology, and other changes in the workplace. Some common age/generational groups are labeled as follows:

- Matures (born before 1946)
- Baby boomers (born 1946–1964)
- Generation Xers (born 1965–1980)
- Generation Yers (millenials) (born 1981–2000)

As the economy and industries have changed, the aging of the U.S. workforce has become a significant concern. Workers over age 55 are delaying retirement more often, working more years, and/or looking for part-time work or phased retirement. Economic conditions are the predominant reasons why these workers are bypassing the "normal" retirement age of 65.[13] As older and more experienced employees retire in the future, employers will face increasing gaps as they try to replace the experience and capabilities of baby boomers.

Generational differences in expectations are likely to add to challenges and conflicts in organizations. For instance, many baby boomers and matures are concerned about security and experience, while younger people have different concerns. Generation Yers are often seen as the "why" generation; they expect to be rewarded quickly, use more technology, and often ask more questions about why managers and organizations make the decisions they do. Consider the dynamics of a mature manager directing generation X and Y individuals, or generation X managers supervising older, more experienced baby boomers as well as generation Y employees. However, it is crucial to be aware that stereotyping these individuals by generations may not reflect how actual individuals view their jobs and produce organizational results.[14]

Managing Multigenerational Workforce What the discussion of generations suggests is that managers must be aware of the possible opportunities as well as the challenges with a multigenerational workforce in an organization. Firms are engaging in activities to enhance multigenerational and managerial effectiveness as described in Figure 4-2. For example, Border's Group bookstores and a Virginia hospital have had good experiences, because of expanded training, with different generations of individuals working together.[15]

The generation gaps may be less severe than many articles suggest. How much such gaps are reduced relates to supervisor/subordinate/coworker relationships and how employees of all types are engaged in the organization through training work teams and by other means.[16]

Gender Workforce Diversity

Women are becoming a greater percentage of workers in the U.S. workforce; they comprise more than 46% of the total employed individuals. However, men average more work time daily than do women.[17] Interestingly, as the economic and labor market has been shifting, the job fields dominated by men have been hit harder than those consisting mostly of women. Male workers

FIGURE 4-2	Positive Multigenerational Management Activities

Positive Multigenerational Management Activities

- Integrating generational individuals
- Recognizing employees' different expectations
- Developing varied mentoring means
- Adapting training methods to reflect generational capabilities

- Utilizing younger persons' technology skills to aid baby boomers
- Supporting individual career expectations that vary by groups
- Openly addressing generational issues
- Establishing multigenerational work groups and projects

are more heavily represented in manufacturing, farming, and other "male-dominated" industries, so male employees have been impacted more severely by the market shifts than women employees with their higher rates of participation in industries such as health care and education.

From this follows some of the gender issues that occur in organizations. First, women overall have lower average pay than men due to the nature of their jobs and work hours. Second, in some industries and countries, women make up a much smaller percentage of senior executives and managers in many organizations and occupations. Over the past decade more women have become managers, but women comprise only about 10% or less of senior level executive and board members.[18] Some of the wage gap between men and women is due to the greater family/home responsibilities that females have to meet. One survey found that more than 40% of working mothers would take pay cuts to have more time with their children.[19]

Both women and men also are increasingly facing the need to aid older family members, as matures and baby boomers encounter health disabilities and other problems. Addressing work and family issues is part of work-life balancing, which is examined later in this chapter in the discussion of workforce flexibility in jobs.

NATURE OF JOBS AND WORK

One way to visualize an organization is as an entity that takes inputs from the surrounding environment and then, through some kind of "work," turns those inputs into goods or services. **Work** is effort directed toward accomplishing results.

Work Effort directed toward accomplishing results.

Work Flow Analysis

Work flow analysis Study of the way work (inputs, activities, and outputs) moves through an organization.

Work flow analysis is the study of the way work moves through an organization. Usually, it begins with an examination of the quantity and quality of the desired and actual *outputs* (goods and services). Then the *activities* (tasks and jobs) that lead to the outputs are evaluated to see if they are achieving the desired outputs. Finally, the *inputs* (people, material, information, data, equipment, etc.) must be assessed to determine if they make the outputs and activities better and more efficient.

An integrating work flow analysis is likely to lead to better employee involvement, greater efficiency, and more customer satisfaction as organizational work is divided into jobs so that it can be coordinated. A **job** is a grouping of the tasks, duties, and responsibilities that constitutes the work assignment for an employee. Tasks, duties, and responsibilities may change over time; therefore, jobs may change and may increase or decrease in number.

If internal changes do not happen, an organization is probably failing to adapt to the shifting business and competitive environment and may be becoming outmoded or noncompetitive. As an example, at Southwest Airlines, organizational values and strategies are tied to having involved employees working in a flexible enjoyable culture that delivers dependable service at low fares. Southwest employees have a high degree of flexibility in how they perform their work as workload demands shift. Other airlines, such as American and United, have higher fares, fewer service amenities, and employees with more narrowly defined jobs. The way work is done and how jobs are designed and performed vary significantly under these two approaches, and the differences impact the number of jobs and people needed.

Technology and Work Flow Analysis A factor that must be considered in work flow analysis in organizations is technology. The information-based systems used by many employees make work flow different from what it was in previous years. Sometimes the differences are positive and highly productive, but technology also can reduce work flow and productivity. For example, consider the amount of time some employees spend on personal use of technology such as text-messaging, twitters, and personal websites such as Facebook. Such usage can distract workers and may reduce work-related productivity.

Business Process Reengineering After work flow analysis provides an understanding of how work is being done, reengineering generates the needed changes in the operations. The purpose of **business process reengineering (BPR)** is to improve such activities as product development, customer service, and service delivery. BPR consists of three phases:

1. *Rethink:* Examine how the current organization of work and jobs affects customer satisfaction and service.
2. *Redesign:* Analyze how jobs are put together, the work flow, and how results are achieved; then redesign the process as necessary.
3. *Retool:* Look at new technologies (equipment, computers, software, etc.) as opportunities to improve productivity, service quality, and customer satisfaction.

Job Grouping of tasks, duties, and responsibilities that constitutes the total work assignment for an employee.

Business process reengineering (BPR) Measures for improving such activities as product development, customer service, and service delivery.

Because of the desire to improve HR efficiency and effectiveness, BPR is increasingly being applied to HR management. Although implementation of reengineering can be difficult, if done well it can aid work success. For instance, firms such as AT&T and a mid-sized Italian bank have done reengineering that has been successful for both the organization and the workforce.[20]

JOB DESIGN

Job design refers to organizing tasks, duties, responsibilities, and other elements into a productive unit of work. Identifying the components of a given job is an integral part of job design. Job design receives attention for three major reasons:

- Job design can influence *performance* in certain jobs, especially those where employee motivation can make a substantial difference.
- Job design can affect *job satisfaction*. Because people are more satisfied with certain job elements than others, identifying what makes a "good" job becomes critical. Reduced turnover and absenteeism also can be linked to effective job design.
- Job design can impact both *physical* and *mental health*. Problems that may require assistance such as hearing loss, backache, leg pain, stress, high blood pressure, and even heart disease sometimes can be traced directly to job design.

Managers play a significant role in job design because often they are the people who establish jobs and their design components. They must make sure that job expectations are clear, that decision-making responsibilities and the accountability of workers are clarified, and that interactions with other jobs are integrated and appropriate.[21]

The nature and characteristics of both jobs and people should be considered when job design is done. As Figure 4-3 indicates, managers can influence or control job characteristics, but not people characteristics.

Job design Organizing tasks, duties, responsibilities, and other elements into a productive unit of work.

FIGURE 4-3   **Some Characteristics of People and Jobs**

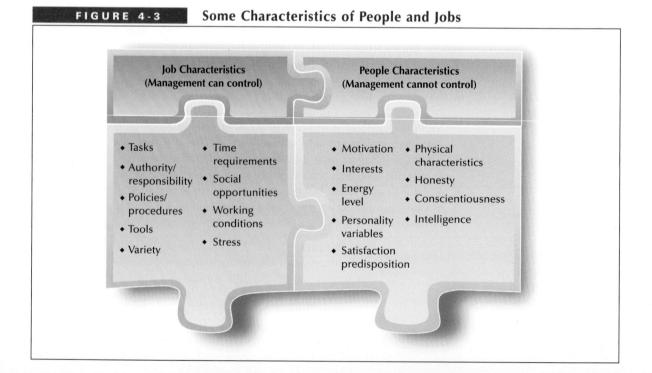

Job Characteristics (Management can control)	People Characteristics (Management cannot control)
◆ Tasks ◆ Authority/ responsibility ◆ Policies/ procedures ◆ Tools ◆ Variety ◆ Time requirements ◆ Social opportunities ◆ Working conditions ◆ Stress	◆ Motivation ◆ Interests ◆ Energy level ◆ Personality variables ◆ Satisfaction predisposition ◆ Physical characteristics ◆ Honesty ◆ Conscientiousness ◆ Intelligence

Workers and Job Design

Organizations are employing a variety of workers, and not just full-time ones. Depending on economic and competitive factors, the types of workers in one firm may include:

- Full-time employees
- Part-time employees
- Independent contractors
- Temporary workers
- Contingent workers

Although some organizations still use the traditional approach of employing full- and part-time workers, many firms are making significant use of independent, temporary, and contingent individuals. These persons are not employees but generally work at-will or on limited contracts, and they may be working for other employers as well. A **contingent worker** is someone who is not an employee, but a temporary or part-time worker for a specific period of time and type of work.

According to the U.S. Bureau of Labor Statistics, contingent workers are a part of "alternative workers" who may be on-call, working through an employment agency, or operating as independent contractors.[22] A number of contingent workers have contracts with employers that establish their pay, hours, job requirements, limitations, and time periods. As mentioned in Chapter 1, more employers are using contingent or temporary workers. Estimates are that up to 50% of some types of jobs are performed by contingent workers who are not regular employees. Nike, Kelly Services, and Earthlink are examples of firms that are using more contingent workers.[23]

Person-Job Fit Not everyone would enjoy being an HR manager, an engineer, a nurse, or a drill-press operator. But some people like and do well at each of these jobs. The **person-job fit** is a simple but important concept of matching characteristics of people with characteristics of jobs. If a person does not fit a job, theoretically either the person can be changed or replaced or the job can be altered. However, though an employer can try to make a "round" person fit a "square" job, it is hard to successfully reshape people. By redesigning jobs, the person-job fit may sometimes be improved more easily. For example, bank tellers talk to people all day; an individual who would rather not talk to others all day may do better in a job that does not require so much interaction because that part of the bank teller job probably cannot be changed. Different people will consider some jobs "good" and others "bad." As a result, people will fit different kinds of work.

Job-Person Match Matching people with jobs they like and fit can have positive consequences. Higher or lower turnover rates in the first few months of employment are often linked to recruiting and selection screening efforts. Then, once individuals have been placed in jobs, other job/work factors affect retention. Because individuals spend significant time on their jobs, they expect to have modern equipment, technology, and good working conditions. Physical and environmental factors such as space, lighting, temperature, noise, and layout can affect retention of employees as well as their work.

Additionally, workers want a safe work environment, in which risks of accidents and injuries have been addressed. That is especially true for employees in such industries as manufacturing, agriculture, utilities, and transportation,

Contingent worker Someone who is not an employee, but a temporary or part-time worker for a specific period of time and type of work.

Person-job fit Matching characteristics of people with characteristics of jobs.

which have higher safety risks than do many service industries and office environments.

Common Approaches to Job Design

One approach for designing or redesigning jobs is to simplify the job tasks and responsibilities. Job simplification may be appropriate for jobs that are to be staffed with entry-level employees. However, making jobs too simple may result in boring jobs that appeal to few people, causing high turnover. Several other approaches also have been used as part of job design.

Job Enlargement and Job Enrichment Attempts to alleviate some of the problems encountered in excessive job simplification fall under the general headings of job enlargement and job enrichment. **Job enlargement** involves broadening the scope of a job by expanding the number of different tasks to be performed. **Job enrichment** is increasing the depth of a job by adding responsibility for planning, organizing, controlling, or evaluating the job. Some examples of job enrichment are:

- Giving the employee an entire job rather than just a piece of the work
- Allowing the employee more flexibility to perform the job as needed
- Increasing the employee's accountability for work by reducing external control
- Expanding assignments for employees to do new tasks and develop special areas of expertise
- Directing feedback reports to the employee rather than only to management

Job Rotation One technique that can break the monotony of an otherwise simple routine job is **job rotation**, which is the process of shifting a person from job to job. There are several advantages to job rotation with one being that it develops an employee's capabilities for doing several different jobs. For instance, some firms have been successful at using job rotation for employees with disabilities in special assembly lines and different work requirement times.[24] Even people without disabilities can be adaptable and change jobs and careers internally in appropriate ways. Clear policies that identify for employees the nature and expectations of job rotations are more likely to make job rotation work.[25]

Job enlargement Broadening the scope of a job by expanding the number of different tasks to be performed.

Job enrichment Increasing the depth of a job by adding responsibility for planning, organizing, controlling, or evaluating the job.

Job rotation Process of shifting a person from job to job.

Job sharing Scheduling arrangement in which two employees perform the work of one full-time job.

Job Sharing Another alternative used is **job sharing**, in which two employees perform the work of one full-time job. For instance, a hospital allows two radiological technicians to fill one job, and each individual works every other week. Such arrangements are beneficial for employees who may not want or be able to work full-time because of family, school, or other reasons. The keys to successful job sharing are that both "job sharers" must work effectively together and each must be competent in meeting the job requirements.

Characteristics of Jobs

A model developed by Hackman and Oldham focuses on five important design characteristics of jobs. Figure 4-4 shows that *skill variety, task identity*, and *task significance* affect the meaningfulness of work; *autonomy* stimulates responsibility; and *feedback* provides knowledge of results. Each aspect can make a job better for the jobholder to the degree that it is present.

| FIGURE 4-4 | Job Characteristics Model |

* **Skill variety** is the extent to which the work requires several different activities for successful completion. For example, lower skill variety exists when an assembly-line worker performs the same two tasks repetitively. Skill variety is not to be confused with *multitasking*, which is doing several tasks at the same time with computers, telephones, personal organizers, and other means. The impact of multitasking for an employee may be never getting away from the job—not a "better" outcome for everyone.

* **Task identity** is the extent to which the job includes a "whole" identifiable unit of work that is carried out from start to finish and that results in a visible outcome. For example, when a customer calls with a problem, a customer specialist can handle the stages from maintenance to repair in order to resolve the customer's problem.

* **Task significance** is the impact the job has on other people. A job is more meaningful if it is important to other people for some reason. For instance, police officers may experience more fulfillment when dealing with a real threat than when merely training to be ready in case a threat arises.

* **Autonomy** is the extent of individual freedom and discretion in the work and its scheduling. More autonomy leads to a greater feeling of personal responsibility for the work.

* **Feedback** is the amount of information employees receive about how well or how poorly they have performed. The advantage of feedback is that it helps employees to understand the effectiveness of their performance and contributes to their overall knowledge about the work.

Skill variety Extent to which the work requires several different activities for successful completion.

Task identity Extent to which the job includes a "whole" identifiable unit of work that is carried out from start to finish and that results in a visible outcome.

Task significance Impact the job has on other people.

Autonomy Extent of individual freedom and discretion in the work and its scheduling.

Feedback The amount of information employees receive about how well or how poorly they have performed.

Using Worker Teams in Jobs

Typically, a job is thought of as something done by one person. However, where appropriate, jobs may be designed for teams to take advantage of the increased productivity and commitment that can follow such a change. Organizations can assign jobs to teams of employees instead of just individuals. Some firms have gone as far as dropping such terms as *workers* and *employees*, replacing them with *teammates, crew members, associates,* and other titles that emphasize teamwork.

As organizations have changed, the types of teams have changed as well. Having global operations with diverse individuals and using technology advances have affected the nature of teams contributing to organizational projects. For example, one survey found that about one-third of the different types of teams possible were used in major HR projects.[26]

Special Types of Teams There are several types of teams that function outside the scope of members' normal jobs and meet from time to time. One is the **special-purpose team**, which is formed to address specific problems, improve work processes, and enhance the overall quality of products and services. Often, special-purpose teams are a mixture of employees, supervisors, and managers.

The **self-directed team** is composed of individuals who are assigned a cluster of tasks, duties, and responsibilities to be accomplished. Unlike special-purpose teams, self-directed work teams become entities that use regular internal decision-making processes. Use of self-directed work teams must be planned well and fit the culture of the organization.

The **virtual team** is composed of individuals who are separated geographically but linked by communications technology. The success of virtual work teams depends on a number of factors, including training of team members, planning and managing virtual tasks and projects, and using technology for expansion of teamwork. However, some research has identified that virtual teams can lead to unresolved problems, less productivity, and miscommunications.[27]

Global Teams Global operations have resulted in an increasing use of virtual teams. Members of these teams seldom or never meet in person. Instead, they "meet" electronically using Web-based systems. With global teams, it is important for managers and HR to address various issues, including who is to be chosen for the teams, how they are to communicate and collaborate online and sometimes in person, and what tasks and work efforts may be done with these teams.[28]

Teams and Work Efforts As the use of teams has grown, creating ones that contribute to organizational performance is important. Factors that affect the work team success and performance increasingly have become part of HR.[29] Figure 4-5 highlights some common team elements related to team performance.

The use of work teams has been a popular form of job redesign in the last decade. Improved productivity, increased employee involvement, greater coworker trust, more widespread employee learning, and greater employee use of knowledge diversity are among the potential benefits.[30] In a transition to work teams, efforts are necessary to define the areas of work, scope of authority, and goals of the teams. Also, teams must recognize and address dissent, conflict, and other problems.[31]

The role of supervisors and managers changes with use of teams because of the emergence or development of team leaders. Rather than giving orders, often the team leader becomes a facilitator to assist the team, to mediate and resolve conflicts among team members, and to interact with other teams and managers elsewhere.

GLOBAL

Special-purpose team
Organizational team formed to address specific problems, improve work processes, and enhance the overall quality of products and services.

Self-directed team
Organizational team composed of individuals who are assigned a cluster of tasks, duties, and responsibilities to be accomplished.

Virtual team Organizational team composed of individuals who are separated geographically but linked by communications technology.

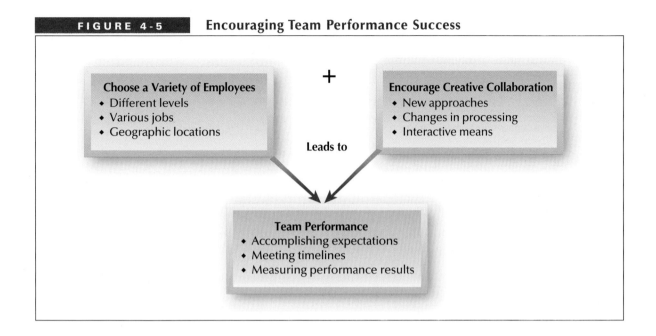

FIGURE 4-5   **Encouraging Team Performance Success**

Choose a Variety of Employees
• Different levels
• Various jobs
• Geographic locations

+

Encourage Creative Collaboration
• New approaches
• Changes in processing
• Interactive means

Leads to

Team Performance
• Accomplishing expectations
• Meeting timelines
• Measuring performance results

LOGGING ON

Team Building, Inc.
This website provides information for team building services and team building training products. Visit the site at www.teambuildinginc.com.

Teams can be enhanced through task responsibility, discussion structures, and cooperation efforts. Age and educational diversity can expand task-relevant information and team performance bases.[32] However, some organizations have noted a lack of willingness of team members to share information with those who are different from themselves. To counteract such problems, diversity training for teams and their members could be part of the design when establishing and managing teams.[33]

JOBS AND WORK SCHEDULING

Considerations that can affect job design for both employers and employees are how the work is to be done, the time during which work is scheduled, and the location of employees when working. One factor changing how and when work is done is technology, including the creation of telework for some people.

Telework

Individuals who may be working at home or at other places illustrate **telework**, which means that employees work via electronic, telecommunications, and Internet means. The use of technology for telework is expected to grow, with almost 70% of private-sector respondents predicting more usage of IT resources in telework.[34] Some employers are allowing employees to *telecommute* one or more days a week. Telecommuting allows employees to work from home when bad weather or widespread health issues (e.g., pandemic flu) prevents them from coming to office facilities.[35] Common advantages of telework for employers are highlighted in Figure 4-6.

Telework Employees work with technology via electronic, telecommunications, and Internet means.

FIGURE 4-6   Telework Advantages for Employers

Business Impacts	Employee Impacts
◆ Improves business/employee productivity ◆ Reduces organizational costs ◆ Saves on paid travel and commuting time ◆ Reduces environmental and energy costs and effects ◆ Provides work services at varied hours	◆ Aids individual retention and reduces turnover ◆ Expands employee recruitment "area" and attractiveness ◆ May enhance employee job satisfaction and morale ◆ Enhances employees' personal lives and health

Teleworking Considerations As more employers use telework, there are both advantages and concerns to consider. Several firms have found that telework can cut costs and raise productivity. For example, Home Shopping Network has 900 telecommuters in three states and has increased productivity and employee applicant desirability. This is why, according to one survey, almost 40% of organizations offer some telecommuting.[36]

However, the working relationship with teleworkers should begin with a carefully worded policy. This is necessary because the fact that managers have less direct supervision of teleworkers raises a number of issues and employee concerns. Such a policy must consider work time use, evaluation of performance, handling of expenses, and other factors.

Additional issues affect employees and their relationships with coworkers and managers. One is overwork when having to balance home and work requirements. Maintaining employee motivation when individuals are not physically present at company facilities also can be challenging and may increase employee stress. This is a special concern for global employees. Also, the 15-hour time zone difference between the United States and some Asian countries may make it difficult for global employees to participate in conference calls or do extensive travel for meetings.

LOGGING ON

The Telework Coalition
This coalition is a nonprofit organization committed to advancing the growth and success of telecommuting. Visit their site at www.telcoa.org.

Work Schedule Alternatives

Different types of work schedules have been developed for employees in different occupations and areas. The traditional U.S. work schedule of 8 hours a day, 5 days a week, is in transition. Workers in various occupations may work less or more than 8 hours at a workplace, and may have additional work at home.

The work schedules associated with jobs vary. Some jobs must be performed during "normal" daily work hours and on weekdays, while others require employees to work nights, weekends, and extended hours. Hours worked vary globally as well. As the HR Perspective indicates, there are significant differences in the hours worked in different countries. Given the global

Global Work Schedule Differences

The number of work hours in a week and a year varies from country to country. Some of the differences in annual work hours are illustrated in the following chart.

Annual Hours Worked by Employed Person by Country

• Korea	2,305 hours	• Canada	1,736 hours
• Mexico	1,871 hours	• Australia	1,722 hours
• Italy	1,824 hours	• France	1,561 hours
• The United States	1,794 hours	• Germany	1,433 hours
• Japan	1,785 hours	• The Netherlands	1,392 hours

These numbers are interesting when other countries are compared with the United States. What is thought of as the "normal" U.S. work schedule is 40 hours per week, up to 50 weeks per year, excluding vacation time,

making about 2,000 hours annually. However, the numbers of 1,794 hours in the United States and those in other countries may be affected by extended time-off polices set by laws and/or policies of employers.[37]

The European Union (EU) has issued the Working Time Directive, which states that employees in EU countries should work a maximum of 48 hours a week. However, EU workers can opt out of the maximum. For instance, France has had a law limiting working hours to 35 hours a week, but because exceptions have been made, the weekly average in different firms sometimes is lower or higher than 35. Notice that workers in other countries average different numbers of work hours.

Given the global organizations in many industries, the differences in work hours must be considered across countries. Doing so means that work scheduling expectations and policies may have to be different for an operation in different countries.

nature of many organizations, HR must adjust to different locations because of the international variations. Organizations are using many different work scheduling arrangements, based on industry demands, workforce needs, and other organizational factors.[38] These different types include shift work and the compressed workweek.

Shift Work A common work schedule design is *shift work*. Many organizations need 24-hour coverage and therefore may schedule three 8-hour shifts per day. Most of these employers provide some form of additional pay, called a *shift differential*, for working the evening or night shifts. Some types of shift work have been known to cause difficulties for some employees personally, such as weariness, irritability, lack of motivation, and illness.[39] Nevertheless, some employers must have 24-hour, 7-day coverage, so shift work is likely to continue to be an option.

Compressed workweek
A workweek in which a full week's work is accomplished in fewer than five 8-hour days.

Compressed Workweek One type of work schedule design is the **compressed workweek**, in which a full week's work is accomplished in fewer than five 8-hour days. Compression usually results in more work hours each day and fewer workdays each week, such as four 10-hour days, a 3-day week, or 12-hour shifts. One survey in chemical industry plants found that 96% of the workers who shifted to 12-hour schedules did not wish to return to 8-hour schedules.[40] However, 12-hour schedules have led to sleep difficulties, fatigue, and an increased number of injuries.

Work Flexibility and Scheduling

Flexible work schedules allow organizations to make better use of workers by matching work demands to work hours. One type of scheduling is **flextime**, in which employees work a set number of hours a day but vary the starting and ending times. In some industries, flextime allows more employees to be available at peak times when more customers and clients are present. The flexibility has aided in recruiting and retaining key staff members.[41]

Employees Working at Home As part of organizational job restructurings, economic conditions, and work-life considerations, a number of individuals work at their home locations. Estimates are that more than 15 million employees work from home either full-time or part-time. While some may be self-employed, others are full-time or part-time employees of firms. For instance, a senior HR professional for Hewlett-Packard leads a team of 40 professionals in compensation and benefits who support full-time employees in more than 50 countries. His approach requires regular teleworking and personal communications, as well as planning and communicating with executives and others primarily from home.[42]

Employer Policies on Flexible Work Schedules Flexible scheduling allows organizational and HR managers to choose when, where, and how workers will perform their jobs, while still covering workloads.[43] With work flexibility and home work, *electronic monitoring* of activities and performance may be necessary. For instance, at a call-service firm, home-based employees are monitored on their use of phones through electronic links and get unpaid time off for taking personal breaks. Restrictions such as these are designed to keep workers meeting employers' requirements.[44] Employers still must comply with federal and state compensation laws when using flexible schedules.

Work-Life Balancing For many employees throughout the world, balancing their work and personal lives is a significant concern. According to several surveys of workers and executives, work-life balance is one of the top ten concerns in most countries.[45] Another survey found that work-life balance is the second most important item for executives, with only compensation being more important. A lack of sufficient work-life balance was cited by more than 40% of surveyed employees, and almost half said they might quit their current employers in an effort to get better work-life balance.[46] Single parents, especially women, may face more work-life balancing issues than some other employees.[47]

Thousands of employees, both in large global firms like IBM and Hewlett-Packard and in many smaller firms, have flexible work schedules and/or use technology to work from locations away from the workplace as a way to help balance work and personal lives. Firms such as Xerox and J.M. Smucker give employees paid time off for community volunteer work. Numerous health care firms allow employees to adjust their work schedules in order to address personal, family, health, and other issues.[48]

Flextime Scheduling arrangement in which employees work a set number of hours a day but vary starting and ending times.

JOB ANALYSIS

While job design attempts to develop jobs that fit effectively into the flow of the organizational work, the more narrow focus of job analysis centers on using a formal system to gather data about what people do in their jobs. The basic

FIGURE 4-7   Job Analysis in Perspective

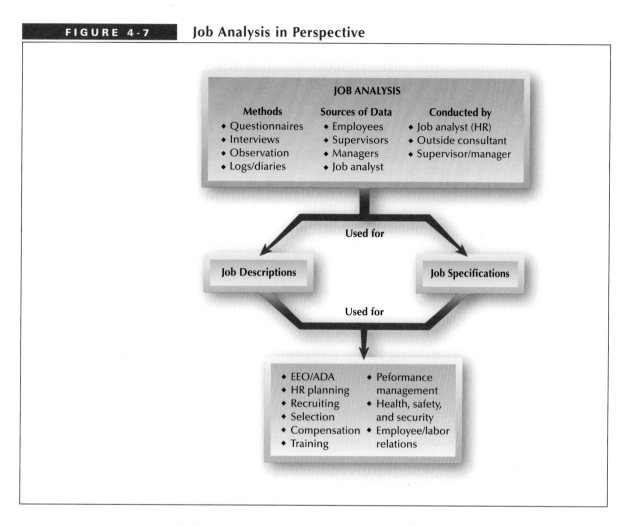

building block of HR management, **job analysis,** is a systematic way of gathering and analyzing information about the content, context, and human requirements of jobs. Most other functions in HR are based on and affected by job analysis.

An overview of job analysis is shown in Figure 4-7. The value of job analysis begins as the information is compiled into *job descriptions* and *job specifications* for use in virtually all HR activities.

Purposes of Job Analysis

Job analysis has grown in importance as the workforce and jobs have changed. To be effective, HR planning, recruiting, and selection all should be based on job requirements and the capabilities of individuals identified by job analysis. In EEO matters, accurate details on job requirements are needed, as the credentials in job descriptions can affect court decisions.[49] Additionally, compensation, training, and employee performance appraisals all should be based on the specific identified needs of the jobs. Job analysis also is useful in identifying job factors and duties that may contribute to workplace health/safety and employee/labor relations issues. Information coming from job analyses that can be helpful in making the distinction among jobs includes the following:

Job analysis Systematic way of gathering and analyzing information about the content, context, and human requirements of jobs.

- Work activities and behaviors
- Interactions with others

- Performance standards
- Financial and budgeting impact
- Machines and equipment used
- Working conditions
- Supervision given and received
- Knowledge, skills, and abilities needed

Job Analysis Responsibilities

Job analysis requires a high degree of coordination and cooperation between the HR unit and operating managers. The assignment of responsibility for job analysis depends on who can best perform various parts of the process. In large companies, the HR unit supervises the process to maintain its integrity and writes the job descriptions and specifications for uniformity. The managers review the efforts of the HR unit to ensure accuracy and completeness. They also may request new job analyses when jobs change significantly. In small organizations, managers may perform all job analysis responsibilities. Figure 4-8 shows a typical division of responsibilities in organizations with an HR unit.

Different types of job analysis are used as part of HR efforts. The most traditionally and widely used method is task-based job analysis. But some have emphasized the need for competency-based job analysis. Both types of job analysis are discussed next. Task-based analysis is still the most widely used method.

Task-Based Job Analysis

Task Distinct, identifiable work activity composed of motions.

Duty Work segment composed of several tasks that are performed by an individual.

Task-based job analysis is the most common form and focuses on the tasks, duties, and responsibilities performed in a job. A **task** is a distinct, identifiable work activity composed of motions, whereas a **duty** is a larger work segment composed of several tasks that are performed by an individual. Because both tasks and duties describe activities, it is not always easy or necessary to distinguish between the two. For example, if one of the employment supervisor's

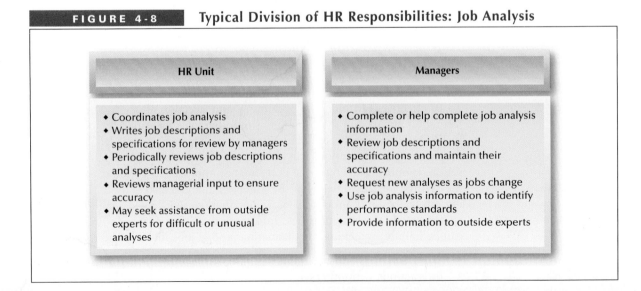

FIGURE 4-8   **Typical Division of HR Responsibilities: Job Analysis**

HR Unit	Managers
• Coordinates job analysis	• Complete or help complete job analysis information
• Writes job descriptions and specifications for review by managers	• Review job descriptions and specifications and maintain their accuracy
• Periodically reviews job descriptions and specifications	• Request new analyses as jobs change
• Reviews managerial input to ensure accuracy	• Use job analysis information to identify performance standards
• May seek assistance from outside experts for difficult or unusual analyses	• Provide information to outside experts

duties is to interview applicants, one task associated with that duty would be asking job-related questions. **Responsibilities** are obligations to perform certain tasks and duties. Task-based job analysis seeks to identify all the tasks, duties, and responsibilities that are part of a job.

Competency-Based Job Analysis

Unlike the traditional task-based approach to analyzing jobs, the competency approach considers how knowledge and skills are used. **Competencies** are individual capabilities that can be linked to performance by individuals or teams.

The concept of competencies varies widely from organization to organization. The term *technical competencies* is often used to refer to specific knowledge and skills of employees. For example, the following have been identified as *behavioral competencies*:

- Customer focus
- Team orientation
- Technical expertise
- Results orientation
- Communication effectiveness
- Leadership
- Conflict resolution
- Innovation
- Adaptability
- Decisiveness

The competency approach attempts to identify the competencies have been identified as driving employee performance.[50] For instance, many supervisors talk about employees' attitudes, but they have difficulty identifying exactly what they mean by "attitude." A variety of methodologies are used to help supervisors articulate examples of competencies and how those factors affect performance.[51]

Responsibilities Obligations to perform certain tasks and duties.

Competencies Individual capabilities that can be linked to enhanced performance by individuals or teams.

Unlike the traditional task-based job analysis, one purpose of the competency approach is to influence individual and organizational behaviors in the future. The competency approach may be more broadly focused on behaviors, rather than just on tasks, duties, and responsibilities. Some of the more comprehensive competency-based job analysis components may extensively include knowledge, skills, abilities, and personality characteristics.[52]

Integrating Technology and Competency-Based Job Analysis As jobs continue to change, technology expands, and workers become more diverse, it may be that there will be a more integrated use of both job analysis approaches. Another factor that will contribute to the use of both types of job analysis is that strategic competencies are identified for some jobs, not just performing job tasks and duties. In the future, people doing jobs are more likely to need integrated job analysis means, rather than just one approach.[53] The decision about whether to use a task-based or competency-based approach to job analysis is affected by the nature of jobs and how work is changing. However, task-based analysis is likely to remain more widely used as it is the most defensible legally, and it is the primary focus of the remainder of this chapter.

LOGGING ON

Job Analysis.net
A resource for conducting a job analysis, including different types of methods, legal issues, questionnaires, and job descriptions, can be found at www.jobanalysis.net.

IMPLEMENTING JOB ANALYSIS

The process of job analysis must be conducted in a logical manner, following appropriate management and professional psychometric practices. Analysts usually follow a multistage process, regardless of the specific job analysis methods used. The stages for a typical job analysis, as outlined in Figure 4-9, may vary somewhat with the number of jobs included. Each of the phases is discussed next.

Planning the Job Analysis

Prior to the job analysis process itself is the planning done to gather data from managers and employees. Probably the most important consideration is to identify the objectives of the job analysis, which might be as simple as updating job descriptions or as comprehensive as revising the compensation programs in the organization. Whatever the purpose identified, the effort needs the support of top management.

FIGURE 4-9   **Stages in the Job Analysis Process**

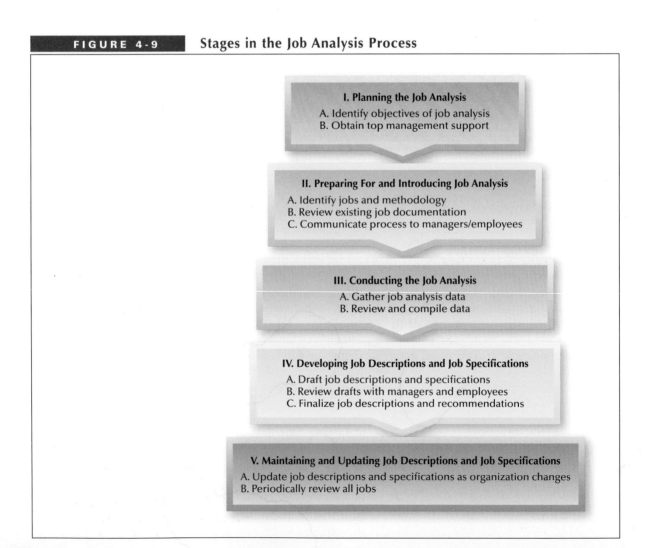

I. Planning the Job Analysis
A. Identify objectives of job analysis
B. Obtain top management support

II. Preparing For and Introducing Job Analysis
A. Identify jobs and methodology
B. Review existing job documentation
C. Communicate process to managers/employees

III. Conducting the Job Analysis
A. Gather job analysis data
B. Review and compile data

IV. Developing Job Descriptions and Job Specifications
A. Draft job descriptions and specifications
B. Review drafts with managers and employees
C. Finalize job descriptions and recommendations

V. Maintaining and Updating Job Descriptions and Job Specifications
A. Update job descriptions and specifications as organization changes
B. Periodically review all jobs

Preparing for and Introducing the Job Analysis

Preparation for job analysis includes identification of the jobs to be analyzed. Next reviewing organization charts, existing job descriptions, previous job analysis information, and other resources is part of the planning. This phase also identifies those who will be involved in conducting the job analysis and the methods to be used. A key part is identifying and communicating the process to appropriate managers, affected employees, and others.

Conducting the Job Analysis

If questionnaires are used, it is often helpful to have employees return them to supervisors or managers for review before giving them back to those conducting the job analysis. Questionnaires should be accompanied by a letter explaining the process and instructions for completing and returning them. If interviews are used, they may occur after the return of the questionnaires, in order to clarify more details. Once data from job analyses are compiled, the information should be sorted by job, organizational unit, and job family.

Developing Job Descriptions and Job Specifications

At the fourth stage, the job analysts draft job descriptions and job specifications. Generally, organizations find that having managers and employees write job descriptions is not recommended for several reasons. First, it reduces consistency in format and details, both of which are important given the legal consequences of job descriptions. Second, managers and employees vary in their writing skills so they may write the job descriptions and job specifications to reflect what they do and what their personal qualifications are, not what the job requires. However, completed drafts should be reviewed with managers and supervisors, and then employees, before they are finalized.

Maintaining and Updating Job Descriptions and Job Specifications

Once job descriptions and specifications have been completed and reviewed by all appropriate individuals, a system must be developed for keeping them current and posted on a firm's intranet source. One effective way to ensure that appropriate reviews occur is to use current job descriptions and job specifications as part of other HR activities. For example, each time a vacancy occurs, the job description and specifications should be reviewed and revised as necessary *before* recruiting and selection efforts begin. Similarly, in some organizations, managers and employees review job descriptions during performance appraisal interviews.

JOB ANALYSIS METHODS

Another consideration is the *method to be used*. Job analysis information about what people are doing in their jobs can be gathered in a variety of ways. Traditionally the most common methods have been observation, interviewing, and questionnaires. However, the expansion of technology has led to computerization and Web-based job analysis information resources. The use of a combination of these approaches depends on the situation and the organization.[54] Each of these methods is discussed next.

Observation

With the observation method, a manager, job analyst, or industrial engineer observes the individual performing the job and takes notes to describe the tasks and duties performed. Use of the observation method is limited because many jobs do not have complete and easily observed job duties or job cycles. Thus, observation may be more useful for repetitive jobs and in conjunction with other methods.

Work Sampling One type of observation, work sampling, does not require attention to each detailed action throughout an entire work cycle. This method allows a manager to determine the content and pace of a typical workday through statistical sampling of certain actions rather than through continuous observation and timing of all actions. Work sampling is particularly useful for routine and repetitive jobs.

Employee Diary/Log Another observation method requires employees to "observe" their own performances by keeping a diary/log of their job duties, noting how frequently those duties are performed and the time required for each one. Although this approach sometimes generates useful information, it may be burdensome for employees to compile an accurate log. The logging approach can be technology-based, reducing some of the problems.

Interviewing

The interview method requires a manager or an HR specialist to talk with the employees performing each job. A standardized interview form is used most often to record the information. Both the employee and the employee's supervisor must be interviewed to obtain complete details on the job.

Sometimes, group or panel interviews are used. A team of subject matter experts (SMEs) who have varying insights about a group of jobs is assembled to provide job analysis information. This option may be particularly useful for highly technical or complex jobs. For instance, the competency approach may use interviewing to identify dimensions that are more than task-based. Because the interview method can be quite time consuming, combining it with one of the other methods is common.

Questionnaires

The questionnaire is a widely used method of gathering data on jobs. A survey instrument is developed and given to employees and managers to complete. The typical job questionnaire often covers the areas shown in Figure 4-10.

The questionnaire method offers a major advantage in that information on a large number of jobs can be collected inexpensively in a relatively short period of time. However, the questionnaire method assumes that employees can accurately analyze and communicate information about their jobs. Using interviewing and observation in combination with the questionnaire method allows analysts to clarify and verify the information gathered in questionnaires.

Position Analysis Questionnaire (PAQ) The Position Analysis Questionnaire is a specialized instrument that incorporates checklists. Each

FIGURE 4-10	Typical Areas Covered in a Job Analysis Questionnaire

Duties and Percentage of Time Spent on Each	Contact with Other People
• Regular duties • Special duties performed less frequently	• Internal contacts • External contacts
Supervision	**Physical Dimensions**
• Supervision given to others • Supervision received from others	• Physical demands • Working conditions
Decisions Made	**Jobholder Characteristics**
• Records and reports prepared • Materials and equipment used • Financial/budget responsibilities	• Knowledge • Skills • Abilities • Training needed

job is analyzed on 27 dimensions composed of 187 "elements." The PAQ has a number of divisions, each containing numerous job elements.

The PAQ focuses on "worker-oriented" elements that describe behaviors necessary to do the job rather than on "job-oriented" elements that describe the technical aspects of the work. Although its complexity may deter potential users, the PAQ can be used to conduct validity studies on selection tests. It also may contribute to internal pay fairness because it considers the varying demands of different jobs.

Managerial Job Analysis Questionnaire Because managerial jobs often differ from jobs with clearly observable routines and procedures, some specialized job analysis methods exist. One well-known method is the Management Position Description Questionnaire (MPDQ). Composed of more than 200 statements, the MPDQ examines a variety of managerial dimensions, including decision making and supervising.

Computerized Job Analysis Systems

With the expansion of information technology and Web-based resources, computerized job analysis systems have been developed. An important feature of technological job analysis is the specificity of data that can be gathered and compiled into a job analysis database. As a result, a technology-based job analysis system can often reduce the time and effort involved in writing job descriptions. These systems often store banks of job duty statements that relate to each of the task and scope statements of the questionnaires. The use of computerized methods will likely continue to grow because of the advantages offered (see the later section on O*Net).

Combination Methods

A number of different ways to obtain and analyze information about a job exist. Each method has strengths and weaknesses, and a combination of methods

O*Net Resources for Employers

Since the recent expansion of the O*Net databases for employers, this resource contains data on more than 800 occupations, classified by industry. Included in the occupational categories are the following:

- Task statements or importance, relevance, and frequency
- Abilities (work activities, knowledge, skills, and work content)
- Training, work experiences, and education
- Interests and work values, work styles, and job zones

O*Net can be used in different ways. For example, one way is to see what abilities will be needed in certain jobs. More than 50 abilities are listed, including arm-hand steadiness, fluency of ideas, time sharing, visualization, written and oral comprehension, and speech clarity. Employers can use the abilities and the other components to generate data for some parts of job analysis and for developing job descriptions.

O*Net also now contains the *Dictionary of Occupational Titles (DOT)* and has hundreds of jobs descriptions. For example, on HR jobs, the DOT and O*Net have listed details on occupations such as Employee Relations Specialist and Human Resource Advisor. For these and all other types of jobs, an extensive list of tasks and detailed work activities is provided. A Spanish version database is available to aid with diverse workers and jobs. The details provided give supervisors, managers, and HR professionals a valuable resource as they develop or revise job descriptions, compare recruiting advertisements, develop training components, and perform other HR activities. In summary, O*Net is a database of worker attributes and job characteristics to describe jobs and the skills workers will need to perform them. It can be accessed at www.onetcenter.org.[55]

generally may be more appropriate than one method alone. Regardless of the methods used, job analysis provides the information necessary to develop job descriptions and job specifications.

Job Analysis and O*Net

A variety of resources related to job analysis are available from the U.S. Department of Labor (DOL). The resources have been developed and used over many years by various entities. *Functional job analysis* uses a competency approach to job analysis. A functional definition of what is done in a job can be generated by examining the three components of *data*, *people*, and *things*. The levels of these components traditionally have been used to identify and compare important elements of more than 120 jobs in the *Dictionary of Occupational Titles (DOT)*. But O*Net is now the main DOL resource available and provides employers with a wide range of useful items, as noted in the HR Online description.

Although not specifically a job analysis, O*Net is a database compiled by the U.S. Department of Labor to provide basic occupational data that covers more than 800 occupations based on the Standard Occupational Classification (SOC) developed by the government. O*Net also provides extensive links to additional resources on workplace issues.

BEHAVIORAL AND LEGAL ASPECTS OF JOB ANALYSIS

Job analysis involves determining what the "core" job is. A detailed examination of jobs, although necessary, sometimes can be a demanding and disruptive experience for both managers and employees, in part because job analysis can identify the difference between what currently is being performed in a job and what *should* be done. This is a major issue about job analysis for some people, but it is not the only concern. Thus, some behavioral factors that can affect job analysis are discussed next.

Current Incumbent Emphasis

A job analysis and the resulting job description and job specifications should not describe just what the person currently doing the job does and that person's qualifications. The incumbent may have unique capabilities and the ability to expand the scope of the job to assume more responsibilities, and the employer might have difficulty finding someone exactly like that individual if the person left. Consequently, it is useful to focus on *core duties* and *necessary knowledge, skills, and abilities* by determining what the job would be if the incumbent were to quit or be moved to a different job.

"Inflation" of Jobs and Job Titles

People have a tendency to inflate the importance and significance of their jobs. Because job analysis information is used for compensation purposes, both managers and employees hope that "puffing up" jobs will result in higher pay levels, greater "status" for résumés, and more promotional opportunities.

Inflated job titles also can be used to enhance employees' images without making major job changes or pay adjustments.[56] For instance, banking and financial institutions often use officer designations to enhance status. In one small Midwestern bank, an employee who had three years' experience as a teller was "promoted" with no pay increase to Second Vice President of Customer Service. In effect, she became the lead teller when her supervisor was out of the bank, and now could sign more customer account forms, but her duties and compensation were basically the same.

An additional concern is the use of offbeat titles. For example, what is a "group idea management director," "chief transformation officer," or "marketing evangelist"? What does a "human character manager" really do? These examples illustrate how job titles may be misleading, both inside and outside the place of employment. Titles should convey a clear view of what a job involves.

Employee and Managerial Anxieties

Both employees and managers have concerns about job analysis. Through job analysis, the job description is supposed to identify what is done in a job. However, it is difficult to capture all facets of a job in which employees perform a variety of duties and operate with a high degree of independence.

Employee Fears One fear that employees may have concerns the purpose of a detailed investigation of their jobs. Some employees fear that an analysis of their jobs will put a straitjacket on them, limiting their creativity and flexibility by formalizing their duties. However, having accurate, well-communicated job descriptions can assist employees by clarifying their roles and the expectations within those roles. One effective way to handle anxieties is to involve the employees in the revision process.

Often the content of a job may reflect the desires and skills of the incumbent employee. For example, in one firm, an employee promoted to customer service supervisor continued to spend considerable time answering customer calls, rather than supervising employees taking the calls. As part of job analysis discussions, the operations manager discussed the need for the supervisor to train the employees on handling special customer requests and to delegate more routine duties to others.

Managerial Straitjacket One primary concern of managers and supervisors is that the job analysis and job descriptions will unrealistically limit managerial flexibility. Because workloads and demands change rapidly, managers and supervisors want to be able to move duties to other employees, cross-train employees, and have more dynamic, flexible means available to accomplish work. If job descriptions are written or used restrictively, some employees may use an omission to limit managerial flexibility. In some organizations with unionized workforces, very restrictive job descriptions exist.

Because of such difficulties, the final statement in many job descriptions is a miscellaneous clause that consists of a phrase similar to "Performs other duties as needed upon request by immediate supervisor." This statement covers unusual situations in an employee's job. However, duties covered by this phrase cannot be considered essential functions under legal provisions including the Americans with Disabilities Act, as discussed next.

Legal Aspects of Job Analysis

Chapter 3 on equal employment laws, regulations, and court cases emphasized that legal compliance must focus on the jobs that individuals perform. The Uniform Guidelines on Employee Selection Procedures make it clear that HR requirements must be tied to specific job-related factors if employers are to defend their actions as a business necessity. This approach has direct impact on job descriptions and persons with disabilities who may apply for those jobs.

Job Analysis and the Americans with Disabilities Act (ADA) One result of the ADA is increased emphasis by employers on conducting job analyses, as well as developing and maintaining current and accurate job descriptions and job specifications.

The ADA requires that organizations identify the *essential job functions*, which are the fundamental duties of a job. These do not include the marginal functions of the positions. **Marginal job functions** are duties that are part of a job but are incidental or ancillary to the purpose and nature of the job. Job analysts, HR staff members, and operating managers must evaluate and make decisions when information on three considerations is not clear. The three major considerations used in determining essential functions and marginal functions are as follows:

- Percentage of time spent on tasks
- Frequency of tasks done
- Importance of tasks performed

Job analysis also should identify the *physical demands* of jobs. For example, the important physical skills and capabilities used on the job of nursing representative could include being able to hear well enough to aid clients and doctors. However, hearing might be less essential for a heavy equipment operator in a quarry.

An important part of job analysis is obtaining information about what duties are being performed and what percentage of time is devoted to each duty. As the ADA suggests, the percentage of time spent on a duty generally indicates its relative importance. Another consideration is the ease or difficulty of assigning a duty to be performed by someone else, or in a different job.

Job Analysis and Wage/Hour Regulations   Typically, job analysis identifies the percentage of time spent on each duty in a job. This information helps determine whether someone should be classified as exempt or nonexempt under the wage/hour laws.

As will be noted in Chapter 11, the federal Fair Labor Standards Act (FLSA) and most state wage/hour laws indicate that the percentage of time employees spend on manual, routine, or clerical duties affects whether they must be paid overtime for hours worked in excess of 40 hours a week. To be exempt from overtime, the employees must perform their *primary duties* as executive, administrative, professional, or outside sales employees. *Primary* has been interpreted to mean occurring at least 50% of the time

Other legal-compliance efforts, such as those involving workplace safety and health, can also be aided through the data provided by job analysis. In summary, it is difficult for an employer to have a legal staffing system without performing job analysis. Truly, job analysis is the most basic HR activity and the foundation for most other HR activities.

JOB DESCRIPTIONS AND JOB SPECIFICATIONS

Marginal job functions
Duties that are part of a job but are incidental or ancillary to the purpose and nature of the job.

The output from analysis of a job is used to develop a job description and its job specifications. Together, these two documents summarize job analysis information in a readable format and provide the basis for defensible job-related actions. They also identify individual jobs for employees by providing documentation from management.

Writing Job Descriptions

Although not the most exciting part of HR management, developing and maintaining current job descriptions is important. Some key suggestions for writing a job description that includes the essential functions and duties of a job follow:

- *Compose specific duty statements that contain most of the following elements:*
  - A precise action verb and its object
  - The frequency of the duties and the expected outcomes
  - The tools, equipment, aids, and processes to be used
- *Be logical:* If the job is repetitive, describe the tasks as they occur in the work cycle. For varied jobs, list the major tasks first and follow those with the less frequent and/or less important tasks in order.
- *Use proper details:* Make sure the description covers all the meaningful duties of the job, but avoids too many details.

- *Be specific:* For example, instead of saying "Lifts heavy packages," say "Frequently lifts heavy packages weighing up to 50 pounds."
- *Use the active voice:* Start each statement with a functional verb in the present tense (third-person singular)—for instance, "Compiles," "Approves," or "Analyzes." Avoid terms like *handles, maintains,* and *processes.*
- *Describe, do not prescribe:* Say "Operates electronic imaging machine," not "Must know how to operate electronic image machine." (The latter is a job specification, not a job description.)
- *Be consistent:* Define terms like *may, occasionally,* and *periodically.*
- *Prepare a miscellaneous clause:* This clause provides flexibility and may be phrased as follows: "Performs other related duties as assigned by supervisory personnel."

Job Descriptions

Job description
Identification of the tasks, duties, and responsibilities of a job.

In most cases, the job description and job specifications are combined into one document that contains several sections. A **job description** identifies the tasks, duties, and responsibilities of a job. It describes what is done, why it is done, where it is done, and, briefly, how it is done. The HR On-the-Job shows suggestions for writing job descriptions.

Job Specifications

Job specifications The knowledge, skills, and abilities (KSAs) an individual needs to perform a job satisfactorily.

While the job description describes activities to be done, the **job specifications** list the knowledge, skills, and abilities (KSAs) an individual needs to perform a job satisfactorily. KSAs include education, experience, work skill requirements, personal abilities, and mental and physical requirements. Accurate job specifications identify what KSAs a person needs to do the job, not necessarily the current employee's qualifications.

Performance Standards

Performance standards
Indicators of what the job accomplishes and how performance is measured in key areas of the job description.

Performance standards flow directly from a job description and indicate what the job accomplishes and how performance is measured in key areas of the job description. If employees know what is expected and how performance is to be measured, they have a much better chance of performing satisfactorily. Unfortunately, performance standards are often not developed as supplemental items from job descriptions. Even if performance standards have been identified and matched to job descriptions, they must be communicated to employees if the job descriptions are to be effective HR tools.

Job Description Components

A typical job description contains several major parts. The following content presents an overview of the most common components.

Identification The first part of the job description is the identification section, in which the job title, department, reporting relationships, location, and date of analysis may be given. Usually, it is advisable to note other information that is useful in tracking jobs and employees through HR systems. Additional items commonly noted in the identification section are job code, pay grade, exempt/nonexempt status under the Fair Labor Standards Act (FLSA), and the EEOC classification (from the EEO-1 form).

General Summary The second part, the general summary, is a concise statement of the general responsibilities and components that make the job different from others. One HR specialist has characterized the general summary statement as follows: "In thirty words or less, describe the essence of the job." Often, the summary is written after all other sections are completed so that a more complete overview is prepared.

Essential Job Functions and Duties The third part of the typical job description lists the essential functions and duties, generally in order of importance. It contains clear, precise statements on the major tasks, duties, and responsibilities performed. Writing this section is the most time-consuming aspect of preparing job descriptions.

Job Specifications The next portion of the job description gives the qualifications needed to perform the job satisfactorily. The job specifications typically are stated as: (1) knowledge, skills, and abilities; (2) education and experience; and (3) physical requirements and/or working conditions. The components of the job specifications provide information necessary to determine what accommodations might and might not be possible under the Americans with Disabilities Act.

Disclaimers and Approvals The final section on many job descriptions contains approval signatures by appropriate managers and a legal disclaimer. This disclaimer allows employers to change employees' job duties or to request employees to perform duties not listed, so that the job description is not viewed as a contract between the employer and the employee. Figure 4-11 contains a sample job description and job specifications for a Customer Service Supervisor. Also, Appendix G has sample HR-related job descriptions.

FIGURE 4-11   Sample Job Description

Identification Section

Position Title: Customer Service Supervisor
Department: Marketing/Customer Service   EEOC Class: O/M
Reports To: Marketing Director   FLSA Status: Exempt

General Summary

Supervises, coordinates, and assigns work of employees to ensure customer
service department goals and customer needs are met.

Essential Job Functions

1. Supervises the work of Customer Service Representatives to enhance performance by
   coordinating duties, advising on issues or problems, and checking work. (55%)
2. Provides Customer Service training for company employees in all departments. (15%)
3. Creates and reviews reports for service orders for new and existing customers. (10%)
4. Performs employee performance evaluations, training, and discipline. (10%)
5. Follows up with customer complaints and issues and provides resolutions. (10%)
6. Conducts other duties as needed by guided by Marketing Director and executives.

Knowledge, Skills, and Abilities

- Knowledge of company products, services, policies, and procedures.
- Knowledge of marketing and customer programs, data, and results.
- Knowledge of supervisory requirements and practices.
- Skill in completing multiple tasks at once.
- Skill in identifying and resolving customer problems.
- Skill in oral and written communication, including Spanish communications.
- Skill in coaching, training, and performance evaluating employees.
- Skill in operating office and technological equipment and software.
- Ability to communicate professionally with coworkers, customers and vendors.
- Ability to work independently and meet managerial goals.
- Ability to follow oral and written instructions.
- Ability to organize daily activities of self and others and to work as a team player.

Education and Experience

Bachelor's degree in business or marketing, plus 3–5 years of industry experience. Supervisory, marketing,
and customer service experience helpful.

Physical Requirements	Percentage of Work Time Spent on Activity			
	0–24%	25–49%	50–74%	75–100%
Seeing: Must be able to see well enough to read reports.				X
Hearing: Must be able to hear well enough to communicate with customers, vendors and employees.				X
Standing/Walking: Must be able to move about department.			X	
Climbing/Stooping/Kneeling: Must be able to stoop or kneel to pick up paper products or directories.	X			
Lifting/Pulling/Pushing: Must be able to lift up to 50 pounds.	X			
Fingering/Grasping/Feeling: Must be able to type and use technical sources.				X

Working Conditions: Normal working conditions absent extreme factors.

Note: *The statements herein are intended to describe the general nature and level of work being performed, but are not to be seen as a complete list of responsibilities, duties, and skills required of personnel so classified. Also, they do not establish a contract for employment and are subject to change at the discretion of the employer.*

SUMMARY

- Diversity management focuses on organizational efforts to ensure that all people are valued regardless of their differences.
- The "business case" for diversity is built on its ability to allow new talent and ideas, aid in employee attraction and retention, allow for an increase in market share, and lead to lower costs.
- The workforce composition is becoming more diverse based on race/ethnicity, age, gender, and other life components.
- Work is organized into jobs for people to do. Work flow analysis and business process reengineering are both approaches used to check how well this has been done.
- Job design involves developing jobs that people like to do. It may include simplification, enlargement, enrichment, rotation, or sharing.
- Designing jobs so that they incorporate skill variety, task identity and significance, autonomy, and feedback is important for both employers and employees.
- The use of work teams and virtual teams is growing in organizations throughout the United States and globally.
- Work-related teams are aiding organizational and managerial productivity and growth, despite some problems that may occur.

- Telework, whereby employees work with technology, is leading to more work flexibility.
- Work scheduling through flextime allows employees to work more at home, which enhances their work-life balancing activities.
- Job analysis is a systematic investigation of the content, context, and human requirements of a job.
- Task-based job analysis focuses on the tasks, duties, and responsibilities associated with jobs.
- Competency-based job analysis focuses on basic characteristics that can be linked to enhanced performance, such as technical and behavioral competencies.
- The job analysis process has five stages, beginning with planning and ending with maintaining and updating job descriptions and job specifications.
- A number of methods of job analysis are used, with interviews and questionnaires being the most popular.
- Both the behavioral reactions of employees and managers and legal-compliance issues must be considered as part of job analysis.
- The end products of job analysis are job descriptions, which identify the tasks, duties, and responsibilities of jobs, and job specifications, which list the knowledge, skills, and abilities needed to perform a job satisfactorily.

CRITICAL THINKING ACTIVITIES

1. Describe how diversity of workers has been impacting organizations, including organizations for which you have worked recently.
2. For many individuals, the nature of work and jobs is changing. Describe these changes, some reasons for them, and how they are affecting both HR management and individuals.
3. Explain how you would conduct a job analysis in a company that has never had job

descriptions. Utilize the O*Net as a resource for your information.

4. You need to convince upper management of the usefulness of a companywide diversity program. How will you define *diversity*, and what arguments can be made for so defining it? Use the website www.diversityinc .com and other sources to gather the necessary information.

HR EXPERIENTIAL PROBLEM SOLVING

You have recently assumed the role of HR Manager in your company. In reviewing the company records, you note that the job descriptions were last updated 5 years ago. The Company President has taken the

position that there is no need to update the job descriptions. However, you also note that the company has grown by 50% during the last 5 years, resulting in many changes, including some in job functions. You want to build a business case to convince the Company President of the need to update the job descriptions. To help you build your case, use the information on the purpose of job descriptions at www.hrtools.com.

1. How can job descriptions be used as a management tool?
2. What role do job descriptions have in helping companies comply with various legal issues?

CASE

ROWE and Flexible Work and Success at Best Buy

Best Buy is a large national retailer with many full-time and part-time employees in more than 1,000 stores. Beginning several years ago, Best Buy has made major changes in its work schedules. Rather than emphasizing fixed hours, Best Buy increased use of flexible work hours in its corporate headquarters and stores. Based on the success of an initial experimental program with 300 employees in some departments, the changes have evolved into a more broadly used program labeled ROWE—Results Only Work Environment.

At the heart of ROWE is the philosophy of focusing on employees getting their work done, not just meeting clock hours. To implement ROWE, managers and employees have had to identify performance result expectations and measures for all jobs. The focus of ROWE has been on how people make judgments on work to be done and the time at work to do it. The core focus of ROWE is employee performance meeting expectations, not just being at work.

The HR payoff of ROWE has been significant. According to metrics, voluntary employee turnover has declined in some divisions by as much as 75% to 90% over several years. Average worker productivity in the same period increased over one-third. Some other key results of the ROWE plan have been:

- Increased customer satisfaction because of the work-results focus of Best Buy employees
- Higher employee morale and engagement because of the ability to place work and life demands in balance
- Higher managerial performance because of the attention to results, not just on training schedules and regulations

For some employees and managers with family responsibilities and personal interests, one of the greatest advantages of the ROWE program is the ability for them to achieve better work-life balance. From mothers of school-aged children to single males involved in hobbies and sports, employees can adjust schedules to meet their personal and professional needs. For instance, one employee left often in early afternoon in order to participate in entertainment activities. Other employees have finished work and gone hunting or golfing during the "normal workweek" because they had completed their work requirements. Obviously, these persons can make expansive use of technology for doing their work anywhere, such as getting messages while at family or sporting events, responding quickly to job-related questions, and providing immediate work-related information.

The ROWE program now has been expanded to include retail store managers and workers. Doing so has meant making some modifications to ensure that sufficient salespersons are available to serve customers at a wide range of days and times. But with Best Buy retail stores previously experiencing a turnover rate of 60% plus, adapting to ROWE has been important. It has helped with recruiting store employees, retaining them so that turnover has decreased, and enhancing customer service.

In summary, the change in the culture at Best Buy to focus on results, employee success, and greater work flexibility has made Best Buy one of the best places for many people to shop and work. How this program will expand and modify as economic, workforce diversity, and jobs change will be interesting to observe.[57]

QUESTIONS

1. Discuss how a ROWE-type program would fit in organizations where you have worked. Explain why it would or would not work.
2. Identify factors in the ROWE program that might make using it for retail employees more difficult than using it for managers and employees in corporate offices, technical centers, and nonretail jobs and locations.

SUPPLEMENTAL CASES

The Reluctant Receptionist

This case illustrates how incomplete job analysis and job descriptions create both managerial and employee problems. (For the case, go to www.cengage.com/management/mathis.)

Jobs and Work at R.R. Donnelley

This case describes how a printing firm had to increase productivity and redesign jobs. (For the case, go to www.cengage.com/management/mathis.)

NOTES

1. Kathleen Koster, "Flex Schedules Key to Corporate Performance," *Employee Benefit News*, May 28, 2009, http://ebn.benefitnews.com/news; "Survey Results: Flexible Work Arrangements," *Institute for Corporate Productivity*, 2008, 3–8, www.i4cp.com.

2. "Employment Projections" *U.S. Bureau of Labor Statistics*, www.bls.gov.

3. David A. Harrison and Katherine L. Klein, "What's the Difference? Diversity Constructs as Separation, Variety, or Disparity in Organizations," *Academy of Management Review*, 22 (2007), 1199–1228.

4. Eddy S.W. Nig, "Why Organizations Choose to Manage Diversity," *Human Resource Development Review*, 7 (2008), 58–78.

5. Robert Rodriguez, "Diversity Finds Its Place," *HR Magazine,* August 2006, 56–61.

6. Kathy Gurchiek, "Putting Diversity into Practice Stymies Many Firms," *HR News*, August 27, 2007, www.shrm.org/hrnews.

7. Bill Leonard, "Diversity Initiatives Must Grow from Key Business Goals," *SHRMOnLine*, April 29, 2009, www.shrm.org/hrdisciplines; Ellen F. Curtis and Janice L. Dreachslin, "Integrative Literature Review: Diverse Management Interventions and Organizational Performance," *Human Resource Development Review*, 7 (2008), 107–134.

8. Lynn M. Shore, et al., "Diversity in Organizations: Where Are We Now and Where Are We Going?" *Human Resource Management Review*, 22 (2007), 1199–1228; Sharon Wong, "Diversity—Making Space for

Everyone at NASA/Goddard Space Flight Center . . .," *Human Resource Management*, 47 (2008), 389–399.

9. Gill Kilton and Anne-Marie Greene, "The Costs and Opportunities of Doing Diversity Work in Mainstream Organizations," *Human Resource Management Journal*, 19 (2009), 159–175; Orlando C. Richard, et al., "The Impact of Racial Diversity on Intermediate and Long-Term Performance," *Strategic Management Journal,* 28 (2007), 1213–1233.

10. Based on Terence F. Shea, "Dismantling Language Barriers," *HR Magazine*, November 2008, 48–52.

11. "An Older and More Diverse Nation by Mid-Century," *U.S. Census Bureau News*, August 14, 2008, www.census.gov.

12. Sherri B. Welch, "Diversity as Business Strategy: Company Faced Racial Tensions Head-on," *Workforce Week*, April 2009, www.workforce.com; G. M. Combs and J. Griffith, "An Examination of Interracial Contact," *Human Resource Development Review*, 6 (2007), 222–244.

13. Tara Kalwarski, "Retirement: Not When It Used to Be?" *Business Week*, November 3, 2008, 96; Stephen Miller, "60 Percent of Older Workers Delay Retirement," *HR Disciplines*, March 23, 2009, www.shrm.org.

14. "Managing Across the Generations," *HR Compliance*, May 14, 2009, www.ceridian.com; "Gen Y Creates Need for Cultural Overhaul," *WorldatWork Newsline*, January 11, 2008, www.worldatwork.org/

waw; "Generation X: Magic or Mayhem in the Middle," 2009, www.talentAnarchy.com.

15. Nancy Lockwood, et al., "The Multigenerational Workforce: Opportunity for Competitive Success," *SHRM Research Quarterly*, First Quarter, 2009, 1–10; Robert J. Grossman, "Keep Pace with Older Workers," *HR Magazine*, May 2008, 39–46.

16. Frank Giancola, "The Generation Gap: More Myth than Reality," *Human Resource Planning*, 29 (2006), 32; Susan A. Murphy, *Leading a Multigenerational Workforce* (Washington, DC: AARP, 2007).

17. *American Time Use Survey*, U.S. Department of Labor, 2008, www.bls.gov/tus/#news.

18. George Desvaux, et al., "A Business Case for Women," *The McKinsey Quarterly*, September 2008, 1ff.; Philip N. Cohen and Matt Huffman, "Working for the Woman? Female Mangers and the Gender Wage Gap," *American Sociological Review*, 72 (2007), 681–704.

19. "43% of Working Moms Would Take Pay Cuts to Spend Time with Kids," May 8, 2008, www.careerbuilder.com; Jean Kimmel and Rachel Connnelly, "Mother's Time Choices," *Journal of Human Resources*, 62 (2007), 643–681.

20. Eugene A. Hall, et al., "How to Make Reengineering Really Work," *The McKinsey Quarterly*, September 2008, www.mckinseyquarterly.com.

21. George McCormick, et al., "The Manager's Impact on Job and Organization Design," *WorldatWork*

Journal, Fourth Quarter, 2007, 82–91.

22. For more details and data on contingent employees, go to www .bls.gov.

23. Fay Hansen, "A Permanent Strategy for Temporary Hires," *Workforce Management*, February 26, 2007, 25–32.

24. Allysson M. Costa and Cristobal Mirrales, "Job Rotation in Assembly Lines Employing Disabled Workers," *International Journal of Production Economics,* 112 (2009), 1016.

25. Margaret Fiester, "Job Rotation, Total Rewards, Measuring Value," *HR Magazine*, August 2008, 33.

26. Kathy Gurchiek, "HR Structure Reflects Organizational Size," *HR News*, June 15, 2009, www.shrm.org.

27. Michael O'Brien, "Long-Distance Relationship Troubles," *Human Resource Executive Online*, July 7, 2009, www.hrexecutive.com.

28. Billie Williamson, "Managing at a Distance," *Business Week*, July 27, 2009, 64–65; Lynda Gratton, "Working Together . . . When Apart," *The Wall Street Journal*, June 16, 2007, R4.

29. "Innovative Work Teams in a Challenging Business Environment," *SHRM Workplace Visions*, 2009, No. 1, 1–6.

30. Ramon Rico, et al., "Team Implicit Coordination Processes," *Academy of Management Review*, 33 (2008), 163–184.

31. Marjo Sinokki, "The Association Between Team Climate at Work and Mental Health," *Occupational and Environmental Medicine*, 66 (2009), 523–526; Christopher M. Barnes and John R. Hollenbeck, "Sleep Deprivation and Decision-Making Teams," *Academy of Management Review*, 34 (2009), 56–66l.

32. Jessica Mesmert-Magnus and Leslie A. DeChurch, "Information Sharing and Team Performance: A Meta-Analysis," *Journal of Applied Psychology*, 94 (2009), 535–546; Erick Kearney, et al., "When and How Diversity

Benefits Teams," *Academy of Management Journal*, 52 (2009), 581–598.

33. Andrew R. McIlvane, "The Problem with Diverse Teams," *Human Resource Executive Online*, June 2, 2009, www.hreonline.com.

34. Rita Zeidner, "Telework Influencing Technology Investments," *HR Magazine*, July 2008, 22.

35. Heidi Russell Rafferty, "Experts: Telework Might Hold Key to Pandemic Solution," *HR News*, May 7, 2009, www.shrm.org/ publications.

36. Lorrie Lykins and Mark Vickers, "Can Telework Cut Costs and Raise Productivity in Today's Economy?" *Trend Watcher*, March 6, 2009, www.i4cp.com.

37. Based on "Annual Hours Worked per Employed Person, 1997 and 2007," *Labor Market Indicators*, Organization for Economic Cooperation and Development, 2009, www.oecd.org.

38. Terrance M. McMenamin, "A Time to Work: Recent Trends in Shift Work and Flexible Schedules," *Monthly Labor Review*, December 2007, 3–14.

39. "Extended Unusual Work Shifts," *U.S. Occupational Safety & Health Administration*, September 7, 2005, www.osha.gov.

40. Martin Moore-Ede, et al., "Advantages and Disadvantages of Twelve-Hour Shifts, A Balanced Perspective," 2007, www.ciridian .com.

41. "Innovative Workplace Flexibility Options for Hourly Workers," *Corporate Voices for Working Families*, 2009, www .cvworkingfamilies.org/ publications.

42. Euan Hutchinson, "'People People' Work at Home, Too," *HR Magazine*, September 2008, 60–62.

43. E. Jeffrey Hill, et al., "Defining and Conceptualizing Work Flexibility," *Community, Work, and Family*, 11 (2008), 149–163.

44. Sue Shellenbarger, "Work at Home: Employers Watch," *The*

Wall Street Journal, July 30, 2008, D1*ff*.

45. Beth A. Heinen and Rebecca R. H. Mulvaney, "Global Factors Influencing Work-Life Policies and Practices," *WorldatWork Journal*, First Quarter, 2008, 34–41; Sheri Gaster and Virginia G. McMorrow, "Expatriates Assignments Influence on Work-Life Balance," *WorldatWork Journal*, Fourth Quarter, 2008, 62–69.

46. Kathleen Koster, "Work-Life Balance Key for Employees," *Employee Benefit News*, May 7, 2009, http://ebn .benefitnews.com; Maggie C. Moore and Nancy R. Lockwood, "Work/Life Balance: A Global Perspective," *HRM Research*, April 1007, www.shrm.org/ research.

47. Jean Kimmel and Rachel Connelly, "Mothers' Time Choices," *Journal of Human Resources*, 62 (2006), 643–681; Melanie A. Hulbert, "Unveiling Gendered Assumptions in the Organizational Implementation of Work-Life Policies," *WorldatWork Journal*, First Quarter, 2009, 42–54.

48. For examples, see Sherry Sullivan and Lisa Mainiero, "Benchmarking Ideas for Fostering Family-Friendly Workplaces," *Organizational Dynamics*, 36 (2006), 45–62; Pamela Babcock, "Elder Care at Work," *HR Magazine*, September 2008, 111–113.

49. *Lamb v. Boeing Co.*, No. 5-18431 (4th Cir., Jan. 11, 2007).

50. Douglas W. Crisman, "Using Competencies to Drive Talent Management," *Workspan*, December 2006, 11.

51. Garry Kranz, "Calling on Experts," *Workforce Management*, June 2008, www .workforce.com.

52. "Competency Modeling and Job Analysis: Current Trends and Debates in the Academic Literature," *ICF International*, 2009, www.icfi.com.

53. Juan L. Sanchez and Edward L. Levine, "What Is (or Should Be) the Difference Between Competency

Modeling and Traditional Job Analysis?" *Human Resource Management Review*, 19 (2009), 53–63.

54. Jason C. Kovac, "The Purpose of Job Analysis," *Workspan*, December 2006, 11.

55. For details, go to the website listed in the boxed feature, as well as www.dol.gov and www.onetcenter.org. The value of O*Net is identified in various publications, including Max Maller, *The Manager's Guide to HR*, Chapter 1 (Alexandria, VA: SHRM, 2009).

56. Arthur D. Martinez, et al., "Job Title Inflation," *Human Resource Management Review*, 18 (2008), 19–27.

57. Based on Lynn Gresham, "Best Buy Puts Work-Life Balance on New Axis," *Employee Benefit Advisor*, March 2007, 24–26; Michelle Conlin, "Smashing the Clock," *BusinessWeek*, December 11, 2006, 60–68.

5

Human Resource Planning and Retention

After you have read this chapter, you should be able to:

- Define HR planning and outline the HR planning process.

- Describe the means for assessing the external and internal workforce in HR planning.

- Identify methods for forecasting HR supply and demand levels.

- Explain the nature of the psychological contract and how motivation is linked to individual performance.

- Describe different kinds of turnover and how turnover can be measured.

- Identify the six drivers of retention and ways retention measurement can occur.

Need More Workers?

(AP Photo/Toby Talbot)

As economic conditions have changed negatively for many organizations, they have had to cut jobs and workers. One industry that has made many reductions has been the automotive industry. Yet, employers in some other industries have had a continuing shortage of workers.

One illustration of such problems is in the milk producing industry as well as other agricultural employers. Many U.S. individuals, even if they are unemployed, do not want to work in jobs such as those in these industries, since they have relatively low pay rates and the working conditions tend to be outdoors or in warehouses. Therefore, U.S. dairy farmers have had to use immigrants from Latin countries to fill 40% of their jobs, but the use of immigrants has created HR issues due to state and federal laws regarding employment of illegal immigrants.

Employers in other industries also are needing workers. Some construction companies, health care organizations, and technology employers are facing shortages of qualified individuals. Attracting, recruiting, and retaining good employees are crucial. For instance, Google, the large technology employer, estimated that it could lose a significant number of employees to technology competitors such as Facebook, Twitter, or new firms. Whatever the industry, where more workers are needed, HR efforts should be expanded.

Employers in different industries face staffing issues emphasizing HR planning and retention. As industry and economic conditions continue to change, planning and retention will only increase in importance.[1]

Staffing an organization is an HR activity that is both strategic and operational in nature. As the HR Headline indicates, HR planning is important in a wide variety of industries and firms. HR planning affects what employers do when recruiting, selecting, and retaining people, and, of course these actions affect organizational results and success.

The challenges caused by changing economic conditions during recent years show why HR workforce planning should occur.[2] A study by Watson Wyatt that found that it does occur in more than 80% of organizations in more than 30 countries. However, only one-fourth of smaller U.S.-based companies had formal HR plans.[3] Planning in small firms is more informal, as shown below.

HUMAN RESOURCE PLANNING

Human resource planning is the process of analyzing and identifying the need for and availability of human resources so that the organization can meet its objectives. The focus of HR planning is to ensure the organization has the *right number of human resources,* with the *right capabilities,* at the *right times,* and in the *right places.* In HR planning, an organization must consider the availability and allocation of people to jobs over long periods of time, not just for the next month or even the next year.[4]

Additionally, as part of the analyses, HR plans can include several approaches. Actions may include shifting employees to other jobs in the organization, laying off employees or otherwise cutting back the number of employees, retraining present employees, and/or increasing the number of employees in certain areas. Factors to consider include the current employees' knowledge, skills, and abilities and the expected vacancies resulting from retirements, promotions, transfers, and discharges. To do this, HR planning requires efforts by HR professionals working with executives and managers. The HR Best Practices box illustrates how several firms have made HR planning important.

Organizational Size and HR Planning

The need for HR planning in larger organizations is especially important. For example, in a review, the U.S. government's Corps of Engineers, with a workforce of 35,000, was found to have an outdated strategic HR plan. Also, it had not done an organization-wide needs analysis for current and future workforce. If adjustments to foreseeable changes were not made, people or even entire divisions could be working at cross-purposes with the rest of the organization.[5]

An illustration of an effective HR planning emphasis can be seen in Walgreens, the large retail drugstore chain. This firm has had an aggressive business plan. Since each Walgreens store must be staffed with pharmacists, managers, and customer service employees, the firm's HR planning has involved identifying how and where to find enough pharmacists to fill openings caused by turnover and retirement, as well as how to staff new stores. Walgreens illustrates that part of HR planning is identifying the knowledge, skills, and abilities (KSAs), as well as experience and other capabilities, for current and future jobs.

Human resource planning Process of analyzing and identifying the need for and availability of human resources so that the organization can meet its objectives.

Effective HR Planning for the Workforce Future

Important HR functions in many organizations revolve around staffing: recruiting, employing, and retaining employees. More than half of the HR professionals in a Society for Human Resource Management (SHRM) survey identified efforts in those areas as the most important HR activities in their firms. Forecasting the need for employees and identifying how to retain them are components of these functions. Several examples illustrate their importance.

At Valero Energy, employee turnover was projected to increase significantly over a 5-year period. This forecast triggered an increase in HR planning. Within 2 years, Valero had established the means, linked to its strategic HR planning, to build its workforce for an additional 3 years.

Another firm that has used HR planning effectively is Corning, Inc., a worldwide technology firm with more than 25,000 employees. This firm used HR planning globally to identify that hiring more engineers in Taiwan instead of the United States would be better and less expensive, given the pay levels and the supply of potential U.S. engineering employees.

In a different industry, Chicago-based CNA Financial identified that it would have an insufficient number of underwriters in 2 years at its current turnover rate, and that more than 80% of its safety engineers were eligible to retire. To address these concerns, extensive planning was undertaken for reducing turnover in both occupations and identifying sources for possible recruits. As a result, the turnover rates at CNA in both groups dropped significantly, and relevant training and development efforts were expanded.

These examples reinforce how HR planning can help meet future workforce supply and demand in terms of employees. Also, increasing employee retention by reducing turnover can aid in enhancing organizational performance and effective HR management.[6]

Small Business HR Planning In a smaller business, even though the owner/manager knows on a daily basis what is happening and what should be done, planning is still important. One difficult area for HR planning in small businesses is family matters and succession. Particular difficulties arise when a growing business is passed from one generation to another, resulting in a mix of family and nonfamily employees.

Key to successful transition in a small business is having a clear HR plan. In small businesses, such a plan includes incorporating key nonfamily members in HR planning efforts because nonfamily members may have important capabilities and expertise that family members do not possess. Planning for the attraction and retention of these "outsiders" may be vital to the future success of smaller organizations.

LOGGING ON

Human Resource Planning Society
Information and resources on building a strategic HR plan are available at www.hrps.org.

Small businesses may use the HR planning process, which is discussed next. But in very small organizations, too often the process is much more intuitive and is done entirely by the top executives, who often are family members, which may eliminate nonfamily members from the process.

HR Planning Process

The steps in the HR planning process are shown in Figure 5-1. Notice that the process begins with considering the organizational strategic planning objectives.

FIGURE 5-1   HR Planning Process

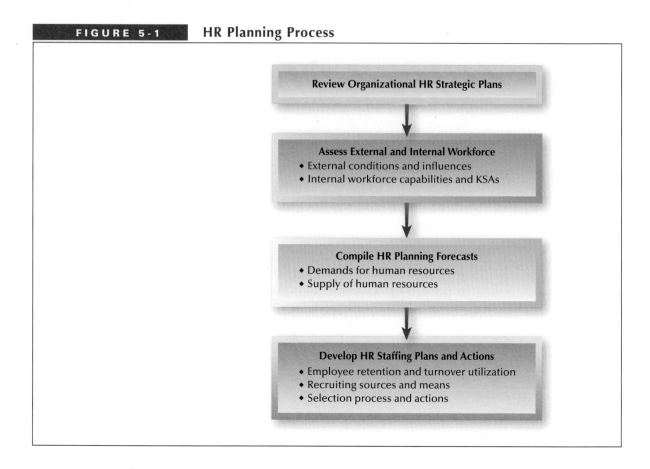

Then the possible *available workforce* must be evaluated by identifying both the external and internal workforce.

Once those assessments are complete, forecasts must be developed to identify both the demand for and supply of human resources. Management then formulates HR staffing plans and actions to address imbalances, both short-term and long-term. One means of developing and measuring HR planning is use of a team of subject matter experts (SMEs) to increase the validity and reliability of the HR planning results.[7] Specific strategies may be developed to fill vacancies or deal with surplus employees. For example, a strategy might be to fill 50% of expected vacancies by training employees in lower-level jobs and promoting them into more advanced anticipated openings.

Finally, HR plans are developed to provide specific direction for the management of HR activities related to employee recruiting, selection, and retention. The most telling evidence of successful HR planning is a consistent alignment of the availabilities and capabilities of human resources with the needs of the organization over shorter or longer periods of time.

ASSESSING THE EXTERNAL WORKFORCE

The first stage of HR planning is to *examine organization objectives and plans.* If a network technology firm plans to double its number of client accounts from 100 to 200 in a 3-year period, that firm also must identify how many and what types of new employees will be needed to staff the expanded services, locations, and facilities. Several common external factors to be considered are highlighted next.

Economic and Governmental Factors

The general cycles of economic recession and economic boom in different businesses affect HR planning. Factors such as interest rates, inflation, and economic decline or growth affect the availability of workers and should figure into organizational and HR plans and objectives. There is a considerable difference between finding qualified applicants in a 4% unemployment market and in a 9% unemployment market. As the unemployment rate rises, the number of qualified people looking for work increases, often making it easier to fill some jobs. But those hired may receive lower pay and benefits than in their previous jobs.

A broad array of government regulations affects the labor supply and therefore HR planning. As a result, HR planning must be done by individuals who understand the legal requirements of various government regulations. In the United States and other countries, tax legislation at local, state, and federal levels affects HR planning. Pension provisions and Social Security legislation may change retirement patterns and funding options. Elimination or expansion of tax benefits for job-training expenses might alter some job-training activities associated with workforce expansions. In summary, an organization must consider a wide variety of government policies, regulations, and laws during the HR planning process.

Competitive Evaluations

When making HR plans, employers must consider a number of geographic and competitive concerns. The *net migration* into a particular region is important. For example, in the past decade, the populations of some U.S. cities in the South, Southwest, and West have grown rapidly and have provided sources of labor. However, areas in the Northeast and Midwest have experienced declining populations.

Direct competitors are another important external force in HR planning. Failure to consider the competitive labor market and to offer pay scales and benefits competitive with those of organizations in the same general industry and geographic location may cost a company dearly in the long run.

Finally, the impact of *international competition* must be considered as part of environmental scanning. Global competition for labor intensifies as global competitors shift jobs and workers around the world, as illustrated by the outsourcing of jobs from the United States to countries with cheaper labor.

Changing Workforce Considerations

As mentioned in the previous chapter, significant changes in the workforce, both in the United States and globally, must be considered when doing external assessments for HR planning. Shifts in the composition of the workforce, combined with the use of different work patterns, have created workplaces and organizations that are notably different from those of a decade ago.

Many organizations face major concerns about having sufficient workers with the necessary capabilities. When scanning the potential and future workforce, it is important to consider a number of variables, including:

- Aging of the workforce
- Growing diversity of workers
- Female workers and work-life balancing concerns
- Availability of contingent workers
- Outsourcing possibilities

When considering these factors, it is important to analyze how they affect the current and future availability of workers with specific capabilities and experience. For instance, in a number of industries, the median age of highly specialized professionals is over 50 years, and the supply of potential replacements with adequate education and experiences is not sufficient to replace such employees as they retire. One global study found that less than 15% of surveyed firms have planned for workforce shortages due to the "brain drain" created by the retirement of existing older workers.[8]

ASSESSING THE INTERNAL WORKFORCE

Analyzing the jobs that will need to be done and the capabilities of people who are currently available in the organization to do them is the next part of HR planning. The needs of the organization must be compared against the labor supply available both inside and outside the organization.

Current and Future Jobs Audit

The starting point for evaluating internal workforce strengths and weaknesses is an audit of the jobs being done in the organization. A comprehensive analysis of all current jobs provides a basis for forecasting what jobs will need to be done in the future. Much of the data in the audit should be available from existing staffing and organizational databases. The following questions may be some key ones addressed during the internal assessment:

- What jobs exist now and how essential is each job?
- How many individuals are performing each job?
- What are the reporting relationships of jobs?
- What are the vital KSAs needed in the jobs?
- What jobs will be needed to implement future organizational strategies?
- What are the characteristics of those anticipated jobs?

Employee and Organizational Capabilities Inventory

As HR planners gain an understanding of the current and future jobs that will be necessary to carry out organizational plans, they can conduct a detailed audit of current employees and their capabilities. The basic source of data on employees is available in the HR records in the organization. The HR Online illustrates the growth of technology in obtaining such data.

An inventory of organizational skills and capabilities may consider a number of elements. The following ones are important:

Technology Expanding Employee Skills Databases

Both employers and employees are using the expansion of technology as part of workforce-related factors. Technological systems and software related to HR planning and talent management are growing about 15% a year. Some examples of the uses of such technology follow.

For employees, dramatic growth in information technology (IT) methods is occurring. Aon Corporation surveyed 800 employees using Web 2.0 social media. The study found that more than two-thirds of both younger and older workers were using technology for job-related purposes. Aon recommended that employees use technology means such as text-messaging, blogs, wikis, and twitters to identify and enhance their skills and productivity.

Skills databases are an increasingly popular tool being used to track employee talent. The concept is simple: Put employees' skills and technical expertise, prior jobs, training, coaching aptitude, certifications, geographical experience, languages, career aspirations, and other topics in a database, and then use analyses of

this information as part of HR forecasting for individual capabilities. These databases also can be evaluated to fill jobs or can be analyzed to identify strengths and weaknesses of a division or even the whole company.

Some systems rely on managers to enter and update employee information in the database, but managers sometimes fail to do so or withhold information, fearing they might lose their most skilled employees to someone else in the company. Other approaches request employees to enter their skills and proficiency levels, and then managers review the reports. However, employees, because of either personal confidentiality concerns or being overworked, may not always enter their skills data accurately.

In spite of such difficulties, obtaining and utilizing IT data on employees' skills can aid both managers and employees in HR planning and forecasting. Then using those HR plans and forecasts may enhance the identification, engagement, and retention of both existing workers and potential employees.[9]

- Individual employee demographics (age, length of service in the organization, time in present job)
- Individual career progression (jobs held, time in each job, education and training levels, promotions or other job changes, pay rates)
- Individual performance data (work accomplishment, growth in skills, working relationships)

All the details on an individual employee's skills that go into a databank may affect that person's career. Therefore, the data and their use must meet the same standards of job-relatedness and nondiscrimination as those met when the employee was initially hired. Furthermore, security measures must ensure that sensitive information is available only to those who have a specific use for it.

Managers and HR staff members can gather data on individual employees and aggregate details into a profile of the current organizational workforce. This profile may reveal many of the current strengths and deficiencies of people in the organization. For instance, a skills mismatch may be identified in which some workers are either overqualified or underqualified for their jobs.[10] The profile also may highlight potential future problems. For example, if some specialized expertise, such as advanced technical skills, is absent in many workers, the organization may find it difficult to take advantage of its changing technological developments; or if a large group of experienced employees are all in the same age bracket, their eventual retirements about the same time might lead to future "gaps" in the organization.

FORECASTING HR SUPPLY AND DEMAND

The information gathered from scanning the external environment and assessing internal strengths and weaknesses is used to predict HR supply and demand in light of organizational objectives and strategies. **Forecasting** uses information from the past and the present to identify expected future conditions. Projections for the future are, of course, subject to error. Fortunately, experienced people usually are able to forecast with enough accuracy to positively affect long-range organizational planning.

Forecasting Using information from the past and the present to identify expected future conditions.

Forecasting Methods and Periods

Forecasting methods may be either judgmental or mathematical, as Figure 5-2 shows. Methods for forecasting human resources range from a manager's best

FIGURE 5-2   **HR Forecasting Example Methods**

Judgmental Methods

- *Estimates* can be either top-down or bottom-up, but essentially people who are in a position to know are asked, "How many people will you need next year?"

- The *rule of thumb* method relies on general guidelines applied to a specific situation within the organization. For example, a guideline of "one operations manager per five reporting supervisors" aids in forecasting the number of supervisors needed in a division. However, it is important to adapt the guideline to recognize widely varying departmental needs.

- The *Delphi technique* uses input from a group of experts whose opinions of forecasted situations are sought. These expert opinions are then combined and returned to the experts for a second anonymous opinion. The process continues through several rounds until the experts essentially agree on a judgment. For example, this approach is used to forecast effects of technology on HR management and staffing needs.

- *Nominal groups*, unlike the Delphi method, require experts to meet face to face. Their ideas may be cited independently at first, discussed as a group, and then compiled as a report.

Mathematical Methods

- *Statistical regression analysis* makes a statistical comparison of past relationships among various factors. For example, a statistical relationship between gross sales and number of employees in a retail chain may be useful in forecasting the number of employees that will be needed if the retailer's sales increase 15% or decrease 10%.

- *Simulation models* are representations of real situations in abstract form. For example, an econometric model of the growth in software usage would lead to forecasts of the need for software developers. Numerous simulation methods and techniques are available.

- *Productivity ratios* calculate the average number of units produced per employee. These averages can be applied to sales forecasts to determine the number of employees needed. For example, a firm could forecast the number of needed sales representatives using these ratios.

- *Staffing ratios* can be used to estimate indirect labor. For example, if the company usually uses one clerical person for every 25 production employees, that ratio can be used to estimate the need for clerical employees.

guess to a rigorous and complex computer simulation. Despite the availability of sophisticated judgmental and mathematical models and techniques, forecasting is still a combination of quantitative methods and subjective judgment. The facts must be evaluated and weighed by knowledgeable individuals, such as managers or HR planners, who use the mathematical models as tools and make judgments to arrive at decisions.

HR forecasting should be done over three planning periods: short range, intermediate range, and long range. The most commonly used planning period of six months to one year focuses on *short-range* forecasts for the immediate HR needs of an organization. Intermediate- and long-range forecasting are much more difficult processes. *Intermediate-range* plans usually project one to three years into the future, and *long-range* plans extend beyond three years.

Forecasting the Demand for Human Resources

The demand for employees can be calculated for an entire organization and/or for individual units in the organization. For example, a forecast might indicate that a firm needs 125 new employees next year, or that it needs 25 new people in sales and customer service, 45 in production, 20 in accounting and information systems, 2 in HR, and 33 in the warehouse. The unit breakdown obviously allows HR planners to better pinpoint the specific skills needed than does the aggregate method.

Demand for human resources can be forecast by considering specific openings that are likely to occur. The openings (or demands) are created when new jobs are being created or current jobs are being reduced. Additionally, forecasts must consider when employees leave positions because of promotions, transfers, turnovers, and terminations.

An analysis is used to develop decision rules (or "fill rates") for each job or level. For example, a decision rule for a financial institution might state that 50% of branch supervisor openings will be filled through promotions from customer service tellers, 25% through promotions from personal bankers, and 25% from new hires. Forecasters must be aware of multiple effects throughout the organization, because as people are promoted from within, their previous positions become available. Continuing the example, forecasts for the need for customer service tellers and personal bankers would also have to be developed. The overall purpose of the forecast is to identify the needs for human resources by number and type for the forecasting period.

Forecasting the Supply of Human Resources

Once human resources needs have been forecast, then availability of qualified individuals must be identified. Forecasting availability considers both *external* and *internal* supplies. Although the internal supply may be somewhat easier to calculate, it is important to calculate the external supply as accurately as possible.

External Supply The external supply of potential employees available to the organization needs to be identified. Extensive use of government estimates of labor force populations, trends in the industry, and many more complex and interrelated factors must be considered. Such information is often available from state or regional economic development offices, including these items:

- Net migration into and out of the area
- Individuals entering and leaving the workforce
- Individuals graduating from schools and colleges
- Changing workforce composition and patterns
- Economic forecasts for the next few years
- Technological developments and shifts
- Actions of competing employers
- Government regulations and pressures
- Circumstances affecting persons entering and leaving the workforce

Internal Supply Figure 5-3 shows in general terms how the internal supply can be calculated for a specific employer. Estimating internal supply considers the number of external hires and the employees who move from their current jobs into others through promotions, lateral moves, and terminations. It also considers that the internal supply is influenced by training and development programs, transfer and promotion policies, and retirement policies, among other factors. In forecasting the internal supply, data from the replacement charts and succession planning efforts are used to project potential personnel changes, identify possible backup candidates, and keep track of attrition (resignations, retirements, etc.) for each department in an organization.

FIGURE 5-3   **Estimating Internal Labor Supply for a Given Unit**

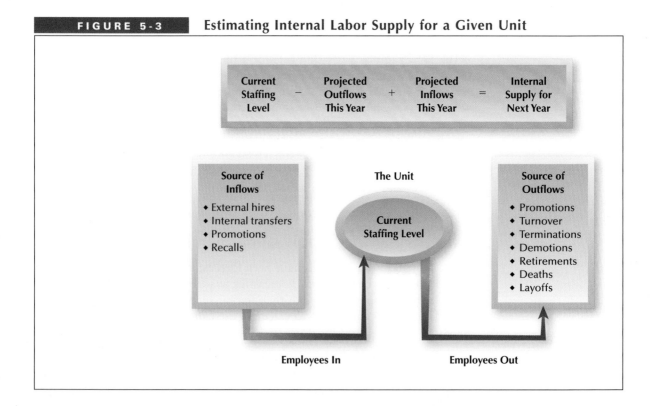

INDIVIDUAL WORKERS AND ORGANIZATIONAL RELATIONSHIPS

Relationships between individuals and their employers can vary widely from favorable to unfavorable. The individual's performance is a major part of why the employer wants the individual to stay or go. Competent employees who are satisfied with their employers, who know what is expected, and who have reduced turnover potential are assets to the organization. But just as individuals in an organization can be a competitive advantage, they can also be a liability. When few employees are satisfied with their jobs, when people are constantly leaving, and when the employees who do remain work ineffectively, the organization faces a *competitive disadvantage.*

Understanding the relationships between individuals and organizations is more than just academically interesting. The economic health of most organizations depends on the efforts of employes with the ability and motivation to do their jobs well. The exchanges in the relationship between an employee and an employer affect both of them.[11] Two considerations in these relationships include the psychological contract and motivation, which can help with understanding employee retention.

Psychological Contract

A concept that has been useful in discussing individuals' relationships with their employers is that of a **psychological contract**, which refers to the unwritten expectations employees and employers have about the nature of their work relationships. The psychological contract can create either a positive or negative relationship between an employer and an individual. It is based on trust and commitment that leads to meeting both the employer's and employee's expectations and needs.[12]

Unwritten psychological contracts between employers and employees encompass expectations about both tangible items (e.g., wages, benefits, employee productivity, and attendance) and intangible items (e.g., loyalty, fair treatment, and job security). Employers may attempt to detail their expectations through handbooks and policy manuals, but those materials are only part of the total "contractual" relationship.

The Changing Psychological Contract Traditionally, employees expected to exchange their efforts and capabilities for secure jobs that offered competitive pay, a solid range of benefits, and career progression within an organization, among other factors. But as some organizations have changed in economic terms, they have had to address various organizational crises by downsizing and eliminating workers who had given long and loyal service. Consequently, in these firms, a growing number of remaining employees are questioning whether they should remain loyal to and stay with their employers.

Psychological contract
The unwritten expectations employees and employers have about the nature of their work relationships.

When individuals feel that they have some control and perceived rights in the organization, they are more likely to be committed to the organization and utilize their knowledge, skills, and abilities to accomplish performance results.[13] A psychological contract recognizes the following components:

Employers Provide	Employees Contribute
• Competitive compensation and benefits	• Continuous skill improvement and increased productivity
• Flexibility to balance work and home life	• Reasonable time with the organization
• Career development opportunities	• Extra efforts and results when needed

Psychological contracts can be strengthened and employee commitment enhanced when the organization is involved in a cause the employee values highly. Conversely, psychological contracts can be violated, not only in reaction to personal mistreatment, but from a perception that the organization has abandoned an important principle or cause. For instance, when unethical or illegal behavior of upper management occurs, the psychological contract is violated. Thus, employees may feel anger, distrust, reduced loyalty and commitment, and increased willingness to leave. Also, social exchange relationships in organizations can be affected by psychological contract breaches and violations.[14]

GLOBAL

Global Psychological Contract Concerns With many organizations having global operations, the psychological contract becomes more complicated. Employees in foreign countries and expatriate employees from the United States have varying psychological contract expectations. For expatriates, if the organizational expectations are not made clear prior to their relocation, more of them will be likely to quit within the first year or demand return to their home country.[15]

An additional concern for multinational firms is to meet the psychological contract expectations of individuals in different cultures and countries. Consider the number of jobs that have been shifted from the United States and Europe to China, India, Romania, Mexico, the Philippines, Brazil, and other countries with different global factors. Being aware of varying psychological contract issues with foreign employees is important if global HR efforts are to be successful.

Individual Employee Performance and Motivation

The idea of a psychological contract between the individual employee and the organization helps clarify why people might stay or leave a job. But for an employer to *want* to keep an employee, that person must be performing well. The HR unit in an organization exists in part to provide ways to analyze and address the performance and motivation of individual employees.

Individual Performance Factors The three major factors that affect how a given individual performs are illustrated in Figure 5-4. They are: (1) individual ability to do the work, (2) effort expended, and (3) organizational support. The relationship of those factors is widely acknowledged in management literature as follows:

$$\text{Performance } (P) = \text{Ability } (A) \times \text{Effort } (E) \times \text{Support } (S)$$

Individual performance is enhanced to the degree that all three components are present with an individual employee, and diminished if any of these factors is reduced or absent. For instance, if several production workers have the abilities to do their jobs and work hard, but the organization provides outmoded equipment

| FIGURE 5-4 | Components of Individual Performance |

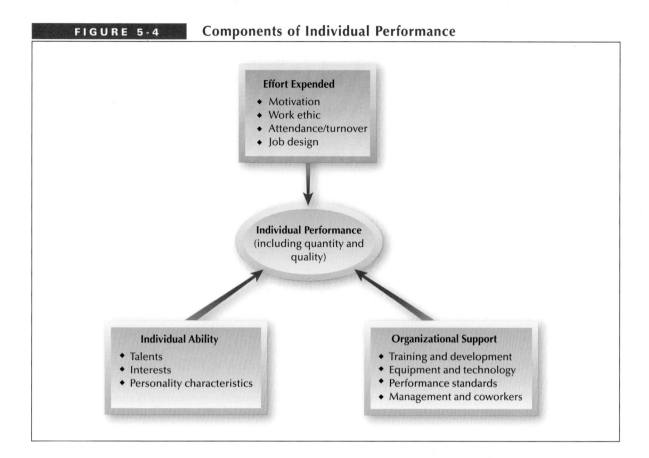

or the management style of supervisors causes negative reactions by the workers, the lack of organizational support may reduce individual performance.

An example of how this performance equation can work in a positive way is seen in the link between individual motivation and organizational support in the form of coworkers. Studies have shown that the motivation of poor-performing employees can be improved when these employees work more intensely with a group of better-performing workers. The link between individual motivation and organizational support has important HR management implications.[16]

Individual Motivation and Management Implications The desire within a person causing that person to act is called **motivation**. People usually act to reach a goal, which means that motivation is a goal-directed drive that seldom occurs in a void. The words *need, want, desire,* and *drive* are all similar to *motive,* from which the word *motivation* is derived. Approaches to understanding motivation vary because different theorists have developed their own views and models.[17] Each approach has contributed to the understanding of human motivation, and details on different approaches can be found in various organizational behavior textbooks.

Motivation is complex and individualized, and managerial strategies and tactics must be broad-based to address the motivation concerns of individuals at work. Factors that can inhibit motivation and work performance include a worker's capacities and determination to get work done regardless of difficulties.[18] For instance, with a poor-performing employee, managers must determine whether inadequate individual behavior is due to employee deficiencies, inconsistent reward policies, or low desire for the rewards offered.

Motivation The desire within a person causing that person to act.

By having supportive supervisors and managers who serve as mentors, concerns about motivations can be better addressed with employees.[19] Understanding motivation is important because employee engagement can affect both performance and retention. Fostering motivation can improve performance and can reduce turnover.

Many organizations spend a considerable amount of money to "motivate" their employees, using a wide range of tactics. For example, some firms hire motivational speakers to inspire employees, and "motivational coaches" command fees of up to $50,000 a speech. Other employers give employees items such as T-shirts, mugs, or books as motivators. However, such efforts may or may not be effective in improving employees' job satisfaction and loyalty.

Many employees rely on the unspoken psychological contract, and their hope that the employer will honor this "agreement" affects their job satisfaction and motivation. One survey found that 45% of the surveyed workers indicated that personal job satisfaction was their main motivation for job performance.[20]

Nature of Job Satisfaction

In its most basic sense, **job satisfaction** is a positive emotional state resulting from evaluating one's job experiences. Job *dissatisfaction* occurs when one's expectations are not met. For example, if an employee expects clean and safe working conditions, that employee is likely to be dissatisfied if the workplace is dirty and dangerous.

Dimensions of job satisfaction frequently mentioned include worker relationships, pay and benefits, performance recognition, and communications with managers and executives. Sometimes job satisfaction is called *morale,* which appears to have declined somewhat in recent years in some firms due to economic factors and changes in the elements of the employee-employer relationship. Frequently cited reasons for decline in morale include more demanding and stressful work, fewer relationships with management, and less confidence in compensation and other rewards.[21] Depending on the job, the work-life balancing mentioned earlier also can lead to either positive or negative effects in workers' job satisfaction.[22]

One way employers address job satisfaction, and ultimately retention, is by regularly surveying employees. One specific type of survey used by many organizations is an **attitude survey**, which focuses on employees' feelings and beliefs about their jobs and the organization. Once the survey results are compiled, management responds to the results. If the employer takes responsive actions, employees may view the employer more positively; however, if management ignores the survey results, their inaction can lead to less employee job satisfaction.[23]

Organizational Commitment and Job Satisfaction The degree to which employees believe in and accept organizational goals and want to remain with the organization is called **organizational commitment**. Job satisfaction influences organizational commitment, which in turn affects employee retention and turnover. As Figure 5-5 depicts, the interaction of the individual and the job determines levels of job satisfaction and organizational commitment.

Engagement and Loyalty A related idea is *employee engagement,* which is the extent to which an employee feels linked to organizational success. Surveys have shown that levels of employee engagement range from 15% to 45% for highly engaged workers, and 5% to 20% for disengaged ones.[24]

Job satisfaction A positive emotional state resulting from evaluating one's job experiences.

Attitude survey A survey that focuses on employees' feelings and beliefs about their jobs and the organization.

Organizational commitment The degree to which employees believe in and accept organizational goals and desire to remain with the organization.

| **FIGURE 5-5** | Factors Affecting Job Satisfaction and Organizational Commitment |

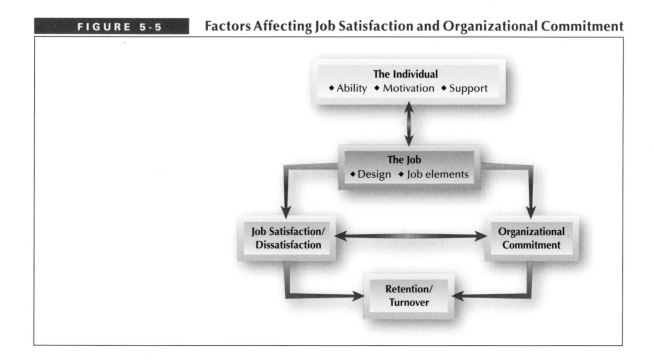

Engaged employees may be seen as "loyal" employees who are more than just satisfied with their jobs; they are pleased with the relationships with their employers. In changing labor markets, employers find that turnover of key people occurs more frequently when employee loyalty is low. For example, the Federal Office of Personnel Management has used engagement efforts with retirement-eligible employees to defer their departures, which reduces turnover.[25] Excessive turnover makes clear the importance of having an engaged and committed workforce.

A logical extension of organizational engagement focuses more specifically on *continuance commitment* factors. These are the factors that influence decisions to remain with or leave an organization, and ultimately they are reflected in employee retention and turnover statistics. The relationships among satisfaction, commitment, and turnover have been affirmed across cultures, full- and part-time workers, genders, and occupations. Organizational engagement and commitment can be seen as essential in retaining employees in organizations. Individuals who are not as satisfied with their jobs or who are not as committed to the organization are more likely to withdraw from the organization. Understanding engagement and commitment in relation to turnover is one facet of retention efforts for managers.

LOGGING ON

Loyalty Research Center
This research center provides employee loyalty/employee engagement research and consulting services. Visit their site at www.loyaltyresearch.com.

EMPLOYEE TURNOVER

Turnover The process in which employees leave an organization and have to be replaced.

Turnover occurs when employees leave an organization and have to be replaced. Many organizations have found that turnover is a costly problem. For instance, health care firms experienced over 30% turnover annually in one state. Just in registered nurse jobs, the turnover cost in the state was more than $125 million per year, with individual nurse turnover costs being $32,000 per person.[26]

The extent to which employers face high turnover rates and costs varies by organization and industry. For higher-level executives and professionals, turnover costs can run as much as two times the departing employees' annual salaries, and rates often are linked to executive job expectations and needed skills changes.[27] In many service industries, the turnover rates and costs are frequently very high. In the retail industry, turnover in some companies averages more than 100% a year for part-time workers and around 75% a year for full-time workers. The U.S. supermarkets, fast-food restaurants, and other retail service industry firms spend billions of dollars each year to deal with worker turnover.

Types of Employee Turnover

Turnover is classified in a number of ways. One classification uses the following categories, although the two types are not mutually exclusive:

- **Involuntary Turnover**

  Employees are terminated for poor performance or work rule violations

- **Voluntary Turnover**

  Employees leave by choice

Involuntary turnover is triggered at all levels by employers terminating workers due to organizational policies and work rule violations, excessive absenteeism, performance standards that are not met by employees, and other issues. Voluntary turnover too can be caused by many factors, some of which are not employer controlled. Common voluntary turnover causes include job dissatisfaction, pay and benefits levels, supervision, geography, and personal/family reasons. Career opportunities in other firms, when employees receive unsolicited contacts, may lead to turnover for individuals, especially those in highly specialized jobs such as IT.[28] Voluntary turnover may increase with the size of the organization, most likely because larger firms are less effective in preventing turnover and have more employees who are inclined to move.

Another view of turnover classifies it based on whether it is good or bad for the organization:

- **Functional Turnover**

  Lower-performing or disruptive employees leave

- **Dysfunctional Turnover**

  Key individuals and high performers leave at critical times

Not all turnover is negative for organizations; on the contrary, functional turnover represents a positive change. Some workforce losses are desirable, especially if those who leave are lower-performing, less reliable, and/or disruptive individuals.[29] Of course, dysfunctional turnover also occurs. That happens when key individuals leave, often at crucial times. For example, a software project leader who leaves in the middle of a system upgrade in order to take a promotion at another firm could cause the system upgrade timeline to slip due to the difficulty of replacing the employee and could also lead other software specialists in the firm to seek out and accept jobs at competitive firms.

Employees quit for many reasons, only some of which can be controlled by the organization, so another classification uses the following terms to describe types of turnover:

- **Uncontrollable Turnover**

  Employees leave for reasons outside the control of the employer

- **Controllable Turnover**

  Employees leave for reasons that could be influenced by the employer

Some examples of reasons for turnover the employer cannot control include: (1) the employee moves out of the geographic area, (2) the employee decides to stay home with young children or an elder relative, (3) the employee's spouse is transferred, and (4) the employee is a student worker who graduates from college. Even though some turnover is inevitable, employers recognize that reducing turnover saves money, and that they must address the turnover that is controllable. Organizations are better able to keep employees if they deal with the concerns of those employees that might lead to the controllable turnover.

Turnover and "Churn" Hiring new workers while laying off others is called **churn**. This practice raises a paradox in which employers complain about not being able to find skilled workers while they are laying off others. As organizations face economic and financial problems that result in layoffs, the remaining employees are more likely to consider jobs at other firms.[30] In this situation, turnover is more likely to occur, and efforts are needed to keep existing employees. HR actions such as information sharing, opportunities for more training/learning, and emphasis on job significance can be helpful in lowering turnover intentions of individuals.[31]

Measuring Employee Turnover

The U.S. Department of Labor estimates that the cost of replacing an employee ranges from one-half to five times the person's annual salary.[32] The turnover rate for an organization can be computed as a monthly or yearly cost. The following formula, in which *separations* means departures from the organization, is widely used:

$$\frac{\text{Number of employee separations during the year}}{\text{Total number of employees at midyear}} \times 100$$

Common turnover rates range from almost 0% to more than 100% a year and vary among industries. As a part of HR management systems, turnover data can be gathered and analyzed in a number of different ways, including the following categories:

- Job and job level
- Department, unit, and location
- Reason for leaving
- Length of service

- Demographic characteristics
- Education and training
- Knowledge, skills, and abilities
- Performance ratings/levels

Two examples illustrate why detailed analyses of turnover are important. A manufacturing organization had a companywide turnover rate that was not severe, but 80% of the turnover occurred within one department. That imbalance indicated that some specific actions on training supervisors and revising pay levels were needed to resolve problems in that unit. In a different organization, a global shipping/delivery firm found ways to reduce turnover of sales and service employees. The actions of that firm reduced its turnover 29%, which contributed to an annual savings of more than $18 million in direct and indirect costs.[33] In both of these examples, the targeted turnover rates declined as a result of employer actions taken in response to the turnover analyses that were done.

Churn Hiring new workers while laying off others.

FIGURE 5-6   **Model for Costing Lost Productivity**

Job Title: _____

A. Typical annual pay for this job   _____
B. Percentage of pay for benefits multiplied by annual pay   _____
C. Total employee annual cost (add A + B)   _____
D. Number of employees who voluntarily quit the job in the past   _____
   12 months
E. Number of months it takes for 1 employee to become fully productive   _____
F. Per person turnover cost (multiply [E ÷ 12] × C × 50%*)   _____
G. Annual turnover cost for this job (multiply F × D)   _____

*Assumes 50% productivity throughout the learning period (E).

MEASURE

HR Metrics: Determining Turnover Costs

A major step in reducing the expense of turnover is to decide how the organization is going to record employee departures and what calculations are necessary to maintain and benchmark the turnover rates. Determining turnover costs can be relatively simple or very complex, depending on the nature of the efforts made and the data used.

Figure 5-6 shows a model for calculating the cost of productivity lost to turnover. If a job pays (A) $20,000 and benefits cost (B) 40%, then the total annual cost for one employee (C) is $28,000. Assuming that 20 employees have quit in the previous year (D) and that it takes three months for 1 employee to be fully productive (E), the calculation results in a per person turnover cost (F) of $3,500. Overall, the annual lost productivity (G) would be $70,000 for the 20 individuals who have left. In spite of the conservative and simple nature of this model, it easily makes the point that turnover is costly. As another example, if 150 tellers in a large bank corporation leave in a year, calculations done according to this model produce turnover costs of more than $500,000 a year.

Detailing Turnover Costing Other areas to be included in calculating detailed turnover costs are also available.[34] Some of the most common areas considered include the following:

- *Separation costs:* HR staff and supervisory time, pay rates to prevent separations, exit interview time, unemployment expenses, legal fees for separations challenged, accrued vacation expenditures, continued health benefits, and others
- *Vacancy costs:* Temporary help, contract and consulting firm usage, existing employee overtime, and other costs until the person is replaced
- *Replacement costs:* Recruiting and advertising expenses, search fees, HR interviewer and staff time and salaries, employee referral fees, relocation and moving costs, supervisor and managerial time and salaries, employment testing costs, reference checking fees, preemployment medical expenses, relocation costs, and others

- *Training costs:* Paid orientation time, training staff time and pay, costs of training materials, supervisor and manager time and salaries, coworker "coaching" time and pay, and others
- *Hidden/indirect costs:* Costs that are not obvious, such as reduced productivity, decreased customer service, additional unexpected employee turnover, missed project deadlines, and others

These turnover metrics illustrate that turnover is a crucial HR and managerial issue that must be constantly evaluated and addressed.

LOGGING ON

TalentKeepers
For Web-based employee retention solutions, visit www.talentkeepers.com.

Not all turnover is negative. Turnover of low performers should be considered positive. There may be an "optimal" amount of useful turnover in order to replace low performers and add part-time or contract workers with special capabilities to enhance workforce performance.[35] HR professionals should take actions to reduce negative turnover and to address the retention of key employees.

RETENTION OF HUMAN RESOURCES

Retention of employees as human resources is part of HR staffing and planning efforts. Turnover, as the opposite of retention, often has been seen as a routine HR matter requiring records and reports. However, what was once a bothersome detail has become a substantial HR issue for many employers. Thus, organizations are being forced to study why employees leave and why they stay. Sometimes an individual in the HR area is assigned to specifically focus on retention to ensure that it receives high priority.

Myths and Realities about Retention

Keeping good employees is a challenge that all organizations share and that becomes even more difficult as labor markets change. Unfortunately, some myths have arisen about what it takes to retain employees. Some of the most prevalent myths and realities are as follows:

1. *Money is the main reason people leave.* Money certainly is a vital HR tool, and if people feel they are being paid inadequately, they may be more likely to leave. But if they are paid close to the competitive level they expect, other parts of the job become more important.
2. *Hiring has little to do with retention.* This is not true. Recruiting and selecting the people who fit the jobs and who are less likely to leave in the first place, and then orienting them to the company, can greatly increase retention. It is important to select for retention.
3. *If you train people, you are only training them for another employer.* Developing skills in employees may indeed make them more marketable, but it also tends to improve retention. When an employer provides employees with training and development assistance, job satisfaction may increase and employees are more likely to stay, particularly if they see more future opportunities internally.
4. *Do not be concerned about retention during organizational change.* That is exactly the time to worry about retention. Although some people's jobs may have to be cut because of economic organizational

factors, the remaining employees that the company would like to keep may have the most opportunity and reason to leave voluntarily. For example, during a merger or acquisition, most workers are concerned about job security and their employer's future. If they do not feel a part of the new organization early on, many may leave or evaluate alternatives.

5. *If solid performers want to leave, the company cannot hold them.* Employees are best viewed as "free agents," who indeed can leave when they want. The key to keeping solidly performing employees is to create an environment in which they want to stay and grow.

Drivers of Retention

Because both people and jobs are so varied, managers and HR professionals need to realize that individuals may remain or leave their employment for both job-related and personal reasons. For instance, if employees choose to leave an organization for family reasons (e.g., because a spouse is transferring or to raise children), there may be a limited number of actions the employer can take to keep them on the job. However, there are significant actions that an employer can take to retain employees in many other circumstances. Figure 5-7 illustrates some of these "drivers" of retention, or areas in which employers can take action to strengthen the possibility of keeping employees.

The actual reasons that people stay or leave vary according to job groupings, industry and organizational issues, geographical global aspects, and other factors. For instance, a survey of executives by Robert Half International found that the most common factors that caused satisfactory employees to quit their jobs were unhappiness with management, limited career advancements and recognition, insufficient pay and benefits, and job boredom.[36] This survey illustrates that many of the factors involved in retention drivers are organizational and management factors within the employer's control.

FIGURE 5-7   **Drivers of Retention**

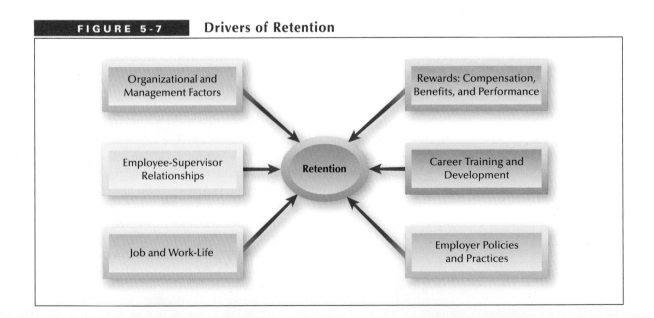

Organizational and Management Factors A number of organizational/ management factors influence individuals in their decisions to stay with or leave their employers. Organizations that have clearly established goals and hold managers and employees accountable for accomplishing results are viewed as better places to work, especially by individuals wishing to progress both financially and career-wise. Further, effective management provides the resources necessary for employees to perform their jobs well.[37] These factors reflect workplace commitment by employees, which leads to more positive organizational views in the industry and communities.

Other organizational components that affect employee retention are related to the management of the organization. Some organizations see external events as threatening, whereas others see changes as challenges requiring responses.[38] The latter approach can be a source of competitive advantage, especially if an organization is in a growing, dynamic industry. Another organizational factor that can affect employee job performance and potential turnover intentions is "organizational politics."[39] This can include managerial favoritism, having to be involved in undesirable activities, taking credit for what others do, and other actions that occur in many departments and organizational settings.

A final factor affecting how employees view their organizations is the quality of organizational leadership. Often, leaders have an identified strategic plan that guides how the firm responds to changes. If a firm is not effectively managed, then employees may be disappointed by the ineffective responses and inefficiencies they deal with in their jobs. A survey of 700 workers identified that "bad bosses" who do not give employees recognition for accomplishments or who fail to keep promises can lead to almost 40% of the workers being dissatisfied and more likely to look for other jobs.[40]

Work Relationships Work relationships that affect employee retention include *supervisory/management support* and *coworker relations*. A supervisor or manager builds positive relationships and aids retention by being fair and nondiscriminatory, allowing work flexibility and work-family balancing, giving feedback that recognizes employee efforts and performance, and supporting career planning and development.

Additionally, many individuals build close relationships with coworkers. Such work-related friendships do not appear on employee records, but these relationships can be an important signal that a workplace is positive. Overall, what this means is that it is not just where people work, but also with whom they work, that affects employee retention. If individuals are not linked with or do not relate well to their coworkers, there is greater likelihood for turnover to occur.[41]

Job and Work-Life Many individuals have seen a decline in job security during the past decade. All the downsizings, layoffs, mergers and acquisitions, and organizational restructurings have affected employee loyalty and retention. As coworkers experience layoffs and job reductions, the anxiety levels of the remaining employees rise. Consequently, employees start thinking about leaving before they too get cut. Organizations in which job continuity and security are high tend to have higher retention rates.

Some jobs are considered "good" and others are thought to be "bad," but not all people agree on which jobs are which. As mentioned previously, the design of jobs and peoples' preferences can vary significantly. Job design factors that can impact retention include the following:

Global Retention

The same core elements that affect retention in the United States are important across the globe according to a McKinsey Global Institute study. Higher turnover and lower retention rates can be seen among expatriate employees working outside their home countries. Also, repatriating those who have been overseas only to return to less-than-ideal situations later in the United States is another source of international retention difficulties.[42]

Retention can also be a challenge in countries where national workers staff the firms. India with its large global economic market illustrates what kinds of difficulties can occur. Estimates are that service industries in India will encounter a shortfall in one year of 500,000 employees who are qualified for jobs in those industries, which include financial services, information technology, and retail, among others.

One would think that given the large Indian population, recruitment and retention would not be problems. But the need for individuals with special skills in cities such as Mumbai, Delhi, and others is creating major issues. Firms are giving 12% to 15% yearly pay increases to many key workers in order to retain them; in addition, they are using both yearly and longer-term incentives for more senior-level employees.

The retention situation in India is expected to expand to other countries as global economic conditions improve and change, and the global market continues to grow. For instance, a survey of 32,000 employers in 26 countries indicated that almost one-third of them would have hired more professional staff members if they had been available. So, global attraction and retention are growing HR concerns.[43]

- A knowledge, skills, and abilities mismatch, either through overqualification or underqualification, can lead to turnover.
- Job accomplishments and workload demands that are dissatisfying or stressful may impact performance and lead to turnover.
- Both timing of work schedules and geographic locations may contribute to burnout of some individuals but not others.
- The ability of employees to balance work and life requirements affects their job performance and retention.

Numerous examples could be given on how each of these items affect retention, but one example comes from a survey of chief financial officers on the impact of these issues in their firms. In this survey, work-life flexibility efforts were seen as creating significant retention, recruitment, and productivity results.[44] This study illustrates that how organizations address jobs can drive retention efforts, including global retention as discussed in the HR Perspective.

Rewards: Compensation, Benefits, and Performance The tangible rewards that people receive for working come in the form of pay, incentives, and benefits. Employees often cite better pay or benefits as the reason for leaving one employer for another. Employers do best if they offer *competitive pay and benefits,* which means they must be close to what other employers are providing and what individuals believe to be consistent with their capabilities, experience, and performance. If compensation is not close, often defined as within 10% to 15% of the "market" rate, turnover is likely to be higher.

However, the reality of compensation is a bit more complex than it seems at first glance. For instance, one study of public-sector employees identified that broad reward programs, not just pay and benefits, aided with workforce retention in difficult economic situations.[45] A number of employers have used a wide range of special benefits and perks to attract and retain employees. For example, Student Media Group in Delaware added work-related plasma television screens, videogame players, and free soda and snacks as part of a special rewards package to create more positive views to aid in retaining employees.[46]

Another part of rewards generally is that individuals need to be satisfied with both the actual levels of pay and the processes used to determine pay. That is why the performance management systems and performance appraisal processes in organizations must be designed so they are linked to compensation increases. To strengthen links between organizational and individual performance, an increasing number of fast-growing private-sector firms are using variable pay and incentives programs.[47] Some programs offer cash bonuses or lump-sum payments to reward extra performance, which also aids with retention efforts.

Another rewards aspect that affects retention is *employee recognition,* which can be both tangible and intangible. Tangible recognition comes in many forms, such as "employee of the month" plaques and perfect-attendance certificates. Intangible and psychological recognition includes feedback from managers and supervisors that acknowledges extra effort and performance, even if monetary rewards are not given. For instance, one firm, Fairmont Hotels and Resorts, is using a "Serviceplus Colleague Recognition Program" to engage its 30,000 employees. Different types of recognitions include "Star of the Month" and "Memory Maker" for significant service. For such recognition, a small amount of money (under $50) and other types of rewards are given. An employee survey has shown significant increases in positive employee views of both their jobs and the Fairmont firm.[48]

Career Training and Development Many employees in all types of jobs consistently indicate that organizational efforts to aid their career training and development can significantly affect employee retention. *Opportunities for personal growth* lead the list of reasons why individuals took their current jobs and why they stay there. In one survey, nearly one-third of workers identified the lack of career advancement opportunities to be the most important reason for potentially changing employers.[49]

Training and development efforts can be designed to indicate that employers are committed to keeping employees' knowledge, skills, and abilities current. Also, training and development can help underused employees attain new capabilities. Such a program at Southwest Airlines has been very successful. Recruiters were reassigned to different departments, which resulted in their generating sales and revenues in flight operations and other areas.[50]

Organizations address training and development in a number of ways. Tuition aid programs, typically offered as a benefit by many employers, allow employees to pursue additional educational and training opportunities. These programs often contribute to higher employee retention rates because the employees' new knowledge and capabilities can aid the employer. Also, through formal career planning efforts, employees discuss with their managers career opportunities within the organization and career development activities that will help them to grow.

Career development and planning efforts may include formal mentoring programs. For instance, information technology (IT) organizations are using career development programs so that IT individuals can expand their skills outside of technical areas. Programs in some firms cover communication and negotiation tactics, which gives the employees additional capabilities that are needed in managerial and other jobs.[51] Companies can help reduce attrition by showing employees that they are serious about career advancement opportunities.

Employer Policies and Practices A final set of factors found to affect retention is based on the employer relations policies that exist. Such areas as the reasonableness of HR policies, the fairness of disciplinary actions, and the means used to decide work assignments and opportunities all affect employee retention. If individuals feel that policies are unreasonably restrictive or are applied inconsistently, they may be more likely to look at jobs offered by other employers.

LOGGING ON

Retensa
For resources and newsletters on current trends in employee retention strategies, visit this site at www.retensa.com.

The increasing demographic diversity of U.S. workplaces makes the *nondiscriminatory treatment* of employees important, regardless of gender, age, and other characteristics. The organizational commitment and job satisfaction of ethnically diverse individuals are affected by perceived discriminatory treatment. A number of firms have recognized that proactive management of diversity issues results in greater retention of individuals of all backgrounds.

MANAGING RETENTION

The foregoing sections summarized the results of many studies and popular HR practices to identify factors that can cause retention difficulties. Retention matters because turnover can cause poor performance in otherwise productive units. Now our focus turns toward the keys to managing retention as part of effective HR management.

MEASURE

Retention Assessment and Metrics

To ensure that appropriate actions are taken to enhance retention, management decisions require data and analyses rather than subjective impressions, anecdotes of selected individual situations, or panic reactions to the loss of key people. Examples of data for analyzing retention are highlighted in Figure 5-8. Discussion on some of these sources follows.

The analysis of turnover data is an attempt to get at the cause of retention problems. Analysis should recognize that turnover is a symptom of other factors that may be causing problems. When the causes are treated, the symptoms can go away.

Some of the first areas to consider when analyzing data for retention include the work, pay/benefits, supervision, and management systems. Common methods of obtaining useful perspectives are employee surveys, exit interviews, and first-year turnover evaluations.

Employee Surveys Employee surveys can be used to diagnose specific problem areas, identify employee needs or preferences, and reveal areas in which HR activities are well received or viewed negatively. Whether the surveys are on general employee attitudes, job satisfaction, or specific issues, the survey results must be examined as part of retention measurement efforts. For

FIGURE 5-8   **Retention Measurement and Assessment Sources**

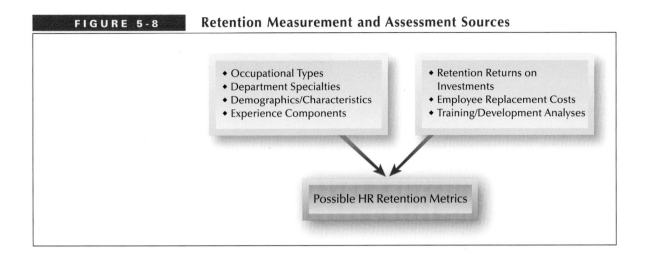

example, a growing number of "mini-surveys" on specific topics are being sent via e-mail questionnaires, blogs, and other means.

Regardless of the topics in a survey, obtaining employee input provides managers and HR professionals with data on the "retention climate" in an organization. By obtaining data on how employees view their jobs, their coworkers, their supervisors, and organizational policies and practices, these surveys can be starting points for reducing turnover and increasing the length of time that employees are retained. Some employers conduct attitude surveys yearly while others do so intermittently.

By asking employees to respond candidly to an attitude survey, management is building employees' expectations that actions will be taken on the concerns identified. Therefore, a crucial part of conducting an attitude survey is providing feedback to those who participated in it. It is especially important that even negative survey results be communicated to avoid fostering the appearance of hiding the results or placing blame.

Exit Interviews One widely used means for assisting retention assessment efforts is the **exit interview**, in which individuals who are leaving the organization are asked to give their reasons. HR must regularly summarize and analyze the data by category (e.g., reasons for leaving, department, length of service, etc.) to provide managers and supervisors with information for improving company efforts. As described in the HR On-the-Job feature, the exit interview process should contain some important aspects.

Many HR departments regularly contact former employees who were valuable contributors, as they may be willing to provide more information on questionnaires that are e-mailed to their homes or in telephone conversations conducted some time after they have left the organization.[52] For instance, one health care firm contacts former employees within 60 days after they have left. Many times these follow-up conversations reveal the "real" reasons for departures, other than what was said in the exit interviews. This health care firm also has a program through which ex-employees are invited to return as "alumni" and have lunch with former coworkers, which has led to a number of departed individuals indicating they would like to return to the firm because the jobs they took elsewhere did not turn out to be as "promising" as they had anticipated. Thus, rehiring can be aided by ongoing efforts such as e-mails, exit interview follow-ups, and continuing contacts with good former employees.

Exit interview An interview in which individuals who are leaving an organization are asked to give their reasons.

Conducting Exit Interviews

Departing employees may be reluctant to divulge their real reasons for leaving. A skilled HR interviewer may be able to gain useful information that departing employees do not wish to share with managers and supervisors. The following suggestions may be useful when conducting exit interviews:

- Decide who will conduct the exit interview and when the discussion will occur. Often these interviews occur on the last day or so of a departing individual's employment.
- Emphasize that the information provided by the departing employee will be treated confidentially and used to make improvements.
- Utilize a checklist or a set of standard questions so that the information can be summarized. Typical areas covered include

reasons for leaving, supervision, pay, training, liked and disliked aspects of the job, and details on the organization to which the employee is moving.

When doing the actual exit interview, numerous questions can be asked. Ones typically asked of individuals include the following:

- Why are you leaving as an employee?
- What have you liked and disliked about your job and managers?
- What company actions have made you and other employees more or less positive?
- What would or would not lead you to recommend the employer to future possible hires?

First-Year Turnover Evaluations A special type of retention assessment focuses on first-year employees. It is not unusual for turnover to be high among newer employees during their first year. Sometimes the cause of departure is voluntary; for example, individuals may identify a mismatch between what they expected in their jobs and managers and what actually occurs, or between their perceptions of the new job and its reality. Other times individuals are involuntarily removed in the first year. Some causes can be excessive absenteeism and poor performance, mismatches with job requirements, and conflicts with other employees and managers. If these situations occur too often, HR may need to reevaluate its recruiting and selection processes, as well as its job previews to make sure they are realistic.[53]

Overall, focus on first-year retention and turnover is useful because individuals who stay for a year are more likely to extend their employment and have greater retention beyond the first year. Also, effective first-year efforts may lead to future career development, higher performance, and other positive retention factors.

Retention Evaluation and Follow-Up

Management can take numerous actions to deal with retention issues. The choice of a particular action depends on the analysis of the turnover and retention problems in a particular organization and should be custom tailored for that organization.

Tracking of intervention results and *adjustment of intervention efforts* should be part of retention evaluation and follow-up. Some firms use pilot programs to see how changes affect retention before extending them to the entire organization. For instance, to test the effect of flextime scheduling on employee turnover, a firm might try flexible scheduling in one department. If the turnover rate in that department drops in comparison to the turnover rates in other departments still working set schedules, the firm might extend the use of flexible scheduling to other departments.

Retention evaluation and follow-up are key facets of the broader organizational HR planning and staffing. Effective retention management can have major impacts on the integrated HR attraction, recruiting, and selection processes.

SUMMARY

- HR planning involves analyzing and identifying the need for and availability of human resources so that the organization can meet its objectives.
- When developing HR plans, it is important to examine potential HR availability, both external and internal.
- When assessing external labor supply sources, economic, governmental, competitive, and workforce composition changes should be analyzed.
- Assessing internal strengths and weaknesses as a part of HR planning requires auditing and inventorying current jobs and employee capabilities.
- The supply and demand for human resources can be forecast with a variety of methods and for differing periods of time.
- Psychological contracts are unwritten expectations that employees and employers have about the nature of their work relationships.
- The components of individual performance are individual ability, effort expended, and organizational support.
- Motivation deals with the needs and desires of human behavior and managerial and organizational factors.

- The interaction between individuals and their jobs affects both job satisfaction and organizational commitment. The extent to which employees feel linked to organizational success can affect employee engagement and loyalty.
- Turnover occurs when employees leave an organization and must be replaced. It can be classified in a number of ways, but it should be measured and its costs determined.
- Increasing employee retention or reducing turnover is important in HR management.
- Drivers of retention include organizational, managerial, and job factors that may affect employees' work-life balancing; compensation and other rewards; career training and development; and employer policies and practices.
- Retention of employees is a major focus of HR management efforts in organizations, as demonstrated by the use of retention measures, including employee surveys and exit interviews.
- Managing retention should include evaluation and tracking of both retention actions and turnover follow-up.

CRITICAL THINKING ACTIVITIES

1. Discuss the major components of HR planning and forecasting efforts.

2. Describe your expectations for a job. How well does your employer meet the expectations you bring to the psychological contract?

3. If you became the new manager at a restaurant with high employee turnover, what actions

would you take to increase retention of employees?

4. As the HR manager, you must provide the senior management team with turnover costs for the following high-turnover position. Use Web sites such as

www.talentkeepers.com and www
.keepemployees.com, to calculate turnover and
analyze the variables involved. Also identify
any other data that might be relevant, and
then discuss how you would reduce the
turnover.

Position: Machine Operator

Number of employees: 250

Number of turnovers: 85

Average wage: $11.50/hour

Cost of benefits: 35% of payroll

HR EXPERIENTIAL PROBLEM SOLVING

Your company has reaped the benefits of having
long-term, tenured employees, but many of them
are now approaching retirement. It is anticipated
that approximately 20% of the company's workforce will retire in the next 3 to 5 years. In reviewing the remaining workforce through HR planning
efforts, you have become aware of work-life balance issues that need to be reviewed and addressed.
The Company President has requested that you
prepare a Retention Plan outlining these issues as
well as ways to address them. Resources to help
you address the issues in the Retention Plan can be
found at www.workfamily.com.

1. What steps will you take to identify key priorities in the work-life balance issues?

2. How will you present a business case to gain
   management support for addressing those issues
   in order to help retain existing workers and to
   fill the positions vacated by retiring employees?

CASE

Accenture—Retaining for Itself

Accenture is a firm that provides a wide range of
consulting and services to organizations worldwide. With more than 170,000 employees, the
firm has clients in 120 countries that receive
many HR and other consulting services. Among
others, these services include organizational, strategic, and change management analyses; leadership training and development; and technology
assistance and supply chain assistance. Large and
small client organizations also outsource various
operational functions to Accenture instead of
performing them internally with employees. Thus,
Accenture has many individuals who serve as consultants and support experts on specialized areas
and industries.

Because of its many professional consulting and support staff members, Accenture has
to manage its own human resources effectively
in order to serve both itself and its clients. The
rapid growth of this widespread firm has caused
Accenture to hire up to 60,000 employees in
just one year due to the expansion of clients and
the need to replace employees who have left to
become employees at other firms, to become independent consultants, or to work as employees at
client firms.

What Accenture does for its own employees
illustrates one reason why it is widely used by
clients. At the heart of Accenture's approach for
itself is to consider its employees as a virtual
workforce. This means that numerous employees work in many different places at different
times, often using work-life balancing, technology
resources, and work-related job flexibility. With
offices in more than 150 cities worldwide, the
work locations and schedules vary so much that
numerous Accenture consultants have to reserve
a desk at an office when they need to be there.
Otherwise, many employees are encouraged to
work outside offices.

The out-of-office environment presents an
extensive HR challenge for Accenture in terms of
engaging its employees. Many consultant employees work intermittently with a variety of managers
and coworkers, in teams as large as 1,000 consultants, throughout multiple countries.

To practice retention in its own firm, Accenture
does extensive training and development of employees. All new Accenture workers participate in "New
Joiner Orientation" where they learn what is expected
of them, do sample client projects with coworkers,
and become linked to personal career counselors.

Career training and development efforts include a wide range of activities, access to Accenture's "Career Marketplace" website, and training in how to work effectively on different types of projects and in global locations. The value of these activities is shown in the fact that almost 39% of Accenture's open U.S. jobs are filled by current employees who change and/or increase their job levels.

What Accenture's employee retention program emphasizes is that the firm does not just consult about HR and other services for clients, but also does for itself what many current and potential clients need to do, which is to view HR planning and retention as crucial for organizational success and growth.[54]

QUESTIONS

1. Identify how some Accenture-type efforts have and have not occurred in your current and previous workplaces. Also, discuss why focusing on employee retention pays off for Accenture clients, and not just for Accenture itself.

2. Go to the Accenture website, www.accenture.com, to research and gather job- and career-related information that might need to be adapted by other employers. As part of this research, examine how Accenture markets itself to current and potential employees.

SUPPLEMENTAL CASES

The Clothing Store

This case describes the approach of one firm to improving employee retention. (For the case, go to www.cengage.com/management/mathis.)

Alegent Health

This case discusses how Alegent, a large nonprofit health care system, improved employee retention and reduced turnover. (For the case, go to www.cengage.com/management/mathis.)

NOTES

1. Based on Susan J. Wells, "Say Hola to the Majority Minority," *HR Magazine*, September 2008, 38–45; Miriam Jordan, "Got Workers? Dairy Farms Run Low on Labor," *The Wall Street Journal*, July 30, 2009, A13; Scott Morrison, "Google Searches for Staffing Answers," *The Wall Street Journal,* May 19, 2009, B1; and Anton Trianovski, "Skilled Trades Seek Workers," *The Wall Street Journal*, August 19, 2008, B1.

2. Fay Hansen, "Strategic Workforce Planning in an Uncertain World," *Workforce Management Online*, July 2009, www.workforce.com.

3. Carol Morrison, "The Time to Plan Is Now," *Trend Watcher*, April 17, 2009, www.i4cp.com.

4. For an overview, see Robert J. Greene, "Ensuring Future Work Viability," *Worldat Work Journal*, Fourth Quarter, 2007, 23–33.

5. "Corps of Engineers Needs to Update Its Workforce Planning . . .," *Human Capital*, U.S. Government Accountability Office, May 2008, www.goa.gov.

6. Based on *HR's Evolving Role in Organizations and Its Impact on Business Strategy*, SHRM, 2008, www.shrm.org/surveys; Carolyn Hirschman, "Putting Forecasting in Focus," *HR Magazine*, March 2007, 44–49.

7. Kenneth J. Zulz and Thomas J. Chernack, "Development and Initial Validation of an Instrument for Human Capital Planning," *Human Resource Development Quarterly*, 19 (2008), 7–33.

8. Pamela Babcock, "Workforce Planning Remains Largely Unaddressed Global Challenge," *SHRM Staffing Management*, December 2007, www.shrm.org/ema.

9. Based on Lydell C. Bridgeford, "Point-and-Click Productivity," *Employee Benefit News*, June 15, 2009, 18–19; Ed Frauenheim, "HR Technology: Talent Tools Still Essential," *Workforce Management*, April 20, 2009, 20.

10. Arne L. Kallenberg, "The Mismatched Worker: When People Don't Fit Their Jobs," *Academy of Management Perspectives*, February 2008, 24–40.

11. Jacqueline A.M. Coyle-Shapiro and Lynn M. Shore, "The Employee-Organization Relationship," *Human Resource Management Review*, 17 (2007), 166–179.

12. S. Lester, et al., "Managing Employee Perceptions of the Psychological Contract over Time," *Journal of Organizational Behavior*, 28 (2007), 191–208.

13. "The Employment Relationship: Implications for the Psychological Contract," *SHRM Research*, May 2008.

14. Tanguy Dulac, et al., "Not All Responses to Breach Are the Same," *Academy of Management Journal*, 51 (2008), 1079–1098.

15. S. Chi and S. Chen, "Perceived Psychological Contract Fulfillment and Job Attitudes Among Repatriates," *International Journal of Manpower*, 28 (2007), 474–488.

16. B. Weber and G. Hertel, "Motivation Gains of Inferior Group Members: A Meta-Analytical Review," *Journal of Personality and Social Psychology*, 93 (2007), 973–993.

17. Piers Steel and Cornelius König, "Integrating Theories of Motivation," *Academy of Management Review*, 31 (2006), 889–913.

18. Brian A. Altman and Mesut Akdere, "Towards a Theoretical Model of Performance Inhibiting Workplace Dynamics," *Human Resource Development Review*, 7 (2008), 408.

19. Thomas Zagenczk, "Mentors, Supervisors, and Role Models: Do They Reduce the Effects of Psychological Contract Breach?" *Human Resource Management Journal*, 19 (2009), 237–259.

20. "Workers Want Personal Satisfaction More than Money," *WorldatWork Newsline*, May 22, 2009, www.worldatwork.org.

21. For a more detailed review of job satisfaction factors, see "2009 Employee Job Satisfaction: Understanding the Factors That Make Work Gratifying," *SHRM Research*, 2009, www.shrm.org.; Daniel C. Ganseter, "Measurement Challenges for Studying Work-Related Stressors and Strains," *Human Resource Management Review*, 18 (2008), 259–270.

22. Remus Ilies, et al., "The Spillover of Daily Job Satisfaction onto Employees' Family Lives," *Academy of Management Journal*, 52 (2009), 87–102.

23. Rebecca R. Hastings, "Employee Surveys: Prepare to Act," *HR Disciplines*, June 15, 2009, www.shrm.org.

24. Frank Giancola, "Employee Engagement: What You Need to Know," *Workspan*, October 2007, 55–59.

25. For more information, see Nancy R. Lockwood, "Leveraging Employee Engagement for Competitive Advantage," *SHRM Research*, No. 1, 2007, 1–11.

26. "Estimating Turnover Costs," www.keepemployees.com.

27. M. D. Burton and C. H. Beckman, "Leaving a Legacy," *American Sociological Review*, 72 (2007), 239–266.

28. Tae Hean Lee, et al., "Understanding Voluntary Turnover," *Academy of Management Journal*, 51 (2008), 651–671.

29. Kris Dunn, "Good Versus Bad Turnover," *Workforce Management Online*, July 2007, www.workforce.com.

30. Charlie O. Trevor and Anthony Nyberg, "Keeping Your Headcount When All About You Are Losing Theirs," *Academy of Management Journal*, 51 (2008), 259–276.

31. Thomas Ng and Marcus M. Butts, "Effectiveness of Organizational Efforts to Lower Turnover Intentions," *Human Resource Management*, 48 (2009), 289–310.

32. For details on industries, types of jobs, and other components, go to www.dol.gov.

33. "Global Shipping and Delivery Giant . . .," *Talent Keepers Retention Case Study*, www.talentkeepers.com.

34. For detailed examples, go to www.talentkeepers.com, www.shrm.org, and www.keepemployees.com. Also see "Tool: The Cost of Turnover," *Workforce Management*, November 2003, www.workforce.com.

35. John Sullivan, "Not All Turnover Is Equal," *Workforce Management*, May 21, 2007, 42; W. S. Siebert and Nikolay Zubanov, "Searching for the Optimal Level of Employee Turnover," *Academy of Management Journal*, 5 (2009), 294–313.

36. "Unhappiness with Management, Limited Advancement Cited as Top Reasons Employees Quit," *WorldatWork Study*, January 21, 2009, www.worldatwork.org.

37. For an overview, see Sandra L. Fornes, et al., "Workplace Commitment: A Conceptual Model Developed from Integrative Review of Research," *Human Resource Development Review*, 7 (2008), 339.

38. Sarah E. Needleman, "Allying Workers Fears During Uncertain Times," *The Wall Street Journal*, October 6, 2008, B5.

39. Chu-Hsiang Chang, et al., "The Relationship Between Perceptions of Organizational Politics, Employee Attitudes, Strain, and Behavior," *Academy of Management Journal*, 52 (2009), 779–801.

40. Kathy Gurchiek, "Bad Bosses—More than Bad Salaries—Drive Workers Away," *HR News*, January 11, 2007, www.shrm.org.

41. David R. Hekman, et al., "Combined Effects of Organizational and Professional Identification on the Reciprocity Dynamics for Professional Employees," *Academy of Management Journal*, 52 (2009), 506–526.

42. Riki Takevchi, et al., "A Model of Expatriate Withdrawal Related Outcomes," *Human Resource Management Review*, 15 (2005), 119–138; Kathryn Tyler, "Retaining Repatriates," *HR Magazine*, March 2006, 1–4.

43. Based on Padmaja Alaganandan, "India's Human Capital Challenge," *Workspan*, November 2008, 111–114; "The World of Work," *BusinessWeek*, January 6, 2007, 57–58.

44. Cali Williams Yost, "CFO's See Business Impacts of Work Flexibility . . . ," *WorldatWork Journal*, Second Quarter 2009, 59–67.

45. Patricia K. Zinghum and Jay R. Schuster, "Workforce Retention, Pay and Rewards Practices in Tough-Market Cities," *WorldatWork Journal*, Fourth Quarter, 2008, 16–27.

46. Raymund Flandez, "Rewards Help Soothe Hard Times," *The Wall Street Journal*, July 7, 2008, B4.

47. Patricia K. Zingheim, et al., "Compensation, Reward, and Retention Practices in Fast-Growth Companies," *WorldatWork Journal*, Second Quarter, 2009, 22–37.

48. Matthew Smith and Derek Irvine, "Employee Recognition Program . . . ," *Workspan*, August 2009, 29–37.

49. Kathy Gurchiek, "Lack of Career Advancement Main Reason Workers Consider Leaving," *HR News*, February 29, 2008, www.shrm.org.

50. Phred Dvorak, "Firms Shift Underused Workers," *The Wall Street Journal*, June 22, 2009, B2.

51. Lisa Cooling, "Keep Your IT People Happy," *Inside Supply Management*, May 2008, 38–40.

52. William Werhane "How Do We Get Better Information from Our Exit Interviews?" *Workforce Management Online*, October 1, 2009, www.workforce.com.

53. "First-Year Turnover Rate," *SHRM Metric of the Month*, October 1, 2006, www.shrm.org/research.

54 Based on Jessica Marquez, "Accentuating the Positive," *Workforce Management*, September 22, 2008, 18–25. Also see information available at www.accenture.com.

6

Recruiting and Labor Markets

After you have read this chapter, you should be able to:

- List different ways that labor markets can be identified and approached.

- Discuss strategic recruiting decisions on recruiting images, outsourcing, and other related areas.

- Explain why Internet recruiting has grown and how it affects recruiting efforts done by employers.

- List and briefly discuss five external recruiting sources.

- Identify three internal sources for recruiting and issues associated with their use.

- Describe three factors to consider when doing recruiting measurement and metrics.

Passive Recruiting Becomes Active

Digital Vision/Photodisc/Jupiter Images

Employed individuals who may not be considering other jobs but who are recruited are called *passive job seekers*. For firms to search to fill jobs with persons who are not actively looking for a job means that they have to use a variety of means to encourage *passives* to become *actives*.

Many passives are approached via Internet tools. This approach is especially used for executive and other hard-to-fill openings, even for passives who do not have current résumés. Search consultants use passive recruiting to locate possible individuals to fill jobs to which the consultants have been assigned. Use of IT networking sites such as Facebook, Linked In, ZoomInfo, and others provides information on passive individuals.

Once information on a "passive candidate" is located, personal contact can be made and conversations held to encourage the passive to consider job openings. Personal communication about certain employers and job openings helps get passives to consider the openings.

This type of recruiting is becoming increasingly common as people use the Internet sites that can be accessed by others to learn about both jobs and individuals. Several Internet sites are adding thousands of individual profiles weekly. More than 20% of the large Fortune 500 firms use such sites along with other ways to find candidates for difficult-to-fill openings and top executive jobs.[1] So, as an employer, are you ready to find passives?

The staffing process used by an employer, based on HR planning and retention as key components, must include successful recruiting and selection efforts. However, as the HR Headline illustrates, new approaches to those actions are evolving. Without significant attention and measurement, recruiting and selection can become just a set of administrative functions: coordinating internal openings, handling the flow of candidate data, dealing with regulatory reporting, and moving candidates through the system.

This chapter examines recruiting, and the next chapter examines selection. **Recruiting** is the process of generating a pool of qualified applicants for organizational jobs. If the number of available candidates equals the number of people to be hired, no real selection is required—the choice has already been made. The organization must either leave some openings unfilled or take all the candidates. One survey of employers in slow labor markets found that almost half of the hiring managers cited less qualified applicants as the biggest recruiting and hiring challenge.[2] It is important to view recruiting broadly as a key part of staffing, and not just as a collection of administrative and operational activities.

RECRUITING

Recruiting is becoming more important as labor markets shift. Although recruiting can be expensive, an offsetting concept that must be considered is the *cost of unfilled jobs*. For example, consider a company in which three operations-related jobs are vacant. Assume these three vacancies cost the company $300 for each business day the jobs remain vacant. If the jobs are not filled for four months, the cost of this failure to recruit in a timely fashion will be about $26,000.

Although cost is certainly an issue, and some employers are quite concerned about cost per hire as well as the cost of vacancies, *quality* might be an important trade-off. For example, if an organizational strategy focuses on quality as a competitive advantage, a company might choose to hire only from the top 15% of candidates for critical jobs, and from the top 30% of candidates for all other positions. Though this approach may raise the cost per hire, it will improve workforce quality.

These examples illustrate that recruiting should not just be seen as an expense, but as part of overall HR planning and strategy. To be effective, recruiters need to integrate efforts involving labor markets, recruiting responsibilities and goals, and recruiting sources, including the Internet. Figure 6-1 highlights key integrative recruiting components.

Strategic Recruiting and HR Planning

It is important that recruiting be treated as a part of strategic HR planning because it is a key mechanism for filling positions necessary to get the work done. Recruiting requires an employer to:

- Know the industry and where to successfully recruit qualified employees.
- Identify keys to success in the labor market, including competitors' recruiting efforts.
- Cultivate relationships with sources of prospective employees.
- Promote the "company brand" so that the employer is known as a good place to work.

Recruiting Process of generating a pool of qualified applicants for organizational jobs.

| **FIGURE 6-1** | **Integrating Recruiting Components** |

- Use recruiting metrics in order to measure the effectiveness of recruiting efforts.

Recruiting decisions can identify not only the kinds and numbers of applicants, but also how difficult or successful recruiting efforts may be by type of jobs. In addition, effective recruiting focuses on discovering talent *before* it is needed.

Training of Recruiters and Managers

Regardless of the methods used, an important recruiting issue is how much training will be given to recruiters and managers. Training on recruiting-related activities, communications skills, and job-specific details is common. Also, those involved in recruiting should learn the types of actions that violate EEO regulations and how to be sensitive to diversity issues with applicants. Such training areas often include appropriate language to use with applicants so that racist, sexist, and other inappropriate remarks do not hurt the image of the employer and result in legal complaints.

Training recruiters may include the importance of employers engaging in ethical behaviors during recruiting efforts. One way to evaluate training efforts in this area is through follow-up activities. For instance, to assess ethical behavior when recruiting college graduates, some employers send follow-up surveys to interviewees asking about the effectiveness of the recruiters and the image the candidates have of the employers as a result of the recruiting contacts.[3]

LABOR MARKETS

Labor markets External supply pool from which employers attract employees.

Because staffing takes place in different labor markets that can vary a great deal, learning some basics about labor markets aids in understanding recruiting. **Labor markets** are the external supply pool from which employers attract employees. To understand where recruiting takes place, one can think of the sources of employees as a funnel, in which the broad scope of labor markets

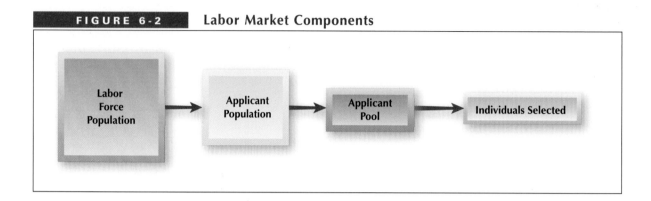

FIGURE 6-2   Labor Market Components

narrows progressively to the point of selection and job offers, as Figure 6-2 shows. Of course, if the selected candidates reject the offers, then HR staff members must move back up the funnel to the applicant pool for other candidates, and in extreme cases may need to reopen the recruiting process.

Labor Market Components

Several different means of identifying labor markets exist. One useful approach is to take a broad view of the labor markets and then narrow them down to specific recruiting sources. The broadest labor market component and measure is the **labor force population**, which is made up of all individuals who are available for selection if all possible recruitment strategies are used. For firms with global locations in multiple countries, the labor force population can be much larger than that of a business operating in only one country. For example, some U.S.-based airlines have customer service centers located in the Philippines, India, and other countries as well as the United States. The labor force population for such businesses is much broader than that of a business operating in a single country.

The **applicant population** is a subset of the labor force population that is available for selection if a particular recruiting approach is used. This population can be broad or narrow depending on the jobs needing to be filled and the approaches used by the employer. For example, if a firm is recruiting highly specialized engineers for multiple geographic locations, the recruiting methods may involve a broad range of approaches and sources, including professional associations, convention attendance, general and specialized websites, using recruiting consulting firms, and offering recruitment incentives to existing employees. However, a smaller firm in a limited geographic location might limit its recruiting for management trainees to MBA graduates from major universities in the area. This recruiting method would result in a different group of applicants from those who might apply if the employer were to advertise the openings for management trainees on a local radio station, post a listing on an Internet jobs board, or encourage current employee referrals and applications. Figure 6-3 illustrates some common items that affect recruiting applicant populations.

The **applicant pool** consists of all persons who are actually evaluated for selection. Many factors can affect the size of the applicant pool, including the reputation of the organization and industry as a place to work, the screening efforts of the organization, the job specifications, and the information available. It is important to develop an *applicant tracking system* when considering

Labor force population
All individuals who are available for selection if all possible recruitment strategies are used.

Applicant population
A subset of the labor force population that is available for selection using a particular recruiting approach.

Applicant pool All persons who are actually evaluated for selection.

FIGURE 6-3	Considerations for Determining Applicant Populations

CONSIDERATIONS FOR DETERMINING APPLICANT POPULATIONS

- Number and type of recruits needed
- Timing of recruiting to ensure timely placement
- External and internal messages on job details
- Qualifications of competent applicants to be considered
- Sources for obtaining qualified applicants
- Outside and inside recruiting means to be used
- Administrative recruiting and application review activities

LOGGING ON

JobWeb
For a special report about labor markets and jobs outlook, visit www.jobweb.com.

the applicant pool. Using such a system, both administratively and electronically, can make the recruiting process more effective.[4] For example, when the applicant pool size increases, recruiters can consistently identify the most effective future employees for several jobs, and not just fill current jobs because of a larger supply.[5]

Unemployment Rates and Applicant Population When the unemployment rate is high in a given market, many people are looking for jobs. When the unemployment rate is low, there are fewer applicants. Unemployment rates vary with business cycles and present very different challenges for recruiting at different times. For instance, in some U.S. states, when many automobile plants closed and workers were laid off, manufacturers in other industries and even retailers experienced a significant increase in their numbers of job applicants, making recruiting easier and larger applicant pools a fact.

Different Labor Markets and Recruiting

The supply of workers in various labor markets differs substantially and affects staffing. Organizations recruit in a number of different labor markets, including industry-specific markets and occupational, educational and technical, and geographic markets. Labor markets can be viewed in several ways to provide information that is useful for recruiting. It is important to understand the broad labor markets from which candidates are identified and attracted. These labor markets can include both internal and external sources, which will be discussed later.

Industry and Occupational Labor Markets Labor markets can be classified by industry and occupation. Depending on economic and industry aspects, recruiting emphases can be changed. For example, the biggest increases in U.S. jobs until the year 2016 are going to be in the positions of registered nurses, retail sales and customer service representatives, home health aides, and postsecondary teachers.[6] These data illustrate that recruiting will be more difficult in filling these jobs during the next few years. Trucking and welding jobs are also expected to present significant recruiting difficulties.[7]

Recruiting for smaller firms can be challenging. For instance, a small certified professional accounting (CPA) firm had to work extensively to identify which CPA professionals would prefer working in a small firm rather than a large one. One key to this firm's recruiting efforts was to clearly identify the unique characteristics of working in a smaller firm, which included greater assignment variety, more work flexibility, and better career possibilities.[8] Those characteristics would appeal to some but not all who might apply.

Educational and Technical Labor Markets Another way to look at labor markets is by considering the educational and technical qualifications that define the people being recruited. Employers may need individuals with specific licenses, certifications, or educational backgrounds. For instance, recruiting physician leaders for a medical organization led to the establishment of a special search committee to set goals for the committee members. Then, as part of recruiting and selection, the top candidates were asked to develop departmental vision statements and three-year goals. That information made the recruiting and selection process more effective.[9]

Another special labor market is suppliers and contractors for U.S. military forces. Firms such as Cintas Corporation, with more than 34,000 employees, and Raytheon, with 77,000 employees, serve as federal government defense contractors. The need to recruit for specialty jobs in engineering and technology by such firms illustrates why considering different types of labor markets is appropriate.[10]

A prominent occupational area that is expected to be extremely tight during the next few years is the *information technology* (IT) labor market. That labor market, which was tight several years ago, is now becoming tight again as IT is used in a wider variety of jobs.[11] Another example of a tight labor market is that of business professors with PhDs, who are forecast to be in short supply in the next few years due to the retirement of baby boomers from faculty positions. Other examples of shortages in specific labor markets include certified auto mechanics, heating and air-conditioning technicians, and network-certified computer specialists.

Geographic Labor Markets One common way to classify labor markets is based on geographic location. Markets can be local, area or regional, national, or international. Local and area labor markets vary significantly in terms of workforce availability and quality, and changes in a geographic labor market may force changes in recruiting efforts. For instance, if a new major employer locates in a regional labor market, other existing area employers may see a decline in their numbers of applicants.

Geographic markets require different recruiting considerations. For example, attempting to recruit locally for a job market that is a national competitive market will likely result in disappointing applicant rates. A catalog retailer that tries to recruit a senior merchandising manager from the small town where the firm is located may encounter difficulties, although it may not need to recruit nationally for workers to fill administrative support jobs. This example shows how varying geographic labor markets must be evaluated as part of recruiting.

GLOBAL

Global Labor Markets Employers in the United States are tapping global labor markets when necessary and expanding export work to overseas labor markets when doing so is advantageous. Firms in different industries are expanding in India, China, Indonesia, Romania, Poland, and other countries.

The migration of U.S. work overseas has been controversial. While many decry the loss of American jobs, some employers respond that they cannot be competitive in a global market if they fail to take advantage of labor savings. For example, at some operations in India and China, U.S. employers pay less than half of what they would pay for comparable jobs to be performed in U.S. facilities. A significant number of U.S. and European firms have farmed out software development and back-office work to India and other countries with lower wages. However, some advancements in American worker productivity have made it possible to have fewer U.S. employees to produce certain items, which has resulted in a cost savings, even at those employees' higher wage rates. Hence, those types of jobs are not being exported to other countries.

The use of the Internet has resulted in global jobs being recruited in many places, but often recruiting employees for global assignments requires different approaches from those used for typical recruiting efforts in the home country. The recruiting processes must consider variations in culture, laws, and language. For instance, in some countries, potential recruits like to work for European and U.S. firms, so recruiters emphasize the "Western" image. But in other countries, cultural employer operational differences change how recruiting is done.

Dealing with foreign labor markets can present challenges. For example, in China recruiting is regulated and generally requires the approval of local personnel or labor authorities. Hiring foreign employees into U.S. jobs must meet certain legal requirements, including H1 visa requirements. Concerns exist about hiring illegal immigrants as well.[12]

STRATEGIC RECRUITING DECISIONS

When there are economic declines in certain geographic areas and occupations, a greater number of talented recruits are available, and recruiting costs can be lower.[13] But whether recruits are plentiful or scarce, employers must decide on several recruiting issues. These important strategic decisions for recruiting are discussed next.

Recruiting Presence and Image

Recruiting efforts may be viewed as either continuous or intensive. *Continuous* efforts to recruit offer the advantage of keeping the employer in the recruiting market. For example, with college recruiting, some organizations may find it advantageous to have a recruiter on a given campus each year. Employers that visit a campus only occasionally are less likely to build a following at that school over time. Also, continuous recruiting may lead to constant Internet job postings, contact with recruiting consultants, and other market-related actions.

Intensive recruiting may take the form of a vigorous recruiting campaign aimed at hiring a given number of employees, usually within a short period of time. Sometimes such efforts are the result of unforeseeable changes in external factors, but they also can result from a failure in the HR planning system to identify needs in advance or to anticipate drastic changes in workforce needs.

Employment "Branding" and Image The "employment brand" or image of an organization is the view of it held by both employees and outsiders.

Effective Recruitment at USDA

Every year Optimas Awards are given by Workforce.com to recognize and highlight how organizations improve results through workforce actions. One federal government entity received the award for its recruiting-related efforts.

The federal agency, the United States Department of Agriculture (USDA) Food Safety and Inspection Service, faced significant competition with private employers for candidates in positions such as science professionals, veterinarians, and other jobs. With position openings at 6,000 sites, the agency had to take significant action. First, more than 100 agency employees were trained to be effective recruiters as an expansion of their regular professional job responsibilities. Next, these "recruiters" annually visited more than 50 universities and colleges to recruit more staff. By using their training, these USDA individuals were able to reduce the time in which jobs were unfilled by more than five days on average.

One occupational group that needed significantly more recruiting was veterinarians. Given a shortage of qualified individuals, the agency took several actions in this area. One was raising the beginning salary level for veterinarians. Also, a hiring incentive was established in the form of 25% of base pay over four years. As a result, the shortage of veterinarians decreased by 50% as approximately 100 veterinarians were hired each year.

The recruiting efforts have significantly changed agency operation as well. Some operational actions that have been implemented are more flexible work scheduling, telework usage, and flexible management. These actions have helped make the USDA Food Safety and Inspection Service more appealing to applicants and employees. That this entity received the Optimas award indicates that governmental and public-sector employers, and not just private-sector ones, must continually adapt and improve their recruiting planning and strategies.[14]

Organizations that are seen as desirable employers are better able to attract qualified applicants than are those with poor reputations. For example, one firm had good pay and benefits, but its work demands were seen as excessive, and frequent downsizings had resulted in some terminations and transfers. The result was high turnover and fewer applicants interested in employment at the company. That firm had a poor brand or image as an employer.

Companies can spend considerable effort and money establishing brand images for their products. Not only can the company brand help generate more recruits, but it also can help with applicant self-selection because it affects whether individuals ever consider a firm and submit applications. Recruiting and employer branding should be seen as part of organizational marketing efforts and linked to the overall image and reputation of the organization and its industry. The HR Best Practices illustrates how a federal government agency changed its recruitment culture to improve its image and be more effective in its recruiting efforts.

Organization-Based versus Outsourced Recruiting

A basic decision is whether the recruiting will be done by the employer or outsourced to someone else. This decision need not be focused on an "either-or" situation entirely. In most organizations, HR staff members handle many of the recruiting efforts. However, because recruiting can be a time-consuming process and HR staff and other managers in organizations have many other responsibilities, outsourcing is a way to decrease the number of staff needed for recruiting and free some of their time for other responsibilities.

Recruitment process outsourcing (RPO) can be done to improve the number and quality of recruiting candidates, as well as to reduce recruiting costs.[15] Estimates are that RPO is expected to grow significantly in the near future. Both large and small employers in different industries outsource such functions as placement of advertisements, initial screening of résumés, and initial telephone contacts with potential applicants. For example, General Electric (GE) uses RPO to save time and efforts of HR staff, as well as to target its recruiting efforts more effectively. Once the RPO activities are done, the employer's HR staff members can take over the rest of the recruiting activities in a cost-effective and timely manner.[16]

Professional Employer Organizations and Employee Leasing A specific type of outsourcing uses professional employer organizations (PEOs) and employee leasing. The employee leasing process is simple: An employer signs an agreement with the PEO, after which the staff is hired by the leasing firm and leased back to the company for a fee. In turn, the leasing firm writes the paychecks, pays taxes, prepares and implements HR policies, and keeps all the required records for the employer.

One advantage of leasing companies for employees is that they may receive better benefits than they otherwise would get in many of the small businesses that use leasing firms. But all this service comes at a cost to employers. Leasing companies often charge employers between 4% and 6% of employees' monthly salaries. Thus, while leasing may save employers money on benefits and HR administration, it also may increase total payroll costs.

The PEO and the employment agency are different types of entities. A PEO has its own workforce, which it supplies by contract to employers with jobs. However, an employment agency provides a "work-finding" service for job seekers and supplies employers with applicants whom they may then hire.

Regular versus Flexible Staffing

Another strategic decision affects how much recruiting will be done to fill staffing needs with regular full-time or part-time employees. Decisions as to which should be recruited hinge on whether to seek regular employees or to use more flexible approaches, which might include temporaries or independent contractors. A number of employers have decided that the cost of keeping a regular workforce has become excessive and is growing worse due to economic, competitive, and governmental considerations. However, not just money is at issue. The large number of employment regulations also constrains the employment relationship, making many employers reluctant to hire new regular full-time employees.

Flexible staffing uses workers who are not traditional employees. Using flexible staffing arrangements allows an employer to avoid some of the cost of full-time benefits such as vacation pay and pension plans. Flexible staffing may lead to recruiting in different markets, since it includes the use of temporary workers and independent contractors.

Temporary Workers Employers who use temporary employees can hire their own temporary staff members or contract with agencies supplying temporary workers on a rate-per-day or rate-per-week basis. Originally developed to provide clerical and office workers to employers, temporary workers in professional, technical, and even managerial jobs are becoming more common. The importance of using temporary workers is illustrated through the use of computer technology by an educational publisher. The publisher utilized an automated employment, recruiting, and screening system to obtain sufficient temporary workers for its firm. That employer obtained sufficient qualified workers which resulted in a return on its hiring investment of $6 for every $1 of cost.[17]

Some employers hire temporary workers as a way for individuals to move into full-time, regular employment. Better-performing workers may move to regular positions when these positions become available. This "try before you buy" approach is potentially beneficial to both employers and employees. However, if individuals come through temporary service firms, those firms typically bill client companies a placement charge if a temporary worker is hired full-time. Also, employing temporary workers as opposed to full-time workers can have implications in regard to federal laws such as the Family Medical Leave Act, the Fair Labor Standards Act, and others.[18]

Independent Contractors Some firms employ independent contractors as workers who perform specific services on a contract basis. These workers must be truly independent as determined by regulations used by the U.S. Internal Revenue Service and the U.S. Department of Labor. Independent contractors are used in a number of areas, including building maintenance, security, advertising, and others. One major reason for the use of independent contractors is that some employers experience significant savings because benefits are not provided to those individuals.

Recruiting and EEO: Diversity Considerations

Recruiters must consider EEO and diversity factors for several reasons, as Figure 6-4 indicates. The following text highlights each of the diversity consideration dimensions.

FIGURE 6-4   **Recruiting and Diversity Considerations**

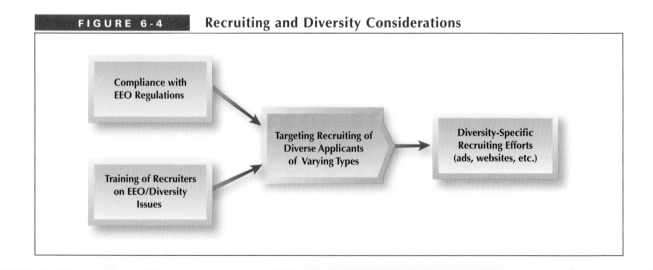

EEO and Recruiting Efforts Recruiting as a key employment-related activity is subject to various considerations, especially equal employment laws and regulations. As part of legal compliance in the recruiting process, organizations must work to reduce external disparate impact, or underrepresentation of protected-class members compared to the labor markets utilized by the employer. If disparate impact exists, then the employer may need to make special efforts to persuade protected-class individuals to apply for jobs. For employers with affirmative action plans (AAPs), special ways to reduce disparate impact can be identified as goals listed in those plans. Also, many employers that emphasize internal recruiting should take actions to obtain protected-class applicants externally if disparate impact exists in the current workforce.

The Equal Employment Opportunity Commission (EEOC) guidelines state that no direct or indirect references implying gender or age are permitted. These guidelines affect interviews, advertisements, and other recruiting activities. Some examples of impermissible terminology are: "young and enthusiastic," "Christian values," and "journeyman lineman." Also, advertisements should contain wording about being an Equal Opportunity Employer (EEO), or even more specific designations such as EEO/M-F/AA/ADA. Employers demonstrate inclusive recruiting by having diverse individuals represented in company materials, in advertisements, and as recruiters.

Recruiting Diversity A broad range of factors applies to recruiting diversity. Many employers have expanded efforts to recruit workers from what, for some, are nontraditional labor pools. Nontraditional diverse recruitees for certain jobs may include:

- Persons with different racial/ethnic backgrounds
- Older workers over 40 years of age
- Single parents
- Workers with disabilities
- Welfare-to-work workers
- Homeless/substance abuse workers

The growth in racial/ethnic workforce diversity means that a wider range of potential employment sources should be utilized. Almost 60% of surveyed employers review their recruitment practices to ensure that they are inclusive, and almost half provide diversity training to managers involved in hiring.[19] The population growth in Hispanics in the United States means that specialized recruiting programs to tap Hispanics as applicants may grow in use. For instance, Goodwill Industries, a large nonprofit organization, provides diversity training of staff members and has partnerships with Hispanic community organizations to aid in the recruitment and retention of Hispanic workers.[20]

Older potential workers may include retirees who have become bored (or need money), those who have been involuntarily laid off, or those who are making career changes and want to try a new field. But some employers prefer younger workers as recruites, even though that can create both legal and recruiting supply issues.[21] Single parents may be attracted to a family-friendly employer that offers flexibility, including part-time work, because it is frequently difficult to balance job and family life. Some firms also recruit stay-at-home parents by using flexibility and work-at-home technology.

Individuals with disabilities are another group of potential resources. More than 21 million people with disabilities are of working age, but only about 8 million of them are employed. Therefore, it is appropriate that employers expand their educational, training, and staffing policies and practices to employ more individuals with disabilities.[22]

Realistic Job Previews

Providing a balanced view of the advantages, demands, expectations, and challenges in an organization or a job may help attract employees with more realistic expectations and reduce the number of employees who quit a few months after being hired because the "reality" they discover does not match what they expected. Thus, recruiting efforts can benefit from *realistic job previews*, but their usage must be monitored. RJPs will be further discussed in the next chapter as part of the selection process.[23]

Recruiting Source Choices: Internal versus External

Most employers combine the use of internal and external recruiting sources. Both promoting from within the organization (internal recruitment) and hiring from outside the organization (external recruitment) come with advantages and disadvantages.

Organizations that face rapidly changing competitive environments and conditions may need to place a heavier emphasis on external sources in addition to developing internal sources. A possible strategy might be to promote from within if a qualified applicant exists and to go to external sources if not. However, for organizations existing in environments that change slowly, emphasis on promotion from within may be more suitable. Once the various recruiting policy decisions have been addressed, the actual recruiting methods can be identified and used for both internal and external recruiting.

INTERNET RECRUITING

The Internet has become the primary means for many employers to search for job candidates and for applicants to look for jobs. The growth in Internet use is a key reason that the following employer actions occur:

- Adjusting general employer recruiting systems to use new approaches
- Identifying new types of recruiting for specific jobs
- Training managers and HR professionals on technical recruiting sources, skills, and responsibilities

E-Recruiting Means

The growth in the Internet has led both employers and employees to use Internet recruiting tools. Internet links, Web 2.0 sites, blogs, twitters, and other types of Internet/Web-based usages have become viable parts of recruiting. One survey of e-recruiting software providers identified numerous firms as e-recruiting clients, and some of them serve more than 1,000 employers.[24] Of the many recruiting sites using special software, the most common ones are Internet job boards, professional/career websites, and employer websites.

Internet Job Boards Numerous Internet job boards, such as Monster and Yahoo! HotJobs, provide places for employers to post jobs or search for candidates. Job boards offer access to numerous candidates. Some Internet locations allow recruiters to search one website, such as MyJobHunter.com, to obtain search links to many other major job sites. Applicants can also use these websites to do one match and then send résumés to all jobs in which they are interested.[25] However, a number of the individuals accessing these sites are "job lookers" who are not serious about changing jobs, but are checking out compensation levels and job availability in their areas of interest. Despite such concerns, HR recruiters find general job boards useful for generating applicant responses.

Professional/Career Websites Many professional associations have employment sections at their websites. As illustration, for HR jobs, see the Society for Human Resource Management site, www.shrm.org, or WorldatWork, www.worldatwork.org. The SHRM organization has established a Job Posting Center that numerous recruiters and employers can use to post a wide range of industry openings.[26] A number of private corporations maintain specialized career or industry websites to focus on IT, telecommunications, engineering, medicine, and other areas. Use of these targeted websites may limit somewhat recruiters' search time and efforts. Also, posting jobs on such websites is likely to target applicants specifically interested in the job field and may reduce the number of applications from less-qualified applicants.

Employer Websites Despite the popularity of job boards and association job sites, many employers have learned that their own websites can be most effective and efficient when recruiting candidates. The most successful of these websites are created by highly prominent firms and take extensive actions to guide job seekers to their firm.[27] Employers include employment and career information on their websites under headings such as "Employment" or "Careers." This is the place where recruiting (both internal and external) is often conducted. On many of these sites, job seekers are encouraged to e-mail résumés or complete online applications.

It is important for the recruiting and employment portions of an employer website to be seen as part of the marketing efforts of the firm.[28] The formatting of the employment section of an organizational website must be shaped to market jobs and organizational careers effectively. A company website should market the employer by outlining information on the organization, including its products and services, organizational and industry growth potential, and organizational operations. The attractiveness, usability, and formatting of an employer's website can affect job seekers' view of that organization positively or negatively.[29] See HR On-the-Job for company website recruiting ideas.

Recruiting and Internet Social Networking

The Internet has led to social networking of individuals on blogs, twitters, and a range of websites. Many people initially use the social media more than job board sites.[30] Internet connections often include people who work together as well as past personal contacts and friends.

The informal use of the Web presents some interesting recruiting advantages and disadvantages for both employers and employees. Social networking sites allow job seekers to connect with employees of potential hirers. For instance, some sites include posts on what it is like to work for a boss, and job hunters can contact the posters and ask questions. An example is LinkedIn, which has a job-search engine that allows people to search for contacts who work for employers with posted job openings.

Effective Recruiting Using an Employer Website

Employers who are effective recruiters through their company websites have sites that enhance the image of their companies and their jobs. Important guidelines to creating an effective website include:

- Make the site easy to navigate. The "Employment" or "Careers" button should be on the home page. Job information should be no more than three clicks away.
- Include information that people want. Describe the company, its products and services, careers in the organization, and advantages of working for the firm.
- Use qualifying categories (location, job function, skills, education, etc.) to help candidates find the jobs for which they are eligible. Use of such categories saves time, especially for companies who are large employers.

- Use self-assessment checklists to ask candidates about experience and interests and to direct them to the jobs that fit them the best.
- Make it easy to apply for a job by providing the means to build a résumé on the site or to paste in an existing résumé. Online applications also should be provided.
- Design the site to provide recruiters with an additional way to post jobs, search for résumés and applications, and screen applicants. Otherwise, it is difficult to manage a busy website.
- Collect metrics on the site. To determine its effectiveness, gather information about the site, such as the number of visitors, hits from ads, actual hires, and other details.

Firms and employers are now engaging in *social collaboration* by joining and accessing social technology networks such as MySpace, Facebook, and many others. Posting job openings on these sites means that millions of website users can see the openings and can make contact online. Often those doing recruiting can send individuals to the company website and then process candidates using electronic résumés or completed online applications.[31]

Job Applicants and Social Network Sites Many individuals see social media and networking websites as a key part of online recruiting. A study of 200 users of one such website indicated that the individuals who were job seeking were doing so for active reasons such as career opportunities, job inquiries, and others; relatively few of them were passive job seekers who were just looking at website information.[32]

Almost half of surveyed employers indicated that instead of using general job boards, they were changing to social networking and niche job sites for recruiting workers with specific skills. However, employers who use social networking sites for recruiting must have plans and well-defined recruiting tools to take full advantage of these sites.[33]

Recruiting Using Special Technology Means

For a number of years, the Internet has been used by people globally. Several special Internet tools that can be used as part of recruiting efforts are blogs, e-videos, and twitters.

Blogs and Recruiting Both employers and individuals have used blogs as part of recruiting to fill jobs. Firms such as Best Buy, Microsoft, Honeywell, and Manpower have used blogs on which individuals could read and provide content. For instance, describing job openings and recruiting needs on the Best Buy blog has resulted in individuals responding to job areas such as finance, marketing, HR, and other specialties. Numerous other employers have used blogs to generate recruiting results as well.[34]

E-Video and Recruiting With video capabilities of all types available, employers are using videos in several ways. Some firms use videos to describe their company characteristics, job opportunities, and recruiting means. Suppliers such as Monstor.com, CareerTV, and others have worked with employer clients to produce online recruitment videos.[35]

Some of the online videos contain "employment games" for both current and potential employees that focus on creating positive employment images. People who are interested in working for the company can then follow up by using online job application documentation and information. For example, MITRE, a systems engineering firm, developed a "Job of Honor" video game that drew more than 5,000 hits in one year; more than 600 people in the United States and from 25 other countries became registered players in the game. Participation levels like this have led employers to increase job-related recruiting and follow-up activities using Web-based linkages.[36]

Recruiting through Twitter Twitter can be used for many different purposes, including personal, social, legal, and employment-related messages. More than 7 million people have joined Twitter.com to become "tweeters." One professional sent a tweet in January 2009, and by June of that year more than 20,000 people had responded by contacting JobAngels with tweets.[37]

The Twitter system limits messages to 140 specific characters, but even so tweeting has rapidly become a social network recruiting method. Recruiters send tweet messages to both active and passive job candidates, and then follow up with longer e-mails to computers, personal contacts, and other actions to facilitate recruiting. Since Twitter is such a relatively new service, how exactly it will be best used for recruiting is still evolving.[38]

LOGGING ON

RecruitingBlogs.com
For HR professional resources and information on using social networks for recruiting, including Twitter, Facebook, and LinkedIn, visit www.recruitingblogs.com.

Legal Issues in Internet Recruiting

With Internet recruiting expanding, new and different concerns have arisen. Several of these issues have ethical and moral as well as legal implications. The following examples illustrate some of these concerns:

- When companies use screening software to avoid looking at the thousands of résumés they receive, are rejections really based on the qualifications needed for the job?
- How can a person's protected-category and other information be collected and analyzed for reports?
- Are too many individuals in protected categories being excluded from the later phases of the Internet recruiting process?
- Which applicants really want jobs? If someone has accessed a job board and sent an e-mail asking an employer about a job opening, does the person actually want to be an applicant?

- What are the implications of Internet recruiting in terms of confidentiality and privacy?

Loss of privacy is a potential disadvantage with Internet recruiting. Sharing information gleaned from people who apply to job boards or even company websites has become common. As a company receives résumés from applicants, it is required to track those applicants and report to the federal government. But the personal information that can be seen by employers on websites such as MySpace, Facebook, LinkedIn, and others may be inappropriate and can possibly violate legal provisions. Also, blogging creates enough possible legal concerns that regulations may be implemented by the U.S. Federal Trade Commission (FTC).[39]

Employment lawyers are issuing warnings to employers about remarks and other characteristics posted on LinkedIn, Facebook, and Twitter. According to one survey of employers, about three-fourths of hiring managers in various-sized companies checked persons' credentials on LinkedIn, about half used Facebook, and approximately one-fourth used Twitter.[40] Some of the concerns raised have included postings of confidential details about an employee's termination, racial/ethnic background, or gender and the making of discriminatory comments. All of these actions could lead to wrongful termination or discrimination lawsuits. Thus, because Internet usage has both advantages and disadvantages for recruiting, legal advice should be obtained, and HR employment-related policies, training, and enforcement should include such advice.

Advantages of Internet Recruiting

Employers have found a number of advantages to using Internet recruiting. A primary one is that many employers have saved money using Internet recruiting versus other recruiting methods such as newspaper advertising, employment agencies, and search firms, all of which can cost substantially more.

Another major advantage is that a very large pool of applicants can be generated using Internet recruiting. Individuals may view an employer more positively and obtain more useful information, which can result in more individual applications.[41] In fact, a large number of candidates may see any given job listing, although exposure depends on which Internet sources are used. One side benefit of Internet recruiting is that jobs literally are posted globally, so potential applicants in other geographic areas and countries can view job openings posted on the Internet. It also improves the ability to target specific audiences, including more diverse persons, through the use of categories, information, and other variables.[42]

Internet recruiting also can save time. Applicants can respond quickly to job postings by sending electronic responses, rather than using "snail mail." Recruiters can respond more rapidly to qualified candidates in order to obtain more necessary applicant information, request additional candidate details, and establish times for further communication, including interviews.[43]

A good website and useful Internet resources also can help recruiters reach "passive" job seekers—those who have a good job and are not really looking to change jobs but who might consider it if a better opportunity were presented. These individuals often do not list themselves on job boards, but they might visit a company website for other reasons and check out the careers or employment section. A well-designed corporate website can help stimulate interest in some passive job seekers, as well as other potential candidates.

Disadvantages of Internet Recruiting

The positive things associated with Internet recruiting come with a number of disadvantages. Because of broader exposure, Internet recruiting often creates additional work for HR staff members and others internally. More online job postings must be sent; many more résumés must be reviewed; more e-mails, blogs, and twitters need to be dealt with; and expensive specialized software may be needed to track the increased number of applicants resulting from Internet recruiting efforts.

Another issue with Internet recruiting is that some applicants may have limited Internet access, especially individuals from lower socioeconomic groups and from certain racial/ethnic groups. In addition, many individuals who access Internet recruiting sources are browsers who may submit résumés just to see what happens, but they are not actively looking for new jobs.

Internet recruiting is only one approach to recruiting, but its use has been expanding. Information about how Internet recruiting methods compare with other, more traditional approaches is relevant. Also, how well the Internet recruiting resources perform must be compared to the effectiveness and integration of other external and internal recruiting sources.

EXTERNAL RECRUITING SOURCES

Even when the overall unemployment rate increases, numerous jobs and/or employers still face recruiting challenges. External recruiting is part of effective HR staffing. Regardless of the methods used, external recruiting involves some common advantages and disadvantages, which are highlighted in Figure 6-5. Some of the prominent traditional and evolving recruiting methods are highlighted next.

Media Sources

Media sources such as newspapers, magazines, television, radio, and billboards typically have been widely used in external recruiting. Some firms have sent

FIGURE 6-5   **Advantages and Disadvantages of External Recruiting**

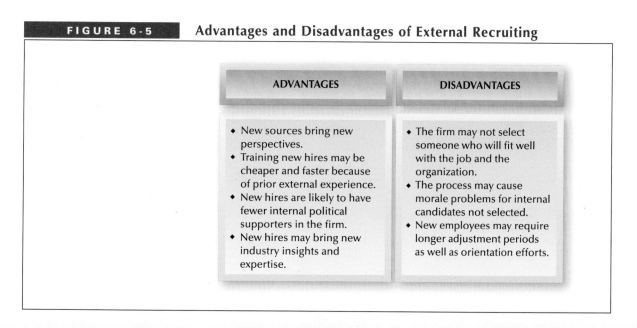

ADVANTAGES	DISADVANTAGES
• New sources bring new perspectives. • Training new hires may be cheaper and faster because of prior external experience. • New hires are likely to have fewer internal political supporters in the firm. • New hires may bring new industry insights and expertise.	• The firm may not select someone who will fit well with the job and the organization. • The process may cause morale problems for internal candidates not selected. • New employees may require longer adjustment periods as well as orientation efforts.

direct mail using purchased lists of individuals in certain fields or industries. Internet usage has led to media sources being available online, including postings, ads, videos, webinars, and many other expanding media services. In some cities and towns, newspaper ads are still very prominent, though they may trigger job searchers to go to an Internet source for more details.

Recruiting differs depending on company and location; for instance, filling jobs at community banks in rural areas might involve different types of recruiting from filling jobs in larger banks in urban areas.[44] Whatever medium is used, it should be tied to the relevant labor market and should provide sufficient information on the company and the job. Thus, one major key is to make the wording of job ads readable and understandable, rather than using extensive abbreviations and omitting appealing details.[45] Figure 6-6 shows the kinds of information a good recruiting ad contains.

Evaluating Media Ads HR recruiters should measure the responses that different media generate in order to evaluate the effectiveness of various sources. The easiest way to track responses to ads is to use different contact names, e-mail addresses, or phone number codes in each ad, so the employer can identify which advertisement has prompted each applicant response that is received.

Although the total number of responses to each ad should be tracked, judging the success of an ad only by this number is a mistake. For example, it is better to have 10 responses with two qualified applicants than 30 responses with only one qualified applicant. Therefore, after individuals are hired, follow-up should be done to see which sources produced the employees who stay longer and perform better.

FIGURE 6-6   **What to Include in an Effective Recruiting Ad**

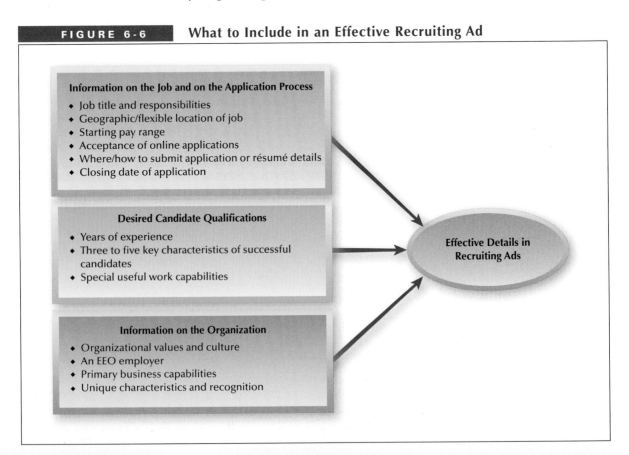

Information on the Job and on the Application Process

- Job title and responsibilities
- Geographic/flexible location of job
- Starting pay range
- Acceptance of online applications
- Where/how to submit application or résumé details
- Closing date of application

Desired Candidate Qualifications

- Years of experience
- Three to five key characteristics of successful candidates
- Special useful work capabilities

Information on the Organization

- Organizational values and culture
- An EEO employer
- Primary business capabilities
- Unique characteristics and recognition

Effective Details in Recruiting Ads

Competitive Recruiting Sources

Other sources for recruiting include professional and trade associations, trade publications, and competitors. Many professional societies and trade associations publish newsletters or magazines and have websites containing job ads. Such sources may be useful for recruiting the specialized professionals needed in an industry.

Some employers have extended recruiting to customers. Retailers such as Wal-Mart and Best Buy have aggressive programs to recruit customers to become employees in stores. While in the store, customers at these firms can pick up applications, apply online using kiosks, and even schedule interviews with managers or HR staff members. Other firms have included employment announcements when sending out customer bills or newsletters.

Employment Agencies

Employment agencies, both public and private, are a recruiting source. Every state in the United States has its own state-sponsored employment agency. These agencies operate branch offices in cities throughout the states and do not charge fees to applicants or employers. They also have websites that potential applicants can use without having to go to the offices.

Private employment agencies operate in most cities. For a fee collected from either the employee or the employer, these agencies do some preliminary screening and put employers in touch with applicants. Private employment agencies differ considerably in the levels of service, costs, policies, and types of applicants they provide. One specific type of private agency, the outplacement firm, is highlighted in the HR Perspective.

"Headhunters" The size of the fees and the aggressiveness with which some firms pursue candidates for executive and other openings have led to such firms being called *headhunters*. These employment agencies focus their efforts on executive, managerial, and professional positions. The executive search firms are split into two groups: (1) *contingency firms* that charge a fee only after a candidate has been hired by a client company, and (2) *retainer firms* that charge a client a set fee whether or not the contracted search is successful. Most of the larger firms work on a retainer basis. However, search firms are generally ethically bound not to approach employees of client companies in their search for job candidates for another employer.[46]

LOGGING ON

Job Agencies.com
For information about employment agencies, including a directory of worldwide agencies spanning many employment industries, visit www.jobagencies.com.

Labor Unions

Labor unions may be a useful source of certain types of workers. For example, in electrical and construction industries, unions traditionally have supplied workers to employers. A labor pool is generally available through a union, and workers can be dispatched from the hiring hall to particular jobs to meet the needs of employers.

In some instances, labor unions can control or influence recruiting and staffing activity. An organization with a strong union may have less flexibility than a nonunion company in deciding who will be hired and where those people will be placed. Unions can benefit employers through apprenticeship and cooperative staffing programs, as they do in the building and printing industries.

Outplacement Firms as Recruiting Sources

Outplacement firms typically aid individuals who have lost jobs with obtaining reemployment. As mentioned in earlier chapters, jobs can be lost because specific employees are removed from their jobs, because broad organizational downsizing or department reorganization occurs, or because people leave their jobs. Causes for eliminating specific persons or for people leaving jobs can include work factors, managerial conflicts, and various personal or work-life reasons.

The outplacement firms offer individuals a number of services, such as career counseling, résumé preparations and revisions, website sourcing, training on interview skills, and other useful job-related activities. By providing this assistance, these firms help individuals improve their job-hunting capabilities. One beneficial service of many outplacement firms

is helping job seekers develop and utilize personal networks, composed of past and present professional industry persons, business contacts from previous jobs, and other people.

A major asset of large outplacement firms such as Right Management and Keystone Partners is that they have contacts with a wide range of employers. They can contact potential employers and ask them to meet with outplaced individuals. These firms also utilize networking contacts with the employers with whom they have worked in the past.

In summary, outplacement firms provide a "recruiting bank" for both job-searching individual clients and employers needing new recruits. Because such firms serve both groups, they are another recruiting source that is widely used.[47]

Job Fairs and Creative Recruiting

Employers in various labor markets needing to fill a large number of jobs quickly have used job fairs and special recruiting events. Job fairs have been held by economic development entities, employer and HR associations, and other community groups to help bring employers and potential job candidates together. For instance, the SHRM chapter in a midwestern metropolitan area annually sponsors a job fair at which 75 to 100 employers can meet applicants. Publicity in the city draws several hundred potential recruits for different types of jobs. However, two cautionary notes are in order: (1) Some employers at job fairs may see attendees who are currently their employees "shopping" for jobs with other employers; and (2) "general" job fairs are likely to attract many people, including attendees who are not only unemployed but also unemployable. Industry- or skill-specific events usually offer more satisfactory candidates. Such job fairs also can attract employed candidates who are casually looking around but may not put their résumés on the Internet.

"Virtual" job fairs with Web-based links have been used by the federal government and others. "Drive-through" job fairs at shopping malls have been used by employers in a number of communities. At one such event, interested persons could drive up to a tent outside the mall, pick up applications from a "menu board" of employers, and then park and interview in the tent with recruiters if time allowed. Such creative recruiting methods sometimes can be used to generate a pool of qualified applicants so that jobs can be filled in a timely manner.

Educational Institutions and Recruiting

College and university students are a significant source of entry-level professional and technical employees. Most universities maintain career placement offices in which employers and applicants can meet. A number of considerations affect an employer's selection of colleges and universities at which to conduct interviews, as Figure 6-7 indicates.

Because college/university recruiting can be expensive and require significant time and effort, employers need to determine whether both current and future jobs require persons with college degrees in specific fields. Despite the economic changes in industries and among employers, a majority of employers who were surveyed still plan to have more than half of their hires be college graduates.[48]

A number of factors determine success in college recruiting. Some employers actively build continuing relationships with individual faculty members and career staff at designated colleges and universities. Maintaining a presence on campus by providing guest speakers to classes and student groups increases the contacts for an employer. Employers with a continuing presence and support on a campus are more likely to see positive college recruiting results.

Desirable Capabilities of College Recruits For many employers, a moderately high grade point average (GPA) is a criterion for considering candidates for jobs during on-campus interviews. Recruiters may use GPA benchmarks to initially screen applicants in college recruiting decisions. Considerations beyond grades include the graduates' leadership potential, interpersonal communication skills, and professional motivation factors.[49] Employers also

FIGURE 6-7   **College Recruiting: Considerations for Employers**

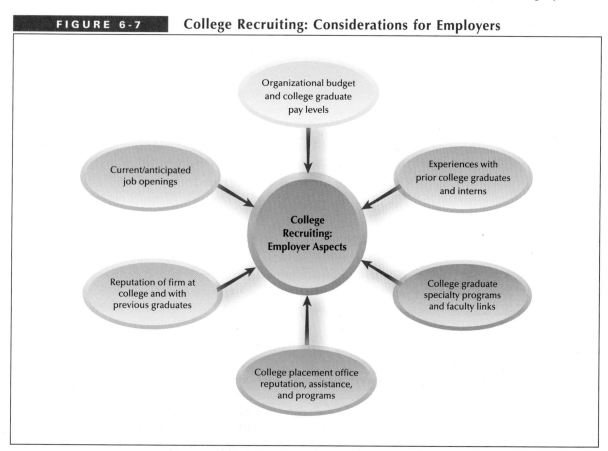

Internships as Part of College Recruiting

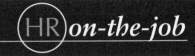

Many employers utilize internships as a basis for recruiting college students and graduates. Companies using internships believe they achieve better retention through the use of internships and cooperative programs. Well-planned internships have the potential to benefit both the individual student interns and the employers.[50] A student gets an opportunity to see if an employer and its culture fit, and the employer gets the equivalent of several months worth of "interview experiences" instead of the short traditional one. The following basic guidelines for the employer can help improve the odds that internships will be rewarding:

- Decide what the company needs in terms of specific jobs and projects, rather than just providing general internships.

- If interns are paid, provide relatively realistic competitive wages, as that will help attract talented individuals.
- Treat the interns like new employees by giving them appropriate work spaces, tools, Internet access, and other resources.
- Effectively manage the interns, including training, mentoring, and performance feedback.

The growth in IT resources has led to some "virtual internships."[51] In these arrangements, interns can access an employer's website, do project work, and interact with managers and others via e-mail, text-messages, and other means. Still, having some personal contact is likely to be useful for establishing the employer and intern images and relationships, which can lead to successful job offers for some interns.

are more likely to hire college candidates with related experience. That is one reason why internships are very important to employers, candidates, and college/university efforts, as the HR On-the-Job indicates.

School Recruiting High schools and vocational/technical schools may be valuable sources of new employees for some organizations. Many schools have a centralized guidance or placement office. Participating in career days and giving company tours to school groups are ways of maintaining good contact with school sources. Cooperative programs, in which students work part-time and receive some school credits, also may be useful in generating qualified future applicants for full-time positions.

Employers recognize that they may need to begin attracting students with capabilities while those students are in high school. For example, GE, IBM, and other corporations fund programs to encourage students with science and math skills to participate in engineering internships during summers. Some employers specifically target talented members of racial/ethnic groups in high schools and provide them with career encouragement, summer internships, and mentoring programs as part of aiding workforce diversity efforts.

INTERNAL RECRUITING METHODS

Filling openings internally may add motivation for employees to stay and grow in the organization rather than pursuing career opportunities elsewhere. The most common internal recruiting methods include: organizational databases, job postings, promotions and transfers, current-employee

| FIGURE 6-8 | Advantages and Disadvantages of Internal Recruiting |

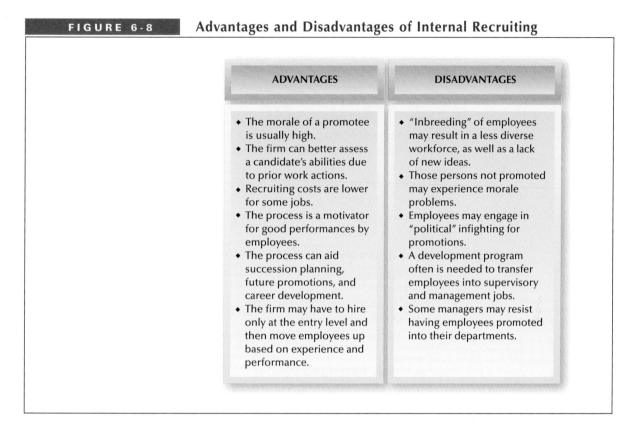

ADVANTAGES	DISADVANTAGES
• The morale of a promotee is usually high. • The firm can better assess a candidate's abilities due to prior work actions. • Recruiting costs are lower for some jobs. • The process is a motivator for good performances by employees. • The process can aid succession planning, future promotions, and career development. • The firm may have to hire only at the entry level and then move employees up based on experience and performance.	• "Inbreeding" of employees may result in a less diverse workforce, as well as a lack of new ideas. • Those persons not promoted may experience morale problems. • Employees may engage in "political" infighting for promotions. • A development program often is needed to transfer employees into supervisory and management jobs. • Some managers may resist having employees promoted into their departments.

referrals, and rerecruiting of former employees and applicants. Some of the common advantages and disadvantages of internal recruiting are highlighted in Figure 6-8.

Internal Recruiting Databases and Internet-Related Sources

HR information technology systems allow HR staff to maintain background and knowledge, skills, and abilities (KSA) information on existing employees. As openings arise, HR can access databases by entering job requirements and then get a listing of current employees meeting those requirements. Employment software can sort employee data by occupational fields, education, areas of career interests, previous work histories, and other variables. For instance, if a firm has an opening for someone with an MBA and marketing experience, the key words *MBA* and *marketing* can be entered in a search field, and the program displays a list of all current employees with these two items identified in their employee profiles.

The advantage of such databases is that they can be linked to other HR activities. Opportunities for career development and advancement are a major reason why individuals stay at or leave their employers. With employee databases, internal opportunities for individuals can be identified. Employee profiles are continually updated to include such items as additional training and education completed, special projects handled, and career plans and desires noted during performance appraisals and career mentoring discussions.

Job Posting

The major means for recruiting current employees for other jobs within the organization is **job posting**, a system in which the employer provides notices of job openings and employees respond by applying for specific openings. Without some sort of job posting system, it is difficult for many employees to find out what jobs are open elsewhere in the organization. In many unionized organizations, job posting and bidding can be quite formal because the procedures are often spelled out in labor agreements. Seniority lists may be used by organizations that make promotions based strictly on seniority.

Regardless of the means used, the purpose of the job posting system is to provide employees with more opportunities to move within the organization. When establishing and managing a job posting system, a number of questions must be addressed:

- What happens if no qualified candidates respond to postings?
- Must employees inform their supervisors that they are applying for another job?
- Are there restrictions on how long an employee must stay in a job before applying for another internal one?
- What types of or levels of jobs will not be posted?

Internet/Web-Based Job Posting While many employers historically have had some kind of job posting system in place for internal jobs, a number of companies are using proactive efforts to get employees to apply through Web-based systems. Kenexa, Oracle, Softscape, LinkedIn, ResumePal, Facebook, and JobFox are just some of the vendors that provide internal recruiting website job posting. The complexity of using such job posting methods varies according to the employer and the technology capabilities and systems available.[52] Employees can log onto a company intranet and create personal profiles, including career objectives, education, skill sets, and pay expectations. They also may attach a résumé. When a job opens, the placement program automatically mines the database for matches. Candidates then are notified by e-mail and go through the regular hiring cycle.

Effective Job Posting For job posting efforts to be effective, especially with better-performing employees, posting wording must be relevant and accurate. Also, the posting should be based on the important characteristics of talented employees. Those people may be most likely to respond because of the organizational reputation, coworkers and bosses, and the possibility of more important and interesting work.[53]

Jobs generally are posted before any external recruiting is done. The organization must allow a reasonable period of time for present employees to check notices of available jobs before it considers external applicants. Employees whose bids are turned down should discuss with their supervisors or someone in the HR area what knowledge, skills, and abilities are needed in order to improve their opportunities in the future.

Promotions and Transfers Many organizations choose to fill vacancies through promotions or transfers from within whenever possible. Firms such as Verizon Communications, Dow Chemical, Microsoft, and IBM have established systems to encourage employees to learn about current and future career needs and opportunities. Some advantages of these programs are reducing

Job posting System in which the employer provides notices of job openings and employees respond by applying for specific openings.

Enhancing Opportunities for Internal Promotion

Recruiting tools can help identify prospective candidates internally. It has been noted that "if you are not recruiting your own employees, someone else will." This is another way of saying that if employees have no internal opportunities for advancement, the best performers will look outside the company.

By taking an electronic look within the company for candidates to promote, firms may not only save money, but also enhance the prospects for retention of current employees. Employers are using HR technology systems to identify employee capabilities for entering management positions from within the company. Some firms have implemented electronic systems for internal

recruiting. The advantage of this Web-based approach can be seen in statistics that show that in one year, a significant number of positions were filled internally, much higher than previously.

When a job opens, Internet programs automatically look in the company database for qualified applicants, and those persons can be notified by e-mail or personal contact. Those individuals can then participate in the firm's hiring process by registering their profiles easily and quickly. Other internal approaches took more time, and fewer people participated. Thus, these technological changes have helped with employee recruiting for promotions and reduced employers' time and costs.[54]

employee turnover, enhancing individuals' skills and talent, and improving productivity.[55] The HR Perspective highlights some of the opportunities of these programs.

Although often successful, internal transfer and promotion of employees within the company may have some drawbacks. For instance, a person's performance on one job may not be a good predictor of performance on another, because different skills may be required on the new job. Also, as employees transfer or are promoted to other jobs, individuals must be recruited to fill the vacated jobs. Planning on how to fill those openings should occur before the job transfers or promotions, not afterward.

Employee-Focused Recruiting

One reliable source of potential recruits is suggestions from current or former employees. Because current and former employees are familiar with the employer, most of them will not refer individuals who are likely to be unqualified or who will make them look bad for giving the referral. Also, follow-up with former employers is likely to be done only with persons who were solid employees previously.

Current-Employee Referrals A reliable source of people to fill vacancies is composed of acquaintances, friends, and family members of current employees. The current employees can acquaint potential applicants with the advantages of a job with the company, furnish e-mails and other means of introduction, and encourage candidates to apply. Word-of-mouth referrals and discussions can positively aid organizational attractiveness and lead to more application decisions by those referred.[56] However, using only word-of-mouth or current-employee referrals can violate equal employment regulations if protected-class individuals are underrepresented in the current organizational workforce. Therefore, some external recruiting might be necessary to avoid legal problems in this area.

Utilizing this source is usually one of the most effective methods of recruiting because many qualified people can be reached at a relatively low cost. Some firms indicate that more than 60% of new hires are due to employee referrals.[57] In an organization with numerous employees, this approach can develop quite a large pool of potential employees. As an example, Integris Health Institute in Oklahoma used a referral program to hire more than 500 medical technicians and nurses in relatively difficult-to-fill jobs. One key component of this program was a referral incentive, whereby the individuals giving the referrals received up to $1,000 per difficult-to-fill job.[58]

Employers in many geographic areas and occupational fields have established employee referral incentive programs similar to that at Integris Health Institute. Mid-sized and larger employers are more likely to use employee referral bonuses. Some referral programs provide different bonus amounts for hard-to-fill jobs compared with common openings; in these situations, appropriate legal concerns should be met.[59]

Rerecruiting of Former Employees and Applicants Former employees and applicants represent another source for recruitment. Both groups offer a time-saving advantage because something is already known about them. Seeking them out as candidates is known as *rerecruiting* because they were successfully recruited previously. Former employees are considered an internal source in the sense that they have ties to the employer; sometimes they are called "boomerangers" because they left and came back.

Individuals who have left for other jobs sometimes are willing to return because the other jobs and employers turned out to be less attractive than initially thought. For example, at Qualcomm, a California-based telecommunications firm, about 70% of former Qualcomm individuals who left voluntarily indicated that they would return if requested.[60] The discussion on follow-up of exit interviews in the previous chapter illustrated that rerecruiting can be a key recruiting contribution.

To enhance such efforts, some firms have established "alumni reunions" to keep in contact with individuals who have left, and also to allow the companies to rerecruit individuals as appropriate openings arise. Key issues in the decision to rerecruit someone include the reasons why the individual left originally and whether the individual's performance and capabilities were good.

Another potential source consists of former applicants. Although they are not entirely an internal source, information about them can be found in the organizational files or an applicant database. Recontacting those who have previously applied for jobs can be a quick and inexpensive way to fill unexpected openings. For instance, one firm that needed two cost accountants immediately contacted qualified previous applicants and was able to hire two persons who were disenchanted with their current jobs at other companies.

RECRUITING EVALUATION AND METRICS

To determine how effective various recruiting sources and methods have been, it is important to evaluate recruiting efforts. But in a survey, a majority of HR executives identified that their firms were not getting sufficient metrics on the quality of hires and how well the new hires fit into the organizations.[61]

The primary way to find out whether recruiting efforts are financially effective is to conduct formal analyses as part of recruiting evaluation. An evaluation done by a consulting firm found that higher shareholder value occured when using time of successful recruiting as a metric. If recruiting was completed within two weeks, the study noted that the total return to shareholders was about 60%, compared to about 10% for companies that needed more than seven weeks to fill job openings. Also, greater use of employee referrals produced a much higher return to shareholders than use of other recruiting means.[62]

Various areas can be measured when evaluating recruiting. Figure 6-9 indicates key recruiting measurement areas in which employers frequently conduct evaluations.

Evaluating Recruiting Quantity and Quality

To evaluate recruiting, organizations can see how their recruiting efforts compare with past patterns and with the recruiting performance of other organizations. Measures of recruiting effectiveness can be used to see whether sufficient numbers of targeted population groups are being attracted.

For example, one area of concern in recruiting might be protected category persons. In Chicago, a network-based recruiting firm received only 16 black and 4 Hispanic applicants out of 276 persons for a customer service job. Yet Chicago has 37% blacks and 26% Hispanics in its population. Clearly, the efforts to increase recruiting in these racial/ethnic groups needed major attention.[63]

Information about job performance, absenteeism, cost of training, and turnover by recruiting source also helps adjust future recruiting efforts. For example, some companies find that recruiting at certain colleges or universities furnishes stable, high performers, whereas recruiting at other schools provides employees who are more prone to leave the organization. General metrics for evaluating recruiting include quantity and quality of applicants.

FIGURE 6-9   **Recruiting Measurement Areas**

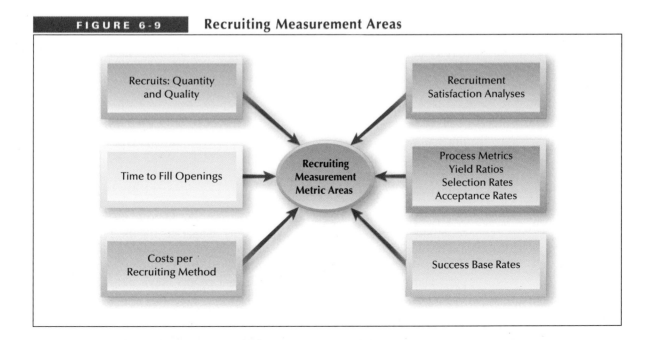

Quantity of Applicants Because the goal of a good recruiting program is to generate a large pool of applicants from which to choose, quantity is a natural place to begin evaluation. The basic measure here considers whether the quantity of recruits is sufficient to fill job vacancies. A related question is: Does recruiting at this source provide enough qualified applicants with an appropriate mix of protected-class individuals?

Quality of Applicants In addition to quantity, a key issue is whether or not the qualifications of the applicant pool are sufficient to fill the job openings. Do the applicants meet job specifications, and do they perform the jobs well after hire? What is the failure rate for new hires for each recruiter? Measures that can be used include items such as performance appraisal scores, months until promotion, production quantity, and sales volume for each hire.

Evaluating Recruiting Satisfaction

The satisfaction of two groups is useful in evaluating recruiting. Certainly the views of managers with openings to fill are important, because they are "customers" in a very real sense. But the applicants (those hired and those not hired) also are an important part of the process and can provide useful input.

Managers can respond to questions about the quality of the applicant pool, the recruiter's service, the timeliness of the process, and any problems that they see. Applicants might provide input on how they were treated, their perceptions of the company, and the length of the recruiting process and other aspects.

Evaluating the Time Required to Fill Openings

Looking at the length of time it takes to fill openings is a common means of evaluating recruiting efforts.[64] If openings are not filled quickly with qualified candidates, the work and productivity of the organization are likely to suffer. If it takes 45 days to fill empty positions, managers who need those employees will be unhappy. Also, as noted earlier, unfilled positions cost money.

Generally, it is useful to calculate the average amount of time it takes from contact to hire for each source of applicants, because some sources may produce recruits faster than others. For example, one firm calculated the following averages for nonexempt, warehouse and manufacturing jobs:

Source	Average Time from Contact to Hire
Internet applicants	32 days
Employment agencies	25 days
Walk-in candidates	17 days
Employee referrals	12 days

These data revealed that, at least for this firm, the Internet methods and use of employment agencies took significantly longer to fill the openings than did relying on other means. Matching the use of sources to the time available showed that employee referrals resulted in faster recruiting results for that particular group of jobs. However, different results might occur when filling executive jobs or highly skilled network technician jobs. Overall, analyses need to be made both organization-wide and by different types of jobs.

Evaluating the Cost of Recruiting

Different formulas can be used to evaluate recruiting costs. The calculation most often used to measure such costs is to divide total recruiting expenses for the year by the number of hires for the year:

$$\frac{\text{Recruiting expenses}}{\text{Number of recruits hired}}$$

The problem with this approach is accurately identifying what details should be included in the recruiting expenses. Should expenses for testing, background checks, relocations, or signing bonuses be included, or are they more properly excluded?

Once those questions are answered, the costs can be allocated to various sources to determine how much each hire from each source costs. It is logical that employers should evaluate the cost of recruiting as a primary metric. Recruiting costs might include costs for employment agencies, advertising, internal sources, external means, and others.[65] The costs also can be sorted by type of job—costs for hiring managers, secretaries, bookkeepers, and sales personnel will all be different.

Certainly, cost is an issue, and some employers are quite concerned about cost per hire, but quality might be the trade-off. For example, if an organizational HR strategy focuses on *quality* as a competitive advantage, a company might choose to hire only from the top 15% of candidates for critical jobs.

General Recruiting Process Metrics

Because recruiting activities are important, the costs and benefits associated with them should be analyzed. A cost–benefit analysis of recruiting efforts may include both direct costs (advertising, recruiters' salaries, travel, agency fees, etc.) and indirect costs (involvement of operating managers, public relations, image, etc.). Cost–benefit information on each recruiting source can be calculated. Comparing the length of time that applicants hired from each source stay in the organization with the cost of hiring from that source also offers a useful perspective.

Yield Ratios One means for evaluating recruiting efforts is **yield ratios**, which compare the number of applicants at one stage of the recruiting process with the number at another stage. The result is a tool for approximating the necessary size of the initial applicant pool. It is useful to visualize yield ratios as a pyramid in which the employer starts with a broad base of applicants that progressively narrows. As Figure 6-10 depicts, to end up with five hires for the job in question, a sample company must begin with 100 applicants in the pool, as long as yield ratios remain as shown.

A different approach to using yield ratios suggests that over the length of time, organizations can develop ranges for crucial ratios. When a given indicator ratio falls outside that range, it may indicate problems in the recruiting process. As an example, in college recruiting the following ratios might be useful:

Yield ratio Comparison of the number of applicants at one stage of the recruiting process with the number at the next stage.

$$\frac{\text{College seniors given second interviews}}{\text{Total number of seniors interviewed}} = \text{Range of } 30\%\text{--}50\%$$

$$\frac{\text{Number who accept offer}}{\text{Number invited to the company to visit}} = \text{Range of } 50\%\text{--}70\%$$

| FIGURE 6-10 | Sample Recruiting Evaluation Pyramid |

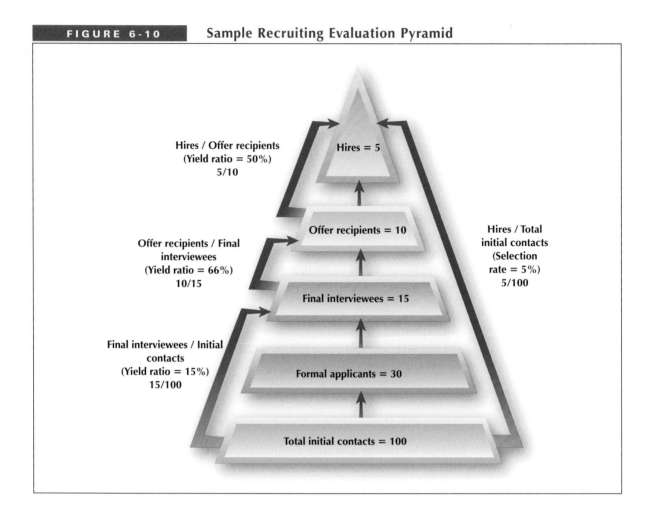

Hires / Offer recipients
(Yield ratio = 50%)
5/10

Hires = 5

Hires / Total
initial contacts
(Selection
rate = 5%)
5/100

Offer recipients / Final
interviewees
(Yield ratio = 66%)
10/15

Offer recipients = 10

Final interviewees = 15

Final interviewees / Initial
contacts
(Yield ratio = 15%)
15/100

Formal applicants = 30

Total initial contacts = 100

$$\frac{\text{Number hired}}{\text{Number offered a job}} = \text{Range of 70\%--80\%}$$

$$\frac{\text{Number finally hired}}{\text{Total number interviewed on campus}} = \text{Range of 10\%--20\%}$$

Selection Rate Another useful calculation is the **selection rate**, which is the percentage hired from a given group of candidates. It equals the number hired divided by the number of applicants; for example, a rate of 30% indicates that 3 out of 10 applicants were hired. The selection rate is also affected by the validity of the selection process. A relatively unsophisticated selection program might pick 8 out of 10 applicants for the job. Four of those might turn out to be good employees. A more valid selection process might pick 5 out of 10 applicants but all perform well. Selection rate measures not just recruiting but selection issues as well. So do acceptance rate and success base rate.

Acceptance Rate Calculating the acceptance rate helps identify how successful the organization is at hiring candidates. The **acceptance rate** is the percent of applicants hired divided by the total number of applicants offered jobs. After the company goes through all the effort to screen, interview, and make job offers, hopefully most candidates accept job offers. If they do not,

Selection rate Percentage hired from a given group of candidates.

Acceptance rate Percent of applicants hired divided by total number of applicants offered jobs.

then HR might want to look at reasons why managers and HR staff cannot "close the deal." It is common for HR staff members to track the reasons candidates turn down job offers. That analysis helps explain the *rejection rate* in order to learn how competitive the employer is compared with other employers and what factors are causing candidates to choose employment elsewhere.

Success Base Rate A longer-term measure of recruiting effectiveness is the success rate of applicants. The *success base rate* can be determined by comparing the number of past applicants who have become successful employees against the number of applicants they competed against for their jobs, using historical data within the organization. Also, the success base rate can be compared with the success rates of other employers in the area or industry using benchmarking data. This rate indicates whether the quality of the employees hired results in employees who perform well and have low turnover. For example, assume that if 10 people were hired at random, it might be expected that 4 of them would be satisfactorily performing employees. Thus, a successful recruiting program should be aimed at attracting the 4 in 10 who are capable of doing well on this particular job.

Realistically, no recruiting program will attract only the people who will succeed in a particular job. However, efforts to make the recruiting program attract the largest proportion possible of those in the base rate group can make recruiting efforts more productive in both the short and long term.

Increasing Recruiting Effectiveness

Evaluation of recruiting should be used to make recruiting activities more effective. Some common activities that are reviewed during evaluation are:

- *Résumé mining*—a software approach to getting the best résumés for a fit from a big database
- *Applicant tracking*—an approach that takes an applicant all the way from a job listing to performance appraisal results
- *Employer career website*—a convenient recruiting place on an employer's website where applicants can see what jobs are available and apply
- *Internal mobility*—a system that tracks prospects in the company and matches them with jobs as they come open
- *Realistic job previews*—a process that persons can use to get details on the employer and the jobs
- *Responsive recruitment*—whereby applicants receive timely responses

Recruiting effectiveness can be increased by using the evaluation data to target different applicant pools, tap broader labor markets, change recruiting methods, improve internal handling and interviewing of applicants, and train recruiters and managers.

Another key way to increase recruiting effectiveness rests with the recruiters themselves. Those involved in the recruiting process can either turn off recruits or create excitement. For instance, recruiters who emphasize positive aspects about the jobs and their employers can enhance recruiting effectiveness. Thus, it is important that recruiters communicate well with applicants and treat them fairly and professionally. Effective recruiting is a crucial factor for HR management, as it leads to selecting individuals for employment who will enhance organizational success.

SUMMARY

- Recruiting is the process of generating a pool of qualified applicants for organizational jobs through a series of activities.
- Recruiting must be viewed strategically as tied to HR planning, and discussions should be held about the relevant labor markets in which to recruit.
- The components of labor markets are labor force population, applicant population, and the applicant pool.
- Labor markets can be categorized by geographic area, industry, occupation, qualifications, and other characteristics.
- Employers must make decisions about organization-based versus outsourced recruiting, regular versus flexible staffing, and other aspects of recruiting.
- Efforts should be made to recruit a diverse workforce, including older workers, individuals with disabilities, women, and members of racial/ethnic groups.
- Internet recruiting has grown in use through job boards, various websites, social networking, and special technology methods.
- While Internet recruiting may be able to save costs and time, it also can generate more unqualified applicants and may not reach certain groups of potential applicants.
- The decision to use internal or external recruiting sources should consider both the advantages and disadvantages of each source.
- The most common external recruiting sources are media sources, competitive sources, labor unions, employment agencies, job fairs and special events, and educational institutions.
- The most common methods of internal recruiting include organizational databases, job postings, promotions and transfers, current-employee referrals, and rerecruiting of former employees and applicants.
- Recruiting efforts should be evaluated as part of utilizing HR measurement to assess the effectiveness of the methods and approaches.
- Recruiting evaluation using recruiting metrics typically includes evaluating recruiting quantity and quality, tracking the time to fill openings, examining the costs and benefits of various recruiting sources, and determining recruiting satisfaction.

CRITICAL THINKING ACTIVITIES

1. What labor markets should be considered when recruiting to fill an opening for a sales representative for a pharmaceutical manufacturer?

2. Discuss ways a regional bank could use the Internet effectively to recruit loan officer professionals.

3. Describe how a local firm might be able to utilize college/university interns to generate future applicants for jobs planned within the next one to two years.

4. Assume you are going to look for a current job of interest to you. Utilize broad websites such as www.Job.com, Yahoo! HotJobs, Monster, Taleo, and others to learn about job possibilities for yourself.

HR EXPERIENTIAL PROBLEM SOLVING

Your small marketing company of about 50 workers has traditionally recruited employees using newspaper print advertisements. Due to diminished recruiting efforts from your ads, the company is interested in using more Internet and social media recruiting. The company President has requested that you, as HR Manager, prepare an overview of how Internet recruiting efforts will be different from the traditional methods used by the company. You will need to make a case for why the company should transition to Internet recruiting and identify the benefits for doing so. To prepare an overview, review the resources found at http://www.recruitersnetwork.com/

1. What will your company need to do differently to actively use Internet recruiting as you compete with other employers for qualified applicants?

2. As you recruit marketing professionals, identify the niche websites that you recommend be used for your Internet postings and the reasons for your recommendations.

C A S E

Recruiting at Kia

As economic conditions became more demanding for some employers, other firms continued to recruit people for jobs. One firm, Kia Motors America, added a large number of jobs at one of its newer facilities. As a subsidiary of a South Korean corporation, Kia Motors America added tons of equipment at its West Point, Georgia, plant, so that ultimately about 300,000 vehicles would be produced annually.

As the firm sought recruits to fill its Georgia plant workforce, more than 40,000 individuals applied for the jobs, the bulk of which were production and maintenance positions. However, the need for people in a variety of other occupations, including air-conditioning service people, cafeteria workers, and medical staff, added to the depth and scope of Kia's recruiting. A limited time frame for applications was set by Kia as part of its recruitment planning.

In the recruiting process, a variety of regional and area sources were contacted as part of the Kia broad publicity and inclusive efforts in the area. Randy Jackson, HR Director, spent a month visiting colleges and churches, appearing on radio and television shows, and using other means to market Kia's recruiting and employment efforts. All of these activities were done to inform applicants about the numerous jobs at Kia and the month-long time frame for application.

To make its recruiting system effective in screening the large number of applicants, Kia established an online-only application process on a special website. As part of its recruiting efforts, Kia and a Georgia Department of Labor agency worked together. One of the agency activities was to make computers available at a local technical college, libraries, and other locations for those

persons without home-based Internet. Having the online system allowed Kia's HR staff to move quickly to identify those applicants who matched available jobs. The use of this system by HR recruiters and managers doing the hiring made the selection process more efficient.

To aid in the selection of employees, recruiting software was used to sort applicants into electronic "buckets," divided by work experiences and education. Then an eight-step process was established to let applicants obtain a realistic job preview of working at Kia. These recruiting actions resulted in the hiring of more than 500 new employees within six months. During the rest of the year, an additional 1,200 workers were hired, primarily for the second shift, and more were hired later.

Although smaller employers might not use such an extensive recruiting process, the Kia process illustrates the kinds of recruiting planning, activities, Internet linkages, and other means that can be used by both large and small employers doing recruiting. The long-term success of Kia's efforts to staff its Georgia operation demonstrates ways in which HR can use both time- and cost-effective recruiting to hire qualified individuals.[66]

QUESTIONS

1. Describe how employing a large number of new workers requires strategic recruiting planning and operational efforts, and discuss what aspects might be different in smaller firms.

2. Discuss how utilizing the Internet, like Kia did and other employers do, is changing how recruiting efforts are occurring for a variety of jobs in employers of different sizes.

SUPPLEMENTAL CASES

Northwest State College

This case shows how recruiting policies can work against successful recruiting when a tight labor market exists. (For the case, go to www.cengage.com/management/mathis.)

Enterprise Recruiting

This case highlights how a large car rental firm uses a range of recruiting approaches successfully. (For the case, go to www.cengage.com/management/mathis.)

NOTES

1. Based on John Flanigan, "Capturing & Captivating the Passive Job Seeker," *Best Practices in Candidate Sourcing, Workforce Management*, 2008; Amitai Givertz, "Passive Candidate Recruiting," *ZoomInfo White Paper*, 2008, www.zoominfo.com.

2. Rick Be, "Employment Doldrums May Be Easing, Survey Notes," *Workforce Management Online*, August 25, 2009, www.workforce.com.

3. "Ethics as Recruiting Tool," *Journal of Accountancy*, January 2009, 21.

4. "What SmBs Should Look for in an Applicant Tracking System," September 25, 2009, www.taleo.com.

5. John Yuva, "Round Up the Recruits," *Inside Supply Management*, July 2008, 23–25; Auren Hoffman, "Why Hiring Is Paradoxically Harder in a Downturn," *HR Leaders*, July 14, 2009, www.hrleaders.org.

6. U.S. Bureau of Labor Statistics, www.bls.gov.

7. Joe Barrett, "Manufacturers Get Top Talent for Hard-to-Fill Jobs," *The Wall Street Journal*, May 30, 2009, A5.

8. "Recruiting for Small Firms," *Journal of Accountancy*, December 2008, 40.

9. Kurt Scott, "The Search for Effective Physician Leaders," *Physician Executive*, March/April 2009, 44–48.

10. Theresa Minton-Eversole, "Mission: Recruitment," *HR Magazine*, January 2009, 43–45.

11. Bill Roberts, "Manage Candidates Right from the Start," *HR Magazine*, October 2008, 73–76.

12. Rita Zeidner, "Does the United States Need Foreign Workers?" *HR Magazine*, June 2009, 42–49;

Paul Gallagher, "H-1B Headaches," *Human Resource Executive*, April 2009, 23–27; Jessica E. Vascellero and Justin Scheck, "Justice Department Probes Hiring Practices in Silicon Valley," *The Wall Street Journal*, June 4, 2009, B3.

13. John Sullivan, "Countercyclical Hiring: The Greatest Recruiting Opportunities in the Last 25 Years," *Electronic Resource Exchange*, August 24, 2009, www.ere.net.

14. Based on Mark Schoeff, Jr., "Managing Change: USDA Food Safety and Inspection Service," *Workforce Management*, October 20, 2008, 26.

15. "What Is Recruitment Process Outsourcing?" *Recruitment Process Outsourcing Association*, June 2009, www.RPOassociation.org.

16. Beth Ellyn Rosenthal, "GE Looks to Recruitment Process Outsourcing . . .," *Outsourcing Journal*, October 2006, 1–4.

17. Justin Lahart, "Employers Shed Fewer Temp Workers," *The Wall Street Journal*, September 5–6, 2009, A2; Patrick Buckley, et al., "The Use of Automated Employment Recruiting and Screening System for Temporary Professional Employees," *Human Resource Management*, 43 (2004), 233–241.

18. Keisha-Ann G. Gray, "Dividing Lines," *Human Resource Executive Online*, September 8, 2009, www.hreonline.com.

19. "Study Ranks Top Diversity Hiring Tools," *WorldatWork Newsline*, August 21, 2008, www.worldatwork.org.

20. Gina Ruiz, "Goodwill Offers Recruiting Ideas on Training Hispanic Workers," *Workforce Management*, May 2007, www.workforce.com.

21. Joanna N. Lahey, "Age, Women, and Hiring," *Journal of Human Resources*, 43 (2008), 30–56.

22. Mark L. Lengnick-Hall, et al., "Overlooked and Underutilized: People with Disabilities Are an Untapped Human Resource," *Human Resource Management*, 47 (2008), 255–273.

23. Brendan J. Morse and Paula M. Popovich, "Realistic Recruitment Practices in Organizations," *Human Resource Management Review*, 19 (2009), 1–8; William Gardner, et al., "Attraction to Organizational Culture Profiles: Effects of Realistic Recruiting . . .," *Management Communication Quarterly*, 22 (2009), 437–472.

24. "E-Recruiting Software Providers," *Workforce Management*, June 22, 2009, 14.

25. "New Job Search Engine Makes Finding a Job Easier," *The Career News*, September 21, 2009, www.thecareernews.com.

26. For details, go to www.shrm.org/jpc.

27. Emma Parry and Shaun Tyson, "An Analysis of the Use and Success of OnLine Recruitment Methodism in the U.K.," *Human Resource Management Journal*, 18 (2008), 257–274.

28. Steven D. Maurer and Yupin Liu, "Developing Effective E-Recruiting Websites: Insights for Managers from Marketers," *Business Horizons*, 50 (2007), 305–314.

29. Lori Foster Thompson, et al., "E-Recruitment and the Benefits of Organizational Web Appeal," *Human Behavior*, 24 (2008), 2384–2398.

30. Dan Schaubel, "Skip Job Boards and Use Social Media Instead," *BusinessWeek Online*, July 29, 2009, 14.

31. Chris Tratar, "Recruiting by Relationship to Fill the Candidate Pipeline," *Workforce Management*, July 20, 2009, S5.

32. Vangie Sison, "Social Media: Attracting Talent in the Age of Web 2.0," *Workspan*, May 2009, 45–49; Sam De Kay, "Are Business-Oriented Social Networking Websites Useful Resources for Locating Passive Job Seekers?" *Business Communications Quarterly*, March 2009, 101–104.

33. Gonzado Hernandez and Ed Frauenheim, "Logging Off of Job Boards," *Workforce Management*, June 22, 2009, 25–28.

34. Juki Hasson, "Blogging for Talent," *HR Magazine*, October 2007, 65–68.

35. Andrew R. McIlvaine, "Lights, Camera, Interview," *Human Resource Executive*, September 16, 2009, 22–25; Rita Zeidner, "Companies Tell Their Stories in Recruitment Videos," *HR Trendbook*, 2008, 28.

36. Michael O'Brien, "Building a Buzz," *Human Resource Executive*, June 16, 2008, 36–38.

37. Adrienne Fox, "Newest Social Medium Has Recruiters All-a-Twitter," *HR Disciplines*, June 24, 2009, www.shrm.org/hrdisciplines.

38. Tracy Cote and Traci Armstrong, "Why Tweeting Has Become an Ad Agency's Main Job Posting Strategy . . .?" *Workforce Management Online*, May 2009, www.workforce.com.

39. For details and current status, go to www.ftc.gov. Also see Ed Fraurnheim and Rich Bell, "A Tighter Rein on HR Blogging?" *Workforce Management Online*, September 2009, www.workforce.com.

40. Tresa Baidas, "Lawyers Warn Employers Against Giving Glowing Reviews on LinkedIn," *National Law Journal*, July 6, 2009, www.nlj.com.

41. Marcel J. H. Van Birgelen, et al., "Effectiveness of Corporate Employment Web Sites," *International Journal of Manpower*, 29 (2008), 731–751.

42. Caren B. Goldberg and David G. Allen, "Black and White and Read All Over: Race Differences in Reactions to Recruitment Web Sites," *Human Resource Management*, 47 (2008), 217–236.

43. Gary Crispin, "The Future of Recruiting," *Human Resource Executive*, September 16, 2009, 32–35.

44. Eric Robbins and Forest Myers, "The Staffing Challenges Lie Ahead for Community Banks," *RMA Journal*, April 2009, 18–23.

45. Mo Edjlali, "The 2 Keys to Killer Job Ads," *Electronic Recruiting Exchange*, July 27, 2006, www.ere.net.

46. Stephanie Overman, "Searching for the Top," *HR Magazine*, January 2008, 47–52.

47. Fay Hansen, "Recruiters Seeking Untapped Talent Among Outplacement Firms," *Workforce Management Online*, March 2009.

48. Theresa Minton-Eversole, "Companies Plan Modest Hiring of 2009 College Graduates," *HR Disciplines*, April 17, 2009, www.shrm.org/hrdisciplines.

49. George Violette and Douglas Chene, "Campus Recruiting: What Local and Regional Accounting Firms Look for in New Hires," *CPA Journal*, December 2008, 66–68.

50. Donna M. Owens, "College Recruiting in a Downturn," *HR Magazine*, April 2009, 51–54.

51. Jonnelle Marte, "An Internship from Your Couch," *The Wall Street Journal*, September 29, 2009, D1.

52. Bill Kutik, "Still Trying to Get Recruiting Right," *Human Resource Executive Online*, April 6, 2009, www.hreonline.com/HRE.

53. Peter Weddle, "The Really Big Impact of a Small Number of Sentient Specifics," *Dice Review*, July 2009, http://marketing.dice.com.

54. Kathryn Tyler, "Helping Employees Step Up," *HR Magazine*, August 1, 2007, 48.

55. Sarah E. Needleman, "New Career, Same Employer," *The Wall Street Journal*, April 21, 2008, B9.

56. Greet Von Hoye and Filip Lievens, "Tapping the Grapevine: A Closer Look at Word-of-Mouth as a Recruitment Source," *Journal of Applied Psychology*, 94 (2009), 341–352.

57. Robert Gandossy and Tina Kao, "The Right People, Right Now . . .," *WorkSpan*, December 2007, 71–74.

58. Leo Jakobson, "Nursing: A Referral Program," *Incentive*, April 2007, 36–39.

59. "What Issue Should We Consider in Implementing Employee Referral Program?" *HRCompliance*, August 15, 2009, www.hrcompliance.cerdian.com.

60. Michael O'Brien, "Gone, But Not Forgotten," *Human Resource Executive*, September 2, 2009, 30–33.

61. Stephanie Overman, "Staffing Management: Measure What Matters," *Staffing Management*, October 1, 2008, www.shrm.org.

62. Ed Emerman, "Effective Recruiting Tied to Strong Financial Performance," *Watson-Wyatt Workside*, 2009, www.watsonwyatt.com/news.

63. Fay Hansen, "Sourcing Disappears as Applications Pile Up for Overwhelmed Recruiters," *Workforce Management Online*, July 23, 2009, www.workforce.com.

64. "Building Championship Recruiting Teams," *Staffing Exclusives*, April 14, 2009, www.StaffingInstitute.org.

65. Alice Snell, "Focus on Process to Reduce Your Recruiting Costs," *Best Practices in Recruitment*, 2009, www.workforce.com, S5.

66. Based on Julie Cook Ramirez, "Engines of Growth," *Human Resource Executive*, August 2009, 36–39; Larry Copeland, "Kia Breathes Life into Old Georgia Textile Mill Town," *USA Today*, March 25, 2010, 5A.

7

Selecting Human Resources

After you have read this chapter, you should be able to:

- Summarize the importance of realistic job previews and application screening efforts to the selection process.

- Diagram the sequence of a typical selection process.

- Discuss how validity and reliability are related to selection.

- Identify three types of selection tests and legal concerns about their uses.

- Contrast several types of selection interviews and some key considerations in conducting these interviews.

- Specify how legal concerns affect background investigations of applicants and use of medical examinations in the selection process.

- Describe the major issues to be considered when selecting candidates for global assignments.

Using Virtual Worlds for Selection

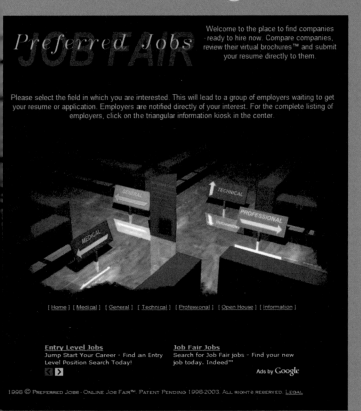

Preferred Jobs
JOB FAIR

Welcome to the place to find companies ready to hire now. Compare companies, review their virtual brochures™ and submit your resume directly to them.

Please select the field in which you are interested. This will lead to a group of employers waiting to get your resume or application. Employers are notified directly of your interest. For the complete listing of employers, click on the triangular information kiosk in the center.

GENERAL
TECHNICAL
PROFESSIONAL
MEDICAL

[Home] [Medical] [General] [Technical] [Professional] [Open House] [Information]

Entry Level Jobs
Jump Start Your Career - Find an Entry Level Position Search Today!

Job Fair Jobs
Search for Job Fair jobs - Find your new job today. Indeed™

Ads by Google

1998 © Preferred Jobs · Online Job Fair™. Patent Pending 1998-2003. All rights reserved. Legal

Some employers are experimenting with a virtual online community to screen possible hires. The program allows job candidates to create a computer-generated image to represent them and to communicate with employers as if text-messaging. The image is called an "avatar." The avatar can be used to interview or to attend virtual job fairs. Company representatives also create avatars. The interactions among these creations in a virtual environment become the basis for screening decisions.

Those who are less tech-savy are finding that they can shoot themselves in their virtual feet. Some people have a difficult time designing and controlling their avatars. For example, one candidate spent 6 hours working on his avatar and could not figure out how to make him sit in a chair; he finally decided to let him sit on top of the chair instead. Other candidates' avatars at an online job fair began floating in the air.

It is not just applicants who have difficulties. Company representatives are not used to recruiting in the virtual world either. One consulting company partner's avatar slumped over by accident and looked like it had gone to sleep during an interview. Mishaps involving avatars are usually viewed as amusing. The mistakes can even be icebreakers. One candidate attending the job fair tried to hand a copy of his résumé to a Hewlett-Packard employee and instead handed her a virtual beer. Luckily they both laughed it off, and the candidate was given an opportunity to continue the interview process.

Using this virtual interaction is cheaper than holding an actual job fair. Higher-ups in the company who might want to attend can do so easily as avatars. Job seekers seem to be much more relaxed in the virtual environment than they would be at a real job fair, since they have time to think

213

before they type their responses rather than having to think and talk at the same time.

Employers say they do not view this as a replacement for traditional selection, but rather as an additional step that can help narrow the field of candidates for some jobs. "This is really a supplement to our regular recruiting practices," says a manager for Hewlett-Packard.[1]

Some would argue that picking the right people for the jobs that need to be done is the most important part of human resource management.[2] Certainly for a business that depends on good people and good performance for the organization to succeed, its importance is very high. For an organization that is failing, improvement may need to come from many different sources, but it is difficult to imagine appropriate changes coming without some new competent people to carry out those changes. In athletic organizations that are not doing well, it is the selection of new coaches and players that creates improvements, if any are to come, and the continued selection of good athletes and coaches that allows ongoing success.

SELECTION AND PLACEMENT

Selection is the process of choosing individuals with the correct qualifications needed to fill jobs in an organization. Without these qualified employees, an organization is far less likely to succeed. A useful perspective on selection and placement comes from two HR observations that underscore the importance of effective staffing:

- "*Hire hard, manage easy.*" The investment of time and effort in selecting the right people for jobs will make managing them as employees much less difficult because many problems are eliminated.
- "*Good training will not make up for bad selection.*" When people without the appropriate aptitudes are selected, employers will have difficulty training them to do those jobs that they do not fit.[3]

Placement

The ultimate purpose of selection is **placement**, or fitting a person to the right job. Placement of human resources should be seen primarily as a matching process. How well an employee is matched to a job can affect the amount and quality of the employee's work, as well as the training and operating costs required to prepare the individual for work life. Further, employee morale is an issue because good fit encourages individuals to be positive about their jobs and what they accomplish.[4]

Selection and placement activities typically focus on applicants' knowledge, skills, and abilities (KSAs), but they should also focus on the degree to which job candidates generally match the situations experienced both on the job and in the company. Psychologists label this *person-environment fit*. In HR it is usually called **person/job fit**. Fit is related not only to satisfaction with work but also to commitment to a company, and to quitting intentions.

Selection The process of choosing individuals with the correct qualifications needed to fill jobs in an organization.

Placement Fitting a person to the right job.

Person/job fit Matching the KSAs of individuals with the characteristics of jobs.

Lack of fit between KSAs and job requirements can be classified as a "mismatch." A mismatch results from poor pairing of a person's needs, interests, abilities, personality, and expectations with characteristics of the job, rewards, and the organization in which the job is located. Five mismatch situations are:[5]

- Skills/job qualifications
- Geography/job location
- Time/amount of work
- Earnings/expectations
- Work/family

Mismatches related to skills/job qualifications and amount of work/time required are likely to cause a person to change jobs to improve fit. The other kinds of mismatches have more to do with conflicts of interests. What makes placement difficult and complex is the need to match people and jobs on multiple dimensions.[6]

People already working in jobs can help identify the most important KSAs for success as part of job analysis. The fit between the individual and job characteristics is particularly important when dealing with overseas assignments because employees must have the proper personalities, skills, and interpersonal abilities to be effective in the international environment.

In addition to the match between people and jobs, employers are concerned about the congruence between people and companies, or the **person/organization fit**.[7] Person/organization fit is important from a "values" perspective, with many organizations trying to positively link a person's principles to the values of the company. Organizations tend to favor job applicants who effectively blend into how business is conducted. Person/organization fit can influence employees' and customers' beliefs about the organization, making this fit a key selection consideration.

LOGGING ON

HR-Guide.com
This website offers links to HR websites relating to selection and staffing resources, including information on methods, best practices, tests, and software programs. Visit the site at www.hr-guide.com.

Selection, Criteria, Predictors, and Job Performance

Regardless of whether an employer uses specific KSAs or a more general approach, effective selection of employees involves using selection criteria and predictors of these criteria. At the heart of an effective selection system must be the knowledge of what constitutes good job performance. When one knows what good performance looks like on a particular job, the next step is to identify what it takes for the employee to achieve successful performance. These are called selection criteria. A **selection criterion** is a characteristic that a person must possess to successfully perform work. Figure 7-1 shows that ability, motivation, intelligence, conscientiousness, appropriate risk, and permanence might be selection criteria for many jobs. Selection criteria that might be more specific to managerial jobs include "leading and deciding," "supporting and cooperating," "organizing and executing," and "enterprising and performing."[8]

To determine whether candidates might possess certain selection criteria (such as ability and motivation), employers try to identify **predictors of selection criteria** that are measurable or visible indicators of those positive characteristics (or criteria). For example, as Figure 7-1 indicates, three good predictors of "permanence" might be individual interests, salary requirements, and tenure on previous jobs. If a candidate possesses appropriate amounts of any or all of these predictors, it might be assumed that the person would stay on the job longer than someone without those predictors.[9]

Person/organization fit
The congruence between individuals and organizational factors.

Selection criterion
Characteristic that a person must possess to successfully perform work.

Predictors of selection criteria Measurable or visible indicators of selection criteria.

| FIGURE 7-1 | Job Performance, Selection Criteria, and Predictors |

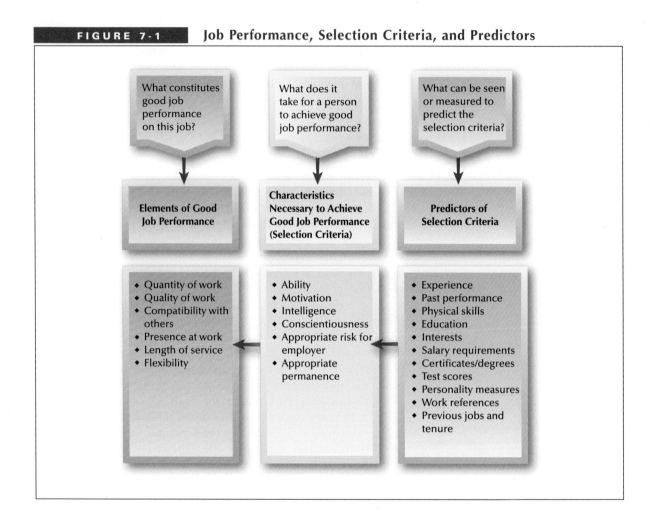

The information gathered about an applicant through predictors should focus on the likelihood that the individual will execute the job competently once hired. Predictors can be identified through many formats such as application forms, tests, interviews, education requirements, and years of experience, but such factors should be used only if they are found to be valid predictors of specific job performance.[10] Using invalid predictors can result in selecting the "wrong" candidate and rejecting the "right" one.

Validity

In selection, validity is the correlation between a predictor and job performance. In other words, validity occurs to the extent that the predictor actually predicts what it is supposed to predict. Several different types of validity are used in selection. Most validity decisions use a **correlation coefficient**, an index number that gives the relationship between a predictor variable and a criterion (or dependent) variable. Correlations always range from −1.0 to +1.0, with higher absolute scores suggesting stronger relationships.

Concurrent validity is one method for establishing the validity associated with a predictor. Concurrent validity uses current employees to validate a predictor or "test." As shown in Figure 7-2, concurrent validity is measured when an employer tests current employees and correlates the scores with

Correlation coefficient
Index number that gives the relationship between a predictor variable and a criterion variable.

Concurrent validity
Measured when an employer tests current employees and correlates the scores with their performance ratings.

FIGURE 7-2   Concurrent and Predictive Validity

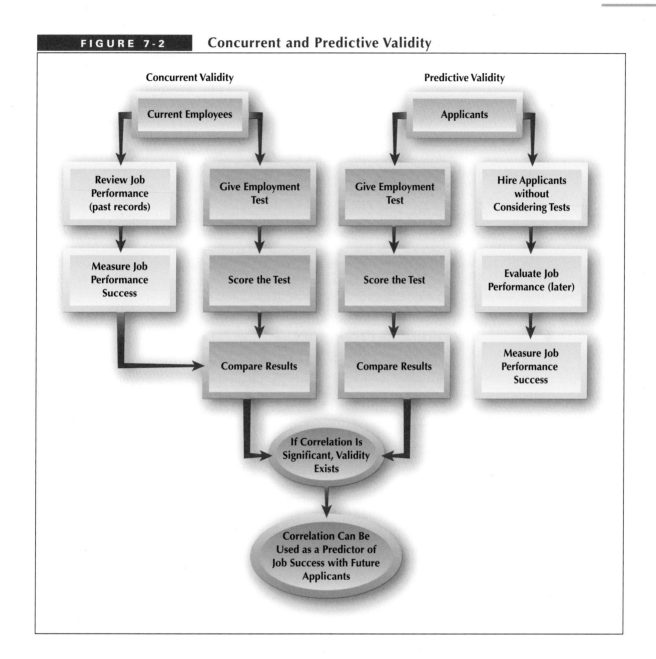

their performance ratings on such measures as their scores on performance appraisals.

A disadvantage of the concurrent validity approach is that employees who have not performed satisfactorily at work are probably no longer with the firm and therefore cannot be tested. Also, extremely good employees may have been promoted or may have left the company for better work situations. Any learning on the job also might confound test scores.

Another method for establishing criterion-related validity is predictive validity. To calculate **predictive validity**, test results of applicants are compared with their subsequent job performance (see Figure 7-2). Job success is measured by assessing factors such as absenteeism, accidents, errors, and performance appraisal ratings. If the employees who had one year of experience at the time of hire demonstrate better performance than those without such

Predictive validity
Measured when test results of applicants are compared with subsequent job performance.

experience, then the experience requirement can be considered a valid predictor of job performance. In addition, individual experience may be utilized as an important "selection criterion" when making future staffing decisions.

The Equal Employment Opportunity Commission (EEOC) has favored predictive validity because it includes the full range of performance and test scores. However, establishing predictive validity can be challenging for managers because a large sample of individuals is needed (usually at least 30) and a significant amount of time must transpire (perhaps one year) to facilitate the analysis. Because of these limitations, other types of validity calculations tend to be more popular.

Reliability Reliability of a predictor or "test" is the extent to which it repeatedly produces the same results over time. For example, if a person took a test in December and scored 75, and then took the same test again in March and scored 76, the exam is probably a reliable instrument. Consequently, reliability involves the consistency of predictors used in selection procedures. A predictor that is not reliable is of no value in selection.

Combining Predictors

If an employer chooses to use only one predictor, such as a pencil-and-paper test, to select the individuals to be hired, the decision becomes straightforward. If the test is valid and encompasses a major dimension of a job, and an applicant does well on the test, then that person should be given a job offer. When an employer uses predictors such as "three years of experience," "possesses a college degree," and "acceptable aptitude test score," job applicants are evaluated on all of these requirements and the multiple predictors must be combined in some way. Two approaches for combining predictors are:

- *Multiple hurdles:* A minimum cutoff is set on each predictor, and each minimum level must be "passed." For example, in order to be hired, a candidate for a sales representative job must achieve a minimum education level, a certain score on a sales aptitude test, and a minimum score on a structured interview.
- *Compensatory approach:* Scores from individual predictors are added and combined into an overall score, thereby allowing a higher score on one predictor to offset, or compensate for, a lower score on another. The combined index takes into consideration performance on all predictors. For example, when admitting students into graduate business programs, a higher overall score on an admissions test might offset a lower undergraduate grade point average.

Selection Responsibilities

Selection is a key responsibility for all managers and supervisors in a company. However, organizations vary in how they allocate selection responsibilities between HR specialists and operating managers. The typical selection responsibilities are shown in Figure 7-3. The need to meet EEO requirements and the inherent strategic implications of the staffing function have caused many companies to place greater emphasis on hiring procedures and techniques and to centralize selection in the HR department. In other companies, each department (or its management team) screens and hires its own personnel. Managers, especially those working in smaller firms, often select their own employees

FIGURE 7-3   **Typical Division of HR Responsibilities: Selection**

HR UNIT	MANAGERS
• Provides initial reception for applicants • Conducts initial screening interview • Administers appropriate employment tests • Obtains background and reference information and sets up a physical examination, if used • Refers top candidates to managers for final selection • Evaluates success of selection process	• Requisition employees with specific qualifications to fill jobs • Participate in selection process as appropriate • Interview final candidates • Make final selection decision, subject to advice of HR specialist • Provide follow-up information on the suitability of selected individuals

because these individuals directly impact their work areas. But the validity and effectiveness of this approach may be questionable because of lack of training in selection among operating managers.

Another approach has HR professionals initially screening the job candidates, and the managers or supervisors making the final selection decisions from the qualified applicant pool. Generally, the higher the positions being filled, the greater the likelihood that the ultimate hiring decisions will be made by operating managers rather than HR professionals.

Selection responsibilities are affected by the existence of a central employment office, which is often housed within a human resources department. In smaller organizations, especially in those with fewer than 100 employees, a full-time employment specialist or group is impractical. But for larger firms, centralizing activities in an employment office might be appropriate.

The employment function in any organization may be concerned with some or all of the following activities: (1) receiving applications, (2) interviewing the applicants, (3) administering tests to applicants, (4) conducting background investigations, (5) arranging for physical examinations, (6) placing and assigning new employees, (7) coordinating follow-up of these employees, (8) conducting exit interviews with departing employees, and (9) maintaining appropriate records and reports.

THE SELECTION PROCESS

Most organizations take a series of consistent steps to process and select applicants for jobs. Company size, job characteristics, the number of people needed, the use of electronic technology, and other factors cause variations on the basic process. Selection can take place in a day or over a much longer period of time, and certain phases of the process may be omitted or the order changed, depending on the employer. If the applicant is processed in one day, the employer usually checks references after selection. Figure 7-4 shows steps in a typical selection process.

FIGURE 7-4   Selection Process Flowchart

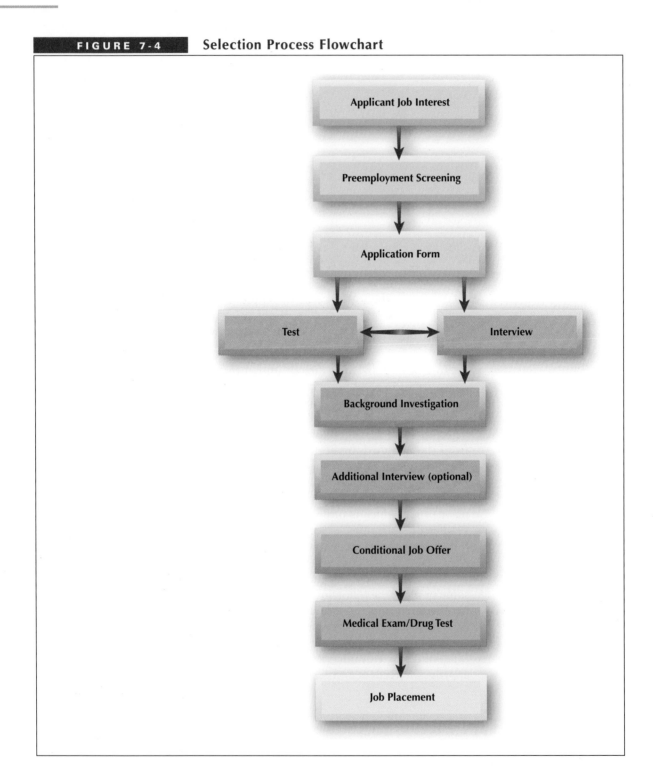

Applicant Job Interest

Individuals wanting employment can indicate interest in a number of ways. Traditionally, individuals have submitted résumés by mail or fax, or applied in person at an employer's location. But with the growth in Internet recruiting, many individuals complete applications online or submit résumés electronically.

Regardless of how individuals express interest in employment, the selection process has an important public relations dimension. Discriminatory hiring practices, impolite interviewers, unnecessarily long waits, unreturned telephone inquiries, inappropriate testing procedures, and lack of follow-up responses can produce unfavorable impressions of an employer. Job applicants' perceptions of the organization will be influenced by how they are treated.

Realistic Job Previews Many individuals know little about companies before applying for employment. Consequently, when deciding whether to accept a job, they pay particularly close attention to the information received during the selection process, including compensation data, work characteristics, job location, and promotion opportunities. Unfortunately, some employers make jobs appear better than they really are. **Realistic job previews** provide potential employees with an accurate introduction to a job so that they can better evaluate the employment situation. Indeed, a realistic job preview can directly enhance individual training and clarify a job role. Also, in global assignments, the use of realistic job previews increases individual confidence and improves decision making about an expatriate position.

A company should consider several strategies when developing a recruiting brand and conveying it to potential employees via realistic job previews. The brand of the company should establish in the minds of recruits the company's overall purpose for being in business, and it should honestly portray the jobs that are performed by individuals already employed in the firm. A project director of a recruiting firm suggests that a firm should evaluate its own strengths and develop a list of employment benefits that would make the company attractive to potential employees. These points may include building human capital, good compensation, and ethics and social responsibility. At the same time, a company needs to convey the less attractive aspects of work, such as difficult work schedules or extensive travel. However, any negative job attributes can be outweighed by the positive factors already covered.

Truth-in-Hiring Lawsuits Recruiters may exaggerate promotional opportunities, pay, or even the company's financial position in an attempt to hire a candidate. However, a candidate who leaves a good job to accept a position and later discovers such exaggerations may choose to sue the company for misrepresenting the job. In some cases, recruiters feel such pressure to "sell" the company that they "oversell" it. The best way to avoid truth-in-hiring lawsuits is to use the realistic job preview correctly.[11]

Preemployment Screening

Many employers conduct preemployment screening to determine if applicants meet the minimum qualifications for open jobs before they have the applicants fill out an application.

Electronic Assessment Screening The use of electronic preemployment screening or assessment has grown. Much of this screening utilizes computer software to review the many résumés and application forms received during the recruiting and selection process. Large companies often use different types of software to receive, evaluate, and track the applications of many potential employees.

When a job posting generates 1,000 or more applications, which is not unusual with large companies or in difficult economic times, responding to each would be a full-time job. Electronic screening can speed up the process.

Realistic job preview
Process through which a job applicant receives an accurate picture of a job.

Cheating on Electronic Assessments

Many retailers make applicants take an assessment online before interviewing them. If they do not do well on this "test," they will not be interviewed. Such tests also are given at in-store kiosks so hiring managers can interview high-scoring persons before they leave the store, but 90% of the time these tests are done online. These assessment tests ask applicants to agree or disagree with statements such as "You have to give up on some things that you start" or "Any trouble you have is your own fault."

The tests cut the amount of time store managers spend interviewing and can improve the levels of measured results in areas such as sales performance, turnover, safety, and so on; but the tests also create a culture of cheating and raise questions for some applicants about their "fairness." Anton Smith took such a test when he applied for hourly work at a sneaker store, but before taking it, he had a friend do a little digging online to find an unauthorized answer key. Then when he took the test, Anton had a good idea how to answer the 130 statements in it. He was hired, but he does not think the test was useful.

The test Smith took is called UNICRV, which is used by about 16% of major retailers. The company that designed it believes the incidence of cheating is low and does not affect the benefits to retailers of using it. CVS Caremark is pleased with the test, according to its head of HR, who says, "I think our field organization is happy with the quality of the candidate."

The more critical the test is to getting a job, the more applicants will try to "game" it. They may take it several times, compare notes with other test takers, consult an online cheat sheet, or have a friend take it for them. Mark Scott took the UNICRV test when applying at Circuit City and did not get hired. A friend told him the test disqualified him. He applied to another chain that uses the test, but this time he had a friend who coached him because the friend had taken and passed the test many times. Scott was hired immediately. He observed that the test process "weeds out people who are honest and selects those who lie." Opportunities to cheat with electronic assessments exist, and people certainly will find them.[12]

This may take several forms: disqualification questions; screening questions to get at KSAs and experience; valid assessment tests; and background, drug, and financial screening. Some of the assessments might include auditions for the job that are based on simulations of specific job-related tasks. For example, in a call center, candidates are given virtual customers with service problems, and branch manager candidates demonstrate their ability to foster relationships with virtual clients and to make quick personnel decisions with virtual employees.[13]

A good strategy is to use simple electronic assessment early to cut down the number of applicants before requiring applications or interviews. That leaves a much more qualified list of remaining applicants with which to work.[14] However, such assessments have a down side as well, as shown in the HR Perspective.

Application Forms

Some employers do not use preemployment screening prior to having applicants fill out an application form. Instead, they have every interested individual complete an application first. These completed application forms then become the basis for prescreening information. But collecting, storing, and tracking these forms can create significant work for HR staff members.

Application forms, which are used universally, can take on different formats. Properly prepared, the application form serves four purposes:

1. It is a record of the applicant's desire to obtain a position.
2. It provides the interviewer with a profile of the applicant that can be used during the interview.
3. It is a basic employee record for applicants who are hired.
4. It can be used for research on the effectiveness of the selection process.

Many employers use only one application form for all jobs, but others use several different forms depending on the position. For example, a hotel might use one form for management and supervisory staff and another for line employees.

Application Disclaimers Application forms should contain disclaimers and notices so that appropriate legal protections are clearly stated. These recommended disclosures include:

- *Employment-at-will:* Indicates the right of the employer or the applicant to terminate employment at any time with or without notice or cause (where applicable by state law)
- *Reference contacts:* Requests permission to contact previous employers listed by the applicant on the application form or résumé
- *Employment testing:* Notifies applicants of required drug tests, pencil-and-paper tests, physical exams, or electronic or other tests that will be used in the employment decision
- *Application time limit:* Indicates how long application forms are active (typically 6 months), and that persons must reapply or reactivate their applications after that period
- *Information falsification:* Conveys to an applicant that falsification of application information can be grounds for serious reprimand or termination

EEO Considerations and Application Forms An organization should retain all applications and hiring-related documents and records for 3 years. Guidelines from the EEOC and court decisions require that the data requested on application forms must be job related. Though frequently found on application forms, questions that ask for the following information are illegal. (See Appendix D for review.)

- Marital status
- Height/weight
- Number and ages of dependents
- Information on spouse
- Date of high school graduation
- Contact in case of emergency

Most of the litigation surrounding application forms has involved questions regarding the gender and age of a potential employee, so special consideration should be dedicated to removing any items that relate to these personal characteristics. Concerns about inappropriate questions stem from their potential to elicit information that should not be used in hiring decisions. Figure 7-5 shows a sample application form containing questions that generally are legal.

FIGURE 7-5   **Sample Application Form**

Application for Employment
An Equal Opportunity Employer*

Today's Date _____

PERSONAL INFORMATION   Please Print or Type

Name (Last) (First) (Full middle name)	Social Security number
Current address City State Zip code	Phone number ( )
What position are you applying for? Date available for employment?	E-mail address

Are you willing to relocate? ☐ Yes ☐ No	Are you willing to travel if required? ☐ Yes ☐ No	Any restrictions on hours, weekends, or overtime? If yes, explain.

Have you ever been employed by this Company or any of its subsidiaries before? ☐ Yes ☐ No	Indicate location and dates

Can you, after employment, submit verification of your legal right to work in the United States? ☐ Yes ☐ No	Have you ever been convicted of a felony? ☐ Yes ☐ No	*Convictions will not automatically disqualify job candidates. The seriousness of the crime and the date of conviction will be considered.*

PERFORMANCE OF JOB FUNCTIONS

Are you able to perform all the functions of the job for which you are applying, with or without accommodation?

☐ Yes, without accommodation   ☐ Yes, with accommodation   ☐ No

If you indicated you can perform all the functions with an accommodation, please explain how you would perform the tasks and with what accommodation.

EDUCATION

School level	School name and address	No. of years attended	Did you graduate?	Course of study
High school				
Vo-tech, business, or trade school				
College				
Graduate school				

PERSONAL DRIVING RECORD

This section is to be completed ONLY if the operation of a motor vehicle will be required in the course of the applicant's employment.

How long have you been a licensed driver?	Driver's license number	Expiration date	Issuing State

List any other state(s) in which you have had a driver's license(s) in the past:

Within the past five years, have you had a vehicle accident? ☐ Yes ☐ No	Been convicted of reckless or drunken driving? If yes, give dates: ☐ Yes ☐ No	Been cited for moving violations? If yes, give dates: ☐ Yes ☐ No

Has your driver's license ever been revoked or suspended? If yes, explain: ☐ Yes ☐ No	Is your driver's license restricted? If yes, explain: ☐ Yes ☐ No

*We are an Equal Opportunity Employer. We do not discriminate on the basis of race, religion, color, gender, age, national origin, or disability.

Résumés as Applications Applicants commonly provide background information through résumés. When the situation arises, EEO standards require that an employer treats a résumé as an application form. As such, if an applicant's résumé voluntarily furnishes some information that cannot be legally obtained, the employer should not use that information during the selection process. Some employers require those who submit résumés to complete an application form as well.

Regardless of how the background information is collected, companies should be dutiful about checking the truthfulness of the information presented on résumés and application forms. Various accounts suggest that a noteworthy percentage of applicants knowingly distort their past work experiences. For example, former RadioShack CEO David Edmondson resigned after it was determined that he had embellished his educational background.[15]

Immigration Verification

Businesses are required to review and record identity documents, such as Social Security cards, passports, and visas, and to determine if they appear to be genuine. It is illegal to knowingly hire employees who are not in the country legally. The consequences for offending businesses are high; penalties range from $375 to $16,000 per incident and 6 months in prison. If HR personnel know they are working with fraudulent documents, corporate liability exists, and seizure of assets and criminal liability for top management can occur.

Immigration and Customs Enforcement (ICE) can audit the records of a business to make certain there has been compliance with employment eligibility laws and rules. Such audits may come from employer filings of government labor documents, disgruntled employees, identity theft complaints, or suspicious patterns of activity.[16]

Employers must use the revised form I-9 for each employee hired after 1986 and must determine within 72 hours whether an applicant is a U.S. citizen, registered alien, or illegal alien. A government program called E-Verify is run by the Department of Homeland Security to help with this process. The use of E-Verify is mandatory for government contractors or subcontractors.[17]

An employer should have a policy to comply with immigration requirements and to avoid knowingly hiring or retaining illegal workers. I-9s should be completed, updated, and audited.

SELECTION TESTING

Many different kinds of tests can be used to help select qualified employees. Literacy tests, skill-based tests, personality tests, and honesty tests are used to assess various individual factors that are important for the work to be performed. These useful employment tests allow companies to predict which applicants will be the most successful before being hired.

However, selection tests must be evaluated extensively before being utilized as a recruiting tool. The development of the test items should be linked to a thorough job analysis. Also, initial testing of the items should include an evaluation by knowledge experts, and statistical and validity assessments of the items should be conducted. Furthermore, adequate security of the testing instruments should be coordinated, and the monetary value of these tests to the firm should be determined. For example, Gerber Products Company was found to be using preemployment selection tests for entry-level positions that did not have sufficient evidence of validity. The tests were negatively impacting minority applicants. Gerber paid 1,912 minority and female applicants $900,000 in back pay and interest.[18]

Ability Tests

Tests that assess an individual's ability to perform in a specific manner are grouped as ability tests. These are sometimes further differentiated into *aptitude tests* and *achievement tests*. **Cognitive ability tests** measure an individual's thinking, memory, reasoning, verbal, and mathematical abilities. Tests such as these can be used to determine applicants' basic knowledge of terminology and concepts, word fluency, spatial orientation, comprehension and retention span, general and mental ability, and conceptual reasoning. The Wonderlic Personnel Test and the General Aptitude Test Battery (GATB) are two widely used tests of this type. Managers need to ensure that these tests assess cognitive abilities that are job related.[19]

Physical ability tests measure an individual's abilities such as strength, endurance, and muscular movement. At an electric utility, line workers regularly must lift and carry equipment, climb ladders, and perform other physical tasks; therefore, testing of applicants' mobility, strength, and other physical attributes is job related. Some physical ability tests measure such areas as range of motion, strength and posture, and cardiovascular fitness. As noted later, care should be taken to limit physical ability testing until after a conditional job offer is made, in order to avoid violating the provisions of the Americans with Disabilities Act (ADA).

Different skill-based tests can be used, including **psychomotor tests**, which measure a person's dexterity, hand–eye coordination, arm–hand steadiness, and other factors. Tests such as the MacQuarie Test for Mechanical Ability can measure manual dexterity for assembly-line workers and others using psychomotor skills regularly.

Many organizations use situational tests, or **work sample tests**, which require an applicant to perform a simulated task that is a specified part of the target job. Requiring an applicant for an administrative assistant's job to type a business letter as quickly as possible would be one such test. An "in-basket" test is a work sample test in which a job candidate is asked to respond to memos in a hypothetical in-basket that are typical of the problems experienced in that job. Once again, these tests should assess criteria that are embedded in the job that is to be staffed.

Situational judgment tests are designed to measure a person's judgment in work settings. The candidate is given a situation and a list of possible solutions to the problem. The candidate then has to make judgments about how to deal with the situation. Situational judgment tests are a form of job simulation.

Assessment Centers An assessment center is not a place but an assessment composed of a series of evaluative exercises and tests used for selection and development. Most often used in the selection process when filling managerial openings, assessment centers consist of multiple exercises and are evaluated by multiple raters. In one assessment center, candidates go through a comprehensive interview, a pencil-and-paper test, individual and group simulations, and work exercises. Individual performance is then evaluated by a panel of trained raters.

It is crucial that the tests and exercises in an assessment center reflect the content of the job for which individuals are being screened, and the types

Margin glossary

Cognitive ability tests Tests that measure an individual's thinking, memory, reasoning, verbal, and mathematical abilities.

Physical ability tests Tests that measure an individual's abilities such as strength, endurance, and muscular movement.

Psychomotor tests Tests that measure dexterity, hand–eye coordination, arm–hand steadiness, and other factors.

Work sample tests Tests that require an applicant to perform a simulated task that is a specified part of the target job.

Situational judgment tests Tests that measure a person's judgment in work settings.

of problems faced on that job. For example, a technology communications organization used a series of assessment centers to hire employees who would interact with clients. The company found that these centers improved the selection process and also provided new employees with a good road map for individual development.

Personality Tests

Personality is a unique blend of individual characteristics that can affect how people interact with their work environment. Many organizations use various personality tests that assess the degree to which candidates' attributes match specific job criteria. For instance, a sporting goods chain offers job applicants a Web-based test. The test evaluates their personal tendencies, and test scores are used to categorize individuals for the hiring decision. Many types of personality tests are available, including the Minnesota Multiphasic Personality Inventory (MMPI) and the Myers-Briggs test.

Although many different personality characteristics exist, some experts believe that there is a relatively small number of underlying *major* traits. The most widely accepted approach to studying these underlying personality traits (although not the only one) is the "Big Five" personality framework. The Big Five traits are generally considered to be useful predictors of various types of job performance in different occupations. The factors are shown in Figure 7-6.

| FIGURE 7-6 | **Big Five Personality Characteristics** |

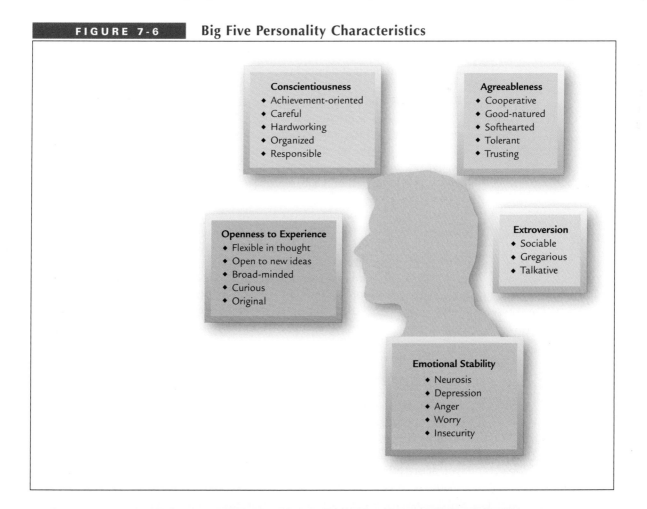

Several of the Big Five traits are related to dimensions such as burnout and accident involvement in both work and nonwork contexts.

Faking Personality Tests "Faking" is a major concern for employers using personality tests. Many test publishers admit that test profiles can be falsified, and they try to reduce faking by including questions that can be used to compute a social desirability or "lie" score. Researchers also favor the use of "corrections" based on components of the test to account for faking—a preference that also constitutes a strong argument for professional scoring of personality tests.[20] Another possibility is use of a "fake warning," which instructs applicants that faking can be detected and can result in a negative hiring impression.

Honesty/Integrity Tests

Companies are utilizing different tests to assess the honesty and integrity of applicants and employees. Employers use these tests as a screening mechanism to prevent the hiring of unethical employees, to reduce the frequency of lying and theft on the job, and to communicate to applicants and employees alike that dishonesty will not be tolerated. Honesty/integrity tests can be valid as broad screening devices for organizations if used properly. About 28% of employers use honesty/integrity testing.[21]

However, these instruments have limitations. For instance, socially desirable responding is a key concern; some questions can be considered overly invasive, insulting, and not job related; sometimes "false positives" are generated (or an honest person is scored as "dishonest"); and test scores might be affected by individual demographic factors such as gender and race.

Polygraphs The polygraph, more generally and incorrectly referred to as the "lie detector," is a mechanical device that measures a person's galvanic skin response, heart rate, and breathing rate. The theory behind the polygraph is that if a person answers a question incorrectly, the body's physiological responses will "reveal" the falsification through the recording mechanisms of the polygraph. As a result of concerns about polygraph validity, Congress passed the Employee Polygraph Protection Act, which prohibits the use of polygraphs for preemployment screening purposes by most employers. Federal, state, and local government agencies are exempt from the act. Also exempted are certain private-sector employers such as security companies and pharmaceutical companies. The act does allow employers to use polygraphs as part of internal investigations of thefts or losses. But in those situations, the polygraph test should be taken voluntarily, and the employee should be allowed to end the test at any time.

Controversies in Selection Testing

Two areas in selection testing generate controversies and disagreements. One is the appropriateness of general mental ability testing, and the other is the validity of personality testing for selection.

General mental ability testing is well established as a valid selection tool for many jobs, but since some minority groups tend to score lower on such exams, there is considerable controversy over whether such tests *ought* to be used.[22] When these tests are used, the case for business necessity must be made, and the instrument used should be validated for the organization using it.

Personality testing for selection flourished during the 1950s. More than 60% of large companies at one time used it for selection.[23] Sears, Standard Oil, and Procter and Gamble used such testing extensively. But in the 1960s researchers concluded that personality is not a good tool for selection, and the use of these tests dropped drastically. In the 1990s, interest in research on personality as a selection tool resurfaced and vendors began selling personality-oriented selection tests. But a seminal research article appearing in *Personnel Psychology* concluded that personality explains so little about actual job outcomes that we should think very carefully about using it *at all* for employment decisions.[24] The study of personality continues in psychology, and as it evolves, the role of personality in selection will undoubtedly continue to be controversial.[25]

SELECTION INTERVIEWING

Selection interviewing of job applicants is done both to obtain additional information and to clarify information gathered throughout the selection process. Interviews are commonly conducted at two levels: first, as an initial screening interview to determine if the person has met minimum qualifications, and then later, as an in-depth interview with HR staff members and/or operating managers to determine if the person will fit into the designated work area. Before the in-depth interview, information from all available sources is pooled so that the interviewers can reconcile conflicting information that may have emerged from tests, application forms, and references.

Interviewing for selection is imperfect and should be focused on gathering valid information that has not been gained in other ways.[26] Because selection interviewing is imperfect, the focus must be on techniques that minimize errors and provide the best information.[27]

Some companies have excessive interview time requirements. For example, one company requires applicants to bring their lunch and spend hours on simulated work tasks, several with tight deadlines.[28] However, a court case in California held that temporary employees were owed overtime pay for time spent in job placement interviews.[29] Although this case dealt with staffing firm employees, the message is that there may be a limit on how long the employment interviewing process can reasonably go on.

Inter-Rater Reliability and Face Validity

Interviews must be reliable and allow interviewers, despite their limitations, to pick the same applicant capabilities again and again. High *intra*-rater reliability (within the same interviewer) can be demonstrated, but only moderate-to-low *inter*-rater reliability (across different interviewers) is generally shown. Inter-rater reliability becomes important when each of several interviewers is selecting employees from a pool of applicants, or if the employer uses team or panel interviews with multiple interviewers.

Employers prefer to use interviews over other selection activities because they have high "face validity" (i.e., interviews make sense to employers). It is often assumed that if someone interviews well and the information obtained in

| FIGURE 7-7 | Validity and Structure in Selection Interviews |

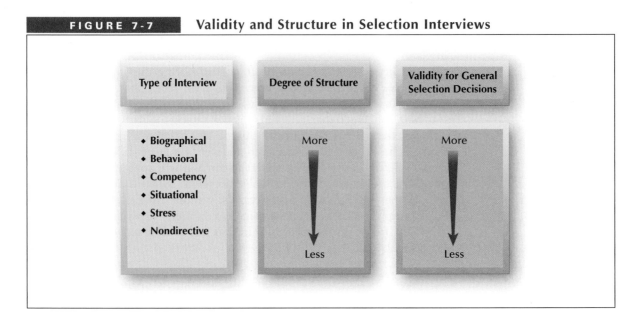

<table>
<tr><td>Type of Interview</td><td>Degree of Structure</td><td>Validity for General Selection Decisions</td></tr>
</table>

Type of Interview
- Biographical
- Behavioral
- Competency
- Situational
- Stress
- Nondirective

Degree of Structure: More → Less

Validity for General Selection Decisions: More → Less

the interview is useful, then the individual will be a good hire.[30] However, an unstructured interview does not always provide much actual validity, causing a growth in the popularity of structured interviews.

As Figure 7-7 shows, various types of selection interviews are used. They range from structured to unstructured, and they vary in terms of appropriateness for selection.

Structured Interviews

A **structured interview** uses a set of standardized questions asked of all applicants so that comparisons can be made more easily. This type of interview allows an interviewer to prepare job-related questions in advance and then complete a standardized interviewee evaluation form that provides documentation indicating why one applicant was selected over another.[31]

The structured interview is useful in the initial screening process because many applicants can be effectively evaluated and compared. However, the structured interview does not have to be rigid. The predetermined questions should be asked in a logical manner but should not be read word for word. The applicants should be allowed adequate opportunity to explain their answers, and interviewers should probe with additional questions until they fully understand the responses. This process can make the structured interview more reliable and valid than other interview approaches.

Structured interviews—in any of several forms, including biographical, behavioral, competency, and situational—are useful when making selection decisions. The structured format ensures that a given interviewer has similar information on each candidate. It also ensures that when several interviewers ask the same questions of applicants, there is greater consistency in the subsequent evaluation of those candidates. In fact, it has been recommended that structured interviews be utilized in selection efforts for federal jobs because individual work performance can be better forecasted. However, companies might have to provide additional guidance to enhance interviewers' implementation of this structure.[32]

Biographical Interview A *biographical interview* focuses on a chronological assessment of the candidate's past experiences. This type of interview is

Structured interview
Interview that uses a set of standardized questions asked of all applicants.

widely used and is often combined with other interview techniques. Overall, the process provides a sketch of past experiences.

Behavioral Interview In the **behavioral interview** technique, applicants are asked to describe how they have performed a certain task or handled a problem in the past, which may predict future actions and show how applicants are best suited for current jobs. A recent study showed that "past behavior" interviews are better at identifying achievement at work than are situational interviews, because they focus on what applicants have actually done in real situations rather than on what they think they might do in hypothetical situations.[33] An example of a behavioral interview line of questioning might be: "Tell me about a time when you initiated a project. What was the situation? What did you do? What were the results?"

Competency Interview The *competency interview* is similar to the behavioral interview except the questions are designed to provide the interviewer with something against which to measure the applicant's response. A *competency profile* for the position is often utilized, which includes a list of competencies necessary to do that particular job. Using competencies as a benchmark to predict job candidate success is useful because interviewers can identify the factors needed in specific jobs. However, these interviews take time and sometimes benefit articulate or impression management-oriented people. Interviewers must be trained in spotting strong answers for the competencies in question.[34]

Situational Interview The **situational interview** contains questions about how applicants might handle specific job situations. Interview questions and possible responses are based on job analysis and checked by job experts to ensure content validity. The interviewer typically codes the suitability of the answer, assigns point values, and adds up the total number of points each interviewee has received. A variation is termed the *case study interview*, which requires a job candidate to diagnose and correct organizational challenges during the interview. Situational interviews assess what the interviewee would consider to be the best option, not necessarily what they did in a similar situation.[35]

Less-Structured Interviews

Some interviews are done unplanned and are not structured at all. Such interviewing techniques may be appropriate for fact finding, or for counseling interviews. However, they are not best for selection interviewing. These interviews may be conducted by operating managers or supervisors who have had little interview training. An *unstructured interview* occurs when the interviewer improvises by asking questions that are not predetermined. A *semistructured interview* is a guided conversation in which broad questions are asked and new questions arise as a result of the discussion. For example: What would you do differently if you could start over again?

A **nondirective interview** uses questions that are developed from the answers to previous questions. The interviewer asks general questions designed to prompt applicants to describe themselves. The interviewer then uses applicants' responses to shape the next question. With a nondirective interview, as with any less-structured interview, difficulties for selection decisions include keeping the conversation job related and obtaining comparable data on various applicants. Many nondirective interviews are only partly organized; as a result, a combination of general and specific questions is asked in no set order, and different questions are asked of different applicants for the

Behavioral interview
Interview in which applicants give specific examples of how they have performed a certain task or handled a problem in the past.

Situational interview
Structured interview that contains questions about how applicants might handle specific job situations.

Nondirective interview
Interview that uses questions developed from the answers to previous questions.

same job. Comparing and ranking candidates is thus more open to subjective judgments and legal challenges, so they are best used for selection sparingly, if at all.

Stress Interview A **stress interview** is designed to create anxiety and put pressure on applicants to see how they respond. In a stress interview, the interviewer assumes an extremely aggressive and insulting posture. Firms using this approach often justify doing so because employees will encounter high degrees of job stress. For example, it might be appropriate in selecting FBI agents or people for high-stress, high-pressure customer complaint positions, but it is not appropriate for most positions. The stress interview can be a high-risk approach for an employer because an applicant is probably already anxious, and the stress interview can easily generate a poor image of the interviewer and the employer. Consequently, an applicant the organization wishes to hire might turn down the job offer.

Who Conducts Interviews?

Job interviews can be conducted by an individual, by several individuals sequentially, or by panels or teams. For some jobs, such as entry-level jobs requiring lesser skills, applicants might be interviewed solely by a human resource professional. For other jobs, employers screen applicants by using multiple interviews, beginning with a human resource professional and followed by the appropriate supervisors and managers. Then a selection decision is made collectively. Managers need to ensure that multiple interviews are not redundant.

Other interview formats are also utilized. In a **panel interview**, several interviewers meet with the candidate at the same time so that the same responses are heard. Panel interviews may be combined with individual interviews. However, without proper planning, an unstructured interview can result, and applicants are frequently uncomfortable with the group interview format. In a **team interview**, applicants are interviewed by the team members with whom they will work. This approach can improve team success, but training is required to educate team members about the selection process, and consensus over the hiring decision should be established.[36]

Effective Interviewing

Many people think that the ability to interview is an innate talent, but this contention is difficult to support. Just being personable and liking to talk is no guarantee that someone will be an effective interviewer. Figure 7-8 lists questions commonly used in selection interviews.

Interviewing skills are developed through training. A number of suggestions for making interviewing more effective are:

- *Plan the interview.* Interviewers should review all information before the interview, and then identify specific areas for questioning. Preparation is critical because many interviewers have not done their research.[37]
- *Control the interview.* This includes knowing in advance what information must be collected, systematically collecting it during the interview, and stopping when that information has been collected. An interviewer should not monopolize the conversation.
- *Use effective questioning techniques.* Utilize questions that will produce full and complete answers that can be evaluated based on job relatedness.

Stress interview Interview designed to create anxiety and put pressure on applicants to see how they respond.

Panel interview Interview in which several interviewers meet with candidate at the same time.

Team interview Interview in which applicants are interviewed by the team members with whom they will work.

| **FIGURE 7-8** | **Questions Commonly Asked in Selection Interviews** |

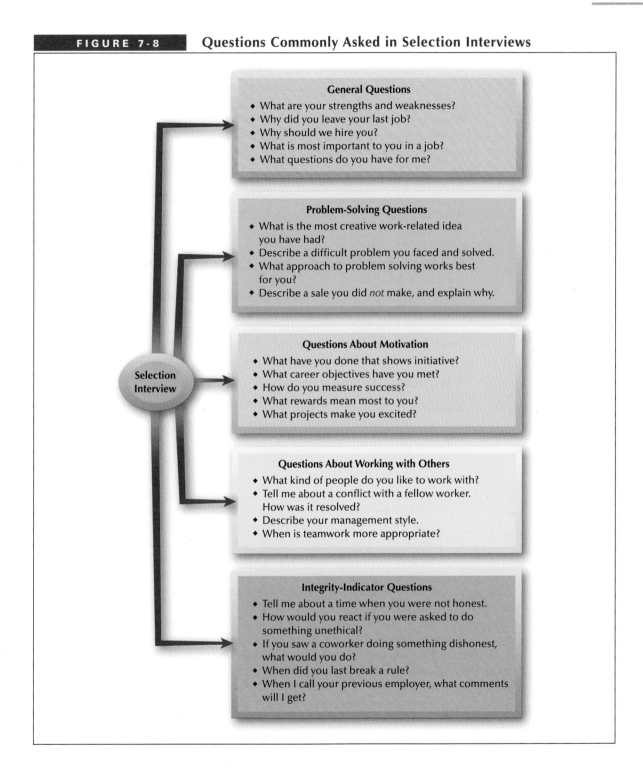

General Questions
- What are your strengths and weaknesses?
- Why did you leave your last job?
- Why should we hire you?
- What is most important to you in a job?
- What questions do you have for me?

Problem-Solving Questions
- What is the most creative work-related idea you have had?
- Describe a difficult problem you faced and solved.
- What approach to problem solving works best for you?
- Describe a sale you did *not* make, and explain why.

Questions About Motivation
- What have you done that shows initiative?
- What career objectives have you met?
- How do you measure success?
- What rewards mean most to you?
- What projects make you excited?

Questions About Working with Others
- What kind of people do you like to work with?
- Tell me about a conflict with a fellow worker. How was it resolved?
- Describe your management style.
- When is teamwork more appropriate?

Integrity-Indicator Questions
- Tell me about a time when you were not honest.
- How would you react if you were asked to do something unethical?
- If you saw a coworker doing something dishonest, what would you do?
- When did you last break a rule?
- When I call your previous employer, what comments will I get?

Selection Interview

Questions to Avoid The following are kinds of questions that should be avoided in selection interviews:

- *Yes/no questions:* Unless verifying specific information, the interviewer should avoid questions that can be answered "yes" or "no." For example, "Did you have good attendance on your last job?" will probably be answered simply "yes."

- *Obvious questions:* An obvious question is one for which the interviewer already has the answer and the applicant knows it.
- *Questions that rarely produce a true answer:* Avoid questions that prompt a less-than-honest response. An example is "How did you get along with your coworkers?" The likely answer is "Just fine."
- *Leading questions:* A leading question is one to which the answer is obvious from the way the question is asked. For example, "How do you like working with other people?" suggests the answer "I like it."
- *Illegal questions:* Questions that involve information such as race, age, gender, national origin, marital status, and number of children are illegal. They are just as inappropriate in the interview as on the application form.
- *Questions that are not job related:* All questions should be directly job related.

Listening Responses to Avoid Effective interviewers avoid listening responses such as nodding, pausing, making casual remarks, echoing, and mirroring. The applicant might try to please the interviewers by examining the feedback provided. However, giving no response to an applicant's answers may imply boredom or inattention. Therefore, interviewers should use friendly but neutral comments when acknowledging the applicant's comments.

Problems in the Interview

Operating managers and supervisors are more likely than HR personnel to use poor interviewing techniques because they do not interview often or lack training. Several problems include:

- *Snap judgments:* Some interviewers decide whether an applicant is suitable within the first two to four minutes of the interview, and spend the rest of the time looking for evidence to support their judgment.
- *Negative emphasis:* When evaluating suitability, unfavorable information about an applicant is often emphasized more than favorable information.
- *Halo effect:* The *halo effect* occurs when an interviewer allows a positive characteristic, such as agreeableness, to overshadow other evidence. The phrase *devil's horns* describes the reverse of the halo effect; this occurs when a negative characteristic, such as inappropriate dress, overshadows other traits.
- *Biases and stereotyping:* "Similarity" bias occurs when interviewers favor or select people that they believe to be like themselves based on a variety of personal factors. Interviewers also should avoid any personal tendencies to stereotype individuals because of demographic characteristics and differences. For instance, age disparities may be a concern as younger executives are interviewing more senior personnel. Additionally, applicants' ethnic names and accents can negatively impact personal evaluations, and older workers are sometimes less likely to get interviewed and hired than are younger applicants.[38]
- *Cultural noise:* Interviewers must learn to recognize and handle cultural noise, which stems from what applicants believe is socially acceptable rather than what is factual.

Other problems that can occur in the interview are demonstrated in the HR Perspective.

Common Interview Mistakes

Bad hiring based on bad interviewing is expensive. It causes poor performance and higher turnover, and results in employing people who are not engaged. Both employers and employees agree that they made the correct hiring decision about *half* of the time. The other half of the decisions were wrong—they were bad choices. At least some errors are due to silly or useless questions that interviewers seem to favor when they have not been properly trained. For example:

- If you were a tree (or a fruit, or an animal, or whatever), what kind would you be?
- Do you like knives?
- How do you make a peanut butter sandwich?
- What is your favorite song?
- What would you do if I gave you an elephant?
- Do you have a girlfriend for me?

There is absolutely no evidence that these and similar questions will help an interviewer pick the best person for the job.

Recent surveys show that illegal questions, as well as stupid ones, are a problem. For example, 32% of interviewers did not know that asking a candidate's age is illegal, 40% did not know it is illegal to ask about marital status, and 44% did not know it is illegal to ask about plans to have children.

Good interviewer behavior can create positive feelings toward the job and the organization. Interviewers who are warm, know the job and company, and have a sense of humor are most successful. With that in mind, how well do these comments from interviewees reflect on their interviewers' behaviors?

- The interviewers were not knowledgeable.
- The interviewer was unenthusiastic and unfriendly.
- She was texting while interviewing.
- The interviewers were arrogant and vague.
- She asked, "Do you like me as a woman?"
- He asked, "What is your natural hair color?"
- He asked, "How strong is your marriage?"
- The interviewer was not smiling.

The interview is the first step in an employment relationship. Questions about trees, songs, or hair color and unfriendly or ignorant remarks from interviewers reduce the chances that the relationship will ever commence.[39]

BACKGROUND INVESTIGATIONS

Failure to check the backgrounds of people who are hired can lead to embarrassment and legal liability. Hiring workers who commit violent acts on the job is one example. While laws vary from state to state, for jobs in certain industries, such as those that provide services to children, vulnerable adults, security, in-home services, and financial services, background checks are mandated in some states. Nationally background checks are required for people with commercial drivers' licenses who drive tractor-trailer rigs and buses interstate.

Negligent Hiring and Retention

Lawyers say that an employer's liability hinges on how well it investigates an applicant's background. Consequently, details provided on the application form should be investigated extensively, and these efforts should be documented.

Negligent hiring occurs when an employer fails to check an employee's background and the employee later injures someone on the job. There is a potential negligent hiring problem when an employer hires an unfit employee, a background check is insufficient, or an employer does not research potential risk factors that would prevent the positive hire decision. Similarly, **negligent retention** occurs when an employer becomes aware that an employee may be unfit for employment but continues to employ the person, and the person injures someone.

Many organizations use outside vendors that specialize in conducting background checks because such outside firms can provide these services much more efficiently and effectively. Background checks have some concern that the information reported might be inaccurate or outdated. For instance, a woman was denied employment by a company because a background report provided by an outside firm contained adverse information. However, after getting the report corrected, she was hired by the company. Consequently, the information provided in criminal record checks should be used judiciously and with caution.

A number of companies are using personal Web pages and the Internet to perform background checks on employees. Many believe that websites provide a more "in-depth" snapshot of a job candidate's individual characteristics, regardless of the information that has been submitted to the company through traditional means with the application form or résumé. Online network sites such as MySpace and Facebook are used to obtain personal information, some of which involves sexual activity, drug use, and other questionable behavior.[40]

Unfortunately, much of the information on personal Web pages appears to be difficult to erase or alter, so some candidates and employees just have to live with less-than-flattering content once it is posted. Also, damaging information can be posted about individuals by anyone on the Internet, further complicating the process of performing fair and legitimate background checks if this information is utilized in job selection.

Background information can be obtained from a number of sources. Some of these sources include past job records, credit history, testing records, educational and certification records, drug tests, Social Security numbers, sex offender lists, motor vehicle records, and military records. Running background checks on every applicant is very expensive. Employers sometimes check only the two or three finalists or the candidate who has received a contingent offer.[41]

The need for background checking can be found in a wide range of positions: pharmacy students, school teachers, janitors, bank tellers, and so on.[42] Consider a car salesman who sexually assaults a young woman while on a test drive. If the salesman failed to tell his employer he was a convicted sex offender, does the employer have the responsibility to do a background check to find out? Probably. Nothing will guarantee that an employee will not commit a violent act at work. But employers can reduce the risk by following a lawful process to screen applicants for signs that a person is not appropriate.[43]

Legal Constraints on Background Investigations

Various federal and state laws protect the rights of individuals whose backgrounds may be investigated during preemployment screening. An employer's most important action when conducting a background investigation is to obtain from the applicant a signed release giving the employer permission to conduct the investigation.

Safeguards are appropriate in background checks because although employee screening has become a big business, it is not always an accurate one.[44]

Negligent hiring Occurs when an employer fails to check an employee's background and the employee injures someone on the job.

Negligent retention Occurs when an employer becomes aware that an employee may be unfit for work but continues to employ the person, and the person injures someone.

When a candidate is an internal candidate, blemishes are likely known. But when candidates come from outside the company, problems are more likely to be hidden, at least at first.[45]

Fair Credit Reporting Act Many employers check applicants' credit histories. The logic is that poor credit histories may signal, either correctly or incorrectly, a certain level of irresponsibility. Firms that check applicants' credit records must comply with the federal Fair Credit Reporting Act. This act basically requires disclosing that a credit check is being made, obtaining written consent from the person being checked, and furnishing the applicant with a copy of the report. Some state laws also prohibit employers from getting certain credit information. Credit history should be checked on applicants for jobs in which use of, access to, or management of money is an essential job function. Commonly, financial institutions check credit histories on loan officers and tellers, and retailers conduct credit checks on cashiers and managerial staff. But unnecessary credit checks may be illegal, according to some EEOC cases.[46]

Medical Examinations and Inquiries

Medical information on applicants may be used to determine their physical and mental capabilities for performing jobs. Physical standards for jobs should be realistic, justifiable, and linked to job requirements. Even though workers with disabilities can competently perform many jobs, they sometimes may be rejected because of their physical or mental limitations.[47]

ADA and Medical Inquiries The ADA prohibits the use of preemployment medical exams, except for drug tests, until a job has been conditionally offered. Also, the ADA prohibits a company from rejecting an individual because of a disability and from asking job applicants any question related to current or past medical history until a conditional job offer has been made. Once a conditional offer of employment has been made, then some organizations ask the applicant to complete a preemployment health checklist or the employer pays for a physical examination of the applicant.[48] It should be made clear that the applicant who has been offered the job is not "hired" until successful completion of the physical inquiry.

Drug Testing Drug testing may be conducted as part of a medical exam, or it may be done separately. Use of drug testing as part of the selection process has increased in the past few years.[49] If drug tests are used, employers should remember that their accuracy varies according to the type of test used, the item tested, and the quality of the laboratory where the test samples are sent. Because of the potential impact of prescription drugs on test results, applicants should complete a detailed questionnaire on this matter before the testing. If an individual tests positive for drug use, then an independent medical laboratory should administer a second, more detailed analysis. Whether urine, blood, saliva, or hair samples are used, the process of obtaining, labeling, and transferring the samples to the testing lab should be outlined clearly and definite policies and procedures should be established.[50]

References

References provided by the candidate are of very limited predictive value. Would someone knowingly pick a reference who would speak poorly of them?

Of course not.[51] Previous supervisors and employers may provide a better prediction. Good questions to ask previous supervisors or employers include:

- Dates of employment
- Position held
- What were the job duties?
- What strengths/weaknesses did you observe?
- Were there any problems?
- Would you rehire?

LOGGING ON

VirtualHRScreening.com

Through its website, this company offers employers comprehensive risk assessments of applicants including background checks, employment references, drug screening, and criminal histories. Visit the site at www.virtualhrscreening.com.

Work-related references from previous employers and supervisors provide a valuable snapshot of a candidate's background and characteristics. Telephoning references is common. Managers should consider using a form that facilitates the factual verification of information given by the applicant. Some organizations send preprinted reference forms to individuals who are giving references for applicants. These forms often contain a release statement signed by the applicant, so that those providing references can see that they have been released from liability on the information they furnish.

Making the Job Offer

The final step of the selection process is offering someone employment. Job offers are often extended over the telephone. Many companies then formalize the offer in a letter that is sent to the applicant. It is important that the offer document be reviewed by legal counsel and that the terms and conditions of employment be clearly identified. Care should be taken to avoid vague, general statements and promises about bonuses, work schedules, or other matters that might change later. These documents should also provide for the individual to sign an acceptance of the offer and return it to the employer, who should place it in the individual's personnel files.

GLOBAL STAFFING ISSUES

GLOBAL

Staffing global assignments involves making selection decisions that impact (or take place in) other countries. When staffing global assignments, cost is a major consideration because establishing a business professional in another country can run as high as $1 million for a 3-year job assignment. Further, if a business professional quits an international assignment prematurely or wants to transfer home, associated costs can be even greater. "Failure" rates for global assignments can run as high as half of those sent overseas in some situations.

Types of Global Employees

Global organizations can be staffed in a number of different ways, including with expatriates, host-country nationals, and third-country nationals. Each staffing option presents some unique HR management challenges.[52] For instance, when staffing with citizens of different countries, different tax laws and other factors apply. HR professionals need to be knowledgeable about the laws and customs of each country represented in their workforce.[53] Experienced expatriates can provide a pool of talent that can be utilized as the firm expands operations into other countries.

Selection Process for Global Assignments

The selection process for an international assignment should provide a realistic picture of the life, work, and culture to which the employee may be sent. HR managers start by preparing a comprehensive description of the job to be done. This description notes responsibilities that would be unusual in the home nation, including negotiating with public officials; interpreting local work codes; and responding to ethical, moral, and personal issues such as religious prohibitions and personal freedoms.[54] Figure 7-9 shows the most frequently cited key competencies for successful global employees. The five areas are as follows:

- *Cultural adjustment:* Individuals who accept foreign job assignments need to successfully adjust to cultural differences.
- *Personal characteristics:* The experiences of many global firms demonstrate that the best employees in the home country may not be the best employees in a global assignment, primarily because of personal characteristics of individuals.
- *Organizational requirements:* Many global employers find that knowledge of the organization and how it operates is important.

FIGURE 7-9   **Selection Factors for Global Employees**

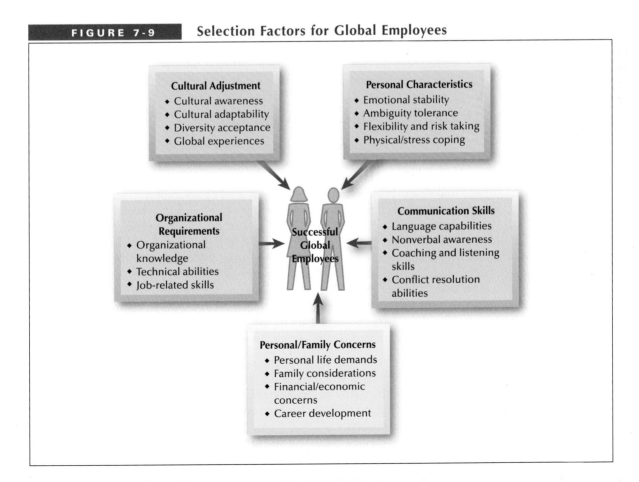

- *Communication skills:* Expatriate employees should be able to communicate in the host-country language both orally and in writing.
- *Personal/family concerns:* The preferences and attitudes of spouses and other family members can influence the success of expatriate assignments.

A growing issue for U.S. firms that hire individuals to fill jobs in other countries is the need for adequate background checks. Global companies want to ensure that their employees have acceptable work histories and personal characteristics. To satisfy this demand, a number of firms have begun to specialize in preemployment screening of global employees.

Some countries have varying government-controlled employment processes that require foreign employers to obtain government approval in order to hire local employees. Many countries such as the United States and Australia require foreign workers to obtain work permits or visas.

For U.S.-based firms, the assignment of women and members of racial/ethnic minorities to international posts involves complying with U.S. EEO regulations and laws. Also, most U.S. EEO regulations and laws apply to foreign-owned firms operating in the United States.

LEGAL CONCERNS IN THE SELECTION PROCESS

Selection is subject to a number of legalities, especially many of the EEO regulations and laws discussed previously. Throughout the selection process, application forms, interviews, tests, background investigations, and any other selection activities must be conducted in a nondiscriminatory manner. But three areas deserve special mention: defining who is an applicant, applicant flow documentation, and selection for "soft skills."

Defining Who Is an Applicant

Employers are required to track applicants who apply for jobs at their companies. It is increasingly important for employers to carefully define exactly who is an applicant and who is not, because many employers are required to track and report applicant information as part of equal employment and affirmative action plans. It is also important because employers may be negatively affected by individuals who claim to have applied for jobs but really just want to file lawsuits. Any person who is interested in a position should be considered an applicant even if no formal posting of the job opening in question has been made, the person has not filed any sort of formal application, and the person does not meet the minimum qualifications for the job.

The EEOC and Office of Federal Contract Compliance Programs (OFCCP) have agreed on this definition of "applicant" to be used when an application has been submitted electronically. An applicant is a person who:[55]

- Has expressed interest through the Internet or electronically and is being considered for a specific position by the employer.
- Has identified that he or she has the basic position qualifications.
- Does not remove his or her interest in the position at anytime during the selection process.
- Has been ranked using "hit features" by employer software or other data techniques that are not linked to assessment qualifications.

Applicant Flow Documentation

Employers must collect applicant data on race, sex, and other demographics to fulfill EEO reporting requirements. Many employers ask applicants to provide EEOC reporting data in a flow form that may be attached to the application form. It is important that employers review this flow form separately and not use it in any selection efforts to avoid claims of impropriety. Because completing the form is voluntary, employers can demonstrate that they tried to obtain the data.

Selecting for "Soft Skills"

Selection in its "scientific" form is about finding valid predictors of what will be needed on a job and picking people who score high on those predictors. These "hard skills" include cognitive skills, education, and technical skills. But these skills may not predict the difference between adequate and outstanding performance. Some argue that "soft skills" provide an important part of the ability to do a job successfully.[56] What are "soft skills"? They are noncognitive abilities that are complementary to outstanding job performance. Examples might include:

Empathy	Leadership
Openness	Integrity
Cooperation	Ethical behavior
Interpersonal style	Effort
Conscientiousness	Emotional intelligence

But selection for soft skills is haphazard.[57] Unlike hard skills, these skills may have to be inferred from past behaviors or from an interview.[58] Tests may be available to help with some soft skills, but the basic process presented in this chapter still must apply. First, identify KSAs, competencies, and job functions through job analysis. Next, decide how those will be identified in an applicant (tests, interviews, experience, etc.). Then use structured behavioral interviewing done by trained interviewers incorporating competency-focused questions. Finally, choose those applicants who are strong in the areas necessary to do the job.[59]

SUMMARY

- Selection is the process that matches individuals and their qualifications to jobs in an organization.
- Placement of people should consider both person/job fit and person/organization fit.
- Mismatches in fit can occur because of skills, geography, time required, earning expectations, and work/family issues.
- Predictors linked to criteria are used to identify the applicants who are most likely to perform jobs successfully.
- The selection process—from applicant interest through preemployment screening, application, testing, interviewing, and background investigation—must be handled by trained, knowledgeable individuals.
- Truth-in-hiring lawsuits may arise from overselling a job.
- Employers are using electronic preemployment screening to cut down applicant pools.
- Application forms must meet EEO guidelines and must ask only for job-related information.
- Selection tests include ability tests, assessment centers, personality tests, and honesty/integrity tests. Some are controversial.

- Structured interviews, including behavioral and situational ones, are more effective and face fewer EEO compliance concerns than do unstructured interviews and nondirective interviews.
- Interviews can be conducted individually, by multiple individuals, or by technology. Regardless of the method, effective interviewing questioning techniques should be used.
- Background investigation can be conducted in a variety of areas. Both when requesting and when giving reference information, employers must take care to avoid potential legal concerns such as negligent hiring and negligent retention.

- Global organizations can be staffed by individuals who are expatriates, host-country nationals, or third-country nationals.
- Selection factors for global employees include cultural adjustment, personal characteristics, communication skills, personal/family concerns, and organizational requirements.
- Selection decisions must be based on job-related criteria in order to comply with various legal requirements.
- HR professionals must be careful to properly identify, track, and document applicants.
- Selecting for "soft skills" must follow the model used for more visible skills.

CRITICAL THINKING ACTIVITIES

1. Develop a set of soft skills necessary for a college professor's job.
2. Put together a structured interview for hiring assistant managers at a large retail store.
3. How would you do a complete background investigation on applicants to minimize concerns about negligent hiring?
4. Your Accounting Manager has decided that a behavioral interview to select accountants will solve many hiring problems. What can you tell the manager about this type of interview and whether it is likely to be effective? Check www.job-interview.net and other sources to gather information.

HR EXPERIENTIAL PROBLEM SOLVING

Your insurance company recently entered into a business contract with a company in the financial industry that requires extensive background checks for all your existing employees and future applicants who will be doing work associated with the contract. Previously your company conducted only employment verification checks in the hiring process. The management team discussions have raised questions and concerns about issues that need to be considered as the company develops and implements a more extensive background screening protocol. Resources to help you identify issues, best practices, and requirements can be found at www.hire-safe.com/Employment_Background_Check_Guidelines.pdf.

1. What concerns does your company need to consider in following background check guidelines?
2. Discuss with the management team the steps your company needs to take to ensure that it complies with the Fair Credit Reporting Act.

C A S E

Full Disclosure on Sex Offenders?

Megan's Law provides that all states are now required to have all convicted sex offenders register so that residents are aware of their presence in a neighborhood. The law is named for Megan Kanka, a 7-year-old who was raped and murdered by a twice-convicted pedophile who moved to her New Jersey neighborhood. He lured her to his house with the promise of showing her a puppy. Megan's Law raises issues around the use of criminal registries in hiring and employee management.

Several issues are involved for an employer in dealing with Megan's Law and employees. For example, in Michigan, the Attorney General released the names of 200 registered sex offenders who had been using MySpace (some in violation of the terms of their parole). Some employers found that the list included the names of some of their employees and had to confront the very real problem of what to do about it.

The presence of a convicted sex offender presents conflicting obligations and concerns. Employers want (and need) to protect other employees and customers from harm based on negligent hiring and negligent retention issues. But is this person a threat? What if the person has an exemplary work record? In some states, it is illegal for employers to use any information found on the Megan's Law website for purposes of employment.

Perhaps the easiest way to proceed would be to keep from hiring convicts in the first place, but federal law limits an employer's ability to do that. The EEOC says that the use of conviction records in employment decisions has an adverse impact on African American and Hispanic males. Using a blanket prohibition against convicts in hiring may allow a plaintiff to demonstrate a disproportionate impact on protected categories of applicants.

Is an employer *required* to check the registry? It depends on the job. Generally the answer is "no," but for certain jobs there is an obligation to check. Those jobs include positions in health care facilities and hospitals (e.g., nurse or aide), day cares and schools (e.g., teacher or aide), security (e.g., guard), social and mental health facilities (e.g., social or mental health worker), taxi and bus services (e.g., drivers), and recreational facilities (e.g., fitness trainer). Virtually any position with access to potential victims is a job with the potential for problems.

Two of the names on the Michigan list presented some difficult management decisions. In one office equipment company, a 34-year-old office equipment repair technician was paroled after serving a 7-year sentence for attacking women on jogging paths. His previous employer offered to rehire him as a field technician who would travel to other offices to repair business machines, as he had been an excellent employee with outstanding repair skills.

In the other case, a new employee was found to be on the list. He was an African American who had served 10 years for child pornography possession. He is driving a school bus for a church and has thus far been a model employee, although he did not list his conviction on the application form even though the question was asked.[60]

QUESTIONS

1. Discuss what a manager should do in each of the two Michigan cases.

2. What circumstances might lead you to make different decisions in different cases under Megan's Law?

SUPPLEMENTAL CASES

Strategic Selection: A Review of Two Companies

This case shows how Hallmark and United Health Group use selection as part of their strategic approach to HR. (For the case, go to www.cengage.com/management/mathis.)

Selecting a Programmer

This case demonstrates how using a test after a pool of candidates has already been interviewed can present some difficulties. (For the case, go to www.cengage.com/management/mathis.)

NOTES

1. Anjali Anthavaley, "A Job Interview You Have to Show Up For," *The Wall Street Journal*, June 20, 2007, D1.
2. Kathy Gurchiek, "Staffing Issues Critical to Business Strategies, SHRM Finds," *HR News*, May 28, 2008, 1–3.
3. Alan Krueger and David Schkade, "Sorting in the Labor Market," *Journal of Human Resources*, 43 (2008), No. 4, 859–883.
4. Melanie Wanzek, "On Second Thought," *Sunday World Herald*, May 10, 2009, CR1.
5. Arne Kalleberg, "The Mismatched Worker: When People Don't Fit Their Jobs," *Academy of Management Perspectives*, February 2008, 24–40.
6. Metin Celik, I. Deha Er, and Y. Ilker Topcu, "Computer-Based Systematic Executive Model of HRM in Maritime Transportation Industry: The Case of Master Selection for Embarking on Board Merchant Ships," *Expect Systems with Applications*, 36 (2009), 1048–1060.
7. Robert Grossman, "Hiring to Fit the Culture," *HR Magazine*, February 2009, 41–50.
8. Dave Bartram, "The Great Eight Competencies: A Criterion-Centric Approach to Validation," *Journal of Applied Psychology*, 90 (2005), 1185–1203.
9. Murray Barrick and Ryan Zimmerman, "Hiring for Retention and Performance," *Human Resource Management*, March–April 2009, 183–206.
10. Peter Cappelli, "The Impact of a High School Diploma," *HR Executive Online*, August 18, 2008, www.hreonline.com, 1–3.
11. Fay Hanson, "Avoiding Truth-in-Hiring Lawsuits," *Workforce Management Online*, December 2007, 1–4.
12. V. O'Connell, "Test for Dwindling Retail Jobs Spawns a Culture of Cheating," *The Wall Street Journal*, January 7, 2009, A1.
13. Aldo Sualdi, "Job Seekers Put Résumé Responders in a Frazzle," *The Denver Post*, November 8, 2009, K1; Gina Ruiz, "Job Candidate Assessment Tests Go Virtual," *Workforce Management Online*, January 2008, 1–4.

14. Adrienne Hedger, "3 Ways to Improve Your Employee Screening," *Workforce Management*, March 16, 2009, 26–30.
15. Gary McWilliams, "RadioShack CEO Agrees to Resign," *The Wall Street Journal*, February 21, 2006, A3.
16. Allison Balvs (ed.), "Employers Beware: ICE Crackdown Target 652 Businesses Nationwide," *Baird Holm Labor and Employment Law Update*, August 2009, 1–2.
17. "Federal Contractors Required to Use E-Verify Beginning Sept. 8, 2009," *Ceridian Abstracts*, www.hrcompliance.ceridian.com, 1.
18. "Gerber Agrees to Pay $900,000 to Minorities and Females for Hiring Discrimination," *Ceridian Abstracts*, August 26, 2009, www.hrcompliance.ceridian.com, 1.
19. Martha Frase, "Smart Selections," *HR Magazine*, December 2007, 63–67.
20. Louis Greenstein, "Web of Deceit," *Human Resource Executive*, June 16, 2008, 57–60.
21. Chris Piotowski and Terry Armstrong, "Current Recruitment and Selection Practices: A National Survey of Fortune 1000 Firms," *North American Journal of Psychology*, 8 (2006), 489–496.
22. Frank Schmidt, et al., "General Mental Ability, Job Performance, and Red Herrings: Responses to Osterman, Hauser, and Schmitt," *Academy of Management Perspectives*, November 2007, 64–76.
23. David Autor and David Scarborough, "Does Job Testing Harm Minority Workers? Evidence from Retail Establishments," *Quarterly Journal of Economics*, February 2008, 219–277; Peter Cappelli, "Assessing Personality," *Human Resource Executive Online*, www.hreonline.com.
24. Frederick Morgeson, et al., "Reconsidering the Use of Personality Tests in Personnel Selection Contexts," *Personnel Psychology*, 60, 2007, 683–729.
25. Benjamin Schneider, "Evolution of the Study and Practice of Personality at Work," *Human Resource Management*, Winter 46 (2007), 583–610.

26. Scott Highhouse, "Stubborn Reliance on Intuition and Subjectivity in Employee Selection," *Industrial and Organizational Psychology*, 1, 2008, 333–341.
27. Jack Welch and Suzy Welch, "Hiring Is Hard Work," *BusinessWeek*, July 7, 2008, 80.
28. Joann Lublin, "What Won't You Do for a Job?" *The Wall Street Journal*, June 2, 2009, B1.
29. Mark McGraw, "Costly Job Interviews," *Human Resource Executive Online*, November 4, 2009, www.hreonline.com, 1–2.
30. Kristen Weirick, "The Perfect Interview," *HR Magazine*, April 2008, 85–88.
31. Chad Van Iddekinge, et al., "Antecedents of Impression Management Use and Effectiveness in a Structured Interview," *Journal of Management*, October 2007, 752–773.
32. Therese Macan, "The Employment Interview: A Review of Current Studies and Directions for Future Research," *Human Resources Management Review*, 19 (2009), 203–218.
33. Henryk T. Krajewski, Richard D. Goffin, Julie M. McCarthy, Mitchell G. Rothstein, and Norman Johnston, "Comparing the Validity of Structured Interviews for Managerial-Level Employees: Should We Look to the Past or Focus on the Future?" *Journal of Occupational & Organizational Psychology*, 79 (2006), 411–432.
34. Kathy Gurchiek, "Behavioral Interviewing Popular but Training in Use Is Urged," *SHRM HR News*, January 28, 2008, www.shrm.org, 1–3.
35. Alexandra Lopez-Pacheco, "How Do I Recruit Great Employees?" *National Post* (Canada), June 8, 2009, FP8; Laura Quinn, and Maxine Dalton, "Leading for Sustainability Implementing the Tasks of Leadership," *Corporate Governance*, 9, 2009, 21–38.
36. Joann Lublin, "For Job Hunters the Big Interview Is Getting Bigger," *The Wall Street Journal*, June 3, 2008, D1.
37. "Failing the Interview," *DD1*, www.ddiworld.com.

38. Joanna Lahey, "Age, Women, and Hiring," *Journal of Human Resources*, XLIII, No. 1, 30–56.

39. Nic Paton, "Half of Hiring Decisions a Mistake, Say Managers," October 7, 2008, www.management-issues.com; Ann Howard and Jehanna Johnson, "If You Were a Tree What Kind Would You Be?" *Development Dimensions International White Paper*, 2008, 1–11.

40. Rita Zeidner, "How Deep Can You Probe?" *HR Magazine*, October 2007, 57–62.

41. Regan Halvorsen, "HR Solutions," *HR Magazine*, September 2008, 36.

42. Cheryl Thompson, "Background Checks for Experiential Education Could Get Centralized," *American Journal of Health System Pharmacy*, September 2009, 1603–1604.

43. Leonard Schloss and J. Gregory Lahr, "Watch Your Back: Smart Hiring and Proper Background Checks," *Employee Relations Law Journal*, Winter 2008, 46–71.

44. Chad Terhune, "The Trouble with Background Checks," *Business Week*, June 9, 2008, 54–57.

45. Lin Grensing-Pophal, "Hiring Inside or Out," *Human Resource Executive Online*, November 10, 2009, www.hreonline.com, 1–3.

46. Allen Smith, "EEOC Challenges Unnecessary Credit Checks," *SHRM HR News*, February 9, 2007, www.shrm.org, 1–2; "Checking Credit of Job Candidates Drives Concern about Civil Rights," *The Wall Street Journal*, January 19, 2007, B2.

47. "Ruling Complicates Return-to-Work Tests," *Business Insurance*, October 5, 2009, 8.

48. "General Communication Guidelines," *Ceridian Abstracts*, April 8, 2009, www.hrcompliance.ceridian.com.

49. Cathy Fyock, "Streamlining the Process," *HR Executive*, November 19, 2007, 49.

50. "The Legal Side of Workplace Drug-Free Policies," *Safety Compliance Letter 2487*, 2008, 7–13; Jo Douglas, "Green Light for Drugs and Alcoholic Testing," *NZ Business*, 22, No. 4, 2008, 84.

51. JoAnn Lublin, "Bulletproofing Your References in the Hunt for a New Job," *The Wall Street Journal*, April 7, 2009, B9.

52. Mary Siegfried, "A New Approach to Global Staffing," *Inside Supply Management*, March 2008, 30–32.

53. Ann Marie Ryan, et al., "Going Global: Cultural Values and Perceptions of Selection Procedures," *Applied Psychology: An International Review*, 2008, 1–37.

54. Ashly Pennington, et al. (eds.), *Human Resource Management: Ethics and Employment* (Oxford: Oxford University Press, 2007), 255.

55. Allen Smith, "OFCCP Updates Guidance on Internet Applicant," *HR News*, November 17, 2006, www.shrm.org/news.

56. Lex Borghans, et al., "Interpersonal Styles and Labor Market Outcomes," *Journal of Human Resources*, 43 (2008) No. 4, 816–855.

57. Dana Mattioli, "Hard Sell on 'Soft' Skills," *The Wall Street Journal*, May 15, 2007, B6.

58. Charles Handler, "Dear Workforce . . .," www.Workforce.com.

59. IRA Blank, "Selecting Employees Based on Emotional Intelligence Competencies: Reap the Rewards and Minimize the Risk," *Employee Relations Law Journal*, Winter 2008, 77–85.

60. Diane Cadrain, "Full Disclosure," *HR Magazine*, September 2007, 60–64.

Training and Development

8

Training Human Resources

After you have read this chapter, you should be able to:

- Define training and discuss why a strategic approach is important.
- Discuss the four phases of the training process.
- Identify three types of analyses used to determine training needs.
- Explain different means of internal and external training delivery.
- Describe the importance of e-learning as part of current training efforts.
- Give an example for each of the four levels of training evaluation.

China's Need for Training

(CNImaging/Newscom)

China has enjoyed an economic bonanza, and with that growth has come a shift toward higher-end manufacturing and services. This shift has led to a greater need for experienced and skilled labor. Local managers need not only technical skills, but skills that are business focused as well. As a result, HR in China faces a large challenge in finding, training, and keeping skilled employees who can thrive in Western-style multinational corporations (MNCs).

China has a workforce of 800 million, but only a small percentage is considered skilled enough to work in MNCs. The Chinese educational system does not teach the range of needed skills, so companies are training workers. A California biomedical testing instrument manufacturer has 270 employees in sales, marketing, and services in China. Five years ago the focus was on technical skills, but now the company wants employees with experience, expertise, and an understanding of the business and relationships.

Chinese culture encourages learning and growing. A Chinese proverb says, "If you want 100 years of prosperity, grow people." And, Chinese employees want the opportunity to be trained. In fact, if they see companies bring in expatriates or non-Chinese workers, they view those companies as having a short-term investment in China and not as likely to be a good place for career growth. Available training is a retention tool that Chinese employees are demanding.

Cisco Systems, which recognized the need to create its own skilled labor pool, now has 220 academies in all provinces in China. The company wants employees to know proposal design, presentation skills, teamwork, products, and sales.

A special administrative region (SAR) of China, Macao, is a good example of an area with specific training needs. Macao's economy is heavily invested in gaming and the hospitality industry. Hotel and gaming companies have grown their training staffs; at the height of training activities, one hotel resort had 30 full-time training people serving thousands of employees. In the gaming industry, training includes training for dealers, security officers, and supervisors. Training is often done on a 24/7 basis to accommodate various work shifts.

Training has become so prominent in many global companies because it is seen as a worthwhile investment. Companies in the United States also have adopted training as a way to retain their talented employees.[1]

Competition forces business organizations to change and adapt in order to compete successfully. Changes in the way things must be done include training or retraining employees and managers. In this sense, training is an ongoing process for most organizations. Organizations in the United States spend more than $126 billion annually on training and development, or more than $1,000 per employee on average.[2]

Training is the process whereby people acquire capabilities to perform jobs. Training provides employees with specific, identifiable knowledge and skills for use in their present jobs. Organizational training may include teaching of "hard" skills, such as teaching sales representatives how to use intranet resources, a branch manager how to review an income statement, or a machinist apprentice how to set up a drill press. "Soft" skills are critical in many instances and can be taught as well. These skills may include communicating, mentoring, managing a meeting, and working as part of a team.

TRAINING AND HR

What kinds of activities usually require training? The most common training topics include, among others, safety, customer service, computer skills, quality initiatives, dealing with sexual harassment, and communication.[3] Training has been studied at length in the United States.[4] The results of these studies show that training is rated as important or very important by 94% of human resources professionals.[5] Further, documented benefits of well-done training include (for both individuals and teams) enhanced skills, greater ability to adapt and innovate, better self-management, and performance improvement. For organizations, research has shown that training brings improvements in effectiveness and productivity, more profitability and reduced costs, improved quality, and increased social capitol.

Training Categories

Training can be designed to meet a number of objectives and can be classified in various ways. As Figure 8-1 shows, some common groupings include the following:

- *Required and regular training*: Complies with various mandated legal requirements (e.g., OSHA and EEO) and is given to all employees (e.g., new employee orientation)

Training Process whereby people acquire capabilities to perform jobs.

| FIGURE 8-1 | Types of Training |

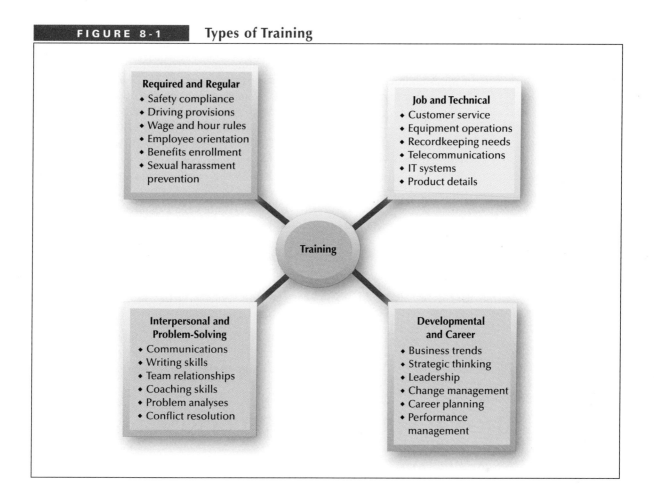

Required and Regular
- Safety compliance
- Driving provisions
- Wage and hour rules
- Employee orientation
- Benefits enrollment
- Sexual harassment prevention

Job and Technical
- Customer service
- Equipment operations
- Recordkeeping needs
- Telecommunications
- IT systems
- Product details

Training

Interpersonal and Problem-Solving
- Communications
- Writing skills
- Team relationships
- Coaching skills
- Problem analyses
- Conflict resolution

Developmental and Career
- Business trends
- Strategic thinking
- Leadership
- Change management
- Career planning
- Performance management

- *Job/technical training*: Enables employees to perform their jobs well (e.g., product knowledge, technical processes and procedures, customer relations)
- *Developmental and career training*: Provides longer-term focus to enhance individual and organizational capabilities for the future (e.g., business practices, executive development, organizational change, leadership)
- *Interpersonal and problem-solving training*: Addresses both operational and interpersonal problems and seeks to improve organizational working relationships (e.g., interpersonal communication, managerial/supervisory skills, conflict resolution)

It is common for a distinction to be drawn between *training* and *development*, with development being broader in scope and focusing on individuals' gaining new capabilities useful for both present and future jobs. Development is discussed in Chapter 9; training is the focus of this chapter.

Legal Issues and Training

A number of legal issues must be considered when designing and delivering training. One concern centers on the criteria and practices used to select individuals for inclusion in training programs. Companies need to make sure those criteria are job related and do not unfairly restrict the participation of protected-category members. Also, failure to accommodate the participation of individuals with disabilities in training can expose organizations to EEO lawsuits.

Another legal issue is employers' requiring employees to sign *training contracts* in order to protect the costs and time invested in specialized employee training. For instance, a telecommunications firm paid $17,000 each to train four network technicians and certify them in specialized equipment. The firm required that each technician sign a training contract whereby one-fourth of the cost would be forgiven each year the employee stayed following the training. A technician who left sooner would be liable to the firm for the unforgiven balance. Health care organizations, IT firms, and other employers often use training contracts, especially for expensive external training.

Finally, the Department of Labor has ruled that employees who are training outside normal working hours (e.g., at home by completing Web-based classes) must be compensated for their time. In one situation, a Web-based class required employees to spend about 10 hours at home completing it; once they did, they performed their job duties better. In this case, the company had to pay the employees for their 10 hours of training under the Fair Labor Standards Act.[6]

LOGGING ON

American Society for Training & Development
This website on training and development contains information on research, education, seminars, and conferences. Visit the site at www.astd.org.

ORGANIZATIONAL STRATEGY AND TRAINING

Training represents a significant expenditure for most employers. But it is too often viewed tactically rather than strategically, which means that training is seen as a short-term activity rather than one that has longer-term effects on organizational success. However, this is changing. For example, during the last recession, unlike previous recessions, some companies chose to maintain training that was necessary for long-term strategic goals.[7]

Strategic Training

Training is used strategically to help the organization accomplish its goals. For example, if sales increases are a critical part of the company's strategy, appropriate training would identify what is causing lower sales and target training to respond as part of a solution.[8]

Strategic training can have numerous organizational benefits. It requires HR and training professionals to get intimately involved with the business and to partner with operating managers to help solve their problems, thus making significant contributions to organizational results. Additionally, a strategic training mind-set reduces the likelihood of thinking that training alone can solve most employee or organizational problems. It is not uncommon for operating managers and trainers to react to most important performance problems by saying, "I need a training program on *X*." With a strategic focus, the organization is more likely to assess whether training actually can address the most important performance issues and what besides training is needed. Training cannot fix all organizational problems.

The value of training can be seen at Walt Disney World where the company has established specific training plans. The implementation of those training plans results in a distinct competitive advantage for the organization. For example, at the Disney Institute, employees (called "cast members") get training experience from their guests' perspectives. As a part of their training, individuals taking hotel reservations stay at a resort as guests in order to gain greater understanding of what they are selling and to experience the services themselves.

Organizational Competitiveness and Training

General Electric, Dell Computers, Motorola, Marriott, Cisco, FedEx, and Texas Instruments all emphasize the importance of training employees and managers. These companies and others recognize that training efforts can be integral to business success. In a sense, for these companies, training is similar to the "continuous improvement" practiced by some manufacturing firms.

The nature of technological innovation and change is such that if employees are not trained all the time, they may fall behind and the company could become less competitive. For example, consider the telecommunications industry today compared with ten years ago, with all the new technologies and the accompanying competitive shifts. Without continual training, organizations may not have staff members with the knowledge, skills, and abilities (KSAs) needed to compete effectively.

Training also can affect organizational competitiveness by aiding in the retention of employees. One reason why many individuals stay or leave organizations is career training and development opportunities. Employers that invest in training and developing their employees may enhance retention efforts.

Figure 8-2 shows how training may help accomplish certain organizational strategies. Ideally, upper management sees the training function as providing valuable intelligence about the necessary core skills.

Knowledge Management For much of history, competitive advantage among organizations was measured in terms of physical capital. However, as

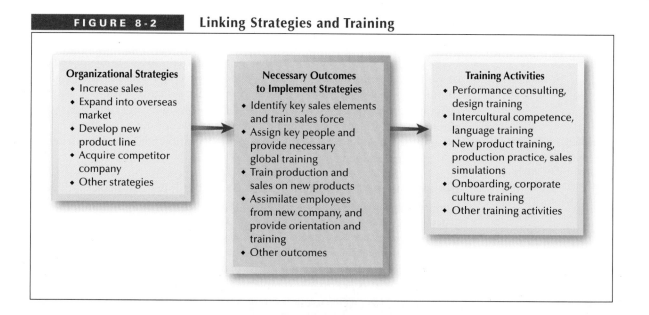

FIGURE 8-2   **Linking Strategies and Training**

Organizational Strategies
- Increase sales
- Expand into overseas market
- Develop new product line
- Acquire competitor company
- Other strategies

Necessary Outcomes to Implement Strategies
- Identify key sales elements and train sales force
- Assign key people and provide necessary global training
- Train production and sales on new products
- Assimilate employees from new company, and provide orientation and training
- Other outcomes

Training Activities
- Performance consulting, design training
- Intercultural competence, language training
- New product training, production practice, sales simulations
- Onboarding, corporate culture training
- Other training activities

the information age has evolved, "intelligence" has become the raw material that many organizations make and sell through their "knowledge workers."[9] **Knowledge management** is the way an organization identifies and leverages knowledge in order to be competitive. It is the art of creating value by using organizational intellectual capital, which is what the organization (or, more exactly, the people in the organization) knows. Knowledge management is a conscious effort to get the right knowledge to the right people at the right time so that it can be shared and put into action.

Training as a Revenue Source Some organizations have identified that training can be a source of business revenue. For instance, Microsoft, Ceridian, Cisco, Hewlett-Packard, and other technology firms bundle customer training with products and services they sell. Also, manufacturers of industrial equipment offer customers training on machine upgrades and new features. Customers of many of these firms pay for additional training either by course, by participant, or as part of equipment or software purchases. Not only are the costs of the trainers' salaries, travel, and other expenses covered, but the suppliers also make a profit on the training through the fees paid by customers. As a side benefit, customer satisfaction and loyalty increase if customers know how to use the products and services purchased. Thus, customer training aids customer retention and enhances future sales revenues.

Performance Consulting Training should result in improved organizational performance. For some companies, ensuring that it does requires a "performance consulting" approach. **Performance consulting** is a process in which a trainer (either internal or external to the organization) and an organization work together to decide how to improve organizational and individual results.[10] That may or may not include training. Performance consulting takes a broad approach by:

- Focusing on identifying and addressing root causes of performance problems
- Recognizing that the interaction of individual and organizational factors influences employee performance
- Documenting the actions and accomplishments of high performers and comparing them with actions and accomplishments of more typical performers

Regardless of whether the trainer is an internal employee or an outside consultant, a performance consulting approach recognizes that training alone cannot automatically solve every employer performance problem. Instead, training is one piece of a larger "bundled solution." For instance, some employee performance issues might be resolved by creating a training program for employees, and others might call for compensation adjustments, job design changes, or reassignment.

Integration of Performance with Training Job performance, training, and employee learning must be integrated to be effective, and HR plays a crucial role in this integration.[11] Organizations find that training experiences that use real business problems to advance employee learning are better than more traditional approaches. Rather than separating the training experience from the context of actual job performance, trainers incorporate everyday business issues as learning examples, thus increasing the realism of training exercises and scenarios. For example, as part of management training at

Knowledge management
The way an organization identifies and leverages knowledge in order to be competitive.

Performance consulting
Process in which a trainer and an organization work together to decide how to improve organizational and individual results.

Business Education at Work

The following is a first-person account from an employee of Graybar Electric Company (an employee-owned company), as she related her experience in a "Mini MBA" set up by Rutgers University. This training program is an excellent example of integrating performance and training.

My employer teamed with Rutgers to produce a new management training program to provide a broad base of business knowledge. Graybar has a long history of promoting people from within and needed a program like this. I was a senior attorney on the company's legal team, and ready for more business education. The training program includes face-to-face meetings as well as online communication. We do most of our work in cross-functional teams. My team in addition to myself includes Graybar employees from Canada (Vice President), Pittsburgh (Operations Manager), and Alabama (Branch Manager). We learn from each other as well as from the formal instruction.

Technology includes e-mail, instant messaging, Webinars, podcasts, conference calls, and the Internet. There are no regularly scheduled classes; we are responsible for reading and finishing assignments at our own pace. For example, a recent assignment was to listen to a podcast by a CEO of an international advertising agency on customer loyalty creation. Our team then drafted an article for the company newsletter, discussing the Graybar brand and how to strengthen the value of the brand with the customers. In another assignment, each team completed an assignment on ethics. The team members identified an ethical issue and designed a 10-minute employee training module based on that incident. This required learning the ethical concepts and translating them into an informative program for employees.

If you take a class at a local college, perhaps you can apply 20% of what you learn to your job. With this program, I probably apply 80–90% directly to my job. We examine real-world challenges affecting Graybar's strategy. The work done by the student is actually used to guide the company's future, as the hands-on learning is presented to senior managers as part of the final exam.[12]

Note: At this writing, Beverly Propst is Vice President of Human Resources at Graybar Electric.

General Electric, managers are given actual business problems to solve, and they must present their solutions to the business leaders in the firm. Using real situations for practice is yet another way of merging the lines between training, learning, and job performance. For another example, see HR Perspective: Business Education at Work.

Chief Learning Officers To emphasize the importance of training and to have internal performance consulting expertise, some organizations have created a position entitled *chief learning officer (CLO)* or *chief knowledge officer (CKO)*. Ideally, the CLO is not just a training director with an inflated new title, but rather a leader who designs knowledge through training for individual employees and the organization. CLOs must demonstrate a high level of comfort in working with boards of directors and the top management team, a track record of success in running some type of business unit, and an understanding of adult learning technologies and processes. If they possess these characteristics, CLOs can take the lead in developing strategic training plans for their organizations.

TRAINING FOR GLOBAL STRATEGIES

GLOBAL

For a global firm, the most brilliant strategies ever devised will not work unless the company has well-trained employees throughout the world to carry them out. A global look at training is becoming more crucial as firms establish and expand operations worldwide. For U.S. employers, the challenge has increased. According to a report, the number of U.S. job skills certifications declined 18% in one year, while there was a 47% increase in similar certifications in India. The conclusion of the study was that U.S. firms may not remain innovative and strategic leaders much longer, due to the decline in specialized skilled and technical workers.[13] Add this problem to the number of global employees with international assignments, and training must be seen as part of global strategic success.[14]

Global Assignment Training

The orientation and training that expatriates and their families receive before departure significantly affect the success of an overseas assignment. When such programs are offered, most expatriates participate in them, and the programs usually produce a positive effect on cross-cultural adjustment. Also, training helps expatriates and their families adjust to and deal with host-country counterparts. A recent survey showed that companies recognize their expatriates often are well trained in skills and technical capabilities but much less well trained in knowledge of the host country culture.[15]

A related issue is the promotion and transfer of foreign citizens to positions in the United States. For example, many Japanese firms operating in the United States conduct training programs to prepare Japanese people for the food, customs, labor and HR practices, and other facets of working and living in the United States. As more global organizations start or expand U.S. operations, more cross-cultural training will be necessary for international employees relocated to the United States.[16]

Intercultural Competence Training

Global employers are providing intercultural competence training for their global employees. Intercultural competence incorporates a wide range of human social skills and personality characteristics. As noted in Figure 8-3, three components of intercultural competence require attention when training expatriates for global assignments:

- *Cognitive*: What does the person know about other cultures?
- *Emotional*: How does the person view other cultures, and how sensitive is the person to cultural customs and issues?
- *Behavioral*: How does the person act in intercultural situations?

Increasingly, global employers are using training methods that allow individuals to behave in international situations and then receive feedback.[17] One method is the Culture Assimilator. Used worldwide, especially by European-based firms, the Culture Assimilator is a programmed training and learning method consisting of short case studies and critical incidents. The case studies describe intercultural interactions and potential misunderstandings involving expatriates and host-country nationals.

FIGURE 8-3   **Intercultural Competence Training**

COMPONENT	POSSIBLE TRAINING
Cognitive	◆ Culture-specific training (traditions, history, cultural customs, etc.) ◆ Language course
Emotional	◆ *Uneasiness:* Social skills training focusing on new/unclear and intercultural situations ◆ *Prejudices:* Coaching may be clarifying ◆ *Sensitivity:* Communication skills course (active listening, verbal/nonverbal cues, empathy)
Behavioral	◆ Culture Assimilator method ◆ International projects ◆ Social skills training focusing on intercultural situations

Source: Developed by Andrea Graf, PhD, and Robert L. Mathis, PhD, SPHR.

PLANNING FOR TRAINING

Whether global or national in scope, training benefits from careful planning before it is done. Planning includes looking at the "big picture" in which the training takes place as well as specifics for the design of a particular training effort. For example, the needs for skills have changed over time and things like adaptability, problem solving, and professionalism have increased in value in some firms.[18] Planning to design training to include changes such as these makes for a more effective training program.

Another training planning issue for some companies is knowledge retention for the firm. When retirees leave, they take everything they have learned during a career. Perhaps a retiree is the only one in the company who knows how to operate a piece of machinery or mix a chemical solution. In some areas technology changes so fast that even young people leaving a company may take with them information that cannot easily be replicated. Companies are responding to this knowledge retention need in various ways, including identifying critical employees, having existing critical employees train and mentor others, producing how-to videotapes, and keeping former employees on call for a period of time after their departure.[19]

Training plans allow organizations to identify what is needed for employee performance *before* training begins so that a fit between training and strategic issues is made.[20] Effective training efforts consider the following questions:

- Is there really a need for the training?
- Who needs to be trained?
- Who will do the training?
- What form will the training take?
- How will knowledge be transferred to the job?
- How will the training be evaluated?

Orientation: Planning for New Employees

A good example of one kind of training that requires planning is orientation. Also called "onboarding," orientation is the most important and widely conducted type of regular training done for new employees. **Orientation**, which is the planned introduction of new employees to their jobs, coworkers, and the organization, is offered by most employers. It requires cooperation between individuals in the HR unit and operating managers and supervisors. In a small organization without an HR department, the new employee's supervisor or manager usually assumes most of the responsibility for orientation. In large organizations, managers and supervisors, as well as the HR department, generally work as a team to orient new employees. Unfortunately, without good planning, new employee orientation sessions can come across as boring, irrelevant, and a waste of time to both new employees and their department supervisors and managers.

Solid academic research indicates that orientation (institutionalized socialization tactics) can be effective—if done well. Orientation reduces role ambiguity, role conflict, and intention to quit; and it increases perceptions of fit, job satisfaction, commitment, and performance.[21] Studies and observations by practicing managers and HR managers confirm this.[22] In addition, evidence from the public sector shows how important orientation is *if done well*.[23] Planning for orientation is reviewed in HR On-the-Job.

Among the decisions to be made during planning are what to present and also, equally important, *when* to present it. Too much information on the first

Orientation Planned introduction of new employees to their jobs, coworkers, and the organization.

Planning for New Employee Orientation

Effective new employee orientation requires planning and preparation. Unfortunately, orientation often is conducted rather haphazardly. To make orientation more effective, the following planning suggestions are useful:

- *Prepare for new employees.* New employees must feel that they belong and are important to the organization. The supervisor, HR unit, and coworkers should be prepared for a new employee's arrival.
- *Consider using mentors.* Some organizations assign coworkers or peers to serve as buddies or mentors as part of the new employees' orientation.
- *Use an orientation checklist.* An orientation checklist can be used to identify what the new employee needs to know now and later.
- *Cover needed information at the proper time.* It is important to give employees information

on the policies, work rules, and benefits of the company *when* they need it. What do they need on the first day? What later?

- *Present orientation information effectively.* Managers and HR representatives should determine the most appropriate ways to present orientation information both in person and using technological means.
- *Avoid information overload.* One common failing of many orientation programs is information overload. New workers presented with too many facts may ignore or inaccurately recall much of the information.
- *Evaluate and follow up.* An HR representative or manager can evaluate the effectiveness of the orientation by conducting follow-up interviews with new employees a few weeks or months after the orientation.

day leads to perceptions of ineffective onboarding. Several shorter sessions over a longer period of time, bringing in information as it is needed, are more effective. Effective orientation achieves several key purposes:

- Establishes a favorable employee impression of the organization and the job
- Provides organization and job information
- Enhances interpersonal acceptance by coworkers
- Accelerates socialization and integration of the new employee into the organization
- Ensures that employee performance and productivity begin more quickly

Electronic Orientation Resources One way of expanding the efficiency of orientation is to use electronic resources. Estimates are that more than 80% of employers have implemented electronic onboarding activities to improve their employee orientation efforts.[24] A number of employers place general employee orientation information on company intranets or corporate websites. New employees log on and go through much of the general material on organizational history, structure, products and services, mission, and other background, instead of sitting in a classroom where the information is delivered in person or by videotape. Specific questions and concerns can be addressed by HR staff and others after employees have reviewed the Web-based information.[25]

Other companies use electronic resources a bit differently. For example, at Mirage Resorts, when candidates accept an offer, they get an e-mail with a link to a password-protected website that welcomes them, and they fill out their I-9, W-2, and other forms on that website. Before reporting to work, they get e-mails daily explaining where to park, where to get uniforms, and where to drop off their dry cleaning. Assigning a desk, getting a computer and security clearance, and many other orientation tasks are all done before the first day on the job by electronic onboarding.[26]

MEASURE

Evaluating Orientation and Metrics

Although orientation is important and can provide many advantages for both the organization and the new employee, it is not always done well. To determine the effectiveness of an orientation training program, evaluation using specific metrics is appropriate. Measurement should be made of the success of both the orientation program *and* the new hires themselves. Suggested metrics include:[27]

- *Tenure turnover rate* — What percentage of new hires of 6 months or less left the organization?
- *New hires failure factor* — What percentage of the total annual turnover was new hires?
- *Employee upgrade rate* — What percentage of new employees received a higher performance rating than previously?
- *Development program participation rate* — What percentage of new employees have moved on to training for or promotion to higher jobs?

Successfully integrating new hires is important, and measuring the degree of success allows the orientation program to be managed.

The way in which a firm plans, organizes, and structures its training affects the way employees experience the training, which in turn influences the

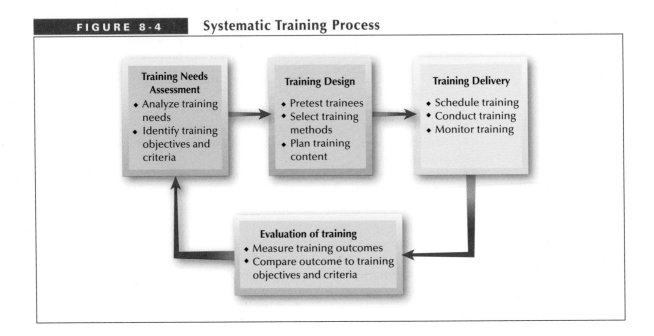

FIGURE 8-4 **Systematic Training Process**

effectiveness of the training. Effective training requires the use of a systematic training process. Figure 8-4 shows the four phases of a systematic approach: assessment, design, delivery, and evaluation. Using such a process reduces the likelihood that unplanned, uncoordinated, and haphazard training efforts will occur. A discussion of the training process follows.

TRAINING NEEDS ASSESSMENT

Assessing organizational training needs is the diagnostic phase of a training plan. This assessment considers issues of employee and organizational performance to determine if training can help. Needs assessment measures the competencies of a company, a group, or an individual as they relate to what is required. It is necessary to find out what is happening and what should be happening before deciding if training will help, and if it will help, what kind is needed. For instance, suppose that in looking at the performance of clerks in a billing department, a manager identifies problems that employees have with their data-entry and keyboarding abilities, and she decides that they would benefit from instruction in these areas. As part of assessing the training needs, the manager has the clerks take a data-entry test to measure their current keyboarding skills. Then the manager establishes an objective of increasing the clerks' keyboarding speed to 60 words per minute without errors. The number of words per minute without errors is the criterion against which training success can be measured, and it represents the way in which the objective is made specific.

Analysis of Training Needs

The first step in training needs assessment is analyzing what training might be necessary. Figure 8-5 shows the three sources used to analyze training needs.

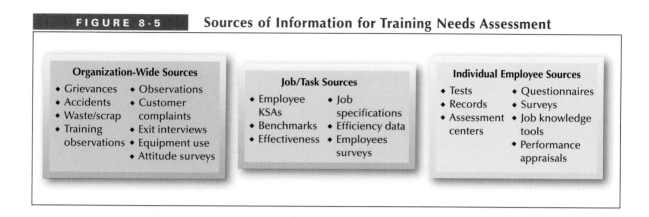

FIGURE 8-5   **Sources of Information for Training Needs Assessment**

Organizational Analysis Training needs can be diagnosed by analyzing organizational outcomes and looking at future organizational needs. A part of planning for training is the identification of the KSAs that will be needed now and in the future as both jobs and the organization change. Both internal and external forces will influence training and must be considered when doing organizational analysis. For instance, the problems posed by the technical obsolescence of current employees and an insufficiently educated labor pool from which to draw new workers should be confronted before those issues become critical.

Organizational analysis comes from various operational measures of organizational performance. Departments or areas with high turnover, customer complaints, high grievance rates, high absenteeism, low performance, and other deficiencies can be pinpointed. Following identification of such problems, training objectives can be developed if training is a solution. During organizational analysis, focus groups of managers can be used to evaluate changes and performance that might require training.

Job/Task Analysis The second way of analyzing training needs is to review the jobs involved and the tasks performed in those jobs. By comparing the requirements of jobs with the KSAs of employees, training needs can be identified. For example, at a manufacturing firm, analysis identified the tasks performed by engineers who served as technical instructors for other employees. By listing the tasks required of a technical instructor, management established a program to teach specific instructional skills; thus, the engineers were able to become more successful instructors.

Another way to pinpoint training gaps in the job or the task being done is to survey employees and have them anonymously evaluate the skill levels of their peers and estimate the skill levels necessary to be successful. This not only identifies job needs but also heightens employees' awareness of their own learning needs.[28] A training needs survey can take the form of questionnaires or interviews with supervisors and employees individually or in groups. The growth of the Internet has resulted in firms using Web-based surveys, requests, and other inputs from managers and employees to identify training needs or jobs.

A good example of needs assessment for a particular job occurred in the construction industry where there was a rash of accidents among Spanish-speaking construction workers. Construction companies recognized the need for training in English as a second language for many people. Restaurants, hospitals, and hotels have faced the same issue for certain (but not all) jobs.[29]

Individual Analysis The third means of diagnosing training needs focuses on individuals and how they perform their jobs. The following sources are examples that are useful for individual analysis:

- Performance appraisals
- Skill tests
- Individual assessment tests
- Records of critical incidents
- Assessment center exercises
- Questionnaires and surveys
- Job knowledge tools
- Internet input

The most common approach for making individual analysis is to use performance appraisal data. In some instances, a good HR information system can be used to identify individuals who require training in specific areas in order to be eligible for promotion. To assess training needs through the performance appraisal process, the organization first determines an employee's performance strengths and inadequacies in a formal review. Then it can design some type of training to help the employee overcome the weaknesses and enhance the strengths.

Another way of assessing individual training needs is to use both managerial and nonmanagerial input about what training is needed. Obtaining this kind of input can be useful in building support for the training from those who will be trained, as they help to identify training needs.

Tests can be a good means of individual-level analysis. For example, a police officer might take a qualification test with her service pistol every 6 months to indicate the officer's skill level. If an officer cannot qualify, training certainly would be necessary.

Establishing Training Objectives and Priorities

Once training requirements have been identified using needs analyses, training objectives and priorities can be established by a "gap analysis," which indicates the distance between where an organization is with its employee capabilities and where it needs to be. Training objectives and priorities are then determined to close the gap. Three types of training objectives can be set:

- *Attitude*: Creating interest in and awareness of the importance of something (e.g., sexual harassment training)
- *Knowledge*: Imparting cognitive information and details to trainees (e.g., understanding how a product works)
- *Skill*: Developing behavioral changes in how jobs and various task requirements are performed (e.g., improving speed on an installation)

The success of training should be measured in terms of the objectives that were set for it. Useful objectives are measurable. For example, an objective for a new sales clerk might be to "demonstrate the ability to explain the function of each product in the department within two weeks." This objective checks *internalization*, that is, whether the person really learned the training content and is able to use the training.

Because training seldom is an unlimited budget item and because organizations have multiple training needs, prioritization is necessary. Ideally, management looks at training needs in relation to strategic organizational plans and as part of the organizational change process. Then the training needs can be prioritized based on organizational objectives. Conducting the training most needed to improve the performance of the organization will produce visible results more quickly.

TRAINING DESIGN

Once training objectives have been determined, training design can start. Whether job-specific or broader in nature, training must be designed to address the specific objectives. Effective training design considers the learners, instructional strategies, and how best to get the training from class to the job.

Working in organizations should be a continual learning process. Different approaches are possible because learning is a complex psychological process. Each of the elements shown in Figure 8-6 must be considered for the training design to be effective and produce learning.

Learner Characteristics

For training to be successful, learners must be ready and able to learn. Learner readiness means that individuals have the ability to learn, which many people certainly have. However, individuals also must have the motivation to learn, have self-efficacy, see value in learning, and have a learning style that fits the training.

Ability to Learn   Learners must possess basic skills, such as fundamental reading and math proficiency, and sufficient cognitive abilities. Companies may discover that some workers lack the requisite skills to comprehend their training. Some have found that a significant number of job applicants and current employees lack the reading, writing, and math skills needed to learn the jobs. Employers might deal with the lack of basic employee skills in several ways:

- Offer remedial training to people in the current workforce who need it.
- Hire workers who are deficient and then implement specific workplace training.[30]
- Work with local schools to help better educate potential hires for jobs.

FIGURE 8-6   **Training Design Elements**

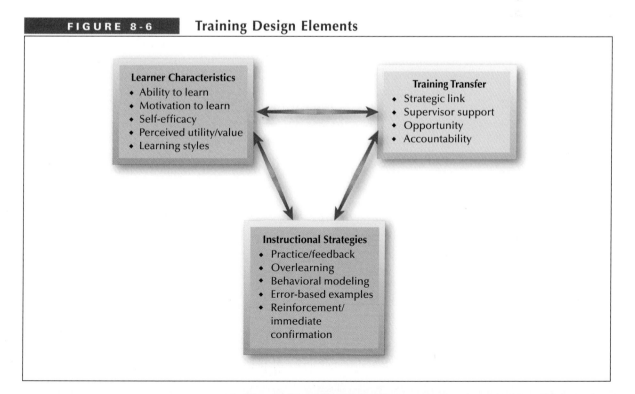

Motivation A person's desire to learn training content, referred to as "motivation to learn," is influenced by multiple factors. For example, differences in gender and ethnicity and the resulting experiences may affect the motivation of adult learners. The student's motivational level also may be influenced by the instructor's motivation and ability, friends' encouragement to do well, classmates' motivational levels, the physical classroom environment, and the training methods used.[31] Regardless of what the motivation is, without it, the student will not learn the material.

Self-Efficacy Learners must possess **self-efficacy**, which refers to people's belief that they can successfully learn the training program content. For learners to be ready for and receptive to the training content, they must feel that it is possible for them to learn it. As an example, some college students' levels of self-efficacy diminish in math or statistics courses when they do not feel adequately able to grasp the material. These perceptions may have nothing to do with their actual ability to learn, but rather reflect the way they see themselves and their abilities. Instructors and trainers must find appropriate ways to boost the confidence of trainees who are unsure of their learning abilities because people with a high level of belief that they can learn perform better and are more satisfied with the training they receive.

Perceived Utility/Value Training that is viewed as useful is more likely to be tried on the job. Perceived utility or value of training is affected by a need to improve, the likelihood that training will lead to improvement, and the practicality of the training for use on the job. Learners must perceive a close relationship between the training and things they want for it to be successful.

Learning Styles People learn in different ways. For example, *auditory* learners learn best by listening to someone else tell them about the training content. *Tactile* learners must "get their hands on" the training resources and use them. *Visual* learners think in pictures and figures and need to see the purpose and process of the training. Trainers who address all these styles by using multiple training methods can design more effective training.

Training design also must sometimes address special issues presented by **adult learning**. Certainly, the training design must consider that all the trainees are adults, but adults come with widely varying learning styles, experiences, and personal goals. For example, training older adults in technology may require greater attention to explaining the need for changes and to enhancing the older trainees' confidence and abilities when learning new technologies. In contrast, younger adults are more likely to be familiar with new technology because of their earlier exposure to computers and technology.

Malcolm Knowles's classic work on adult learning suggests five principles for designing training for adults.[32] According to that work and subsequent work by others, adults:

- Have the need to know why they are learning something.
- Have a need to be self-directed.
- Bring more work-related experiences into the learning process.
- Enter into a learning experience with a problem-centered approach to learning.
- Are motivated to learn by both extrinsic and intrinsic factors.

Self-efficacy People's belief that they can successfully learn the training program content.

Adult learning Ways in which adults learn differently than younger people.

LOGGING ON

Learnativity.com
For articles and other resources on adult learning, training, and evaluation, visit this website at www.learnativity.com.

Instructional Strategies

An important part of designing training is to select the right mix of strategies to fit the learners' characteristics. Practice/feedback, overlearning, behavioral modeling, error-based examples, and reinforcement/immediate confirmation are some of the prominent strategies available in designing the training experience.

Practice/Feedback For some kinds of training, it is important that learners practice what they have learned and get feedback on how they have done so they can improve. **Active practice** occurs when trainees perform job-related tasks and duties during training. It is more effective than simply reading or passively listening. For instance, assume a person is being trained as a customer service representative. After being given some basic selling instructions and product details, the trainee calls a customer and uses the knowledge received.

Active practice can be structured in two ways. The first, **spaced practice**, occurs when several practice sessions are spaced over a period of hours or days. The second, **massed practice**, occurs when a person performs all the practice at once. Spaced practice works better for some types of skills and for physical learning that requires muscle memory, whereas massed practice is usually more effective for other kinds of learning, such as memorizing tasks. Imagine the difficulty of trying to memorize the lists of options for 20 dishwasher models if memorized at a rate of one model a day for 20 days. By the time the appliance distribution salespeople had learned the last option, they likely would have forgotten the first one.

Overlearning Overlearning is repeated practice even after a learner has mastered the performance. It may be best used to instill "muscle memory" for a physical activity in order to reduce the amount of thinking necessary and make responses automatic. But overlearning also produces improvement in learner retention. Research suggests that even with overlearning, refreshers are still sometimes necessary to reduce the effect of response delay.[33]

Behavioral Modeling The most elementary way in which people learn—and one of the best—is through **behavioral modeling,** or copying someone else's behavior. The use of behavioral modeling is particularly appropriate for skill training in which the trainees must use both knowledge and practice. It can aid in the transfer of skills and the usage of those skills by those who are trained.[34] For example, a new supervisor can receive training and mentoring on how to handle disciplinary discussions with employees by observing as the HR director or department manager deals with such problems.

Behavioral modeling is used extensively as the primary means for training supervisors and managers in interpersonal skills. Fortunately or unfortunately, many supervisors and managers end up modeling behaviors they see their bosses use. For that reason, supervisor training should include good role models to show how to handle interpersonal interactions with employees.

Error-Based Examples The error-based examples method involves sharing with learners what can go wrong when they do not use the training properly. A good example is sharing with pilots what can happen when they are not aware of a situation they and their aircraft are entering. Situational awareness training that includes error-based examples has been shown to improve air crew situational awareness.[35] Error-based examples have been incorporated in military, firefighting, and police training as well as aviation training. Case studies that show negative consequences of errors are a good tool for communicating error-based examples.

Active practice
Performance of job-related tasks and duties by trainees during training.

Spaced practice Practice performed in several sessions spaced over a period of hours or days.

Massed practice Practice performed all at once.

Behavioral modeling
Copying someone else's behavior.

Reinforcement and Immediate Confirmation The concept of **reinforcement** is based on the *law of effect*, which states that people tend to repeat responses that give them some type of positive reward and to avoid actions associated with negative consequences. Positively reinforcing correct learned responses while providing negative consequences at some point for wrong responses can change behavior. Closely related is an instructional strategy called **immediate confirmation**, which is based on the idea that people learn best if reinforcement and feedback are given as soon as possible after training. Immediate confirmation corrects errors that, if made throughout the training, might establish an undesirable pattern that would need to be unlearned. It also aids with the transfer of training to the actual work done.

Transfer of Training

Finally, trainers should design training for the highest possible transfer from the class to the job. Transfer occurs when trainees actually use on the job what knowledge and information they learned in training. The amount of training that effectively gets transferred to the job is estimated to be relatively low, given all the time and money spent on training. It is estimated that about 40% of employees apply training to their jobs immediately after training. Among those who do not use the training immediately, the likelihood of it being used decreases over time.[36]

Effective transfer of training meets two conditions. First, the trainees can take the material learned in training and apply it to the job context in which they work. Second, employees maintain their use of the learned material over time. A number of things can increase the transfer of training. Offering trainees an *overview of the training content* and how it links to the strategy of the organization seems to help with both short-term and longer-term training transfer. Another helpful approach is to ensure that the *training mirrors the job* context as much as possible. For example, training managers to be better selection interviewers should include role-playing with "applicants" who respond in the same way that real applicants would.

One of the most consistent factors in training transfer is the *support* new trainees receive *from their supervisors* to use their new skills when they return to the job.[37] Supervisor support of the training, feedback from the supervisor, and supervisor involvement in training are powerful influences in transfer.

Opportunity to use the training also is important. To be trained on something but never to have the opportunity to use it obviously limits transfer. Learners need the opportunity to use new skills on the job if the skills are to remain.

Finally, *accountability* helps transfer training from class to job. Accountability is the extent to which someone expects the learner to use the new skills on the job and holds them responsible for doing so. It may require supervisory praise for doing the task correctly and sanctions for not showing proper trained behavior, but making people accountable for their own trained behavior is effective.[38]

Reinforcement Based on the idea that people tend to repeat responses that give them some type of positive reward and to avoid actions associated with negative consequences.

Immediate confirmation Based on the idea that people learn best if reinforcement and feedback are given as soon as possible after training.

TRAINING DELIVERY

Once training has been designed, the actual delivery of training can begin. Regardless of the type of training done, a number of approaches and methods can be used to deliver it. The growth of training technology continues to expand the available choices, as Figure 8-7 shows.

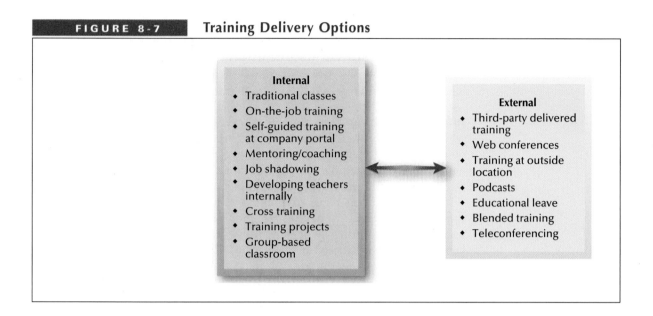

FIGURE 8-7   **Training Delivery Options**

Internal
- Traditional classes
- On-the-job training
- Self-guided training at company portal
- Mentoring/coaching
- Job shadowing
- Developing teachers internally
- Cross training
- Training projects
- Group-based classroom

External
- Third-party delivered training
- Web conferences
- Training at outside location
- Podcasts
- Educational leave
- Blended training
- Teleconferencing

Whatever the approach used, a variety of considerations must be balanced when selecting training delivery methods. The common variables considered are:

- Nature of training
- Subject matter
- Number of trainees
- Individual versus team
- Self-paced versus guided
- Training resources/costs
- E-learning versus traditional learning
- Geographic locations
- Time allotted
- Completion timeline

To illustrate, a large firm with many new hires may be able to conduct employee orientation using the Internet, videotapes, and specific HR staff members, while a small firm with few new hires may have an HR staff member meet individually with the new hires for several hours. A medium-sized company with three locations in a geographic area may bring supervisors together for a two-day training workshop once a quarter. However, a large, global firm may use Web-based courses to reach supervisors throughout the world, with content available in several languages. Frequently training is conducted internally, but some types of training use external or technological training resources.

Further, training can be formal or informal. Formal training is very visible, as it consists of planned learning activities. Informal training takes place when learning may not be the primary focus, but it occurs anyway. The informal learning may be the result of some sort of self-initiated effort or simply serendipitous, but it often occurs as needed.[39]

Internal Training

Internal training generally applies very specifically to the organization and its jobs. It is popular because it saves the cost of sending employees away for training and often avoids the cost of outside trainers. Skills-based technical training is usually conducted inside organizations. Training materials are often created internally as well.[40] Due to rapid changes in technology, the building and updating of technical skills may become crucial internal training needs.

Basic technical skills training is also being mandated by federal regulations in areas where the Occupational Safety and Health Administration (OSHA), the Environmental Protection Agency (EPA), and other agencies have jurisdiction. Three types of internal delivery options will be discussed here: informal training, on-the-job training (OJT), and cross training.

Informal Training One internal source of training is **informal training**, which occurs through interactions and feedback among employees. Much of what employees know about their jobs they learn informally from asking questions and getting advice from other employees and their supervisors, rather than from formal training programs.

Informal learning tends to occur as a result of a learning need in the context of working.[41] It may involve group problem solving, job shadowing, coaching, or mentoring; or it may evolve from employees seeking out other people who have the needed knowledge. Although "informal training" may seem to be a misnomer, a great deal of learning occurs informally in work organizations, and some of it happens by design.

On-the-Job Training The most common type of training at all levels in an organization is *on-the-job training (OJT)* because it is flexible and relevant to what employees do.[42] Well-planned and well-executed OJT can be very effective.[43] Based on a guided form of training known as job instruction training (JIT), OJT is most effective if a logical progression of stages is used, as shown in Figure 8-8. In contrast with informal training, which often occurs spontaneously, OJT should be planned. The supervisor or manager conducting the training must be able to both teach and show the employees what to do.

However, OJT has some problems. Often, those doing the training may have no experience in training, no time to do it, or no desire to participate in it. Under such conditions, learners essentially are on their own, and training likely will not be effective. Another problem is that OJT can disrupt regular work. Unfortunately, OJT can amount to no training at all in some circumstances, especially if the trainers simply abandon the trainees to learn the job alone. Also, bad habits or incorrect information from the supervisor or manager can be transferred to the trainees.

Informal training
Training that occurs through interactions and feedback among employees.

| FIGURE 8-8 | **Stages for On-the-Job Training** |

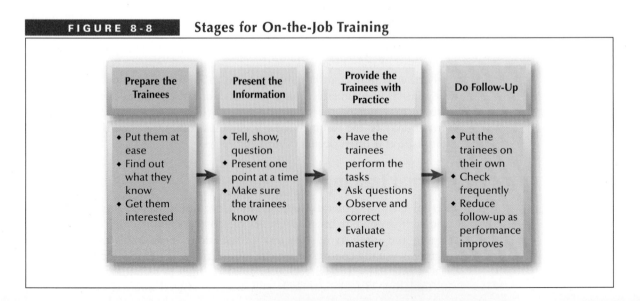

Cross Training "Universal Agents"

As technology has matured in the banking business, ATMs, debit cards, online banking, and direct deposit have changed the job of the bank teller and reduced the need for teller-processed transactions. Cross training can combine the duties of a teller with the duties of a member service representative (MSR), which helps by retaining jobs, making the jobs more interesting and varied, and saving the bank costs.

A "universal agent" is an employee who is cross-trained as both a teller and an MSR. This employee can cover employee absences and lunch breaks for either tellers or MSRs. The universal agent can be scheduled for either position during periods of peak activity, such as Friday afternoons. But to make these advantages become possible, the bank or credit union must provide support with cross training and technology that allows the employee to shift from one job to the other.

The universal agent should be able to serve as a transaction processor, financial counselor, and service provider. Universal agents can approach customers and get them to the proper place/person or handle their needs themselves. If customers need checks cashed, the agent can take them to the teller station. If customers need CDs renewed, the agent can do that at a work station. If customers need loans, the agent can begin the process and call the loan manager for consultation if necessary.

Two technological changes are necessary to make this work. First, the traditional teller's position has to be redesigned to allow the agent to move between the teller's work station and the sales and service work station. Employees circulate through the bank, and every customer receives a sit-down interaction with an agent for all activities.

The second technological change necessary to make the universal agent position work is acquisition of a machine called a "cash recycler." This machine accepts, stores, and dispenses currency and coins similar to an ATM. It allows the universal agent to get away from the traditional teller's cash drawer, which must be closed, reconciled, and locked anytime it is left.

Teller and MSR skill sets differ, and cross training is critical to teach someone in one position the duties of an employee in the other. Tellers may need sales training to be able to do the MSR job, and MSRs will need teller training. However, when properly done, the universal agent approach can provide a better sales and service experience for the customer and keep transaction costs to a minimum.[47]

Cross Training Cross training occurs when people are trained to do more than one job—theirs and someone else's.[44] For the employer, the advantages of cross training are flexibility and development.[45] However, although cross training is attractive to the employer, it is not always appreciated by employees, who often feel that it requires them to do more work for the same pay. To counteract such responses and to make it more appealing to employees, learning "bonuses" can be awarded for successfully completing cross training.

In some organizations, the culture may be such that people seek cross-training assignments to grow or prepare for a promotion, but that is not the case in all organizations.[46] Unions typically are not in favor of cross training because it threatens job jurisdiction and broadens jobs. Cross training may require scheduling work differently during training, and temporarily decreased productivity may result from it as people learn. Overall, an effective cross-training program can overcome the concerns mentioned and has the potential to be good for both employer and employee, as the HR Perspective: Cross Training Universal Agents illustrates.

Cross training Training people to do more than one job.

External Training

External training, or training that takes place outside the employing organization, is used extensively by organizations of all sizes. Large organizations use external training if they lack the capability to train people internally or when many people need to be trained quickly. External training may be the best option for training in smaller firms due to limitations in the size of their training staffs and in the number of employees who need various types of specialized training. Whatever the size of the organization, external training occurs for several reasons:

- It may be less expensive for an employer to have an outside trainer conduct training in areas where internal training resources are limited.
- The organization may have insufficient time to develop internal training materials.
- The HR staff may not have the necessary level of expertise for the subject matter in which training is needed.
- There are advantages to having employees interact with managers and peers in other companies in training programs held externally.

Outsourcing of Training Many employers of all sizes outsource training to external training firms, consultants, and other entities. Perhaps one-third of training expenditures go to outside training sources. The reasons more outside training is not used may be cost concerns, and a greater emphasis on internal linking of training to organizational strategies. However, outsourcing of training is used more frequently when mergers and acquisition occur.[48]

A popular route for some employers is to use vendors and suppliers to train employees. Several computer software vendors offer employees technical certifications on their software. For example, being a Microsoft Certified Product Specialist gives employees credentials that show their level of technical expertise. Such certifications provide employees with items to put on their résumés should they decide to change jobs. These certifications also benefit employers, who can use them as job specifications for hiring and promotion.

Many suppliers host users' conferences, where employees from a number of firms receive detailed training on using products, services, and features that are new to the employees. Some vendors will conduct the training inside an organization as well if sufficient numbers of employees are to be trained.

Government-Supported Job Training Federal, state, and local governments provide a wide range of external training assistance and funding. The Workforce Investment Act (WIA) provides states with block grant programs that target adult education, disadvantaged youth, and family literacy. Employers hiring and training individuals who meet the WIA criteria receive tax credits and other assistance for 6 months or more, depending on the program regulations.

At state and local levels, employers that add to their workforces can take advantage of a number of programs that provide funding assistance to offset training costs. As an example, a number of states offer workforce training assistance for employers. Quick Start (Georgia), Smart Jobs (Texas), and Partnership (Alabama) are three well-known training support efforts. Often such programs are linked to two-year and four-year colleges throughout the state.

Educational Assistance Programs Some employers pay for additional education for their employees. Typically, the employee pays for a course that applies to a college degree and is reimbursed upon successful completion of the course. The amounts paid by the employer are considered nontaxable income for the employee up to amounts set by federal laws.

Lifelong Learning Accounts (LiLA) programs can be offered by employers. These accounts are like 401(K) plans—employers and employees contribute to a fund for adult education. The employee owns the plan and keeps it even if the employee leaves the company. It can be used to further one's education, perhaps in order to move to a different job in the company.[49]

One concern about traditional forms of employee educational programs is that they may pose risks for the employer. Upon completion of the degree, the employee may choose to take the new skills and go elsewhere. Employers must plan to use these skills upon employee graduation to improve the retention of those employees.

LOGGING ON

Quick Start Technical College System of Georgia
The Quick Start system provides information on delivering workforce training in a broad range of industry sectors. Visit the website at www.georgiaquickstart.org.

Combination Training Approaches

Whether training is delivered internally or externally, appropriate training must be chosen. The following overview identifies two common training approaches that often integrate internal and external means. Some are used more for job-based training, while others are used more for development.

Cooperative Training Cooperative training approaches mix classroom training and on-the-job experiences. This training can take several forms. One form, generally referred to as *school-to-work transition*, helps individuals move into jobs while still in school or on completion of formal schooling. Such efforts may be arranged with high schools or community colleges.

Another form of cooperative training used by employers, trade unions, and government agencies is *apprentice training*. An apprenticeship program provides an employee with on-the-job experience under the guidance of a skilled and certified worker. Certain requirements for training, equipment, time length, and proficiency levels may be monitored by a unit of the U.S. Department of Labor. Figure 8-9 indicates the most common areas that use apprenticeships to train people for jobs. Apprenticeships usually last 2 to 5 years, depending on the occupation. During this time, the apprentice usually receives lower wages than the certified individual.

A form of cooperative training called *internship* usually combines job training with classroom instruction from schools, colleges, and universities.[50] Internships benefit both employers and interns. Interns get real-world exposure, a line on their résumés, and a chance to closely examine a possible

FIGURE 8-9   **Most Common Apprenticeship Occupations**

- Electrician (construction)
- Carpenter
- Plumber
- Pipe fitter
- Sheet metal worker

- Structural-steel worker
- Elevator constructor
- Roofer
- Sprinkler fitter
- Bricklayer

employer. Employers get a cost-effective source of labor and a chance to see an intern at work before making a final hiring decision.[51]

E-Learning: Online Training

E-learning is use of the Internet or an organizational intranet to conduct training online. E-learning is popular with employers. The major advantages are cost savings and access to more employees. Estimates are that corporate training conducted through learning technology will increase in the next few years.[52] Almost 30% of learning hours today are totally technology based, according to an ASTD report, and e-learning is preferred by workers under the age of 30.[53]

However, e-learning is advancing gradually, not explosively. It has found favor as part of a "blended" solution that combines it with other forms of learning. By itself, e-learning is not rated among the top effective training practices by training professionals.[54] Changes in technology appear to make possible in the future some things that were not possible in the first years of e-learning. For example, Web 2.0 tools such as instant messaging and Web conferencing may allow trainers to expand to "soft skills" electronic training,[55] and the ability to have reasonably priced video conferencing may make training via this medium more acceptable.[56]

The method is certainly fast and flexible. For example, after Hurricane Katrina, a Red Cross volunteer was able to design and make an online course to train volunteers available in 4 days. When volunteers signed up to help, they were immediately directed to the online training course.[57] Three areas where online learning has proved to be beneficial are distance training/learning, simulations, and blended learning.

Distance Training/Learning Many college and university classes use some form of Internet-based course support. Blackboard and WebCT are two popular support packages that thousands of college professors use to make their lecture content available to students. These packages enable virtual chat and electronic file exchange among course participants, and also enhance instructor-student contact.

Many large employers use interactive two-way television to present classes. The medium allows an instructor in one place to see and respond to a "class" in any number of other locations. With a fully configured system, employees can take courses from anywhere in the world.[58]

Simulations and Training Computer-based training involves a wide array of multimedia technologies—including sound, motion (video and animation), graphics, and hypertext—to tap multiple learner senses. Computer-supported simulations within e-learning can replicate the psychological and behavioral requirements of a task, often in addition to providing some amount of physical resemblance to the trainee's work environment.

From highly complicated systems that replicate difficult landing scenarios for pilots to programs that help medical trainees learn to sew sutures, simulations allow for safe training when the risks associated with failure are high. For example, sanitation workers can get practice driving on slick roads and down tight alleys without damaging anything. A $450,000 computer simulation uses videos, movement, and sound to simulate driving a dump truck. Accidents from poor truck handling skills include damage to fences, posts, and buildings. The safety training simulation reduces such accidents.[59]

Simulations and Games

A young woman walks into a restaurant in a busy city, sets down a purse, and leaves. Moments later a bomb explodes, and people are screaming and injured as the restaurant goes up in flames. Fire trucks and police go to work to deal with the mess. This did not really happen; it is a training simulation made to teach emergency response initiatives. Such real-time virtual training forces employees to apply their knowledge in the real world, and to make quick decisions in difficult situations.

Many people play computer games for fun, but games in various forms also are becoming a very useful part of training. For years military and government workers have used games and simulations to prepare for combat, improve the use of military equipment, and prepare for natural and human-caused disasters. Now many private employers of all types are using gaming situations for both new and existing employees.

For example, a company in Pittsburg uses a virtual training environment in which employees learn to operate a forklift to move loads from the loading area to another area. They must check their equipment before starting, and a wrong move may result in a forklift crashing into another employee or driving off the dock. The simulation allows learning without tying up the dock for training or hurting anyone.

Railroads, trucking companies, banks, retailers, technology firms, hotels, and many others are using gaming simulations. Doing so appears to increase employee interest in training, promises better training transfer, and improves performance. A younger workforce seems to appreciate the training method. Game-based learning (GBL) can present realistic, complete, and captivating experiences for employees. For many, "winning the game" is more motivating than answering questions or taking a test.

However, GBL requires the same needs analysis and planning as any other training effort. While the games may be more interesting than some classes, they do not automatically provide good training. The right game must be used to teach the right things.[60]

Virtual reality is also used to create an artificial environment for trainees so that they can participate in the training. Gaming is a growing e-learning tool, as the HR Perspective describes.

The new technologies incorporated into training delivery affect the design, administration, and support of training. Some companies have invested in electronic registration and recordkeeping systems that allow trainers to register participants, record exam results, and monitor learning progress.

Generally, technology is moving from center stage to becoming embedded in the learning and training processes. As learning and work merge even closer in the future, technology is likely to integrate seamlessly into the work environment of more employees. This integration will allow employees to spend less time in the future learning how to use technology, and more time on learning the desired content. For example, screening passenger bags in airports has been improved by using a simulation tied to the X-ray machine that is used to screen.[61]

Blended learning Learning approach that combines methods, such as short, fast-paced, interactive computer-based lessons and teleconferencing with traditional classroom instruction and simulation.

Blended Learning E-learning cannot be the sole method of training, according to the findings of a number of employers.[62] Therefore, the solution seems to be **blended learning**, which might combine short, fast-paced, interactive computer-based lessons and teleconferencing with traditional classroom instruction and simulation.[63] Deciding which training is best handled by which medium is important. A blended learning approach can use e-learning for building knowledge of certain basics, a Web-based virtual classroom for building skills, and significant

| FIGURE 8-10 | Advantages and Disadvantages of E-Learning |

Advantages	Disadvantages
• Is self-paced; trainees can proceed on their own time • Is interactive, tapping multiple trainee senses • Enables scoring of exercises/ assessments and the appropriate feedback • Incorporates built-in guidance and help for trainees to use when needed • Allows trainers to update content relatively easily • Can enhance instructor-led training • Is good for presenting simple facts and concepts • Can be paired with simulation	• May cause trainee anxiety • Some trainees may not be interested in how it is used • Requires easy and uninterrupted access to computers • Is not appropriate for some training (leadership, cultural change, etc.) • Requires significant upfront investment both in time and costs • Requires significant support from top management to be successful • Some choose not to do it even if it is available

in-person traditional instructor-led training sessions and courses. Use of blended learning provides greater flexibility in the use of multiple training means and enhances the appeal of training activities to different types of employees.[64]

Advantages and Disadvantages of E-Learning The rapid growth of e-learning makes the Internet or an intranet a viable means for delivering training content. But e-learning has both advantages and disadvantages that must be considered.[65] In addition to being concerned about employee access to e-learning and desire to use it, some employers worry that trainees will use e-learning to complete courses quickly but will not retain and use much of what they learned. Taking existing training materials, putting them on the Internet, and cutting the training budget is not the way to succeed with e-learning. An important question to ask is: Can this material be learned as well online as through conventional methods? In some cases, the answer is no.

E-learning is the latest development in training delivery. Some of the biggest obstacles to using it will be keeping up with the rapid changes in technological innovation and designing e-courses appropriately. E-learning has had a major impact on HR and training, but there are no "ten easy steps" to making e-learning successful. Figure 8-10 presents a listing of the most commonly cited advantages and disadvantages of e-learning.

TRAINING EVALUATION

Evaluation of training compares the post-training results to the pre-training objectives of managers, trainers, and trainees. Too often, training is conducted with little thought of measuring and evaluating it later to see how well it worked. Because training is both time consuming and costly, it should be evaluated.[66]

| FIGURE 8-11 | Levels of Training Evaluation |

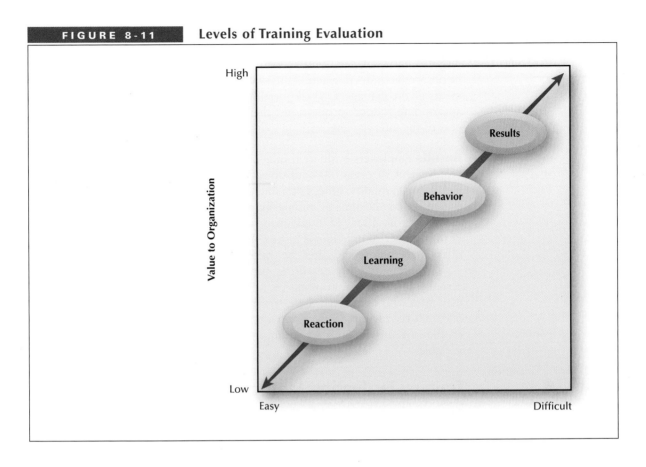

Levels of Evaluation

It is best to consider how training is to be evaluated before it begins. Donald L. Kirkpatrick identified four levels at which training can be evaluated. As Figure 8-11 shows, the evaluation of training becomes successively more difficult to do as it moves from measuring reaction to measuring learning to measuring behavior and then to measuring results. But the training that affects behavior and results versus reaction and learning provides greater value in viewing training as a strategic performance contributor.[67]

Reaction Organizations evaluate the reaction levels of trainees by conducting interviews with or administering questionnaires to the trainees. Assume that 30 managers attend a two-day workshop on effective interviewing skills. A reaction-level measure could be gathered by having the managers complete a survey that asked them to rate the value of the training, the style of the instructors, and the usefulness of the training to them.

Learning Learning levels can be evaluated by measuring how well trainees have learned facts, ideas, concepts, theories, and attitudes. Tests on the training material are commonly used for evaluating learning, and they can be given both before and after training to provide scores that can be compared. If test scores indicate learning problems, then instructors get feedback and courses can be redesigned so that the content can be delivered more effectively. Of course, learning enough to pass a test does not guarantee that trainees will remember the training content months later or that it will change job behaviors.[68]

Behavior Evaluating training at the behavioral level means measuring the effect of training on job performance through observing job performance. For instance, the managers who participated in an interviewing workshop might be observed conducting actual interviews of applicants for jobs in their departments. If the managers asked questions as they had been trained to and used appropriate follow-up questions, then behavioral indicators of the effectiveness of the interviewing training exist.

Results Employers evaluate results by measuring the effect of training on the achievement of organizational objectives. Because results such as productivity, turnover, quality, time, sales, and costs are relatively concrete, this type of evaluation can be done by comparing records before and after training. For the managers who attended interviewing training, evaluators could gather records of the number of individuals hired compared with the number of employment offers made before and after the training.

The difficulty with measuring results is pinpointing whether changes were actually the result of training or of other major factors. For example, the managers who completed the interviewing training program can be measured on employee turnover before and after the training, but turnover also depends on the current economic situation, the demand for workers, and many other variables.

Training Evaluation Metrics

MEASURE

Training is expensive, and it is an HR function that requires measurement and monitoring. Cost–benefit analysis and return-on-investment (ROI) analysis are commonly used to measure training results, as are various benchmarking approaches.

Cost–Benefit Analysis Training results can be examined through **cost–benefit analysis**, which is comparison of costs and benefits associated with training. There are four stages in calculating training costs and benefits:[69]

1. *Determine training costs.* Consider direct costs such as design, trainer fees, materials, facilities, and other administration activities.
2. *Identify potential savings results.* Consider employee retention, better customer service, fewer work errors, quicker equipment production, and other productivity factors.
3. *Compute potential savings.* Gather data on the performance results and assign dollar costs to each of them.
4. *Conduct costs and savings benefits comparisons.* Evaluate the costs per participant, the savings per participant, and how the costs and benefits relate to business performance numbers.

One firm uses HR metrics for many aspects of evaluating how general managers and their stores are performing. Scoring results are produced annually, quarterly, and monthly.

Figure 8-12 shows some costs and benefits that may result from training. Even though some benefits (such as attitude changes) are hard to quantify, comparison of costs and benefits associated with training remains a way to determine whether training is cost-effective. For example, one firm evaluated a traditional safety training program and found that the program did not lead to a reduction in accidents. Therefore, the safety training was redesigned, and better safety practices resulted.

Cost–benefit analysis
Comparison of costs and benefits associated with training.

FIGURE 8-12   **Possible Costs and Benefits in Training**

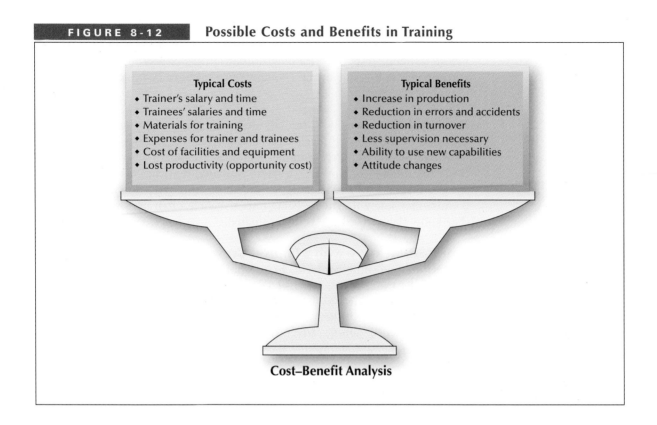

Cost–Benefit Analysis

Return-on-Investment Analysis and Benchmarking In organizations, training is often expected to produce an ROI. Still, too often, training is justified because someone liked it, rather than on the basis of resource accountability. ROI simply divides the return produced because of the training by the cost (or investment) of the training.

In addition to evaluating training internally, some organizations use benchmark measures to compare it with training done in other organizations. To do benchmarking, HR professionals gather data on training in their organization and compare them with data on training at other organizations in the same industry and in companies of a similar size. Comparison data are available through the American Society for Training and Development and its Benchmarking Service. This service has training-related data from more than 1,000 participating employers who complete detailed questionnaires annually. Training also can be benchmarked against data from the American Productivity & Quality Center and the Saratoga Institute.

Training Evaluation Designs

With or without benchmarking data, internal evaluations of training programs can be designed in a number of ways. The rigor of the three designs discussed next increases with each level.

Post-Measure The most obvious way to evaluate training effectiveness is to determine after the training whether the individuals can perform the way management wants them to perform. Assume that a customer service manager has 20 representatives who need to improve their data-entry speeds. After a one-day training session, they take a test to measure their speeds. If the representatives can all type the required speed after training, was the training beneficial? It is difficult to say; perhaps most of them could have done as well before training. Tests after training do not always clearly indicate whether a performance is a result of the training or could have been achieved without the training.

Pre-/Post-Measure By differently designing the evaluation just discussed, the issue of pretest skill levels can be considered. If the data-entry speed is measured before and after training, then it will indicate whether the training made any difference. However, a question would remain: Was any increase in speed a response to the training, or did these employees simply work faster because they knew they were being tested? People often perform better when they know their efforts are being evaluated.

Pre-/Post-Measure with a Control Group Another evaluation design can address the preceding problem. In addition to testing the 20 representatives who will be trained, the manager can test another group of representatives who will not be trained, to see if they do as well as those who are to be trained. This second group is called a control group. After training, if the trained representatives work significantly faster than those who were not trained, the manager can be reasonably sure that the training was effective.

SUMMARY

- Training is the process that provides people with the capabilities they need to do their jobs.
- Four types of training are regular/required, job/technical, interpersonal/problem solving, and developmental/career in nature.
- A strategic approach to training links organizational strategies and HR planning to various training efforts.
- Training affects factors such as organizational competitiveness, knowledge management, revenue, and performance.
- Performance consulting compares desired and actual results in order to identify needed training and nontraining actions.
- Global strategies must consider training as a key component, including intercultural competence training to prepare employees to respond more appropriately to situations encountered during global assignments.
- The training process consists of four phases: assessment, design, delivery, and evaluation.
- Training needs can be assessed using organizational, job/task, and individual analyses, and then training objectives can be set to help the organization meet those needs.

- Training design must consider learner readiness, learning styles, and learning transfer.
- Training can be delivered internally (e.g., OJT training) or through external means, and formally (e.g., through classes) or informally.
- Common training approaches include cooperative training and classroom/conference training.
- Orientation is a form of onboarding designed to help new employees learn about their jobs.
- E-learning is training conducted using the Internet or an intranet, and both its advantages and its disadvantages must be considered in its development.
- Various organizations are taking advantage of training that uses technology, such as Web-based multimedia, video streaming, simulation, and virtual reality.
- Training can be evaluated at four levels: reaction, learning, behavior, and results.
- Training evaluation metrics may include cost–benefit analysis, ROI analysis, and benchmarking.
- A pre-/post-measure with a control group is the most rigorous design for training evaluation; other, less rigorous designs can be used as well.

CRITICAL THINKING ACTIVITIES

1. Identify training needs for a group of new salespeople in a high-end jewelry store.
2. Why is evaluating training an important part of strategic training?
3. Develop an orientation checklist based on one first-day session and a second session of 4 hours each to cover 30-days later.
4. Make a briefing for division managers showing the advantages and disadvantages of e-learning and how to "blend" it with other teaching techniques. Use websites, including www.ASTD.org.

HR EXPERIENTIAL PROBLEM SOLVING

Due to rapid growth of your technology company, the executive team has asked HR to develop an internal training program. The purpose of the program is to help employees recently promoted to supervisory positions develop the leadership skill sets they need to be successful as supervisors. This will be the first formal training program for your small company. As part of the process, you want to consider the learning styles of the new supervisors. To assist you in developing a successful, results-oriented program, review various training websites, including www.agelesslearner.com.

1. To meet the needs of the varied learning styles and maximize the learning potential of the participants, what training techniques should be implemented?
2. Identify the content topics that you will recommend be included in the program to ensure the development of successful leaders.

CASE

21st-Century Onboarding

New employees at Sun Microsystems begin their orientation sessions after being hired with a computer game. It is part of an attempt to integrate new people, improve the image of the company, get feedback, and start training. Looking over the shoulder of a new employee, one would see the person playing a computer game called "Dawn of the Shadow Spectors," battling evil forces that are trying to destroy Sun's network.

Before Sun changed its orientation program, an employee's first day at work consisted mostly of filling out paperwork, as in most companies. Some new employees waited 2 weeks to get e-mail, and people who worked remotely sometimes waited weeks or months before meeting their managers.

The chief learning officer at Sun said, "We wanted to make a better first impression," unlike that made on an employee's first day if the company/manager is not ready and the person just sits there. That can make a bad impression that is lasting. Now at Sun the onboarding starts as soon as a person accepts a job. The new employee logs on to the company's new hire website and learns about the company by playing video games. The person sees a welcome video from the CEO and connects with other employees via social networks. New employees also fill out their W-4s, I-9s, and other paperwork on the website. Sun, which has about 34,000 employees, believes orientation should start the moment a person is hired and continue until the person is productive.

A Houston-based company, El Paso Corporation, which employs about 5,000, has a different onboarding process. New hires attend a first-day orientation and then another a month later. During their first week at the company, they get an e-mail with links to everything from ordering business cards to joining the credit union. Before the new system was instituted, employees sometimes waited to even get a computer. One company official noted that new employees "were here but just sitting around because they didn't have the tools to work." Now they have a workspace, computer, and network access on their first day.

An advertising agency in Fort Lauderdale, Florida, takes yet a different approach. Zimmerman Advertising, which has about 1,000 employees, wants employees to understand the company, so new hires log on and learn from the new hire website what the company does, its client philosophy, and about its leadership. Then they meet for an hour with the CEO who talks about how he built the company. New hires get a 30-, 60-, and 90-day training checklist that must be completed on time and signed by their supervisor. They also have an opportunity to provide feedback via the website. Modern onboarding systems help new employees understand what the company is all about so they are prepared to integrate into it, says Zimmerman's Vice President of HR.[70]

QUESTIONS

1. The case introduces three companies of very different sizes with three different onboarding approaches. What differences do you see in their approaches? What similarities?

2. Are there important ideas missing from all three approaches? If so, what are they?

3. Which approach sounds best to you? Why?

SUPPLEMENTAL CASES

Training Crucial for Hotels

This case illustrates the increased role training is playing in large U.S. hotel chains. (For the case, go to www.cengage.com/management/mathis.)

New Payroll Clerk

This case shows the frustration that often accompanies the first day at work, and why orientation is important in reducing turnover. (For the case, go to www.cengage.com/management/mathis.)

NOTES

1. Based on Adrienne Fox, "China: Land of Opportunity and Challenge," *HR Magazine*, September 2007, 38–44; Z.A.S. Udani, "International Briefing 21: Training and Development in MACAO," *International Journal of Training and Development*, 12, No. 4 (2009), 280–296.

2. Herman Aquinis and Kurt Kraiger, "Benefits of Training and Development for Individuals and Teams, Organizations and Society," *Annual Review of Psychology*, 60 (2009), 451–474.

3. Julie Bos, "Maximize Every Training Dollar," *Workforce Management*, November 17, 2008, 39.

4. Gilad Chan and Richard Klimoski, "Training and Development of Human Resources at Work," *Human Resource Management Review*, 17 (2007), 180–190.

5. Michael Felton-O'Brien, "Taking the Pulse," *Human Resource Executive*, November 19, 2007, 9.

6. James Hall and Marty Denis, "Compensability of Job Related Training," *Workplace Management*, April 6, 2009, 10.

7. Charlotte Huff, "Training Adapts to the Downturn," *Workforce Management*, March 16, 2009, 22.

8. "Tying Training and Development to Competitive Strategy," *Workforce Management*, May 18, 2009, 53.

9. "Strategic Training and Development," *SHRM Research Quarterly*, First Quarter 2008, 1–9.

10. Julie Bos, "Top Trends in Training and Leadership Development," *Workforce Management*, November 19, 2007, 36.

11. Phyllis Thaenou, et al., "A Review and Critique of Research on Training and Organizational Level Outcomes," *Human Resource Management Review*, 17 (2007), 251–273.

12. Based on Beverly Propst, "Business Education á la Carte," *HR Magazine*, October 2008, 52–54.

13. J. J. Smith, "U.S. Workers Tech Skills Declined While India, Eastern Europe Grew," *SHRM Global HR News*, September 2006, www.shrm.org/global.

14. Paula Caligirvir and Saba Calakoglv, "A Strategic Contingency Approach to Expatriate Assignment Management," *Human Resource Management Journal*, 17, 2007, 393–410.

15. Ann Tace, "Training for the Leap Overseas," *T + D*, August 2009, 18.

16. Andrea Edmundson, "Culturally Accessible E-Learning," *T + D*, April 2009, 41–45.

17. Shedeh Tavakoli, et al., "Effects of Assertiveness Training and Expressive Writing on Acculturative Stress in International Students," *Journal of Counseling Psychology*, 56 (2009), 590–596.

18. Stephan Miller, "Skills Critical for a Changing Workforce," *HR Magazine*, August 2008, 24.

19. Jean Thilmany, "Passing on Know-How," *HR Magazine*, June 2008, 100–104.

20. Danielle D'Amour, "Knowledge to Action: The Development of Training Strategies," *Healthcare Policy*, 3, 2008, 68–79.

21. Alan M. Saks, et al., "Socialization Tactics and Newcomer Adjustment,"

Journal of Vocational Behavior, 70, 2007, 413–446.

22. Bridget Testa, "Early Engagement Long Relationship?" *Workforce Management*, September 22, 2008, 27–31; Jerry Newman, "The Undercover Secrets to Successful Onboarding," *Workspan*, February 2009, 22–28.

23. Patricia D'Aurizio, "Onboarding: Delivering on the Process," *Nursing Economics*, July–August 2007, 228–229; Fay Hansen, "Onboarding for Greater Engagement," *Workforce Management Online*, October 2008, www.workforce.com, 1–3.

24. Kathy Gurchiek, "Orientation Programs Help New Hires Find Bearings," *SHRM HR News*, May 25, 2007, www.shrm.org, 1–3.

25. D. J. Chhabra, "What Web-Based Onboarding Can Do for Your Company," *Workspan*, May 2008, 111–114.

26. Louis Greenstein, "Beyond Day One," *Human Resource Executive*, October 2, 2007, 1–26.

27. Bill Gilmyers and Amir Assadi, "What Your New Hires Are Telling You," *Workspan*, July 2009, 30–38.

28. Pierre Gudjian and Oliver Triebel, "Identifying Employee Skill Gaps," *The McKinsey Quarterly*, May 2009, 1–12.

29. Rita Zeidner, "One Workforce Many Languages," *HR Magazine*, January 2009, 33–37.

30. Martha Frase, "An Underestimated Talent Pool," *HR Magazine*, April 2009, 55–58.

31. Sara B. Kimmel and Mary N. McNeese, "Barriers to Business Education: Motivating Adult Learners," *Journals of Behavioral and Applied Management*, 7 (2006), 292.

32. Malcolm S. Knowles, Elwood F. Holton III, and Richard A. Swanson, *The Adult Learner*, 6th ed. (New York: Elsevier, 2005).

33. Lisa Burke and Holly Hutchins, "Training Transfer: An Integrative Literature Review," *Human Resource Development Review*, 6 (2007), 275.

34. John-Paul Hatala and Pamela Fleming, "Making Transfer Climate Visible: Utilizing Social Network Analysis to Facilitate Transfer of Training," *Human Resource Development Review*, 6 (2007), 33–62.

35. Simon Branbury, et al., "FASA: Development and Validation of a Novel Measure to Assess the Effectiveness of Commercial Airline Pilot Situation Awareness Training,"

International Journal of Aviation Psychology, 17 (2007), 131–152.

36. Raquel Velada, et al., "The Effect of Training Design, Individual Characteristics and Work Environment on Transfer of Training," *International Journal of Training and Development*, 11 (2007), 282–294.

37. Burke and Hutchins, *op. cit.*, 28.

38. *Ibid.*, 281.

39. Ronald Jacobs and Yoonhee Park, "A Proposed Conceptual Framework of Workplace Learning," *Human Resource Development Review*, 8 (2009), 133–150.

40. Mark Partridge, "Copyrights and Wrongs," *HR Magazine*, November 2008, 101–104.

41. Jacobs and Park, *op. cit.*, 140–141.

42. Kathryn Tyler, "15 Ways to Train on the Job," *HR Magazine*, September 2008, 105–108.

43. Maite Blazquez and Wiemer Salverda, "Low Wage Employment and the Role of Education and On-the-Job Training," EALE Annual Conference (Amsterdam), September 2008, 1–27.

44. Jennifer Arnould, "Kicking Up Cross-Training," *HR Magazine*, August 2008, 96–100.

45. Eylem Tekin, et al., "Pooling Strategies for Call Center Agent Cross-Training," *IEEE Transactions*, 41, 2009, 546–561.

46. Frada Mozenter, et al., "Perspective on Cross Training Public Service Staff in the Electronic Age: I Have to Learn to Do WHAT?" *Journal of Academic Librarianship*, 29, 2008, 339–404.

47. "Cross Training Boosts Efficiency," *CU 360*, 35, July 27, 2009, 6–7.

48. Marianne Langlois, "Doing Learning Right," *Workforce Management*, May 2008, 53.

49. Susan Ladika, "When Learning Lasts a Lifetime," *HR Magazine*, May 2008, 57–60.

50. Beth Mirza, "Interns Experience the Real World of HR," *HR Magazine*, September 2008, 144–145.

51. Julie Cook Ramirez, "Internal Affairs," *Human Resource Executive*, November 19, 2007, 15–17.

52. Jeanne Meister, "Web Based Corporate Learning Takes Off," *Human Resource Executive*, November 17, 2007, 15–17.

53. American Society of Training and Development, www.astd.org.

54. Sue Weekes, "May E-Learning Pay and Play," *Training Magazine*, May 20, 2008, 1–2.

55. Bill Roberts, "Hard Facts About Soft-Skills E-Learning," *HR Magazine*, January 2008, 76–78.

56. Jim Ware and Charlie Granthom, "Is Video Conferencing Finally about to Take Off?" *Workspan*, December 2008, 18–20; Elizabeth Agnvall, "Meetings Go Virtual," *HR Magazine*, January 2009, 74–78.

57. Sarah Fister Gale, "Do It Yourself E-Learning," *Workforce Management Online*, May 2008, 1–2.

58. Elisabeth Bennett, "Virtual HRD: The Intersection of Knowledge Management, Culture, and Intranets," *Advances in Developing Human Resources*, 11, 2009, 363–372.

59. *Casper Star Tribune*, October 4, 2009, F1B.

60. Sara Gale, "Virtual Training with Real Results," *Workforce Management*, December 2008, 1–3; "Let the Games Begin," *Workforce Management*, December 2008, 54.

61. Adrian Schwaninger, "Adaptive Computer Based Training Increases On-the-Job Performance of X-Ray Screeners," *IEEF Xplore*, 2007, 117–124.

62. Ed Frauenheim, "Your Coworker, Your Teacher," *Workforce Management*, 86, No. 2, 2007, 19–23.

63. Ji-Hye Park, "Factors Associated with Transfer of Training in Workplace E-Learning," *Journal of Workplace Learning*, 19 (2007), 311–329.

64. Laura Aionso Diaz and Florentino Entonado, "Are the Functions of E-Learning and Face-to-Face Environments Really Different?" *Educational Technology and Society*, 12, 2009, 331–343.

65. Kurt Kraiger, "Transforming Our Models of Learning and Development: Web Based Instruction as Enabler of Third Generation Instruction," *Industrial and Organizational Psychology*, 1, 2008, 454–467.

66. Joe Ruff, "Helping Firms Measure Worker Training Results," *Omaha World Herald*, January 21, 2008.

67. Katharine Shobe and Barbara Curtis, "Training Assessment Challenges in a Military Environment: A U.S. Navy Example," *Performance Improvement*, March 2007, 42–46.

68. Yiching Chen, "Learning to Learn: The Impact of Strategy Training," *ELT Journal*, January 2007, 20–28.

69. "Calculate the Cost and Benefits of Training," *Workforce Management*, 2007, www.workforce.com.

70. Leslie Klaff, "New Emphasis on First Impressions," *Workforce Management Online*, March 2008, www.workforce.com, 1–3.

9

Talent Management

After you have read this chapter, you should be able to:

- Identify the importance of talent management and discuss two reasons it may be difficult.

- Explain what succession planning is and its steps.

- Differentiate between organization-centered and individual-centered career planning.

- Discuss three career issues that organizations and employees must address.

- List options for development needs analyses.

- Identify several management development methods.

How Top Companies Develop Stars

(© McDonald's Corporation)

The CEO at American Express says, "Most companies maintain their office copiers better than they build the capabilities of their people." But the world is changing and many companies are being forced to change as well. An examination of companies reveals that some of the best at managing talent include American Express, General Electric, McDonald's, and Eli Lily. These so-called "Academy Companies" offer more training to their executives, and their alumni become leaders at other firms.

American Express has built a rigorous leadership development program with metrics, incentives, goals, values, and calendars. But the biggest investment in leadership for these businesses is the time spent by the CEO and other executives. McDonald's CEO personally reviews the development of the company's top 200 managers. At GE, the CEO reviews the top 600. As the CEO's subordinates see the importance the boss puts on development, they too spend time developing their subordinates. The result is a cascading emphasis on talent management. Indeed, at American Express 25% of a manager's bonus is tied to talent development.

GE requires new hires to intern at least one summer before hiring, and evaluation of their potential begins then. At Eli Lilly about two-thirds of development comes from job experience, one-third from mentoring and coaching, and a small bit from the classroom. Eli Lilly is also trying to deal with the problems associated with rotational assignments; the company is trying short-term additional work assignments where managers do not leave their jobs, but take on a project outside their field to aid development.

The companies on the "Academies" list are also passionate about providing candidate performance feedback along with mentoring and support. Certainly that is not always the case in many organizations, but how can you improve if you don't know how well you have done? Without feedback, managers stop caring.[1]

Workforce planning is concerned with having the correct number of employees in the organization as they are needed. Talent management focuses on having the right individuals ready for the jobs when needed, and a pipeline full of talented people who are being developed for future organizational needs. The focus in talent management is on key positions, key job families, skills that will be needed, competency models, talent pools, and assessments for employees.

The need for talent management is brought on by a demographic landscape dominated by the impending retirement of experienced baby boomers, a shortage of young people entering the workforce in western Europe and a decline in the 35–44 age group in the United States.[2] Issues are further complicated by the number of high school graduates who lack writing and verbal communication skills, as well as a work ethic, and the number of college graduates who are weak in writing, leadership, critical thinking, and creativity skills.[3] Where will the successful workforce of the future come from? Additionally, problems with talent management programs seem to be common.[4] Research shows that a high percentage of companies are not prepared for a sudden loss of leadership, and most managers and executives are not held accountable for developing their direct reports.[5]

The levels of an organization most likely to be included in a talent management program are the executive and director levels, followed by CEOs and Vice Presidents.[6]

TALENT MANAGEMENT IN PERSPECTIVE

The idea that human capital can be a source of competitive advantage for some organizations is gaining ground, but most organizations are not designed or managed to optimize talent performance.[7] Choices for dealing successfully with talent needs are to: (1) emphasize stability in employment and develop talent internally, (2) develop agility as an organization and buy talent as needed, or (3) use some combination of 1 and 2. So the nature of the business and the environment in which it operates to some extent define appropriate strategies for talent management.

Talent management has other characteristics that make it challenging as well. A major one is the nature of "talent" or people. For example, a "deep bench" of talent can be thought of as inventory. But unlike boxes full of empty bottles, talent does not always stay on the shelf until needed—it walks out the door for better opportunities.[8] The shelf life of promising managers and specialists is short if they do not have opportunities where they are currently. Further, job candidates indicate that they are most attracted to opportunities to learn and grow. In fact, career development ranks higher than work-life balance and compensation/benefits for most job seekers.[9] This makes the need for a successful talent management program even greater.

Managing talent in global organizations is complex because movement of managers between countries is limited. Global leadership is especially challenging, as HR processes in different countries are often very different, and employees often expect to be demoted if they return to their home location.[10] Global talent management is an even greater challenge than domestic talent management.

One way to think of talent management is as a process that moves people from recruiting and selection to meeting the need of the organization for talent. Along the way, all the elements of talent management are encountered:

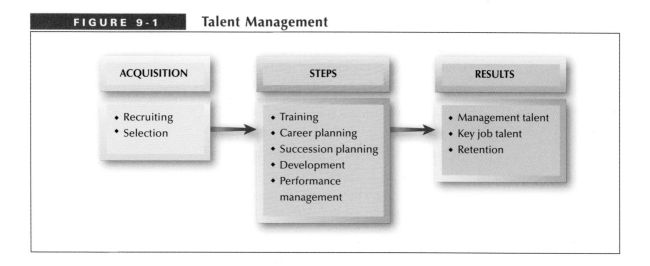

FIGURE 9-1 Talent Management

ACQUISITION	STEPS	RESULTS
◆ Recruiting ◆ Selection	◆ Training ◆ Career planning ◆ Succession planning ◆ Development ◆ Performance management	◆ Management talent ◆ Key job talent ◆ Retention

training, succession planning, career planning, development, and performance management. Figure 9-1 shows the idea. Training and performance management are covered in other chapters but succession planning, career planning, and development are covered in this chapter.

Talent Management "Systems"

Talent management seems to lend itself to the use of various software-based systems that purport to integrate all the pieces of talent management into one manageable whole. For example, one company used a talent management system in:

- Documenting new employee orientations and the onboarding training, regardless of how and where it was done.
- Tracking classroom training and certifications completed by all store employees.
- Automating registration of participants for training and development activities.
- Reporting on completions of training certifications for store employees.
- Compiling and reporting the training and development history of individuals for use with career planning and development.

However, according to one survey, although many companies are planning to use talent management technology, about half still use a manual approach.[11]

One reason for the demand for automated talent management systems is the situation that arose during the last recession. Many talented people were cut from the workforce, and some companies cut more of them than was necessary. Some employers view information from automation as a way to avoid this problem in the future.[12] As an example of the potential in these automated systems, Comcast Corporation can run a search across the entire organization to find people with certain qualifications who are strong in specific skills. If a person is needed for a business development position with strong customer communication and strategic skills, a search of the system will locate a dozen people in the company with excellent performance reviews in those areas during the last year.[13]

The drive to automate talent management also comes in part from the desire to pull together HR, finance, and operations data to get insights on talent that are otherwise difficult to obtain. Whether current systems do this in a way that deals with the key issues is still unclear. A study found that almost half of the companies using automated talent management systems had trouble getting employees and managers to use them. Speculation on why this is so centered on the idea that managers "don't like to use computers to manage people."[14] However, regardless of the current state of the art, the potential for automated talent management systems in the future is great as a tool to aid decision making, but not the whole solution.

Scope of Talent Management

As talent management has evolved, a variety of approaches and tools have come along. The HR perspective discusses some groundbreaking talent management programs.

Groundbreaking Talent Management Programs

How do you develop good managers? Several companies try to grow talent internally by hiring people they view as "high potentials" right out of college and developing them. For example, a program at Lehn and Fink Products (maker of Lysol) is designed to develop general managers from college recruits by using predictors of leadership through extracurricular activities, especially athletics, rather than grades. New recruits begin in low-level jobs and are moved every 6 months.

Curtis Lighting in Chicago rotates new college graduates through each of the 10 departments in the company while they take a program of 100 modular classes led by department heads. Public Service Company of Northern Illinois has a high-potential program to identify employees with aptitude for senior management positions. The program is open to every employee; criteria for selection are performance on the job and evidence of leadership behavior.

General Electric uses peer feedback. After classroom training and 3-month rotational assignments, newly hired candidates get formal peer feedback in an attempt to grow emotional intelligence skills. Another company uses assessment testing of IQ, vocational interest, aptitude, and vocabulary along with structured interviews to select management trainees.

The McCormick Company has created a "junior board of directors." Young executives consider the same problems the board of directors is considering and then make presentations to the real board. The U.S. Army has used forced-ranking systems to identify enlisted personnel who should be promoted to officers. The Navy has used 360-degree feedback systems on performance to identify pilots with the abilities to advance in training. Assessment centers were first used by the CIA and later by industry. Executive coaching, succession planning, rotational development, and assessments of managerial potential all have been widely used.

The talent management programs mentioned above are from 60 to 85 years old. They were well established by the 1950s, gone by the 1990s, and are reappearing in the early part of the twenty-first century as "new" and "novel" approaches to talent management. What happened?

The 1950s practices of long-term planning, succession planning, and management development were based on the assumptions that companies could predict personnel needs a decade in advance and that the talent in their pipelines would stay there. These pipelines turned out more talent than was needed, and when the 1981 recession hit, the development apparatus was dismantled. When the economy recovered, there was plenty of talent on the market to be hired. That surplus was gone by the end of the 1990s, and most organizations today again want an alternative to simply hiring their talent from outside.[15]

Target Jobs The first issue is to identify the types of jobs that will be the focus of talent management efforts. In some organizations, talent management focuses on the CEO and other executive jobs, rather than more broadly. Other organizations target senior management jobs, mid-level managers, and other key jobs. However, those groups only represent about one-third of the total workforce, which raises the question of whether talent management efforts would be more useful if they were more widely implemented.

High-Potential Individuals Some organizations focus talent management efforts primarily on "high-potential" individuals, often referred to as "high-pos." Attracting, retaining, and developing high-pos have become the emphases for some talent management efforts. Some firms classify individuals as being in the top 10% and then set limits on the number of people who can participate in intensive talent management efforts. Other organizations view talent management more broadly. Targeting primarily high-pos may lead to many other employees seeing their career opportunities as being limited. Thus, talent management may need to include more than the top 10% in some cases.

Competency Models What does a person who is ready to be moved up look like? What competencies should the person have? Competency models show knowledge, skills, and abilities (KSAs) for various jobs. An employer must ask, what talent do we need to achieve this? The answer can be found in a competency model. Competency models help to identify talent gaps. Some companies maintain libraries of competency models. One has more than 900 such models.[16] These libraries create a clear path for talent planning. Competency models might be created for executives, managers, supervisors, salespeople, technical professionals, and others.

Talent Pools Talent pools are a way to reduce the risk that the company may not need a certain specialty after developing it. The idea is to avoid developing for a narrow specialized job and instead develop a group or pool of talented people with broad general competencies that could fit a wide range of jobs. Once developed, they can be allocated to specific vacancies. Just-in-time training and coaching can make the fit work.[17]

Career Tracks Career tracks include a series of steps that one follows to become ready to move up. For example, a potential branch manager in a bank might take rotational assignments in customer sales, teller supervisor, credit cards, and other positions before being considered ready to handle the branch manager's job.

Assessment Assessment most often involves tests of one sort or another. Tests for IQ, personality, aptitude, and other factors are used. A portfolio of tests to help predict a person's potential for a job is called an "assessment center," which will be discussed in more detail later.

Development Risk Sharing The employer always runs the risk in developing talent that an employee who has been developed will leave with the valuable skills gained through development. An alternative to this risk is to have promising employees volunteer for development on their own time. Executive

LOGGING ON

Taleo Corporation
For a research library on talent management resources, including articles and interactive tools, visit the Taleo website at www.taleo.com/resources/research.

MBA programs that can be attended on evenings or weekends, extra projects outside a person's current assignment, volunteer projects with nonprofit organizations, and other paths can be used. The employer might contribute through tuition reimbursement or some selected time away from the job, but the risk is at least partly shared by the employee. The rest of this chapter deals with the major elements of talent management in more detail: succession planning, careers, and development.

SUCCESSION PLANNING

The basis for dealing successfully with staffing surprises is succession planning. When a sudden loss of a manager occurs, the void is a serious problem.[18] At that point it is too late to begin to develop a replacement. "Bench strength" and the leadership "pipeline" are metaphors for ways to prevent the void by having replacements ready.

However, succession planning involves more than simply replacement planning. Replacement planning usually develops a list of replacements for given positions. Succession planning must include a well-designed employee development system to reach its potential. Succession planning is the process of identifying a plan for the orderly replacement of key employees.

Succession Planning Process

Whether in small or large firms, succession planning is linked to strategic planning through the process shown in Figure 9-2. The process consists of first defining positions that are critical to the strategy,[19] and then making certain top management is involved personally with mentoring, coaching, and talent identification. It may be appropriate to tie some level of reward to executive success in the process. The next step is to assess the talent available in the organization and determine which have the potential, which are ready now for promotion, and which need additional development. The development practices can vary but should be aimed at specific needs in specific individuals. Finally, evaluating the success of the process is important, and appropriate measures are necessary to do so.[20]

All the work involved in the succession planning process should result in two products: (1) identification of potential emergency replacements for critical positions and (2) other successors who will be ready with some additional development. The development necessary should be made clear to the people involved, along with a plan for getting the development.[21]

Role of HR in Succession Planning Often HR has the primary responsibility for succession planning organization-wide. However, for CEO and senior management succession efforts, top executives and board members often have major involvement. In this case, HR commonly performs the following actions:

- Identifying development needs of the workforce
- Assisting executives/managers in identifying needed future job skills
- Participating in identifying employees who might fill future positions

FIGURE 9-2	Succession Planning Process

INTEGRATE WITH STRATEGY

- ◆ What competencies will be needed?
- ◆ Which jobs will be critical?
- ◆ How should critical positions be filled?
- ◆ Will international assignments be needed?

INVOLVE TOP MANAGEMENT

- ◆ Is CEO personally involved?
- ◆ Are top executives mentoring/coaching?
- ◆ Are there authority and accountability for succession goals?

ASSESS KEY TALENT

- ◆ Does this person have the competencies?
- ◆ What competencies are missing?
- ◆ Are assessments/performance evaluations/etc. valid?
- ◆ Is a results orientation used to identify high positions?
- ◆ Are individuals and career goals/interests compatible?

FOLLOW DEVELOPMENT PRACTICES

- ◆ How can missing competencies be developed?
- ◆ Are there opportunities for those in higher positions to interact with executives/board members?
- ◆ Can talent pools be created for job pools?
- ◆ What are the rewards to subordinate development?
- ◆ Are high position/successors to be told?

MONITOR/EVALUATE

- ◆ Are multiple metrics used?
- ◆ Are positions filled internally?
- ◆ Is the process viewed favorably?

- Communicating succession planning process to employees
- Aiding in tracing and regularly updating succession plan efforts

GLOBAL

Global Succession Planning Succession planning is not just a U.S. issue. In fact, the percentage of the aging population in the workforce is even higher in countries such as Japan, Germany, Italy, and England. In those countries, as well as the United States, the growth of immigrants has added to the population, which also means that employers are facing both legal and workforce diversity issues. Even in countries with growing native workforces, such as China and India, succession planning is important. Having younger workers who can replace senior managers with international experiences and contacts is a growing concern faced worldwide by employers of different sizes and industries.[22]

Succession in Small and Closely Held Organizations Succession planning can be especially important in small and medium-sized firms, but few of these firms formalize succession plans. In fact, the lack of succession planning is frequently viewed as the biggest threat facing small businesses. In closely held family firms (those that are not publicly traded on stock exchanges), multiple family members may be involved. But in others, the third- and fourth-generation family members are not employees and many do not want to be involved, other than as owners or as members of the board of directors.[23]

Even if many CEOs plan to pass the business leadership on to a family member, most of these firms would benefit from planning for orderly succession, particularly if nonfamily members or owners are involved. Addressing the development needs of the successor also helps to avoid a host of potential problems for both the organization and family-member relationships.

Succession Planning Decisions

A number of decision areas should be considered as part of succession planning. Coming to the answer stage on these decisions takes analysis, as the best answer varies depending on the situation.

"Make" or "Buy" Talent? Employers face a "make-or-buy" choice: develop ("make") competitive human resources, or hire ("buy") them already developed from somewhere else. Many organizations show an apparent preference for buying rather than making scarce employees in today's labor market. Current trends indicate that technical and professional people usually are "bought" because of the amount of skill development already achieved, rather than internal individuals being picked because of their ability to learn or their behavioral traits. However, hiring rather than developing internal human resource capabilities may not fit certain environments, and puts the responsibility for development on the employee.

Other organizations are focusing on growing their own leaders.[24] Like any financial decision, the make-or-buy decision can be quantified and calculated when some assumptions are made about time costs, availability, and quality.

Potential versus Performance Another focus of succession planning is shown in Figure 9-3. Note that when developing succession plans for jobs and identifying candidates, focusing only on potential may be too narrow.

FIGURE 9-3   Assessing Potential and Current Performance

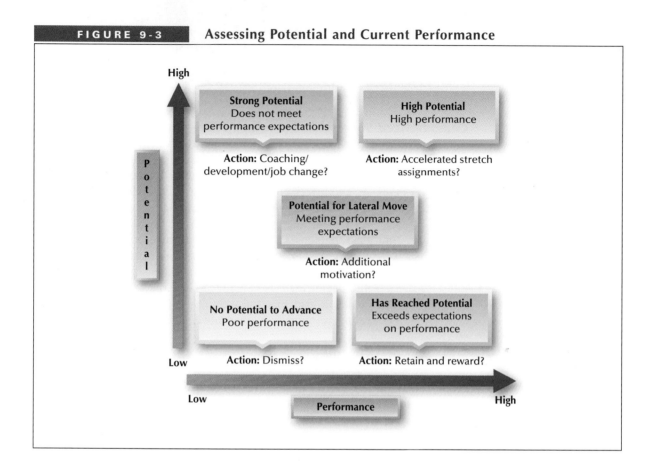

The competency model for a job might be much more complex. For example, assume that succession planning for a Vice President of Operations at a hospital is being done. That position needs candidates who have industry contacts, community involvement, leadership and management capabilities, and other competencies. These items are especially important if the current VP has extensive experience and outstanding performance. To combine potential and performance, a two-dimensional graph like the one shown in Figure 9-3 can be used.

Metrics and Succession Planning Some organizations measure the impact of succession planning. A wide range of metrics are used depending on the company plans. The proper metric should be picked early on in the succession decision process. One key measure is identifying the reduced costs of turnover, which is related to employee retention. For instance, in a mid-sized bank, turnover of "high-potential" employees declined significantly after conducting an organization-wide succession plan. Estimates of the turnover savings were done by the HR Director, and the median per key employee "saved" was more than $15,000 per person.

Another factor to consider is how succession planning and its follow-up may lead to higher performance and organizational profitability. Organizations such as Apple Computers, General Electric, Merck, Hewlett-Packard, Motorola, Verizon, and other companies use benchmark and quantitative measures to show that succession planning provides significant financial returns.

Other common useful metrics are:[25]

- Percentage of key vacancies filled internally
- Job performance of promoted successors
- Bench strength breadth and depth

Computerized Succession Planning Models The expansion of information technology capabilities has resulted in employers being able to have succession planning components available electronically to staff members. Skills tracking systems, performance appraisals, and other databases can be linked to succession plans. As employees complete training and development activities, their data can be updated and viewed as career openings occur in the company.

LOGGING ON

Business & Decision
This website provides an overview of succession planning. Visit the site at www.businessdecision.com.

Via intranet systems, employees can access and update their databases, review job and career opportunities, and complete skill and career interest self-surveys and numerous other items. Another aid in leadership development is 360-degree reviews of managers by others.[26] One such system creates a grid that links employee performance ratings and results to potential career movements.

Benefits of Formal Succession Planning

Employers are doing succession planning formally and informally. As companies become larger, the benefits of formal succession planning become greater. For larger companies, formal planning is recommended. Even government organizations can benefit from formal succession planning.[27] Key benefits include:

- Having a supply of talented employees to fill future key openings
- Providing career paths and plans for employees, which aids in employee retention and performance motivation
- Continually reviewing the need for individuals as organizational changes occur more frequently
- Enhancing the organizational "brand" and reputation of the company as a desirable place to work

Common Succession Planning Mistakes CEO succession should be a focus of the boards of directors. One reason why boards have increased the priority of CEO succession is the Sarbanes–Oxley Act provisions that have added more demands that boards do CEO succession planning.

But focusing only on CEO and top management succession is one of the most common mistakes made. Other mistakes include:

- Starting too late, when openings are already occurring
- Not linking well to strategic plans
- Allowing the CEO to direct the planning and make all succession decisions
- Looking only internally for succession candidates

All of these mistakes are indicative of poor succession planning.[28]

An example of the importance of succession planning is seen in the banking industry. Regulatory provisions and auditors are requiring banks to have succession plans identified for top management jobs. Also, law firms are recognizing the importance of succession planning as more senior partners retire.

Longer-term succession planning should include mid-level and lower-level managers, as well as other key nonmanagement employees. Some firms target key technical, professional, and sales employees as part of succession planning. Others include customer service representatives, warehouse specialists, and additional hourly employees who may be able to move up into other jobs or departments.

Succession planning is an important part of employers doing talent management well. Actions such as career planning and development efforts follow from succession planning efforts.

CAREERS AND CAREER PLANNING

A **career** is the series of work-related positions a person occupies throughout life. People pursue careers to satisfy their individual needs. Careers are an important part of talent management, but individuals and organizations view careers in distinctly different ways.[29] Changes in employer approaches to planning for replacement managers based upon a less predictable business environment have put much of the responsibility for a career on the shoulders of individual employees.

However, companies have found that the lack of a career development plan leaves them vulnerable to turnover, and hiring from outside can have drawbacks.[30] When a company attempts to manage careers internally, there may be a typical career path that is identified for employees. Despite major investments by employers over the last decade to improve company-sponsored career planning, a high percentage (41%) of managers surveyed felt the employer's approach to career development failed to meet their personal needs.[31]

Changing Nature of Careers

The old model of a career in which a person worked up the ladder in one organization is becoming rarer in reality. Indeed, in a few industries, changing jobs and companies every few years is becoming more common. Many U.S. workers in high-demand jobs, such as information technologists and pharmacists, dictate their own circumstances to some extent. For instance, the average 30- to 35-year-old in the United States may have already worked for up to seven different firms. Physicians, teachers, economists, and electricians do not change jobs as frequently. However, as would be expected, even in some of these professions valuable employees who are given offers to switch jobs do so at a higher rate than in the past.

Different Views of Careers Various signs indicate that the patterns of individuals' work lives are changing in many areas: more freelancing, more working at home, more frequent job changes, and more job opportunities but less security. Rather than letting jobs define their lives, more people set goals for the type of lives they want and then use jobs to meet those goals. However, for dual-career couples and working women, balancing work demands with personal and family responsibilities is difficult to do.

Labels for different views of careers include the following:

- *Protean career:* assumes individuals will drive their careers and define goals to fit their life
- *Career without boundaries:* views a manager as having many possible trajectories for a career, and many are across organizational boundaries

Career Series of work-related positions a person occupies throughout life.

- *Portfolio career:* careers are built around a collection of skills and interests and are self-managed
- *Authentic career:* people achieve a high level of personal insight and use this to follow a "true-to-self" career

All these different views of careers have merit for different individuals, but they all show that an organization-centered career planning effort will have to consider the unique needs of the individual employee.

Organization-Centered Career Planning

Careers are different than they were in the past, and managing them puts a premium on career development by both employers and employees. Effective career planning considers both organization-centered and individual-centered perspectives. Figure 9-4 summarizes the perspectives and interaction between the organizational and individual approaches to career planning.

Organization-centered career planning frequently focuses on identifying career paths that provide for the logical progression of people between jobs in an organization. Individuals follow these paths as they advance in organizational units. For example, the right person might enter the sales department as a sales representative, then be promoted to account director, to district sales manager, and finally to vice president of sales.

A good career planning program includes the elements of talent management, performance appraisal, development activities, opportunities for transfer and promotion, and planning for succession. To communicate with employees about opportunities and to help with planning, employers frequently use career workshops, a career "center" or newsletter, and career counseling. Individual managers often play the role of coach and counselor in their direct contact with individual employees and within an HR-designed career management system.

The systems that an employer uses should be planned and managed to guide managers in developing employees' careers.[32] One such system is the career path, or "map," which is created and shared with the individual employee.

Organization-centered career planning Career planning that focuses on identifying career paths that provide for the logical progression of people between jobs in an organization.

FIGURE 9-4   **Organizational and Individual Career Planning Perspectives**

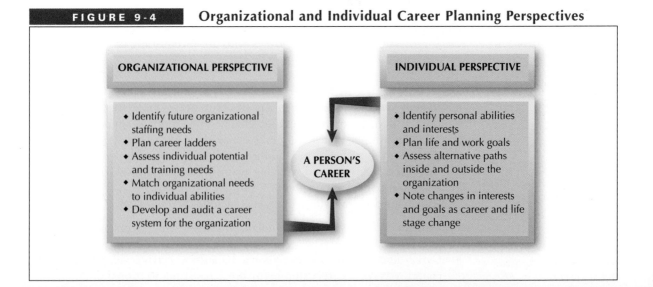

ORGANIZATIONAL PERSPECTIVE

- Identify future organizational staffing needs
- Plan career ladders
- Assess individual potential and training needs
- Match organizational needs to individual abilities
- Develop and audit a career system for the organization

A PERSON'S CAREER

INDIVIDUAL PERSPECTIVE

- Identify personal abilities and interests
- Plan life and work goals
- Assess alternative paths inside and outside the organization
- Note changes in interests and goals as career and life stage change

Career Paths Employees need to know their strengths and weakness, and they often discover those through company-sponsored assessments. Then, career paths to develop the weak areas and fine-tune the strengths are developed. For example, Ed Santry, VP of HR in Pittsburgh for Nisource Inc., had three good candidates for a position. The outside candidate had more experience and was hired. But after the decision, Ed had a discussion with the internal candidates. He presented ideas for them to work on over the next few years to improve their chances of getting one of the positions later.[33]

Career paths represent employees' movements through opportunities over time. Although most career paths are thought of as leading upward, good opportunities also exist in cross-functional or horizontal directions.

Working with employees to develop career paths has aided employers in retaining key employees. At a call center, use of a career path program has led to greater retention of entry-level call center employees. Career progression opportunities are identified to employees who perform well and who see the company as a place to stay and grow a career.

Employer Websites and Career Planning Many employers have careers sections on their websites. Such sections can be used to list open jobs for current employees looking to change jobs. An employer's website is a link to the external world, but should also be seen as a link to existing employee development. Sites also can be used for career assessment, information, and instruction. When designing websites, firms should consider the usefulness of the careers section for development as well as recruitment.

Accommodating Individual Career Needs As noted earlier, not everyone views a career the same way. Further, the way people view their careers depends upon the stage of the career. Some research suggests that if employers expect employees to invest more of their personal resources of time and effort in career self-management, they may find it causes conflict with efforts to balance work and life off the job. Most people cannot both invest great amounts of time beyond their job in career management and have a satisfactory work-life balance as well.[34] This seems especially true for younger employees.

Permitting telecommuting for fast-track employees unwilling to relocate is a way to keep talent in the succession pipeline by accommodating individual needs. Such flexibility is often the difference between continuing a career at a firm and moving on. For example, the CEO of a multimillion dollar business in the Midwest lived primarily in Atlanta. He would live in the Midwestern town for two weeks at a time and return to Atlanta every other weekend, thus telecommuting.[35]

Individual-Centered Career Planning

Organizational changes have altered career plans for many people. Individuals have had to face "career transitions"—in other words they have had to find new jobs. These transitions have identified the importance of **individual-centered career planning**, which focuses on an individual's responsibility for a career rather than on organizational needs.

Individual Actions for Career Planning For individuals to successfully manage their own careers, they should be able to perform several activities. Three key ones are as follows:

Career paths Represent employees' movements through opportunities over time.

Individual-centered career planning Career planning that focuses on an individual's responsibility for a career rather than on organizational needs.

- *Self-assessment*: Individuals need to think about what interests them, what they do not like, what they do well, and their strengths and weaknesses. Career advisors use a number of tools to help people understand themselves. Common professional tests include the Strong Interest Inventory to determine preferences among vocational occupations, and the Allport-Vernon-Lindzey Study of Values to identify a person's dominant values.
- *Feedback on reality*: Employees need feedback on how well they are doing, how their bosses see their capabilities, and where they fit in organizational plans for the future. One source of this information is through performance appraisal feedback and career development discussions.
- *Setting of career goals*: Deciding on a desired path, setting some timetables, and writing down these items all set the stage for a person to pursue the career of choice. These career goals are supported by short-term plans for the individual to get the experience or training necessary to move forward toward the goals.[36]

Individual Career Choices Four general individual characteristics affect how people make career choices:

- *Interests*: People tend to pursue careers that they believe match their interests. But over time, interests change for many people, and career decisions eventually are made based on special skills, abilities, and career paths that are realistic for the individual.
- *Self-image*: A career is an extension of a person's self-image, as well as a molder of it. People follow careers they can "see" themselves in and avoid those that do not fit with their perceptions of their talents, motives, and values.
- *Personality*: An employee's personality includes that individual's personal orientation (e.g., inclination to be realistic, enterprising, or artistic) and personal needs (including affiliation, power, and achievement needs). Individuals with certain personality types gravitate to different clusters of occupations.
- *Social backgrounds*: Socioeconomic status and the educational levels and occupations of a person's parents are included in an individual's social background. Children of a physician or a welder know from a parent what that job is like and may either seek or reject it based on how they view the parent's job.

Less is known about how and why people choose specific organizations than about why they choose specific careers. One obvious factor is timing—the availability of a job when the person is looking for work. The amount of information available about alternatives is an important factor as well. Beyond these issues, people seem to pick an organization on the basis of a "fit" of the climate of the organization as they view it and their own personal characteristics, interests, and needs.

LOGGING ON

Career Planning
This website is a resource for individual career planning. Visit the site at www.careerplanning.org.

Career Progression Considerations

The typical career for individuals today includes more positions, transitions, and organizations—more so than in the past, when employees were less

- *Time*: School has short (quarter/semester) time cycles, whereas time horizons are longer at work.
- *The work*: Problems are more tightly defined at school; at work, the logistical and political aspects of solving problems are less certain.

Job loss as a career transition has been most associated with downsizing, mergers, and acquisitions. Losing a job is a stressful event in one's career, frequently causing depression, anxiety, and nervousness. The financial implications and the effects on family can be extreme as well. Yet the potential for job loss continues to increase for many individuals, and effectively addressing their concerns should be considered in career transition decision making.

Retirement Issues Whether retirement comes at age 50 or age 70, it can require a major adjustment for many people. Some areas of adjustment faced by many retirees include self-direction, a need to belong, sources of achievement, personal space, and goals. To help address concerns over these issues, as well as anxieties about finances, some employers offer preretirement planning seminars for employees.

Companies in the United States will face a severe shortage of badly needed skills in the coming decade unless they act now to convince top-performing older employees to delay or phase in their retirement.[42] Career development for people toward the ends of their careers may be managed in a number of ways. Phased-in retirement, consulting arrangements, and callback of some retirees as needed all act as means for gradual disengagement between the organization and the individual. However, phased-in retirement (which is widely seen as a good situation for all involved) faces major obstacles in current pension laws. Under many pension plans, employees who are working may not receive pension benefits until they reach a normal retirement age.[43]

Early retirement often occurs as a result of downsizings and organizational restructurings. These events have required thousands of individuals, including many managers and professionals, to determine what is important to them while still active and healthy. As a result, some of these people begin second careers rather than focusing primarily on leisure activities or travel.[44] To be successful with early retirement, management must avoid several legal issues, such as forced early retirement and pressuring older workers to resign.

COMMON INDIVIDUAL CAREER ISSUES

Four career issues are sufficiently common as to need individual treatment. These are issues with technical and professional workers, women, dual-career couples, and individuals with global careers.

Technical and Professional Workers

Technical and professional workers, such as engineers, scientists, and IT systems experts, present a special challenge for organizations. Many of these individuals want to stay in their technical areas rather than enter management; yet advancement in many organizations frequently requires a move into management. Most of these people like the idea of the responsibility and opportunity associated with professional advancement, but they do not want to leave the professional and technical puzzles and problems at which they excel.

An attempt to solve this problem, a **dual-career ladder**, is a system that allows a person to advance up either a management or a technical/professional ladder. Dual-career ladders are now used at many firms, most commonly in technology-driven industries such as pharmaceuticals, chemicals, computers, and electronics. For instance, a telecommunications firm created a dual-career ladder in its IT department to reward talented technical people who do not want to move into management. Different tracks, each with attractive job titles and pay opportunities, are provided. Some health care organizations are using "master" titles for senior experienced specialists such as radiologists and neonatal nurses who do not want to be managers. The masters often are mentors and trainers for younger specialists. Unfortunately, the technical/professional ladder may be viewed as "second-class citizenship" within some organizations.

Women and Careers

According to the U.S. Bureau of Labor Statistics, the percentage of women in the workforce has more than doubled since 1970, and will reach almost 50% in the decade following 2010. Women are found in all occupations and jobs, but their careers may have a different element than those of men. Women give birth to children, and in most societies they are also primarily responsible for taking care of their children. The effect of this biology and sociology is that women's careers are often interrupted for childbirth and child rearing.[45]

Work, Family, and Careers The career approach for women frequently is to work hard before children arrive, plateau or step off the career track when children are younger, and go back to career-focused jobs that allow flexibility when they are older. This approach is referred to as sequencing. But some women who sequence are concerned that the job market will not welcome them when they return, or that the time away will hurt their advancement chances. And indeed, many women's careers are stifled due to their career interruptions.[46]

The interaction and conflicts among home, family, and a career affect the average woman differently than they do men. By the time men and women have been out of school for 6 years, on average women have worked much less time than men. These and other career differences provide different circumstances for many females. Employers can tap into the female labor market to a greater extent with child-care assistance, flexible work policies, and a general willingness to be accommodating.

Glass Ceiling Another concern specifically affecting women is the "glass ceiling." This issue describes the situation in which women fail to progress into top and senior management positions. Nationally, women hold about half of managerial/ professional positions but only 10% to 15% of corporate officer positions.[47] Some organizations provide leaves of absence, often under FMLA provisions, but take steps to keep women who are away from work involved in their companies. Some have used e-mentoring for women temporarily off their jobs. Other firms use "phased returns" whereby women employees return to work part-time and then gradually return to full-time schedules. Consequently, in the United States, women are making slow but steady strides into senior management and executive positions.

Dual-Career Couples

As the number of women in the workforce continues to increase, particularly in professional careers, so does the number of dual-career couples. The

Dual-career ladder
System that allows a person to advance up either a management or a technical/professional ladder.

U.S. Bureau of Labor Statistics estimates that more than 80% of all couples are dual-career couples. Marriages in which both mates are managers, professionals, or technicians have doubled over the past two decades.[48] Problem areas for dual-career couples include family issues and job transfers that require relocations.

Family-Career Issues For dual-career couples with children, family issues may conflict with career progression. Thus, one partner's flexibility may depend on what is "best" for the family.[49] Additionally, it is important that the career development problems of dual-career couples be recognized as early as possible. Whenever possible, having both partners involved in planning, even when one is not employed by the company, may enhance the success of such efforts.

Relocation of Dual-Career Couples Traditionally, employees accepted transfers as part of upward mobility in organizations. However, for some dual-career couples, the mobility required because of one partner's transfer often interferes with the other's career. In addition to having two careers, dual-career couples often have established support networks of coworkers, friends, and business contacts to cope with both their careers and their personal lives. Relocating one partner in a dual-career couple may mean upsetting this carefully constructed network for the other person or creating a "commuting" relationship. Recruiting a member of a dual-career couple to a new location may mean HR assistance in finding an equally attractive job available for the candidate's partner at the new location through assistance for the nonemployee partner.[50] The HR On-the-Job highlights the common global relocation issues faced by firms with employees having dual-career jobs.

Handling Global Dual-Career Situations

GLOBAL

Special difficulties exist when individuals transfer to overseas jobs. For example, a spouse who wants to work may not be able to get a work permit, may find that local residents have priority in the job market, or may find incompatible certification/ licensing. In particular, women partners may have difficulty finding employment opportunities in certain countries due to cultural and religious considerations. Only a small percentage of spouses and partners of expatriates are employed during their partners' international assignments. This disparity is one reason why a number of expatriates do not complete the full term of their overseas jobs.

When setting HR policies for global employee relocation assistance, organizations must consider the concerns of dual-career couples. The following approaches can help them reduce the problems faced in such situations:

- Pay employment agency fees for the relocating partner.
- Compensate for a designated number of trips for the partner to look for a job in the proposed new location.
- Help the partner find a job in the same company or in another division or subsidiary of the company in the new geographic location.
- Develop computerized job banks to share with other global companies and employers in the new area that list partners available for job openings.

GLOBAL

Global Career Concerns

Insecurity caused by layoffs and downsizings marks a trend that contrasts with the trend toward personal control over career goals. A number of older male American workers express fear of losing their jobs. But this situation is not just a U.S. phenomenon. Many Japanese workers who have typically worked for the same company their entire lives are experiencing similar job insecurity. In Europe, employers are pressuring governments to dismantle outmoded labor rules that make eliminating employees difficult, while workers are pressuring the same governments to alleviate high unemployment rates. As a result, careers for many individuals worldwide contain both more flexibility and more insecurity.[51]

Many global employees experience anxiety about their continued career progression. Therefore, the international experiences of expatriates must offer benefits both to the employer and to expatriates in terms of their careers.[52] Firms sometimes address this issue by bringing expatriates back to the home country for development programs and interaction with other company managers and professionals. Another potentially useful approach is to establish a mentoring system that matches an expatriate with a corporate executive at the headquarters.

Repatriation The issue of **repatriation** involves planning, training, and reassignment of global employees back to their home countries. For example, after expatriates are brought home, often they no longer receive special compensation packages available to them during their assignments. The result is that they experience a net decrease in total income, even if they receive promotions and pay increases. In addition to dealing with concerns about personal finances, returning expatriates often must reacclimate to U.S. lifestyles, transportation services, and other cultural circumstances, especially if they have been living in less-developed countries.

Many expatriates have had a greater degree of flexibility, autonomy, and independent decision making while living overseas than their counterparts in the United States. Back in the home organization, repatriated employees must readjust to closer working and reporting relationships with other corporate employees.

Another major concern focuses on the organizational status of expatriates upon return. Many expatriates wonder what jobs they will have, whether their international experiences will be valued, and how they will be accepted back into the organization. Unfortunately, many global employers do a poor job of repatriation. To counter this problem, some companies provide career planning, mentoring programs, and even guarantees of employment on completion of foreign assignments.

Global Development Global managers are more expensive than home-country managers, and more problematic as well.[53] Most global firms have learned that it is often a mistake to staff foreign operations with only personnel from headquarters, and they quickly hire nationals to work in a country. For this reason, global management development must focus on developing local managers as well as global executives. Development areas typically include such items as cultural issues, running an international business, leadership/management skills, handling problematic people, and personal qualities.

Repatriation Planning, training, and reassignment of global employees back to their home countries.

DEVELOPING HUMAN RESOURCES

Development represents efforts to improve employees' abilities to handle a variety of assignments and to cultivate employees' capabilities beyond those required by the current job. Development can benefit both organizations and individuals. Employees and managers with appropriate experiences and abilities may enhance organizational competitiveness and the ability to adapt to a changing environment. In the development process, individuals' careers also may evolve and gain new or different focuses.

Development differs from training. It is possible to train people to answer customer service questions, drive a truck, enter data in a computer system, set up a drill press, or assemble a television. However, development in areas such as judgment, responsibility, decision making, and communication presents a bigger challenge. These areas may or may not develop through ordinary life experiences of individuals. A planned system of development experiences for all employees, not just managers, can help expand the overall level of capabilities in an organization. Figure 9-7 profiles development and compares it with training.

Possible Development Focuses

Some important and common management capabilities that may require development include an action orientation, quality decision-making skills, ethical values, and technical skills. Abilities to build teams, develop subordinates, direct others, and deal with uncertainty are equally important but much less commonly developed capabilities for successful managers. For some tech specialties (tech support, database administration, network design, etc.), certain nontechnical abilities must be developed as well: ability to work under pressure, to work independently, to solve problems quickly, and to use past knowledge in a new situation.

Development Efforts to improve employees' abilities to handle a variety of assignments and to cultivate employees' capabilities beyond those required by the current job.

| FIGURE 9-7 | **Development versus Training** |

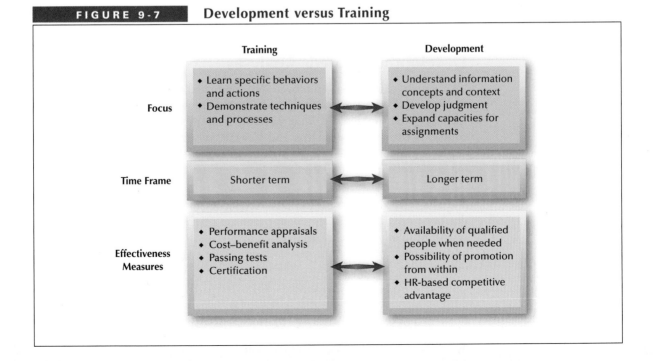

	Training	Development
Focus	• Learn specific behaviors and actions • Demonstrate techniques and processes	• Understand information concepts and context • Develop judgment • Expand capacities for assignments
Time Frame	Shorter term	Longer term
Effectiveness Measures	• Performance appraisals • Cost–benefit analysis • Passing tests • Certification	• Availability of qualified people when needed • Possibility of promotion from within • HR-based competitive advantage

One point about development is clear: in numerous studies that asked employees what they want out of their jobs, training and development ranked at or near the top. The primary assets that individuals have are their knowledge, skills, and abilities (KSAs), and many people view the development of their KSAs as an important part of their jobs.

Lifelong Learning Learning and development are closely linked. For most people, lifelong learning and development are likely and desirable. For many professionals, lifelong learning may mean meeting continuing education requirements to retain certificates. For example, lawyers, CPAs, teachers, dentists, and nurses must complete continuing education requirements in most states to keep their licenses to practice. For other employees, learning and development may involve training to expand existing skills and to prepare for different jobs, for promotions, or even for new jobs after retirement.

Assistance from employers for needed lifelong development typically comes through programs at work, including tuition reimbursement programs. However, much of lifelong learning is voluntary, takes place outside work hours, and is not always formal. Although it may have no immediate relevance to a person's current job, learning often enhances an individual's confidence, ideas, and enthusiasm.

Redevelopment Whether due to a desire for career change or because the employer needs different capabilities, people may shift jobs in midlife or mid-career. Redeveloping people in the capabilities they need is logical and important. In the last decade, the number of college enrollees over the age of 35 has increased dramatically. But helping employees go back to college is only one way of redeveloping them. Some companies offer redevelopment programs to recruit experienced workers from other fields. For example, different firms needing truck drivers, reporters, and IT workers have sponsored second-career programs. Public-sector employers have used redevelopment opportunities as a recruiting tool.

LOGGING ON

The Community Training & Development Centre
For specialized programs and services for learning and lifelong development, visit this website at www.ctdclearningplace.com.

Development Needs Analyses

Like employee training, employee development begins with analyses of the needs of both the organization and the individuals. Either the company or the individual can analyze what a given person needs to develop. The goal, of course, is to identify strengths and weaknesses. Methods that organizations use to assess development needs include assessment centers, psychological testing, and performance appraisals.

Assessment Centers Collections of instruments and exercises designed to diagnose individuals' development needs are referred to as **assessment centers**. Organizational leadership uses assessment centers for both developing and selecting managers. Many types of employers use assessment centers for a wide variety of jobs.

In a typical assessment-center experience, an individual spends two or three days away from the job performing many assessment activities. These activities might include role-playing, tests, cases, leaderless-group discussions, computer-based simulations, and peer evaluations. Frequently, they also include in-basket exercises, in which the individual handles typical work and

Assessment centers
Collections of instruments and exercises designed to diagnose individuals' development needs.

management problems. For the most part, the exercises represent situations that require the use of individual skills and behaviors. During the exercises, several specially trained judges observe the participants.

Assessment centers provide an excellent means for determining individual potential.[54] Management and participants often praise them because they are likely to overcome many of the biases inherent in interview situations, supervisor ratings, and written tests. Experience shows that key variables such as leadership, initiative, and supervisory skills cannot be measured with tests alone. Assessment centers also offer the advantage of helping to identify employees with potential in large organizations. Supervisors may nominate people for the assessment center, or employees may volunteer. For talented people, the opportunity to volunteer is invaluable because supervisors may not recognize their potential interests and capabilities.

Assessment centers also can raise concerns. Some managers may use the assessment center to avoid making difficult promotion decisions. Suppose a plant supervisor has personally decided that an employee is not qualified for promotion. Rather than being straightforward and informing the employee, the supervisor sends the employee to the assessment center, hoping the report will show that the employee is unqualified for promotion. Problems between the employee and the supervisor may worsen if the employee earns a positive report. Using the assessment center for such purposes does not aid in the development of employees, but such uses do occur.

Psychological Testing Psychological tests have been used for several years to determine employees' developmental potential and needs. Intelligence tests, verbal and mathematical reasoning tests, and personality tests are often given. Psychological testing can furnish useful information on individuals about such factors as motivation, reasoning abilities, leadership style, interpersonal response traits, and job preferences.

The biggest problem with psychological testing lies in interpretation, because untrained managers, supervisors, and workers usually cannot accurately interpret test results. After a professional scores the tests and reports the scores to someone in the organization, untrained managers may attach their own meanings to the results. Also, some psychological tests are of limited validity, and test takers may fake desirable responses. Thus, psychological testing is appropriate only when the testing and feedback processes are closely handled by a qualified professional.

Performance Appraisals Well-done performance appraisals can be a source of development information. Performance data on productivity, employee relations, job knowledge, and other relevant dimensions can be gathered in such assessments. In this context, appraisals designed for development purposes, discussed in more detail in Chapter 10, may be different and more useful in aiding individual employee development than appraisals designed strictly for administrative purposes.

HR DEVELOPMENT APPROACHES

Common development approaches can be categorized under three major headings, as Figure 9-8 depicts. Investing in human intellectual capital can occur on or off the job and in "learning organizations." Development becomes imperative as "knowledge work," such as research skills and specialized technology

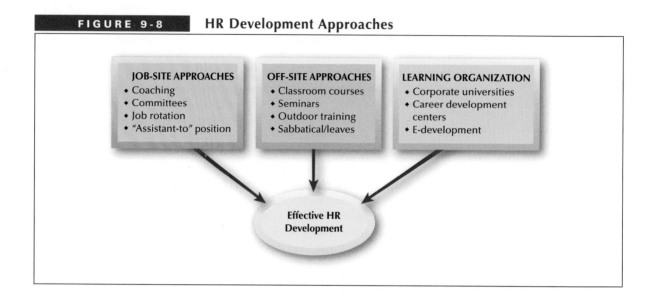

FIGURE 9-8   **HR Development Approaches**

expertise, increases for almost all employers. But identifying the right mix of approaches for development needs requires analyses and planning.

Job-Site Development Approaches

All too often, unplanned and perhaps useless activities pass as development on the job. To ensure that the desired development actually occurs, managers must plan and coordinate their development efforts. Managers can choose from various job-site development methods.[55]

Coaching The oldest on-the-job development technique is coaching, which is the training and feedback given to employees by immediate supervisors. Coaching involves a continual process of learning by doing. For coaching to be effective, employees and their supervisors or managers must have a healthy and open relationship. Many firms conduct formal courses to improve the coaching skills of their managers and supervisors.[56]

The success of coaching is being seen in companies throughout the world. One type of coaching that is growing is team coaching. This approach focuses on coaching groups of individual employees on how to work more effectively as parts of workforce teams. Such team efforts may utilize outside consultants and cover many different areas. Group coaching on leadership may help create high-performance teams.

Unfortunately, organizations may be tempted to implement coaching without sufficient planning. Even someone who is good at a job or a particular part of a job will not necessarily be able to coach someone else to do it well. "Coaches" can easily fall short in guiding learners systematically, even if they know which experiences are best.[57] Often the coach's job responsibilities take priority over learning and coaching of subordinates. Also, the intellectual component of many capabilities might be better learned from a book or a course before coaching occurs. Outside consultants may be used as coaches at the executive level.

Committee Assignments Assigning promising employees to important committees may broaden their experiences and help them understand the personalities, issues, and processes governing the organization. For instance, employees on a safety committee can gain a greater understanding of safety management, which would help them to become supervisors. They also may experience the problems involved in maintaining employee safety awareness. However, managers need to guard against committee assignments that turn into time-wasting activities.

Job Rotation The process of moving a person from job to job is called **job rotation**. It is widely used as a development technique. For example, a promising young manager may spend 3 months in a plant, 3 months in corporate planning, and 3 months in purchasing. When properly handled, such job rotation fosters a greater understanding of the organization and aids with employee retention by making individuals more versatile, strengthening their skills, and reducing boredom. When opportunities for promotion within a smaller or medium-sized organization are scarce, job rotation through lateral transfers may help rekindle enthusiasm and develop employees' talents. A disadvantage of job rotation is that it can be expensive because a substantial amount of time is required to acquaint trainees with the different people and techniques in each new unit.

Assistant Positions Some firms create assistant positions, which are staff positions immediately under a manager (e.g., Assistant to HR Director). Through such jobs, trainees can work with outstanding managers they might not otherwise have met. Some organizations set up "junior boards of directors" or "management cabinets" to which trainees may be appointed. These assignments provide useful experiences if they present challenging or interesting tasks to trainees.

Off-Site Development Approaches

Off-the-job development techniques give individuals opportunities to get away from their jobs and concentrate solely on what is to be learned. Moreover, contact with others who are concerned with somewhat different problems and come from different organizations may provide employees with new and different perspectives. Various off-site methods can be used.

Classroom Courses and Seminars Most off-the-job development programs include some classroom instruction. Most people are familiar with classroom training, which gives it the advantage of being widely accepted. But the lecture system sometimes used in classroom instruction encourages passive listening and reduced learner participation, which is a distinct disadvantage. Sometimes trainees have little opportunity to question, clarify, and discuss the lecture material. The effectiveness of classroom instruction depends on multiple factors: group size, trainees' abilities, instructors' capabilities and styles, and subject matter.

Organizations often send employees to externally sponsored seminars or professional courses, such as those offered by numerous professional and consulting entities. Many organizations also encourage continuing education by reimbursing employees for the costs of college courses. Tuition reimbursement programs provide incentives for employees to study for advanced degrees through evening and weekend classes that are outside their regular workdays and hours.

Job rotation Process of moving a person from job to job.

Outdoor Development Experiences Some organizations send executives and managers off to the wilderness, called *outdoor training* or outdoor development. The rationale for u. ag these wilderness excursions, which can last one day or even seven days or longer, is that such experiences can increase self-confidence and help individuals reevaluate personal goals and efforts. For individuals in work groups or teams, shared risks and challenges outside the office environment can create a sen e of teamwork. The challenges may include rock climbing in the California de rt, whitewater rafting on a river, backpacking in the Rocky Mountains, or ha dling a longboat off the coast of Maine.

Survival-type management development courses may have more impact than many other management seminars. But companies must consider the inherent perils. Some participants have been unable to handle the physical and emotional challenges associated with rappelling down a cliff or climbing a 40-foot tower. The decision to sponsor such programs should depend on the capabilities of the employees involved.

Sabbaticals and Leaves of Absence A **sabbatical** is time off the job to develop and rejuvenate oneself. Some employers provide paid sabbaticals while others allow employees to take unpaid sabbaticals. Popular for many years in the academic world, sabbaticals have been adopted in the business community as well.[58] Some firms give employees 3 to 6 months off with pay to work on "socially desirable" projects. Such projects have included leading training programs in urban ghettos, providing technical assistance in foreign countries, and participating in corporate volunteer programs to aid nonprofit organizations.[59]

Companies that offer sabbaticals speak well of the results. Positive reasons for sabbaticals are to help prevent employee burnout, offer advantages in recruiting and retention, and boost individual employee morale. Women employees have made use of sabbaticals or leaves for family care reasons. The value of this time off to employees is seen in better retention of key women, who also often return more energized and enthusiastic about their work-life balancing act. One obvious disadvantage of paid sabbaticals is the cost. Also, the nature of the learning experience generally falls outside the control of the organization, leaving it somewhat to chance.

Learning Organizations and Development

As talent management becomes more important, employers may attempt to become *learning organizations*. These organizations encourage development efforts through shared information, culture, and leadership that stress the importance of individual learning. This approach focuses on employees who want to develop new capabilities, and they can learn from others in the organization because informal (and formal) teaching and learning is the norm in such organizations.[60] A learning mind-set is probably difficult to introduce into an organization where it does not exist. But where it does exist, it represents a significant potential for development. Figure 9-9 depicts some possible means for developing employees in a learning organization.

Knowledge-based organizations that deal primarily with ideas and information must have employees who are experts at one or more conceptual tasks. These employees continuously learn and solve problems in their areas of expertise. Developing such employees requires an "organizational learning capacity" based on solving problems and learning new ways not previously used. Encouraging them to pass their knowledge on to others is the basis for a learning organization.

Sabbatical Time off the job to develop and rejuvenate oneself.

| FIGURE 9-9 | Possible Means for Developing Employees in a Learning Organization |

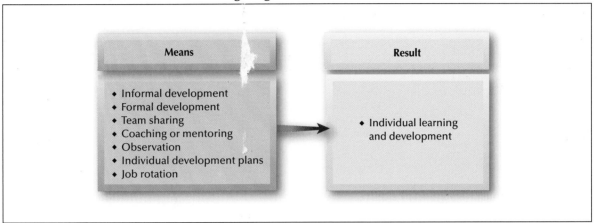

Corporate Universities and Career Development Centers Large organizations may use corporate universities to develop managers and other employees. Corporate universities take various forms.[61] Sometimes regarded as little more than fancy packaging for company training, they may not provide a degree, accreditation, or graduation in the traditional sense. A related alternative, partnerships between companies and traditional universities, can occur where the universities design and teach specific courses for employers.

Career development centers are often set up to coordinate in-house programs and programs provided by suppliers. They may include assessment data for individuals, career goals and strategies, coaching, seminars, and online approaches.

E-Development The rapid growth in technology has led to more use of e-development. Online development can take many forms, such as video conferencing, live chat rooms, document sharing, video and audio streaming, and Web-based courses. HR staff members can facilitate online development by providing a *learning portal*, which is a centralized website for news, information, course listings, business games, simulations, and other materials.

Online development allows participation in courses previously out of reach due to geographic or cost considerations. It allows costs to be spread over a larger number of people, and it can be combined with virtual reality and other technological tools to make presentations more interesting. It can eliminate travel costs as well. When properly used, e-development is a valuable HR development tool. However, the lack of realism can diminish the learning experience. The focus must be learning, not just "using the technology."

MANAGEMENT DEVELOPMENT

Although development is important for all employees, it is essential for managers. Without appropriate development, managers may lack the capabilities to best deploy and manage resources (including employees) throughout the organization.

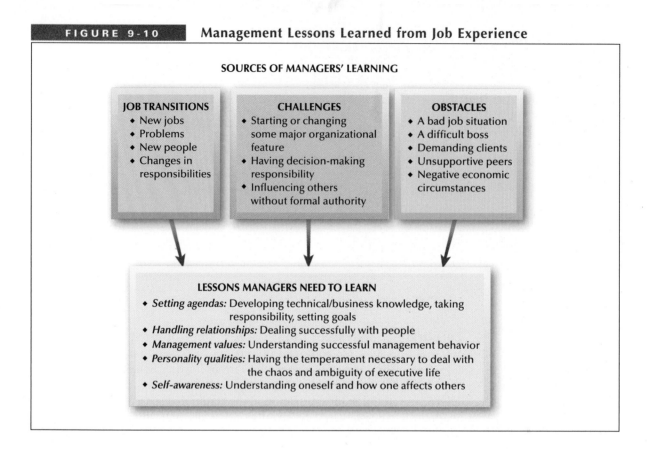

FIGURE 9-10   **Management Lessons Learned from Job Experience**

Experience plays a central role in management development.[62] Indeed, experience often contributes more to the development of senior managers than does classroom training, because much of it occurs in varying circumstances on the job over time. Yet, in many organizations it is difficult to find managers for middle-level jobs. Some individuals refuse to take middle-management jobs, feeling that they are caught between upper management and supervisors. Similarly, not all companies take the time to develop their own senior-level managers. Instead, senior managers and executives often are hired from the outside. Figure 9-10 shows experience-based sources of managers' learning and lists some lessons important in effectively developing supervisors, middle managers, and senior-level executives.

A number of approaches are used to mold and enhance the experiences that managers need to be effective.[63] The most widely used methods are supervisor development, leadership development, management modeling, management coaching, management mentoring, and executive education.

Supervisor Development

At the beginning level for managerial development is the first-line supervisory job. It is often difficult to go from being a member of the work group to being the boss. Therefore, the new supervisors who are used to functioning as individual contributors often require new skills and mind-sets to be successful supervisors.

A number of employers conduct *presupervisor training*. This effort is done to provide realistic job previews of what supervisors will face and to convey to individuals that they cannot just rely on their current job skills and experience in their new positions.

Development for supervisors may vary but usually contains common elements. The usual materials for supervisor training and development include several topics: basic management responsibilities, time management, and human relations.

Human Relations Training This type of training attempts to prepare supervisors to deal with "people problems" brought to them by their employees. The training focuses on the development of the human relations skills a person needs to work well with others. Most human relations programs are aimed at new or relatively inexperienced first-line supervisors and middle managers. They cover motivation, leadership, employee communication, conflict resolution, team building, and other behavioral topics.

The most common reason employees fail after being promoted to management is poor teamwork with subordinates and peers. Other common reasons for management failure include not understanding expectations, failure to meet goals, difficulty adjusting to management responsibilities, and inability to balance work and home lives.

Leadership Development

Organizations are aware that effective leaders create positive change and are important for organizational success. Firms such as Johnson & Johnson, General Electric, and 3M Company are among the top firms in leadership development. Leadership development is expanding a person's capacity to be effective in leadership roles. This development occurs in many ways: classroom programs, assessments, modeling, coaching, job assignments, mentoring, and executive education.

While it is difficult to develop good leaders in one's home country, it is even more difficult to do so in another country.[64] Also, although universities produce smart, ambitious graduates with good technical skills, many graduates face a very steep learning curve when making the change from school into leadership positions.[65] The material that follows examines common ways to help individuals in many different circumstances transition successfully into leadership roles.

Modeling A common adage in management development says that managers tend to manage as they were managed. In other words, managers learn by behavior modeling, or copying someone else's behavior. This tendency is not surprising, because a great deal of human behavior is learned by modeling. Children learn by modeling the behaviors of parents and older children. Management development efforts can take advantage of natural human behavior by matching young or developing managers with appropriate models and then reinforcing the desirable behaviors exhibited by the learners. The modeling process involves more than straightforward imitation or copying. For example, one can learn what not to do by observing a model who does something wrong. Thus, exposure to both positive and negative models can benefit a new manager as part of leadership development efforts.

Coaching In the context of management development, coaching involves a relationship between two individuals for a period of time as they perform their jobs. Effective coaching requires patience and good communication skills.[66]

Coaching combines observation with suggestions. Like modeling, it complements the natural way humans learn. An outline of good coaching pointers will often include the following:

- Explain appropriate behaviors.
- Make clear why actions were taken.
- Accurately state observations.
- Provide possible alternatives/suggestions.
- Follow up and reinforce behaviors used.

A specific application of coaching is the use of *leadership coaching*. Companies use outside experts as executive coaches to help managers improve interpersonal skills or decision-making skills. Sometimes these experts are used to help deal with problematic management styles. Consultants serving as executive coaches predominantly come from a psychology or counseling background and can serve many roles for a client by providing key questions and general directions. Sometimes they meet with employees in person, but many do their coaching by phone or electronically. Research on the effectiveness of coaching suggests that coaching can be beneficial in dealing with chronic stress, psychological difficulties, and even physiological problems faced by executives and managers.

Management Mentoring   A method called **management mentoring** is a relationship in which experienced managers aid individuals in the earlier stages of their careers.[67] Such a relationship provides an environment for conveying technical, interpersonal, and organizational skills from a more-experienced person to a designated less-experienced person. Not only does the inexperienced employee benefit, but the mentor also may enjoy having the opportunity and challenge of sharing wisdom.[68]

Fortunately, many individuals have a series of advisors or mentors during their careers and may find advantages in learning from the different mentors. For example, the unique qualities of individual mentors may help less-experienced managers identify key behaviors in management success and failure.[69] Additionally, those being mentored may find previous mentors to be useful sources for networking. Figure 9-11 describes the four stages in most successful mentoring relationships.

In virtually all countries in the world, the proportion of women holding management jobs is lower than the proportion of men holding such jobs. Similarly, the number of racial and ethnic minorities who fill senior management positions is less than 10%. Unfortunately, younger minority employees and managers may have difficulty finding mentors.[70] Company mentoring programs that focus specifically on women and individuals of different racial/ethnic backgrounds have been successful in a number of larger firms. Based on various narratives of successful women executives, breaking the glass ceiling requires developing political sophistication, building credibility, and refining management styles aided by mentoring.

Management mentoring
Relationship in which experienced managers aid individuals in the earlier stages of their careers.

Executive Education   Executives in an organization often face difficult jobs due to changing and unknown circumstances. "Churning" at the top of organizations and the stresses of executive jobs contribute to increased turnover in these positions. In an effort to decrease turnover and increase management development capabilities, organizations are using specialized

FIGURE 9-11   **Stages in Management Mentoring Relationships**

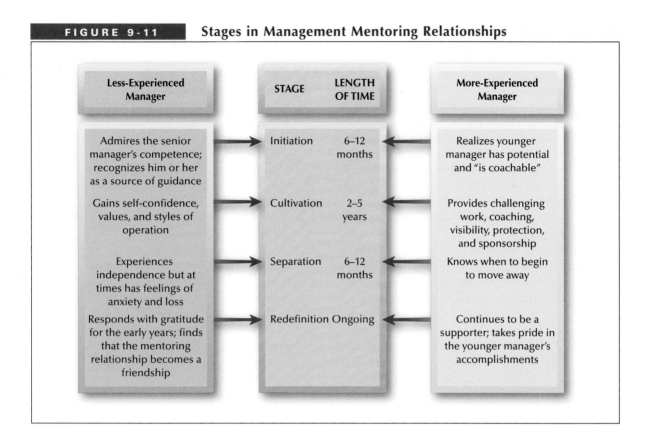

education for executives. This type of training includes executive education traditionally offered by university business schools and adds strategy formulation, financial models, logistics, alliances, and global issues. Enrollment in Executive Masters of Business Administration (EMBA) degree programs is popular also.

Problems with Management Development Efforts

Development efforts are subject to certain common mistakes and problems. Many of the management development problems in firms have resulted from inadequate HR planning and a lack of coordination of HR development efforts. Common problems include the following:

- Failing to conduct adequate needs analysis
- Trying out fad programs or training methods
- Substituting training for selecting qualified individuals

Another common management problem is *encapsulated development*, which occurs when an individual learns new methods and ideas, but returns to a work unit that is still bound by old attitudes and methods. The development was "encapsulated" in the classroom and is essentially not used on the job. Consequently, in this situation, it is common for individuals who participate in development programs paid for by their employers to become discouraged and move to new employers that allow them to use their newly developed capabilities more effectively.

SUMMARY

- Talent management is growing in importance because it is concerned with the attraction, development, and retention of human resources.
- Training, succession planning, career planning, and performance management are crucial parts of talent management.
- Succession planning is the process that identifies how key employees are to be replaced, including deciding whether to make or buy talent and how to use electronic and Web-based succession planning programs.
- A number of different mistakes can occur in succession planning, including focusing only on CEO and senior management succession.
- The nature of careers is changing, as retention of employees and work-life balance have become more important.
- Career planning may focus on organizational needs, individual needs, or both; and career paths and employer websites are part of career planning.
- A person chooses a career according to interests, self-image, personality, social background, and other factors.
- Several special individual career issues must be addressed, including those related to technical and professional workers.
- Career issues for women may include work-family balancing and glass ceiling concerns, as well as being part of dual-career couples.
- Global career development has special challenges, including relocations of dual-career couples, global development, and repatriation.
- Development differs from training because it focuses on less tangible aspects of performance, such as attitudes and values.
- Developing specific competencies may require lifelong learning and redevelopment of employees.
- Needs analyses for development may include assessment centers, psychological testing, and performance appraisals.
- HR development approaches can involve job-site, off-site, and learning organization activities.
- On-the-job development methods include coaching, committee assignments, job rotation, and "assistant-to" positions.
- Off-site development means often include classroom courses, seminars, and degrees; outdoor experiences; and sabbaticals and leaves of absences.
- Learning organization development efforts reflect knowledge-based means, such as corporate universities and centers and e-development efforts.
- Management development is a special focus in many organizations, including supervisor development and leadership development.
- Management modeling, coaching, and mentoring are valuable parts of management development efforts.

CRITICAL THINKING ACTIVITIES

1. Discuss what talent management is and why it is a consideration addressed by a growing number of employers.

2. Describe the broad range of talent management efforts that use software applications by going to www.learn.com. Then give some examples of firms that have successfully used these applications.

3. How has the increase in uncertainty in business affected the "make-or-buy" decision, and is this trend likely to change?

4. Design a management development program for first-level supervisors in an electric utility company. What courses and experiences do they need?

HR EXPERIENTIAL PROBLEM SOLVING

You are the HR Director of a large manufacturing company that is approximately 50 years old. The company has reaped the benefits of a mostly tenured workforce, and many of the key workers are now approaching retirement age. It is anticipated that approximately 20% of the company's workforce will retire in the next 3 to 5 years. You also are planning to retire within that period of time. To assist the company with the retirement transition process, you want to present a business case to the President for a succession plan for several key positions, including the Chief Financial Officer and Director of Operations. To develop an effective succession plan, visit www.score.org/article_succession_plan .html.

1. Identify the outside company advisors who should be included in the succession planning process.

2. The successor employee for the replacement of the Director of Operations should have an advanced level of work experience in what key essential functions?

CASE

Leadership Leverage

Gunderson Lutheran Health System in La Crosse, Wisconsin, is a health care delivery company that includes a 325-bed hospital, several specialty medical practices, and 41 clinics. In a recent year, they saw 1.4 million outpatient visits. The network has 6,834 employees including physicians, medical staff, managers and supervisors, and senior leaders. The age of their health care managers was a concern when asked whether they had a ready supply of leaders to step in. Upper management felt that growing leaders internally made sense from the standpoint of continuity and cultural fit.

The HR staff researched best practices in talent management and development. The result was the establishment of a Talent Development Review Group including the top leaders. This group became accountable for developing leaders, making necessary development happen, and overseeing the growth of *high-potential (high-po)* talent. The Review Group followed five steps in their process.

1. They spent two years *building a tiered leadership competency model* that included criteria for executives, directors, and managers to ensure the right mix of KSAs. The tiered model defined behaviors and competencies necessary to demonstrate excellence in each role. The competencies were used for behavioral interview questions and for position descriptions, and they formed the basis for 360-degree feedback.

2. The next step was to *identify high-potential talent.* The Review Group picked candidates for consideration in each of four pools. Pool members had to demonstrate willingness to:

   • Advance
   • Participate in leadership assessment
   • Receive feedback and coaching
   • Take on development opportunities
   • Invest the necessary time

In the five years after the program began, 60 high-po employees at all levels of leadership were identified, assessed, and had their career paths discussed.

3. Once high-pos had been identified and invited into a pool, it was time to *assess the talent.* The high-pos took assessment tools to identify strengths and development needs. Each candidate and the Review Group determined an initial strategy for closing gaps in the candidate's readiness.

4. A variety of tools were used to *develop plans for individual high-pos,* including stretch assignments, role expansion, job rotations, coaching, onboarding, continuing education, mentoring, project assignments, and committee assignments.

5. *Tracking progress* included setting milestones and success metrics to make sure candidates would build the necessary skills. The effect of the development activities on performance was measured as well, with feedback from peers, colleagues, and superiors. The Review Group continues to look at progress annually.

While numbers tell a positive story, another big change has been in the culture among the top leaders, who now see talent development as a strategic necessity.[71]

QUESTIONS

1. The top managers are very busy people. Why was it necessary to involve them in leadership leverage?

2. The program took 5 years to get to the end point. Is that realistic, or did it take too long? Explain why the timing may vary.

3. Would you let the names of the high-pos out to the rest of the organization? Why or why not?

SUPPLEMENTAL CASES

Equipping for the Future

This case shows how one company in the oil industry started a succession planning program. For the case, go to www.cengage.com/management/mathis.)

Developed Today, Gone Tomorrow

This case illustrates a serious concern some employers have about developing employees only to have them leave. For the case, go to www.cengage.com/management/mathis.)

NOTES

1. Geoff Colvin, "How Top Companies Breed Stars," *CNN Money*, September 20, 2007, 1–5.
2. Matthew Guthridge, et al., "Making Talent a Strategic Priority," *The McKinsey Quarterly*, January 2008, 2–9; David Semb, "The Upcoming Crisis in Talent Management," *Chief Learning Officer*, October 2009, 54–56.
3. Mark Schoeff, Jr., "Skills of Recent High School Graduates Leave Employers Cold," *Workforce Management*, April 13, 2007, 1–2.
4. Guthridge, *op. cit.*, 54, 55.
5. "Two-Thirds of Companies Are Not Prepared for Sudden Loss of Leadership," *WorldatWork*, August 14, 2008, 1; "Few Companies Can Execute Their Talent Management Plan," *WorldatWork*, October 30, 2008, 1.
6. *Ibid.*
7. Edward Lawler, *Talent: Making People Your Competitive Advantage* (Jossey-Bass, 2008).
8. Peter Cappelli, "A Supply Chain Model for Talent Management," *People and Strategy*, 32 (2009), 5.
9. Helene Cavalli, "Development Opportunities Most Important to Job Seekers," *LinkedIn*, December 1, 2009, 1–3.
10. Matthew Guthridge and Asmus Komm, "Why Multi-Nationals Struggle to Manage Talent," *The McKinsey Quarterly*, May 2008, 2.
11. "Talent Management Continues to Go High Tech," *HR Focus*, October 2009, 8–9.
12. Ed Fravenheim, "Special Report on HR Technology—Talent Planning for the Times," *Workforce Management*, October 19, 2009, 37–43.
13. Grae Yohe, "The Talent Solution," *Human Resource Executive*, June 2, 2009, 1ff.
14. Ed Fravenheim, "Style Over Substance?" *Workforce Management*, May 19, 2008, 30.
15. Peter Cappelli, "The Great Circle of Talent Management," *Human Resource Executive Online*, August 20, 2007, www.hreonline.com, 1–3; Peter Cappelli, "Talent Management Cycles: Part II," *Human Resource Executive Online*, September 17, 2007, www.hreonline.com, 1–3.
16. Adrienne Hedger, "How to Improve Talent Management?" *Workforce Management*, September 8, 2008, 54; Jon Younger, et al., "Developing Your Organization's Brand as a Talent Developer," *Human Resource Planning*, 30 (2007), 23.
17. P. Cappelli, 2009, 6.
18. B. Behan, "Lesson from VOA: Avoiding a Succession Debate," *BusinessWeek Online*, October 7, 2009, 1.
19. Stephan Miles and Theodore Dysart, "Road Map for Successful Succession Planning," *Directors and Boards*, First Quarter 2008, 57–59.
20. Dan Dalton and Catherine Dalton, "CEO Succession: Best Practices in a Changing Environment," *Journals of Business Strategy*, 28 (2007), 11–13.
21. Charles Greer and Meghna Virick, "Diverse Succession Planning Lessons from the Industry Leaders," *Human Resource Management* (2009), 351–367.
22. Jennifer Robison, "Scientific, Systematic Succession Planning," *Gallup Management Journal*, June 2, 2009, 1–6.
23. Steve Schumacher, "Passing the Torch," *Rock Products*, October 2008, 32–34.
24. Matt Boyle, "The Art of Succession," *BusinessWeek*, May 11, 2009, 30–32.
25. Jayson Saba and Kevin Martin, "Succession Management," *Aberdeen Group*, 2008, 2–28.
26. "Succession Success," *Human Resource Executive*, July 2008, 22–27.
27. Karen Jarrell and Kyle Pewitt, "Succession Planning in Government," *Review of Public Personnel Administration*, 27 (2007), 297–309.
28. Paula Ketter, "Sounding Succession Alarms," *T + D*, January 2009, 20.
29. Traci McCready and Chris Hatcher, "How to Align Career Development and Succession Planning," *Workspan*, March 2009, 61–63.
30. Edward Lawler III, "Choosing the Right Talent," *Workspan*, July 2008, 73–75.
31. Kathy Gurchiek, "Career Development Gets Failing Grade from Many Workers," *2008 HR Trendbook*, 49–50.
32. Ronan Carbery and Thomas Garavan, "Conceptualizing the Participation of Managers in Career-Focused Learning and Development," *Human Resource Development Journal*, 6 (2007), 396–397.
33. Kathryn Tyler, "Helping Employees Step Up," *HR Magazine*, August 2007, 49.
34. Jane Sturges, "All in a Day's Work?" *Human Resource Management Journal*, 18 (2008), 132.
35. Kathy Gurchiek, "Telecommuting Becomes Succession Planning Tool," *HR News*, July 14, 2008, www.shrm.org, 1–3.
36. Yongho Park and William Rothwell, "The Effects of Organizational Learning Climate, Career Enhancing Strategy, and Work Orientation on the Protean Career," *Human Resource Development International*, 8 (2009), 387–405.

37. Lindsey Gerdes, "The Best Places to Launch a Career," *BusinessWeek*, September 15, 2008, 37–44.

38. Dennis Laker and Ruth Laker, "The Five Year Resume: A Career Planning Exercise," *Journal of Management Education*, 31 (2007), 128–141.

39. Johannes Thijssen, et al., "Toward the Employability Link Model," *Human Resource Development Review*, 7 (2008), 164–183.

40. Nancy Wendlandt and Aaron Rochler, "Addressing the College to Work Transition," *Journal of Career Development*, 35 (2008), 151–165.

41. Thomas Ng and Daniel Feldman, "The School to Work Transition: A Role Identity Perspective," *Journal of Vocational Behavior*, 71 (2007), 114–134.

42. Marjorie Armstrong-Stassen, "Organizational Practices and the Post Retirement Employment Experience of Older Workers," *Human Resource Management Journal*, 18 (2008), 36–53.

43. Collin Barr, "Pension Tension on the Rise," *Fortune CNN Money*, November 30, 2009, 1–3.

44. "Millions Now in 'Encore' Careers," *WorldatWork Newsline*, June 18, 2008, www.worldatwork.org, 1.

45. Sherry Sullivan and Lisa Mainiero, "Benchmarking Ideas for Fostering Family Friendly Workplaces," *Organizational Dynamics*, 36, 2007, 45–62.

46. Cari Tuna, "Initiative Moves Women Up the Corporate Ladder," *The Wall Street Journal*, October 20, 2008, B4.

47. Jessica Marquez, "Gender Discrimination Begins Much Earlier than Exec Levels, Report Shows," *Workforce Management*, May 12, 2009, 1–3.

48. Cathy Arnst, "Women Want Careers Just as Much as Men," *BusinessWeek*, March 27, 2009, 1.

49. Joy Pixley, "Life Course Patterns of Career Prioritizing Decisions and Occupational Attainment in Dual-Earner Couples," *Work and Occupations*, 35 (2008), 127–162.

50. Michael Harvey, et al., "Global Dual-Career Exploration and the Role of Hope and Curiosity," *Journal of Management Psychology*, 24 (2009), 178–197.

51. Jena McGregor and Steve Hamm, "Managing the Workforce," *BusinessWeek*, January 28, 2008, 34–51.

52. Jean-Luc Cerdin and Marie Le Pargneux, "Career and International Assignment Fit," *Human Resource Management*, January–February 2009, 5–25.

53. Bill Leisy and N. S. Rajan, "Global Talent Management," *Workspan*, March 2009, 39–45.

54. Jayson Saba, et al., "Assessments in Talent Management," *Aberdeen Group*, 2009, www.aberdeen.com, 1–23.

55. Alina Dizik, "Training Without a Campus," *The Wall Street Journal*, April 15, 2009, D4.

56. "Employees Want to Be Challenged by Coaches," *WorldatWork Newsline*, December 12, 2008, 1–2.

57. "What Is a Coaching Culture?" *Coaching Conundrum 2009 Global Executive Summary*, Blessing White, 2009, 5–23.

58. Frank Giancola, "Making Sense of Sabbaticals," *Workspan*, July 2006, 39–41.

59. Beth Mirza, "Build Employee Skills, Help Non Profits," *HR Magazine*, October 2008, 30.

60. Jia Wang, "Developing Organizational Learning Capacity in Crises Management," *Advances in Developing Human Resources*, 10 (2008), 425–444; Paul Tosey and Jane Mathison, "Do Organizations Learn?" *Human Resource Management Review*, 7 (2008), 13–31.

61. Desda Moss, "A Lesson in Learning," *HR Magazine*, November 2007, 31–52.

62. Donna Owens, "Success Factors," *HR Magazine*, August 2008, 87–89.

63. Lisa Dragoni, et al., "Understanding Management Development," *Academy of Management Journal*, 52 (2009), 731–743.

64. Mary Siegfried, "Filling the Leadership Void," *Inside Supply Management*, April 2007, 22–26.

65. E. Norman, "Develop Leadership Talent During a Recession," *Workspan*, May 2009, 35–42.

66. Robert Hooijberg and Nancy Lane, "Using Multisource Feedback Coaching Effectively in Executive Education," *Academy of Management Learning and Education*, 8 (2009), 483–493.

67. Lillian Eby, et al., "Does Mentoring Matter?" *Journal of Vocational Behavior*, 72 (2008), 254–267.

68. Susan Wells, "Tending Talent," *HR Magazine*, May 2009, 53–56.

69. Sarah Hazlett and Sharon Gibson, "Linking Mentoring and Social Capitol," *Advances in Developing Human Resources*, 9 (2007), 384–411.

70. Mario Gardiner, et al., "Show Me the Money," *Higher Education Research and Development*, 27 (2007), 425–442.

71. Based on Nancy Noelke, "Leverage the Present to Build the Future," *HR Magazine*, March 2009, 34–36.

10

Performance Management and Appraisal

After you have read this chapter, you should be able to:

- Identify the components of performance management systems.

- Distinguish between performance management and performance appraisal.

- Explain the differences between administrative and developmental uses of performance appraisal.

- Describe the advantages and disadvantages of multisource (360-degree) appraisals.

- Discuss the importance of training managers and employees about performance appraisal, and give examples of rater errors.

- Identify several concerns about appraisal feedback and ways to make it more effective.

Performance Management Does Not Focus Enough on Ethics

(Ryan McVay/Photodisc/Getty Images)

A recent study determined that many organizations do not focus enough on ethics when managing performance. For instance, only 43% of HR practitioners indicated that their employers included measures of ethics on performance evaluations. Making matters worse, professionals claimed that they were expected to take an active role in managing ethics, but many felt disconnected from the process. Further, many companies do not have a comprehensive program that raises awareness of ethics, and some companies have developed no ethics policies whatsoever. Such findings are troubling considering that problems are common. Organizations need to develop standards governing how employees are expected to behave.[1]

Given these realities, HR professionals should be involved in the development of those standards. Performance management practices such as evaluation forms should include measures that identify positive behaviors. HR professionals also need to create comprehensive programs that increase the motivation to take appropriate actions. Developing codes of conduct that outline company guidelines, offering training that teaches employees important workplace values, and increasing communication of important job standards can all work together to promote an ethical culture. In additon, reinforcement programs should be developed so that positive behaviors are rewarded and undesirable behaviors are punished. HR managers need to be in the "driver's seat" when it comes to encouraging ethics.

Employers want employees who perform their jobs well and contribute to the mission and objectives of the organization, but managers have to provide the proper context for such high productivity. Performance management is the primary tool used to identify, communicate, measure, and reward employees so that they can make these contributions, and the process is one that supports a company's strategic direction. Properly designing the performance management system is therefore a key method for increasing overall organizational performance.

THE NATURE OF PERFORMANCE MANAGEMENT

The performance management process starts by identifying the strategic goals an organization needs to accomplish to remain competitive and profitable. After these ideas are crystallized, managers identify how they and their employees can help support organizational objectives by successfully completing work. In a sense, the sum of the work completed in all jobs should advance the strategic plan. By adopting a "big-picture" quantitative approach, managers can successfully combine individual efforts in a manner that provides practical measures of organizational effectiveness. Performance management can also provide a unified approach to dealing with individual career development.[2]

As Figure 10-1 shows, performance management links organizational strategy to ultimate results. Performance management enables a company to convert overall strategy into results that support the mission and objectives. However, just having a strategic plan does not guarantee that results will be achieved and objectives will be satisfied. When organizational strategies have been defined, they must be translated into department- or unit-level actions. Then these actions must be assigned to individuals who are held accountable for efficient and effective goal accomplishment.[3]

Often performance management is confused with one of its key components—performance appraisal. **Performance management** is a series of activities designed to ensure that the organization gets the performance it needs from its employees. **Performance appraisal** is the process of determining how well employees do their jobs relative to a standard and communicating that information to them.

An effective performance management system should do the following:

- Make clear what the organization expects
- Provide performance information to employees
- Identify areas of success and needed development
- Document performance for personnel records

Performance management starts with the development and understanding of organizational strategy, and then dovetails into a series of steps that involves identifying performance expectations, providing performance direction, encouraging employee participation, assessing job performance, and conducting the performance appraisal. As Figure 10-2 suggests, successful performance management is a circular process that requires a system of administrative tools that effectively structures the dialogue between managers and their employees, and the motivation to utilize the system in a productive way.[4]

A successful performance management system allows managers to better prepare employees to tackle their work responsibilities by focusing on

Performance management Series of activities designed to ensure that the organization gets the performance it needs from its employees.

Performance appraisal Process of determining how well employees do their jobs relative to a standard and communicating that information to them.

FIGURE 10-1   **Performance Management Linkage**

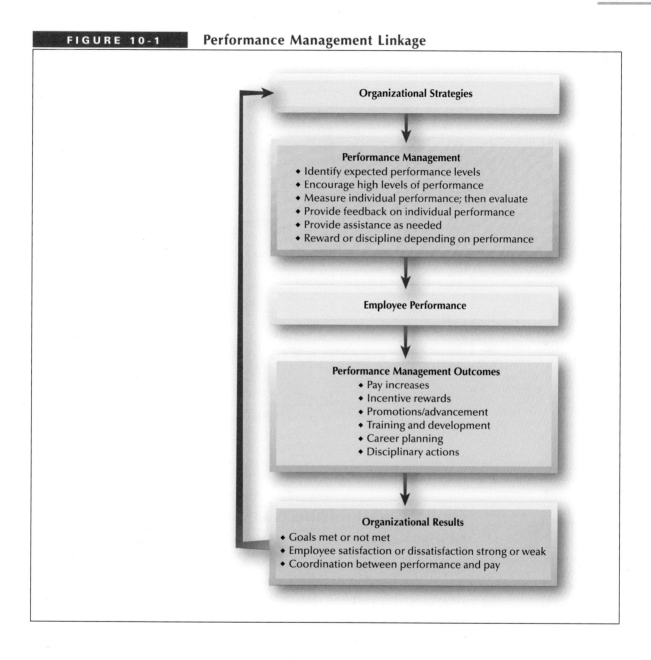

these activities. For example, the software company CA recently revised its performance review procedures so that the process would better facilitate individual motivation and growth. Employees are rated on standardized job criteria, complete self-evaluations, and are given completed evaluation forms several days ahead of appraisal meetings to consider ratings. "Performance agreements" explicitly connect individual actions to corporate goals, and the whole process of performance management is strengthened through positive communication.[5]

Even well-intentioned employees do not always know what is expected or how to improve their performance, which also makes performance management necessary. Additionally, dismissal of an employee may become necessary, and without evidence that the employee has been advised of performance issues, legal problems may result.

FIGURE 10-2   Components of Performance Management

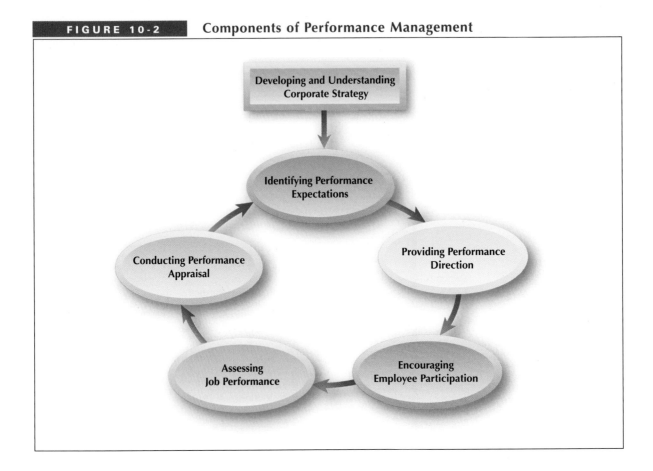

Global Cultural Differences in Performance Management

Global Cultural Differences in Performance Management

Performance management systems and appraisals are very common in the United States and some other countries. However, challenges can be experienced when performance management approaches are used in other countries where multinational organizations have operations, or when they are used with employees who have diverse cultural backgrounds with characteristics very different from those of an American background.

In some countries and cultures, it is uncommon for managers to rate employees or to give direct feedback, particularly if some points are negative. For instance, in several countries, including China and Japan, there is a high respect for authority and age. Consequently, expecting younger subordinates to engage in joint discussions with their managers through a performance appraisal process is uncommon. Use of such programs as multisource/360-degree feedback (discussed later in this chapter) would be culturally inappropriate.

In various other cultures, employees may view criticism from superiors as personally devastating rather than as useful feedback that highlights individual training and development needs. Therefore, many managers do not provide feedback, nor do employees expect it.

Even in the physical settings for appraisal discussions, "cultural customs" associated with formal meetings may need to be observed. For example, in some Eastern European countries, it is common to have coffee and pastries or an alcoholic drink before beginning any formal discussion. These examples illustrate that performance management processes may need to be adapted or even dropped in certain global settings.

Performance-Focused Organizational Cultures

Organizational cultures vary on many dimensions, and one of these differences involves the degree to which performance is emphasized. Some corporate cultures are based on an *entitlement* approach, meaning that *adequate* performance and stability dominate the organization. Employee rewards vary little from person to person and are not based on individual performance differences. As a result, performance appraisal activities are seen as having few ties to performance and as being primarily a "bureaucratic exercise."

At the other end of the spectrum is a *performance-driven* organizational culture focused on results and contributions. In this context, performance appraisals link results to employee compensation and development. This approach is particularly important when evaluating CEO performance because companies want to hold top leaders accountable for corporate outcomes and motivate them to improve operational and financial results. CEO performance evaluations should therefore provide structure to the performance appraisal process (i.e., descriptions and dates), establish CEO roles and responsibilities, and identify important performance objectives.[6]

Studies have shown the benefits of developing a performance-focused culture throughout the organization. One longitudinal study of 207 companies in 22 industries found that firms with performance-focused cultures had significantly higher growth in company revenue, employment, net income, and stock prices than did companies with different cultures. Another study also found that firms with strong performance cultures had dramatically better results.[7] Figure 10-3 shows the components of a successful performance-focused culture.

However, a pay-for-performance approach can present several challenges to organizations, particularly in educational institutions. The teacher pay-for-performance plan recently implemented in the Houston school district has increased perceptions that the system creates inequity, with some teachers getting bonuses and others receiving no extra compensation.[8] Denver Public Schools implemented a similar plan several years ago that ties bonuses to criteria such as students' performance on tests/achievement, teaching evaluations, and professional growth/education, but the plan is being met with harsh criticism because it allegedly favors less senior teachers who accept challenging teaching assignments.[9]

Despite these setbacks, it appears that where possible, a performance-based-pay culture is desirable. One study found that 33% of managers and 43% of nonmanagers felt their company was not doing enough about poor performers. The nonmanagers felt that failure to deal with poor performance was unfair to those who worked hard.[10] In one financial services company that did not give poor performance reviews, a new CEO instituted a performance system that gave star performers raises as high as 20% and poor performers nothing. The tougher performance system encouraged poor performers to leave the company voluntarily, increased the performance of many other employees, and enhanced company profitability.[11] Additionally, performance-based pay can strengthen the link between employee and organizational goals, increase individual motivation, and augment worker retention, especially when an organization develops sound compensation, performance, and strategic plans.[12]

FIGURE 10-3   Components of a Performance-Focused Culture

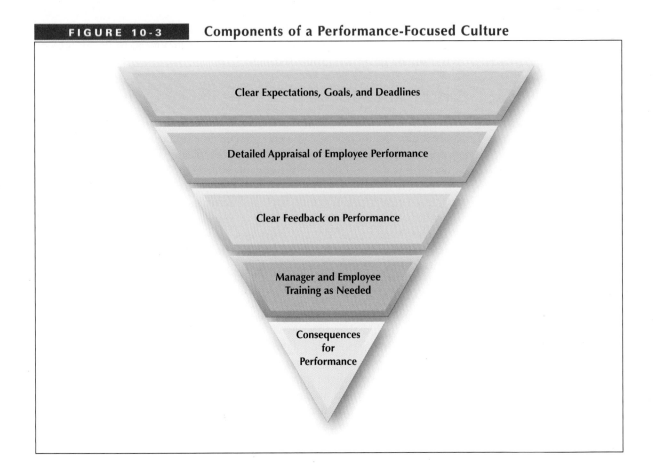

Clear Expectations, Goals, and Deadlines

Detailed Appraisal of Employee Performance

Clear Feedback on Performance

Manager and Employee
Training as Needed

Consequences
for
Performance

IDENTIFYING AND MEASURING EMPLOYEE PERFORMANCE

Performance criteria vary from job to job, but the most common employee performance measures associated with many jobs include the following:

- Quantity of output
- Quality of output
- Timeliness of output
- Presence/attendance on the job
- Efficiency of work completed
- Effectiveness of work completed

Specific **job duties** identify the most important elements in a given job. For example, a salesperson must know a company's products and services, identify the needs of customers, and actively sell in order to be successful at work. Since such actions are so important, duties are identified from job descriptions that contain the most important parts of individual jobs. They help to define what the organization pays employees to do. Therefore, the performance of individuals on those important job duties should be measured and compared against appropriate standards, and the results should be communicated to the employee.

To complicate matters, multiple job duties are the rule rather than the exception in most jobs. An individual might demonstrate better performance

Job duties Important
elements in a given job.

on some duties than others, and some duties might be more important than others to the organization. For example, professors are broadly required to conduct research, teach classes, and provide service to important university stakeholders. Some professors focus heavily on one area of work over the others, which can cause performance management issues when their universities value all the different parts of the job.

Weights can be used to show the relative importance of several duties in one job. For example, in a management job at a company that wants to improve customer service feedback, control operational costs, and encourage quality improvements, weights might be assigned as follows:

Weighting of Management Duties at Sample Firm	Weight
Improve customer feedback	50%
Control operational costs	30%
Encourage quality improvements	20%
Total Management Performance	**100%**

Types of Performance Information

Managers can use three different types of information about employee performance, as Figure 10-4 shows. *Trait-based information* identifies a character trait of the employee—such as attitude, initiative, or creativity—and may or may not be job related. For example, one study concluded that conscientiousness was an important determinant of job performance.[13] Because traits tend to be ambiguous, and favoritism of raters can affect how traits are viewed, court decisions generally have held that trait-based performance appraisals are too vague to use when making performance-based HR decisions such as promotions or terminations. Also, fixating too much on characteristics such as "potential" can lead managers to ignore the important behaviors and outcomes that help organizations reach their objectives.[14]

FIGURE 10-4	Types of Performance Information

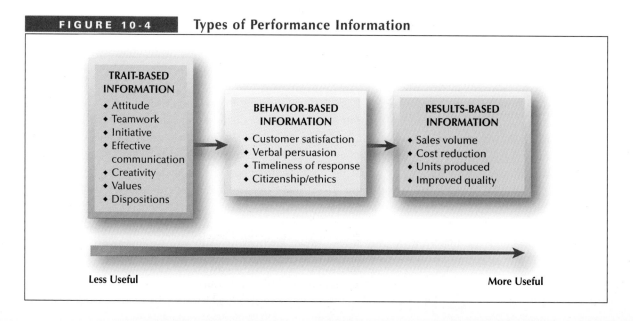

Behavior-based information focuses on specific behaviors that lead to job success. For a waitperson, the behavior "menu up-selling" can be observed and used as performance information. Additionally, a human resource director who institutes an "open-door policy" behaves in a manner that likely increases communication with employees. Behavioral information clearly specifies the behaviors management wants to see. A potential problem arises when any of several behaviors can lead to successful performance, and employees rely on these different behaviors to complete work. For example, salespeople might use different verbal persuasion strategies with customers because no one approach can be utilized successfully by all individuals.

Results-based information considers employee accomplishments. For jobs in which measurement is easy and obvious, a results-based approach works well. For instance, a professor might receive extra compensation for securing grants or publishing papers in academic journals, or a salesperson in a retail outlet might receive extra commission pay based on how many products are sold. However, in this approach, that which is measured tends to be emphasized, which may leave out equally important but difficult-to-measure parts of work. For example, a car salesperson who gets paid *only* for sales may be unwilling to do paperwork and other work not directly related to selling cars. Further, ethical or even legal issues may arise when only results are emphasized, and *how* the results were achieved is not considered, so care should be taken to balance the different types of information. For a study on behavior-based and results-based information, see the HR Perspective.

Behaviors or Results . . . Why Not Both?

A study of human resource professionals conducted by *Human Resource Executive* determined that a majority of organizations focused on a balance of behavioral and results criteria when managing individual performance.[15] A smaller number (34%) focused on objectives and results, and even fewer professionals (11%) stated that their companies relied just on behaviors. The percentage breakdowns were similar for assessments of top managers, and a majority of professionals reported that corporate performance objectives originated from the top organizational ranks. According to Scott Cohen, a leader at Watson Wyatt Worldwide in Boston, even though results are extremely important, it is important for a business to focus on the kinds of actions and employee behaviors that ensure sustained viability from a long-range perspective, with a particular eye toward the promotion of behaviors that are considered to be ethical in nature.

Companies should therefore consider developing a performance management process that takes into consideration the many different employee behaviors that bring about high levels of organizational performance. For instance, recognizing members of the organization for ethical conduct (i.e., helping others, doing the right thing, complying with the company's codes of conduct), particularly when such conduct results in positive outcomes for the company, would serve to reinforce the notion that both behaviors and results are important employee considerations. Many of these behaviors can be emphasized in the company's value statements so that employees realize the importance of positive action on the job, making them more likely to function in a manner consistent with the company's expectations.

Performance measures can be viewed as objective or subjective. The *objective measures* can be observed—for example, the number of cars sold or the number of invoices processed can be counted. *Subjective measures* require judgment on the part of the evaluator and are more difficult to determine. One example of a subjective measure is a supervisor's ratings of an employee's "attitude," which cannot be seen directly. Consequently, both objective and subjective measures should be used carefully.

Relevance of Performance Criteria

Measuring performance requires focusing on the most important aspects of employees' jobs. For example, measuring the initiative of customer service representatives in an insurance claims center may be less relevant than measuring the number of calls the representatives handle properly. Likewise, evaluating how well a hotel manager is liked by peers is likely to be less relevant than evaluating the policies created by the manager to increase hotel profitability. These examples stress that the most important job criteria or duties should be identified in job descriptions and then conveyed to employees.

Performance measures that leave out some important job duties are considered *deficient*. For example, measurement of an employment interviewer's performance is likely to be deficient if it evaluates only the number of applicants hired and not the quality of those hired or how long those hired stay at the company. On the other hand, including irrelevant criteria in performance measures *contaminates* the measures. For example, appearance might be a contaminating criterion in measuring the performance of a telemarketing sales representative whom customers never see. Managers need to guard against using deficient or contaminated performance measures.

Overemphasis on one or two criteria also can lead to problems. For example, overstressing the number of traffic tickets written by a police officer or the revenue generated by a sales representative may lead to the employee ignoring other important performance areas. In addition, cheating can become an issue when goals are set to support such criteria because individuals might act unethically to reach objectives, especially when the objectives are linked to specific rewards.[16] The scandals involving Enron, Qwest, and Tyco and the financial crisis in the first decade of the twenty-first century clearly illustrate this concern.

Performance Standards

Performance standards define the expected levels of employee performance. Sometimes they are labeled *benchmarks*, *goals*, or *targets*—depending on the approach taken. Realistic, measurable, clearly understood performance standards benefit both organizations and employees. In a sense, performance standards define what satisfactory job performance is, so performance standards should be established *before* work is performed. Well-defined standards ensure that everyone involved knows the levels of accomplishment expected. For example, a business college might require each of its faculty members to publish at least one academic article a year to be considered in good standing as an employee.

Both numerical and nonnumerical standards can be established. Sales quotas and production output standards are familiar numerical performance standards. A standard of performance can also be based on nonnumerical criteria. Assessing whether someone has met a performance standard, especially a

Performance standards
Define the expected levels of employee performance.

FIGURE 10-5   **ACTFL Performance Standards for Speaking Proficiency**

PERFORMANCE LEVEL	DEMONSTRATED ABILITY
Superior	• Participates fully in conversations relating to needs and professional interests • Discusses topics both concretely and abstractly • Can deal effectively with unfamiliar speaking situations
Intermediate	• Can participate in simple conversations on predictable topics • Can satisfy simple needs to survive in the language's culture • Can ask and answer questions
Novice	• Can respond to simple questions • Can convey minimal meaning by using isolated words or memorized phrases • Can satisfy a limited number of immediate needs

nonnumerical one, can be difficult, but usually can be done. For example, how would you correctly measure someone's ability to speak a foreign language before the person was sent overseas? Figure 10-5 lists a number of performance standards that facilitate such measurement and make assessing a person's performance level, even nonnumerical performance, much more accurate.[17]

MEASURE

Performance Metrics in Service Businesses

Measuring performance in service businesses is difficult, but the process is important. Measuring service performance is difficult because services are very individualized for customers, there is typically great variation in the services that can be offered, and service quality is somewhat subjective. Yet the performance of people in service jobs is commonly evaluated along with the basic productivity measure used in the industry. Some of the most useful sources of performance differences among managers in service businesses are:

- Regional differences in labor costs
- Service agreement differences
- Equipment/infrastructure differences
- Work volume

On an individual employee level, common measures are: cost per employee, incidents per employee per day, number of calls per product, cost per call, sources of demand for services, and service calls per day.

Once managers have determined appropriate measures of the service variance in their company, they can deal with waste and service delivery. *Performance that is measured can be managed.*[18]

PERFORMANCE APPRAISALS

Performance appraisals are used to assess an employee's performance and provide a platform for feedback about past, current, and future performance expectations. Performance appraisal is variously called *employee rating*, *employee evaluation*, *performance review*, *performance evaluation*, or *results appraisal*.

Performance appraisals are widely used for administering wages and salaries, giving performance feedback, and identifying individual employee strengths and weaknesses. Most U.S. employers use performance appraisals for office, professional, technical, supervisory, middle management, and non-union production workers, and there are many reasons for this widespread use. According to a recent report issued by Bersin & Associates, performance management, which comprised self, manager, and multisource reviews and goal setting, benefits an organization with increased operational competence, legal compliance, enhanced corporate growth, and heightened transformational processes and performance.[19]

Indeed, performance appraisals can provide answers to a wide array of work-related questions, and by advancing a road map for success, poor performance can be improved. Even after a positive appraisal, employees benefit if appraisals help them to determine how to improve job performance. In addition, even though an employer may not need a reason to terminate an employee, as a practical matter, appraisals can provide justification for such actions should that become necessary.

However, appraisal programs must be carefully developed to fully capitalize on the talents and efforts of employees. For instance, research has indicated that a gap often exists between actual job performance and the ratings of the work.[20] Poorly done performance appraisals lead to disappointing results for all concerned, and there is reason to believe that evaluations can cause bad feelings and damaged relationships if not managed well.[21] Some believe that performance evaluations are an unnecessary part of work because of vague rating terms, self-interest, and/or deception on the part of rating managers.[22]

Managers need to display courage and honesty when they evaluate the performance of their workers.[23] One study concluded that some of the top reasons for ineffective evaluations were: "unclear performance criteria/bad rating instrument" (78%), "poor working relationship with your boss" (72%), "lack of ongoing performance feedback" (67%), "superior lacks information on actual performance" (63%), and "perceived political reviews" (59%).[24] Indeed, performance reviews can be politically oriented and highly subjective in nature, which can adversely impact the relationships between managers and their employees.[25] However, having no formal performance appraisal can weaken discipline and harm an employee's ability to improve.

Uses of Performance Appraisals

Organizations generally use performance appraisals in two potentially conflicting ways. One use is to provide a measure of performance for consideration in making pay or other administrative decisions about employees. This *administrative* role often creates stress for managers doing the appraisals and employees as well. The other use focuses on the *development* of individuals. In this role, the manager acts more as a counselor and coach than as a judge, a perspective that can change the overall tone of the appraisal process. The developmental

FIGURE 10-6 Uses for Performance Appraisals

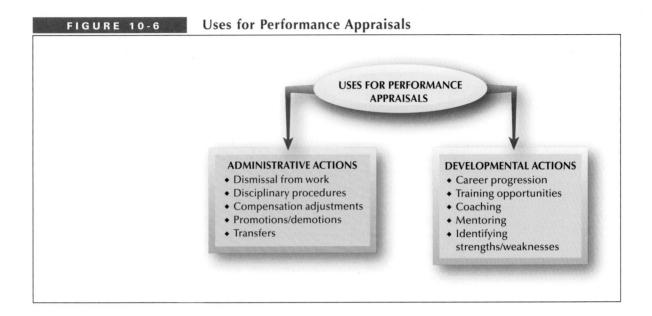

performance appraisal emphasizes identifying current training and development needs, as well as planning employees' future opportunities and career directions. Figure 10-6 shows both uses for performance appraisals.

Administrative Uses of Appraisals Three administrative uses of appraisal impact managers and employees the most: (1) determining pay adjustments; (2) making job placement decisions on promotions, transfers, and demotions; and (3) choosing employee disciplinary actions up to and including termination of employment.

A performance appraisal system is often the link between additional pay and rewards that employees receive and their job performance. Performance-based compensation affirms the idea that pay raises are given for performance accomplishments rather than based on length of service (seniority) or granted automatically to all employees at the same percentage levels. In pay-for-performance compensation systems, historically supervisors and managers have evaluated the performance of individual employees and also made compensation recommendations for the same employees. If any part of the appraisal process fails, better-performing employees may not receive larger pay increases, and the result is perceived inequity in compensation.

Many U.S. workers say that they see little connection between their performance and the size of their pay increases due to flaws in performance appraisals.[26] However, the use of such appraisals to determine pay is common. Consequently, many people argue that performance appraisals and pay discussions should be done separately. Two major realities support this view. One is that employees often focus more on the pay received than on the developmental appraisal feedback. The other is that managers sometimes manipulate ratings to justify the pay they wish to give individuals or the amount the market or budget situation suggests should be given.[27] As a result, many employees view the appraisal process as a "game," because compensation increases have been predetermined before the appraisal.

To address these issues, numerous organizations have managers first conduct performance appraisals and discuss the results with employees, and then several weeks later hold a shorter meeting to discuss pay issues. For example,

Belimo Aircontrols developed an approach like this by creating different performance appraisal and compensation forms that are considered separately at different times.[28] By adopting such an approach, the results of the performance appraisal can be considered before the amount of the pay adjustment is determined. Also, the performance appraisal discussions between managers and employees can focus on the developmental uses of appraisals.

Employers are interested in the administrative uses of performance appraisals as well, such as decisions about promotions, terminations, layoffs, and transfer assignments. Promotions and demotions based on performance must be documented through performance appraisals; otherwise, legal problems can result.

To improve the administrative processes of performance appraisals, many employers have implemented software so that managers can prepare appraisals electronically. As the HR Online indicates, many firms are using such HR technology not only to administer appraisals but also to facilitate employee development and talent management in a fully integrated capacity.[29] For instance, Porsche Cars North America utilizes a performance review system called Vurv Express Performance that facilitates employee participation in performance management.[30] The Zoological Society of San Diego also uses a Web-based performance management program that enables employees to better understand the linkages between organizational and employee goals.[31] Finally, Belkin International Inc., an electronic accessories provider located in Los Angeles, uses software developed by SuccessFactors to reduce administrative inefficiencies and enhance the strategic flavor of evaluations.[32]

Using Technology to Enhance Performance Appraisals

Proper performance management requires considerable time, resources, and paperwork, so companies are using more technology to become more efficient in the management of human resources. A performance appraisal system that uses technology to automate processes can provide many advantages to organizations, so human resource professionals should consider utilizing electronic methods to facilitate the manner in which appraisal procedures are administered and managed.

Automated systems offered by vendors provide common formats, sample text, integration with compensation, and development and succession planning. These systems also can provide information on individuals, units, and the performance of entire companies. All of these features serve to enhance the effectiveness of a company's performance management processes.

In addition, automated systems can help managers identify which of a company's thousands of employees are its top performers, or provide a breakdown of workers with certain competencies and the best performers among them. The systems may use "dashboards," which are advanced technologies that provide indicators of the current performance levels of the organization. Aggregating performance information can provide "big picture," overarching perspectives on performance management that are difficult for human resource professionals to get otherwise. Finally, online performance assessment can minimize face-to-face meetings and reduce time, perhaps allowing for more frequent reviews.

One survey found that about 28% of organizations surveyed had automated their performance systems. Those that had done so confirmed that ease of use, time savings, and ability to track performance had improved. Other companies should therefore find ways to better utilize technology to enhance performance management.[33]

Developmental Uses of Appraisals For employees, a performance appraisal can be a primary source of information and feedback that builds their future development in an organization. By identifying employee strengths, weaknesses, potentials, and training needs through performance appraisal feedback, supervisors can inform employees about their progress, discuss areas in which additional training may be beneficial, and outline future developmental plans.

The manager's role in performance appraisal meetings parallels that of a coach, discussing good performance, explaining what improvements are needed, and showing employees how to improve. It is clear that employees do not always know where and how to improve, and managers should not expect improvement if they are unwilling to provide developmental feedback. Many firms, such as the diesel engine parts distributor Cummins Mid-South LLC, are combining performance and learning management processes with technological support programs that prompt more effective evaluations, increased employee development, and reduced turnover.[34]

Positive reinforcement for desired behaviors contributes to both individual and organizational growth. The purpose of the feedback is both to reinforce satisfactory employee performance and to address performance deficiencies. The developmental function of performance appraisal can also identify areas in which the employee might wish to grow. For example, in a performance appraisal interview targeted exclusively to development, an employee found out that the only factor keeping her from being considered for a management job in her firm was the lack of a working knowledge of cost accounting. Her supervisor suggested that she consider taking some night courses at the local college.

The use of teams provides a different set of circumstances for developmental appraisals. The manager may not see all of an employee's work, but the employee's team members do. Teams can provide important feedback. However, it is still an open question as to whether teams can handle administrative appraisals. When teams are allowed to design appraisal systems, they tend to "get rid of judgment" and avoid differential rewards. Thus, group appraisal may be best suited to developmental, not administrative, purposes.

Decisions about the Performance Appraisal Process

A number of decisions must be made when designing performance appraisal systems. Some important ones are identifying the appraisal responsibilities of the HR unit and of the operating managers, the type of appraisal system to use, the timing of appraisals, and who conducts appraisals.

Appraisal Responsibilities The appraisal process can benefit both the organization and the employees, if done properly. As Figure 10-7 shows, the HR unit typically designs a performance appraisal system. The operating managers then appraise employees using the appraisal system. During development of the formal appraisal system, managers usually offer input as to how the final system will work.

It is important for managers to understand that appraisals are *their* responsibility. Through the appraisal process, effective employee performance can be developed to be even better, and poor employee performance can be improved or poor performers can be removed from the organization. Performance

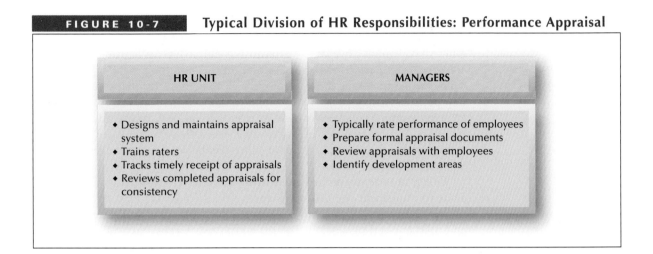

FIGURE 10-7 **Typical Division of HR Responsibilities: Performance Appraisal**

HR UNIT

- Designs and maintains appraisal system
- Trains raters
- Tracks timely receipt of appraisals
- Reviews completed appraisals for consistency

MANAGERS

- Typically rate performance of employees
- Prepare formal appraisal documents
- Review appraisals with employees
- Identify development areas

appraisal must not be simply an HR requirement but also a management process, because guiding employees' performance is among the most important responsibilities of managers.

Informal versus Systematic Appraisal Processes Performance appraisals can occur in two ways: informally and/or systematically. A supervisor conducts an *informal appraisal* whenever necessary. The day-to-day working relationship between a manager and an employee offers an opportunity for the employee's performance to be evaluated. A manager communicates this evaluation through conversation on the job, over coffee, or by on-the-spot discussion of a specific occurrence. For instance, a restaurant manager might discuss a waiter's table service while they both eat lunch in the break room. Although such informal feedback is useful and necessary, it should not take the place of formal appraisal.

Frequent informal feedback to employees can prevent "surprises" during a formal performance review. However, informal appraisal can become *too* informal. For example, a senior executive at a large firm so dreaded face-to-face evaluations that he delivered one manager's review while both sat in adjoining stalls in the men's room.

A *systematic appraisal* is used when the contact between a manager and employee is formal, and a system is in place to report managerial impressions and observations on employee performance. This approach to appraisals is quite common, and one survey found that almost 90% of employers have a formal performance management system or process.[35] Systematic appraisals feature a regular time interval, which distinguishes them from informal appraisals. Both employees and managers know that performance will be reviewed on a regular basis, and they can plan for performance discussions. For example, a front desk supervisor in a large hotel chain may wish to provide more formalized feedback to a bell captain, so a systematic appraisal session will be scheduled so that both individuals can prepare ahead of time to discuss performance issues.

Timing of Appraisals Most companies require managers to conduct appraisals once or twice a year, most often annually. Employees commonly receive an appraisal 60 to 90 days after hiring, again at 6 months, and annually thereafter. *Probationary* or *introductory employees*, who are new and in a trial period, should be informally evaluated often—perhaps weekly for the first month, and monthly thereafter until the end of the introductory period. After that, annual reviews are typical. For employees in high demand, some employers use accelerated appraisals—every 6 months instead of every year. This is done to retain those employees so that more feedback can be given and pay raises may occur more often. In some organizations, meeting more frequently with employees can enhance individual performance. For instance, Whirlpool Corp. requires managers to meet with employees on a quarterly basis, but because some want even more feedback, some managers schedule meetings every few weeks.[36]

One way to separate the administrative and developmental uses of appraisals is to implement the following appraisal schedule: (1) First hold a performance review and discussion; (2) later hold a separate training, development, and objective-setting session; and (3) within two weeks, have a compensation adjustment discussion. Having three separate discussions provides both the employee and the manager with opportunities to focus on the administrative, developmental, and compensation issues. Using this framework is generally better than addressing all three areas in one discussion of an hour or less, once a year.

Legal Concerns and Performance Appraisals

Because appraisals are supposed to measure how well employees are doing their jobs, it may seem unnecessary to emphasize that performance appraisals must be job related. However, it is important for evaluations to adequately reflect the nature of work, and employees should have fair and nondiscriminatory performance appraisals. Companies need to have appraisal systems that satisfy the courts, as well as performance management needs.[37] The HR On-the-Job shows the elements of a legal performance appraisal system.

Elements of a Legal Performance Appraisal System

The elements of a performance appraisal system that can survive court tests can be determined from existing case law. It is generally agreed that a legally defensible performance appraisal should include the following:

- Performance appraisal criteria based on job analysis
- Absence of disparate impact
- Formal evaluation criteria that limit managerial discretion
- A rating instrument linked to job duties and responsibilities

- Documentation of the appraisal activities
- Personal knowledge of and contact with each appraised individual
- Training of supervisors in conducting appraisals
- A review process that prevents one manager, acting alone, from controlling an employee's career
- Counseling to help poor performers improve

Of course, having all these components is no guarantee against lawsuits. However, including them does improve the chance of winning any lawsuits that might be filed.

WHO CONDUCTS APPRAISALS?

Performance appraisals can be conducted by anyone familiar with the performance of individual employees. Possible rating situations include the following:

- Supervisors rating their employees
- Employees rating their superiors
- Team members rating each other
- Employees rating themselves
- Outside sources rating employees
- A variety of parties providing multisource, or 360-degree, feedback

Supervisory Rating of Subordinates

The most widely used means of rating employees is based on the assumption that the immediate supervisor is the person most qualified to evaluate an employee's performance realistically and fairly. To help themselves provide accurate evaluations, some supervisors keep performance logs noting their employees' accomplishments so that they can reference these notes when rating performance. For instance, a sales manager might periodically observe a salesperson's interactions with clients so that constructive performance feedback can be provided at a later date. Figure 10-8 shows the traditional

---

FIGURE 10-8   **Traditional Performance Appraisal Process**

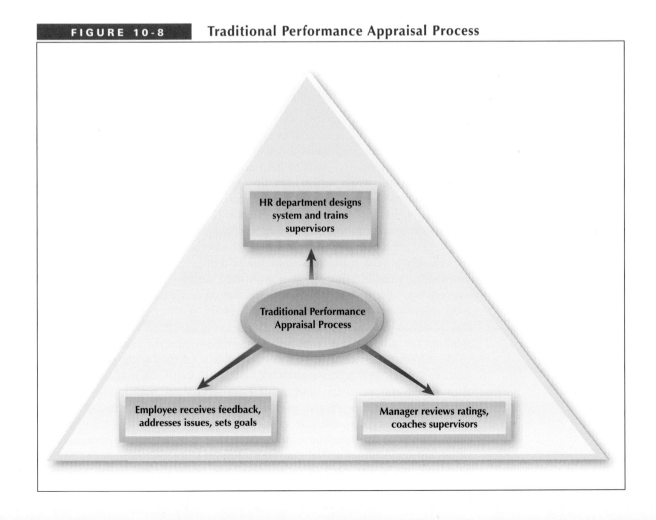

- HR department designs system and trains supervisors
- Traditional Performance Appraisal Process
- Employee receives feedback, addresses issues, sets goals
- Manager reviews ratings, coaches supervisors

review process by which supervisors conduct performance appraisals on employees.

Employee Rating of Managers

A number of organizations today ask employees to rate the performance of their immediate managers. A prime example of this type of rating takes place in colleges and universities, where students evaluate the teaching effectiveness of professors in the classroom. Another example is HCL Technologies in India, which requires employees to rate their bosses as part of a multisource review process that posts evaluations on the intranet.[38] These performance appraisal ratings are generally used for management development purposes.

Having employees rate managers provides three primary advantages. First, in critical manager-employee relationships, employee ratings can be quite useful for identifying competent managers. The rating of leaders by combat soldiers is one example of such a use. Second, this type of rating program can help make a manager more responsive to employees. This advantage can quickly become a disadvantage if the manager focuses on being "nice" rather than on managing; people who are nice but have no other qualifications may not be good managers in many situations. Finally, employee appraisals can contribute to career development efforts for managers by identifying areas for growth.

A major disadvantage of having employees rate managers is the negative reaction many superiors have to being evaluated by employees. Also, the fear of reprisals may be too great for employees to give realistic ratings. This may prompt workers to rate their managers only on the way the managers treat them, not on critical job requirements. The problems associated with this appraisal approach limit its usefulness to certain situations, including managerial development and improvement efforts.[39]

Team/Peer Rating

Having employees and team members rate each other is another type of appraisal with potential both to help and to hurt. Peer and team ratings are especially useful when supervisors do not have the opportunity to observe each employee's performance but other work group members do. For instance, some of the advanced training programs in the U.S. military use peer ratings to provide candidates more extensive feedback about their leadership qualities and accomplishments. Peer evaluations are also common in collegiate schools of business where professors commonly require students to conduct peer evaluations after the completion of group-based projects. One challenge of this approach is how to obtain ratings with virtual or global teams, in which the individuals work primarily through technology, not in person (i.e., an online college class). Another challenge is obtaining ratings from and for individuals who are on different special project teams throughout the year.

Some contend that any performance appraisal, including team/peer ratings, can negatively affect teamwork and participative management efforts. Although team members have good information on one another's performance, they may not choose to share it in the interest of sparing feelings; alternatively, they may unfairly attack other group members. Some organizations attempt to overcome such problems by using anonymous appraisals and/or having a consultant or HR manager interpret team/peer ratings. Despite the problems, team/peer performance ratings are probably inevitable, especially where work teams are used extensively.[40]

Self-Rating

Self-appraisal works in certain situations. As a self-development tool, it requires employees to think about their strengths and weaknesses and set goals for improvement. Employees working in isolation or possessing unique skills may be particularly suited to self-ratings because they are the only ones qualified to rate themselves. Overall, the use of self-appraisals in organizations has increased. For instance, the YMCA located in Greater Rochester, New York, successfully incorporated self-ratings into a traditional rating approach that presumably did not generate enough dialogue and direction for individual development; reactions from both workers and supervisors have been favorable.[41]

However, employees may use quite different standards and not rate themselves in the same manner as supervisors. Research exploring how people might be more lenient or more demanding when rating themselves is mixed, with self-ratings being frequently higher than supervisory ratings. Still, employee self-ratings can be a useful source of performance information for development.[42]

Outsider Rating

People outside the immediate work group may be called in to conduct performance reviews. This field review approach can include someone from the HR department as a reviewer, or completely independent reviewers from outside the organization. Examples include a review team evaluating a college president or a panel of division managers evaluating a supervisor's potential for advancement in the organization. A disadvantage of this approach is that outsiders may not know the important demands within the work group or organization.

The customers or clients of an organization are good sources for outside appraisals. For sales and service jobs, customers may provide useful input on the performance behaviors of employees. For instance, many hospitality organizations such as restaurants and hotels use customer comments cards to gather feedback about the service provided by customer contact personnel, and this information is commonly used for job development purposes.

Multisource/360-Degree Feedback

The use of multisource rating, or 360-degree feedback, has grown in popularity in organizations. Multisource feedback recognizes that for many jobs, employee performance is multidimensional and crosses departmental, organizational, and even global boundaries. Therefore, information needs to be collected from many different sources to adequately and fairly evaluate an incumbent's performance in one of these jobs.

The major purpose of 360-degree feedback is *not* to increase uniformity by soliciting like-minded views. Instead, it is designed to capture evaluations of the employee's different roles to provide richer feedback during an evaluation. Figure 10-9 shows graphically some of the parties who are often involved in 360-degree feedback. For example, an HR manager for an insurance firm deals with seven regional sales managers, HR administrators in five claims centers, and various corporate executives in finance, legal, and information technology. The Vice President of HR uses 360-degree feedback to gather data on all facets of the HR manager's job before completing a performance appraisal on the

FIGURE 10-9   **Multisource Appraisal**

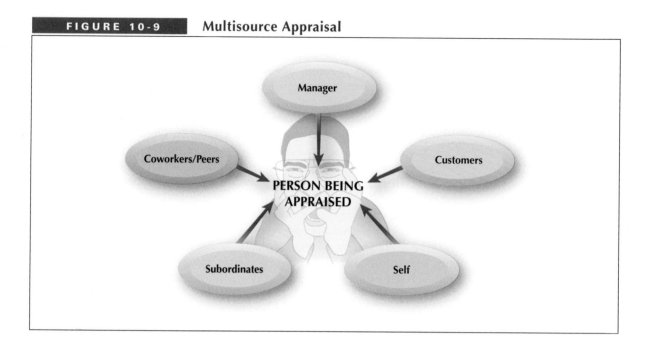

manager. Similar examples can be cited in numerous managerial, professional, technical, operational, and administrative jobs.

Significant administrative time and paperwork are required to request, obtain, and summarize feedback from multiple raters. Using electronic systems to summarize the information can greatly reduce the administrative demands of multisource ratings and increase the effectiveness (i.e., privacy and expediency) of the process.[43]

Developmental Use of Multisource Feedback As originally designed and used, multisource feedback focuses on the use of appraisals for future development of individuals. Conflict resolution skills, decision-making abilities, team effectiveness, communication skills, managerial styles, and technical capabilities are just some of the developmental areas that can be examined. Even in a multisource system, the manager remains a focal point, both to receive the feedback initially and to follow up with the employee appropriately.

Administrative Use of Multisource Feedback The popularity of 360-degree feedback systems has led to the results being used for compensation, promotion, termination, and other administrative decisions. When using 360-degree feedback for administrative purposes, managers must anticipate potential problems. Differences among raters can present a challenge, especially when using 360-degree ratings for discipline or pay decisions. Bias can just as easily be rooted in customers, subordinates, and peers as in a boss, and the lack of accountability of those sources can affect the ratings. "Inflation" of ratings is common when the sources know that their input will affect someone's pay or career. At one manufacturing firm, the apparent "back scratching" associated with multisource reviews led the company to drop the program.[44] Also, issues of confidentiality and anonymity have led to lawsuits. Even though multisource approaches offer possible solutions to the well-documented dissatisfaction associated with performance appraisals, a number of questions have arisen as multisource appraisals have become more common.

Evaluating Multisource Feedback Research on multisource/360-degree feedback has revealed both positives and negatives. More variability than expected may be seen in the ratings given by the different sources. Thus, supervisor ratings must carry more weight than peer or subordinate input to resolve the differences. One concern is that those peers who rate poor-performing coworkers tend to inflate the ratings so that the peers themselves can get higher overall evaluation results.[45]

Another concern is whether 360-degree appraisals improve the process or simply multiply the number of problems by the total number of raters. Also, some wonder whether multisource appraisals really create better decisions that offset the additional time and investment required. These issues appear to be less threatening when the 360-degree feedback is used *only for development*, so companies should consider using multisource feedback primarily as a developmental tool to enhance future job performance[46] while effectively reducing the use of multisource appraisals as an administrative tool.

LOGGING ON

Personnel Decisions International
This is a website for a firm specializing in the development of people utilizing many different development tools, including managing performance data. Visit the site at
www.personneldecisions.com.

TOOLS FOR APPRAISING PERFORMANCE

Performance can be appraised by a number of methods. Some employers use one method for all jobs and employees, some use different methods for different groups of employees, and others use a combination of methods. The following discussion highlights different tools that can be used and some of the advantages and disadvantages of each approach.

Category Scaling Methods

The simplest methods for appraising performance are category scaling methods, which require a manager to mark an employee's level of performance on a specific form divided into categories of performance. A *checklist* uses a list of statements or words from which raters check statements that are most representative of the characteristics and performance of employees. Often, a scale indicating perceived level of accomplishment on each statement is included, which becomes a type of graphic rating scale.

Graphic Rating Scales

Graphic rating scale Scale that allows the rater to mark an employee's performance on a continuum.

The **graphic rating scale** allows the rater to mark an employee's performance on a continuum indicating low to high levels of a particular characteristic. Because of the straightforwardness of the process, graphic rating scales are commonly used in performance evaluations.[47] Figure 10-10 shows a sample appraisal form that combines graphic rating scales with essays. Three aspects of performance are appraised using graphic rating scales: *descriptive categories* (such as quantity of work, attendance, and dependability), *job duties* (taken from the job description), and *behavioral dimensions* (such as decision making, employee development, and communication effectiveness).

| FIGURE 10-10 | Sample Performance Appraisal Form |

Date sent: 4/19/11   Return by: 5/01/11

Name: Joe Hernandez   Job title: Receiving Clerk

Department: Receiving   Supervisor: Marian Williams

Employment status (check one): Full-time __X__ Part-time _____   Date of hire: 5/12/02

Rating period: From: 4/30/10   To: 4/30/11

Reason for appraisal (check one): Regular interval __X__   Introductory ____   Counseling only ____   Discharge ____

Using the following definitions, rate the performance as I, M, or E.

I—Performance is below job requirements and **improvement is needed.**

M—Performance **meets** job requirements and standards.

E—Performance **exceeds** job requirements and standards **most** of the time.

SPECIFIC JOB RESPONSIBILITIES: List the prinicipal activities from the job summary, rate the performance on each job duty by placing an X on the rating scale at the appropriate location, and make appropriate comments to explain the rating.

I ———————————————— M ———————————————— E

Job Duty #1: Inventory receiving and checking
Explanation: _____

_____

I ———————————————— M ———————————————— E

Job Duty #2: Accurate recordkeeping
Explanation: _____

_____

I ———————————————— M ———————————————— E

Attendance (including absences and tardies):   Number of absences ____   Number of tardies ____
Explanation: _____

_____

Overall rating: In the box provided, place the letter—I, M, or E—that best describes the employee's overall performance.

Explanation: _____

_____

Each of these types can be used for different jobs. How well employees meet established standards is often expressed either numerically (e.g., 5, 4, 3, 2, 1) or verbally (e.g., "outstanding," "meets standards," "below standards"). If two or more people are involved in the rating, they may find it difficult to agree on the exact level of performance achieved relative to the standard in evaluating employee performance. Notice that each level specifies performance standards or expectations in order to reduce variation in interpretations of the standards by different supervisors and employees.

Concerns with Graphic Rating Scales Graphic rating scales in many forms are widely used because they are easy to develop and provide a uniform set of criteria to equally evaluate the job performance of different employees. However, the use of scales can cause rater error because the form might not accurately reflect the relative importance of certain job characteristics, and some factors might need to be added to the ratings while others might need to be deleted. If they fit the person and the job, the scales work well. However, if they fit poorly, managers and employees who must use them frequently complain about "the rating form."

A key point must be emphasized. Regardless of the scales used, the focus should be on the job duties and responsibilities identified in job descriptions. The closer the link between the scales and what people actually do, as identified in current and complete job descriptions, the stronger the relationship between the ratings and the job, as viewed by employees and managers. Also, should the performance appraisal results be challenged by legal actions, the closer performance appraisals measure what people actually do, the more likely employers are to prevail in those legal situations.

An additional drawback to graphic rating scales is that often separate traits or factors are grouped together, and the rater is given only one box to check. For example, "dependability" could refer to meeting deadlines for reports, or it could refer to attendance and tardiness. If a supervisor gives an employee a rating of 3, which aspect of "dependability" is being rated? One supervisor might rate employees on meeting deadlines, while another rates employees on attendance.

Another drawback is that the descriptive words sometimes used in scales may have different meanings to different raters.[48] Terms such as *initiative* and *cooperation* are subject to many interpretations, especially if used in conjunction with words such as *outstanding*, *average*, and *poor*. Also, as Figure 10-11 shows, the number of scale points can be defined differently.

FIGURE 10-11   **Sample Terms for Defining Standards**

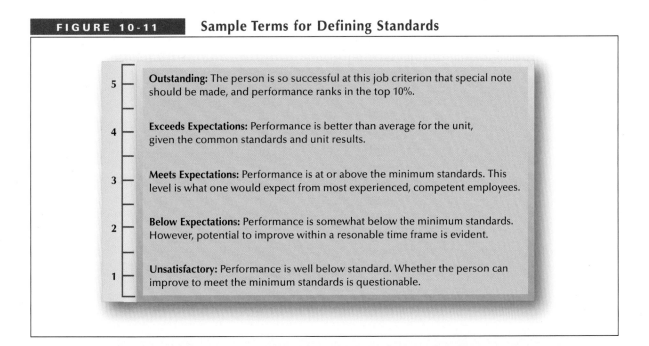

5 — Outstanding: The person is so successful at this job criterion that special note should be made, and performance ranks in the top 10%.

4 — Exceeds Expectations: Performance is better than average for the unit, given the common standards and unit results.

3 — Meets Expectations: Performance is at or above the minimum standards. This level is what one would expect from most experienced, competent employees.

2 — Below Expectations: Performance is somewhat below the minimum standards. However, potential to improve within a resonable time frame is evident.

1 — Unsatisfactory: Performance is well below standard. Whether the person can improve to meet the minimum standards is questionable.

Behavioral Rating Scales In an attempt to overcome some of the concerns with graphic rating scales, employers may use behavioral rating scales designed to assess individual actions instead of personal attributes and characteristics.[49] Different approaches are used, but all describe specific examples of employee job behaviors. In a behaviorally–anchored rating scale (BARS), these examples are "anchored" or measured against a scale of performance levels.

When creating a BARS system, identifying important *job dimensions*, which are the most important performance factors in a job description, is done first. Short statements describe both desirable and undesirable behaviors (anchors). These are then "translated," or assigned, to one of the job dimensions. Anchor statements are usually developed by a group of people familiar with the job. Assignment to a dimension usually requires the agreement of 60% to 70% of the group. The group then assigns each anchor a number that represents how good or bad the behavior is, and the anchors are fitted to a scale. Figure 10-12 contains an example that rates customer service skills for individuals taking orders for a national catalog retailer. Spelling out the behaviors associated with each level of performance helps minimize some of the problems noted for the graphic rating scale.

Several problems are associated with the behavioral approaches. First, creating and maintaining behaviorally–anchored rating scales requires extensive time and effort. In addition, various appraisal forms are needed to accommodate different types of jobs in an organization. For instance, because nurses, dietitians, and admissions clerks in a hospital all have distinct job descriptions, a separate BARS form needs to be developed for each.

FIGURE 10-12   **Behaviorally–Anchored Rating Scale for Customer Service Skills**

The Customer Service Representative

Outstanding	5	← Used positive phrases to explain product
	4	← Offered additional pertinent information when asked questions by customer
Satisfactory	3	← Referred customer to another product when requested item was not available
	2	← Discouraged customer from waiting for an out-of-stock item
Unsatisfactory	1	← Argued with customer about suitability of requested product

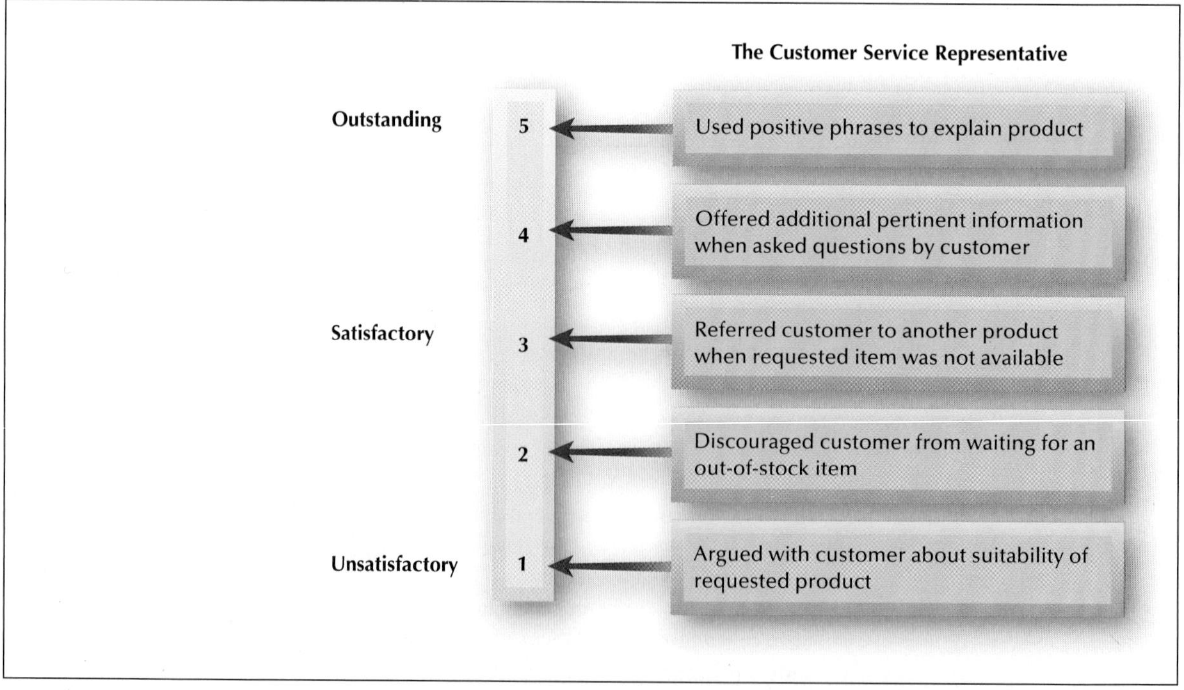

Comparative Methods

Comparative methods require that managers directly compare the performance levels of their employees against one another, and these comparisons can provide useful information for performance management. A recent study found that performance evaluations that utilize social comparisons provide more valid assessments of employee performance than do absolute measures.[50] However, there are other issues. An example of this process would be an information systems supervisor comparing the performance of a programmer with that of other programmers. Comparative techniques include ranking and forced distribution.

Ranking The **ranking** method lists the individuals being rated from highest to lowest based on their performance levels and relative contributions.[51] One disadvantage of this process is that the sizes of the performance differences between employees are often not fully investigated or clearly indicated. For example, the performances of individuals ranked second and third may differ little, while the performances of those ranked third and fourth differ a great deal. This limitation can be mitigated to some extent by assigning points to indicate performance differences. Ranking also means someone must be last, which ignores the possibility that the last-ranked individual in one group might be equal to the top-ranked employee in a different group. Further, the ranking task becomes unwieldy if the group to be ranked is large.

Forced Distribution Forced distribution is a technique for distributing ratings that are generated with any of the other appraisal methods and comparing the ratings of people in a work group. With the **forced distribution** method, the ratings of employees' performance are distributed along a bell-shaped curve. For example, a medical clinic administrator ranking employees on a 5-point scale would have to rate 10% of the employees as a 1 ("unsatisfactory"), 20% as a 2 ("below expectations"), 40% as a 3 ("meets expectations"), 20% as a 4 ("above expectations"), and 10% as a 5 ("outstanding").

Forced distribution has been used in some form by an estimated 30% of all firms with performance appraisal systems. At General Electric, in the "20/70/10" program, managers identify the top 20% and reward them richly so that few will leave. The bottom 10% are given a chance to improve or leave. The forced distribution system is controversial because of both its advantages and its disadvantages, which are discussed next.[52]

Advantages and Disadvantages of Forced Distribution One reason why firms have mandated the use of forced distributions for appraisal ratings is to deal with "rater inflation." If employers do not require a forced distribution, performance appraisal ratings often do not match the normal distribution of a bell-shaped curve (see Figure 10-13).

The use of a forced distribution system forces managers to identify high, average, and low performers. Thus, high performers can be rewarded and developed, while low performers can be "encouraged" to improve or leave. Advocates of forced ranking also state that forced distribution ensures that compensation increases truly are differentiated by performance rather than being spread somewhat equally among all employees. Forced rankings may also enhance a company's level of talent, instill a high-performance work environment, and increase workers' self-confidence.[53]

Ranking Performance appraisal method in which all employees are listed from highest to lowest in performance.

Forced distribution Performance appraisal method in which ratings of employees' performance levels are distributed along a bell-shaped curve.

FIGURE 10-13   **Forced Distribution on a Bell-Shaped Curve**

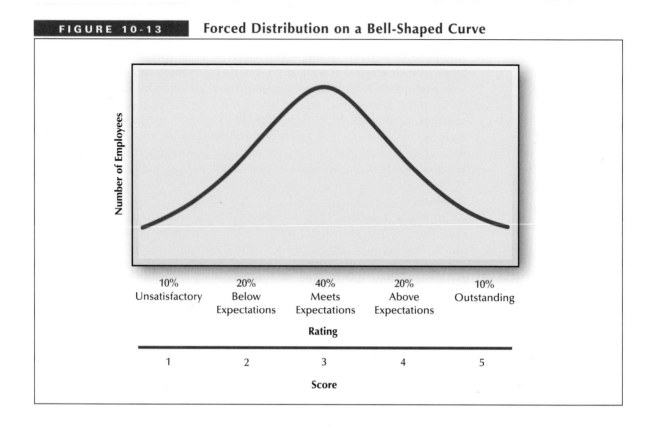

But the forced distribution method suffers from several drawbacks. One problem is that a supervisor may resist placing any individual in the lowest (or the highest) group. Difficulties also arise when the rater must explain to an employee why the employee was placed in one group and others were placed in higher groups. Further, particularly with small groups, the nature and magnitude of rating scores often may not conform to a bell-shaped distribution, possibly due to leniency bias.[54] In some cases, the manager may make false distinctions between employees. By comparing people against each other, rather than against a standard of job performance, supervisors trying to fill the percentages may end up giving employees subjective ratings. Finally, forced ranking structures can increase anxiety in employees, promote conformity, and encourage gaming of the system.[55] Consequently, a number of firms such as Ford and Goodyear Tire & Rubber have been involved in lawsuits about forced distribution performance appraisal processes.[56]

A number of actions are recommended to address these problems if a forced distribution system is to be used, including many that are similar to those for making other methods of appraisals more legal and effective[57]:

- Use specific, objective criteria and standards to evaluate employees.
- Involve employees in program development.
- Ensure that sufficient numbers of individuals are being rated, so that ranking profiles are relevant.
- Train managers, and review their ratings to ensure job relatedness (no favoritism).

Narrative Methods

Managers and HR specialists often are required to provide written appraisal information. However, some appraisal methods are entirely written, rather than relying on predetermined rating scales or ranking structures. Documentation and descriptive text are the basic components of the critical incident method and the essay method.

Critical Incident In the critical incident method, the manager keeps a written record of both highly favorable and unfavorable actions performed by an employee during the entire rating period. When a "critical incident" involving an employee occurs, the manager writes it down. For instance, when a sales clerk at a clothing store spends considerable time with a customer helping him purchase a new suit, a manager might document this exceptional service for later review during an annual evaluation. The critical incident method can be used with other methods to document the reasons why an employee was given a certain rating.

Essay The essay method requires a manager to write a short essay describing each employee's performance during the rating period. Some "free-form" essays are without guidelines; others are more structured, using prepared questions that must be answered. The rater usually categorizes comments under a few general headings. The essay method allows the rater more flexibility than other methods do. As a result, appraisers often combine the essay with other methods.

The effectiveness of the essay approach often depends on a supervisor's writing skills. Some supervisors do not express themselves well in writing and as a result produce poor descriptions of employee performance, whereas others have excellent writing skills and can create highly positive impressions. If well composed, essays can provide highly detailed and useful information about an employees' job performance.

Management by Objectives

Management by objectives (MBO) specifies the performance goals that an individual and manager identify together. Each manager sets objectives derived from the overall goals and objectives of the organization; however, MBO should not be a disguised means for a superior to dictate the objectives of individual managers or employees. Other names for MBO include *appraisal by results*, *target coaching*, *work planning and review*, *performance objective setting*, and *mutual goal setting*.

MBO Process Implementing a guided self-appraisal system using MBO is a four-stage process. The stages are as follows:

1. *Job review and agreement:* The employee and the superior review the job description and the key activities that constitute the employee's job. The idea is to agree on the exact makeup of the job.
2. *Development of performance standards:* Together, the employee and the employee's superior develop specific standards of performance and determine a satisfactory level of performance that is specific and measurable. For example, a quota of selling five cars a month may be an appropriate performance standard for a salesperson.

Management by objectives (MBO)
Performance appraisal method that specifies the performance goals that an individual and manager identify together.

3. *Setting of objectives:* Together, the employee and the superior establish objectives that are realistically attainable.
4. *Continuing performance discussions:* The employee and the superior use the objectives as bases for continuing discussions about the employee's performance. Although a formal review session may be scheduled, the employee and the supervisor do not necessarily wait until the appointed time to discuss performance. Objectives can be mutually modified as warranted.

The MBO process seems to be most useful with managerial personnel and employees who have a fairly wide range of flexibility and control over their jobs. When imposed on a rigid and autocratic management system, MBO often has failed. Emphasizing penalties for not meeting objectives defeats the development and participative nature of MBO.

Combinations of Methods

No single appraisal method is best for all situations. Therefore, a performance measurement system that uses a combination of methods may be sensible in certain circumstances. Using combinations may offset some of the advantages and disadvantages of individual methods. Category scaling methods sometimes are easy to develop, but they usually do little to measure strategic accomplishments. Further, they may make inter-rater reliability problems worse. Comparative approaches help reduce leniency and other errors, which makes them useful for administrative decisions such as determining pay raises. But comparative approaches do a poor job of linking performance to organizational goals, and by themselves do not provide feedback for improvement as well as other methods do.

Narrative methods work well for development because they potentially generate more feedback information. However, without good definitions of performance criteria or standards, they can be so unstructured as to be of little value. Also, these methods work poorly for administrative uses. The MBO approach works well to link performance to organizational goals, but it can require much effort and time for defining objectives and explaining the process to employees. Narrative and MBO approaches may not work as well for lower-level jobs as for jobs with more varied duties and responsibilities.

When managers can articulate what they want a performance appraisal system to accomplish, they can choose and mix methods to realize those advantages. For example, one combination might include a graphic rating scale of performance on major job criteria, a narrative for developmental needs, and an overall ranking of employees in a department. Different categories of employees (e.g., salaried exempt, salaried nonexempt, and maintenance) might require different combinations of methods.

TRAINING MANAGERS AND EMPLOYEES IN PERFORMANCE APPRAISAL

Court decisions on the legality of performance appraisals and research on appraisal effectiveness both stress the importance of training managers and employees on performance management and on conducting performance appraisals. Managers with positive views of the performance appraisal system are more likely to use the system effectively. Unfortunately, such training occurs only sporadically or not at all in many organizations.

For employees, performance appraisal training focuses on the purposes of appraisal, the appraisal process and timing, and how performance criteria and standards are linked to job duties and responsibilities. Some training also discusses how employees might rate their own performance and use that information in discussions with their supervisors and managers.

Most systems can be improved by training supervisors in how to do performance appraisals.[58] Because conducting the appraisals is critical, training should center around minimizing rater errors and providing raters with details on documenting performance information. Training is especially essential for those who have recently been promoted to jobs in which conducting performance appraisals is a new experience for them. Without training, managers and supervisors often "repeat the past," meaning that they appraise others much as they have been appraised in the past, whether accurately or inaccurately. The following list is not comprehensive, but it does identify some topics covered in appraisal training:

- Appraisal process and timing
- Performance criteria and job standards that should be considered
- How to communicate positive and negative feedback
- When and how to discuss training and development goals
- Conducting and discussing the compensation review
- How to avoid common rating errors

Rater Errors

There are many possible sources of error in the performance appraisal process. One of the major sources is the raters. Although completely eliminating errors is impossible, making raters aware of them through training is helpful. Figure 10-14 lists some common rater errors.

Varying Standards When appraising employees, a manager should avoid applying different standards and expectations to employees performing the same or similar jobs. Such problems often result from the use of ambiguous criteria and subjective weightings by supervisors.

Recency and Primacy Effects The **recency effect** occurs when a rater gives greater weight to recent events when appraising an individual's performance. Examples include giving a student a course grade based only on the student's performance in the last week of class and giving a drill press operator a high rating even though the operator made the quota only in the last two weeks of the rating period. The opposite of the recency effect is the **primacy effect**, which occurs when a rater gives greater weight to information received first when appraising an individual's performance.

Central Tendency, Leniency, and Strictness Errors Ask students, and they will tell you which professors tend to grade easier or harder. A manager may develop a similar *rating pattern*. Appraisers who rate all employees within a narrow range in the middle of the scale (i.e., rate everyone as "average") commit a **central tendency error**, giving even outstanding and poor performers an "average" rating.

Rating patterns also may exhibit leniency or strictness. The **leniency error** occurs when ratings of all employees fall at the high end of the scale. The

Recency effect Occurs when a rater gives greater weight to recent events when appraising an individual's performance.

Primacy effect Occurs when a rater gives greater weight to information received first when appraising an individual's performance.

Central tendency error Occurs when a rater gives all employees a score within a narrow range in the middle of the scale.

Leniency error Occurs when ratings of all employees fall at the high end of the scale.

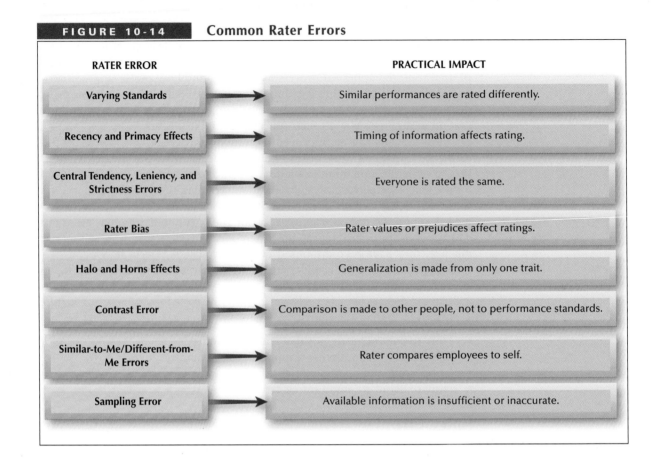

FIGURE 10-14   **Common Rater Errors**

RATER ERROR	PRACTICAL IMPACT
Varying Standards	Similar performances are rated differently.
Recency and Primacy Effects	Timing of information affects rating.
Central Tendency, Leniency, and Strictness Errors	Everyone is rated the same.
Rater Bias	Rater values or prejudices affect ratings.
Halo and Horns Effects	Generalization is made from only one trait.
Contrast Error	Comparison is made to other people, not to performance standards.
Similar-to-Me/Different-from-Me Errors	Rater compares employees to self.
Sampling Error	Available information is insufficient or inaccurate.

strictness error occurs when a manager uses only the lower part of the scale to rate employees. To avoid conflict, managers often rate employees higher than they should. This "ratings boost" is especially likely when no manager or HR representative reviews the completed appraisals.

Rater Bias When a rater's values or prejudices distort the rating, this is referred to as **rater bias**. Such bias may be unconscious or quite intentional. For example, a manager's dislike of certain ethnic groups may cause distortion in appraisal information for some people. Use of age, religion, seniority, sex, appearance, or other "classifications" also may skew appraisal ratings if the appraisal process is not properly designed. A review of appraisal ratings by higher-level managers may help correct this problem.

Halo and Horns Effects The **halo effect** occurs when a rater scores an employee high on all job criteria because of performance in one area. For example, if a worker has few absences, the supervisor might give the worker a high rating in all other areas of work, including quantity and quality of output, without really thinking about the employee's other characteristics separately. The opposite is the *horns effect*, which occurs when a low rating on one characteristic leads to an overall low rating.

Contrast Error Rating should be done using established standards. One problem is the **contrast error**, which is the tendency to rate people relative to one another rather than against performance standards. For example, if

Strictness error Occurs when ratings of all employees fall at the low end of the scale.

Rater bias Occurs when a rater's values or prejudices distort the rating.

Halo effect Occurs when a rater scores an employee high on all job criteria because of performance in one area.

Contrast error Tendency to rate people relative to others rather than against performance standards.

everyone else performs at a mediocre level, then a person performing only somewhat better may be rated as "excellent" because of the contrast effect. But in a group where many employees are performing well, the same person might receive a lower rating. Although it may be appropriate to compare people at times, the performance rating usually should reflect comparison against performance standards, not against other people.

Similar-to-Me/Different-from-Me Errors Sometimes, raters are influenced by whether people show characteristics that are the same as or different from their own. For example, a manager with an MBA degree might give subordinates with MBAs higher appraisals than those with only bachelor's degrees. The error comes in measuring an individual against another person rather than measuring how well the individual fulfills the expectations of the job.

Sampling Error If the rater has seen only a small sample of the person's work, an appraisal may be subject to sampling error. For example, assume that 95% of the reports prepared by an employee have been satisfactory, but a manager has seen only the 5% that had errors. If the supervisor rates the person's performance as "poor," then a sampling error has occurred. Ideally, the work being rated should be a broad and representative sample of all the work done by the employee.

APPRAISAL FEEDBACK

After completing appraisals, managers need to communicate results in order to give employees a clear understanding of how they stand in the eyes of their immediate superiors and the organization. Organizations commonly require managers to discuss appraisals with employees. The appraisal feedback interview provides an opportunity to clear up any misunderstandings on both sides. In this interview, the manager should focus on coaching and development, and not just tell the employee, "Here is how you rate and why." Emphasizing development gives both parties an opportunity to consider the employee's performance as part of appraisal feedback.[59]

Appraisal Interview

The appraisal interview presents both an opportunity and a danger. It can be an emotional experience for the manager and the employee because the manager must communicate both praise and constructive criticism. A major concern for managers is how to emphasize the positive aspects of the employee's performance while still discussing ways to make needed improvements. If the interview is handled poorly, the employee may feel resentment, which could lead to future conflict. Consequently, a manager should identify how employees add value to the organization and show appreciation when employees make valuable contributions.[60] When poor performance must be discussed, managers might consider using a "self-auditing" approach that relies on questions that encourage employees to identify their own performance deficiencies.[61]

Employees usually approach an appraisal interview with some concern. They may feel that discussions about performance are both personal and

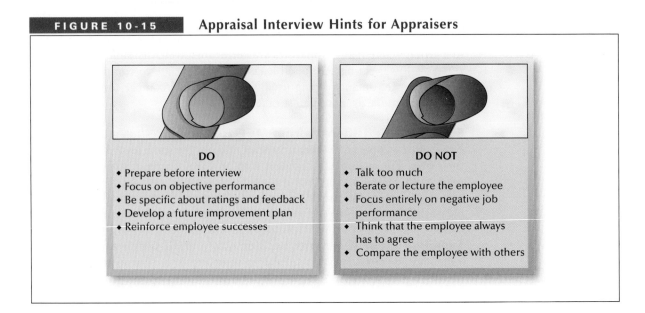

FIGURE 10-15   Appraisal Interview Hints for Appraisers

DO
- Prepare before interview
- Focus on objective performance
- Be specific about ratings and feedback
- Develop a future improvement plan
- Reinforce employee successes

DO NOT
- Talk too much
- Berate or lecture the employee
- Focus entirely on negative job performance
- Think that the employee always has to agree
- Compare the employee with others

important to their continued job success. At the same time, they want to know how their managers feel about their performance. Figure 10-15 summarizes hints for an effective appraisal interview for supervisors and managers.

Feedback as a System

The three commonly recognized components of a feedback system are data, evaluation of that data, and some action based on the evaluation. *Data* are factual pieces of information regarding observed actions or consequences. Most often, data are facts that report what happened, such as "Charlie solved a purchasing problem" or "Mary spoke harshly to an engineer." Data alone rarely tell the whole story. For instance, Mary's speaking harshly may have been an instance of poor communication and reflective of a lack of sensitivity, or it may have been a proper and necessary action. Someone must evaluate the meaning or value of the data.

Evaluation is the way the feedback system reacts to the facts, and it requires performance standards. Managers might evaluate the same factual information differently than would customers (e.g., regarding merchandise exchange or credit decisions) or coworkers. Evaluation can be done by the person supplying the data, by a supervisor, or by a group.

For feedback to cause change, some decisions must be made regarding subsequent *action*. In traditional appraisal systems, the manager makes specific suggestions regarding future actions the employee might take. Employee input often is encouraged as well. In 360-degree feedback, people from whom information was solicited might also suggest actions that the individual may consider. It may be necessary to involve those providing information if the subsequent actions are highly interdependent and require coordination with the information providers.[62] Regardless of the process used, the feedback components (data, evaluation, and action) are necessary parts of a successful performance appraisal feedback system.

Reactions of Managers

Managers who must complete appraisals of their employees often resist the appraisal process.[63] Many feel that their role calls on them to assist, encourage, coach, and counsel employees to improve their performance. However, being a judge on the one hand and a coach and a counselor on the other hand may cause internal conflict and confusion for managers.

Knowing that appraisals may affect employees' future careers also may cause altered or biased ratings. This problem is even more likely when managers know that they will have to communicate and defend their ratings to the employees, their bosses, or HR specialists. Managers can easily avoid providing negative feedback to an employee in an appraisal interview and thus avoid unpleasantness in an interpersonal situation by making the employee's ratings positive. But avoidance helps no one. A manager owes an employee a well-done appraisal, no matter how difficult an employee is, or how difficult the conversation about performance might be.[64]

Reactions of Appraised Employees

Employees may well see the appraisal process as a threat and feel that the only way for them to get a higher rating is for someone else to receive a low rating. This win-lose perception is encouraged by comparative methods of rating. Emphasis on the self-improvement and developmental aspects of appraisal appears to be the most effective way to reduce this reaction.[65]

Another common employee reaction resembles students' response to tests. A professor may prepare a test that the professor feels is fair, but it does not necessarily follow that students will believe the test is fair; they simply may see it differently. Likewise, employees being appraised may not necessarily agree with the manager doing the appraising. However, in most cases, employees will view appraisals done well as what they are meant to be—constructive feedback.

Effective Performance Management

Regardless of the approach used, managers must understand the intended outcome of performance management.[66] When performance management is used to develop employees as resources, it usually works. When one key part of performance management, a performance appraisal, is used to punish employees, performance management is less effective. In its simplest form as part of performance management, performance appraisal is a manager's observation: "Here are your strengths and weaknesses, and here is a way to develop for the future."

Done well, performance management can lead to higher employee motivation and satisfaction. To be effective, a performance management system, including the performance appraisal processes, should be:

- Consistent with the strategic mission of the organization
- Beneficial as a development tool
- Useful as an administrative tool
- Legal and job related
- Viewed as generally fair by employees
- Effective in documenting employee performance

Calibration Is the Key to Better Employee Evaluations and Performance Management

When conducting employees' performance evaluations, managers often make difficult decisions about job performance, many times without a strong reference point about how the company really defines what is acceptable and what is unacceptable. Many evaluators also do not have a real understanding of how other managers rate their employees, making relative comparisons of job performance difficult to implement throughout the organization. Consequently, ratings might not adequately or fairly convey how well employees are progressing in their jobs, which can present many different human resource challenges. Such inaccurate evaluations have the potential to derail a company's ability to effectively manage motivation because employees are not given adequate feedback, and personnel decisions are not properly linked to performance the way it is defined by the company.

Performance calibration mitigates many of these challenges and concerns by developing a more consistent understanding about how employees' job performance should be assessed. This understanding can be strengthened with company-sponsored training for evaluators that demonstrates how to properly rate individuals, thus developing a more uniform understanding about the rating process that should occur in the different operational areas of the organization. In other words, calibration sessions explore how ratings should be used to more effectively document current job performance according to company standards, while emphasizing how ratings across different work areas should be uniform. The resulting appraisals are often times more consistent and comparative across company ranks, and employees become more confident in the process as a whole, which serves to increase motivation and effort on the job.[67]

Many of these factors can be enhanced through the effective development of the performance management process. The HR Best Practices explores one approach called calibration, which enables organizations to establish more specific and consistent guidelines about how employee performance should be rated across different jobs and work areas during a rating cycle. Consequently, feedback provided to employees is more consistent and fair, which can enhance employees' motivation to tackle their work responsibilities. By making sure that raters understand how to consistently evaluate job performance, managers should be able to increase support for the performance management process throughout the organization.

SUMMARY

- Performance management systems attempt to identify, measure, communicate, develop, and reward employee performance.
- Performance management has a broad organizational focus, whereas performance appraisals are the processes used to evaluate how employees perform their jobs and then communicate that information to employees.

- Effective performance management has a number of components, beginning with a performance-focused organizational culture.
- Job criteria identify important elements of a job, and the relevance of job criteria affects the establishment of performance standards.

- Federal employment guidelines and numerous court decisions affect the design and use of the performance appraisal process.
- Appraising employee performance serves both administrative and developmental purposes.
- Performance appraisals can be done either informally or systematically.
- Appraisals can be conducted by superiors, employees (rating superiors or themselves), teams, outsiders, or a variety of sources.
- Appraisal methods include: category scaling, comparative, narrative, and management by objectives.
- Category scaling methods, especially graphic rating scales and behavioral rating scales, are widely used.
- Comparative methods include ranking and forced distribution, both of which raise methodological and legal concerns.
- Narrative methods include the critical incident technique and the essay approach.
- Training managers and employees on how to conduct performance appraisals can contribute to the effectiveness of a performance management system.
- Many performance appraisal problems are caused by a number of different rater errors.
- The appraisal feedback interview is a vital part of any appraisal system, and the reactions of both managers and employees must be considered when evaluating the system.

CRITICAL THINKING ACTIVITIES

1. Describe how an organizational culture and the use of performance criteria and standards affect the remaining components of a performance management system.

2. Suppose you are a supervisor. What errors might you make when preparing the performance appraisal on a clerical employee? How might you avoid those errors?

3. Based on your experiences, as well as the chapter information, what are some good "rules of thumb" for conducting successful performance appraisal interviews?

4. Review the performance appraisal process and appraisal form used by a current or former employer, and compare them with those provided by other students. Also review other appraisal issues by going to www.workforce.com and searching for articles on *performance appraisals*. Develop a report suggesting changes to make the performance appraisal form and process you reviewed more effective.

HR EXPERIENTIAL PROBLEM SOLVING

As the new HR Director of a company in the behavioral health industry, you have the responsibility to develop a performance management system. You need to present a business case to senior executives that the performance management system does not stand alone and must be integrated into the company's strategic plan, business needs, and measurements. For information on performance management best practices, review various publications in the articles tab at www.insala.com.

1. Given several key practices for a successful performance management system, which ones should be implemented first?

2. Identify key measurements to transition the company from the current system of looking at personality factors to a new system of looking at performance factors.

C A S E

Building Performance Management through Employee Participation

A process of performance management is developed in companies to better shape how employees execute their job responsibilities and complete their work. Ideally, employees should feel comfortable with this process, believing that the communication occurring between managers and workers facilitates the completion of important workplace goals. Unfortunately, many employees become dissatisfied with how their organizations encourage goal-directed behavior, which can result in poor job attitudes, decreased motivation, and reduced effort on the job. These negative factors lead some companies to seek alternative ways to design and implement performance management systems so that employees are encouraged to work hard in their jobs.

Jewelers Mutual Insurance Company (JMI) is one such company that has actively improved its performance management approach, and the results have been very encouraging. Employees were initially dissatisfied with the feedback and goal-setting approaches that were being utilized to manage job performance, so company leaders decided to involve employees in the redesign efforts to create a more viable program that would be satisfactory for all the parties involved. An outside consultant started the process by interviewing top leaders in the company, and focus groups were used to solicit feedback from various other members of the organization. By utilizing a more participative and inclusive approach, the company was able to identify the problems with the current performance management system and generate greater support for the proposed changes that would ultimately fix these issues. This case illustrates how important employee participation is in the effective management of human resources, particularly when developing a viable performance management system.

Several key changes were made to the performance management system based on the feedback received from managers and employees. In particular, inconsistencies in the administration of the performance management system, problems with the rating techniques and forms, and various challenges linking pay to performance were specifically targeted as part of the redesign effort. Such reflection and self-assessment prompted a number of specific improvements to management of job performance within the company. Evaluations are now based on narratives, various metrics of accountability, and job goals. Further, feedback is provided to employees on a quarterly basis, compensation is more strongly linked to individual effort, and the performance management system functions in concert with the other elements of human resource management. The changes made to the performance management processes at JMI Company demonstrate how human resource professionals can work with other staff members to create a system that excites employees and, ultimately, yields greater job performance.[68]

QUESTIONS

1. Discuss how this case illustrates how greater support for a performance management system can be developed through employee participation.

2. Identify some of the ways that performance management systems can be improved based on the experiences at JMI.

S U P P L E M E N T A L   C A S E S

Performance Management Improvements for Bristol-Myers Squibb

This case identifies how performance management systems might be redesigned. (For the case, go to www.cengage.com/management/mathis.)

Unequal/Equal Supervisors

This case identifies the consequences of giving appraisal ratings that may not be accurate. (For the case, go to www.cengage.com/management/mathis.)

NOTES

1. Based on "Performance Reviews Often Skip Ethics, HR Professionals Say," June 13, 2008, www.worldatwork.org.

2. Paul Falcone, "Big-Picture Performance Appraisal: Tying Individual Ratings to an Overall Team Score Shows Senior Executives Organizational Performance," *HR Magazine*, August 2007, 97–100.

3. Herman Aguinis, *Performance Management* (Upper Saddle River, NJ: Pearson/Prentice Hall, 2007), 50–51.

4. Adapted from Elaine D. Pulakos, "Performance Management: A Roadmap for Developing, Implementing and Evaluating Performance Management Systems," *Effective Practice Guidelines*, SHRM Foundation, 2004.

5. Amy Joyce, "Bosses Strive for Fair Job Reviews," *Omaha-World Herald*, November 20, 2006, D1.

6. Patrick Shannon, Colleen O'Neill, Nanci R. Hibschman, and J. Carlos Rivero, "CEO Performance Evaluation: Getting It Right," *Perspective*, Mercer Human Resource Consulting, April 21, 2005.

7. Brian E. Becker, Mark A. Huselid, and Dave Ulrich, *The HR Scorecard: Linking People, Strategy, and Performance* (Boston, MA: Harvard Business School Press, 2001).

8. "Into the Hornet's Nest," *The Economist*, May 12, 2007, 30–31.

9. Stephanie Simon, "Denver Teachers Object to Changes in Pay-for-Performance Plan," *The Wall Street Journal*, August 18, 2008, A3.

10. "Survey: Failure to Deal with Poor Performers May Decrease Engagement of Other Employees," *Newsline*, June 22, 2006.

11. Susan J. Wells, "No Results, No Raise," *HR Magazine*, May 2005, 76–80.

12. "The Missing Link: Driving Business Results Through Pay-for-Performance," Best Practices in Performance Management, Special Advertising Supplement to *Workforce Management* (Success Factors), S4.

13. Frank L. Schmidt and John E. Hunter, "Development of a Causal Model of Processes Determining Job Performance," *Current Directions in Psychological Science*, 1 (1992), 89–92.

14. Keith Rosen, "The Seduction of Potential," *HR Magazine*, May 2009, 85–87.

15. Anne Freedman, "Performance Management: Balancing Values, Results in Reviews," *Human Resource Executive*, August 2006, 62–63.

16. Peter Cappelli, "More Lessons from the Financial Crisis," *Human Resource Executive Online*, October 13, 2008, http://hreonline.com/HRE; Wayne F. Cascio and Peter Cappelli, "Lessons from the Financial Services Crisis," *HR Magazine*, January 2009, 47–50.

17. Adapted from American Counsel on the Teaching of Foreign Languages (ACTFL), *Oral Proficiency Interview Tester Training Manual* (Stamford, CT: ACTFL Inc., 2006), 81–109.

18. Eric Harmon, Scott Hensel, and T. E. Lukes, "Measuring Performance in Services," *The McKinsey Quarterly*, February, 2006, 2–7.

19. Josh Bersin, "The Business Case for Performance Management Systems: A Handbook for Human Resources Executives and Managers," *Bersin & Associates Research Report*, January 2008.

20. Kevin R. Murphy, "Explaining the Weak Relationship Between Job Performance and Ratings of Job Performance," *Industrial and Organizational Psychology*, 1, (2008), 148–160.

21. Gerald R. Ferris, Timothy R. Munyon, Kevin Basik, and M. Ronald Buckley, "The Performance Evaluation Context: Social, Emotional, Cognitive, Political, and Relationship Components," *Human Resource Management Review*, 18 (2008), 146–163; Adrienne Fox, "Curing What Ails Performance Reviews," *HR Magazine*, January 2009, 52–56.

22. Jared Sandberg, "Performance Reviews Need Some Work, Don't Meet Potential," *The Wall Street Journal*, October 20, 2007, B1.

23. *WorldatWork* Staff, "Courage Is Critical to Success of Performance Appraisals," Headlines, NewsEdge Enterprise Solutions Content Solutions, May 8, 2007, http://dialog.newsedge.com/newsedge.

24. Clinton Longnecker, "Managerial Performance Appraisals: The Good, The Bad, and The Ugly," *HR Advisor*, May/June 2005, 19–26.

25. Samuel A. Culbert, "Get Rid of the Performance Review!" *The Wall Street Journal*, October 20, 2008, R4.

26. "Communicating Beyond Ratings Can Be Difficult," *Workforce Management*, April 24, 2006, 35.

27. Samuel A. Culbert, "Get Rid of the Performance Review!" *The Wall Street Journal*, October 20, 2008, R4.

28. Adrienne Fox, "Curing What Ails Performance Reviews," *HR Magazine*, January 2009, 52–56.

29. Lisa Hartley, "Unified Talent Management and the Holy Grail," Best Practices in Performance Management, Special Advertising Supplement to *Workforce Management* (Taleo), S5; Paul Loucks, "The Need for Web-Based Talent & Performance Management," *Workspan*, October 2007, 68–70.

30. "Performance Tuning at Porsche," Best Practices in Performance Management, Special Advertising Supplement to *Workforce Management* (Vurv), S3.

31. Paul Loucks, "The Need for Web-Based Talent & Performance Management," *Workspan*, October 2007, 68–70.

32. Drew Robb, "Appraising Appraisal Software," *HR Magazine*, October 2008, 65–66, 68, 70.

33. "9 Critical Reasons to Automate Performance Management: For Small and Mid-Sized Businesses," Success Factors, www.successfactors.com; "Performance Management," *HR Magazine*, November 2005, 135; "Performance Tuning at Porsche," Best Practices in Performance Management,

Special Advertising Supplement to *Workforce Management* (Vurv), S3; Dawn S. Onley, "Using Dashboards to Drive HR," *HR Magazine*, April 2006, 109–115; Erin White, "For Relevance Firms Revamp Worker Reviews," *The Wall Street Journal*, July 17, 2006, B1; Anne Freedman, "Balancing Values, Results in Reviews," *Human Resource Executive*, August 2006, 62.

34. Jennifer Taylor Arnold, "Two Needs, One Solution," *HR Magazine*, May 2009, 75–77.

35. "Performance Management Practices," www.ddi.com.

36. Erin White, "For Relevance Firms Revamp Worker Reviews," *The Wall Street Journal*, July 17, 2006, B1.

37. Gerard P. Panaro, "The Two-Edged Sword of Employee Job Evaluations," *HR Advisor*, May/June 2005, 39–43.

38. Jena McGregor, "The Employee Is Always Right," *BusinessWeek*, November 19, 2007, 80–82.

39. Clinton Longnecker, "Managerial Performance Appraisals: The Good, The Bad, and The Ugly," *HR Advisor*, May/June 2005, 19–26.

40. Aguinis, *Performance Management*, 256–265.

41. Adrienne Fox, "Curing What Ails Performance Reviews," *HR Magazine*, January 2009, 52–56.

42. W. H. Berman, J. C. Scott, and D. Finch, "Assessments: Connecting Employees with the Performance Improvement Process," *Workforce Performance Solutions*, June 2005, 20–24.

43. Leanne Atwater, John F. Brett, and Atira Cherise Charles, "Multisource Feedback: Lessons Learned and Implications for Practice," *Human Resource Management*, 46 (2007), 285–307.

44. Jared Sandberg, "Performance Reviews Need Some Work, Don't Meet Potential," *The Wall Street Journal*, October 20, 2007, B1.

45. "360° Evaluation of Managers," *Omaha World-Herald*, May 9, 2005, D1.

46. Leanne Atwater, John F. Brett, and Atira Cherise Charles, "Multisource Feedback: Lessons Learned and Implications for Practice," *Human Resource Management*, 46 (2007), 285–307; Anne Freedman, "Performance Management: Balancing Values, Results in Reviews," *Human Resource Executive*, August 2006, 62–63.

47. Leslie A. Weatherly, "Performance Management: Getting It Right from the Start," *SHRM Research Quarterly*, 2004.

48. "What Is the 'Rating Scale' Method of Performance Evaluation?" *Ceridian HR Compliance Reference System*, http://hrcompliance.ceridian.com/www/content/10/12487/15884.

49. Leslie A. Weatherly, "Performance Management: Getting It Right from the Start," *SHRM Research Quarterly*, 2004.

50. Richard D. Goffin, R. Blake Jelley, Deborah M. Powell, and Norman G. Johnston, "Taking Advantage of Social Comparisons in Performance Appraisal: The Relative Percentage Method," *Human Resource Management*, 48 (2009), 251–268.

51. Leslie A. Weatherly, "Performance Management: Getting It Right from the Start," *SHRM Research Quarterly*, 2004.

52. Jena McGregor, "The Struggle to Measure Performance," *BusinessWeek*, January 9, 2006, 26–28.

53. Michael O'Malley, "Forced Ranking: Proceed Only with Great Caution," *WorldatWork*, First Quarter 2003, 31–39.

54. Leslie A. Weatherly, "Performance Management: Getting It Right from the Start," *SHRM Research Quarterly*, 2004.

55. Michael O'Malley, "Forced Ranking: Proceed Only with Great Caution," *WorldatWork*, First Quarter 2003, 31–39.

56. Dick Grote, "Making Forced Rankings Work," *Workforce Management Online*, November 2005, www.workforce.com.

57. Steve Scullen, Paul Bergey, and Lynda Aiman-Smith, "Forced Distribution Rating Systems and the Improvement of Workforce Potential," *Personnel Psychology*, 58 (2005), 1–31.

58. Aguinis, *Performance Management*, 155–162.

59. Steve Hamm, "Motivating the Troops," *BusinessWeek*, November 21, 2005, 88–92.

60. "A Positive Psychology Handbook for Entrepreneurs," *BusinessWeek, Small Biz*, February/March 2009, 47.

61. "Can You Suggest Constructive Techniques for Discussing an Employee's Poor Performance?" *Ceridian HR Compliance Reference System*, http://hrcompliance.ceridian.com.

62. D. Van Fleet, T. Peterson, and E. Van Fleet, "Closing the Performance Feedback Gap with Expert Systems," *Academy of Management Executive*, August 2005, 38–53.

63. G. Adler and M. Ambrose, "Toward Understanding Fairness Judgments Associated with Computer Performance Monitoring," *Human Resource Management Review*, 15 (2005), 43–67.

64. Carol Hymowitz, "What to Do When Your Favorite Workers Don't Make the Grade," *The Wall Street Journal*, April 11, 2000, B1.

65. Laura Roberts, et al., "How to Play to Your Strengths," *Harvard Business Review*, January 2005, 74–80; Peter Drucker, "Managing Oneself," *Harvard Business Review*, January 2005, 100–109.

66. Aileen MacMillan, "Raising the Bar on Performance Management Practices to Optimize Performance Reviews and Goal Management," *HR.com*, April 2006, 2–12.

67. Adrienne Fox, "Curing What Ails Performance Reviews," *HR Magazine*, January 2009, 52–56; Jim Kochanski and Angelita Becom, "Four Key Steps to Performance Management," *Workspan*, February 2008, 32–36.

68. "An 'Inside-Out' Approach to Enhancing Performance Management," *HR Focus*, September 2006, 3–5.

4

Compensation

11

Total Rewards and Compensation

After you have read this chapter, you should be able to:

- Identify the three general components of total rewards and give examples of each.
- Discuss four compensation system design issues.
- List the basic provisions of the Fair Labor Standards Act (FLSA).
- Outline the process of building a base pay system.
- Describe the two means of valuing jobs.
- Explain two ways individual pay increases are determined.

Rewarding Employees to Encourage Positive Behaviors

(© Erik Snyder/Jupiter Images)

A recent interview with Steve Kerr, author of the popular article "On the Folly of Rewarding A While Hoping for B," indicated that companies often fail to properly implement positive compensation approaches. This is because active steps are not taken to make sure that rewards prompt the kinds of behaviors the company wants to see. According to Kerr, the employer has to find a way to measure job performance so that productivity can be properly supported with adequate rewards and other compensation. Companies also have to articulate what levels of performance are expected in different jobs, especially given that many types of work present ambiguous definitions about what is "good" and "bad" performance. In addition, top leadership needs to determine how to break down mission statements in a manner that enables employees to understand how their behaviors can support the accomplishment of corporate objectives.[1]

Given Kerr's insightful comments, HR professionals need to better identify the types of behaviors that reward systems are promoting. HR professionals also need to create comprehensive compensation programs that motivate the kinds of actions needed to help organizations prosper and grow. By explicitly linking fair compensation to positive employee behaviors, companies can expect to see increased individual satisfaction and job performance.

In order to remain competitive, companies need to develop reward packages that satisfy people. These reward packages, commonly known as **total rewards**, include all the monetary and nonmonetary rewards provided by a company to attract, motivate, and retain employees. The success of a pay system depends on linking organizational objectives and strategies to compensation so that individuals are encouraged to work in a manner that benefits the company and its stakeholders. For example, Forensic Technology, a Canadian firm specializing in weapons and ballistic identification, recently improved employee retention and engagement by connecting the rewards program to broad strategic goals focusing on social responsibility, improving business operations, and becoming a valued employer.[2]

Critical to an effective total rewards approach to pay is the need to balance the interests and costs of the employers with the needs and expectations of employees. This can be a difficult process. On the one hand, employee payroll and benefits represent a large portion of total operating costs in some industries such as financial services, health care, education, and hospitality. On the other hand, recent surveys suggest that there is growing concern among HR professionals that total rewards programs can be used more effectively to obtain good talent in organizations, and that these programs should be more clearly communicated to employees.[3] Effective management of total rewards can be accomplished by evaluating expenses and determining the value of compensation. An optimal relationship between costs and employee impact must be achieved while considering many financial and operational factors.[4]

Additionally, the concept of total rewards requires a much broader understanding of pay or compensation than has traditionally occurred in business organizations. The total rewards concept emphasizes *both* indirect and direct compensation, which strengthens a company's ability to motivate employees, particularly in challenging financial situations such as those sometimes faced by companies.[5] Indeed, a lagging economy will likely require employers to make calculated adjustments to total rewards to reflect new business conditions.[6] Emphasizing nonmonetary rewards such as training and development, work-life programs, employee recognition, and career management should enable companies to remain competitive from an employment perspective despite decreasing compensation budgets.[7] Broadly defining compensation should also help companies develop creative policies that keep employees motivated. Examples include bringing pets to work at Google, providing day-care support at Nordstrom, and honoring "your special blend" at Starbucks.[8]

LOGGING ON

WorldatWork
This website provides information on products and services as well as research on compensation and benefits. Visit the site at www.worldatwork.org.

NATURE OF TOTAL REWARDS AND COMPENSATON

Because so many organizational funds are spent on employees, top management and HR executives should match total rewards systems and practices with what the organization is trying to accomplish. To do so, several decisions must be made:

Total rewards Monetary and nonmonetary rewards provided by companies to attract, motivate, and retain employees.

- Legal compliance with all appropriate laws and regulations
- Cost-effectiveness for the organization
- Internal, external, and individual equity for employees
- Performance enhancement for the organization

- Performance recognition and talent management for employees
- Enhanced recruitment, involvement, and retention of employees

Employers must balance their costs at a level that rewards employees sufficiently for their knowledge, skills, abilities, and performance accomplishments. During the past several years, total rewards have been a significant focus in HR, and different frameworks have been developed.[9] One prominent approach has been developed by *WorldatWork*, a leading professional association that focuses on compensation.[10] The model shows how a company's strategic and cultural characteristics influence various elements of compensation such as work-life, recognition, and career development—all of which ultimately strengthen the positive nature of the employment relationship and generate increased business performance.[11]

To combine severale leading approaches into a simplified view, Figure 11-1 identifies three primary groups. What the figure illustrates is that total rewards must be seen more broadly than just compensation and benefits. The importance of performance management and talent management has been discussed in detail in the previous two chapters. The focus of the next three chapters is on compensation, variable pay, and benefits.

The development of viable total reward programs containing the critical elements specified in Figure 11-1 requires companies to evaluate policies on a regular basis. After assessing current compensation paradigms using a variety of methodologies, new approaches that better reflect current demands must be developed and put into action. Finally, these new programs should be evaluated over time to determine relative effectiveness, as well as the impact on employee satisfaction.[12] The relationship between organizational culture and pay policy needs to be particularly recognized during these steps because compensation should support and complement a firm's current business values and practices.[13]

FIGURE 11-1   **Total Rewards Components**

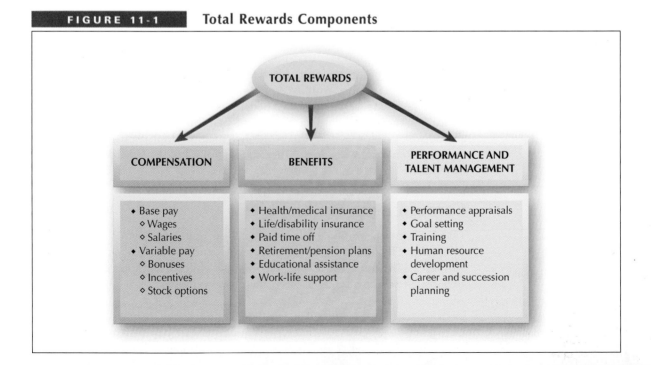

Types of Compensation

One of the distinctions not formally a part of Figure 11-1 is that rewards can be either intrinsic or extrinsic. *Intrinsic rewards* may include praise for completing a project or meeting performance objectives. Other psychological and social forms of compensation also reflect intrinsic type of rewards. *Extrinsic rewards* are tangible and take both monetary and nonmonetary forms. One tangible component of a compensation program is *direct compensation*, whereby the employer provides monetary rewards for work done and performance results achieved. *Base pay* and *variable pay* are the most common forms of direct compensation. The most common indirect compensation is employee *benefits*.

Base Pay The basic compensation that an employee receives, usually as a wage or a salary, is called **base pay**. Many organizations use two base pay categories, *hourly* and *salaried*, which are identified according to the way pay is distributed and the nature of the jobs. Hourly pay is the most common means and is based on time.

Employees paid hourly receive **wages**, which are payments calculated based on time worked. In contrast, people paid **salaries** receive the same payment each period regardless of the number of hours worked. Being paid a salary has typically carried higher status for employees than has being paid a wage. However, overtime may have to be paid to certain salaried employees as well as most wage earners as defined by federal and state laws.

Variable Pay Another type of direct pay is **variable pay**, which is compensation linked directly to individual, team, or organizational performance. The most common types of variable pay for most employees are bonuses and incentive program payments. Executives often receive longer-term rewards such as stock options. There is reason to believe that performance-based policies for rewarding top managers that link equity-based incentives to performance are effective. Some companies such as Best Buy and Kimberly Clark are already using such programs.[14] Variable pay, including executive compensation, is discussed in Chapter 12.

Benefits Many organizations provide rewards in an indirect manner. With indirect compensation, employees receive the tangible value of the rewards without receiving actual cash. A **benefit** is a reward—for instance, health insurance, vacation pay, or a retirement pension—given to an employee or a group of employees for organizational membership, regardless of performance. Often employees do not directly pay for all of the benefits they receive. Benefits are discussed in Chapter 13.

Compensation Philosophies

Two basic compensation philosophies lie on opposite ends of a continuum, as shown in Figure 11-2. At one end of the continuum is the *entitlement* philosophy; at the other end is the *performance* philosophy. Most compensation systems fall somewhere in between these two extremes.

Entitlement Philosophy The **entitlement philosophy** assumes that individuals who have worked another year are entitled to pay increases, with little regard for performance differences. Many traditional organizations that give

Base pay Basic compensation that an employee receives, usually as a wage or salary.

Wages Payments calculated directly from the amount of time worked by employees.

Salaries Consistent payments made each period regardless of the number of hours worked.

Variable pay Compensation linked directly to individual, team, or organizational performance.

Benefit Indirect reward given to an employee or group of employees as part of membership in the organization.

Entitlement philosophy Assumes that individuals who have worked another year are entitled to pay increases, with little regard for performance differences.

| FIGURE 11-2 | Continuum of Compensation Philosophies |

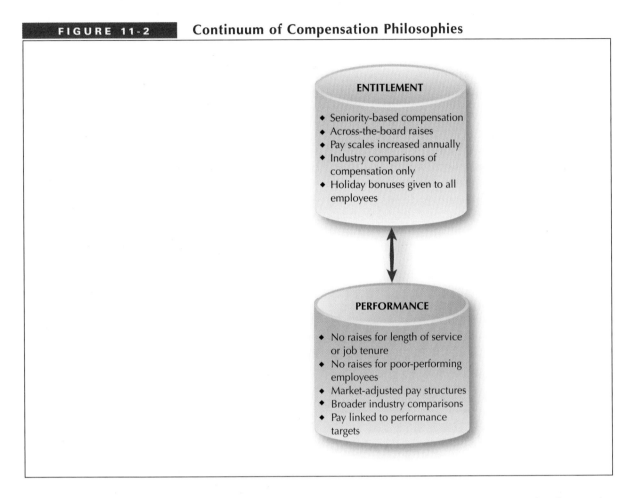

automatic increases to their employees every year are practicing the entitlement philosophy. These automatic increases are often referred to as *cost-of-living raises*, even if they are not tied specifically to economic indicators. Further, most of those employees receive the same or nearly the same percentage increase each year. One of the challenges associated with cost-of-living increases is that employees are given the same adjustments without any regard for performance, a process that can undermine the purpose of compensation.[15] As such, bonuses in many entitlement-oriented organizations are determined in a manner that often fails to reflect operating results. Employees "expect" the bonuses, which become another form of entitlement.

Performance Philosophy A **pay-for-performance philosophy** requires that compensation changes reflect performance differences. Organizations operating under this philosophy do not guarantee additional or increased compensation simply for completing another year of organizational service. Instead, they structure pay and incentives to reflect performance differences among employees. Employees who perform satisfactorily maintain or advance their compensation levels more than marginal performers. The bonuses and incentives are based on individual, group, and/or organizational performance.

Few organizations totally follow all performance-oriented compensation practices, but the overall trend is toward greater use of pay-for-performance systems, with more and more companies turning to performance criteria to shape rewards for all employees.[16] Such plans may help to reduce employee

Pay-for-performance philosophy Requires that compensation changes reflect performance differences.

Using Rewards to Effectively Develop Talent

Even though the recent downturn in the economy has given companies some leverage when attracting and retaining employees, it is still in employers' best interests to link together pay strategies and talent management approaches in a manner that best satisfies workers. A research study determined that combining these two HR functions can pay large dividends when it comes to managing the employment environment. In fact, evidence suggests that linking compensation with talent management can increase a firm's ability to encourage people to seek employment in the company, as well as retain them once they are hired.

The key to this process is developing an "employee value proposition," demonstrating the combined benefits received by working for an organization. Another key is human resource planning that clearly shows how the organization must support its business goals with HR programs such as talent and rewards administration. Finally, companies should evaluate the effectiveness of the reward programs offered to employees, which should include assessments of market position, competitiveness, and the use of performance-based pay.

Evaluating base pay is particularly important because employees value this component of compensation above many others, and it is critical that base pay be competitive so that the firm can retain high-performing individuals. Incentive pay is also important because it reinforces the kinds of performance that directly support corporate goals, and companies should not ignore the benefits of recognition compensation because these incentives are more immediate in nature. All of these components of compensation enable the company to more effectively manage talent.[17]

turnover and increase employee commitment, motivation, and retention.[18] However, performance-based plans need to be evaluated periodically to determine whether performance is being fairly measured and linked to rewards.[19] Also, merit- and performance-based systems do not always lead to increased employee performance because of inappropriate pay differentials, equity concerns, and poor teamwork. As a result, some organizations might consider using more group-based plans.[20]

The total rewards approach reflects a more performance-oriented philosophy because it tends to place more value on individuals' performance, rather than just paying them based on having a job. When determining compensation, managers consider elements such as how much an employee knows or how competent an employee is. Some organizations use both compensation and variable pay programs as part of a total rewards approach for all levels of employees. Widespread use of various incentive plans, team bonuses, organizational gainsharing programs, and other designs links growth in compensation and variable pay to results.

Regularly communicating to employees and managers the compensation philosophy helps to reinforce the organizational commitment to it.[21] A recent study found that communication of profit-sharing information increased knowledge, which influenced commitment and satisfaction.[22] Communication also can enhance understanding and perceptions of pay policies, encouraging greater generalized pay satisfaction and career development.[23] Finally, establishing a dialogue with employees about total rewards enables them to be more involved with the development of pay systems that enhance talent and return on investment.[24] A company's compensation philosophy can be used to develop individual talent in an organization, a strategy covered in the HR Best Practices.

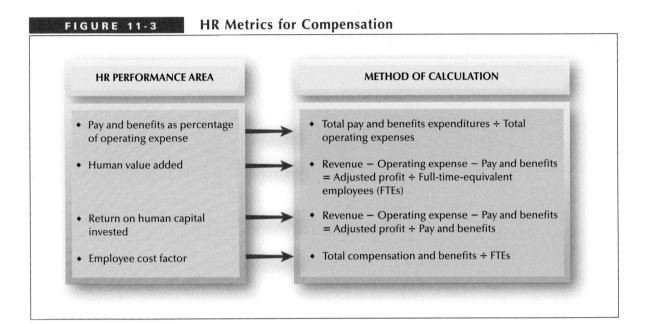

FIGURE 11-3   **HR Metrics for Compensation**

HR PERFORMANCE AREA	METHOD OF CALCULATION
• Pay and benefits as percentage of operating expense	• Total pay and benefits expenditures ÷ Total operating expenses
• Human value added	• Revenue − Operating expense − Pay and benefits = Adjusted profit ÷ Full-time-equivalent employees (FTEs)
• Return on human capital invested	• Revenue − Operating expense − Pay and benefits = Adjusted profit ÷ Pay and benefits
• Employee cost factor	• Total compensation and benefits ÷ FTEs

MEASURE

HR Metrics and Compensation

Employers spend huge amounts of money for employee compensation. Just like any other area of cost, compensation expenditures should be evaluated to determine their effectiveness. Many measures can be used to do this.[25] Employee turnover/retention is one widely used factor. It assumes that how well compensation systems operate affects employees' decisions about staying or leaving the organization. Other more specific measures are used as well, such as the ones shown in Figure 11-3.[26]

The numbers for calculating various measures are readily available to most HR professionals and chief financial officers, but such calculations are not made in many firms. Often the importance of using these numbers is not a priority for managers or CFOs. Ideally, compensation metrics should be computed each year, and then compared with metrics from past years to show how the rate of compensation changes compares with the rate of changes in the organization overall (revenues, expenses, etc.).

Compensation Responsibilities

To administer compensation expenditures wisely, HR specialists and operating managers must work together. A typical division of compensation responsibilities is illustrated in Figure 11-4. HR specialists guide the development and administration of an organizational compensation system and conduct job evaluations and wage surveys. Also, because of the complexity involved, HR specialists typically assume responsibility for developing base pay programs and salary structures and policies. HR specialists may or may not do actual payroll processing. This labor-intensive responsibility is typically among the first to be outsourced. Operating managers evaluate the performance of employees and consider their performance when deciding compensation increases within the policies and guidelines established by the HR unit and upper management.

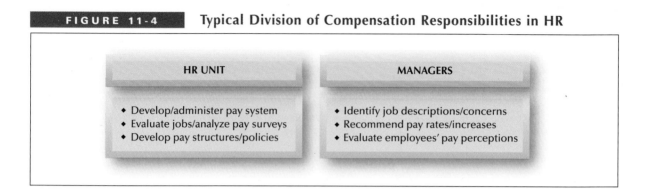

FIGURE 11-4   **Typical Division of Compensation Responsibilities in HR**

HR UNIT	MANAGERS
• Develop/administer pay system	• Identify job descriptions/concerns
• Evaluate jobs/analyze pay surveys	• Recommend pay rates/increases
• Develop pay structures/policies	• Evaluate employees' pay perceptions

COMPENSATION SYSTEM DESIGN ISSUES

Depending on the compensation philosophies, strategies, and approaches identified for an organization, a number of decisions are made that affect the design of the compensation system. Some important ones are highlighted next.

Compensation Fairness and Equity

Most people in organizations work to gain money for their efforts. Whether employees receive base pay or variable pay, the extent to which they perceive their compensation to be fair often affects their performance, how they view their jobs, and their employers. This factor may lead to lower or higher turnover rates. Pay satisfaction also has been found to be linked to organizational-level performance outcomes.[27]

Equity The perceived fairness of what a person does (inputs) and what the person receives (outcomes) is called **equity**. Individuals judge equity in compensation by comparing their input (effort and performance) against the effort and performance of others and against the outcomes (the rewards received). These comparisons are personal and are based on individual perceptions, not just facts. A study by Salary.com found that almost 60% of the workers surveyed believed they were underpaid. But according to reviews of compensation databases, less than 20% were actually underpaid.[28] These findings illustrate how the perceptions of individuals are critical in how equity is viewed.

External Equity If an employer does not provide pay that employees view as equitable compared to other employees performing similar jobs in other organizations, that employer is likely to experience higher turnover. Another drawback is greater difficulty in recruiting qualified and high-demand individuals. By not being competitive, the employer is more likely to attract and retain individuals with less knowledge and fewer skills and abilities, resulting in lower overall organizational performance. Organizations track external equity by using pay surveys, which are discussed later in this chapter, and by looking at the compensation policies of competing employers.

Internal Equity in Compensation Internal equity means that employees receive compensation in relation to the knowledge, skills, and abilities (KSAs) they use in their jobs, as well as their responsibilities and accomplishments. Two key issues—procedural justice and distributive justice—relate to internal equity.

Equity Perceived fairness between what a person does and what the person receives.

Procedural justice is the perceived fairness of the process and procedures used to make decisions about employees, including their pay. As it applies to compensation, the entire process of determining base pay for jobs, allocating pay increases, and measuring performance must be perceived as fair.

A related issue that must be considered is **distributive justice**, which is the perceived fairness in the distribution of outcomes. As one example, if a hardworking employee whose performance is outstanding receives the same across-the-board raise as an employee with attendance problems and mediocre performance, then inequity may be perceived. Likewise, if two employees have similar performance records but one receives a significantly greater pay raise, the other may perceive an inequity due to supervisory favoritism or other factors not related to the job.

To address concerns about both types of justice, some organizations establish compensation appeals procedures. Typically, employees are encouraged to contact the HR department after discussing their concerns with their immediate supervisors and managers.

Procedural justice
Perceived fairness of the process and procedures used to make decisions about employees.

Distributive justice
Perceived fairness in the distribution of outcomes.

Pay Secrecy Another equity issue concerns the degree of secrecy that organizations have regarding their pay systems. Pay information that may be kept secret in "closed" systems includes how much others make, what raises others have received, and even what pay grades and ranges exist in the organization. Some firms have policies that prohibit employees from discussing their pay with other employees, and violations of these policies can lead to disciplinary action.[29] Several court decisions have ruled that these policies violate the National Labor Relations Act, but many employees simply avoid discussing pay with coworkers because it can make the workplace uncomfortable.[30]

Quantitative Techniques Facilitate Compensation Management

HR*perspective*

In order to more effectively manage employee compensation, it is often necessary for HR professionals to conduct quantitative assessments of reward information. This can be a challenging endeavour because many professionals have not been given the training required to assess numerical compensation data. Despite this reality, HR persons need to understand some basic statistical concepts and calculations so that organizations can develop more competitive pay structures to attract talent, increase job satisfaction, and reduce turnover.

Central tendency measures can be utilized to identify important numbers. Examples include mean scores (averages), median values (middle numbers in lists), and mode numbers (numbers appearing more frequently in groups). *Distribution statistics* indicate how numbers are distributed across a particular grouping. Examples include quartiles (placing numbers into quarters), percentiles

(placing numbers into hundredths), and frequency distribution (using histograms to show how frequently numbers occur). Finally, a number of *relationship measures* can be used to evaluate data, which include correlations that show the relationships between two or more variables and regression analyses that indicate how well a set of variables can predict another factor.

Other important issues that HR professionals must understand include internal and external validity. *Internal validity* indicates the degree to which findings are acceptable based on the use of a good research program, while *external validity* refers to the degree to which the findings will occur based on different sets of conditions. In summary, companies should encourage HR staff to seek out additional statistical materials and training, as well as provide the proper resources when necessary.[31]

Statistical Analysis The management of different fairness and equity issues requires managers to understand the various statistical methodologies that can be used to evaluate current compensation levels. For instance, HR professionals need to check how corporate pay programs compare to the compensation being offered by competing firms so that compensation can be adjusted to reflect the company's pay philosophy. HR professionals also must determine the degree to which compensation is distributed fairly within the organization based on such factors as job level, experience, training, and other human capital factors. All of these issues require a firm understanding of basic statistics. Some of the specific calculations that can facilitate compensation management are covered in the HR Perspective on the previous page.

Market Competitiveness and Compensation

The market competitiveness of compensation has a significant impact on how equitably employees view compensation. Providing competitive compensation to employees, whether globally, domestically, or locally, is a concern for all employers.[32] Some organizations establish specific policies about where they wish to be positioned in the labor market. These policies use a *quartile strategy*, as illustrated in Figure 11-5. Data in pay surveys reveal that the dollar differential between quartiles is generally 15% to 20%.

"Meet the Market" Strategy Most employers choose to position themselves in the *second quartile* (median), in the middle of the market, as identified by pay data from surveys of other employers' compensation plans. Choosing this level attempts to balance employer cost pressures and the need to attract and retain employees, by providing mid-level compensation scales that "meet the market" for the employer's jobs.

"Lag the Market" Strategy An employer using a *first-quartile* strategy may choose to "lag the market" by paying below market levels, for several reasons. If the employer is experiencing a shortage of funds, it may be unable to pay

| FIGURE 11-5 | **Compensation Quartile Strategies** |

Third Quartile: Above-Market Strategy

(Employer positions pay scales so that 25% of other firms pay above and 75% pay below)

Maximum

Second Quartile: Middle-Market Strategy

(Employer positions pay scales so that 50% of other firms pay above and 50% pay below)

Median

First Quartile: Below-Market Strategy

(Employer positions pay scales so that 75% of other firms pay above and 25% pay below)

Minimum

more. Also, when an abundance of workers is available, particularly those with lower skills, a below-market approach can be used to attract sufficient workers at a lesser cost. Some employers hire illegal immigrants at below-market rates because of the large numbers of those individuals who want to work in the United States. The downside of this strategy is that it increases the likelihood of higher worker turnover. If the labor market supply tightens, then attracting and retaining workers becomes more difficult.

"Lead the Market" Strategy A *third-quartile* strategy uses an aggressive approach to "lead the market." This strategy generally enables a company to attract and retain sufficient workers with the required capabilities and to be more selective when hiring. Because it is a higher-cost approach, organizations often look for ways to increase the productivity of employees receiving above-market wages.

Selecting a Quartile The pay levels and pay structures used can affect organizational performance.[33] Individual employee pay levels will vary around the quartile level, depending on experience, performance, and other individual factors. Deciding in which quartile to position pay structures is a function of a number of considerations. The financial resources available, competitiveness pressures, and the market availability of employees with different capabilities are external factors. For instance, some employers with extensive benefits programs or broad-based incentive programs may choose a first-quartile strategy so that their overall compensation costs and levels are not excessive.

Competency-Based Pay

The design of most compensation programs rewards employees for carrying out their tasks, duties, and responsibilities. The job requirements determine which employees have higher base rates. Employees receive more for doing jobs that require a greater variety of tasks, more knowledge and skills, greater physical effort, or more demanding working conditions. However, the design of some compensation programs emphasizes competencies rather than the tasks performed.

Competency-based pay rewards individuals for the capabilities they demonstrate and acquire. In knowledge-based pay (KBP) or skill-based pay (SBP) systems, employees start at a base level of pay and receive increases as they learn to do other jobs or gain additional skills and knowledge and thus become more valuable to the employer.[34] For example, a printing firm operates two-color, four-color, and six-color presses. The more colors, the more skills required of the press operators. Under a KBP or SBP system, press operators increase their pay as they learn how to operate the more complex presses, even though sometimes they may be running only two-color jobs. A recent study determined that receiving SBP is related to learning and skill enhancement, which demonstrates that such pay systems can be effective.[35]

When an organization moves to a competency-based system, considerable time must be spent identifying the required competencies for various jobs. Reliance on items such as college diplomas and degrees may need to change such that more emphasis is placed on demonstrated knowledge and competencies rather than degrees.[36] *Progression* of employees must be possible, and employees must be paid appropriately for all their competencies. Any *limitations* on the numbers of people who can acquire more competencies should be clearly identified. *Training* in the appropriate competencies is particularly

Competency-based pay
Rewards individuals for the capabilities they demonstrate and acquire.

important. Also, a competency-based system needs to acknowledge or certify employees as they acquire certain competencies, and then to verify the maintenance of those competencies. In summary, use of a competency-based system requires significant investment of management time and commitment.

Individual versus Team Rewards

As some organizations have shifted to using work teams, they have faced the logical concern of how to develop compensation programs that build on the team concept. At issue is how to compensate the individuals whose performance may be evaluated on team achievements.[37] For base pay, employers often compensate individuals on the basis of competencies, experience, and other job factors. Then many organizations use team incentive rewards on top of base pay. Variable pay rewards for teams are most frequently distributed annually as specified dollar amounts, not as percentages of base pay. Team-based incentives are discussed in Chapter 12.

GLOBAL

Global Compensation Issues

All of the issues discussed here can become more complex when dealing with global compensation. The growing world economy has led to many more employees working internationally. Some are located and work in multiple countries, while others may be based in a home country such as the United States or Germany, but have international responsibilities. Therefore, organizations with employees working throughout the world face some special compensation issues.

Variations in laws, living costs, tax policies, and other factors all must be considered in establishing the compensation for local employees and managers, as well as managers and professionals brought in from other countries. Even fluctuations in the values of various currencies must be tracked and adjustments made as the currencies rise or fall in relation to currency rates in other countries. With these and numerous other concerns, developing and managing a global compensation system becomes extremely complex.[38] The components of one possible global compensation package are illustrated in Figure 11-6.

FIGURE 11-6   **Possible Components of Global Employee Compensation**

GLOBAL EMPLOYEE COMPENSATION

- Foreign Service and Hardship Premiums
- Relocation and Moving Allowances
- Housing and Utilities Allowances
- Cost-of-Living Adjustments
- Tax Equalization Payments
- Educational Allowance for Children
- Home Leave and Travel Allowances

One significant global issue in compensation design is how to compensate the employees from different countries. Local wage scales vary significantly between countries. For instance, in some less-developed countries, pay levels for degreed professionals may range from $15,000 to $30,000 a year, whereas in Europe and the United States, individuals with the same qualifications are paid $50,000 to $80,000 a year. Lower-skilled local workers may make as little as $300 a month in less-developed countries, whereas comparable employees make $1,800 to $2,500 a month in the United States and Europe. These large compensation differences have led to significant "international outsourcing" of jobs to lower-wage countries. The movement of call-center and information technology (IT) jobs to India and manufacturing jobs to China, the Philippines, and Mexico are examples.

Many organizations have started to globalize many of their pay policies in order to attract and retain the talent located within the footprint of global operations. This process requires custom-tailoring of the compensation approach to suit the needs of the central organization, while providing the proper incentives and benefits to drive motivation at local units.[39] For instance, Cox Communications developed a variable pay framework that provides flexibility to HR professionals to customize compensation policies to fit the needs of local worksites, and while this program is used domestically, it serves as a positive benchmark for other international companies.[40] Total rewards also can be used to motivate employees in diverse global environments because HR professionals can combine packages with the best practices of other nations to develop appropriate compensation strategies.[41]

Compensating Expatriates

Expatriates are citizens of one country who are working in a second country and employed by an organization headquartered in the first country. It has been estimated that the aggregate employer costs for an expatriate, including all allowances, is three to four times the expatriate's salary. Thus, if an expatriate's salary is $200,000, the actual cost of employing that person is likely $600,000 to $800,000. The overall costs for many senior-level expatriates can be near $1 million.[42]

Balance-sheet approach
Compensation plan that equalizes cost differences between the international assignment and the same assignment in the home country.

The two primary approaches to international compensation for expatriates are the balance-sheet approach and the global market approach. The **balance-sheet approach** is a compensation plan that equalizes cost differences between the international assignment and the same assignment in the home country of the individual or the corporation. Reviews have found that the balance-sheet approach can result in higher employer costs and more administrative complexity than other plans.[43] These considerations have led more multinational firms to use a different means. Some firms also have decreased the amount of compensation provided to expatriates using a benchmark approach, with extensive communication to boost employee support for the reduced plans.[44]

Global market approach
Compensation plan that attempts to be more comprehensive in providing base pay, incentives, benefits, and relocation expenses regardless of the country to which the employee is assigned.

Unlike the balance-sheet approach, the **global market approach** attempts to be more comprehensive in providing base pay, incentives, benefits, and relocation expenses regardless of the country to which the employee is assigned. This approach to compensation requires significant flexibility, detailed analyses, and extensive administrative effort. Almost 60% of multinational firms use this approach.[45]

Tax equalization plan
Compensation plan used to protect expatriates from negative tax consequences.

Many international compensation plans attempt to protect expatriates from negative tax consequences by using a **tax equalization plan**. Under such a plan, the company adjusts an employee's base income downward by the amount of estimated home-country tax to be paid for the year. Thus, the employee pays only the foreign-country tax. For instance, a tax equalization plan attempts to ensure that U.S. expatriates will not pay any more or less in taxes than if they were working in the United States. Major changes in the U.S. tax law in 2006 changed the tax provisions that may affect the 300,000 U.S. expatriates working abroad.[46] Because of the variation in tax laws and rates from country to country, tax equalization too can be very complex.

LEGAL CONSTRAINTS ON PAY SYSTEMS

Pay systems must comply with many government constraints. The important areas addressed by the laws include minimum-wage standards and hours of work. The following discussion examines the laws and regulations affecting base compensation. Laws and regulations affecting incentives and benefits are examined in later chapters.

Fair Labor Standards Act (FLSA)

The major federal law affecting compensation is the Fair Labor Standards Act (FLSA), which was originally passed in 1938. Compliance with FLSA provisions is enforced by the Wage and Hour Division of the U.S. Department of Labor. To meet FLSA requirements, employers must keep accurate time records and maintain those records for 3 years. Penalties for wage and hour violations often include awards of up to 2 years of back pay for affected current and former employees.

The provisions of both the original act and subsequent revisions focus on the following major areas:

- Establish a minimum wage.
- Discourage oppressive use of child labor.
- Encourage limits on the number of hours employees work per week, through overtime provisions (exempt and nonexempt statuses).

Minimum Wage The FLSA sets a minimum wage to be paid to the broad spectrum of covered employees. The actual minimum wage can be changed only by congressional action. A lower minimum wage is set for "tipped" employees, such as restaurant servers, but their compensation must equal or exceed the minimum wage when average tips are included. Minimum-wage levels have sparked significant political discussions and legislative maneuvering at both the federal and state levels for the past decade. Consequently, a three-stage increase in the federal minimum wage occurred beginning in 2007 as part of the Fair Minimum Wage Act of 2007, which recently was set with the current minimum wage of $7.25 an hour. Note that if a state's minimum wage is higher, employers must meet the state level rather than the federal level. Some research suggests that minimum wage increases will create a compensation ripple effect, possibly raising the pay rates for more than 10% of jobs and encouraging companies to downsize employment.[47]

Discussion also surrounds the payment of a "living wage" versus the minimum wage. A **living wage** involves earnings that are supposed to meet the basic needs of an individual working for an organization, including food, clothing,

Living wage Earnings that are supposed to meet the basic needs of an individual working for an organization.

and shelter. In the United States, many cities have passed local living-wage legislation.

Child Labor Provisions The child labor provisions of the FLSA set the minimum age for employment with unlimited hours at 16 years. For hazardous occupations (see Chapter 14), the minimum is 18 years of age. Individuals 14 to 15 years old may work outside school hours with certain limitations. Many employers require age certificates for employees because the FLSA makes the employer responsible for determining an individual's age. A representative of a state labor department, a state education department, or a local school district generally issues such certificates.

Exempt and Nonexempt Statuses Under the FLSA, employees are classified as exempt or nonexempt. **Exempt employees** hold positions for which employers are not required to pay overtime. **Nonexempt employees** must be paid overtime. The current FLSA regulations used to identify whether or not a job qualifies for exempt status classifies exempt jobs into five categories:

- Executive
- Administrative
- Professional (learned or creative)
- Computer employees
- Outside sales

As Figure 11-7 indicates, the regulations identify several factors to be considered in exempt status: salaried pay levels per week, duties and responsibilities, and other criteria that must exist for jobs to be categorized as exempt. To review the details for each exemption, go to the U.S. Department of Labor's website at www.dol.gov.

In base pay programs, employers often categorize jobs into groupings that tie the FLSA status and the method of payment together. Employers are required to pay overtime for *hourly* jobs in order to comply with the FLSA. Employees in positions classified as *salaried nonexempt* are covered by the overtime provisions of the FLSA and therefore must be paid overtime. Salaried nonexempt positions sometimes include secretarial, clerical, and salaried blue-collar positions. A common mistake made by employers is to avoid paying

Exempt employees
Employees who are not paid overtime.

Nonexempt employees
Employees who must be paid overtime.

| FIGURE 11-7 | Determining Exempt Status under the FLSA |

CATEGORIES FOR EXEMPT STATUS

- Executive
- Administrative
- Professional (learned and creative)
- Computer employee
- Outside sales

MAJOR CRITERIA FOR EXEMPT STATUS

- Pay level per week
- Job duties and responsibilities (testing)
  - Primary duties
  - Decision discretion/ judgment
  - Authority/work responsibilities
  - Other factors
- Paid on salary basis

overtime to any salaried employees, even though some do not qualify for exempt status. Misclassifying certain assistant managers is one example.[48] A number of large organizations in the United States have faced lawsuits recently over the misclassification of workers, so managers should make sure that jobs are properly classified.[49]

The FLSA does not require employers to pay overtime for *salaried exempt* jobs, although some organizations have implemented policies to pay a straight rate for extensive hours of overtime. For instance, some electric utilities pay first-line supervisors extra using a special rate for hours worked over 50 a week during storm emergencies. A number of salaried exempt professionals in various IT jobs also receive additional compensation for working extensively more than 40 hours per week.

Overtime The FLSA establishes overtime pay requirements. Its provisions set overtime pay at one and one-half times the regular pay rate for all hours over 40 a week, except for employees who are not covered by the FLSA. Overtime provisions do not apply to farm workers, who also have a lower minimum-wage schedule.

The workweek is defined as a consecutive period of 168 hours (24 hours × 7 days) and does not have to be a calendar week. If they wish to do so, hospitals and nursing homes are allowed to use a 14-day period instead of a 7-day week, as long as overtime is paid for hours worked beyond 8 in a day or 80 in a 14-day period. No daily number of hours requiring overtime is set, except for special provisions relating to hospitals and other specially designated organizations. Thus, if a manufacturing firm operates on a 4-day/10-hour schedule, no overtime pay is required by the act.

The most difficult part is distinguishing who is and is not exempt.[50] Some recent costly settlements have prompted more white-collar workers to sue for overtime pay. Retail managers, reporters, sales reps, personal bankers, engineers, computer programmers, and claims adjusters have won in some cases, as being nonexempt workers.

Common Overtime Issues For individuals who are nonexempt, employers must consider a number of issues. These include the following:

- *Compensatory time off:* "Comp" hours are given to public-sector nonexempt employees in lieu of payment for extra time worked at the rate of one and one-half times the number of hours over 40 that are worked in a week. Comp time is currently not available in the private sector and cannot be legally offered to employees working for private for-profit organizations. Also, comp time cannot be carried over from one pay period to another. The only major exception to these provisions is for some public-sector employees, such as fire and police officers, and a limited number of other workers.
- *Incentives for nonexempt employees:* Employers must add the amount of direct work-related incentives to a person's base pay. Then overtime pay should be calculated as one and one-half times the higher (adjusted) rate of pay.
- *Training time:* Time spent in training must be counted as time worked by nonexempt employees unless it is outside regular work hours, not directly job-related, or falls under various other aspects. College degree programs may not be affected by these provisions.
- *Travel time:* Travel time must be counted as work time if it occurs during normal work hours, even on nonworking days, unless the nonexempt

person is a passenger in a car, bus, train, airplane, or other similar mode of transportation. The complex clarifications regarding travel regulations affecting overtime should be reviewed by HR specialists to ensure compliance.

The complexity of overtime determination can be confusing for managers, employees, and HR professionals. To review the areas listed above and additional ones, examine sections 541, 775, 785, and other sections listed on the U.S. Department of Labor's website at www.dol.gov.

Independent Contractor Regulations

The growing use of contingent workers by many organizations has focused attention on another group of legal regulations—those identifying the criteria that independent contractors must meet.[51] For an employer, classifying someone as an independent contractor rather than an employee offers a major advantage. The employer does not have to pay Social Security, unemployment, or workers' compensation costs. These additional payroll levies may add 10% or more to the costs of hiring the individual as an employee. Most federal and state entities rely on the criteria for independent contractor status identified by the Internal Revenue Service (IRS). However, the misclassification of employees as independent contractors is becoming an increasingly significant legal concern for organizations.[52] Firms such as Wal-Mart, Allstate, Microsoft, and FedEx have settled lawsuits for misclassifying individuals as independent contractors,[53] although recently a court determined that FedEx had properly classified a large group of its drivers.[54]

Behavioral Control Some key differences between an employee and an independent contractor have been identified by the IRS. The first set of factors consists of behavioral control factors, which indicate the extent to which an employer can control what a worker does and how a worker performs. One key area includes *business instructions given to the worker*, such as where and when to work, in what sequences, and with what tools and equipment, as well as how to purchase supplies and services. The other area is *business training given to the worker*, such as when someone must be trained to perform in a specific manner, rather than accomplishing results.

Financial Control This set of factors focuses on the extent to which an employer can control the business facets of a worker's job. Considerations include how many *unreimbursed business expenses* a worker has and what investments a worker makes independently to do the job. Other financial factors include whether a worker *provides services to other firms*, how the *business pays the worker*, and if the worker can make a *profit or loss*.

Relationship-Type Factors A number of other items can help clarify whether a relationship is truly independent or not, such as having *written contracts* and the *extent of services provided*. Also, if the employer *provides benefits*, such as insurance or pensions, it is more likely that the person is an employee, and not an independent contractor. For additional details, go to www.irs.gov.

Acts Affecting Government Contractors

Several compensation-related acts apply to firms having contracts with the U.S. government. The Davis-Bacon Act of 1931 affects compensation paid by firms engaged in federal construction projects valued at over $2,000. It deals only with federal construction projects and requires that the "prevailing" wage be paid on all such projects. The *prevailing wage* is determined by a formula that considers the rate paid for a job by a majority of the employers in the appropriate geographic area.

Two other acts require firms with federal supply or service contracts exceeding $10,000 to pay a prevailing wage. Both the Walsh-Healy Public Contracts Act and the McNamara-O'Hara Service Contract Act apply only to those who are working directly on a federal government contract or who substantially affect its performance.

Legislation on Equal Pay and Pay Equity

Various legislative efforts have addressed the issue of wage discrimination on the basis of gender. The Equal Pay Act of 1963 applies to both men and women and prohibits using different wage scales for men and women performing substantially the same jobs.[55] Pay differences can be justified on the basis of merit (better performance), seniority (longer service), quantity or quality of work, experience, or factors other than gender. Similar pay must be given for jobs requiring equal skills, equal responsibilities, equal efforts, or jobs done under similar working conditions.

"Pay equity" is not the same as equal pay for equal work; instead, it is similar to an idea called comparable worth. **Pay equity** is the concept that the pay for all jobs requiring comparable KSAs should be the same even if actual job duties and market rates differ significantly. A few states and the Canadian province of Ontario have laws requiring pay equity for public-sector jobs. However, simply showing the existence of pay disparities for jobs that are significantly different has not been sufficient to prove discrimination in many court cases.

State and Local Laws

Many states and municipalities have enacted modified versions of federal compensation laws. If a state has a higher minimum wage than that set under the FLSA, the higher figure becomes the required minimum wage in that state. On the other end of the spectrum, many states once limited the number of hours women could work, but these laws have been held to be discriminatory in a variety of court cases, and thus states have dropped such laws.

Garnishment Laws

Garnishment occurs when a creditor obtains a court order that directs an employer to set aside a portion of an employee's wages to pay a debt owed a creditor. Regulations passed as a part of the Consumer Credit Protection Act have established limitations on the amount of wages that can be garnished. Also, the act restricts the right of employers to discharge employees whose pay is subject to a single garnishment order. All 50 states have laws applying to wage garnishments.

Lilly Ledbetter Fair Pay Act

As a result of limited time allowed under law for claiming pay discrimination based on sex, religion, color, disability, and other protected characteristics, the Lilly Ledbetter Fair Pay Act was signed by President Obama in January

Pay equity The concept that the pay for all jobs requiring comparable knowledge, skills, and abilities should be the same even if actual job duties and market rates differ significantly.

Garnishment A court order that directs an employer to set aside a portion of an employee's wages to pay a debt owed to a creditor.

of 2009. Before the law was passed, individuals had to submit complaints of pay discrimination to the EEOC within a 180- or 300-day window, which was based on the state where the person was employed. This new legislation effectively negates any statute of limitations for filing a complaint, so claims of pay discrimination can now be made at any time after the alleged misconduct.[56]

DEVELOPMENT OF A BASE PAY SYSTEM

As Figure 11-8 shows, a base compensation system is developed using current job descriptions and job specifications. These information sources are used when *valuing jobs* and analyzing *pay surveys*—activities that are designed to ensure that the pay system is both internally equitable and externally competitive. The data compiled in these two activities are used to design *pay structures*, including *pay grades* and minimum-to-maximum *pay ranges*. After pay structures are established, individual jobs must be placed in the appropriate pay grades and employees' pay must be adjusted according to length of service and performance. Finally, the pay system must be monitored and updated.

FIGURE 11-8   **Compensation Administration Process**

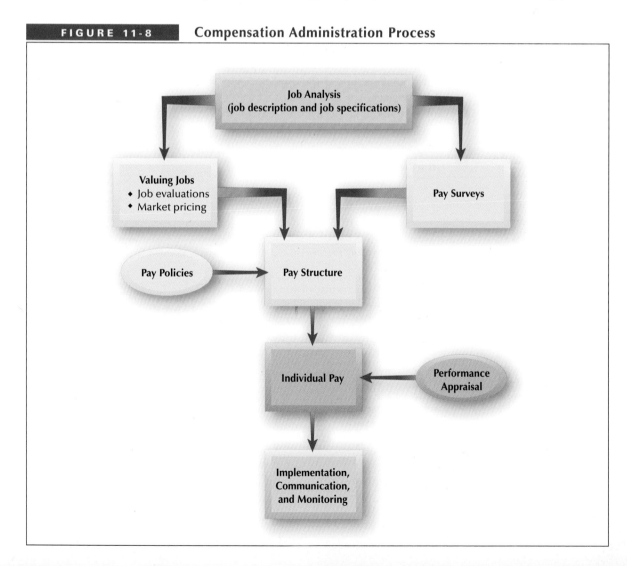

Employers want their employees to perceive their pay levels as appropriate in relation to pay for jobs performed by others inside the organization. Frequently, employees and managers make comments such as "This job is more important than that job in another department, so why are the two jobs paid about the same?" Two general approaches for valuing jobs are available: job evaluation and market pricing. Both approaches are used to determine the values of jobs in relation to other jobs in an organization, and they are discussed next.

Valuing Jobs with Job Evaluation Methods

Job evaluation is a formal, systematic means to identify the relative worth of jobs within an organization. Several job evaluation methods are available for use by employers of different sizes.[57]

Point Method   The most widely used job evaluation method, the point method, looks at compensable factors in a group of similar jobs and places weights, or *points*, on them. A **compensable factor** identifies a job value commonly present throughout a group of jobs. Compensable factors are derived from job analysis and reflect the nature of different types of work performed in the organization, as illustrated in Figure 11-9.

A special type of point method, the Hay system, uses three factors and numerically measures the degree to which each of these factors is required in a job. The three factors are *know-how*, *problem-solving ability*, and *accountability*.

The point method is the most popular because it is relatively simple to use and it considers the components of a job rather than the total job. However, point systems have been criticized for reinforcing traditional organizational

Job evaluation Formal, systematic means to identify the relative worth of jobs within an organization.

Compensable factor Job value commonly present throughout a group of jobs within an organization.

| FIGURE 11-9 | **Examples of Compensable Factors for Different Job Families in a Hotel** |

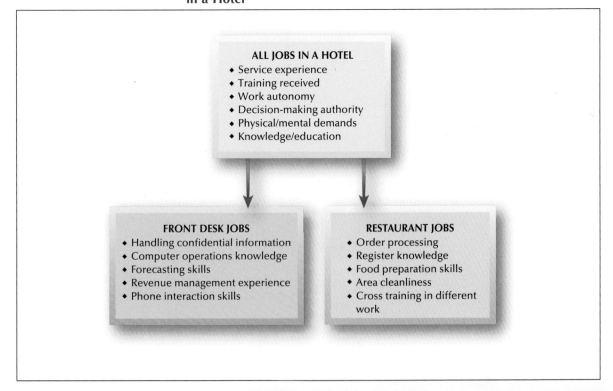

structures and job rigidity. Although not perfect, the point method of job evaluation is generally better than the ranking and classification methods because it quantifies job elements.

Other Job Evaluation Methods Several job evaluation methods are available that are used for different reasons. Common ones include the following:

- The *ranking method* is a simple system that places jobs in order, from highest to lowest, by their value to the organization. The entire job is considered rather than the individual components. The ranking method generally is more appropriate in a small organization having relatively few jobs.
- In the *classification method* of job evaluation, descriptions of each class of jobs are written, and then each job in the organization is put into a grade according to the class description it best matches. The major difficulty with the classification method is that subjective judgments are needed to develop the class descriptions and to place jobs accurately in them.
- The *factor-comparison method* is a quantitative complex combination of the ranking and point methods. Each organization must develop its own key jobs and its own factors. The major disadvantages of the factor-comparison method are that it is difficult to use and time-consuming to establish and develop.

Legal Issues and Job Evaluation Because job evaluation affects the employment relationship, specifically the pay of individuals, some legal issues are of concern.[58] Critics have charged that traditional job evaluation programs place less weight on knowledge, skills, and working conditions for many female-dominated jobs in office and clerical areas than on the same factors for male-dominated jobs in craft and manufacturing areas. Employers counter that because they base their pay rates heavily on external equity comparisons in the labor market, they are simply reflecting rates the "market economy" sets for jobs and workers, rather than discriminating on the basis of gender.

Valuing Jobs Using Market Pricing

Some employers have scaled back their use of "internal valuation" through traditional job evaluation methods. They have instead switched to **market pricing,** which uses market pay data to identify the relative value of jobs based on what other employers pay for similar jobs. Jobs are arranged in groups tied directly to similar survey data amounts.

Key to market pricing is identifying relevant market pay data for jobs that are good "matches" with the employer's jobs, geographic considerations, and company strategies and philosophies about desired market competitiveness levels. That is why some firms have used market pricing as part of strategic decisions in order to ensure market competitiveness of their compensation levels and practices. There is also growing interest in the market pricing of critical individual skills that enable companies to reach important business goals.[59] Finally, organizations should plan to review market-based pay policies every 2 to 3 years to verify that compensation is adequately matched to market conditions.[60]

Market pricing Use of market pay data to identify the relative value of jobs based on what other employers pay for similar jobs.

Advantages of Market Pricing The primary advantage cited for the use of market pricing is that it closely ties organizational pay levels to what is actually occurring in the market, without being distorted by "internal" job evaluation. An additional advantage of market pricing is that it allows an employer to communicate to employees that the compensation system is truly "market linked," rather than sometimes being distorted by internal issues. Employees often see a compensation system that was developed using market pricing as having "face validity" and as being more objective than a compensation system that was developed using the traditional job evaluation methods.[61]

Disadvantages of Market Pricing The foremost disadvantage of market pricing is that for numerous jobs, pay survey data are limited or may not be gathered in methodologically sound ways. A closely related problem is that the responsibilities of a specific job in a company may be somewhat different from those of the "matching" job identified in the survey.[62]

Finally, tying pay levels to market data can lead to wide fluctuations based on market conditions. For evidence of this, one has only to look back at the extremes of the IT job market during the past decade, when pay levels varied significantly. For these and other types of jobs, the debate over the use of job evaluation versus market pricing is likely to continue because both approaches have pluses and minuses associated with them.

Pay Surveys

A **pay survey** is a collection of data on compensation rates for workers performing similar jobs in other organizations. Both job evaluation and market pricing are tied to surveys of the pay that other organizations provide for similar jobs.

Because jobs may vary widely in an organization, it is particularly important to identify **benchmark jobs**—ones that are found in many other organizations. Often these jobs are performed by individuals who have similar duties that require similar KSAs. For example, benchmark jobs commonly used in clerical/office situations are accounts payable processor, customer service representative, and receptionist. Benchmark jobs are used because they provide "anchors" against which individual jobs can be compared.

An employer may obtain surveys conducted by other organizations, access Internet data, or conduct its own survey. Many different surveys are available from a variety of sources. National surveys on many jobs and industries come from the U.S. Department of Labor's Bureau of Labor Statistics, professional and national trade associations, and various management consulting companies. In many communities, employers participate in wage surveys sponsored by the local chamber of commerce or local HR associations.

Internet-Based Pay Surveys HR professionals can access a wide range of pay survey data online. In many cases, pay survey questionnaires are distributed electronically rather than as printed copies, and HR staff members complete the questionnaires electronically. It is anticipated that during the next 5 years, most pay surveys will be conducted using electronic, Web-based technology.

The Internet provides a large number of pay survey sources and data.[63] However, use of these sources requires caution because their accuracy and completeness may not be verifiable or may not be applicable to individual firms and employees. The HR Online discusses how to address employee questions regarding pay survey data that are accessible from the Internet.

Pay survey Collection of data on compensation rates for workers performing similar jobs in other organizations.

Benchmark jobs Jobs found in many organizations that can be used for the purposes of comparison.

Responding to Internet Pay Survey Data Questions

Employees who are dissatisfied with their pay may bring Internet data to HR professionals or their managers and ask why their current pay is different from the pay reported in the Internet data. Responding to such questions from employees requires addressing a number of areas. Salary.com includes sample explanations on its website. Points to be made in discussing employee concerns include the following:

- *Job titles and responsibilities:* Comparison should be made against the employee's full job description, not just job titles and the brief job summaries on the websites.
- *Experience, KSAs, and performance:* Most pay survey data on the Internet are averages of

multiple companies and of multiple employees in those companies with varying experience, KSA levels, and performance.

- *Geographic differences:* Many pay survey sites on the Internet use geographic index numbers, not the actual data from employers in a particular area.
- *Company size and industry:* Pay levels may vary significantly by company size, with smaller firms often having lower pay. Also, pay levels may be lower in certain industries, such as retail and nonprofits.
- *Base pay versus total compensation:* Employers have different benefits and incentive compensation programs. However, Internet data usually reflect only base pay amounts.

Using Pay Surveys The proper use of pay surveys requires evaluating a number of factors to determine if the data are relevant and valid. The following questions should be answered for each survey:

- *Participants:* Does the survey cover a realistic sample of the employers with whom the organization competes for employees?
- *Broad-based:* Does the survey include data from employers of different sizes, industries, and locales?
- *Timeliness:* How current are the data (determined by the date the survey was conducted)?
- *Methodology:* How established is the survey, and how qualified are those who conducted it?
- *Job matches:* Does the survey contain job summaries so that appropriate matches to job descriptions can be made?

Pay Surveys and Legal Issues One reason for employers to use outside sources for pay surveys is to avoid charges that the employers are attempting "price fixing" on wages. One such case involved an HR group and nine hospitals in the Salt Lake City area. The consent decree that resulted prohibited health care facilities in Utah from cooperating when developing or conducting a wage survey. The hospitals can participate in surveys conducted by independent third-party firms only if privacy safeguards are met. Cases in other industries have alleged that by sharing wage data, the employers attempted to hold wages down artificially in violation of the Sherman Antitrust Act.[64]

LOGGING ON

Institute of Management and Administration (IOMA)

For information on salary sources that are reviewed by the IOMA, visit the website at www.ioma.com.

PAY STRUCTURES

Once job valuations and pay survey data are gathered, pay structures can be developed using the process identified in Figure 11-10. Data from the valuation of jobs and the pay surveys may lead to the establishment of several different pay structures for different job families, rather than just one structure for all jobs. A **job family** is a group of jobs having common organizational characteristics. Organizations can have a number of different job families. Examples of some common pay structures based on different job families include: (1) hourly and salaried; (2) office, plant, technical, professional, and managerial; and

Job family Group of jobs having common organizational characteristics.

FIGURE 11-10   **Establishing Pay Structures**

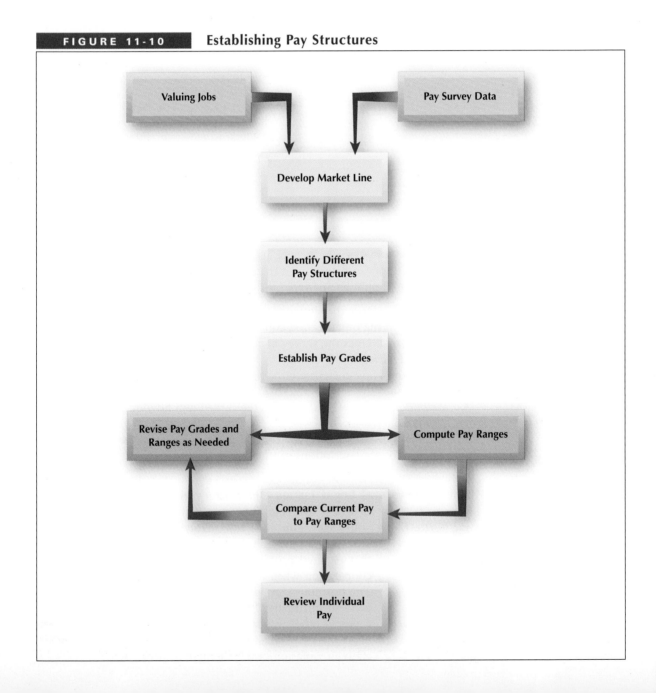

(3) clerical, IT, professional, supervisory, management, and executive. The nature, culture, and structure of the organization are considerations for determining how many and which pay structures to have.

Pay Grades

In the process of establishing a pay structure, organizations use **pay grades** to group individual jobs having approximately the same job worth. Although no set rules govern the establishment of pay grades, some overall suggestions can be useful. Generally, 11 to 17 grades are used in small and medium-sized companies, such as companies with fewer than 500 to 1,000 employees. Two methods are commonly used to establish pay grades: job evaluation data and use of job market banding.

Setting Pay Grades Using Job Evaluation Points One approach to determining pay grades uses job evaluation points or other data generated from the traditional job evaluation methods discussed earlier in the chapter. This process ties pay survey information to job evaluation data by plotting a **market line** that shows the relationship between job value as determined by job evaluation points and job value as determined by pay survey rates. The statistical analysis done when determining market lines focuses particularly on the r^2 levels from the regression when the data are analyzed by different job families and groups. Generally, an r^2 of 0.85 or higher is desired. (Details on the methods and statistical analyses can be found in compensation texts.)[65]

A market line uses data to place jobs having similar point values into pay grades. Pay ranges can then be computed for each pay grade.

Setting Pay Grades Using Market Banding Closely linked to the use of market pricing to value jobs, **market banding** groups jobs into pay grades based on similar market survey amounts. Figure 11-11 shows two "bands" for jobs in a community bank. The midpoint of the survey average is used to develop pay range minimums and maximums, the methods of which are discussed later in this chapter.

Pay Ranges

Once pay grades are determined, the pay range for each pay grade must be established. Using the market line as a starting point, the employer can determine minimum and maximum pay levels for each pay grade by making the market line the midpoint line of the new pay structure (see Figure 11-12). For example, in a particular pay grade, the maximum value may be 20% above the midpoint located on the market line, and the minimum value may be 20% below it. Once pay grades and ranges have been computed, then the current pay of employees must be compared with the draft ranges. A number of employers are reducing the number of pay grades and expanding pay ranges by broadbanding.

Broadbanding The practice of using fewer pay grades with much broader ranges than in traditional compensation systems is called **broadbanding**. Combining many grades into these broadbands is designed to encourage horizontal movement and therefore more skill acquisition. About one-quarter of all employers in one survey are using broadbanding.[66] The main advantage of

---

Pay grades Groupings of individual jobs having approximately the same job worth.

Market line Graph line that shows the relationship between job value as determined by job evaluation points and job value as determined pay survey rates.

Market banding Grouping jobs into pay grades based on similar market survey amounts.

Broadbanding Practice of using fewer pay grades with much broader ranges than in traditional compensation systems.

| FIGURE 11-11 | Market-Banded Pay Grades for Community Bank |

Grade	Job	Pay Survey Summary	Pay Grade		
			Minimum	**Midpoint***	**Maximum**
1	Mail Clerk / Messenger	$19,167			
	Proof Machine Operator	$18,970	$15,600	$18,703	$22,444
	General Office Clerk	$18,594			
	Receptionist	$17,810			
2	Bookkeeper	$22,913			
	Loan Clerk	$22,705			
	Customer Service Representative	$22,337	$17,966	$22,458	$26,950
	Data Entry / Computer Operator	$22,309			
	Head Teller	$22,305			
	Special Teller	$22,179			

*Computed by averaging the pay survey summary data for the jobs in each pay grade.

broadbanding is that it is more consistent with the flattening of organizational levels and the growing use of jobs that are multidimensional. The primary reasons for using broadbanding are: (1) to create more flexible organizations, (2) to encourage competency development, and (3) to emphasize career development.

A problem with broadbanding is that many employees expect a promotion to be accompanied by a pay raise and movement to a new pay grade. As a result of removing this grade progression, the organization may be seen as offering fewer upward promotional opportunities. An additional concern identified by a research study on broadbanding of IT jobs is that it can significantly impact salary levels and costs. Therefore, HR must closely monitor the effects of broadbanding.[67] Despite these and other problems, it is likely that broadbanding will continue to grow in usage.

Individual Pay

Once managers have determined pay ranges, they can set the pay for specific individuals. Setting a range for each pay grade gives flexibility by allowing individuals to progress within a grade instead of having to move to a new grade each time they receive a raise. A pay range also allows managers to reward the better-performing employees while maintaining the integrity of the pay system. Regardless of how well a pay structure is constructed, there usually are a few individuals whose pay is lower than the minimum or higher than the maximum due to past pay practices and different levels of experience and performance. Two types of such employees are discussed next.

Red-circled employee
Incumbent who is paid above the range set for a job.

Red-Circled Employees A red-circled employee is an incumbent who is paid above the range set for the job. For example, assume that an employee's

FIGURE 11-12   **Example of Pay Grades and Pay Ranges**

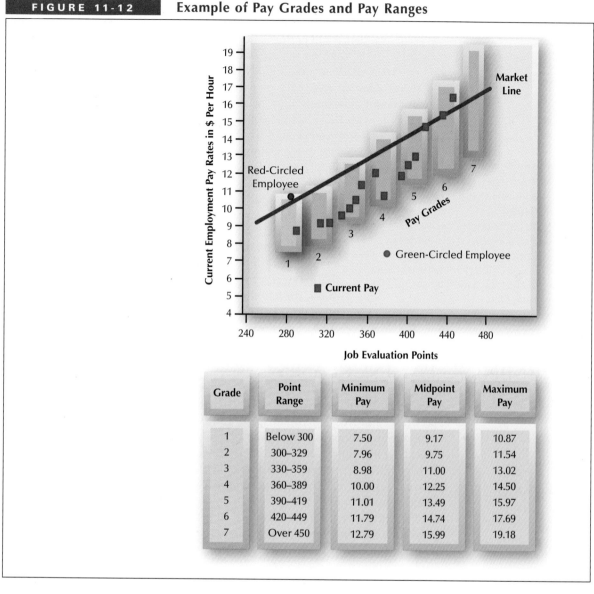

Grade	Point Range	Minimum Pay	Midpoint Pay	Maximum Pay
1	Below 300	7.50	9.17	10.87
2	300–329	7.96	9.75	11.54
3	330–359	8.98	11.00	13.02
4	360–389	10.00	12.25	14.50
5	390–419	11.01	13.49	15.97
6	420–449	11.79	14.74	17.69
7	Over 450	12.79	15.99	19.18

current pay is $11.92 an hour, but the pay range for that person's pay grade is $7.96 to $11.54 an hour. The person would be red-circled. Management would try over a year or so to bring the employee's rate into grade.

Several approaches can be used to bring a red-circled person's pay into line. Although the fastest way would be to cut the employee's pay, that approach is not recommended and is seldom used. Instead, the employee's pay may be frozen until the pay range can be adjusted upward to get the employee's pay rate back into the grade. Another approach is to give the employee a small lump-sum payment but not adjust the pay rate when others are given raises.

Green-Circled Employees An individual whose pay is below the range set for a job is a **green-circled employee**. Promotion is a major contributor to this situation. Generally, it is recommended that the green-circled individual receive fairly rapid pay increases to reach the pay grade minimum. More frequent increases can be used if the minimum is a large amount above the incumbent's current pay.

Green-circled employee
Incumbent who is paid below the range set for a job.

Pay Compression One major problem many employers face is **pay compression**, which occurs when the pay differences among individuals with different levels of experience and performance become small. Pay compression occurs for a number of reasons, but the major one involves situations in which labor market pay levels increase more rapidly than current employees' pay adjustments.[68]

In response to shortages of particular job skills in a highly competitive labor market, managers may occasionally have to pay higher amounts to hire people with those scarce skills. For example, suppose the job of specialized information systems analyst is identified as a $48,000 to $68,000 salary range in one company, but qualified individuals are in short supply and other employers are paying $70,000. To fill the job, the firm likely will have to pay the higher rate. Suppose also that several good analysts who have been with the firm for several years started at $55,000 and have received 4% increases each year. These current employees may still be making less than the $70,000 paid to attract and retain new analysts with less experience from outside. Making certain that pay rates for company jobs are market-based and pay raises are based on performance-based reviews are ways to mitigate salary compression.[69]

DETERMINING PAY INCREASES

Decisions about pay increases are often critical ones in the relationships between employees, their managers, and the organization. Individuals express expectations about their pay and about how much of an increase is "fair," especially in comparison with the increases received by other employees. This is why HR professionals must be actively involved in the communication of pay increases to help manage perceptions of any changes made to employees' compensation.[70]

Pay increases can be determined in several ways: performance, seniority, cost-of-living adjustments, across-the-board increases, and lump-sum increases. These methods can be used separately or in combination.

Performance-Based Increases

As mentioned earlier, some employers have shifted to more pay-for-performance philosophies and strategies. Consequently, they have adopted the following means to provide employees with performance-based increases.

Targeting High Performers This approach focuses on providing the top-performing employees with significantly higher pay raises. Some organizations target the top 10% of employees for significantly greater increases while providing more standard increases to the remaining satisfactory performers. According to a survey by Hewitt Associates, average raises for the best performers in 1 year were 9.9%, satisfactory performers got 3.6%, and low performers got 0% to 1.3%.[71]

The primary reason for having such significant differentials focuses on rewarding and retaining the critical high-performing individuals.[72] Key to rewarding exceptional performers is identifying how much their accomplishments have been above the normal work expectations. The more "standard"

Pay compression Occurs when the pay differences among individuals with different levels of experience and performance become small.

increases for the average performers are usually aligned with labor market pay adjustments, so that those individuals are kept competitive. The lower performers are given less because of their performance issues, which "encourages" them to leave their organizations.

Pay Adjustment Matrix A system for integrating appraisal ratings and pay changes must be developed and applied equally. Often, this integration is done through the development of a *pay adjustment matrix*, or *salary guide chart*. Use of pay adjustment matrices bases adjustments in part on a person's **compa-ratio**, which is the pay level divided by the midpoint of the pay range. To illustrate, the following is an example of the compa-ratio for an employee called *J:*

$$\text{Employee } J = \frac{\$13.35 \text{ (current pay)}}{\$15.00 \text{ (midpoint)}} \times 100 = 89 \text{ (Compa-ratio)}$$

Salary guide charts reflect a person's upward movement in an organization. That movement often depends on the person's performance, as rated in an appraisal, and on the person's position in the pay range, which has some relation to experience as well. A person's placement on the chart determines what pay raise the person should receive. According to the chart shown in Figure 11-13, if employee *J* is rated as exceeding expectations (3) with a compa-ratio of 89, that person is eligible for a raise of 7% to 9%.

Two interesting elements of the sample matrix illustrate the emphasis on paying for performance. First, individuals whose performance is below

Compa-ratio Pay level divided by the midpoint of the pay range.

FIGURE 11-13   **Pay Adjustment Matrix**

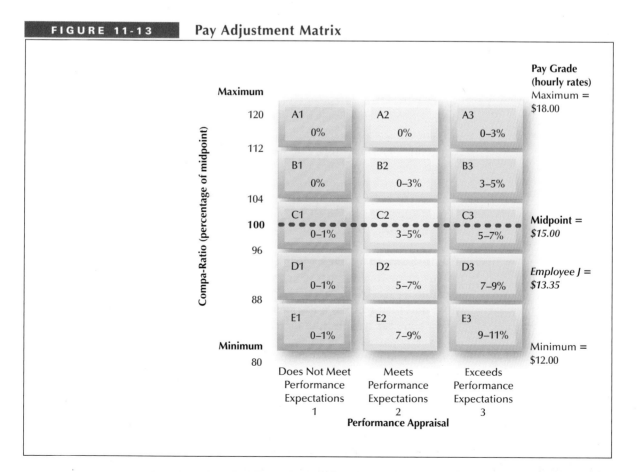

expectations receive small to no raises. This approach sends a strong signal that poor performers will not continue to receive increases just by completing another year of service. Second, as employees move up the pay range, they must exhibit higher performance to obtain the same percentage raise as those lower in the range performing at the "meets performance expectations" level (see Figure 11-13). This approach is taken because the firm is paying above the market midpoint but receiving only satisfactory performance rather than above-market performance. Charts can be constructed to reflect the specific pay-for-performance policies and philosophy in an organization.

Standardized Pay Adjustments

Several different methods are used to provide standardized pay increases to employees. The most common ones are discussed next.

Seniority The time spent in an organization or on a particular job, called **seniority**, can be used as the basis for pay increases. Many employers have policies that require a person to be employed for a certain length of time before being eligible for pay increases. Pay adjustments based on seniority often are set as automatic steps once a person has been employed the required length of time, although performance must be at least satisfactory in many nonunion systems.

Cost-of-Living Adjustments A common pay-raise practice is the use of a *cost-of-living adjustment* (COLA). Often, these adjustments are tied to changes in the Consumer Price Index (CPI) or some other general economic measure. However, numerous studies have revealed that the CPI overstates the actual cost of living, and, as stated previously, COLA increases do little to recognize employees for their relative contributions to the organization.

Across-the-Board Increases Unfortunately, some employers give across-the-board raises and call them *merit raises,* which they are not. Usually the percentage raise is based on standard market percentage changes or financial budgeting determinations not specifically linked to the COLA. If all employees get the same percentage pay increase, it is legitimately viewed as having little to do with merit or good performance. For this reason, employers should reserve the term *merit* for any amount above the standard raise, and they should state clearly which amount is for performance and which amount is the "automatic" portion.

Lump-Sum Increases Most employees who receive pay increases, either for merit or for seniority, receive an increase in the amount of their regular monthly or weekly paycheck. For example, an employee who makes $12.00 an hour and then receives a 3% increase will move to $12.36 an hour.

In contrast, a **lump-sum increase (LSI)** is a one-time payment of all or part of a yearly pay increase. The pure LSI approach does not increase the base pay. Therefore, in the example of a person making $12.00 an hour, if an LSI of 3% is granted, the person receives a lump sum of $748.80 ($0.36 an hour × 2,080 working hours in the year). However, the base rate remains at $12.00 an hour, which slows down the progression of the base wages.

An LSI plan offers advantages and disadvantages.[73] The major advantage of an LSI plan is that it heightens employees' awareness of what their performance levels "merited." Another advantage is that the firm can use LSIs

Seniority Time spent in an organization or on a particular job.

Lump-sum increase (LSI) One-time payment of all or part of a yearly pay increase.

to slow down the increase of base pay and thus reduce or avoid the compounding effect on succeeding raises. One disadvantage of LSI plans is that workers who take a lump-sum payment may become discouraged because their base pay has not changed. Unions generally resist LSI programs because of their impact on pensions and benefits, unless the total amount used in those computations includes the LSI.

SUMMARY

- The concept of *total rewards* has become a crucial part of HR management, and includes compensation, benefits, and performance and talent management.
- Compensation provided by an organization can come directly through base pay and variable pay and indirectly through benefits.
- A continuum of compensation philosophies exists, ranging from an entitlement philosophy to a performance philosophy.
- HR metrics can and should be used to measure the effectiveness of compensation.
- For compensation expenditures to be administered effectively, compensation responsibilities of both HR specialists and managers must be performed well.
- When designing and administering compensation programs, internal and external equity, organizational justice, and pay openness all must be considered.
- Decisions about compensation must always consider market competitiveness and positioning, use of competency-based pay, and team rewards.
- Compensation practices for international employees are much more complex than those for domestic employees, because they are affected by many more factors.

- The Fair Labor Standards Act (FLSA), as amended, is the major federal law that affects pay systems. It requires most organizations to pay a minimum wage and to comply with overtime provisions, including appropriately classifying employees as exempt or nonexempt and as independent contractors or employees.
- A base pay system is developed using information from valuations of jobs and pay surveys, both of which are designed to ensure that the pay system is internally equitable and externally competitive.
- The valuation of jobs can be determined using either job evaluation or market pricing.
- Once a firm has collected pay survey data, it can develop a pay structure, which is composed of pay grades and pay ranges.
- Broadbanding, which uses fewer pay grades with wider ranges, has grown in popularity.
- Individual pay must take into account the placement of employees within pay grades.
- Problems involving "red-circled" jobs, whose rates are above the applicable pay range, and "green-circled" jobs, whose rates are below the applicable pay range, can be addressed in a number of ways.
- Individual pay increases can be based on performance, seniority, cost-of-living adjustments, across-the-board increases, lump-sum increases, or a combination of different approaches.

CRITICAL THINKING ACTIVITIES

1. Discuss the compensation philosophies and approaches that have been used at organizations where you have worked. What have been the consequences of those philosophies and approaches?

2. You have been named Human Resources Manager for a company that has 180 employees and no formal base pay system. What steps will you take to develop such a coordinated system?

3. You are the HR Director for an insurance company with regional offices in several states. For each office, you want to be sure that the administrative assistants reporting to the regional manager are paid appropriately. Go to www.salary.com to find geographic pay survey data for this job in Hartford, Connecticut; Atlanta, Georgia; Omaha, Nebraska; and Phoenix, Arizona. Then recommend pay ranges,

identifying the low, median, and high rates for each pay range. To present the data, list each of the offices in order from lowest median pay to highest median pay.

4. If you had to develop a list of compensation best practices, what practices would be on your list? Develop the list, and compare your findings with those of your classmates.

HR EXPERIENTIAL PROBLEM SOLVING

You have recently been given the responsibility to update all of the company's job descriptions to comply with the Fair Labor Standards Act (FLSA) classifications. The company president believes his secretary is an exempt employee and she is not eligible for overtime pay when she works more than 40 hours in a workweek. You need to prepare a memorandum outlining the essential job functions/duties and giving an opinion about whether the secretary position qualifies for an exempt status

classification. To assist you in making this determination, go to www.dol.gov/whd/flsa.

1. What would the HR professional identify as required key essential functions for the position to qualify for an exempt classification?

2. Assuming you identify that the secretarial position would not be qualified as exempt, what approach will you take to inform the president of your determination?

CASE

Pay for Performance Enhances Employee Management at Scripps Health

Scripps Health is a long-standing and prominent nonprofit health-based organization that is based in the greater San Diego area. The organization experienced a severe financial downturn that led to increased employee discontent and turnover, as well as the exit of the firm's CEO. In an effort to fix these problems, CEO and President Chris Van Gorder implemented a new strategic plan that was used to enhance how the employees were treated.

The new strategic plan contained several components that encouraged employees to work more effectively in their jobs. For example, administrators were to utilize a more participatory leadership approach to create "buy-in" among staff members, and a natural extension of this approach was the development of a physician leadership cabinet that improved how personnel interacted with each other, and that strengthened firm coordination through widespread communication. Top managers also focused on improving individual satisfaction and productivity by enhancing work efficiency levels.

A major part of these more streamlined operations stemmed from implementation of a beneficial performance management plan. In particular, this plan outlined how managerial talent would be developed, employees would be recognized for a job well done, and motivation would be orchestrated through a competitive compensation approach.

Reorganizing the compensation policies of the organization was one of the primary areas targeted for improvement by the firm's leadership. Part of this redesign process involved periodic reviews of job content, the use of annual appraisals to enhance communication, and the assessment of experience and education to properly adjust compensation amounts. Further, the organization strives to offer competitive compensation that rests at the 65th percentile of the relevant labor markets, which positions the firm squarely in the middle between the top and bottom levels of competitive compensation. The company also tests the pay markets twice a year so that it can remain competitive with regard to compensation. Finally, workers can tap into extra money based on ratings given vis-à-vis the annual performance appraisal sessions; if employees do well on their performance reviews, they can earn as much 5% of their salaries as merit-based compensation.[74]

QUESTIONS

1. Discuss how this case illustrates how compensation can be used as a method for improving employee satisfaction and motivation.

2. Identify some of the ways that performance-based pay systems should be developed based on the experiences at Scripps Health.

S U P P L E M E N T A L   C A S E S

Compensation Changes at JC Penney

This case identifies how performance management systems might be redesigned. (For the case, go to www.cengage.com/management/mathis.)

Scientific Turmoil

This case discusses the concerns associated with having a formal base pay system and communication issues that occur. (For the case, go to www.cengage.com/management/mathis.)

N O T E S

1. Adapted from "Targeting Rewards," *Human Resource Executive*, July 2, 2009, 33, 36.
2. Bob King, "Revised Total Rewards Package," *Workspan*, April 2009, 44–48.
3. Deloitte Consulting Report, "2007 Top Five Total Rewards Priorities," 2007 Deloitte Development LLC.
4. Pat Gurren, "Managing Compensation and Benefits in Turbulent Times," Workspan Weekly, April 2009, www.worldatwork.org/waw.
5. Frank Giancola, "Total Rewards: A Current Assessment," *WorldatWork Journal*, Fourth Quarter 2008, 50–60.
6. Juan Pablo Gonzales, "Refocusing Total Rewards When the Economy Is a Blur," *Workspan*, January 2009, 27–32.
7. Marc Drizin, "Broaden the Impact of Recognition and Rewards," *Workspan*, November 2008, 54–58; Leah Carlson Shepard, "Employers Broaden Definition of Total Rewards," *Employee Benefits News*, May 2008, 1*ff*.
8. Jean Kristofferson and Bob King, "The 'It' Factor: A New Total Rewards Model Leads the Way," *Workspan*, April 2006, 18–27.
9. Richard Kantor and Tina Kao, "Total Rewards: Clarity from Confusion and Chaos," *WorldatWork Journal*, Third Quarter 2004, 7–15.
10. To view this model, go to WorldatWork Total Rewards Model: Strategies to Attract, Motivate, and Retain Employees, http://www.worldatwork.org/pub/total_rewards_model.pdf.

11. "What Is Total Rewards?" www.worldatwork.org.
12. Robert L. Heneman, "Implementing Total Rewards Strategies," *SHRM Foundation's Effective Practice Guidelines Series*, 2007.
13. Frank Giancola, "Linking Rewards with Organizational Culture," *WorldatWork Journal*, First Quarter 2008, 55–65.
14. Donald P. Delves, "Taking a Holistic Approach," *Human Resource Executive*, November 19, 2007, 92–96.
15. Paul Weatherhead, "Why CPI-Based Pay Policies Are Not the Answer," *Workspan*, November 2008, 48–53.
16. Charles Coy, "The Road to Total Compensation Management," *Workforce Management* (Special Advertising Supplement).
17. Laura Sejen, "Merging Reward and Talent Management to Strengthen Company Performance," *Workspan*, January 2009, 66–69.
18. Brad Hill and Christine Tande, "Total Rewards: The Employment Value Proposition," *Workspan*, October 2006, 18–22; Success Factors, "3 Steps to Building a Pay-for-Performance Culture," *Workforce Management* (Special Advertising Supplement).
19. Jude Sotherlund and Chris Gokturk, "Pay for Performance: Walking a Legal Fine Line," *Workspan*, January 2007, 36–40.
20. Fay Hansen, "Merit-Pay Payoff?" *Workforce Management*, November 3, 2008, 33–39; Fay Hansen, "Lackluster Performance," *Workforce Management*, November 5, 2007, 39–45; Lisa Hartley, "Can Pay Really Make a Difference?" *Workforce Management* (Special Advertising Supplement).

21. Charlotte Garvey, "Philosophizing Compensation," *HR Magazine*, January 2005, 73–76.
22. Christina Sweins and Panu Kalmi, "Pay Knowledge, Pay Satisfaction and Employee Commitment: Evidence from Finnish Profit-Sharing Schemes," *Human Resource Management Journal*, 18 (2008), 366–385.
23. "Pay Communication: A Reality Check," *Workspan*, October 2008, 52–59; Terry Satterfield, "Pay Satisfaction: A Practical Approach to a Challenging Issue," *Workspan*, August 2008, 47–50.
24. Greg Stoskopf, Leah Reynolds, and David Buck, "A Rewarding Approach: Transforming Your Total Rewards Strategy for Maximum Effect," *Workspan*, April 2009, 36–41.
25. For examples, see Dow Scott, Dennis Morajda, and Thomas D. McMillien, "Evaluating Pay Program Effectiveness," *WorldatWork Journal*, Second Quarter 2006, 50–59.
26. Jac Fitz-Enz and Barbara Davison, *How to Measure Human Resources Management*, 3rd ed. (New York: McGraw-Hill, 2002); www.shrm.org/hrtools.
27. S. C. Currell, et al., "Pay Satisfaction and Organizational Outcomes," *Personnel Psychology*, 58 (2005), 613–640.
28. For details of various compensation surveys and studies, go to www.salary.com.
29. Jonathan A. Segal, "Labor Pains for Union-Free Employers," *HR Magazine*, March 2004, 113–118.
30. Brian Hindo, "Mind If I Peek at Your Paycheck," *BusinessWeek*, June 18, 2007, 40, 42.

31. Based on Robert J. Greene, "Applying Analytics to Rewards Management" (Part 1), *Workspan*, January 2009, 47–51; Robert J. Greene, "Applying Analytics to Rewards Management" (Part 2), *Workspan*, February 2009, 83–86.

32. Mark Reilly and Lisa Audi, "Does It Still Make Sense to Use Geographic Pay Rates?" *Workspan*, December 2006, 52–56.

33. Mark P. Brown, Michael C. Sturman, and Marcia J. Simmering, "Compensation Policy and Organizational Performance: The Efficiency, Operational, and Financial Implications of Pay Levels and Pay Structures," *Academy of Management Journal*, 46 (2003), 752–762.

34. Carri Baca and Gary Starzmann, "Clarifying Competencies: Powerful Tools for Driving Business Success," *Workspan*, March 2006, 44–47.

35. Erich C. Dierdorff and Eric A. Surface, "If You Pay for Skills, Will They Learn? Skill Change and Maintenance Under a Skill-Based Pay System," *Journal of Management*, 34 (2008), 721–743.

36. R. Eugene Hughes, "Skill or Diploma? The Potential Influence of Skill-Based Pay Programs on Sources of Skills Acquisition and Degree Programs," *WorkStudy*, 45 (2003), 179.

37. Larry S. Carlton, "Finding the Right Method of Team Compensation," *SHRM White Paper*, December 2004, www.shrm.org.

38. Geoffrey W. Latta, "The Future of Expatriate Compensation," *WorldatWork Journal*, Second Quarter 2006, 42–49.

39. Stephen Barlas, "Making Global Pay Pay Off," *Human Resource Executive*, October 16, 2008, 52–54.

40. David J. Cichelli and Angie Keller, "Cox Communications Tackles Central vs. Local Compensation Design," *Workspan*, September 2007, 53–56.

41. J. J. Smith, "Total Rewards Package Is Tool in Global War for Talent," www.shrm.org/global.

42. T. T. Runnion, "Expatriate Programs from Preparation to Success," *Workspan*, July 2005, 21.

43. B. W. Watson and G. Singh, "Global Pay Systems in Support of a Multinational Strategy," *Compensation and Benefits Review*, January/February 2005, 33–37.

44. Carlos Mestre, Anne Rossier-Renaud, and Madeleine Berger, "Better Benchmarks for Global Mobility," *Workspan*, April 2009, 73–77.

45. Fay Hansen, "Many Countries, One Compensation System," *Workforce Management*, October 23, 2006, 28.

46. Kelley M. Butler, "Foreign Income Tax Hikes Squeeze Expats, Employers," *Employee Benefit News*, October 2006, 18.

47. Peter Coy, "More Ammo for a Higher Minimum Wage," *BusinessWeek*, November 17, 2006, 38.

48. Steven Siegel, "Top Five Employer Mistakes Under the FLSA," *Workforce Management*, September 2006, www.workforce.com.

49. Amy Onder, "Retail Store Employees Misclassified as Exempt," *HR Magazine*, March 2009, 72; Michael Orey, "Wage Wars," *BusinessWeek*, October 1, 2007, 50–60.

50. "The Overtime Rules: Are You Truly in Compliance?" *The HR Specialist*, December 2006, 1–2.

51. Andrew E. Schultz, "Are Your Independent Contractors Really Employees in Disguise?" *Workspan*, April 1, 2006, 57–60.

52. Thomas R. Bundy, "Worker Misclassification: The Next Big Legal Concern?" *Employee Relations Law Journal*, 33 (2007), 18–26.

53. Dean Faust, "The Ground War at FedEx," *BusinessWeek*, November 28, 2005, 42–43.

54. Alex Roth, "Verdict Backs FedEx in Labor Case," *The Wall Street Journal*, April 2, 2009, B4.

55. For example, see Norman L. Tolle, "Court Affirms Decision Holding Employer Liable for Violating Equal Pay Act," *Employee Benefit Plan Review*, July 2006, 24.

56. Bill Leonard, "President Signs Wage Bias Law," *HR Magazine*, March 2009, 13; Towers Perrin, "New Law Makes Companies More Vulnerable to Complaints of Pay Discrimination," www.towersperrin.com.

57. For additional details on different methods, see *Job Evaluation: Methods to the Process* (Scottsdale, AZ: WorldatWork), 2005, 159 pp.

58. Kay Gilbert, "The Role of Job Evaluation in Determining Equal Value in Tribunals: Tool, Weapon, or Cloaking Device?" *Employee Relations*, 27 (2005), 7–20.

59. Doug Sayed, "Market Pricing and Compensating 'Hot' and 'Critical' Skills," *Workspan*, January 2009, 53–57.

60. Elizabeth A. Chidichimo, "Improving Your Market-Based Programs," *Workspan*, June 2009, 38–44.

61. Kimberly Merriman, "A Fairness Approach to Market-Based Pay," *Workspan*, March 2006, 48–50.

62. Charles H. Fay and Madhura Tare, "Market Pricing Concerns," *WorldatWork Journal*, Second Quarter 2007, 61–69.

63. Marty Orgel, "Web Sites That Provide Salary Help," *The Wall Street Journal*, October 16, 2008, B4.

64. *District of Utah, U.S. District Court v. Utah Society for Healthcare Human Resources Administration, et al.*, No. 14203, *Federal Register*, March 1994.

65. For example, see Richard I. Henderson, *Compensation Management in a Knowledge-Based World*, 10th ed. (Upper Saddle River, NJ: Prentice Hall, 2006).

66. Mercer Human Resource Consulting, *2006 Compensation Planning Survey* (New York: Mercer Corporation, 2006).

67. C. H. Fay, et al., "Broadbanding— Pay Ranges and Labor Costs," *WorldatWork Journal*, Second Quarter 2004, 8–23.

68. Susan Ladika, "Decompressing Pay," *HR Magazine*, December 2005, 79–82.

69. Linda Ulrich, "Money Talks: Identifying, Preventing, and Alleviating Systematic Salary Compression Issues," *Workspan*, November 2008, 42–46.

70. Lin Grensing-Pophal, "And Now, a Word About Salary Increases," *HR Magazine*, November 2008, 93–98.

71. Erin White, "The Best vs. the Rest," *The Wall Street Journal*, January 30, 2006, B1.

72. Jessica Marquez, "Raising the Performance Bar," *Workforce Management*, April 24, 2006, 31–32.

73. Bob Fulton, "What Are the Pro's and Con's of Switching to Lump-Sum Payments as Compensation?" *Workforce Management Research Center*, January 12, 2004, www.workforce.com.

74. Based on Susan J. Wells, "Prescription for a Turnaround," *HR Magazine*, June 2009, 88–94.

12

Incentive Plans and Executive Compensation

After you have read this chapter, you should be able to:

- Define variable pay and identify three elements of successful pay-for-performance plans.
- Discuss three types of individual incentives.
- Identify key concerns that must be addressed when designing group/team variable pay plans.
- Discuss why profit sharing and employee stock ownership are common organizational incentive plans.
- Explain three ways that sales employees are typically compensated.
- Identify the components of executive compensation and discuss criticisms of executive compensation levels.

Variable Pay at Cox Communications

ox Communications is a well-known large firm with 20 local markets. Even though the company offers many of the same services in all of its markets, each market has differences in terms of services, customer growth, and operational factors. Cox allows local management to develop incentive plans for employees based on the different market areas, but provides a basic variable pay framework as a guide.

Although Cox has more than 400 different incentive plans, managers review the plans using four major guidelines. One guideline is used to determine the applicability of various incentives to different types of jobs. Another is to measure performance on local job tasks and unusual demands. This can identify jobs and unique aspects in each. Additionally, the variable pay framework considers the mechanics used to make payouts, including selected performance measures and formulas used for the payouts. The final factor considers two components of timing: the periods for both the performance measures and the payouts.

The Cox incentive programs serve all types and locations of employees well. Varying incentives reflects the differences faced by service technicians, sales representatives, telephone contact workers, executives, managers, HR professionals, and other employees. However, by developing and administering the unique variable pay framework, Cox ties an effective approach to variable pay and incentives to the company's organizational success efforts.[1]

Pay for performance can be a part of total rewards. As discussed in the previous chapter, more employers are moving toward systems providing base pay for performance using matrixes and other means, rather than just giving all workers a standard percentage increase in pay. If the question is whether people work harder because pay is tied to performance, the answer is yes.

Tying pay to performance holds a promise that both employers and employees find attractive. For employees, it can mean more pay; for employers, it can mean more output per employee and therefore more productivity. However, it is much more difficult to design a successful variable pay or special incentive system than to simply pay employees a set hourly wage or salary.

Variable pay programs are very popular, with more than 80% of organizations using them, according to a WorldatWork annual survey. The most widely used of these programs involve awards based on individual, unit, and organizational performance and success.[2] Common types of variable pay programs are based on factors such as sales, customer service, productivity, attendance, safety, and executive incentives.

VARIABLE PAY: INCENTIVES FOR PERFORMANCE

Variable pay is compensation linked to individual, group/team, and/or organizational performance. Variable pay plans attempt to provide tangible rewards, traditionally known as *incentives,* to employees for performance beyond normal expectations. The philosophical foundation of incentives rests on several basic assumptions:

- Some jobs contribute more to organizational success than others.
- Some people perform better and are more productive than others.
- Employees who perform better should receive more compensation.
- Many employees' total compensation should be tied directly to performance and results.

Pay for performance has a different philosophical base than does a more traditional compensation system, in which differences in job responsibilities are recognized through different amounts of base pay. In many organizations, length of service is a primary differentiating factor. However, giving additional rewards to some people and not others is seen as potentially divisive and as hampering employees' working together. This is why many labor unions oppose pay-for-performance programs. In contrast, high-performing workers expect extra rewards for outstanding performance that increases organizational results.

Incentives can take many forms. For example, they can include simple praise, "recognition and reward" programs that award trips and merchandise, bonuses for performance accomplishments, and rewards for successful results for the company. A variety of possibilities are discussed later in this chapter. A successful plan will include a combination of different types of incentives.

Developing Successful Pay-for-Performance Plans

Employers adopt variable pay or incentive plans for a number of reasons. Key reasons that many employers adopt these plans are as follows:

- Link strategic business goals and employee performance
- Enhance organizational results and reward employees financially for their contributions

Variable pay Compensation linked to individual, group/team, and/or organizational performance.

- Recognize different levels of employee performance through different rewards
- Achieve HR objectives, such as increasing retention, reducing turnover, recognizing training, and rewarding safety

As economic conditions have changed in industries and among employers, the use of variable pay incentives has changed as well. Under variable pay programs, employees can have a greater sharing of the gains or declines in organizational performance results. Even in organizations where the number of staff members has been reduced, such as investment firms, employers are switching from base pay to variable compensation means.[3]

Variable pay plans can be considered successful if they meet the objectives the organization had for them when they were initiated and if they work with the organizational culture and the financial resources of the organization. Both financial and nonfinancial rewards for performance are important in pay-for-performance plans. The manner in which targets are set and measured is important.[4] Three elements that affect the success of variable pay systems are discussed next. These are highlighted in Figure 12-1.

Does the Plan Fit the Organization? The success of any incentive pay program relies on its consistency with the culture of the organization.[5] For example, if an organization is autocratic and adheres to traditional rules and procedures, an incentive system that rewards flexibility and teamwork is likely to fail. In such a case, the incentive plan has been "planted" in the wrong growing environment.

When it comes to variable pay-for-performance plans, one size does not fit all.[6] A plan that has worked well for one company will not necessarily work well for another. For instance, in professional service firms, performance measures such as client progress and productivity, new business development revenues, client satisfaction, and profit contributions are typically linked to pay-for-performance programs.[7] These measures might not work as well in a different industry. For an incentive plan to work, it must be linked to the objectives of the organization, its financial resources, and its desired performance results. However, when these criteria are met, many employers find that

---

FIGURE 12-1   **Effective Variable Pay Plans**

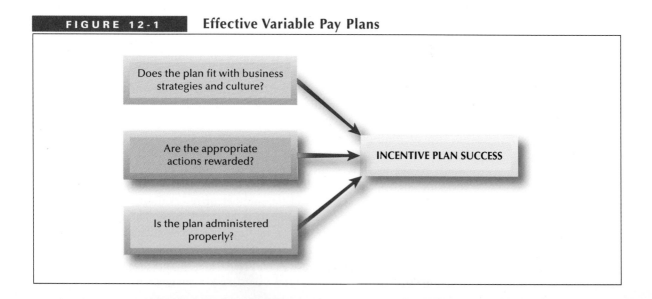

Awarding Points for Staff Efforts

One incentive that is widely used is award points. For taking certain actions or accomplishing designated results, the individual employees can get point-based incentive awards in addition to their pay. Examples from different industries illustrate the potential effectiveness of using this type of incentive.

One of the staffing concerns in hospitals is staffing certain work shifts. Instead of using independent contract persons to cover some shifts, some health care facilities are using award points and other incentives to encourage employees to be the extra shift workers. For example, at a Hawaiian hospital, employees who request night shifts or 8-hour days get awarded extra award points in addition to their pay. The employees can use their points for gasoline cards, tuition benefits, gift cards, and other awards. The impact of this system

for the hospital is that about 70% of the firm's unfilled shift hours are being covered by employees who get the award-point incentives. Over an extended period of time, more than 100,000 extra shift hours by workers were aligned with the awards.

Similar programs have been used in other industries. For instance, one airline used point-based awards to reward customer service personnel for getting more fees on overweight checked passenger bags. Also, the airline employees received such awards for community service, nonprofit volunteer activities, and other behaviors.

Different types of incentive systems have grown in usage in numerous other firms, industries, and organizational settings. This discussion illustrates how custom tailoring incentives can reward employees for desired actions.[8]

variable pay plans make performance results a higher priority than just how employees behave in their jobs, thus contributing to positive organizational results.

Does the Plan Reward Appropriate Actions? Variable pay systems should be tied as much as possible to desired performance. Employees must see a direct relationship between their efforts and their financial and nonfinancial rewards, as the HR Perspective illustrates.

Because people tend to produce what is measured and rewarded, organizations must make sure that what is being rewarded is clearly linked to what is needed. For instance, in a highly innovative firm, incentives may be very motivating for managers, given economic and other organizational performance impacts.[9] Performance measures need to give appropriate emphasis and weights for calculating incentives in order for the programs to be effective. If incentive measures are manipulated or inappropriate, the variable pay systems may not be as effective.[10]

Use of multiple measures helps to ensure that important performance dimensions are not omitted. For example, assume a hotel reservation center wants to set incentives for employees to increase productivity by lowering the time they spend on each call. If that reduction is the only measure, the quality of customer service and the number of reservations made might drop as employees rush callers in order to reduce talk time. Therefore, the center should consider basing rewards on multiple measures, such as talk time, reservations booked, and the results of customer satisfaction surveys.

Linking pay to performance may not always be appropriate. For instance, if the output cannot be measured objectively, management may not be able to correctly reward the higher performers with more pay. Managers may not even be able to accurately identify the higher performers. For example, in an office where tasks are to provide permits for building renovations, individual contributions may not be identifiable or appropriate.

Is the Plan Administered Properly? A variable pay plan may be complex or simple, but it will be successful only if employees understand what they have to do to be rewarded. The more complicated a plan is the more difficult it will be to communicate it meaningfully to employees. Experts generally recommend that a variable pay plan include several performance criteria. But having multiple areas of focus should not overly complicate the calculations necessary for employees to determine their own incentive amounts. Managers also need to be able to explain clearly what future performance targets need to be met and what the rewards will be.

Global Variable Pay

GLOBAL

Variable pay is expanding in global firms, as well as among foreign-country employers. In Europe, Asia, and Latin America, more than 80% of management professionals and general staff are eligible for broad-based variable pay plans. Many programs are similar to those at U.S.-based companies, but global programs must accommodate cultural, legal, and economic differences.[11] For firms with operations in multiple countries, having widely spread incentives requires that local managers be trained to control the reward programs and that the different choices in the programs are beneficial for success.[12]

Although administering any incentive plan can be difficult, global incentive programs can be especially complex. A company may have an overarching strategy, such as growing market share or increasing the bottom line, but that strategy frequently works out to different goals in different geographical regions. Also, laws and regulations differ from one country to the next. For example, in Latin America, there are mandatory profit-sharing regulations, so variable pay must reflect that. Countries such as China and India use individual incentives more widely than do the United States and Europe. However, to attract and retain expatriates, who are persons from one country working in another one, both salaries and incentives must be considered.

Metrics for Variable Pay Plans

MEASURE

Firms in the United States are spending significant amounts on variable pay plans as incentives. For instance, according to one survey, incentive expenditures in one year totaled $46 billion. Interestingly, more than $30 billion was paid on incentive merchandise and about $13 billion was spent on travel incentives. With such incentive expenditures increasing each year, it is crucial that the results of variable pay plans be measured to determine the success of the programs.[13]

Various metrics can be used, depending on the nature of the plan and the goals set for it. Figure 12-2 shows some examples of different metrics that can be used to evaluate variable play plans.

A common metric for incentive plans is return on investment (ROI). One firm, Leapfrog Group, has developed an ROI Estimator for its hospital pay-for-performance plan on health care activities, such as heart bypass, angioplasty, and others.[14] To illustrate a general ROI example, suppose a company decides that using a program to provide rewards in the form of lottery drawing

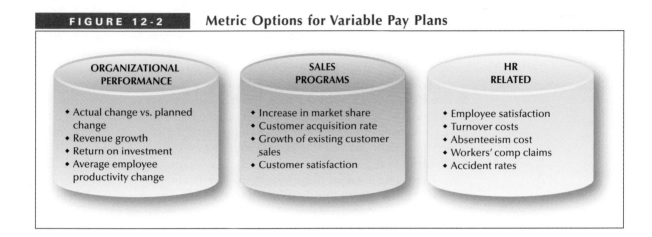

FIGURE 12-2   Metric Options for Variable Pay Plans

ORGANIZATIONAL PERFORMANCE

- Actual change vs. planned change
- Revenue growth
- Return on investment
- Average employee productivity change

SALES PROGRAMS

- Increase in market share
- Customer acquisition rate
- Growth of existing customer sales
- Customer satisfaction

HR RELATED

- Employee satisfaction
- Turnover costs
- Absenteeism cost
- Workers' comp claims
- Accident rates

chances each month for employees who were not absent during the month will reduce absenteeism. An ROI metric would look at the dollar value of the improvement minus the cost of the program divided by the total cost. So if the value of the reduction in absenteeism was $100,000 per year, and the program cost $85,000, calculations would be $(100,000 - 85,000) \div 85,000$, for just over a 17% return on the investment.

Other metrics also can be used to evaluate programs for management decision making. Regardless of the variable pay plan, employers should gather and evaluate data to determine if the expenditures are justified by increased organizational operating performance.[15] If the measures and analyses show positive results, the nature of the plan is truly a pay-for-performance one. If not, the plan should be changed to one that is more likely to be successful.

Successes and Failures of Variable Pay Plans

Even though variable pay has grown in popularity, some attempts at incentives have succeeded while others have not. Incentives *do* work, but they are not a panacea because their success depends on multiple factors.[16] The positive view that many employers have of variable pay is not shared by all workers. If individuals see incentives as desirable, they are likely to put forth the extra effort to attain the performance objectives that trigger the incentive payouts. But not all employees believe that they are rewarded when doing a good job, and not all employees are motivated by their employers' incentive plans.

Some employees prefer increases in their pay over noncash incentives, but noncash incentives do motivate some workers to perform better than cash rewards do. In addition, a research study concluded that the incentives employees say they desire may not be ones that actually lead to higher performance results.[17]

One factor that can lead to failure of a variable pay plan is having an incentive plan that is too complex for employees and management to understand. If the plan is too complicated to follow, the focus may not be on successful performance, employee misunderstanding and miscommunications can occur, and lower performance may be the result.[18]

Given these dynamics and the complexity of these plans, providing a variable pay plan that will be successful requires significant, continuing efforts.[19] Some factors that contribute to the success of incentive plans are as follows:

- Develop clear, understandable plans that are continually communicated.
- Use realistic performance measures.
- Keep the plans current and linked to organizational objectives.
- Clearly link performance results to payouts that truly recognize performance differences.
- Identify variable pay incentives separately from base pay.

Three Categories of Variable Pay

The incentives offered in variable pay plans can be classified into three categories: individual, group/team, and organizational. There are advantages and disadvantages to each.

Individual incentives are given to reward the effort and performance of individuals. Some common means of providing individual variable pay are piece-rate systems, sales commissions, and individual bonuses. Others include special recognition rewards such as trips or merchandise. However, with individual incentives, employees may focus on what is best for them personally, which may inhibit the performance of other individuals with whom they are competing. For this reason, in some situations, group/team incentives may be more appropriate.

When an organization rewards an entire group/team for its performance, cooperation among the members may increase. The most common *group/team incentives* are gainsharing or goalsharing plans, in which the employees on a team that meets certain goals, as measured against performance targets, share in the gains. Often such programs focus on quality improvement, cost reduction, and other measurable results.

Organizational incentives reward people according to the performance results of the entire organization. This approach assumes that all employees working together can generate improved organizational results that lead to better financial performance. These programs often share some of the financial gains made by the firm with employees through payments calculated as a percentage of the employees' base pay. The most prevalent forms of organization-wide incentives are profit-sharing plans and employee stock plans.

Figure 12-3 shows some of the programs that fall under each type of incentive or variable pay plan. These programs are discussed in the following sections.

LOGGING ON

Wilson Group
The Wilson Group provides consulting services on variable pay compensation systems. Visit its website at www.wilsongroup.com.

| FIGURE 12-3 | **Categories of Variable Pay Plans** |

INDIVIDUAL	GROUP/TEAM	ORGANIZATIONAL
• Piece-rate systems • Bonuses • Special incentive programs (trips, merchandise, awards) • Sales compensation	• Group team results • Gainsharing/goalsharing • Quality improvement • Cost reduction	• Profit sharing • Employee stock plans • Executive stock options • Deferred compensation

INDIVIDUAL INCENTIVES

Individual incentive systems tie personal effort to additional rewards. Conditions necessary for the use of individual incentive plans are as follows:

- *Individual performance must be identified.* The performance of each individual must be measured and identified because each employee has job responsibilities and tasks that can be separated from those of other employees.
- *Individual competitiveness must be desired.* Because individuals generally pursue the incentives for themselves, competition among employees often occurs. Therefore, independent competition in which some individuals "win" and others do not must be something the employer can tolerate.
- *Individualism must be stressed in the organizational culture.* The culture of the organization must be one that emphasizes individual growth, achievements, and rewards. If an organization emphasizes teamwork and cooperation, then individual incentives may be counterproductive.

Piece-Rate Systems

The most basic individual incentive systems are piece-rate systems. Under **straight piece-rate system**, wages are determined by multiplying the number of units produced (such as garments sewn or service calls handled) by the piece rate for one unit. Because the cost is the same for each unit, the wage for each employee is easy to figure, and labor costs can be accurately predicted.

A *differential piece-rate system* pays employees one piece-rate wage for units produced up to a standard output and a higher piece-rate wage for units produced over the standard. Managers often determine the quotas or standards by using time and motion studies. For example, assume that the standard quota for a worker is set at 300 units per day and the standard rate is 14 cents per unit. However, for all units over the standard, the employee receives 20 cents per unit. Under this system, the worker who produces 400 units in one day would get \$62 (300 × 14¢) + (100 × 20¢). Many possible combinations of straight and differential piece-rate systems can be used, depending on situational factors.

Despite their incentive value, piece-rate systems can be difficult to apply because determining standards is a complex and costly process for many types of jobs. In some instances, the cost of determining and maintaining the standards may be greater than the benefits derived. Also, jobs in which individuals have limited control over output or in which high standards of quality are necessary may be unsuited to piecework unless quality can be measured.

Bonuses

Individual employees may receive additional compensation in the form of a **bonus**, which is a one-time payment that does not become part of the employee's base pay. Individual bonuses are used at all levels in some firms and are the most popular short-term incentive plan.

A bonus can recognize performance by an employee, a team, or the organization as a whole. When performance results are good, bonuses go up. When performance results are not met, bonuses go down. Most employers base part of an employee's bonus on individual performance and part on

Straight piece-rate system Pay system in which wages are determined by multiplying the number of units produced by the piece rate for one unit.

Bonus One-time payment that does not become part of the employee's base pay.

company results, as appropriate. Numerous CEOs receive bonuses based on specific results.[20]

Bonuses also can be used to reward employees for contributing new ideas, developing skills, or obtaining professional certifications. When helpful skills or certifications are acquired by an employee, a pay increase or a one-time bonus may follow. For example, a financial services firm provides the equivalent of two weeks' pay to employees who master job-relevant computer skills. Another firm gives one week of additional pay to members of the HR staff who obtain professional certifications such as Professional in Human Resources (PHR), Senior Professional in Human Resources (SPHR), or Certified Compensation Professional (CCP).

"Spot" Bonuses A unique type of bonus used is a "spot" bonus, so called because it can be awarded at any time. Spot bonuses are given for a number of reasons, perhaps for extra time worked, extra efforts, or an especially demanding project. For instance, a spot bonus may be given to an information technology employee who installed a computer software upgrade that required extensive time and effort.

Often, spot bonuses are given in cash, although some firms provide managers with gift cards, travel vouchers, or other noncash rewards. Noncash rewards vary in types and levels, but they need to be immediately visible and useful to be seen as desirable by individuals.[21] The keys to successful use of spot bonuses are to keep the amounts reasonable and to provide them only for exceptional performance accomplishments. The downside to their use is that they can create jealousy and resentment in other employees who feel that they deserved a spot bonus but did not get one.

Special Incentive Programs

Numerous special incentive programs can be used to reward individuals, ranging from one-time contests for meeting performance targets to awards for performance over time. For instance, safe-driving awards are given to truck drivers with no accidents or violations on their records during a year. Although special programs can be developed for groups and for entire organizations, they often focus on rewarding individuals. Special incentives are used for several purposes, as noted in Figure 12-4.

FIGURE 12-4   **Purposes of Special Incentives**

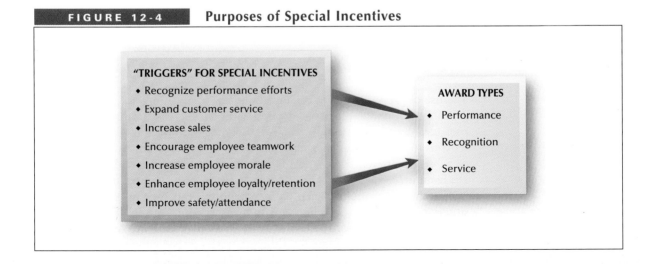

"TRIGGERS" FOR SPECIAL INCENTIVES
- Recognize performance efforts
- Expand customer service
- Increase sales
- Encourage employee teamwork
- Increase employee morale
- Enhance employee loyalty/retention
- Improve safety/attendance

AWARD TYPES
- Performance
- Recognition
- Service

Performance Awards Cash, merchandise, gift certificates, and travel are the most frequently used incentive rewards for significant performance. Cash is still highly valued by many employees because they can decide how to spend it. However, noncash incentives may be stronger motivators, based on a study that considered awards such as vacation cruises, home kitchen equipment, groceries, and other noncash items.[22] For instance, travel awards appeal to many U.S. employees, particularly trips to popular destinations such as Disney World, Las Vegas, Hawaii, and international locations. These examples indicate that many employees appreciate the "trophy" value of such awards as much as the actual monetary value.

Recognition Awards Another type of program recognizes individual employees for their performance. For instance, many organizations in industries such as hotels, restaurants, and retailers have established "employee of the month" and "employee of the year" awards. Hotels often use favorable guest comment cards as the basis for providing recognition awards to front desk representatives, housekeepers, and other hourly employees.

Recognition awards often work best when given to acknowledge specific efforts and activities that the organization has targeted as important. Global employers may use recognition awards that reflect cultural differences in various countries. The criteria for selecting award winners may be determined subjectively in some situations. However, formally identified criteria provide greater objectivity and are more likely to be seen as rewarding performance rather than as favoritism. When giving recognition awards, organizations should use specific examples to describe clearly how those receiving the awards were selected.

Service Awards Another type of reward given to individual employees is the service award. Although service awards often are portrayed as rewarding performance over a number of years, in reality the programs in most firms recognize length of service (e.g., 1, 3, 5, or 10 years) more than employees' actual performance. Many of these awards increase in value as the length of service increases, and often they are made as dollar amounts rather than as gifts.

Some firms give recipients gift cards to retail or restaurant locations, while others let qualifying employees select items from a range of merchandise choices (e.g., cameras, watches, and other items). Different firms offer employees of certain lengths of service special trips to resorts or social events. The overall goal of these awards is to give appreciation to employees for service.[23]

GROUP/TEAM INCENTIVES

The use of groups/teams in organizations has implications for incentive compensation. Although the use of groups/teams has increased substantially in the past few years, the question of how to compensate their members equitably remains a significant challenge. Many firms provide rewards for work groups or teams in different ways and for several reasons, as Figure 12-5 notes.

Team incentives can take the form of either cash bonuses for the team or items other than money, such as merchandise or trips. But group incentive situations may place social pressure on members of the group. Everyone in the group succeeds or fails. Therefore, some argue that team incentives should be given to team members equally, although not everyone agrees.

FIGURE 12-5   **Teams and Variable Pay Plan Results**

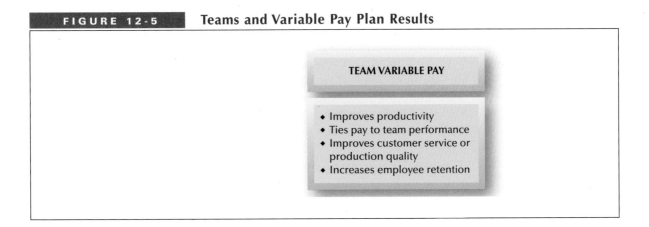

Design of Group/Team Incentive Plans

In designing group/team incentive plans, organizations must consider a number of issues. The main concerns are how and when to distribute the incentives, and who will make decisions about the incentive amounts.

Distribution of Group/Team Incentives Several decisions about how to distribute and allocate group/team rewards must be made. The two primary ways for distributing those rewards are as follows:

1. *Same-size reward for each member:* All members receive the same payout, regardless of job level, current pay, seniority, or individual performance differences.
2. *Different-size reward for each member:* Employers vary individual rewards depending on such factors as contribution to group/team results, current pay, years of experience, and skill levels of jobs performed.

Generally, more organizations use the first approach. The combination of equal team member award payouts and individual pay differences rewards performance by making the group/team incentive equal while also recognizing that individual differences exist and are important to many employees. The size of the group/team incentive can be determined either by using a percentage of base pay for the individuals or the group/team as a whole, or by offering a specific dollar amount. For example, one firm pays members individual base rates that reflect years of experience and any additional training that they have. Additionally, the group/team reward is distributed to all as a flat dollar amount.

Timing of Group/Team Incentives How often group/team incentives are paid out is another important consideration. Choices seen in firms with group/team incentives are monthly, quarterly, semiannually, and annually, although the most common period used is annually. However, the shorter the time period, the greater the likelihood that employees will see a closer link between their efforts and the performance results that trigger the award payouts. For instance, employers may limit the group/team rewards to $1,000 or less, allowing them to pay out rewards more frequently. The nature of the teamwork, measurement criteria, and organizational results must all be considered when determining the appropriate time period.

Decision Making about Group/Team Incentive Amounts To reinforce the effectiveness of working together, some group/team incentive programs allow members to make decisions about how to allocate the rewards to individuals. In some situations, members vote; in some, a group/team leader decides. In other situations, the incentive "pot" is divided equally, thus avoiding conflict and recognizing that all members contributed to the team results. However, many companies have found group/team members unwilling to make incentive decisions about coworkers.

Group/Team Incentive Challenges

The difference between rewarding team members *equally* and rewarding them *equitably* triggers many of the problems associated with group/team incentives. Rewards distributed in equal amounts to all members may be perceived as "unfair" by employees who work harder, have more capabilities, or perform more difficult jobs. This problem is compounded when an individual who is performing poorly prevents the group/team from meeting the goals needed to trigger the incentive payment. Also, employees working in groups/teams may have less satisfaction with rewards that are the same for all, versus rewards based on performance, which often are viewed as more equitable.

Generally, managers view the concept of people working in groups/teams as beneficial. But to a large extent, many employees still expect to be paid according to individual performance. Until this individualism is recognized and compensation programs that are viewed as more equitable by more "team members" are developed, caution should be used when creating and implementing group/team incentives.

Group size is another consideration in team incentives. If a group becomes too large, employees may feel that their individual efforts have little or no effect on the total performance of the group and the resulting rewards. But group/team incentive plans also may encourage cooperation in small groups where interdependence is high. Therefore, in those groups, the use of group/team performance measures is recommended. Such plans have been used in many industries. Conditions for successful team incentives are shown in Figure 12-6. If these conditions cannot be met, then either individual or organizational incentives may be more appropriate.

Types of Group/Team Incentives

Group/team reward systems use various ways of compensating individuals. The components include individual wages and salaries in addition to the other rewards. Most organizations that use group/team incentives continue to pay individuals based either on the jobs performed or the individuals' competencies and capabilities. The two most common types of group/team incentives are team results and gainsharing.

Group/Team Results Pay plans for groups/teams may reward all members equally on the basis of group output, cost savings, or quality improvement. The design of most group/team incentives is based on a "self-funding" principle, which means that the money to be used as incentive rewards is obtained through improvement of organizational results. A good example is gainsharing, which can be structured as either a group or company-wide incentive.

FIGURE 12-6   **Conditions for Successful Group/Team Incentives**

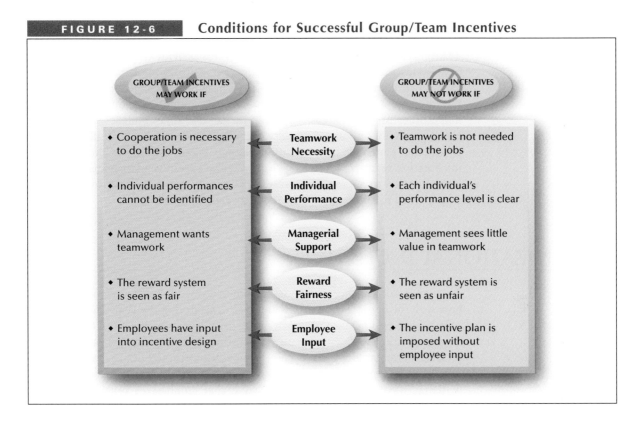

Gainsharing The system of sharing with employees greater-than-expected gains in profits and/or productivity is **gainsharing**. Also called *teamsharing* or *goalsharing*, the focus is to increase "discretionary efforts," which are the difference between the maximum amount of effort a person can exert and the minimum amount of effort that person needs to exert to keep from being fired.

Workers in many organizations are not paid for discretionary efforts, but are paid to meet the minimum acceptable level of effort required. When workers do demonstrate discretionary efforts, the organization can afford to pay them more than the going rate, because the extra efforts produce financial gains over and above the returns of minimal efforts. Some organizations have linked Lean Six Sigma programs together with gainsharing to emphasize the attainment of results. For example, in a global pharmaceutical plant, this kind of program was seen as contributing to improved productivity and lower direct labor costs.[24]

To develop and implement a gainsharing or goalsharing plan, management must identify the ways in which increased productivity, quality, and financial performance can occur and decide how some of the resulting gains should be shared with employees. Measures such as labor costs, overtime hours, and quality benchmarks often are used. Both organizational measures and departmental measures may be targeted, with the weights for gainsharing split between the two categories. Plans frequently require that an individual must exhibit satisfactory performance to receive the gainsharing payments.

Two older approaches similar to gainsharing exist. One, called *Improshare,* sets group piece-rate standards and pays weekly bonuses when those standards are exceeded. The other, the *Scanlon plan,* uses employee committees and passes on savings to the employees.

Gainsharing System of sharing with employees greater-than-expected gains in profits and/or productivity.

Group/Team Incentives and Information Sharing

Team incentives such as gainsharing programs provide money to be used as a cash bonus for employees based on cost savings from implementing employee ideas. The increased usage of employee-based knowledge in a gainsharing program may enhance organizational results, reduce production costs, and make other useful changes. For example, at one time, bonuses at IBM were based primarily on individual performance. The result was a number of "fiefdoms" that paralyzed information exchange. People would not share valuable information because "knowledge is power," so executive management changed compensation to a team-based model. The result was better information flow, which aided the growth of IBM in the decade that followed.[25]

ORGANIZATIONAL INCENTIVES

An organizational incentive system compensates all employees according to how well the organization as a whole performs during the year. The basic concept behind organizational incentive plans is that overall results may depend on organization-wide efforts and cooperation. The purpose of these plans is to produce better results by rewarding cooperation throughout the organization. For example, conflict between marketing and production can be overcome if management uses an incentive system that emphasizes organization-wide profit and productivity. To be effective, an organizational incentive program should include everyone from nonexempt employees to managers and executives. Two common organizational incentive systems are profit sharing and employee stock plans.

Profit Sharing

As the name implies, **profit sharing** distributes some portion of organizational profits to employees. One research study found that profit-sharing plans in small firms can help to enhance employee commitment and increase job-related performances of individuals.[26] The primary objectives of profit-sharing plans can include the following:

- Increase productivity and organizational performance
- Attract or retain employees
- Improve product/service quality
- Enhance employee morale

Typically, the percentage of the profits distributed to employees is set by the end of the year before distribution, although both timing and payment levels are considerations. In some profit-sharing plans, employees receive portions of the profits at the end of the year; in others, the profits are deferred, placed in a fund, and made available to employees on retirement or on their departure from the organization.[27] Figure 12-7 shows how profit-sharing plans can be funded and allocated. Often the level of profits is influenced by factors not under the employees' control, such as accounting decisions, marketing efforts, competition, and elements of executive compensation. In recent years, some labor unions have supported profit-sharing plans that tie employees' pay increases to improvements against broader organizational performance measures, not just the "bottom-line" numbers.

Profit sharing System to distribute a portion of the profits of an organization to employees.

| FIGURE 12-7 | Framework Choices for a Profit-Sharing Plan |

FUNDING CHOICES

- Fixed percentage of profits
- Sliding percentage based on sales or return assests
- Unit profits
- Some other formula

ALLOCATION CHOICES

- Equally to all employees
- Based on employee earnings
- Based on earnings or years of service
- Based on contribution and performance

Drawbacks of Profit-Sharing Plans When used throughout an organization, including with lower-level workers, profit-sharing plans can have some drawbacks. First, employees must trust that management will disclose accurate financial and profit information. As businesspeople know, both the definition and level of profit can depend on the accounting system used and on decisions made. To be credible, management must be willing to disclose sufficient financial and profit information to alleviate the skepticism of employees, particularly if profit-sharing levels fall from those of previous years. If profit-sharing communication is done well, employee pay satisfaction and commitment can be improved.[28] Second, profits may vary a great deal from year to year, resulting in windfalls or losses beyond the employees' control. Third, payoffs are generally far removed by time from employees' efforts; therefore, higher rewards may not be obviously linked to better performance.

Employee Stock Plans

Two types of organizational incentive plans use stock ownership in the organization to reward employees. The goal of these plans is to get employees to think and act like "owners."

A **stock option plan** gives employees the right to purchase a fixed number of shares of company stock at a specified exercise price for a limited period of time. If the market price of the stock exceeds the exercise price, employees can then exercise the option and buy the stock. The number of firms giving stock options to nonexecutives has declined in recent years, primarily due to changing laws and accounting regulations.

Stock option plan Plan that gives employees the right to purchase a fixed number of shares of company stock at a specified price for a limited period of time.

Employee stock ownership plan (ESOP) Plan designed to give employees significant stock ownership in their employers.

Employee Stock Ownership Plans Firms in many industries have an **employee stock ownership plan (ESOP)**, which is designed to give employees significant stock ownership in their employers. According to the National Center for Employee Ownership, an estimated 11,000 firms in the United States offer broad employee-ownership programs covering about 13 million workers.[29] Firms in many industries have ESOPs. For example, a clothing designer in New York, Eileen Fisher, has an ESOP for about 600 employees. The account was established when Fisher transferred about 30% of her total shares to the ESOP. Doing this gave her employees more incentive to enhance the performance of the firm, which hopefully would raise its stock value.[30]

Globally, employees stock purchase plans (ESPPs) are expanding in companies operating outside the United States. However, in some countries, such as Hong Kong, Austria, and the European Union, regulations are more limiting.[31]

Establishing an ESOP creates several advantages. The major one is that the firm can receive favorable tax treatment on the earnings earmarked for use in the ESOP. Another is that an ESOP gives employees a "piece of the action" so that they can share in the growth and profitability of their firm. Employee ownership may motivate employees to be more productive and focused on organizational performance.[32]

Many people approve of the concept of employee ownership as a kind of "people's capitalism." However, the sharing also can be a disadvantage for employees because it makes their wages/salaries and retirement benefits dependent on the performance of their employers. This concentration poses even greater risk for retirees because the value of pension fund assets is also dependent on how well the company does or does not perform.[33] The financial downturns, bankruptcies, and other travails of some firms in tough economic conditions have illustrated that an ESOP does not necessarily guarantee success for the employees who become investors.

Salespeople and executives are unique in many ways from other employees and their pay is different as well. Both of these types of employees are typically tied to variable pay incentives more than other employees. Therefore, a consideration of sales and executive pay follows.

LOGGING ON

myStockOptions.com
For tools to communicate with, educate, and train employees about stock options, visit this website at www.mystockoptions.com.

SALES COMPENSATION

The compensation paid to employees involved with sales and marketing is partly or entirely tied to individual sales performance. Salespeople who sell more products and services receive more total compensation than those who sell less. Sales incentives are perhaps the most widely used individual incentives. The intent is to stimulate more effort from salespeople so they earn more money.

Jobs in sales in many organizations have changed greatly in the last 20 years. Certainly the sales department is still responsible for bringing in revenue for a company, but today's customers have more choices and more information, and so the distribution of power has changed. Because of the pressure to make sales and the international environment in which competition is taking place, ethical issues have arisen in the sales area, as discussed in the HR Perspective.

Types of Sales Compensation Plans

Sales compensation plans can be of several general types, depending on the degree to which total compensation includes some variable pay tied to sales performance. A look at three general types of sales compensation and some challenges to sales compensation follows.

Salary Only Some companies pay salespeople only a salary. The *salary-only approach* is useful when an organization emphasizes serving and retaining

Ethical Concerns and Sales Compensation

Sales commission programs can effectively drive the behavior of sales representatives, especially if the sales performance measures are based wholly or mostly on sales volume and revenues. However, some sales incentives programs may encourage unethical behavior, particularly when compensation of sales representatives is based solely on commissions. For instance, there have been consistent reports that individuals in other countries buying major industrial equipment have received bribes or kickbacks from sales representatives. The bribes are paid from the incentives received by the sales representatives. This criticism may apply especially with major transactions that generate large revenues, such as aircraft contracts or large insurance coverage products.

One way of addressing sales compensation ethical issues uses a mixture of guaranteed base salary and lowered commission rates. Other approaches use other sales-related dimensions, such as customer service, repeat business, and customer satisfaction.

A key consideration for management is to have ongoing communications with sales professionals, so that the salespeople themselves can identify what is unfair or inappropriate in sales incentive plans. Also, it is important for salespeople to view a sales incentive plan as fair when they compare it to what other sales representatives are paid in relation to their own pay. Thus, numerous activities can influence ethical issues when developing and managing sales incentive plans.[34]

existing accounts over generating new sales and accounts. This approach is frequently used to protect the income of new sales representatives for a period of time while they are building up their clientele. Generally, the employer extends the salary-only approach for new sales representatives to no more than six months, at which point it implements one of the other systems discussed later in this section. Salespeople who want additional rewards often function less effectively in salary-only plans because they are less motivated to sell without additional performance-related compensation.

Straight Commission A widely used individual incentive system in sales jobs is the **commission**, which is compensation computed as a percentage of sales in units or dollars. Commissions are integrated into the pay given to sales workers in three common ways: straight commission, salary-plus-commission, and bonuses.

In the *straight commission system*, a sales representative receives a percentage of the value of the sales the person has made. Consider a sales representative working for a consumer products company who receives no compensation if that person makes no sales, but who receives a percentage of the total amount of all sales revenues that person has generated. The advantage of this system is that it requires the sales representative to sell in order to earn. The disadvantage is that it offers no security for the sales staff.

To offset this insecurity, some employers use a **draw** system, in which sales representatives can draw advance payments against future commissions. The amounts drawn are then deducted from future commission checks. Arrangements must be made for repayment of drawn amounts if individuals leave the organization before earning their draws in commissions.

Commission Compensation computed as a percentage of sales in units or dollars.

Draw Amount advanced against, and repaid from, future commissions earned by the employee.

Salary-Plus-Commission or Bonuses The form of sales compensation used most frequently is the *salary-plus-commission,* which combines the stability of a salary with the performance aspect of a commission. A common split is 80–20% or 70–30% salary to commission, although the split varies by industry and can be based on numerous other factors.[35] Some organizations also pay salespeople salaries and then offer bonuses that are a percentage of the base pay, tied to how well each employee meets various sales targets or other criteria. A related method is using *lump-sum bonuses,* which may lead to salespeople working more intensively to get more sales results than the package approach.[36]

Sales Compensation Challenges

Sales incentives work well, especially when they are tied to the broad strategic initiatives of the organization and its specific marketing and sales strategies. However, as economic and competitive changes have become more complex and shifted in nature, employers in many industries have faced challenges in their sales. Therefore, firms need to analyze more thoroughly their sales compensation costs, assess how the sales pay is increasing or decreasing performance efforts by employees, and then evaluate the extent to which the sales and profit goals are being met.[37] HR must be actively involved in meeting these challenges.

Technology and Sales Compensation Programs The last few years have seen the growth of sales compensation plans with different design features. Many of them are multitiered and can be rather complex. Selling over the Internet brings challenges to incentive compensation as well. Some sales organizations combine individual and group sales bonus programs. In these programs, a portion of sales incentive is linked to the attainment of group sales goals.

Internet-based software has helped employers administer programs and post results daily, weekly, or monthly. Salespeople can use this information to track their results. Administering incentives globally is difficult, but HR technology has helped as incentive management software has become widespread. These systems are advantageous because they can track the performance of numerous employees worldwide who may be covered by different incentive plans. Consider a company that has different product lines, geographic locations, and company subsidiaries, and imagine tracking the performance of hundreds or thousands of sales representatives for a sales incentive program. Or imagine manually tracking attendance, safety, and training incentives for firms with employees worldwide. The development of software systems to measure and record such things has been important in helping executives and managers support and manage their global sales forces more effectively.

MEASURE

Sales Performance Metrics Successfully using variable sales compensation requires establishing clear performance criteria and measures. Figure 12-8 shows some of the possible sales metrics. Generally, no more than three sales performance measures should be used in a sales compensation plan. Otherwise, sales commission plans can become too complex to motivate sales representatives.[38] On the other hand, some plans may be too simple, focusing only on the salesperson's pay, and not on wider organizational objectives. Many companies measure performance primarily by comparing

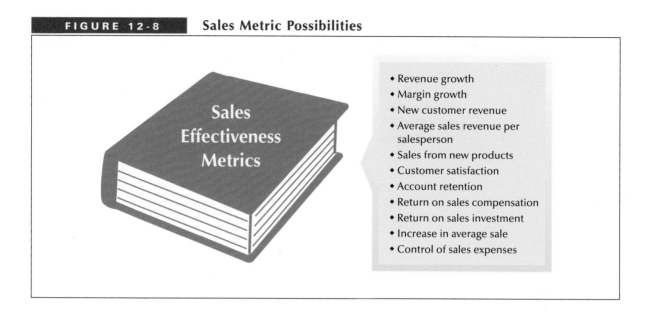

FIGURE 12-8   Sales Metric Possibilities

Sales Effectiveness Metrics

- Revenue growth
- Margin growth
- New customer revenue
- Average sales revenue per salesperson
- Sales from new products
- Customer satisfaction
- Account retention
- Return on sales compensation
- Return on sales investment
- Increase in average sale
- Control of sales expenses

an individual's sales revenue against established quotas. These plans would be better if the organizations used a variety of criteria, including total revenue, obtaining new revenue, and selling specific and new products or services.[39]

Effectiveness of Sales Incentive Plans So many organizations have sales incentive plans that it would be logical to think those plans are effective. However, many sales compensation plans are not seen as effective by either salespeople or managers and executives. One problem that can occur is constantly making too many changes in sales incentives, resulting in confusion by many people. Frequent changes reduce the effectiveness of plans and create problems with the sales representatives and managers. HR professionals may be involved in designing, revising, and communicating sales incentive plans, as well as responding to the complaints and concerns of sales representatives.

Effective sales incentives ideally should provide extra compensation for making sales, but sales managers warn that incentive systems will fail when an "entitlement culture" takes hold in the sales force. An entitlement culture is the idea that bonuses are *deferred salary* rather than extra pay for extra sales performance. When sales incentives designed to be extra pay for top performers become reliable paychecks on which everyone can count, entitlement has taken root and motivation drops.[40]

Failure to deal with incentive programs that no longer motivate salespeople causes variable costs (pay for performance) to actually become fixed costs (salary) from the perspective of the employer. Pay without performance, poor quota setting, and little difference in pay between top and bottom performers cause problems. Therefore, significant efforts are needed to establish and maintain effective sales incentive plans.

EXECUTIVE COMPENSATION

Most organizations administer compensation for executives somewhat differently than compensation for other employees. An executive typically is someone in the top two levels of an organization, such as Chief Executive Officer

(CEO), President, Senior Vice President, Chief Operating Officer, Executive Vice President, Chief Financial Officer, or Senior HR Executive. As HR has become more strategic and important, top HR executives also may be covered by executive compensation.

At the heart of most executive compensation plans is the idea that executives should be rewarded if the organization grows in profitability and value over a period of years. Therefore, variable pay distributed through different types of incentives is a significant part of executive compensation components in both U.S. and global organizations.

Changing worldwide economic conditions have influenced executive compensation throughout many jobs. In some firms, executive compensation has been frozen or reduced due to declining performance in the United States and globally. For example, a survey of U.S. companies identified that more than 60% were not planning to restore the executive pay levels, and about 40% were putting more emphasis on performance incentives.[41] In addition, criticisms of executive pay in U.S. firms have increased as plants have been closed, firms have gone bankrupt, and unemployment rates have increased. Undoubtedly, the major elements of executive compensation will continue to be part of how employers and HR address these concerns.

Elements of Executive Compensation

Because many executives are in high tax brackets, their compensation often is provided in ways that offer significant tax savings, which means that their total compensation packages may be more significant than just their base pay. Thus, executives often are interested in current compensation and the mix of items in the total package. Figure 12-9 illustrates the components of executive compensation packages.

Executive Salaries Salaries of executives vary by the type of job, size of organization, the industry, and other factors. In some organizations, particularly nonprofits, salaries often make up 90% or more of total compensation. In contrast, in large corporations, salaries may constitute less than half of the total package. Survey data on executive salaries are often reviewed by boards of directors to ensure that their organizations are competitive.

FIGURE 12-9   **Components of Executive Compensation Packages**

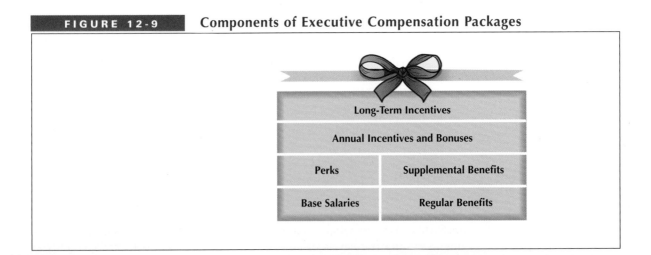

Executive Benefits Many executives are covered by *regular benefits plans* that are also available to nonexecutive employees, including traditional retirement, health insurance, and vacation plans. In addition, executives may receive *supplemental benefits* that other employees do not receive. For example, corporate-owned insurance on the life of the executive is popular; this insurance pays both the executive's estate and the company in the event of death. One supplemental benefit that has grown in popularity is company-paid financial planning for executives. Also, trusts of various kinds may be designed by the company to help executives deal with estate-planning and tax issues. *Deferred compensation* is another way of helping executives with tax liabilities caused by incentive compensation plans.

Executive Perquisites (Perks) In addition to the regular benefits received by all employees, perquisites often are received by executives. **Perquisites (Perks)** are special benefits—usually noncash items—for executives. Many executives value the status enhancement of these visible symbols, which allow the executives to be seen as "very important people" both inside and outside their organizations. Perks also can offer substantial tax savings because some of them are not taxed as income. Some commonly used executive perks are company cars, health club and country club memberships, first-class air travel, use of private jets, stress counseling, and chauffeur services.

Annual Executive Incentives and Bonuses Annual incentives and bonuses for senior managers and executives can be determined in several ways. One way is to use a discretionary system whereby the CEO and the board of directors decide bonuses; the absence of formal, measurable targets detracts significantly from this approach. Another way is to tie bonuses to specific measures, such as return on investment, earnings per share, and net profits before taxes. More complex systems create bonus pools and thresholds above which bonuses are computed. Whatever method is used, it is important to describe it so that executives attempting to earn additional compensation understand the plan; otherwise, the incentive effect will be diminished.

Long-Term Executive Performance Incentives Executive performance-based incentives tie executive compensation to the long-term growth and success of the organization. However, whether these incentives really emphasize the long term or merely represent a series of short-term rewards is controversial. Short-term rewards based on quarterly or annual performance may not result in the kind of long-run-oriented decisions necessary for the company to perform well over many years. As would be expected, the total amount of pay-for-performance incentives varies by management level, with CEOs receiving significantly more than subsidiary or other senior managers.

A *stock option* gives individuals the right to buy stock in a company, usually at an advantageous price. Various types of stock option plans are the most widely used executive incentive. A survey by Watson Wyatt identified that about two-thirds of companies granted stock equity awards to employees who were paid $100,000 to $125,000, and those who were paid higher amounts were given such participation opportunities also. Several types of stock option plans are used for executives, with *restricted stock options* becoming more prevalent. A *restricted stock option* indicates that company stock shares will be paid as a grant of shares to individuals, usually linked to achieving specific performance criteria.[42] Other types of stock options include *phantom stock*, *performance shares*, and other specialized technical forms that are beyond the scope of this discussion.

Perquisites (Perks) Special benefits—usually noncash items—for executives.

Despite the prevalence of such plans, research has found little relationship between providing CEOs with stock options and subsequent firm performance. The two items may not be closely linked in some firms. Because of the numerous corporate scandals involving executives at Enron, WorldCom, Tyco, and elsewhere who received outrageously high compensation due to stock options and the backdating of those options, the use of stock options has been changing. Also, the recent economic difficulties in the automobile, banking, financial, investment, manufacturing, and other industries have led to more governmental and regulatory oversight of these plans. One outcome of the corporate abuses by executives has been the passage of the Sarbanes–Oxley Act. This act has numerous provisions that have affected the accounting and financial reporting requirements of different types of executive compensation. Also, the Financial Accounting Standards Board (FASB) has adopted rules regarding the expensing of stock options and related types of executive compensation.

LOGGING ON

Graef Crystal: The Crystal Report
The Crystal Report evaluates executive compensation levels and issues. Visit the website at www.crystalreport.com.

GLOBAL

Global Executive Compensation

The expansion of global business by firms based in both the United States and other countries has raised executive compensation issues. Numerous executives have responsibilities for operations throughout the world, and they are compensated for those expanded responsibilities. However, senior executives in the United States continue to earn higher salaries than similar executives in other countries.

In the United States, critics of executive pay levels point out that many U.S. corporate CEOs have a ratio value of more than 350 times that of the average workers in their firms, while in Britain the ratio is 22, in Canada it is 20, and in Japan it is 11.[43] Even though executives in other countries often have lower base pay, they also may have valuable incentives at percentage rates similar to those of U.S. executives. However, in some global firms, long-term incentives may be reduced for foreign executives to be more similar to U.S. practices in their countries.[44] This example illustrates that global compensation programs for executives can be complex and extensive.

"Reasonableness" of Executive Compensation

The notion of providing monetary incentives that are tied to improved performance results makes sense to most people. However, in the United States, there is an ongoing debate about whether executive compensation, especially that of CEOs, is truly linked to performance. Given the astronomical amounts of some executive compensation packages, this concern is justified, as highlighted in the HR Perspective.

The reasonableness of executive compensation is often justified by comparison to compensation market surveys, but these surveys usually provide a range of compensation data that requires interpretation. One study found that a 60% increase in the U.S. CEO compensation over two decades could be linked to the market capital in large companies in that same period.[45] Despite this methodological analysis, there is continued concern about the overall levels of executive compensation. Some useful questions that have been suggested for determining whether executive pay is "reasonable" include the following:

- Would another company hire this person as an executive?
- How does the executive's compensation compare with that for executives in similar companies in the industry?

CEO Executives Overpaid?

HR perspective

The staggeringly large amounts of some annual compensation packages for executives have raised ethical questions. A primary question is whether any single CEO is really deserving of annual compensation totaling more than $20 million plus stock option profits, retirement bonuses, and other payments.

With the recent economic problems in the financial, banking, and related industries, many people have been angered to learn that a Goldman Corporation CEO received more than $50 million in pay, bonuses, and stock incentives, and that a former Merrill Lynch CEO received a $15 million signing bonus plus a pay package for several years valued at $50 to $120 million. In some nonfinancial firms, CEOs have received compensation totals ranging from $30 to $322 million per year!

Such compensation packages for executives have led many to question the ethical implications. A significant issue for both board members and governmental investigators is whether any single CEO is really deserving of compensation totaling more than $50 million when a range of executives are included in an organization.

As large as they are, these compensation packages provide little meaning unless they are put into context. If the company is doing well and performing better than competitors and above expectations, such packages *might* be justifiable to stockholders. But these large numbers have created increased emphases by legislators and regulators to change federal compensation rules regarding banks and some other industries.

Excluding the most highly paid executives from a survey of smaller companies, median total executive compensation has been found to be about $2.5 million.[46] Even at this level, the question that still must be addressed by boards of directors, stockholders, and executives is this: How realistic is it to provide an amount to one person, when other managers and executives contribute to organizational performance and do not receive such payouts? Is company performance really dependent on one person's performance? What do you think?

- Is the executive's pay consistent with pay for other employees within the company?
- What would an investor pay for the level of performance of the executive?

Link between Executive Compensation and Corporate Performance

Of all the executive compensation issues that have been raised, the one that is discussed most frequently is whether executive compensation levels, especially for CEOs, are sufficiently linked to organizational performance. Board members of some organizations have viewed CEO compensation as not being as closely linked to performance as needed, resulting in CEO total compensation being seen as too high.[47]

The most important reason for giving pay as incentives is that it is thought to be effective in motivating employees and increasing corporate performance and stock values. Another common reason for using variable compensation is related to the ability to attract and keep employees. These reasons apply to executives as well as to other employees. But in order for compensation based on these reasons to be effective, executive compensation packages must be linked to performance.

One key aspect in evaluating this topic is the performance measures used. In many settings, financial measures such as return on equity, return to shareholders, earnings per share, and net income before taxes are used to measure performance. However, a number of firms also incorporate nonfinancial organizational measures of performance when determining executive bonuses and incentives. Customer satisfaction, employee satisfaction, market share, productivity, and quality are other areas measured for executive performance rewards.

Measurement of executive performance varies from one employer to another. Some executive compensation packages use a short-term focus of one year, which may lead to large rewards for executive performance in a given year even though corporate performance over a multiyear period is mediocre, especially if the yearly measures are not carefully chosen. Executives may manipulate earnings per share due to stock-based incentives by selling assets, liquidating inventories, or reducing research and development expenditures.[48] All of these actions may make organizational performance look better in the short run but impair the long-term growth of the organization.

A number of other executive compensation issues and concerns exist. Figure 12-10 highlights some of the criticisms and counterarguments in regard to executive compensation.

One of the more controversial issues is that some executives seem to get large awards for negative actions. It seems contradictory to some to reward executives who improve corporate results by cutting staff, laying off employees, changing pension plans, or increasing the deductible on the health insurance, although sometimes cost-cutting measures are necessary to keep a company afloat. However, a sense of reasonableness must be maintained. If rank-and-file employees suffer, giving bonuses and large payouts to executives appears counterproductive and even hypocritical.

Compensation committee
Subgroup of the board of directors that is composed of directors who are not officers of the firm.

Executive Compensation and Boards of Directors In most organizations, the board of directors is the major policy-setting entity and must approve executive compensation packages. Corporate directors receive compensation for board and committee meetings and other activities.[49] The **compensation committee**

FIGURE 12-10   Common Executive Compensation Criticisms

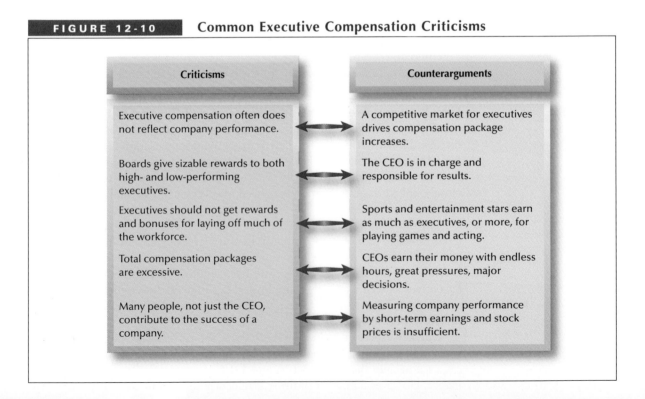

Criticisms	Counterarguments
Executive compensation often does not reflect company performance.	A competitive market for executives drives compensation package increases.
Boards give sizable rewards to both high- and low-performing executives.	The CEO is in charge and responsible for results.
Executives should not get rewards and bonuses for laying off much of the workforce.	Sports and entertainment stars earn as much as executives, or more, for playing games and acting.
Total compensation packages are excessive.	CEOs earn their money with endless hours, great pressures, major decisions.
Many people, not just the CEO, contribute to the success of a company.	Measuring company performance by short-term earnings and stock prices is insufficient.

usually is a subgroup of the board of directors that is composed of directors who are not officers of the firm. A compensation committee generally makes recommendations to the board of directors on overall pay policies, salaries for top officers, supplemental compensation such as stock options and bonuses, and additional perquisites for executives.

One major concern voiced by many critics is that the base pay and bonuses of CEOs are often set by the members of board compensation committees, many of whom are CEOs or executives of other companies with similar compensation packages. Also, the compensation advisors and consultants to the CEOs often collect large fees, and critics charge that those fees distort the objectivity of the advice given.

To counter criticism, some corporations have changed the composition of the compensation committees by taking actions such as prohibiting "insider" company officers from serving on them. Also, some firms have empowered the compensation committees to hire and pay compensation consultants without involving executive management. Finally, better disclosure can provide the board with a fuller picture of a chief's entire compensation package.

SUMMARY

- Variable pay, also called incentives, is compensation that can be linked to individual, group/team, and/or organizational performance.
- Effective variable pay plans fit both business strategies and organizational cultures, appropriately award actions, and are administered properly.
- Metrics for measuring the success of variable pay plans are crucial.
- Piece-rate and bonus plans are the most commonly used individual incentives.
- The design of group/team variable pay plans must consider how the incentives are to be distributed, the timing of the incentive payments, and who will make decisions about the variable payout.
- Organization-wide rewards include profit sharing and stock ownership plans.

- Sales employees may have their compensation tied to performance on a number of criteria. Sales compensation can be provided as salary only, commission only, or salary-plus-commission or bonuses.
- Measuring the effectiveness of sales incentive plans is a challenge that may require the plans to be adjusted based on success metrics.
- Executive compensation must be viewed as a total package composed of salaries, bonuses, benefits, perquisites (perks), and both short- and long-term performance-based incentives.
- Performance-based incentives often represent a significant portion of an executive's compensation package.
- A compensation committee, which is a subgroup of the board of directors, generally has authority over executive compensation plans.

CRITICAL THINKING ACTIVITIES

1. Discuss why variable pay-for-performance plans have become popular and what elements are needed to make them successful.

2. Give examples of individual incentives used by an organization in which you were employed, and then describe why those plans were or were not successful.

3. Describe the nature and components of, and the issues currently facing, executive compensation in various U.S. industries.

4. Suppose you have been asked to lead a taskforce to develop a sales incentive plan at your firm. The taskforce is to generate a list of strategies and issues to be evaluated by upper management. Using details from www.salescompensation.org and other related websites, identify and develop preliminary materials for the taskforce.

HR EXPERIENTIAL PROBLEM SOLVING

Your insurance company needs to update the sales incentive program for its sales/marketing representatives. Due to growth in the volume and diversity of the products being sold, the existing system of having one incentive program for all sales marketers no longer meets the needs of the company. To maximize sales in each of the product lines, the system needs to provide an incentive and reward system to encourage employees to focus on their specific product lines while also cross-marketing the company's portfolio of other products. To identify the key facets of a sales commission program, visit websites including www.8020salesperformance .com/sales_compensation.html.

1. Would a compensation program that offered only commission work for your company? Why or why not?
2. What other incentives would assist the company in motivating the sales staff?

CASE

Sodexo Incentives

Many employers offer incentives to employees working in different jobs. Often, the incentives are to reward employee performance, both in the short and the long term. But some company incentive plans are viewed negatively by employees, while others are seen as highly positive by employees at all levels.

One firm that has a well-regarded, broad-based incentive plan is Sodexo, a large food and facilities service firm with more than 350,000 employees in 80 countries. Being such a large firm, Sodexo has a variety of clients, including many corporate and governmental entities, hospitals, manufacturing firms, and universities. Thus, the firm's client services are varied, with many of them being basic ones such as cleaning offices, maintenance of all types of facilities, doing landscaping, and managing other basic and professional activities. In North America, including the United States, Sodexo has almost 125,000 staff members. More than 40,000 of the North American staff members work in health care, including clinics, offices, and hospital sites.

Being such a large firm with employees doing many different types of jobs, a key part of Sodexo's organizational and HR cultures involves engaging its employees in many ways. One aspect is having a widely based employee rewards program containing recognition and incentives. The company's "Spirit of Sodexo" program focuses on three general-award facets: service, teamwork, and progress. To operate this program, the company has required executives, including the top HR officer, to develop processes for the nomination of employees who make significant contributions, locally and regionally, as well as in business and corporate divisions of the firm.

Some of the recognitions and awards provided to employees are interesting. Because the biggest division of workers is in health care locations, a special incentive program called Sodexo CARES has been used for several years for employees who accomplish especially unique results. At one hospital, a small group of dieticians developed a new system for ordering medication and devices online, something that is not done in most hospitals. These dieticians received recognition and incentive awards for their job-related accomplishments.

Another incentive reward for exceptional efforts went to a female employee who worked as a food caterer and prepared special meals for a young foreign hospital patient who had difficulty eating typical U.S. foods. The employee home-cooked various items for that patient when the patient had surgery. Her efforts were increasingly recognized throughout Sodexo, and she received a national incentive award. Both she and her husband attended a national meeting in a different city where she was recognized and became the subject of a short video. She also received a $500 gift card and a lot of publicity.

Numerous other examples exist showing how Sodexo uses employee incentives as part of its culture in many different industry jobs. To learn more about Sodexo and its organizational and HR culture, go to www.sodexo.com. The overall picture of such widely focused incentive recognition efforts illustrates how incentives can significantly influence the motivation and performance of employees.[50]

both the culture and employee retention efforts in a firm.

QUESTIONS

1. Based on the Sodexo example, discuss the importance of widespread incentives in improving

2. How might having employees receive recognition and incentives at a national level impact the performance of their coworkers and colleagues?

SUPPLEMENTAL CASES

Cash Is Good, Card Is Bad

Both the positive and negative issues associated with the use of an incentive plan are discussed in this case. (For the case, go to www.cengage .com/management/mathis.)

Incentive Plans for Fun and Travel

This case discusses incentive plans that stimulate employee interest and motivate them to perform well. (For the case, go to www.cengage .com/management/mathis.)

NOTES

1. Based on David J. Cichelli and Angie Keller, "Cox Communications Tackles Central vs. Local Compensation Design," *Workspan*, September 2007, 53–56.
2. Allison Avalos, "Salary Budget Increases," *Workspan*, September 2009, 27–30.
3. M. Rush Benton, "Hope Is Not a Business Strategy . . ." *Investment News*, June 1, 2009, 1.
4. Bruce Ellig, "What Pay for Performance Should Measure," *WorldatWork Journal*, Second Quarter, 2008, 64–75.
5. Brad Hill and Christine Tande, "Incentive Pay: Short-Term Change Agent or Long-Term Success?" *Workspan*, September 2009, 61–64.
6. Ken Abosch, "The Past, Present, and Future of Variable Pay," *Workspan*, July 2009, 27–30.
7. Eric Chapman, "Where Executive and Employee Compensation Is Headed in the Next 12 Months," *Workspan*, July 2009, 23–25; Robert J. Fulton, Jr., "How Do Professional Services Firms Tie Pay to Performances?" *Dear Workforce Newsletter*, April 30, 2009, www .workforce.com.
8. Based on Susan Lackey, "Fill Those Unpopular Shifts," *HR Magazine*, April 2009, 63–66.
9. Jinyu He and Heli C. Wang, "Innovative Knowledge Assets and

Economic Performance," *Academy of Management Journal*, 52 (2009), 919–938.
10. M. J. Gibbs, et al., "Performance Measure Properties and Incentive System Design," *Industrial Relations*, 48 (2009), 237–264.
11. Ken Abosch, et al., "Broad-Based Variable Pay Goes Global," *Workspan*, 56–62.
12. Tyler Gentry and Karl Glotzbach, "Incentives Without Borders," *The Power of Incentives*, 2007, 77–82.
13. Leo Jakobson, "$46 Billion Spent on Incentives," *Incentive*, November 2007, 27–28.
14. Chris Silva, "An Incentive to Provide Incentives," *Employee Benefit News*, May 2007, 11–12.
15. Michael Marino and Steve Van Putter, "Four Cardinal Directions for Navigating Incentive Design in Uncertain Times," *Workspan*, December 2008, 57–61.
16. Patricia K. Zinghelm and Jay R. Schuster, "Revisiting Effective Incentive Design," *WorldatWork Journal*, First Quarter, 2005, 50–58.
17. Scott A. Jeffrey, "Justifiability and the Motivational Power of Tangible Noncash Incentive," *Human Performance*, 22 (2009), 143–155.
18. Peter A. Lupo, "Keep It Simple," *Workspan*, October 2009, 65–68.
19. Jean VanRensselar, "Designing an Incentive Program for Non-

Sales Employees," *The Power of Incentives*, 2007, 87–96.
20. Bonnie Schindler, "Understanding Private Company Incentive Pay Practices," *Workspan*, March 2008, 43–48; Dan Kleinman, "Getting Our Bonus Expectations Right," *Workspan*, July 2009, 75–76.
21. Christopher Cabera, "Non-Cash Rewards . . .," *Workspan*, July 2008, 25–26.
22 Leo Jakobson, "Don't Show Me the Money," *Incentive*, September 2009, 14–19.
23. Rebecca R. Hastings, "Length-of-Service Awards Becoming More Personal," *HR Magazine Supplement on SHRM's 2009 HR Trend Book*, www.shrm.org, 43–48.
24. Robert Masternak, "Gainsharing and Lean-Six Sigma—Perfect Together," *WorldatWork Journal*, First Quarter, 2005, 44–49.
25. M. W. Van Alstyne, "Create Colleagues Not Competitors," *Harvard Business Review*, September 2005, 24–28.
26. A. Bayo-Moriones and M. Larraa-Kintana, "Profit-Sharing Plans and Affective Commitment," *Human Resource Management*, March–April 2009, 207–226.
27. "In Depth Profit Sharing: Share Peace of Mind," *Employee Benefits Magazine*, January 2006, 42.

28. Christina Sweins and Panu Kalmi, "Pay Knowledge, Pay Satisfaction, and Employee Commitment," *Human Resource Management Journal*, 18 (2008), 366–385.

29. *A Statistical Profile of Employee Ownership*, February 2009, www.nceo.org.

30. Theo Francis, "Inside Eileen Fisher's Employee Stock Plan," *The Wall Street Journal*, January 22, 2007, B3.

31. Jennifer Kirk, "Employee Stock Purchase Programs Go Global," *Workspan*, July 2008, 10–12.

32. "How an Employee Ownership Plan (ESOP) Works," *National Center for Employee Ownership*, 2009, www.nceo.org.

33. Jim Hein and Michael Enos, "Navigating Underwater Stock Options," *Workspan*, May 2009, 28–33.

34. Based on Chad Albrecht, "Sales Compensation and the Fairness Question," *Workspan*, August 2009, 16–20.

35. For details on survey results, see *Sales Compensation Practices 2008* (Scottsdale, AZ: WorldatWork, 2008), 8.

36. Thomas J. Steenburgh, "Effort or Timing: The Effect of Lump-Sum Bonuses," *QuantMarkEcon*, 6 (2008), 235–256.

37. Andris A. Zoltners, et al., "Sales Force Effectiveness," *Journal of Personal Selling and Sales Management*, 28 (2008), 115–131; Tom Knight and Mark Masson, "Compensation Planning for a Down Economy," *Workspan*, May 2008, 78–83.

38. Jerry Colletti and Mary S. Fiss, "Five Common Flaws in Sales Compensation Formula Design and How to Address Them," *Colletti-Fiss, LLC*, 2008.

39. Jim Stoeckman, "Change of the Horizon: An Analysis of Sales Compensation Practices," *Workspan*, April 2007, 41–43.

40. D. Bello and S. Barnes, "The Sales-Incentive Entitlement Culture," *Workspan*, August 2006, 40–43.

41. Stephen Miller, "Most Companies Not Ready to Restore Executive Pay Cuts," *HR Disciplines*, October 12, 2009, www.shrm.org.

42. For details, go to *Watson-Wyatt Data Services Long-Term Incentive Database*, 2008, www.watsonwyatt.com; David Seitz, "The Tide Is Shifting: LTI Developments in the United States," *Workspan*, July 2008, 41–50.

43. For details, go to www.standardand-poors.com.

44. Peter Acker and John Cummings, "What in the World Is Happening with Long-Term Incentives?" *Workspan*, September 2008, 64–68.

45. Xavier Gabaix and Augustin Landier, "Why Has CEO Pay Increased So Much?" *Quarterly Journal of Economics*, February 2008, 49–98.

46. Based on Robert J. Grossman, "Executive Pay: Perception and Reality," *HR Magazine*, April 2009, 26–32; Aaron Lucchetti, et al., "Fed Hits Banks with Sweeping Pay Limits," *The Wall Street Journal*, October 23, 2009, A1ff.

47. Steven N. Kaplan, "Are U.S. CEOs Overpaid?" *Academy of Management Perspectives*, May 2008, 5–20; Edward Lawler III and David Finegold, "CEO Compensation: What Board Members Think," *WorldatWork Journal*, Third Quarter, 2007, 38–47.

48. Xiamoneg Zhang, et al., "CEOs on the Edge: Earnings Manipulation and Stock-Based Incentives," *Academy of Management Journal*, 51 (2008), 241–258.

49. "Compensation for Corporate Directors Rose Modestly in 2008," *Towers-Perrin Monitor*, October, 2009, www.towersperrin.com.

50. Based on information from news releases and information at www.sodexo.com; Alex Palmer, "Their Real Award Winners," *Incentive*, July 2009, 16–20; Mark Schoeff, Jr., "Sodexo—2008 Winner Service," *Workforce Management*, October 20, 2008, 23.

13

Managing Employee Benefits

After you have read this chapter, you should be able to:

- Define a benefit and identify four strategic benefits considerations.

- Summarize why benefits management and communications efforts are important.

- Distinguish between mandated and voluntary benefits and list three examples of each.

- Explain the importance of managing the costs of health benefits and identify some methods of doing so.

- Discuss the shift of retirement plans from defined-benefit to defined-contribution and cash balance programs.

- Describe the growth of financial, family-oriented, and time-off benefits and their importance to many employees.

Behavioral Economics Guides Benefits Administration

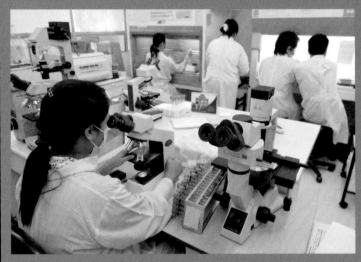

(JAY DIRECTO/AFP/Getty Images)

Research shows that employees do not always make the right choices about how to use the benefits provided to them by their employers. In fact, employees' behaviors can be outright counterproductive and counterintuitive when it comes to taking advantage of benefits programs. As a result, the benefit portfolios are less likely to improve employees' opinions of the organization and, more importantly, less likely to enhance individual well-being. Many top managers have become highly interested in the psychological and behavioral aspects of benefits administration, and the field of behavioral economics. This field, which assumes that people are consistently irrational, is growing dramatically in the human resource management arena.

Many companies are starting to incorporate elements of behavioral economics (rewards, punishments, peer pressure, etc.) in the management of employee benefits. For instance, companies such as Lowe's participate in a program called Select Home Delivery, which provides employees mail-order pharmacy benefits and home delivery. In order to protect individuals from making poor health care decisions, employees must opt out of the program if they want to fill prescriptions at local pharmacies. Other companies such as Abbott Laboratories use a program called Know Your Numbers, which encourages individuals to evaluate their personal health compared to certain benchmarks.[1]

FIGURE 13-1 **Employer Compensation and Benefits Costs per Hour**

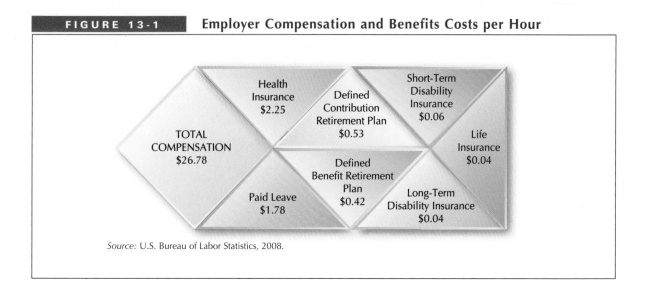

Source: U.S. Bureau of Labor Statistics, 2008.

An employer provides benefits to workers for being part of the organization. A **benefit** is an indirect reward given to an employee or group of employees for organizational membership. Benefits often include retirement plans, vacations with pay, health insurance, educational assistance, and many more programs.

In the United States, employers often fill the role of major provider of benefits for citizens. In many other nations, citizens and employers are taxed to pay for government-provided benefits, such as health care and retirement programs. Although federal regulations require U.S. employers to provide certain benefits, U.S. employers voluntarily provide many others.

Benefits are costly for the typical U.S. employer, averaging from 30% to 40% of payroll expenses. In highly unionized manufacturing and utility industries, they may be over 70% of payroll. Figure 13-1 shows the per-hour costs employers expend for average wages and salary amounts, as well as different types of benefits, as reported by *BenefitsMarketplace*. Health insurance represents the largest percentage of total compensation (7.9%) and is the most costly for the average employer, followed by paid leave (7.0%), defined-benefit retirement plans (2.6%), and defined-contribution retirement plans (1.8%). Notice that of the average total compensation of $26.86, employers are paying $8.04 for benefits, 25% of which are for health insurance benefits.[2] Surveys conducted nationally and in various states indicate that the costs of benefits are increasing, sometimes faster than inflationary rates, causing some organizations to require employees to help pay for these benefits.[3] These numbers illustrate why benefits have become a strategic concern in HR management.

Benefit An indirect reward given to an employee or group of employees for organizational membership.

BENEFITS AND HR STRATEGY

In the United States, a challenge for employers is how to best manage the balancing act between the growing costs of benefits and the use of those benefits in accomplishing organizational goals. For instance, organizations can choose to compete for or retain employees by providing different levels of base compensation, variable pay, and benefits. Indeed, several recent surveys determined that while the lagging economy caused organizations to downsize or cut various programs, some companies have remained focused on benefits, exploring new benefits options and adopting a more comprehensive approach to compensation management.[4] This is why benefits should be looked at as a vital part of the total rewards "package" when determining organizational strategies regarding compensation.

The benefits approach chosen to be part of total rewards depends on many factors, such as workforce competition, organizational life cycle, and corporate strategic approach. For example, a relatively new technology firm may choose to have slightly lower base pay and use highly variable incentives to attract new employees, but keep the cost of benefits as low as possible for a while. Or an organization that hires predominantly female employees might choose a family-friendly set of benefits, such as child-care assistance, to attract and retain employees, but offer little variable pay and only market-level base pay.

The reasons why employers offer benefits are multifaceted and tie into strategic considerations. As Figure 13-2 indicates, there are several aspects to looking at benefits strategically.

Benefits as Competitive Advantage

It is important that benefits be used to help create and maintain competitive advantages.[5] Benefits should not be viewed entirely as cost factors because they can positively affect HR efforts. Given the intense competition for competent workers, companies should consider investing in benefits packages that are attractive for those employees. Recent research indicates that company benefits are linked to individual job satisfaction in the United States.[6] Despite this finding, evidence also suggests that benefits do not always meet the needs of both employers and workers, so more efforts are needed to successfully position benefits as a driver of employee relations.[7]

FIGURE 13-2   **Strategic Benefits Considerations**

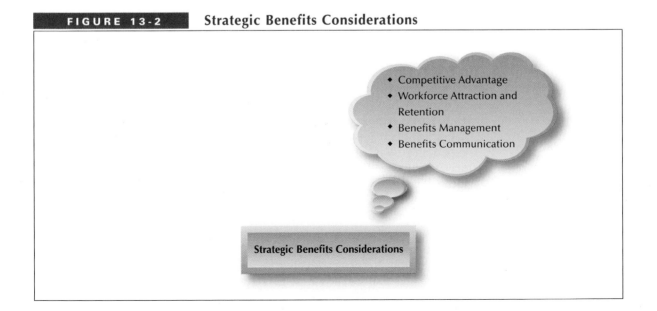

- Competitive Advantage
- Workforce Attraction and Retention
- Benefits Management
- Benefits Communication

Strategic Benefits Considerations

Employers may offer benefits to aid recruiting and retention, impact organizational performance, and meet legal requirements. Also, some employers see benefits as reinforcing the company philosophy of social and corporate citizenship. Employers that provide good benefits are viewed more positively within a community and the industry by customers, civic leaders, current employees, and workers in other firms. Conversely, employers who are seen as skimping on benefits, cutting benefits, or taking advantage of workers may be viewed more negatively. A list of excellent employers indicated that companies such as Google and Genentech offered innovative benefits including healthy workplace initiatives, work-family balance programs, and sabbaticals, and these benefits have increased profitability and retention.[8]

Another company that has used benefits as part of a total rewards strategy is Jackson's Food Stores, based in Idaho, with 87 stores. The firm has expanded its variable pay and benefits package for both full-time and part-time employees. Consequently, employee retention has increased, which has resulted in better customer service and enhanced organizational results. Other firms such as Howalt-McDowell Insurance, ITA Group, and Argon ST have been recognized for offering benefits packages that have enhanced several components of organizational performance.[9]

The primary reasons executives see for offering benefits is to attract and retain talent and meet responsibilities to employees. According to a survey by an international consulting firm, 48% of executives see benefits as extremely important to a company's competitive effectiveness and another 41% saw benefits as somewhat important. This survey and others confirm that benefits are viewed by both employers and employees as a part of being an "employer of choice" when attracting and retaining individuals.[10]

GLOBAL

Global Benefits Benefits vary from country to country. In many countries, retirement, health, and other benefits are provided as part of government services. Employers are taxed heavily to pay into government funds that cover the benefits. This model is very different from the one in the United States, where most benefits are provided by employers directly.

Retirement and pension systems are provided by the government in many countries as well. National pension programs in Germany, France, and Japan, among other countries, are facing significant financial pressures due to their aging workforces and populations. Such challenges also face the Social Security and Medicare systems in the United States.

Health care benefits also differ significantly worldwide. Many countries, including Great Britain and Canada, have national health services. Some global firms require employees to use the medical services available from host countries, whereas other global employers provide special coverage that allows expatriates to receive health care from private providers. Arranging quality private coverage becomes an especially important issue for global employees located in various underdeveloped countries where the availability and quality of medical facilities and treatment vary widely.

The amount of leave and vacation time also vary significantly around the globe. Of all of the major countries, only the United States, Australia, and Ethiopia do not provide paid leave for new parents. Additionally, the annual leave/vacation in European countries averages 36 days per year, whereas the United States and Canada average about 10 to 12 days, the lowest amounts

LOGGING ON

International Society of Certified Employee Benefit Specialists (ISCEBS)

For information on benefit program research surveys, visit the ISCEBS website at www.iscebs.org/surveys.

of annual vacation leave among developed countries. These examples illustrate the benefits challenges faced by firms that have employees located in different countries.[11] How these challenges are handled impacts global attraction of employees for the international employers.

Role of Benefits for Workforce Attraction and Retention

As stated previously, benefits can influence employees' decisions about which particular employer to work for, whether to stay with or leave an employer, and when to retire. What benefits are offered, the competitive level of benefits, and how those benefits are viewed by individuals all affect employee attraction and retention efforts of employers. An additional concern is that the composition of the U.S. workforce is changing, and expectations about benefits by different generations of employees are affecting benefit decisions.[12] For instance, many baby boomers who are approaching retirement age are concerned about retirement benefits and health care, while the younger generation of workers is more interested in flexible and portable benefits. However, all generations have concerns about the nature of and changes in health insurance. Having benefits plans that appeal to the different groups is vital to attracting and retaining all different types of employees.

A major advantage of benefits is that they generally are not taxed as income to employees. For this reason, benefits represent a somewhat more valuable reward to employees than an equivalent cash payment. For example, if employees categorized in a 25% tax bracket earn an extra $400 working on a special team project, they must pay $100 in taxes on this amount (disregarding exemptions). But if their employer provides prescription drug coverage in a benefits plan, and they receive the $400 as payments for prescription drugs, they are not taxed on the amount, and they receive the entire value of $400, not just $300. This feature makes benefits a desirable form of compensation to employees if they understand the value provided by the benefits.

BENEFITS MANAGEMENT AND COMMUNICATIONS

Based on the strategic benefits decisions made, benefits programs must be designed, administered, measured, and communicated. Figure 13-3 highlights the key components of effective benefits management.

Benefits Design

Benefits plans can provide flexibility and choices for employees, or they can be standardized for all employees. Increasingly, employers are finding that providing employees with some choices and flexibility allows individuals to tailor their benefits to their own situations. However, the more choices available, the higher the administrative demands placed on organizations.[13] A number of key decisions are part of benefits design:

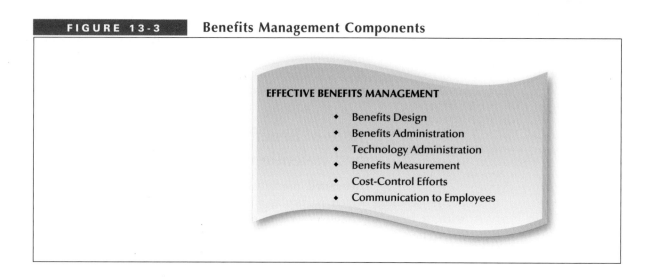

FIGURE 13-3   **Benefits Management Components**

EFFECTIVE BENEFITS MANAGEMENT

- Benefits Design
- Benefits Administration
- Technology Administration
- Benefits Measurement
- Cost-Control Efforts
- Communication to Employees

- How much total compensation, including benefits, can be provided?
- What part of the total compensation of individuals should benefits constitute?
- Which employees should be provided which benefits?
- What expense levels are acceptable for each benefit offered?
- What is being received by the organization in return for each benefit?
- How flexible should the package of benefits be?

Part-Time Employee Benefits Another key design issue is whether or not to provide benefits coverage to part-time employees. Many employers do not provide part-time employee benefits, except some time-off leave benefits. According to data from the U.S. Bureau of Labor Statistics, about one-fourth of part-time workers are involved in company retirement plans, and a minority of them is eligible for health care benefits.[14] Part-time employees who do receive benefits usually do so in proportion to the percentage of full-time work they provide. Companies such as Barnes and Noble, Whole Foods, and Starbucks have been recognized as exceptional employers because they offer various benefits to part-time workers.[15]

Flexible Benefits As mentioned, as part of both benefits design and administration, many employers offer employees choices for benefits. A **flexible benefits plan** allows employees to select the benefits they prefer from groups of benefits established by the employer. Sometimes called a *flex plan* or *cafeteria plan*, these plans have a variety of "dishes," or benefits, available so that each employee can select an individual combination of benefits within some overall limits.

As a result of the changing composition of the workforce, flexible benefits plans have grown in popularity. Flexible benefits systems recognize that individual employee situations differ because of age, family status, and lifestyle. For instance, dual-career couples may not want the same benefits from two different employers. Under a flex plan, one of them can forgo some benefits that are available in the partner's plan and take other benefits instead.

Flexible benefits plan
Program that allows employees to select the benefits they prefer from groups of benefits established by the employer.

A problem with flexibility in benefits choice is that an *inappropriate benefits package* may be chosen by an employee. A young construction worker may not choose a disability benefit, but if that person is injured, the family may suffer financial hardship. Part of this problem can be overcome by requiring employees to select a core set of benefits (life, health, and disability insurance) and then offering options on other benefits.

Another problem can be **adverse selection** by employees, whereby *only* higher-risk employees select and use certain benefits. For example, only employees with chronic illnesses might choose health insurance. Because insurance plans are based on a group rate, the employer may face higher rates if insufficient numbers of healthy employees select an insurance option.

Because many flexible plans have become so complex, they require more administrative time and information systems to track the different choices made by employees. Despite the disadvantages, flex plans will likely continue to grow in popularity.

HR and Benefits Administration

With the myriad of benefits, it is easy to see why many organizations must make coordinated efforts to administer benefits programs. Figure 13-4 shows how benefits administration responsibilities can be split between HR specialists and operating managers. HR specialists play the more significant role, but managers must assume responsibility for some of the communication aspects of benefits administration.

Adverse selection Situation in which *only* higher-risk employees select and use certain benefits.

One significant trend affecting HR is that outsourcing of benefits administration may be necessary. A sizable majority of corporations in one study indicated that they were outsourcing more benefits functions.[16] The most frequently outsourced item is Employee Assistance Plans. Administrative activities related to retiree benefits, 401(k) plans, and flexible spending accounts also are often outsourced.

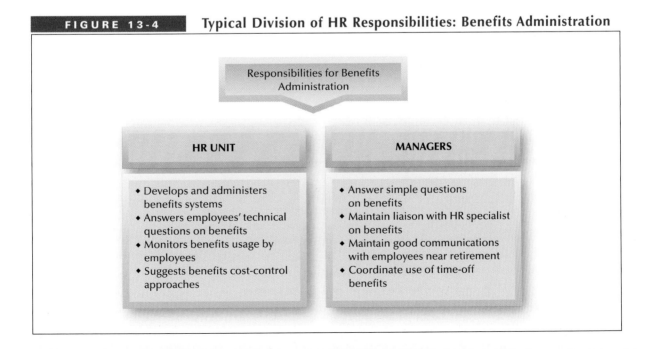

FIGURE 13-4   **Typical Division of HR Responsibilities: Benefits Administration**

Responsibilities for Benefits Administration

HR UNIT	MANAGERS
• Develops and administers benefits systems • Answers employees' technical questions on benefits • Monitors benefits usage by employees • Suggests benefits cost-control approaches	• Answer simple questions on benefits • Maintain liaison with HR specialist on benefits • Maintain good communications with employees near retirement • Coordinate use of time-off benefits

HR Technology and Benefits

The spread of HR technology, particularly Internet-based systems, has significantly changed the benefits administration time and activities for HR staff members. Internet and computer-based systems are being used to communicate benefits information, conduct employee benefits surveys, and facilitate benefits administration. Recent research shows that these systems can decrease expenses, increase positive communication, and effectively connect people across many different HR functions, including benefits management.[17]

Information technology allows employees to change their benefits choices, track their benefits balances, and submit questions to HR staff members and external benefits providers. Some systems such as Workday provide prepackaged connections with benefits providers so that information technology requirements are minimized. Use of the Internet for benefits enrollment has increased significantly in a three-year period. The greatest use has been to allow employees to sign up for, change, or update their benefits choices through Web-based systems. Previously, HR departments had to send out paper forms, hold numerous benefits meetings, and answer many phone calls from employees. The switch to online enrollment and communications has led to reductions in HR staff and benefits administration costs. Interest in virtual benefits fairs is also increasing because information about available services can be delivered more conveniently to employees. Finally, as part of the recent stimulus plan's push for electronic health documents, many companies such as Wal-Mart, Intel, BP, and IBM are using digitized employee health records and information to facilitate individual wellness management.[18] These efforts should all serve to streamline the efforts required to deliver benefits to employees.

MEASURE

Benefits Measurement

The significant costs associated with benefits require that analyses be conducted to determine the payoffs for the benefits. With the wide range of benefits that are offered, numerous HR metrics can be used.[19] Some examples are shown in Figure 13-5.

Other metrics are used to measure the return on the expenditures for various benefits programs provided by employers. Some common benefits that employers track using HR metrics are workers' compensation, wellness

---

FIGURE 13-5   **Common Benefits Metrics**

COMMON BENEFITS METRICS

- Benefits as a percentage of payroll (pattern over a multiyear period)
- Benefits expenditures per full-time-equivalent (FTE) employee
- Benefits costs by employee group (full-time vs. part-time, union vs. nonunion, management, professional, technical, office, etc.)
- Benefits administration costs (including staff time multiplied by the staff pay and benefits costs per hour)
- Health care benefits costs per participating employee

programs, prescription drug costs, leave time, tuition aid, and disability insurance. The overriding point is that both benefits expenditures generally, and costs for individual benefits specifically, need to be measured and evaluated as part of strategic benefits management.

Benefits Cost Control

Because benefits expenditures have risen significantly in the past few years, particularly for health care, employers are focusing more attention on measuring and controlling benefits costs, even reducing or dropping benefits offered to employees. For example, Goodyear Tire & Rubber cut contributions to employee 401(k) accounts in 2003, and while the company recently reimplemented a modest 401(k) match program, it halted some pension programs. Likewise, General Motors, Sears Holdings, and Eastman Kodak have initiated cutbacks to retirement benefits.[20]

Another common means of benefits cost control is cost sharing, which refers to having employees pay for more of their benefits costs. Almost 60% of firms use this means. The next three means of health care cost control are using wellness programs, adding employee health education efforts, and changing prescription drug programs. Sometimes it is more cost effective for individuals to purchase benefits directly from providers, and some companies also are negotiating contracts with providers to offer benefits at reduced rates. Companies might also consider consolidating benefits packages into more streamlined offerings so that costs can be minimized.[21]

Benefits Communication

Employees generally do not know much about the values and costs associated with the benefits they receive from employers. This ignorance is illustrated by a survey in which only 5% of HR executives identified that their employees appreciated their total compensation package. More than one-third stated that employees do not understand the dollar value of benefits. However, other research suggests that some companies are communicating extensively with employees because individuals are now expected to make their own decisions about benefits and generalized health.[22]

Benefits communication and satisfaction of employees with their benefits are linked. For instance, employees often do not fully understand their health benefits, a situation that can cause individual dissatisfaction. Consequently, many employers should consider developing special benefits communication systems to inform employees about the monetary value of the benefits they provide. Employers can use various means, including videos, CDs, emails, electronic alerts, newsletters, and employee meetings. All these efforts are done to ensure that employees are knowledgeable about their benefits. Some of the important information to be communicated includes the value of the plans offered, why changes have to be made, and the fundamental financial costs of the plans. The Employee Retirement Income Security Act (ERISA) also requires sponsors of health programs to write a *summary plan description* that details the rights and benefits associated with particular plans, and these documents must be easy to understand.[23]

When planning benefits communication efforts, it is important to consider factors such as the timing and frequency, the communication sources, and the specialized content. Any significant changes to benefits, such as cuts to 401(k) matches, should be communicated by the top managers in the organization,

Using Online Technology to Combat Presenteeism

Presenteeism, which occurs when employees report to work but do not accomplish their assigned tasks effectively, can be a serious problem for organizations. Examples of presenteeism include working through an illness, dealing with personal problems on the job, and managing various medical conditions while on the clock. Unfortunately, presenteeism is becoming more common in organizations because of the recent economic turndown and increased stress related to work-life balance. Companies can offer different benefits to reduce the likelihood that workers will be adversely affected by presenteeism.

One of the best ways to combat presenteeism is the development and institutionalization of a companywide employee health and wellness program. Encouraging employees to take ownership of their physical and mental well-being can, under many circumstances, reduce stress and increase quality of work life. The major obstacle in creating such a program involves getting individuals to actually participate in the benefit plan, and technology is proving to be a valuable tool for increasing awareness of company health benefits. For instance, Web portals can be used to educate employees about health and wellness programs and various medical issues. In addition, mobile technology can be utilized by different providers to give employees quick and easy access to insurance records, medical appointments, and other administrative information. Using online technology can be beneficial for both employers and employees because presenteeism can be decreased.[24]

and these communications should be supported by HR professionals and other key managers who are well-informed to answer any questions. HR professionals should also collect feedback about benefits programs. Some companies are using Twitter, an online communication network of brief messages, to gather important opinions about their benefits.[25] The HR Online describes a similar use of Internet communications to increase participation in health and wellness programs that can reduce employee "presenteeism."

Benefits Statements Some employers give individual employees a "personal statement of benefits" that translates benefits into dollar amounts. Increasingly, firms are using the Internet to provide statements, with estimates that 60% of employers are doing so.[26] These statements often are used as part of a total rewards education and communication effort. The Employee Retirement Income Security Act (ERISA) also requires that employees receive an annual pension-reporting statement, which also can be included in the personal benefits statement.

LOGGING ON

BenefitNews.Com
This website is a resource for surveys, archived articles, and the latest trends and information regarding employee benefits. Visit the site at www.benefitnews.com.

TYPES OF BENEFITS

A wide range of benefits are offered by employers. Some are mandated by laws and government regulations, while others are offered voluntarily by employers as part of their HR strategies. Figure 13-6 shows how the typical employer dollar is spent on different types of benefits.

FIGURE 13-6   **How the Typical Benefits Dollar Is Spent**

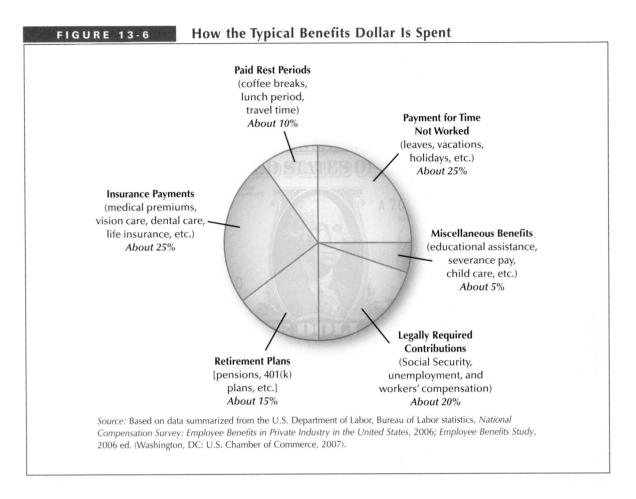

Paid Rest Periods
(coffee breaks,
lunch period,
travel time)
About 10%

**Payment for Time
Not Worked**
(leaves, vacations,
holidays, etc.)
About 25%

Insurance Payments
(medical premiums,
vision care, dental care,
life insurance, etc.)
About 25%

Miscellaneous Benefits
(educational assistance,
severance pay,
child care, etc.)
About 5%

Retirement Plans
[pensions, 401(k)
plans, etc.]
About 15%

**Legally Required
Contributions**
(Social Security,
unemployment, and
workers' compensation)
About 20%

Source: Based on data summarized from the U.S. Department of Labor, Bureau of Labor statistics, *National Compensation Survey: Employee Benefits in Private Industry in the United States,* 2006; *Employee Benefits Study,* 2006 ed. (Washington, DC: U.S. Chamber of Commerce, 2007).

Government-Mandated Benefits

There are many mandated benefits that employers in the United States must provide to employees by law. Social Security (federal) and unemployment insurance (state) are funded through a tax paid by the employer based on the employee's compensation. Workers' compensation laws exist in all states. In addition, under the Family and Medical Leave Act (FMLA), employers must offer unpaid leave to employees with certain medical or family difficulties. Other mandated benefits are funded in part by taxes, through Social Security. The Consolidated Omnibus Budget Reconciliation Act (COBRA) mandates that an employer continue to provide health care coverage—albeit paid for by the employees—for a time after employees leave the organization. The Health Insurance Portability and Accountability Act (HIPAA) requires that most employees be able to obtain coverage if they were previously covered in a health plan and provides privacy rights for medical records.

A major reason for additional mandated benefits proposals is that federal and state governments would like to shift many of the social costs for health care and other expenditures to employers. This shift would relieve some of the budgetary pressures facing government entities that otherwise might have to raise taxes and/or cut spending.

The federal plan for universal health care benefits for individuals has been passed, but given the complexity of the bill and uncertainty over exactly how it will work, it is unclear exactly how such coverage will impact organizations, sponsors of health benefits, and health care providers. Additional mandated benefits have been proposed for many other areas but not adopted are as follows:

- Child-care assistance
- Pension plan coverage that can be transferred by workers who change jobs
- Core benefits for part-time employees working at least 500 hours a year
- Paid time off for family leave
- Paid time off for pregnancy and child bearing

Voluntary Benefits

Employers voluntarily offer other types of benefits to help them compete for and retain employees. By offering additional benefits, organizations are assuming a need to provide greater security and benefits support to workers with widely varied personal circumstances. In addition, as jobs become more flexible and varied, both workers and employers recognize that choices among benefits are necessary, as evidenced by the growth in flexible benefits and cafeteria benefit plans. Figure 13-7 lists seven types of mandated and voluntary benefits. The following sections describe them by type.

FIGURE 13-7   **Types of Benefits**

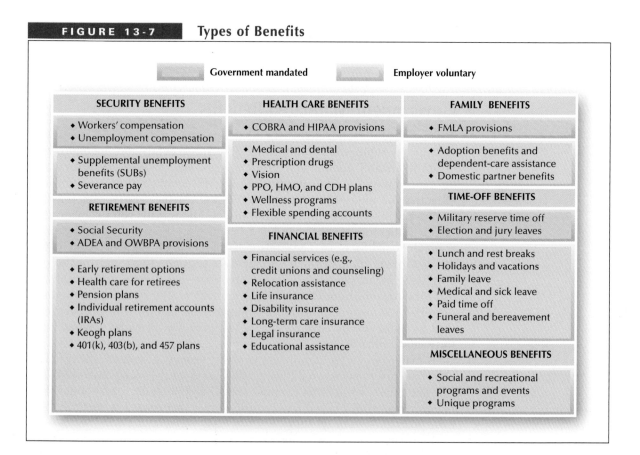

| Government mandated | Employer voluntary |

SECURITY BENEFITS
- Workers' compensation
- Unemployment compensation

- Supplemental unemployment benefits (SUBs)
- Severance pay

RETIREMENT BENEFITS
- Social Security
- ADEA and OWBPA provisions

- Early retirement options
- Health care for retirees
- Pension plans
- Individual retirement accounts (IRAs)
- Keogh plans
- 401(k), 403(b), and 457 plans

HEALTH CARE BENEFITS
- COBRA and HIPAA provisions

- Medical and dental
- Prescription drugs
- Vision
- PPO, HMO, and CDH plans
- Wellness programs
- Flexible spending accounts

FINANCIAL BENEFITS
- Financial services (e.g., credit unions and counseling)
- Relocation assistance
- Life insurance
- Disability insurance
- Long-term care insurance
- Legal insurance
- Educational assistance

FAMILY BENEFITS
- FMLA provisions

- Adoption benefits and dependent-care assistance
- Domestic partner benefits

TIME-OFF BENEFITS
- Military reserve time off
- Election and jury leaves

- Lunch and rest breaks
- Holidays and vacations
- Family leave
- Medical and sick leave
- Paid time off
- Funeral and bereavement leaves

MISCELLANEOUS BENEFITS
- Social and recreational programs and events
- Unique programs

SECURITY BENEFITS

A number of benefits provide employee security. These benefits include some mandated by laws and others offered by employers voluntarily. The primary benefits found in most organizations include workers' compensation, unemployment compensation, and severance pay.

Workers' Compensation

Workers' compensation provides benefits to persons who are injured on the job. State laws require most employers to supply workers' compensation coverage by purchasing insurance from a private carrier or state insurance fund or by providing self-insurance. Government employees in the United States are covered under the Federal Employees Compensation Act, administered by the U.S. Department of Labor.

The workers' compensation system requires employers to give cash benefits, medical care, and rehabilitation services to employees for injuries or illnesses occurring within the scope of their employment. In exchange, employees give up the right to pursue legal actions and awards. The costs to employers for workers' compensation average about 1.8% of total payroll, and about $0.47 per hour in wages per worker.[27] However, it is much higher in some states. Workers' compensation is a part of HR risk management and worker protection.

Unemployment Compensation

Another benefit required by law is unemployment compensation, established as part of the Social Security Act of 1935. Because each U.S. state operates its own unemployment compensation system, provisions differ significantly from state to state. The tax is paid to state and federal unemployment compensation funds. The percentage paid by individual employers is based on "experience rates," which reflect the number of claims filed by workers who leave.

An employee who is out of work and is actively looking for employment normally receives up to 26 weeks of pay, at the rate of 50% to 80% of normal pay. Most employees are eligible. However, workers fired for misconduct or those not actively seeking employment generally are ineligible. Only about 40% of eligible people use the unemployment compensation system. This underutilization may be due both to the stigma of receiving unemployment and the complexity of the system, which some feel is simply not worth the effort.

Supplemental unemployment benefits (SUBs) are closely related to unemployment compensation, but they are not required by law. A provision in some union contracts requires organizations to contribute to a fund that supplements the unemployment compensation available to employees from federal and/or state sources.

Criticisms of Unemployment Insurance Two problems explain changes in unemployment insurance laws proposed at state and federal levels: (1) abuses are estimated to cost billions each year, and (2) many state unemployment funds are exhausted during economic slowdowns. Also, some states allow striking

Workers' compensation
Security benefits provided to persons who are injured on the job.

union workers to collect unemployment benefits despite strike fund payments from the union. This provision is bitterly opposed by many employers.

Severance Pay

As a security benefit, **severance pay** is voluntarily offered by employers to individuals whose jobs are eliminated or who leave by mutual agreement with their employers. Employer severance pay provisions often provide severance payments corresponding to an employee's level within the organization and the person's years of employment. The Worker Adjustment and Retraining Notification Act (WARN) of 1988 requires that many employers give 60 days' notice if a mass layoff or facility closing is to occur. The act does not require employers to give severance pay.

Some employers have offered reduced amounts of cash severance and replaced some of the severance value with continued health insurance and out-placement assistance. Through *outplacement assistance*, ex-employees receive résumé writing instruction, interviewing skills workshops, and career counseling.

Severance pay Security benefit voluntarily offered by employers to individuals whose jobs are eliminated or who leave by mutual agreement with their employers.

HEALTH CARE BENEFITS

Employers provide a variety of health care and medical benefits, usually through insurance coverage. A recent national survey indicated that health plans are considered by employees to be the most important benefit that companies offer, and another study found that slightly more than half of individuals are satisfied with the current health insurance offered.[28] The most common plans cover medical, dental, prescription drug, and vision care expenses for employees and their dependents. Figure 13-8 notes the percentage of private industry workers receiving different types of health benefits.

FIGURE 13-8   Private Industry Workers with Health Benefits

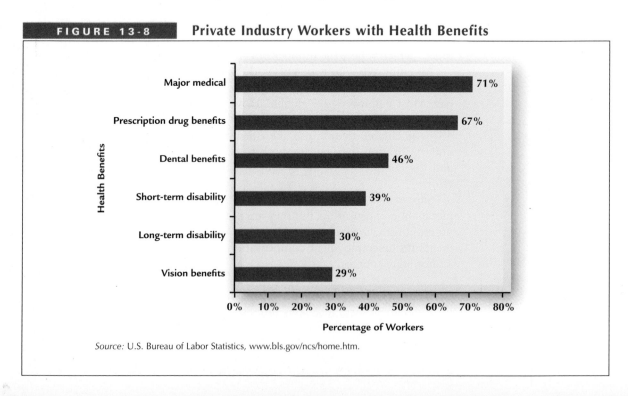

Source: U.S. Bureau of Labor Statistics, www.bls.gov/ncs/home.htm.

Increases in Health Benefits Costs

For several decades, the costs of health care have escalated at rates well above those of inflation and changes in workers' earnings. For instance, the reduction in the number of obstetricians caused by litigation fears and the price of malpractice insurance has increased costs due to higher premiums and diagnostic testing. In addition, the costs of health care have increased by two percentage points over increases in the GDP across many developed nations for close to 50 years. As a result of large increases such as these, many employers find that dealing with health care benefits is time consuming and expensive. This is especially frustrating for employers who have found that many employees seem to take their health benefits for granted. Consequently, a growing number of firms, particularly smaller ones, have asked, "Why are we offering these benefits anyway?" About 10% of all employers have answered the question by discontinuing or dramatically cutting health benefits.[29] Two major groups of workers that have contributed to the increasing costs are uninsured workers and retirees.

Uninsured Workers Some of the health benefits cost pressures are due to health care providers having to cover the costs for the rising number of individuals in the United States without health insurance coverage. A number of uninsured workers are illegal immigrants; others work for employers that do not provide benefits. About 15% to 20% of the U.S. population lacks health coverage, and covering those costs forces hospitals, pharmacies, and other health care providers to raise their rates on all patient services. Thus, the costs are shifted to those with health insurance paid for by employers, making this a high-profile political issue that has driven attention to health care reform.[30]

Retirees' Health Benefits Costs Another group whose benefits costs are rising is retirees whose former employers still provide health benefits coverage. For instance, at General Motors, there are 2.4 retired employees for every active employee. Increasing the problem at GM is that health care usage rates for older retirees are significantly higher than those of current employees. GM has to add almost $1,500 per vehicle to cover employee and retiree health care costs, which amounts to more than the steel used to build the cars.[31]

To control retiree health benefits costs, some firms are cutting their benefits or requiring retirees to pay higher rates for health benefits. Approximately 75% of employers in one survey have increased health insurance premiums in recent years. In addition, one company has frozen health care benefits for thousands of its retirees. Future increased costs will be paid for by the individual retirees, not the employer. Naturally, such efforts by firms have faced resistance and even lawsuits from disgruntled retirees. At these and other firms, this issue raises troubling ethical concerns. Many of the retirees worked for their employers for 20, 30, or more years, yet the reward for their long service increasingly is a reduction in health care benefits. As a result, many individuals are delaying retirement until age 65 so that Medicare coverage can be secured.[32]

LOGGING ON

America's Health Insurance Plans
For current information on legislative and regulatory health care issues affecting American consumers, visit this website at www.ahip.org.

Controlling Health Care Benefits Costs

Employers offering health care benefits are taking a number of approaches to controlling their costs. The most prominent ones are changing copayments and employee contributions, using managed care, switching to mini-medical plans or consumer-driven health plans, and increasing health preventive and wellness efforts.

Changing Copayments and Employee Contributions The **copayment** strategy requires employees to pay a portion of the cost of insurance premiums, medical care, and prescription drugs. Requiring new or higher copayments and employee contributions is the most prevalent cost-control strategy identified by many employers surveyed. For instance, employers who raise the per-person deductible from $50 to $250 realize significant savings in health care expenses due to decreasing employee usage of health care services and prescription drugs.

These changes are facing significant resistance by employees, especially those who have had *first-dollar coverage*. With this type of coverage, all expenses, from the first dollar of health care costs, are paid by the employee's insurance. Experts claim that when first-dollar coverage is included in a basic health plan, many employees see a doctor for even minor illnesses, which results in an escalation of the benefits costs.

Using Managed Care Several other types of programs attempt to reduce health care costs paid by employers. **Managed care** consists of approaches that monitor and reduce medical costs through restrictions and market system alternatives. Managed care plans emphasize primary and preventive care, the use of specific providers who will charge lower prices, restrictions on certain kinds of treatment, and prices negotiated with hospitals and physicians.

The most prominent managed care approach is the **preferred provider organization (PPO)**, a health care provider that contracts with an employer or an employer group to supply health care services to employees at a competitive rate. Employees have the freedom to go to other providers if they want to pay the differences in costs. *Point-of-service plans* are somewhat similar, offering financial incentives to encourage employees to use designated medical providers.

Another managed care approach is a **health maintenance organization (HMO)**, which provides services for a fixed period on a prepaid basis. The HMO emphasizes both prevention and correction. An employer contracts with an HMO and its staff of physicians and medical personnel to furnish complete medical care, except for hospitalization. The employer pays a flat rate per enrolled employee or per enrolled family. The covered individuals may then go to the HMO for health care as often as needed. Supplemental policies for hospitalization also are provided. While HMOs remain widely used, a growing number of employers are focusing on other means to control the costs of health care benefits.

Many employers have found that some of the health care provided by doctors and hospitals is unnecessary, incorrectly billed, or deliberately overcharged. Consequently, both employers and insurance firms often require that medical work and charges be audited through a **utilization review**. This process may require a second opinion, a review of the procedures done, and a review of charges for the procedures.

Mini-Medical Plans Another type of plan that has grown in usage in the past few years is the *mini-medical plan*. This type of plan provides limited health benefits coverage for employees. In the past, these plans have been used more with part-time and lower wage level employees. But more employers are using these plans for full-time employees of all types. A typical mini-medical plan limits the number of doctor visits paid per year to fewer than 10, covers

Copayment Strategy of requiring employees to pay a portion of the cost of insurance premiums, medical care, and prescription drugs.

Managed care Approaches that monitor and reduce medical costs through restrictions and market system alternatives.

Preferred provider organization (PPO) A health care provider that contracts with an employer or an employer group to supply health care services to employees at a competitive rate.

Health maintenance organization (HMO) Plan that provides services for a fixed period on a prepaid basis.

Utilization review Audit of services and costs billed by health care providers.

Mini-Medical Plans on the Rise

Mini-medical plans are becoming more and more popular among organizations looking to provide more economical health care coverage to employees. Minimal coverage plans typically offer individuals scaled-down health care benefits, and because coverage is limited, the plans are offered at a highly discounted rate. Management can negotiate different coverage caps depending on the needs of workers, and premium prices, which may or may not be paid completely by employees, tend to rise as the caps increase. Additionally, plans often do not include deductibles, and when they do, out-of-pocket costs are fixed at a low rate. Given these parameters, mini-medical plans are particularly suited to smaller companies that employ predominantly younger, hourly, part-time workers who do not need regular and/ or extensive health care coverage. Mini-medical plans have become popular because managers believe that offering even modest programs that facilitate positive health management is better than offering nothing.

However, are mini-medical plans really adequate for companies seeking to provide modest health care benefits to employees? Some critics believe that the money spent on minimal health care coverage could be better used to cover items such as personal and family necessities. Mini-plans might also sound better than they really are depending on the details of the individual coverage accounts. For instance, a plan might only cover expenses for certain procedures, and there may be daily coverage caps. An organization must therefore carefully and diligently evaluate the terms of mini-plans so that there are no misunderstandings about how medical expenses will be covered by insurance companies. Employers also must be proactive about communicating to employees the terms of different plans so that employees can take full advantage of their health care benefits. By making sure individuals understand their coverage options, companies should be able to take greater advantage of the many benefits of mini-medical plans.[33]

only certain prescription drugs, provides very limited hospital coverage, and caps total annual health benefits costs at $10,000 or less. These limitations result in significantly fewer benefits for employees, but dramatically lower costs for employers.[34] The HR Best Practices discusses the increasing popularity of mini-medical plans.

Consumer-Driven Health Plans

Some employers are turning to employee-focused health benefits plans. The most prominent is a **consumer-driven health (CDH) plan**, which provides employer financial contributions to employees to help cover their health-related expenses. Various surveys of companies have identified that a growing number of employers have switched to CDH plans, and that others are actively considering switching to these plans. Recent figures also suggest that an increasing number of CDH plans are being offered by both large and small businesses and that more workers are signing up for them. For instance, Humana, the health benefits company located in Louisville, Kentucky, implemented a successful consumer-directed program based on principles such as individual health management and mutual accountability.[35]

Consumer-driven (CDH) plan Health plan that provides employer financial contributions to employees to help cover their health-related expenses.

In these plans, which are also called *defined-contribution health plans*, an employer places a set amount into each employee's "account" and identifies a number of health care alternatives that are available. Then individual employees select from those health care alternatives and pay for part of the costs from their accounts.

There are two advantages to such plans for employers. One is that more of the increases in health care benefits costs are shifted to employees, because the employer contributions need not increase as fast as health care costs. Second, the focus of controlling health care usage falls on employees, who may have to choose when to use and not use health care benefits. Figure 13-9 highlights the components of CDH plans.

Health Savings Accounts Often **Health savings accounts (HSAs)** are combined with high-deductible insurance to cut employer costs. Such insurance is defined as plans that have between $1,150 and $5,800 in deductibles for individuals, and between $2,300 and $11,600 in deductibles for families.[36] Other components of an HSA include the following:

- Both employees and employers can make contributions to an account.
- Individual employees can set aside pretax amounts for medical care into an HSA.
- Unused amounts in an individual's account can be rolled over annually for future health expenses.
- Incentives are included to encourage employees to spend less on health expenses.
- Contributions must be uniform for all employees enrolled in HSA accounts unless they are based on a cafeteria program.[37]

Health accounts (HSAs)
High-deductible health plans with federal tax advantages.

The key component of HSA accounts is that employees may get more health benefits choices, but their insurance usually has higher annual deductibles. These plans often result in employers having lower overall expenditures because higher employee deductibles result in lower costs for the employers. For example, at one firm an employee has a $3,000 annual deductible to meet, compared with a $1,000 amount previously under a PPO plan. With the

---

FIGURE 13-9 **Components of Consumer-Driven Health Plans**

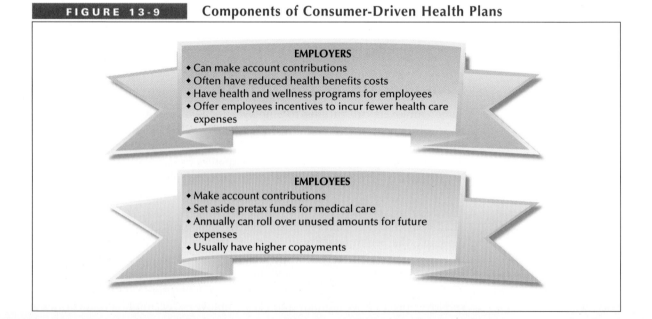

EMPLOYERS
- Can make account contributions
- Often have reduced health benefits costs
- Have health and wellness programs for employees
- Offer employees incentives to incur fewer health care expenses

EMPLOYEES
- Make account contributions
- Set aside pretax funds for medical care
- Annually can roll over unused amounts for future expenses
- Usually have higher copayments

higher deductible amounts, employers often cut or limit their contributions, reducing their costs by 10% to 30%. Because of these shifts in costs, less than 7% of employees are voluntarily switching to these plans, even though many employers have added HSAs to their benefits plan mix.[38]

Health Reimbursement Arrangements Closely related to an HSA is a health reimbursement arrangement. This type of plan also may be called a *health reimbursement account* or a *personal care account*. Under a **health reimbursement arrangement (HRA)**, the employer sets aside money in a health reimbursement account to help employees pay for qualified medical expenses. The definition of "qualified medical expenses" can be determined by the employer within tax law limitations. A key difference from an HSA is that employees cannot contribute money to an HRA. The employer also can decide if employees must pay deductibles first or if they can utilize funds in their HRA to pay for first-dollar expenses. If an employee does not utilize all of the funds available in the HRA during the plan year, the employee may be allowed to roll all or a portion of the balance into the next plan year.[39]

Health Care Preventive and Wellness Efforts

Preventive and wellness efforts can occur in a variety of ways. Many employers offer programs to educate employees about health care costs and how to reduce them. Newsletters, formal classes, and many other approaches are all designed to help employees understand why health care costs are increasing and what they can do to control them. For instance, Avivia Health provides health coaching to employees so that they can develop more positive wellness strategies, and some companies are using "Walkstations," treadmills linked to work areas, to encourage greater exercise in the workplace. Many employers have programs that offer financial incentives to improve health habits. These wellness programs, discussed more in Chapter 14, reward employees who stop smoking, lose weight, and participate in exercise programs, among other activities. For example, employees at Ottawa Dental Labs, a small dental technology firm located in Ottawa, Illinois, are given "Vitality Bucks" that can be used to obtain different gifts and bonuses. An online health program called "DASH" (Dietary Approach to Stop Hypertension Program) was successfully implemented at EMC Corp. without any employee incentives, indicating that incentives might not always be needed to increase participation.[40]

Employee Reactions to Cost-Control Efforts As would be expected, many employees are skeptical about or even hostile to employer efforts to reduce health benefits costs and raise employees' contributions. Surveys of employees have found that they are more dissatisfied with changes to their health benefits than with the moderation of base pay increases. In fact, about 75% of the employees in one survey said that they would forgo any pay increase to keep their health benefits unchanged.[41]

For cost-control efforts to work for employers, the gap between employees' and employers' views on benefits must be bridged, which requires significant communication with and education of employees to counter their negative reactions. Key in communicating about controlling health benefits costs is sharing information and having a continuing and effective benefits communications plan.

Health reimbursement arrangement (HRA) Health plan in which the employer sets aside money in a health reimbursement account to help employees pay for qualified medical expenses.

Health Care Legislation

The importance of health care benefits to employers and employees has led to a variety of federal and state laws being created. The passage of a nationalized health care plan that insures all individuals is one such example. Some laws have been enacted to provide protection for employees who leave their employers, either voluntarily or involuntarily. To date, the two most important laws passed that govern issues related to the protection of former workers are COBRA and HIPAA.

COBRA Provisions The Consolidated Omnibus Budget Reconciliation Act (COBRA) requires that most employers (except churches and the federal government) with 20 or more full-time and/or part-time employees (partial count based on hours needed to work for full-time status, or hours worked/full-time hours) offer extended health care coverage to certain groups, as follows:[42]

- Employees who voluntarily quit or are terminated
- Widowed or divorced spouses and dependent children of former or current employees
- Retirees and their spouses and dependent children whose health care coverage ends
- Any child who is born or adopted by a covered employee
- Other individuals involved in the plan such as independent contractors and agents/directors

A company has 30 days to tell plan managers about certain qualifying events (i.e., employment termination, decreased hours, employee death, Medicare coverage, or bankruptcy), eligible individuals have 60 days to inform the plan managers after other qualifying events (i.e., divorce, legal separation, loss of dependent status), the plan must send individuals an election notice or denial of coverage continuation within 14 days after receiving notice, and entitled individuals have 60 days to move forward with COBRA coverage.[43] The chart in Figure 13-10 shows the duration of coverage that is offered depending on the

FIGURE 13-10   **Overview of COBRA Provisions**

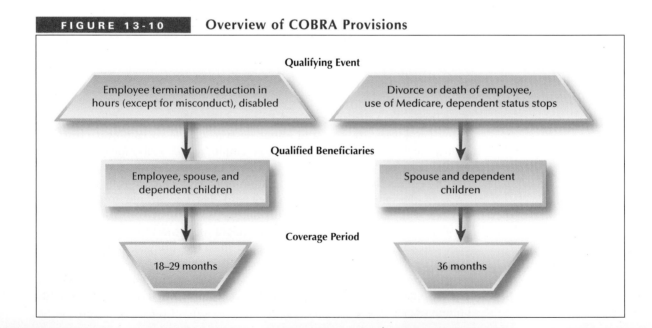

qualifying circumstances.[44] The individual no longer employed by the organization must pay the premiums, but the employer may charge this individual no more than 102% of the premium costs to insure a similarly covered employee. The 2% premium addition generally does not cover all relevant costs, because those costs often run several percentage points more.

Compliance with COBRA regulations can be very complex, and noncompliance with the law can lead to lawsuits and corporate payments of health care bills. Consequently, COBRA requirements often mean additional paperwork and related costs for many employers. For example, firms must not only track the former employees but also notify their qualified dependents. In addition, the American Recovery and Reinvestment Act of 2009 recently waived 65% of qualified persons' COBRA costs for involuntary separation of work that occurred from September 1, 2008, through February 28, 2010, and the decreased costs could run for up to 15 months for health care benefits that started on or after February 17, 2009.[45]

HIPAA Provisions The Health Insurance Portability and Accountability Act (HIPAA) of 1996 allows employees to switch their health insurance plans when they change employers, and to get new health coverage with the new company regardless of preexisting health conditions. The legislation also prohibits group insurance plans from dropping coverage for a sick employee and requires them to make individual coverage available to people who leave group plans.

One of the greatest impacts of HIPAA comes from its provisions regarding the privacy of employee medical records. These provisions require employers to provide privacy notices to employees. They also regulate the disclosure of protected health information without authorization.[46]

Flexible Spending Accounts Under current tax law (specifically, section 125 of the Internal Revenue Code), employees can divert some pretax income into **flexible spending accounts** to fund certain additional benefits. Under tax law at the time of this writing, the funds in the account can be used to purchase only the following: (1) additional health care (including offsetting deductibles), (2) life insurance, (3) disability insurance, and (4) dependent-care benefits. An example illustrates the advantage of these accounts to employees. Assume an employee earns $3,000 a month and has $100 a month deducted to put into a flexible spending account. That $100 does not count as gross income for tax purposes, so the employee's taxable income is reduced. The employee uses the money in the account to purchase additional benefits.

Other Important Health Care Legislation Several other key laws also should be understood by HR professionals. For instance, the Mental Health Parity and Addiction Equity Act, which was passed along with the Wall Street bailout legislation, requires employers to provide "equal and fair" health care coverage to those individuals adversely affected by mental disorders and substance problems. Comparisons should be made with benefits provided to employees who experience physical ailments to determine the parity of coverage.[47] Also, the Children's Health Insurance Program Reauthorization Act of 2009 gives states the opportunity to provide financial assistance for the defraying of costs associated with employer-based health care programs to (1) children of low-income families or (2) individuals below the age of 19 who are entitled to receive Medicare. Employers can request that payments be made directly to individuals instead of the business receiving subsidies from the government.[48]

Flexible spending accounts Benefits plans that allow employees to contribute pretax dollars to fund certain additional benefits.

RETIREMENT BENEFITS

The aging of the workforce in many countries is affecting retirement planning for individuals and retirement plan costs for employers and governments. In the United States, the number of citizens at least 55 years or older has increased significantly in recent years, and older citizens currently constitute a large portion of the population. Simultaneously, the age of retirement has declined, as it has been doing for decades. With more people retiring earlier and living longer, retirement benefits are becoming a greater concern for employers, employees, and retired employees.

Unfortunately, most U.S. citizens have inadequate savings and retirement benefits for funding their retirements. According to a study by the Employee Benefit Research Institute, almost 70% of individuals over age 55 have inadequately saved for retirement.[49] These individuals are heavily dependent on employer-provided retirement benefits. But many employers with fewer than 100 workers do not offer retirement benefits. Also, the economic downturn caused a reduction in the value of worker retirement accounts and contributions, leading many older employees to continue with their employment.[50] Therefore, individuals must rely on Social Security payments, which were not designed to provide full retirement income.

Social Security

The Social Security Act of 1935, with its later amendments, established a system providing *old-age, survivor's, disability*, and *retirement* benefits. Administered by the federal government through the Social Security Administration, this program provides benefits to previously employed individuals. Employees and employers share in the cost of Social Security through a tax on employees' wages or salaries.

Social Security Changes Since the inception of the system, the Social Security payroll taxes have risen to 15.3% currently, with employees and employers each paying 7.65% up to an established maximum. In addition, Medicare taxes have more than doubled, to 2.9%.

Because the Social Security system affects a large number of individuals and is government operated, it is a politically sensitive program. The U.S. Congress has responded to public pressure by raising payments and introducing cost-of-living adjustments. Now, it is likely that legislative action will have to respond to widespread criticisms that the system is not financially sound and must consider alternatives to ensure the future viability of the Social Security system.

Pension Plans

Pension plan Retirement program established and funded by the employer and employees.

A **pension plan** is a retirement program established and funded by the employer and employees. Organizations are not required to offer pension plans to employees, and fewer than half of U.S. workers are covered by them. Small firms offer pension plans less often than do large ones.

Defined-benefit plan Retirement program in which employees are promised a pension amount based on age and service.

Defined-Benefit Pension Plans A "traditional" pension plan, in which the employer makes the contributions and the employee will get a defined amount each month upon retirement, is no longer the norm in the private sector. Through a **defined-benefit plan**, employees are promised a pension amount based on age and service. The employees' contributions are based on actuarial calculations on the *benefits* to be received by the employees after retirement and the *methods* used to determine such benefits. A defined-benefit plan gives employees greater assurance of benefits and greater predictability in the amount of benefits that will be available for retirement. Defined-benefit plans are often preferred by workers with longer service, as well as by small business owners.

If the funding in a defined-benefit plan is insufficient, the employer may have to make up the shortfall. Therefore, many employers have dropped defined-benefit plans in favor of defined-contribution plans (discussed next) so that their contribution liabilities are known. Notice in Figure 13-11 that unionized employees participate to a greater extent in defined-benefit plans than any other category. A study also found that high affective commitment among employees led them to work beyond an age that was advantageous financially in a defined-benefit pension plan, while high continuance commitment led individuals to retire earlier within a time frame that was more financially beneficial.[51]

Defined-contribution plan Retirement program in which the employer makes an annual payment to an employee's pension account.

Defined-Contribution Pension Plans In a **defined-contribution plan,** the employer makes an annual payment to an employee's pension account. The key to this plan is the *contribution rate*; employee retirement benefits depend on fixed contributions and employee earnings levels. Profit-sharing

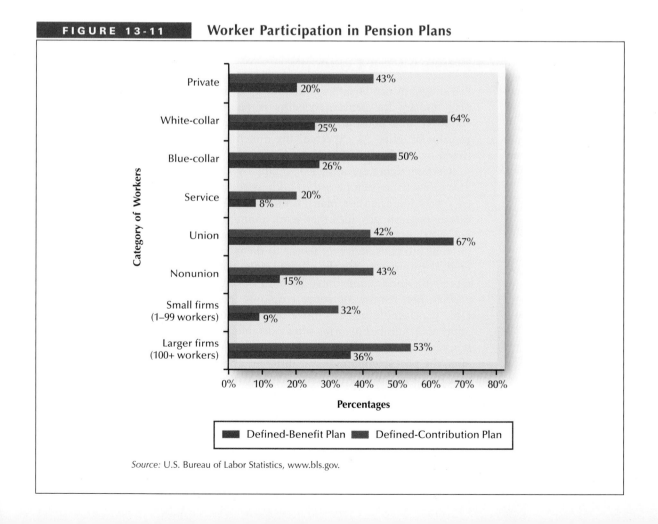

FIGURE 13-11   Worker Participation in Pension Plans

Source: U.S. Bureau of Labor Statistics, www.bls.gov.

plans, employee stock ownership plans (ESOPs), and 401(k) plans are common defined-contribution plans. Because these plans hinge on the investment returns on the previous contributions, the returns can vary according to profitability or other factors. Therefore, employees' retirement benefits are somewhat less secure and predictable. But because of their structure, these plans are sometimes preferred by younger, shorter-service employees.

Cash Balance Pension Plans Some employers have changed traditional pension plans to hybrids based on ideas from both defined-benefit and defined-contribution plans. One such plan is a **cash balance plan**, in which retirement benefits are based on an accumulation of annual company contributions, expressed as a percentage of pay, plus interest credited each year. With these plans, retirement benefits accumulate at the same annual rate until an employee retires. Because cash balance plans spread funding across a worker's entire career, these plans work better for mobile younger workers.

However, conversions to cash balance plans have caused discontent and even lawsuits among older employees at AT&T, EDS, and most notably IBM. At IBM, workers in the age 40 group would have lost a significant amount of retirement under the plan. Court decisions in *Cooper v. IBM Personal Pension Plan* ruled in favor of IBM. Consequently, in 2006, IBM and other firms proceeded with freezing their old plans and making the conversion to cash balance plans.[52]

Many smaller employers do not offer pension plans for a number of reasons. The primary reason, in addition to their cost, is the administrative burdens imposed by government legislation, discussed later in the chapter.

Pension Plan Concepts

Pension plans can be either contributory or noncontributory. In a **contributory plan**, money for pension benefits is paid in by both employees and the employer. In a **noncontributory plan**, the employer provides all the funds for pension benefits. As expected, the noncontributory plans are generally preferred by employees and labor unions.

Certain rights are attached to employee pension plans. Various laws and provisions have been passed to address the right of employees to receive benefits from their pension plans. Called **vesting**, this right assures employees of a certain pension, provided they work a minimum number of years. If employees resign or are terminated before they have been employed for the required vesting time, no pension rights accrue to them except the funds they have contributed. If employees stay the allotted time, they retain their pension rights and receive the funds contributed by both the employer and themselves.

Another feature of some employee pensions is **portability**. In a portable plan, employees can move their pension benefits from one employer to another. A number of firms offer portable pension plans. Instead of requiring workers to wait until they retire to move their traditional pension plan benefits, the portable plan takes a different approach. Once workers have vested in a plan for a period of time, such as five years, they can transfer their fund balances to other retirement plans if they change jobs.

Individual Retirement Options

The availability of several retirement benefit options makes the pension area more complex. The most prominent options are individual retirement accounts (IRAs) and 401(k), 403(b), 457, and Keogh plans. These plans may

Cash balance plan
Retirement program in which benefits are based on an accumulation of annual company contributions plus interest credited each year.

Contributory plan Pension plan in which the money for pension benefits is paid by both employees and the employer.

Noncontributory plan Pension plan in which all the funds for pension benefits are provided by the employer.

Vesting Right of employees to receive certain benefits from their pension plans.

Portability A pension plan feature that allows employees to move their pension benefits from one employer to another.

be available in addition to company-provided pension plans and usually are contributory plans.

The **401(k) plan** gets its name from section 401(k) of the federal tax code. This plan is an agreement in which a percentage of an employee's pay is withheld and invested in a tax-deferred account. Many employers match employee 401(k) contributions, up to a percentage of the employee's pay. As a result, a significant number of employees contribute to 401(k) plans. The use of 401(k) plans and of the assets in them has grown significantly in the past few years. Employers frequently have programs to encourage employees to contribute to 401(k) plans. Some employers are making employee participation in 401(k) plans automatic, unless the employees specifically opt out of them.[53] The advantage to most employees is that they can save pretax income toward their retirement.

A special type of 401(k), the *Roth IRA*, was established effective 2006. This is a modification of the traditional 401(k) that allows participants to be taxed in the current year for contributions. That means that under the Roth IRA, the taxed gains in the value of the 401(k) over years are not as much as with regular 401(k) but are not taxed when withdrawn. Employers may offer both types of plans.[54]

401(k) plan Agreement in which a percentage of an employee's pay is withheld and invested in a tax-deferred account.

LOGGING ON

401k Retirement Plan Online Guide

This website provides investors with information on 401(k) plans. Visit the site at www.401k-site.com.

LEGAL REQUIREMENTS FOR RETIREMENT BENEFITS

A number of laws and regulations affect retirement plans. Some of the key ones are highlighted next.

Employee Retirement Income Security Act

The widespread criticism of many pension plans led to passage of the Employee Retirement Income Security Act (ERISA) in 1974. The purpose of this law is to regulate private pension plans so that employees who put money into them or depend on a pension for retirement funds actually receive the money when they retire.

ERISA essentially requires many companies to offer retirement plans to all employees if they offer retirement plans to any employees. Accrued benefits must be given to employees when they retire or leave. The act also sets minimum funding requirements, and plans not meeting those requirements are subject to financial penalties imposed by the IRS. Additional regulations require that employers pay plan termination insurance to ensure payment of employee pensions should the employers go out of business. To spread out the costs of administration and overhead, some employers use plans funded by multiple employers.

Retirement Equity in Pension Plans The U.S. Supreme Court decision in *Arizona Governing Committee v. Norris* forced pension plan administrators to use "unisex" mortality tables, which do not reflect the gender differential in mortality.[55] To bring legislation in line with this decision, in 1984, Congress passed the Retirement Equity Act as an amendment to ERISA and the Internal Revenue Code. It liberalized pension regulations that affect women, guaranteed access to benefits, prohibited pension-related penalties due to absences from work such as maternity leave, and lowered the vesting age.

Qualified Domestic Relations Order Created by provisions of ERISA, a *qualified domestic relations order (QDRO)* is an agreement made by a divorcing couple that identifies who gets assets in a retirement plan. Use of a QDRO provides protection for both individuals and their children in a divorce. Also, use of a QDRO provides some beneficial tax provisions.[56]

Retiree Benefits and Legal Requirements

Some employers choose to offer retiree health benefits that may be paid for by the retirees, the company, or both. The costs of such coverage have risen dramatically. To ensure that firms adequately reflect the liabilities for retiree health benefits, the Financial Accounting Standards Board issued Rule 106, which requires employers to establish accounting reserves for funding retiree health care benefits. For instance, one problem with retiree pension benefits is that a number of firms are facing unfunded pension liabilities.

Pension Protection Act of 2006 The Pension Protection Act of 2006 has numerous reporting requirements that must be met by employers. These requirements make employers disclose the assets and liabilities of pension plans. The act also requires that employers increase funding to cover unfunded liabilities they face. Many of the provisions focus specifically on the deficit created by defined-benefit plans that employers must cover.[57]

Retirement Benefits and Age Discrimination

According to a 1986 amendment to the Age Discrimination in Employment Act (ADEA), most employees cannot be forced to retire at a specific age. As a result, employers have had to develop policies to comply with these regulations. In many employer pension plans, "normal retirement" is the age at which employees can retire and collect full pension benefits. Employers must decide whether individuals who continue to work past normal retirement age (perhaps 65) should receive the full benefits package, especially pension credits. Some changes in Social Security regulations have increased the age for full benefits past age 65, so modifications in policies may occur. Another issue involves the amount health care benefits provided to retirees, and recent EEOC guidelines indicate that companies can spend less on benefits for retirees who are 65 and older compared to their younger counterparts without committing age discrimination.[58]

Early Retirement Many pension plans include provisions for early retirement to give workers voluntary opportunities to leave their jobs. After spending 25 to 30 years working for the same employer, individuals may wish to use their talents in other areas. Phased-in and part-time retirements are alternatives being used by individuals and firms.

Some employers use early retirement buyout programs to cut back their workforces and reduce costs. Employers must take care to make these early retirement programs truly voluntary. Forcing workers to take advantage of an early retirement buyout program led to the passage of the federal law discussed next.

Older Workers Benefit Protection Act Passed in 1990, the Older Workers Benefit Protection Act (OWBPA) amended the ADEA and overturned a decision by the U.S. Supreme Court in *Public Employees Retirement System of Ohio v. Betts.*[59] This act requires equal treatment for older workers in early retirement or severance situations. It also sets forth some specific criteria that must be met when older workers sign waivers promising not to sue for age discrimination.

FINANCIAL BENEFITS

Employers may offer workers a wide range of special benefits that provide financial support to employees. Figure 13-12 illustrates some common financial benefits. Employers find that such benefits can be useful in attracting and retaining employees. Workers like receiving these benefits, which often are not taxed as income.

Insurance Benefits

In addition to health-related insurance, some employers provide other types of insurance. These benefits offer major advantages for employees because many employers pay some or all of the costs. Even when employers do not pay any of the costs, employees still benefit because of the lower rates available through group programs. The most common types of insurance benefits are the following:[60]

- *Life insurance*: Bought as a group policy, the employer pays all or some of the premiums. A typical level of coverage is one and one-half or two times an employee's annual salary.
- *Disability insurance*: Both *short-term* and *long-term disability insurance* provide continuing income protection for employees who become disabled and unable to work. Long-term disability insurance is much more common because many employers cover short-term disability situations through sick leave programs.

| FIGURE 13-12 | **Common Types of Financial Benefits** |

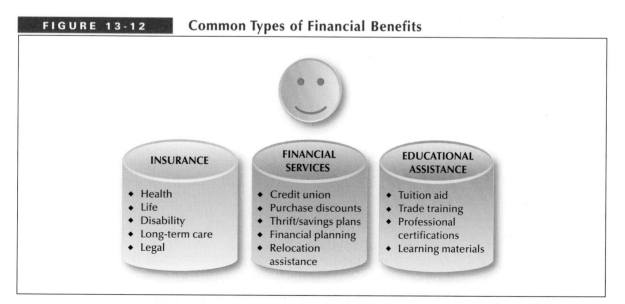

- *Long-term care insurance*: Usually voluntary, these plans allow employees to purchase insurance to cover costs for long-term health care in a nursing home, an assisted-living facility, or at home. Though employees pay for the premiums, they may get cheaper rates through employer-sponsored group plans.
- *Legal insurance*: In these plans employees (or employers) pay a flat fee for a set amount of legal assistance time each month. In return, they have the right to use the service of a network of lawyers to handle their legal problems.

Financial Services

Financial benefits include a wide variety of items. A *credit union* sponsored by the employer provides saving and lending services for employees. *Purchase discounts* allow employees to buy goods or services from their employers at reduced rates. For example, a furniture manufacturer may allow employees to buy furniture at wholesale cost plus 10%, or a bank may offer employees use of a safe deposit box and free checking.

Employee *thrift plans, savings plans,* or *stock investment plans* of different types may be available. To illustrate, in a **stock purchase plan,** the employer provides matching funds equal to the amount invested by the employee for the purchase of stock in the company. Often, employees may buy the stock at a discount. This type of plan allows employees to benefit from the future growth of the corporation. The intent of such a plan is to develop greater employee loyalty and interest in the organization and its success.

Financial planning and counseling are especially valuable services for executives, many of whom may need information on investments and tax shelters, as well as comprehensive financial counseling, because of their higher levels of compensation. The importance of these financial planning benefits likely will grow as a greater percentage of workers approach retirement age and need to plan financially for retirement.

Relocation Assistance Relocation benefits of various types are offered by many firms. Some employers offer temporary relocation benefits, while others provide assistance in finding a job for the spouse of a transferred employee. Numerous other financial-related benefits may be offered as well, including the use of a company car, company expense accounts, and assistance in buying or selling a house.

Educational Assistance

Another benefit that saves financial resources of employees comes in the form of educational assistance and tuition aid, which pays some or all of the costs associated with formal education courses and degree programs. Some employers pay for schooling on a proportional schedule, depending on the grades received; others simply require a passing grade of C or above. Often the costs of books and laboratory materials are covered. Unless the education paid for by the employer meets certain conditions, the cost of educational aid must be counted as taxable income by employees.

Stock purchase plan
Plan in which the employer provides matching funds equal to the amount invested by the employee for the purchase of stock in the company.

ROI of Tuition Aid Providing educational benefits through tuition aid programs is a very popular benefit with employers. More than 90% of employers offer some form of educational assistance to their employees, according to one survey. Two concerns in this area are lack of participation by employees and lack of evaluation of these programs by employers. Some employers are offering incentives such as free tuition or bonuses upon completion of degrees to encourage greater participation by employees. Also, although U.S. employers spend more than $10 billion for tuition aid in one year, only 2% of those firms conduct HR analyses to determine the return on their investment in these programs.[61] To make educational benefits programs more effective, employers need to measure the effect of these programs on employee retention, internal promotions, increased employee satisfaction, and other factors.

FAMILY-ORIENTED BENEFITS

The composition of families in the United States has changed significantly in the past few decades. The number of traditional families, in which the man goes to work and the woman stays home to raise children, has declined significantly, while the percentage of two-worker families has more than doubled. The growth in dual-career couples, single-parent households, and work demands on many workers has increased the emphasis some employers are placing on family-oriented benefits. As mentioned in earlier chapters, balancing family and work demands presents a major challenge to many workers at all levels of organizations. Therefore, employers have established a variety of family-oriented benefits. Since 1993, employers also have been required to provide certain benefits to comply with the Family and Medical Leave Act (FMLA).

Family and Medical Leave Act

The FMLA covers all federal, state, and private employers with 50 or more employees who live within 75 miles of the workplace. Only employees who have worked at least 12 months and 1,250 hours in the previous year are eligible for leave under the FMLA.

FMLA Leave Provisions   The law requires that employers allow eligible employees to take a total of 12 weeks' leave during any 12-month period for one or more of three situations:[62]

- Birth, adoption, or foster care placement of a child
- Caring for a spouse, a child, or a parent with a serious health condition
- Serious health condition of the employee

A **serious health condition** is one requiring in-patient, hospital, hospice, or residential medical care or continuing physician care, or problems that exist beyond three days including treatment provided.[63] An employer may require an employee to provide a certificate from a doctor verifying such an illness. The FMLA provides a number of guidelines regarding employee leaves:[64]

- Employees taking family and medical leave must be able to return to the same job or a job of equivalent status or pay.
- Health benefits must be continued during the leave at the same level and conditions. If, for a reason other than serious health problems, the employee does not return to work, the employer may collect the employer-paid portion of the premiums from the nonreturning employee.

Serious health condition
Health condition requiring in-patient, hospital, hospice, or residential medical care or continuing physician care.

- The leave may be taken intermittently rather than in one block, subject to employee and employer agreements, when birth, adoption, or foster child care is the cause. For serious health conditions, employer approval is not necessary.
- Employees can be required to use all paid-up vacation and personal leave before taking unpaid leave.
- Employees are required to give 30-day notice, where practical.

Some provisions associated with the FMLA started January 16, 2009, expanding coverage for some employees and revising specific criteria of the regulations. For instance, a company representative other than an employee's immediate supervisor may call a health care provider to verify the cause of medical leave. An employer also can require returning employees to complete fitness-for-duty tests that verify important job duties can be completed or that mitigate safety concerns. In addition, companies can require employees to use FMLA leave in the same manner as other time-off programs, and employees are required to follow corporate leave notification procedures. Despite a multitude of other changes, one of the most noteworthy revisions to the FMLA involves providing 26 weeks of leave to individuals providing care to injured family members who served in the military.[65]

Results of the FMLA Since the passage of the act, several factors have become apparent. A significant percentage of employees take family and medical leave. Additionally, many employers have not paid enough attention to the FMLA or do not fully understand it,[66] resulting in numerous lawsuits. Also, although employers are not required to pay employees for leave taken under the FMLA (other than for sick leave or accumulated unused vacation time), some states have complicated this process by passing or considering laws requiring *paid family leave*. Finally, employers have to cover the workload for employees on family leave. This difficulty is compounded because the law requires that workers on these leaves be offered similar jobs at similar levels of pay when they return to work. Balancing work demands for many different employees and their family and medical situations has placed significant demands on HR professionals to ensure compliance with FMLA provisions.

Family-Care Benefits

Family issues are growing in importance for many organizations and for many workers. One repercussion of this emphasis is that employees without families may feel some resentment against those who seem to get special privileges because they have families. Many employees do not have children under the age of 18 and are offered fewer opportunities to use personal days off, flexible scheduling, telecommuting, and other features. Further, they are more frequently asked to travel or put in overtime because they "don't have a family." Nevertheless, a variety of family benefits are available in many organizations.

Adoption Benefits Many employers provide maternity and paternity benefits to employees who give birth to children. A comparatively small number of employees adopt children, and in the interest of fairness and life enrichment, some organizations such as Wendy's, Subaru of America, General Mills, Avon Products, and Timberland provide reimbursement benefits for them. Estimates are that anywhere from 35% to approximately 47% of firms provide some type of adoption benefits.[67]

Child-Care Assistance Balancing work and family responsibilities is a major challenge for many workers. Whether they are single parents or dual-career couples, these employees often experience difficulty obtaining high-quality, affordable child care. Employers are addressing the child-care issue in the following ways:

- Providing referral services to help parents locate child-care providers
- Establishing discounts at day-care centers, which may be subsidized by the employer
- Arranging with hospitals to offer sick-child programs partially paid for by the employer
- Developing after-school programs for older school-age children, often in conjunction with local public and private school systems
- Offering on-site child-care centers

Elder-Care Assistance Another family issue of importance is caring for elderly relatives. An increasing number of organizations are offering benefits that help employees more effectively balance their work and elder-care responsibilities. Besides time off provided by the FMLA, some of these benefits include subsidies for elder-care expenses, referrals to elder-care providers, and elder-care assistance for emergencies.[68]

Measuring the Effectiveness of Family Benefits

Employers that have provided child-care and other family-friendly assistance have found the programs beneficial for several reasons. The greatest advantage is in aiding employee retention.[69] Employees are more likely to stay with employers who aid them with work-life balancing. Child-care benefits can produce significant savings, primarily due to decreased employee absenteeism and turnover. Analyses of elder-care costs-benefits show similar results. To determine such metrics, costs for recruiting, training, turnover, and lost productivity often are included.

Benefits for Domestic Partners

As lifestyles change in the United States, employers are being confronted with requests for benefits from employees who are not married but have close personal relationships with others. The terms often used to refer to individuals with such arrangements are *domestic partners* and *spousal equivalents*. The employees who are submitting these requests are: (1) unmarried employees who are living with individuals of the opposite sex and (2) gay and lesbian employees who have partners.

The argument made by these employees is that if an employer provides benefits for the spouses of married employees, then benefits should be provided for employees without spouses but with alternative lifestyles and relationships.[70] This view is reinforced by data showing that a significant percentage of heterosexual couples live together before or instead of formally marrying. Also, gay employees are being increasingly more open about their lifestyles.

The debate about *same-sex marriages* has amplified the issue for HR professionals and their employers. In some states and cities, laws have been enacted to require employers to grant domestic partners the same benefits rights that they give to traditional married couples. Employers providing domestic partner benefits usually have policies that define what the qualifying relationship is and what documentation is required to verify eligibility. At some firms, both the employee and the "eligible partner" must sign an Affidavit of Spousal Equivalence. With this affidavit, the employee and the partner are asked to affirm the following:

- Each is the other's only spousal equivalent.
- They are not blood relatives.
- They are living together and jointly share responsibility for their common welfare and financial obligations.

However, in states such as Michigan, Nebraska, Ohio, and Kentucky where gay marriage is not allowed, the benefits provided to the domestic partners of public workers are being taken away.[71]

TIME-OFF AND OTHER BENEFITS

Time-off benefits represent a significant portion of total benefits costs. Employers give employees paid time off for a variety of circumstances. Paid lunch breaks and rest periods, holidays, and vacations are common. But time off is given for a number of other purposes as well. As Figure 13-13 indicates, these time-off benefits also include various leaves of absence. The United States does not require organizations to offer the same generous amounts of leave required

| FIGURE 13-13 | Percentage of Companies with Various Paid-Time-Off Plans |

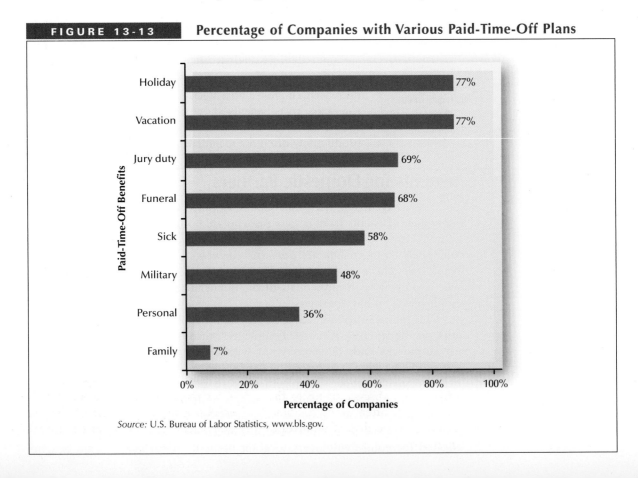

Source: U.S. Bureau of Labor Statistics, www.bls.gov.

by many other nations. However, there is a stronger emphasis in many states such as Colorado and Nevada to offer employees more leave so that they can focus on personal obligations.[72]

Holiday Pay

Most employers provide pay for a variety of holidays. In the United States, employers commonly offer 10 to 12 holidays annually. Employers in many other countries are required to provide a significantly higher number of holidays, approaching 20 to 30 days in some cases. In both the United States and other countries, the number of holidays offered can vary depending on state/provincial laws and union contracts.

As an abuse-control measure, employers commonly require employees to work the last scheduled day before a holiday and the first scheduled workday after a holiday to be eligible for holiday pay. Some employers pay time-and-a-half to hourly employees who must work holidays. Also, some employers provide company holiday parties and holiday bonus programs such as food gifts (e.g., turkeys at Thanksgiving) or holiday gift cards.

Vacation Pay

Paid vacations are a common benefit. Employers often use graduated vacation-time scales based on employees' lengths of service. Some organizations have a "use it or lose it" policy whereby accrued vacation time cannot be carried over from year to year. One survey found that workers on average forfeit three vacation days per year.[73]

Some employers have policies to "buy back" unused vacation time. Other employers, such as banks, may have policies requiring employees to take a minimum number of vacation days off in a row. Regardless of the vacation policies used, employees are often required to work the day before and the day after vacation time off.

Leaves of Absence

Employers grant *leaves of absence*, taken as time off with or without pay, for a variety of reasons. All the leaves discussed here add to employer costs even if unpaid. That is because the missing employee's work must be covered, either by other employees working additionally or by temporary employees working under contract.

Leaves are given for a variety of purposes. Some, such as *military leave, election leave*, and *jury leave*, are required by various state and federal laws. Employers commonly pay the difference between the employee's regular pay and the military, election, or jury pay. Some firms grant the employees military time off and provide regular pay while the employees also receive military pay. Federal law prohibits taking discriminatory action against military reservists by requiring them to take vacation time when deployed or in training. However, the leave request must be reasonable and truly required by the military.

Funeral leave or *bereavement leave* is another common type of leave offered. An absence of up to three days for the death of immediate family members is often granted. Some policies also give unpaid time off for the death of more distant relatives or any permanent resident of an employee's home.[74]

Family Leave As mentioned earlier in the chapter, the passage of the Family and Medical Leave Act clarified the rights of employees and the responsibilities of most employers. Even though *paternity leave* for male workers is available under the FMLA, a relatively low percentage of men take it. The primary reason for the low usage is a perception that it is not as socially acceptable for men to stay home for child-related reasons. That view has begun changing as the number of dual-career couples in the workforce has risen.[75]

Sick Leave Medical and sick leave are closely related. Many employers allow employees to miss a limited number of days because of illness without losing pay. More than 50% of all U.S. workers receive paid sick leave. But U.S. employers do not provide paid sick leave to as many workers percentagewise as do the employers in other developed countries.

Some employers allow employees to accumulate unused sick leave, which may be used in case of catastrophic illnesses. Others pay their employees for unused sick leave. A problem employers face is that only about 35% of unscheduled employee absences are due to illnesses.[76] Some organizations have shifted the emphasis to reward people who do not use sick leave by giving them **well pay**—extra pay for not taking sick leave. Another approach is to use a paid-time-off plan.

Paid-Time-Off Plans

A growing number of employers have made use of a **paid-time-off (PTO) plan**, which combines all sick leave, vacation time, and holidays into a total number of hours or days that employees can take off with pay. Studies have found that about 37% of all employers have PTO plans. More importantly, many of those employers have found PTO plans to be more effective than other means of reducing absenteeism and in having time off scheduled more efficiently. Other advantages cited by employers with PTO plans are ease of administration and as an aid for recruiting and retention and for increasing employee understanding and use of leave policies. Alternatively, PTO plans might increase absenteeism rates in companies and can make workers think that managers do not trust them to effectively manage their time off.[77]

Miscellaneous Benefits

Employers offer a wide variety of miscellaneous benefits. Some of the benefits are voluntary, meaning that employees can participate in them and pay for the costs themselves, often at group discount rates. Various types of voluntary insurance programs are the most common offered.[78] Others are unique to employers and are provided at little or no cost to employees.

Some benefits and services are social and recreational in nature, such as tennis courts, bowling leagues, picnics, parties, employer-sponsored athletic teams, organizationally owned recreational lodges, and other sponsored activities and interest groups. As interest in employee wellness has increased, more firms are providing recreational facilities and activities. The idea behind social and recreational programs is to promote employee happiness and team spirit. Employees may appreciate this type of benefit, but managers should not necessarily expect increased job productivity or job satisfaction as a result. Further, employers should retain control of all events associated with their organizations because of possible legal responsibility.

Well pay Extra pay for not taking sick leave.

Paid-time-off (PTO) plan Plan that combines all sick leave, vacation time, and holidays into a total number of hours or days that employees can take off with pay.

SUMMARY

- Benefits provide additional compensation to some employees as a reward for organizational membership. Because benefits generally are not taxed, they are highly desired by employees.
- Strategic considerations for benefits include their value in creating a competitive advantage and aiding in attracting and retaining employees.
- Benefits design and cost-control actions are crucial to strategic benefits efforts.
- Flexible benefits plans, which can be tailored to individual needs and situations, are increasing in popularity.
- Because of the variety of benefit options available and the costs involved, employers must develop effective systems to communicate benefits information to their employees.
- Benefits can be viewed as mandatory or voluntary. The general types of benefits include security, health care, retirement, financial, family oriented, and time off.
- Three prominent security benefits are workers' compensation, unemployment compensation, and severance pay.
- Because health care benefits costs have increased significantly, employers are managing their health benefits costs more aggressively.

- Efforts to control the costs of health benefits have included changing employee copayments and employee contributions, using managed care, and switching to consumer-driven health (CDH) plans.
- Organizations provide retirement benefits through defined-benefit, defined-contribution, or cash balance plans.
- The pension area is a complex one that is governed by the Employee Retirement Income Security Act (ERISA) and other laws.
- Use of defined-contribution plans and individual retirement accounts is growing.
- Various types of financial services, insurance benefits, relocation assistance, educational assistance, and other benefits enhance the appeal of an organization to employees.
- Family-oriented benefits include complying with the Family and Medical Leave Act (FMLA) of 1993 and offering adoption benefits, child-care assistance, and elder-care assistance.
- Holiday pay, vacation pay, various leaves of absence, and paid-time-off plans are another means of providing benefits to employees.

CRITICAL THINKING ACTIVITIES

1. Why are benefits strategically important to employers, and what are some key strategic considerations?

2. Discuss the following statement: "Health care costs are out of control in the United States, and increasing conflicts between employers and employees are likely as employers try to reduce their health benefits costs."

3. Assume that as an HR staff member, you have been asked to research consumer-driven health

plans because your employer is considering implementing one. Go to a leading benefits information resource, *Employee Benefit News*, at www.benefitnews.com, and identify the elements of a successful CDH plan and some examples of firms that use such a plan.

4. Based on the information discussed in the chapter, how would you oversee the design (or redesign) of a benefits program in a large organization? What issues would you consider?

HR EXPERIENTIAL PROBLEM SOLVING

Your company now has more than 60 employees. The controller has been handling all of the HR functions including administration of the company's benefits. The benefits package includes health, dental, 401(k) and other voluntary benefits. You are

considering outsourcing the benefits administration function to enable the controller to focus more on the company's accounting needs. The terms *human resources outsourcing (HRO), administrative services organization (ASO),* and *professional employer organization (PEO)* have been used in discussions of outsourcing employer HR benefit functions. Information to assist you in determining the type of services to best meet the company's needs can be found at www.corbanone.com.

1. What are the differences between the services offered by an HRO, ASO, and PEO?
2. Based upon the company's size and the types of benefits offered, which service will best meet the needs of the company?

CASE

Strategic Benefits at KPMG Canada

Companies need to offer competitive benefits to employees or risk having employees become dissatisfied with their current job situations. KPMG Canada recently faced such a challenge when the company's portfolio of benefits was viewed by employees as uncompetitive compared to packages offered by other high-performing organizations. Despite its People Matters program that offered leave for adoption, flex-time, workout opportunities, and other perquisites, employee survey results indicated that generalized satisfaction with benefits was low. These results were not alarming to managers, given that KPMG had not revised employee benefits for some time. However, what was needed to fix this problem was a comprehensive overhaul of the company's benefits program using a strategic approach guided by employee feedback, leadership direction, and innovation. Top leadership also wanted the new plan to be congruent with the organizational approach to total rewards and to incorporate a sufficient "wow factor" to satisfy employees.

KPMG started the strategic planning process by comparing current benefits to the packages offered by other competing organizations, and the results verified that the company had to make up some ground in the area of benefits administration. A benefits consultant was hired to facilitate the redesign effort, and a steering committee comprised of top managers was developed to oversee the proposed changes, garner greater support for the new benefits throughout the company, ensure that many different employee needs were being met, and make sure the plan was competitive overall.

After working on the project for more than two years, KPMG successfully developed a new benefits package that delighted employees. For instance, individuals were given many coverage options for dental, medical, disability, and life insurance. In addition, employees could dedicate pools of flex dollars to certain benefits programs that best suited their needs. Individuals are given a set amount of flex dollars, but more can be earned based on pay, different lifestyle incentives, and tax-free bonus incentives. Recent employee survey results show that people prefer the new benefits package over the old plan, which has enhanced how employees feel about the organization as a whole.[79]

QUESTIONS

1. Why is having a competitive benefits package important for KPMG Canada?
2. In your opinion, did top leadership at KPMG Canada manage the benefits redesign effort well? What else could the company have offered its employees to keep them satisfied?

SUPPLEMENTAL CASES

Delivering Benefits

This case explores how FedEx provides benefits to its employees. (For the case, go to www.cengage .com/management/mathis.)

Benefiting Connie

This case describes the problems that can occur when trying to coordinate time-off leaves for employees. (For the case, go to www.cengage.com/ management/mathis.)

N O T E S

1. Based on Jeremy Smerd, "In Workers' Heads," *Workforce Management*, July 22, 2009, 34–39.

2. "Benefits Barometer," *BenefitsMarketplace*, 2009, 7–26.

3. Steve Jordan, "Health Care Costs Rise for Businesses, Employees," *Omaha World-Herald*, November 19, 2007, Section D, 1–2.

4. Lydell C. Bridgeford, "Recession Sends Employers into Strategic Mode," *Employee Benefit News*, April 21, 2009, http://ebn .benefitnews.com.

5. Stephen Miller, "Alternative Benefit Strategies: Not Whether but Which," *SHRM Compensation and Benefit News*, June 2006, www.shrm.org/ rewards.

6. "Benefits Trends and Employee Satisfaction," *Workplace Visions*, SHRM, 2007, 1–8.

7. Towers Perrin, 2007, www .towersperrin.com.

8. Leah Carlson Shepard, "*Fortune* Hails '100 Best Companies to Work For,'" *Employee Benefit News*, April 1, 2007, 1ff.

9. Linda Lisanti, "Happy Employees, Happy Customers," *Convenience Store News*, September 18, 2006, 97; "Benefits Can Improve Business Success," *Employee Benefit News*, February 13, 2007, www .benefitnews.com.

10. "An Executive Perspective on Employee Benefits," *McKinsey Quarterly Survey*, April 2006, 1, www.mckinseyquarterly.com; "Incorporate 'Employer of Choice' Goals into Strategic, Benefits Planning," *Best Practices in HR*, September 22, 2006, 3.

11. Kevin Sweeney, "Around the Benefits World," *Employee Benefit News*, October 2003, 35–36.

12. "A Strong Benefits Mix May Be Answer to Recruiting, Retention Woes," *Workindex.com*, May 3, 2006, www.workindex.com.

13. For an overview and details, see Jerry S. Rosenbloom, *The Handbook of Employee Benefits: Design, Funding, and Administration*, 6th ed. (New York: McGraw-Hill, 2005).

14. U.S. Bureau of Labor Statistics, www.bls.gov.

15. "Top Part-Time Employers," *OfficeSolutions*, Fall 2009, 12.

16. Karen Lee, "Study Shows Six Out of Ten Companies Outsource Benefits," *Employee Benefit News*, October 2004, 11.

17. Thomas W. Gainey and Brian S. Klaas, "The Use and Impact of e-HR: A Survey of HR Professionals," *People and Strategy*, 31 (2008), 50–55.

18. "Building a Better Benefits Experience," Workday, Special Advertising Supplement to *Workforce Management*, S5; "Online Benefits Expected to Become Predominant," *Best's Review*, April 2005, 106; Chris Silva, "Virtually Beneficial: HR Going Virtual with Online Benefits Fairs," *Employee Benefit News*, November 2006, 1ff.; Jeremy Smerd, "Digitally Driven," *Workforce Management*, April 6, 2009, 23–29.

19. Examples of metrics for benefits can be found in Jim Simon, "Weighing the Cost of Employee Benefits," *Workspan*, March 2003, 56–57; Jac Fitz-Enz and Barbara Davidson, *How to Measure Human Resources Management*, 3rd ed. (New York: McGraw-Hill, 2002), 141–156.

20. Laura Petrecca, "Employee Benefits Squeezed: Financially Pinched Companies Cutting Back," *USA Today*, April 7, 2009, 1B–2B.

21. "Cost Control Is Shifting to a Long-Term View," *HR Focus*, September 2006, 1; M. P. McQueen, "The Shifting Calculus of Workplace Benefits," *The Wall Street Journal*, January 16, 2007, D1–D2; Peter Miller, Melanie Langsett, and Susan Hogan, "Giving HR the One-Two Punch: Consolidating Benefits as a Bridge to Shared Services," *Workspan*, May 2009, 50–54.

22. "Few Employees Understand and Appreciate Their Total Compensation Package," *WorldatWork News*, November 29, 2006. For details, go to www .charltonconsulting.com; Lisa Patten, "Communicating the New Benefits Deal," *Benefits Quarterly*, Second Quarter 2007, 33–36.

23. Robert Whiddon, "Ranking Health Plans on Satisfaction," *Employee Benefits News*, June 15, 2008, 1ff.;

Dennis Ackley, "Communication: The Key to Putting the Benefit Back in Benefits," *Workspan*, February 2006, 31–34; Betty Sosnin, "What's in Your Summary Plan Description?" *HR Magazine*, August 2007, 63–70.

24. Based on Lilian Myers, "Transforming Presenteeism into Productivity," *Workspan*, July 2009, 41–43.

25. Michal Kisilevitz, Shub Debgupta, and Daniel Metz, "Improving Employee Benefits Through Effective Communication," *WorldatWork Journal*, First Quarter 2006, 52–60; Jessica Marquez, "Breaking the Bad News on 401(k)s," *Workforce Management*, June 22, 2009, 30ff.; Jennifer Benz, "Say It All in 140 Characters: Everything You Need to Know Before Joining 'Twitterverse,'" *Employee Benefit News*, July 2009, 12ff.

26. Jill Elswick, "Loaded Statements: Web-Based Total Compensation Statements Keep Employees in the Know," *BenefitNews.com*, May 2005, www.benefitnews.com.

27. U.S. Bureau of Labor Statistics, www.bls.gov.

28. Jeremy Smerd, "You Can Do Anything but Don't Mess with My Health Insurance," April 12, 2007, www.workforce.com; Kelley M. Butler, "J.D. Power Releases Results from First-Ever Health Plan Satisfaction Survey," *Employee Benefit News*, April 15, 2007, 1ff.

29. Susan J. Wells, "When OBs Are Scarce," *HR Magazine*, August 2007, 55–60; Jean P. Drouin, "Health Care Costs: A Market-Based View," www .mckinseyquarterly.com; Richard Breeden, "Firms Consider End to Employee Health Insurance," *The Wall Street Journal*, August 14, 2006, B8.

30. Deborah Solomon, David Wessel, and Kris Maher, "Health-Insurance Gap Surges as a Political Issue," *The Wall Street Journal*, January 19, 2007, A1, A12.

31. "Retiree Health-Care Costs Climb to $63.4 Billion at GM," *Omaha World-Herald*, March 12, 2004, B1.

32. "Health Benefit Costs to Keep Growing for Retirees," *Omaha World-Herald*, December 14, 2006, 7A; Bryce G. Hoffman, "Ford to

Freeze Health Plans," *The Denver Post*, December 14, 2005, 3C; Dallas Salisbury, "Crunching the Numbers," *Human Resource Executive Online*, www.hreonline.com.

33. Based on Martha J. Frase, "Minimalist Health Coverage," *HR Magazine*, June 2009, 107–112.

34. Vanesa Fuhrmans, "More Employers Try Limited Health Plans," *The Wall Street Journal*, January 17, 2006, D1; Chris Silva, "Employers Turn to Mini-Med Plans as Stop Gaps," *Employee Benefit News*, December 2006, 39.

35. "More Firms Adopting Consumerism," *Benefits News .com*, September 14, 2006, www .employeebenefitnews.com; Sander Domaszewicz, "A Considered Approach," *Human Resource Executive Online*, May 2, 2009, www.hreonline.com;

36. Robert J. Grossman, "Redirecting Health Coverage," *HR Magazine*, June 2009, 51–55.

37. Christine Keller and Christopher E. Condeluci, "Tax Relief and Health Care Act Should Prompt Re-examination of HSAs," *SHRM HR Legal Report*, July–August 2007, 1–8.

38. Steve Neeleman, "Making Health Savings Accounts Work," *Compensation and Benefits Review*, March/April 2005, 33; Leah Carlson Shepard, "Enrollment in New CDHPs Remains Low," *Benefits News.com*, June 15, 2006, www .employeebenefitnews.com.

39. "Health Insurance Lexicon," *HR Magazine*, August 2008, 61–84.

40. "Two-Thirds of Large Employers Now Offering Incentives to Improve Employees' Health," *Management Barometer*, April 10, 2006, www .barometersurveys.com; Bruce Shutan, "Avivia Health Reveals Ways to Engage Patients in Healthy Living, Sustain Behavioral Change," www. benefitnews.com; Kristen B. Frasch, "A Step Ahead: New Wellness Initiative that Keeps Employees Walking While They Work Is Starting to Catch on in Corporate America," *Human Resource Executive*, February 2009, 30–35; Abhijit Chakraverty, Shwetanuj Saha, Sonal Kathuria, and Chris Vojta, "Understanding and Designing Health-Care Incentive Programs," *Workspan*, January 2008, 48–55; Joanie Bretag, "Health Enhancement Program Shaves Costs," *Workspan*, February 2009, 77–80; Lydell C. Bridgeford, "Sold on Science: Evidence-Based Wellness Program Gains Employee Acceptance Without Incentives," *Employee Benefit News*, June 1, 2007, 44ff.

41. Jeremy Smerd, "You Can Do Anything but Don't Mess with My Health Insurance," *Workforce Management*, April 12, 2007, www.workforce.com.

42. "FAQs for Employees about COBRA Continuation Health Coverage," Employee Benefits Security Administration, www.dol.gov.

43. "An Employee's Guide to Health Benefits under COBRA: The Consolidation Omnibus Budget Reconciliation Act of 1986," U.S. Department of Labor Manual, Employee Benefits Security Administration, www.dol.gov.

44. "Can You Provide Us with a Brief Overview of COBRA?" *Ceridian Abstracts*, www.hrcompliance .ceridian.com.

45. Amy Barrett, "Blindsided: Five H.R. Mistakes You Can't Afford to Make," *BusinessWeek SmallBiz*, April/May 2007, 40–46; Darli Dunkelberger, "Avoiding COBRA's Bite: Three Keys to Compliance," *Compensation and Benefits Review*, March/April 2005, 44; "COBRA Continuation Coverage Assistance under ARRA," Employee Benefits Security Administration, www .dol.gov; "DOL Issues New Model COBRA Notices and Additional Guidance," *Ceridian Abstracts*, May 18, 2009, www.hrcompliance .ceridian.com; Cheryl Risley Hughes, "The COBRA Subsidy Scramble: A Race to Comply," *Employee Benefit News Alert*, ebnbenefitnews@e.benefitnews .com; "IRS Guides Employers on COBRA Rule Change," *Workforce Management*, April 7, 2009, www .workforce.com.

46. For details on HIPAA, see www.hhs .gov/ocr/hipaa.

47. Lydell C. Bridgeford, "Mental Health Parity and Addiction Equity Act Signed into Law," *Employee Benefits News*, December 2008, 44.

48. Amy Erlbacher-Anderson, Gary Clatterbuck, and Adam Cockerill, *Labor Law Forum 2009*, Employee Benefits Law Update, Baird Holm Attorneys at Law, 45–64.

49. *EBRI 2010 Retirement Confidence Study*, www.ebri.org.

50. The Wharton School, "Not So Golden," *Human Resource Executive Online*, www.hreonline .com.

51. Stephanie L. Costo, "Trends in Retirement Plan Coverage over the Last Decade," *Monthly Labor Review*, February 2006, 58–64; Andrew A. Luchak, Dionne M. Pohler, and Ian R. Gellatly, "When Do Committed Employees Retire? The Effects of Organizational Commitment on Retirement Plans under a Defined-Benefit Pension Plan," *Human Resource Management*, 47 (2008), 581–599.

52. Ellen E. Schultz and Theo Francis, "What You Need to Know About Pension Changes," *The Wall Street Journal*, August 15, 2006, D1; A. J. Bianchi, "Futurecast: Cash Balance Retirement Plans After *Cooper v. IBM*," *Employee Benefit News*, October 2006, 72.

53. Eleanor Laise, "Employers Grab Reins of Workers' 401(k)s," *The Wall Street Journal*, April, 25, 2007, D1ff.

54. Rachel D. Kugelmass and Richard Koski, "The Roth 401(k)," *Workspan*, December 2005, 36.

55. *Arizona Governing Committee v. Norris*, 103 S. Ct. 3492, 32 FEP Cases 233 (1983).

56. John Nownes, "What Every Plan Administrator Needs to Know About QDROs," *HRAM Highlights*, October 2003, 8.

57. Debbie Powell, "Reporting and Disclosure Requirements Under the Pension Protection Act of 2006," *Employee Benefit News*, December 2006, 52; Anoinette M. Pilzner, "Pension Protection Act of 2006: Mandates and Options for Retirement Plans," *SHRM HR Legal Report*, October/November, 2006, 1ff.

58. Stephanie Armour, "Rule on Retiree Benefits Changes: Reactions Vary on Health Care Limits for Those 65 and Up," *USA Today*, January 28, 2007, B1.

59. *Public Employees Retirement System of Ohio v. Betts*, 109 S. Ct. 256 (1989).

60. Angela Maas, "Legal Transformation," *Employee Benefit News*, April 15, 2005, 27.

61. "Participation Remains Low for Tuition Assistance Programs," *BenefitNews.com*, June 20, 2006,

www.benefitnews.com; Matt Bolch, "Bearing Fruit," *HR Magazine*, March 2006, 57–60; Andy Meister, "A Matter of Degrees," *Workforce Management*, May 2004, 32–38.

62. "An Overview of the 2007 FMLA Survey," *SHRM Survey Brief*, 1–4.

63. "Workplace Flexibility," *HR Public Policy Issue*, SHRM Governmental Affairs Department, March/April 2007.

64. "An Overview of the 2007 FMLA Survey," *SHRM Survey Brief*, 1–4; "Workplace Flexibility," *HR Public Policy Issue*, SHRM Governmental Affairs Department, March/April 2007.

65. Stephanie Armour, "Rules Clamp Down on Family Leave," *USA Today*, November 14, 2008, A1; "Department of Labor Publishes Final FMLA Regulations," *Labor and Employment Law Alert*, Baird Holm Attorneys at Law, November 17, 2008; Diane Cadrain, "Leave Law Spurs Policy Changes: Revision of the Family and Medical Leave Act Creates Opportunities for Positive Change," *HR Magazine*, March 2009, 47–48; Cara Woodson Welch, Esq. and Carrie Clark, "What You Need to Know about the New Final FMLA Regulations," *Workspan*, March 2009, 17–18.

66. Sara Schaefer Munoz, "A Good Idea, But . . . ," *The Wall Street Journal*, January 24, 2005, R6.

67. Stephanie Armour, "More Companies Add Benefits for Employees Who Adopt," *USA Today*, June 20, 2007, B1; Candice

E. Blair, "Policies That Work for Your Company," *Workspan*, October 2008, 43–46; Leah Carlson Shepard, "Happiness Money Can't Buy: In Tough Economic Times, Adoption Benefits Strengthen Employee Satisfaction, Loyalty," *Employee Benefit News*, May 2009, 66ff.; Carrie Boerio, "Adoption Benefits: Why They're Good for Business," *Workspan*, October 2007, 65–66; Lydell C. Bridgeford, "Employers Honored for Best Adoption Benefits," *Employee Benefit News*, May 2008, 1ff.; Lynn Gresham, "Employers Honored for Adoption Benefits," *Employee Benefit News*, May 2007, 1ff.

68. Stephanie Armour, "Juggling Work, Care for Aging Parent: Some Companies Help Their Workers," *USA Today*, June 26, 2007, 3B.

69. Reagan Baughman, Daniela DiNardi, and Douglas Holtz-Eakin, "Productivity and Wage Effects of 'Family Friendly' Fringe Benefits," *International Journal of Manpower*, 24 (2003), 247.

70. M. A. Ash and M. V. Lee Badgett, "Separate and Unequal: The Effect of Unequal Access to Employment-Based Health Insurance on Same-Sex and Unmarried Different-Sex Couples," *Contemporary Economic Policy*, 24 (2006), 582.

71. Marisol Bello, "Unmarried Couples Lose Legal Benefits: Laws on Gay Marriage Also Apply to Domestic Unions," *USA Today*, June 20, 2007, 1A.

72. "U.S. Lags in Leave, Sick Days, Other Worker Protections," WorldatWork Staff, NewsEdge Enterprise Solutions Content Solutions, http://dialog.newsedge.com; Michael Sanserino, "Push for Time Off Gains in Many States," *The Wall Street Journal*, June 22, 2009, A3.

73. Leah Carlson, "Surveys Show Fewer Vacation Days Taken, Offered," *Employee Benefit News*, November 2004, 20.

74. "Can You Provide Us with a Sample Policy Dealing with Employee Leave Due to a Death in the Family?" *Ceridian Abstracts*, www.hrcompliance.ceridian.com.

75. Ron Lieber, "The Next Frontier: Paternity Leave," *The Wall Street Journal*, July 8, 2006, B1.

76. "Too Many Workers Take Advantage of Sick Days," October 31, 2006, www.benefitnews.com.

77. George Faulkner, "Absent and Accounted For," *Human Resource Executive*, May 2, 2006, 56–57; M. Michael Markowich, *Paid Time-Off Banks* (Scottsdale, AZ: WorldatWork, 2007); Frank Giancola, "Are PTO Plans Really All They're Cracked Up to Be," *Workspan*, June 2008, 21–27.

78. Carolyn Hirschman, "Employees' Choice," *HR Magazine*, February 2006, 95.

79. Based on Steve Spencer and Tim Clarke, "Satisfying Employee Needs and Employer Objectives with a Strategic Benefits Plan," *Workspan Focus*, January 2009, 97–99.

Employee Relations

14

Risk Management and Worker Protection

After you have read this chapter, you should be able to:

- Identify the components of risk management.
- Discuss three legal areas affecting safety and health.
- Identify the basic provisions of the Occupational Safety and Health Act of 1970 and recordkeeping and inspection requirements.
- Discuss the activities that constitute effective safety management.
- List three workplace health issues and how employers are responding to them.
- Explain workplace violence as a security issue and describe some components of an effective security program.
- Describe the nature and importance of disaster preparation and recovery planning for HR.

$1.6 Million Fine When Young Worker Suffocates

(© Nigel Cattlin/Alamy)

In a statement regarding Tempel Grain Elevators in Colorado, the U.S. Department of Labor said that teenage workers were being exposed to hazards. The federal investigation, which followed the death of a 17-year-old Tempel employee, uncovered many safety violations regarding employees aged 14 to 17 years old. In addition, the company had employed a 13-year-old, which was a clear violation of federal law. Teens were driving front-end loaders, forklifts, and other dangerous equipment.

The company was fined for both safety violations and violations of child labor laws. A press release from the Secretary of Labor said the company was "well aware of the hazards and knowingly put its young workers in harm's way." "From safety to wage and hour issues the company created a hazardous and illegal working environment for its workers."

The 17-year-old employee who was killed fell inside a grain bin and was suffocated by grain. Other hazards OSHA found included unguarded conveyors, fall hazards, lack of first aid supplies and trained medical personnel, incomplete fire extinguisher inspections, use of extension cords instead of wiring, and failure to inspect electrical equipment. Tempel Grain received 22 "willful" and 13 "serious" violations. Willful violations included not providing an emergency action plan, no training in safe bin entry, and failure of shut-off and lockout equipment when employees were in the bins. In addition, the wage and hour division found 77 child labor violations involving 15 minors.

The largest OSHA fine to date was $86 million against BP Products North America for safety violations in a Texas City, Texas, refinery that exploded and killed 15 people while injuring 170. Those citations are still being appealed.[1]

Preparing an employer for the variety of potential problems that can occur when doing business is the focus of *risk management*. For human resources, risk management includes:

- Preventing accidents and health problems at work
- Preparing for natural disasters
- Planning for terrorism attacks
- Anticipating global disease outbreaks
- Protecting against workplace violence
- Ensuring HR data are secure

In the United States and most developed nations, the concept of using prevention and control to minimize or eliminate a wide range of risks in workplaces has been expanding.

Effective risk management also is a key component of strategic management.[2] **Risk management** involves responsibilities to consider physical, human, and financial factors to protect organizational and individual interests.[3] Its scope can range from workplace safety and health to disaster preparation. A well-done HR risk management program can affect the bottom line through direct savings in workers' compensation costs, civil liability damages, and litigation expenses, as well as by increasing the likelihood of winning bids and government contracts.

The first emphasis in HR risk management in most organizations is health, safety, and security. The terms *health*, *safety*, and *security* are closely related. The broader and somewhat more nebulous term is **health**, which refers to a general state of physical, mental, and emotional well-being. A healthy person is free from illness, injury, or mental and emotional problems that impair normal human activity. Health management practices in organizations strive to maintain employees' overall well-being.

Typically, **safety** refers to a condition in which the physical well-being of people is protected. The main purpose of effective safety programs in organizations is to prevent work-related injuries and accidents. The purpose of **security** is protecting employees and organizational facilities. With the growth of workplace violence and other risk management issues, security has become an even greater concern for employers and employees alike.

Risk management
Involves responsibilities to consider physical, human, and financial factors to protect organizational and individual interests.

Health General state of physical, mental, and emotional well-being.

Safety Condition in which the physical well-being of people is protected.

Security Protection of employees and organizational facilities.

CURRENT STATE OF HEALTH, SAFETY, AND SECURITY

In a recent year in the United States, about 4 million nonfatal injuries and illnesses occurred at work. That was down from previous years. Specific rates vary depending on the industry, type of job, and other factors. The number of workplace injuries also varies by employer size, with smaller employers having more injuries per employee. The three major causes of injury (overextending, falling, and bodily reaction) were responsible for almost half of the direct costs

FIGURE 14-1   Hidden Costs of Accidents

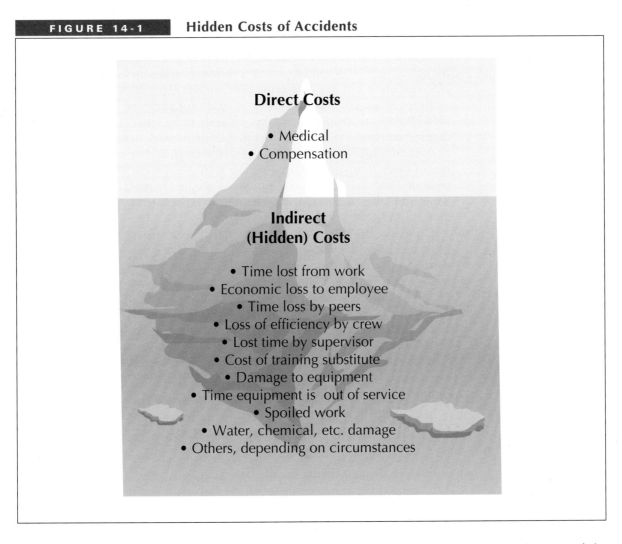

Direct Costs

- Medical
- Compensation

Indirect (Hidden) Costs

- Time lost from work
- Economic loss to employee
- Time loss by peers
- Loss of efficiency by crew
- Lost time by supervisor
- Cost of training substitute
- Damage to equipment
- Time equipment is out of service
- Spoiled work
- Water, chemical, etc. damage
- Others, depending on circumstances

of injuries. Accident costs have gone up faster than inflation because of the rapid increase in medical costs, even though the total number of accidents has been decreasing for some time. Figure 14-1 shows that the direct costs of accidents are only a small part of the total costs. More serious injuries involving days away from work occurred in about half the cases, or 2.1 per 100 workers.[4]

Trends

While injury accidents in general are down, injuries resulting in disabilities among American workers are growing. The problem seems to be related partly to unhealthy lifestyles.[5] The aging workforce also is a factor. Older workers have lower frequencies of disability, but when they are out of work, it is usually for a longer period of time.[6]

Deaths from accidents among Hispanic workers are on the rise. Many work in low-wage jobs with higher risk factors. In addition, poor English communication skills, lack of training, and other factors contribute to this situation, which runs counter to the trends for other groups.[7]

One interesting finding is that it appears more accidents occur in the spring on the day after the change to daylight savings time. Employees had almost 6% more workplace injuries on the Monday following the change to daylight savings time, presumably because of the "lost" hour of sleep. However, no significant change has been shown in the fall when everyone "gains" an hour.[8]

Self-employed workers have higher accident rates than do those who work for others. Although self-employed individuals make up less than 8% of the U.S. civilian workforce, self-employed workers have 20% of the workplace fatalities. When compared to those working for someone else, self-employed individuals were almost three times as likely to be killed. One explanation is that self-employed individuals are more likely to work in industries and occupations with higher fatality rates, especially farming. For instance, more than one of every four self-employed people who died on the job were farmers. A possible conclusion is that self-employed people are more willing to work in dangerous circumstances, and therefore they are more vulnerable to illnesses, injuries, and death.

To reduce risk of lawsuits, a number of companies have turned to employment practices liability insurance (EPLI), mandatory arbitration, and internal conflict resolution programs.[9] EPLI can provide some protection from employment-related lawsuits, but generally it is available only if employment practices, policies, recordkeeping, past claims, training, complaints, and problems pass muster. Mandatory arbitration requires all employees to agree, as a condition of employment, that they will participate in arbitration rather than instituting a lawsuit to settle any employment differences. Alternative conflict resolution programs, such as peer review panels, are designed to solve problems before they become lawsuits, thereby reducing risk for the employer.

Global Health, Safety, and Security

GLOBAL

Safety and health laws and regulations vary from country to country, ranging from virtually nonexistent to more stringent than those in the United States. The importance placed on health, safety, and security relates somewhat to the level of regulation and other factors in each country.

International Emergency Health Services With more and more expatriates working internationally, especially in some less-developed countries, significant health and safety issues require attention. One consideration is provision of emergency evacuation services. For instance, evacuating and caring for an expatriate employee who sustains internal injuries in a car accident in the Ukraine or Sierra Leone may be a major issue. Many global firms purchase coverage for their international employees from an organization that provides emergency services, such as International SOS, Global Assistance & Healthcare, or U.S. Assist. If an emergency arises, the emergency services company dispatches physicians or even transports employees by chartered aircraft. If adequate medical assistance can be obtained locally, the emergency services company maintains a referral list and arranges for the expatriate to receive treatment. Emergency services firms may also provide legal counsel in foreign countries, emergency cash for medical expenses, and assistance in reissuing lost documents.

International Security and Terrorism As more U.S. firms operate internationally, the threat of terrorist actions against those firms and their employees increases. The extent to which employees are likely to experience security problems and violence depends on the country. The employer must regularly check the security conditions in countries where expatriates are traveling and working.

GLOBAL

Global firms take a variety of actions to address security concerns. For example, one U.S. firm removed signs identifying its offices and facilities in a Latin American country in order to reduce the visibility of the firm and reduce its potential as a target for terrorist acts. Many international firms screen entry by all employees, and use metal detectors to scan all packages, briefcases, and other items. Firms commonly use physical barriers such as iron security fences, concrete barricades, bulletproof glass, and electronic surveillance devices in offices as part of their security efforts. Long-term effects of such attacks have been to change attitudes toward travel and security and to increase concern about being able to encourage international assignments and travel.[10]

Kidnapping Not all violence occurs at work. Kidnapping, murder, home invasion, robberies, and carjackings happen relatively frequently in some cities, such as Mexico City. In a number of countries throughout the world, U.S. citizens are especially vulnerable to extortion, kidnapping, bombing, physical harassment, and other terrorist activities.

To counter such threats, many global firms have *kidnap and ransom insurance.* This insurance covers the costs of paying ransoms to obtain releases of kidnapped employees and family members, paying for the bodily injuries suffered by kidnap victims, and dealing with negotiations and other expenses.

LOGGING ON

National Institute for Occupational Health and Safety (NIOSH)

For a list of links to information on a variety of safety and health topics, visit this website at www.cdc.gov/niosh.

Individual employees and their family members working and living abroad must constantly be aware of security concerns. Both predeparture and ongoing security training should be given to all expatriates, their dependents, and employees of global firms working internationally, especially if located in high-risk areas.

LEGAL REQUIREMENTS FOR SAFETY AND HEALTH

Employers must comply with a variety of federal and state laws when developing and maintaining healthy, safe, and secure workforces and working environments. Three major legal areas are workers' compensation legislation, the Americans with Disabilities Act, and child labor laws.

Workers' Compensation

First passed in the early 1900s, workers' compensation laws in some form are on the books in all states today. Under these laws, employers contribute to an insurance fund to compensate employees for injuries received while on the job. Premiums paid reflect the accident rates of the employers, with employers that have higher incident rates being assessed higher premiums. These laws usually provide payments to replace wages for injured workers, depending on the amount of lost time and the wage level. They also provide payments to cover medical bills and for retraining if a worker cannot go back to the current job.[11] Most state laws also set a maximum weekly amount for determining workers' comp benefits. Figure 14-2 shows some of the injuries covered and time lost for each.

Workers' compensation coverage has been expanded in many states to include emotional impairment that may have resulted from physical injury, as well as job-related strain, stress, anxiety, and pressure. Some cases of suicide

| FIGURE 14-2 | Sample of Worker's Comp Covered Injuries |

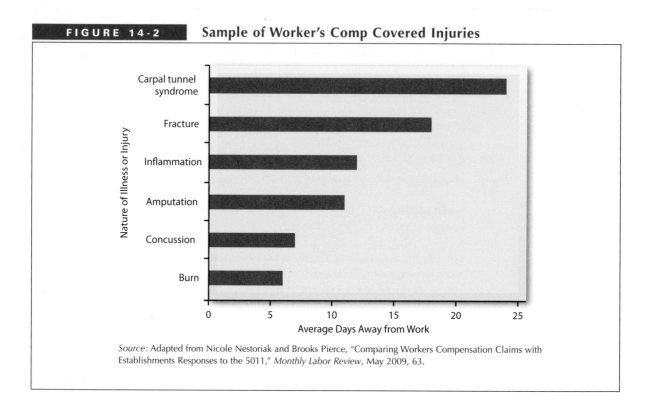

Source: Adapted from Nicole Nestoriak and Brooks Pierce, "Comparing Workers Compensation Claims with Establishments Responses to the 5011," *Monthly Labor Review,* May 2009, 63.

have also been ruled to be job related in some states, with payments due under workers' compensation.

Another aspect of workers' compensation coverage relates to the use of telecommuting by employees. In most situations, while working at home for employers, individuals are covered under workers' compensation laws. Therefore, if an employee is injured while doing employer-related work at home, the employer likely is liable for the injury.

Controlling Workers' Compensation Costs Workers' compensation costs have become a major issue for many employers. These costs usually represent from 2% to 10% of payroll for most employers. The major contributors to increases have been higher medical costs and litigation expenses.[12] However, the frequency of workers' compensation claims for lost time has decreased some in all industry groups.[13]

Key to these reductions has been *return-to-work plans*. These plans monitor employees who are off work due to injuries and illness. Also, the plans focus on returning the individuals to do *light-duty work* that is less physically demanding until they are able to perform their full range of job duties.

Workers' compensation fraud is a fast-growing and expensive problem. It has been estimated that about one fourth of the workers' compensation claims filed are fraudulent. False and exaggerated claims make up the bulk of the fraud—costing employers billions of dollars annually. Employers must continually monitor their workers' compensation expenditures. Efforts to reduce workplace injuries, illnesses, and fraud can reduce workers' compensation premiums and claims costs. Many of the safety and health management suggestions discussed later in this chapter can contribute to reducing workers' compensation costs. Further, research has shown a clear

LOGGING ON

WorkersCompensation.com
This is a national website providing workers' compensation news and information for employers, employees, insurers, and medical providers. Visit the site at www.workerscompensation .com.

linear relationship between obesity and the rate of workers compensation claims.[14]

The Family and Medical Leave Act (FMLA) affects workers' compensation as well. Because the FMLA allows eligible employees to take up to 12 weeks of leave for their serious health conditions, injured employees may ask to use that leave time in addition to the leave time allowed under workers' comp, even if it is unpaid. Some employers have policies that state that FMLA leave runs concurrently with any workers' comp leave.

Americans with Disabilities Act and Safety Issues

Employers sometimes try to return injured workers to light-duty work in order to reduce workers' compensation costs. However, under the Americans with Disabilities Act (ADA), when making accommodations for injured employees through light-duty work, employers may undercut what are really essential job functions. Also, making such accommodations for injured employees for a period of time may require employers to make similar accommodations for job applicants with disabilities.

Health and safety recordkeeping practices have been affected by an ADA provision that requires all medical-related information to be maintained separately from all other confidential files. Specific access restrictions and security procedures must be adopted for medical records of all types, including employee medical benefits claims and treatment records.

HR professionals understand the ADA guidelines as they affect physical disabilities. However, it becomes more difficult where mental illness is at issue. Employees may not be aware of the extent to which their disability may impact their performance. To the extent workplace misconduct is the issue, management should follow normal procedure. Depending on the seriousness of the complaint, it should be determined if the employee presents a risk of violence, but concerns must be based on objective facts. Although no one should ignore a threat to safety, an overreaction to "odd" behavior could be a liability under the ADA.[15]

Child Labor Laws

Safety concerns are reflected in restrictions affecting younger workers, especially those under the age of 18. Child labor laws, found in section XII of the Fair Labor Standards Act (FLSA), set the minimum age for most employment at 16 years. For "hazardous" occupations, 18 years is the minimum. Figure 14-3 lists 17 occupations that the federal government considers hazardous for children who work while attending school.

Two examples illustrate violations of the child labor law provisions. At a fast-food restaurant specializing in roast beef sandwiches, a teenage worker operated a meat slicer, which is a hazard covered by the FLSA. At a national discount retailer, teenage workers were found to have operated the mechanical box crushers. Both situations resulted in enforcement actions and fines for violating the FLSA.

Work-related injuries of younger workers are a significant issue for employers with many youth employees. Industries such as retail and fast food consistently face safety and health issues with these workers. One characteristic

| FIGURE 14-3 | **Selected Child Labor Hazardous Occupations (minimum age: 18 years)** |

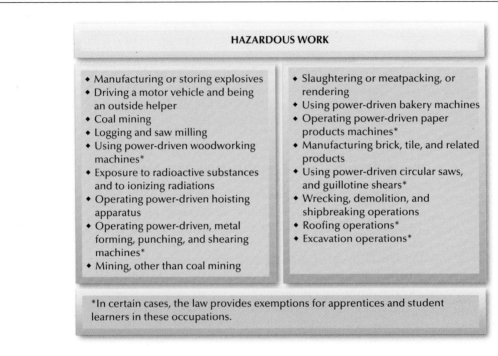

HAZARDOUS WORK

- Manufacturing or storing explosives
- Driving a motor vehicle and being an outside helper
- Coal mining
- Logging and saw milling
- Using power-driven woodworking machines*
- Exposure to radioactive substances and to ionizing radiations
- Operating power-driven hoisting apparatus
- Operating power-driven, metal forming, punching, and shearing machines*
- Mining, other than coal mining

- Slaughtering or meatpacking, or rendering
- Using power-driven bakery machines
- Operating power-driven paper products machines*
- Manufacturing brick, tile, and related products
- Using power-driven circular saws, and guillotine shears*
- Wrecking, demolition, and shipbreaking operations
- Roofing operations*
- Excavation operations*

*In certain cases, the law provides exemptions for apprentices and student learners in these occupations.

of many young workers is to take more risks at work, much like they do when they drive cars. The degree to which workers engage in work-related risks is a significant factor that affects the types and rates of injuries and safety practices of younger workers.

In addition to complying with workers' compensation, ADA, and child labor laws, most employers must comply with the Occupational Safety and Health Act of 1970. This act has had a tremendous impact on the workplace. The act is administered by the Occupational Safety and Health Administration.

OCCUPATIONAL SAFETY AND HEALTH ACT

The Occupational Safety and Health Act of 1970 was passed "to assure so far as possible every working man or woman in the Nation safe and healthful working conditions and to preserve our human resources." Every employer that is engaged in commerce and has one or more employees is covered by the act. Farmers having fewer than 10 employees are exempt. Employers in specific industries, such as coal mining, are covered under other health and safety acts. Federal, state, and local governments are covered by separate statutes and provisions.

The Occupational Safety and Health Act of 1970 established the Occupational Safety and Health Administration, known as OSHA, to administer its provisions. The act also established the National Institute for Occupational Safety and Health (NIOSH) as a supporting body to do research and develop standards. In addition, the Occupational Safety and Health Review Commission (OSHRC) has been established to review OSHA enforcement actions and to address disputes between OSHA and employers who have been cited by OSHA inspectors.

| FIGURE 14-4 | **Distribution of Nonfatal Occupational Injuries versus Illnesses by Private Industry Sector, 2008** |

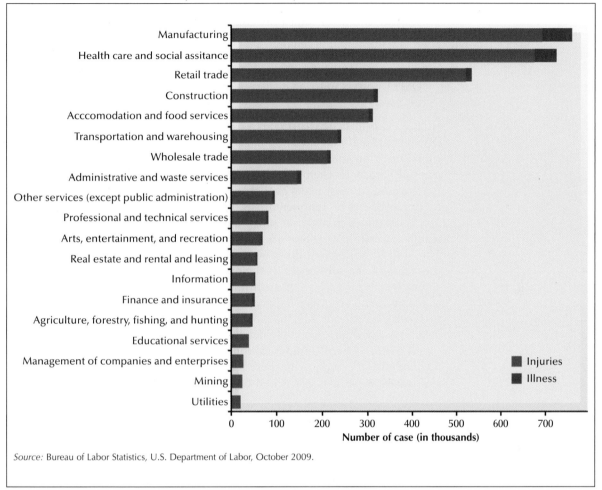

Source: Bureau of Labor Statistics, U.S. Department of Labor, October 2009.

By making employers and employees more aware of safety and health considerations, OSHA has significantly affected organizations. OSHA regulations appear to have contributed to reductions in the number of accidents and injuries in some cases. But in other industries, OSHA has had little or no effect. Figure 14-4 indicates the percentage of workplace illnesses and injuries by industry. In the figure, legal, hospitality, education, and other services are grouped in the services category.

OSHA Enforcement Standards

To implement OSHA regulations, specific standards were established to regulate equipment and working environments. National standards developed by engineering and quality control groups are often used. OSHA rules and standards are frequently complicated and technical. Small business owners and managers who do not have specialists on their staffs may find the standards difficult to read and understand. In addition, the presence of many less important minor standards has hurt the credibility of OSHA.

Some provisions have been recognized as key to employers' responsibility to comply with OSHA. Two basic ones are as follows:

- *General duty*: The act requires that the employer has a "general duty" to provide safe and healthy working conditions, even in areas where OSHA standards have not been set. Employers who know or reasonably should know of unsafe or unhealthy conditions can be cited for violating the general duty clause.
- *Notification and posters*: Employers are required to inform their employees of safety and health standards established by OSHA. Also, OSHA posters must be displayed in prominent locations in workplaces.

Hazard Communication OSHA has established *process safety management* (PSM) standards that focus on hazardous chemicals. As part of PSM, hazard communication standards require manufacturers, importers, distributors, and users of hazardous chemicals to evaluate, classify, and label those substances. Employers also must make available information about hazardous substances to employees, their representatives, and health professionals. This information is contained in material safety data sheets (MSDSs), which must be kept readily accessible to those who work with chemicals and other substances. The MSDSs indicate antidotes or actions to be taken should someone come in contact with the substances. If the organization employs a number of workers for whom English is not the primary language, then the MSDSs should be available in the necessary languages. Also, workers should be trained in how to access and use the MSDS information. The HR On-the-Job describes one means for providing accessible details.

As part of hazard communications, OSHA has established *lockout/tag-out regulations*. To comply with these regulations, firms must provide mechanics and tradespeople with locks and tags to use to make equipment inoperative

Hazard Communication

The availability of the Internet has made it much quicker and easier for employers to meet OSHA's hazard communication requirements. First, employers can access safety information produced by vendors and suppliers on hazardous materials and chemicals. Many of the firms that sell the supplies have websites that contain safety, treatment, and antidote specifications. An employer can immediately access and download updated information and details on new or revised chemicals.

Additionally, information technology allows employers to use the Internet to maintain MSDSs on chemicals and workplace substances. Using MSDS software, firms can update electronic MSDSs regularly rather than having to reissue printed manuals regularly. An employer can place all MSDSs on an intranet, through an Internet link, or access manufacturers' information sheets.

Many MSDSs also can be found on websites. For example, at a warehouse for a company, an employee was injured when a chemical spilled on him. The company used an online link to retrieve the MSDS for that chemical. Coworkers took the employee to the hospital. By the time they got there, the current version of the MSDS had been faxed to the hospital, and a company safety person was on the phone with the hospital staff to provide information about the chemical and the injured employee's treatment.

for repair or adjustment to prevent accidental start-up of defective machinery. Only the person whose name is printed on the tag or engraved on the lock may remove the device.

Bloodborne Pathogens OSHA has issued a standard regarding exposure to the hepatitis B virus (HBV), the human immunodeficiency virus (HIV), and other bloodborne pathogens. This regulation was developed to protect employees who regularly are exposed to blood and other such substances from contracting AIDS and other serious diseases. Obviously, health care laboratory workers, nurses, and medical technicians are at greatest risk. However, all employers covered by OSHA regulations must comply in workplaces where cuts and abrasions are common. Regulations require employers with the most pronounced risks to have written control and response plans and to train workers in following the proper procedures.

Personal Protective Equipment One goal of OSHA has been to develop standards for personal protective equipment (PPE). These standards require that employers analyze job hazards, provide adequate PPE to employees in hazardous jobs, and train employees in the use of PPE items. Common PPE items include safety glasses, hard hats, and safety shoes. Employers are required to provide PPE to all employees who are working in an environment that presents hazards or who might have contact with hazardous chemicals and substances on the job.[16]

Pandemic Guidelines In addition to regulations, OSHA issues guidelines that can help to protect people at work. The guidelines are suggestions that employers can use to deal with a health or safety issue. One such set of guidelines can help employers to prepare for a pandemic disease. These guidelines present information on how a virus is likely to spread among the workforce and include information on engineering controls, work practices, and the use and value of PPE such as respirators and surgical masks. The guidelines also recommend planning to deal with a depleted workforce.[17]

Ergonomics and OSHA

Ergonomics is the study and design of the work environment to address physical demands placed on individuals. In a work setting, ergonomic studies look at such factors as fatigue, lighting, tools, equipment layout, and placement of controls. Ergonomics can provide economic value to employers.

For a number of years, OSHA focused on the large number of work-related injuries due to repetitive stress and repetitive motion, such as cumulative trauma disorders, carpal tunnel syndrome, and other injuries. **Cumulative trauma disorders (CTDs)** are muscle and skeletal injuries that occur when workers repetitively use the same muscles to perform tasks. *Carpal tunnel syndrome*, a cumulative trauma disorder, is an injury common to people who put their hands through repetitive motions such as typing, playing certain musical instruments, cutting, and sewing.

Problems caused by repetitive and cumulative injuries occur in a variety of work settings. The meatpacking industry has a very high level of CTDs. Grocery cashiers experience CTDs from repetitively twisting their wrists when they scan bar codes on canned goods. Office workers experience CTDs too, primarily from doing extensive typing and data entry on computers and computer-related equipment. Most recently, attention has focused on the

Ergonomics Study and design of the work environment to address physical demands placed on individuals.

Cumulative trauma disorders (CTDs) Muscle and skeletal injuries that occur when workers repetitively use the same muscles to perform tasks.

application of ergonomic principles to the design of work stations where workers extensively use personal computers, portable message devices, cell phones, and video display terminals for extended periods of time.

OSHA has approached ergonomics concerns by adopting voluntary guidelines for specific problem industries and jobs, identifying industries with serious ergonomic problems, and giving employers tools for identifying and controlling ergonomics hazards. Among the industries receiving guidelines are nursing homes, poultry processors, and retail grocery stores.

Successful Ergonomics Programs A successful ergonomics program has several components. First, management must commit to reducing injuries caused by repetition and cumulative trauma, including providing financial and other resources to support the efforts. Involvement of employees is key to getting employee support. Other actions should include reviewing jobs where CTD problems could exist and ensuring that proper equipment, seating, lighting, and other engineering solutions are utilized. Also, supervisors and managers should be trained to observe signs of CTD and on how to respond to employee complaints about musculoskeletal and repetitive motion problems.

LOGGING ON

Occupational Safety & Health Administration

Access to OHSA regulations for compliance, newsroom, and much more can be found at the OSHA home page by visiting the website at www.osha.gov.

Work Assignments and OSHA

The rights of employees regarding work assignments have been addressed as part of OSHA regulations. Two prominent areas where work assignments and concerns about safety and health meet are reproductive health and unsafe work.

Work Assignments and Reproductive Health Assigning employees to work in areas where their ability to have children may be affected by exposure to chemical hazards is an issue. Women who are able to bear children or who are pregnant have presented the primary concerns, but in some situations the possibility that men might become sterile also has been involved.

In a court case involving reproductive health, the Supreme Court held that Johnson Controls violated the Civil Rights Act and the Pregnancy Discrimination Act through a policy of keeping women of childbearing capacity out of jobs that might expose them to lead.[18] Although employers have no absolute protection from liability, the following actions can help:

- Maintain a safe workplace for all by seeking the safest working methods.
- Comply with all state and federal safety laws.
- Inform employees of any known risks.
- Document employee acceptance of any risks.

Refusing Unsafe Work Both union and nonunion workers have refused to work when they considered the work unsafe. In many court cases, that refusal has been found to be justified. The conditions for refusing work because of safety concerns include the following:

- The employee's fear is objectively reasonable.
- The employee has tried to have the dangerous condition corrected.
- Using normal procedures to solve the problem has not worked.

OSHA Recordkeeping Requirements

Employers are generally required to maintain a detailed annual record of the various types of injuries, accidents, and fatalities for inspection by OSHA representatives and for submission to the agency. OSHA guidelines state that facilities whose accident records are below the national average rarely need inspecting. But those with high "days away from work scores" may get letters from OSHA and perhaps an inspection.[19] Many organizations must complete OSHA Form 300 to report workshop accidents and injuries. These organizations include firms having frequent hospitalizations, injuries, illnesses, or work-related deaths, and firms in a labor statistics survey conducted by OSHA each year. However, no one knows how many industrial accidents go unreported. It may be more than half, despite increased surveillance of accident-reporting records by OSHA. Immigrants typically do not report accidents, and more workers classified as independent contractors may contribute to lack of reporting.[20]

Reporting Injuries and Illnesses Four types of injuries or illnesses are defined by the Occupational Safety and Health Act. They are as follows:

- *Injury- or illness-related deaths*: fatalities at workplaces or caused by work-related actions
- *Lost-time or disability injuries*: job-related injuries or disabling occurrences that cause an employee to miss regularly scheduled work on the day following the accident
- *Medical care injuries*: injuries that require treatment by a physician but do not cause an employee to miss a regularly scheduled work turn
- *Minor injuries*: injuries that require first aid treatment and do not cause an employee to miss the next regularly scheduled work turn

The recordkeeping requirements for these injuries and illnesses are summarized in Figure 14-5. Notice that only very minor injuries do not have to be recorded for OSHA. For example, an employee was repairing a conveyor belt when his hand slipped and hit the sharp edge of a steel bar. His hand was cut, and he was rushed to the hospital. He received five stitches and was told by the doctor not to use his hand for three days. This injury was recorded and reported to OSHA because the stitches and restricted duty required that it be recorded.

OSHA Inspections

The Occupational Safety and Health Act provides for on-the-spot inspections by OSHA representatives, called compliance officers or inspectors. In *Marshall v. Barlow's, Inc.*, the U.S. Supreme Court held that safety inspectors must produce a search warrant if an employer refuses to allow an inspector into the plant voluntarily. The Court also ruled that an inspector does not have to show probable cause to obtain a search warrant. A warrant can be obtained easily if a search is part of a general enforcement plan.[21]

Dealing with an Inspection When an OSHA compliance officer arrives, managers should ask to see the inspector's credentials. Next, the HR representative for the employer should insist on an opening conference with the compliance officer. The compliance officer may request that a union representative, an employee, and a company representative be present while

FIGURE 14-5   **Guide to Recordability of Cases under the Occupational Safety and Health Act**

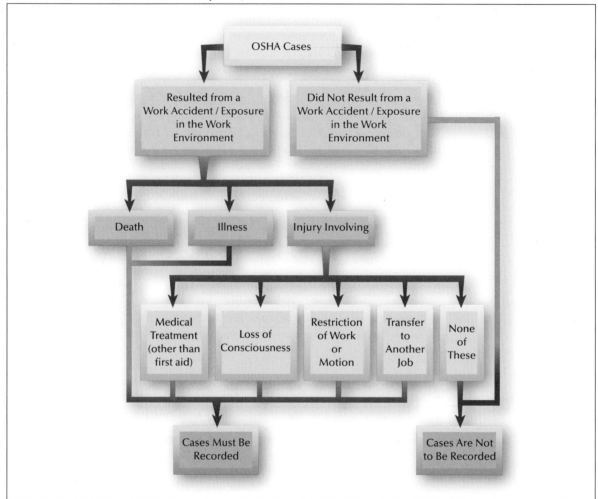

the inspection is conducted. During the inspection, the officer checks organizational records to see if they are being maintained and to determine the number of accidents that have occurred. Following this review of the safety records, the officer conducts an on-the-spot inspection and may use a wide variety of equipment to test compliance with standards. After the inspection, the compliance officer can issue citations for any violations of standards and provisions of the act.

Citations and Violations Although OSHA inspectors can issue citations for violations of the provisions of the act, whether or not a citation is issued depends on the severity and extent of the problems, and on the employer's knowledge of them. In addition, depending on the nature and number of violations, penalties can be assessed against employers. The nature and extent of the penalties depend on the type and severity of the violations as determined by OSHA officials.

A number of different types of violations are cited by OSHA. Ranging from the most severe to minimal, including a special category for repeated violations, the most common are as follows:

- *Imminent danger*: When there is reasonable certainty that the condition will cause death or serious physical harm if it is not corrected immediately, an imminent-danger citation is issued and a notice posted by an inspector. Imminent-danger situations are handled on the highest-priority basis. They are reviewed by a regional OSHA director, and the condition must be corrected immediately. If the condition is serious enough and the employer does not cooperate, a representative of OSHA may obtain a federal injunction to close the company until the condition is corrected. The absence of guardrails to prevent employees from falling into heavy machinery is one example of an imminent danger.
- *Serious*: When a condition could probably cause death or serious physical harm, and the employer should know of the condition, OSHA issues a serious-violation citation. Examples of serious violations are the absence of a protective screen on a lathe and the lack of a blade guard on an electric saw.
- *Other than serious*: Violations that could impact employees' health or safety but probably would not cause death or serious harm are called "other than serious." Having loose ropes in a work area might be classified as an other-than-serious violation.
- *De minimis*: A *de minimis* condition is one not directly and immediately related to employees' safety or health. No citation is issued, but the condition is mentioned to the employer. Lack of doors on toilet stalls is a common example of a *de minimis* violation.
- *Willful and repeated*: Citations for willful and repeated violations are issued to employers who have been previously cited for violations. If an employer knows about a safety violation or has been warned of a violation and does not correct the problem, a second citation is issued. The penalty for a willful and repeated violation can be high. For example, if death results from an accident that involves such a safety violation, a jail term of six months can be imposed on the executives or managers who were responsible.

Consider a case in which a metal manufacturer instructed its employees to operate the machines differently than usual when OSHA conducted an inspection. It also hid pieces of equipment, and management lied about its usual practices. These actions led to a "willful" violation and large fines for numerous violations, primarily because the firm tried to cover up its noncompliance.

Critique of OSHA

OSHA has been criticized on several fronts. Because the agency has so many worksites to inspect, employers have only a relatively small chance of being inspected. Some suggest that employers pay little attention to OSHA enforcement efforts for this reason. Labor unions and others have criticized OSHA and Congress for not providing enough inspectors. For instance, it is common to find that many of the worksites at which workers suffered severe injuries or deaths had not been inspected in the previous five years.

Employers, especially smaller ones, continue to complain about the complexity of complying with OSHA standards and the costs associated with penalties and with making changes required to remedy problem areas. Larger firms can afford to hire safety and health specialists and establish more proactive programs. However, smaller firms that cannot afford to do so still have to comply with the regulations, which leads to managers needing to be more involved in safety management.

SAFETY MANAGEMENT

Well-designed and well-managed safety programs can pay dividends in reduced accidents and associated costs, such as workers' compensation and possible fines. Further, accidents and other safety concerns usually decline as a result of management efforts that emphasize safety.[22] Often, the difference between high-performing firms with good occupational safety records and other firms is that the former have effective safety management programs. As Figure 14-6 indicates, both HR and operating managers must be involved in coordinating health, safety, and security efforts.

Successful safety management has been researched extensively. A summary of what is known about managing safety effectively and reducing accidents includes the following necessary components:

- Organizational commitment
- Policies, discipline, and recordkeeping
- Training and communication
- Participation (safety committees)
- Inspection, investigation, and evaluation

Organizational Commitment and a Safety Culture

At the heart of safety management is an organizational commitment to a comprehensive safety effort that should be coordinated at the top level of management and include all members of the organization. It also should be reflected in managerial actions. A president of a small electrical manufacturing firm who does not wear a hard hat in the manufacturing shop can hardly expect to enforce a requirement that all employees wear hard hats in the shop.

| FIGURE 14-6 | Typical Division of HR Responsibilities: Health, Safety, and Security |

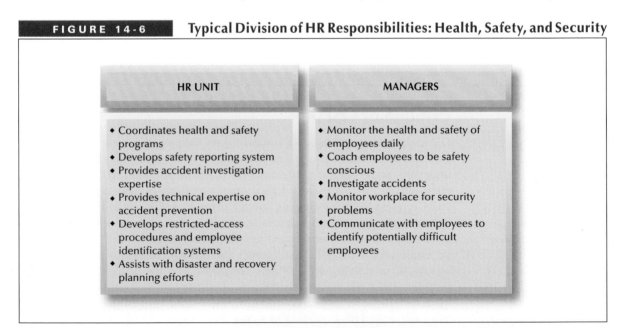

HR UNIT	MANAGERS
• Coordinates health and safety programs • Develops safety reporting system • Provides accident investigation expertise • Provides technical expertise on accident prevention • Develops restricted-access procedures and employee identification systems • Assists with disaster and recovery planning efforts	• Monitor the health and safety of employees daily • Coach employees to be safety conscious • Investigate accidents • Monitor workplace for security problems • Communicate with employees to identify potentially difficult employees

FIGURE 14-7   **Approaches to Effective Safety Management**

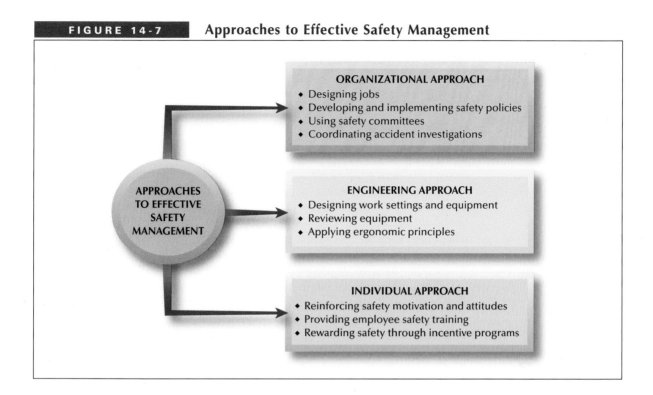

One result of a strong commitment to safety is that a "safety culture" pervades the organization. Firms such as Johnson & Johnson, DuPont Chemical and Energy Operations, and Frito-Lay are well known for emphasizing safety as part of their organizational cultures.

Three approaches are used by employers in managing safety. Figure 14-7 shows the organizational, engineering, and individual approaches and their components. Successful programs may use all three in dealing with safety issues.

Safety and Engineering Employers can prevent some accidents by designing machines, equipment, and work areas so that workers who perform potentially dangerous jobs cannot injure themselves and others. Providing safety equipment and guards on machinery, installing emergency switches, installing safety rails, keeping aisles clear, and installing adequate ventilation, lighting, heating, and air conditioning can all help to make work environments safer.

Designing a job properly requires consideration of the physical setting of the job. The way the work space surrounding a job is utilized can influence the worker's performance of the job itself. Several factors that affect safety have been identified, including size of work area, kinds of materials used, sensory conditions, distance between work areas, and interference from noise and traffic flow.

Individual Considerations in Accidents Engineers approach safety from the perspective of redesigning the machinery or the work area. Industrial psychologists and "human factors" experts see safety differently. They address the proper match of individuals to jobs and emphasize employee training in safety methods, fatigue reduction, and health awareness.

Numerous field studies with thousands of employees, have looked at the human factors in accidents. The results have shown a definite relationship between cognitive factors and occupational safety. Behavior-based safety (BBS) approaches are efforts to reduce *risky behavior* and increase safe behavior by defining unsafe behavior and attempting to change it. While BBS is beneficial, it does not constitute a complete approach to dealing with safety.

Work schedules can be another cause for accidents. The relationship between work schedules and accidents can be explained as follows: Fatigue based on physical exertion sometimes exists in the industrial workplace of today. Boredom, which occurs when a person is required to do the same tasks for a long period of time, is rather common. As fatigue increases, motivation decreases; when motivation decreases, workers' attention wanders, and the likelihood of accidents increases. A particular area of concern is overtime in work scheduling. Overtime work has been consistently related to accident incidence because the more overtime worked, the higher the incidence of severe accidents.

Another area of concern is the relationship of accident rates to different shifts, particularly late-night shifts.[23] Because there tend to be fewer supervisors and managers working the "graveyard" shifts, workers tend to receive less training and supervision. Both of these factors lead to higher accident rates.

Safety Policies, Discipline, and Recordkeeping

Designing safety policies and rules and disciplining violators are important components of safety efforts. Frequently reinforcing the need for safe behavior and frequently supplying feedback on positive safety practices are also effective ways of improving worker safety. Such safety-conscious efforts must involve employees, supervisors, managers, safety specialists, and HR staff members.

For policies about safety to be effective, good recordkeeping about accidents, causes, and other details is necessary. Without records, an employer cannot track its safety performance, compare benchmarks against other employers, and may not realize the extent of its safety problems.

Safety Training and Communication

Good safety training reduces accidents. Supervisors should receive the training first, and then employees should receive it as well, because untrained workers are more likely to have accidents. Safety training involving behavioral modeling, lots of practice, and dialogue is most effective.[24]

Safety training can be done in various ways. Regular sessions with supervisors, managers, and employees are often coordinated by HR staff members. Communication of safety procedures, reasons why accidents occurred, and what to do in an emergency is critical. Without effective communication about safety, training is insufficient. To reinforce safety training, continuous communication to develop safety consciousness is necessary. Merely sending safety memos is not enough. Producing newsletters, changing safety posters, continually updating bulletin boards, and posting safety information in visible areas are also recommended.

Employers may need to communicate in a variety of media and languages. Such efforts are important to address the special needs of workers who have vision, speech, or hearing impairments; who are not proficient in English; or who are challenged in other ways.

Safety Committees

Employees frequently participate in safety planning through safety committees, often composed of workers from a variety of levels and departments. A safety committee generally meets at regularly scheduled times, has specific responsibilities for conducting safety reviews, and makes recommendations for changes necessary to avoid future accidents. Usually, at least one member of the committee comes from the HR department.

Companies must take care to ensure that managers do not compose a majority on their safety committees. Otherwise, they may be in violation of provisions of the National Labor Relations Act, commonly known as the Wagner Act. That act, as explained in detail in Chapter 16, prohibits employers from "dominating a labor organization." Some safety committees have been ruled to be labor organizations because they deal with working conditions.

In approximately 32 states, all but the smallest employers may be required to establish safety committees. From time to time, legislation has been introduced at the federal level to require joint management/employee safety committees. But as yet, no federal provisions have been enacted.

Inspection, Investigation, and Evaluation

It is not necessary to wait for an OSHA inspector to check the work area for safety hazards. Inspections may be done by a safety committee or by a company safety coordinator regularly. Problem areas should be addressed immediately in order to keep work productivity at the highest possible levels. Also, OSHA inspects organizations with above-average rates of lost workdays more frequently.

The phases of accident investigation are in Figure 14-8. Identifying why an accident occurred is useful; taking steps to prevent similar accidents from occurring is even more important.

Closely related to accident investigation is research to determine ways of preventing accidents. Employing safety engineers or having outside experts evaluate the safety of working conditions may be useful. If many similar accidents seem to occur in an organizational unit, a safety training program may be necessary to emphasize safe working practices. As an example, a medical center reported a greater-than-average number of back injuries among employees who lifted heavy patients. Installation of patient lifting devices and safety training on the proper way to use them was initiated. As a result, the number of worker injuries was reduced.

FIGURE 14-8   **Phases of Accident Investigation**

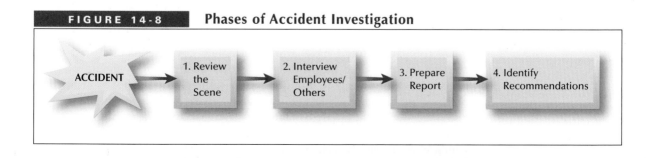

MEASURE

Measuring Safety Efforts

Organizations should monitor and evaluate their safety efforts. Just as organizational accounting records are audited, a firm's safety efforts should be audited periodically as well. Accident and injury statistics should be compared with previous accident patterns to identify any significant changes. This analysis should be designed to measure progress in safety management.

Various safety efforts can be measured. Some common ones are workers' compensation costs per injury/illness; percentage of injuries/illnesses by department, work shifts, and job categories; and incident rate comparisons with industry and benchmark targets. Regardless of the specific measures used, it is critical to be able to track and evaluate safety management efforts using relevant HR metrics.

Employers in a variety of industries have found that emphasizing health and safety pays off in a number of ways. Lower employee benefits costs for health care, fewer work-related accidents, lower workers' compensation costs, and more productive employees can all be results of employer efforts to stress health and safety.

EMPLOYEE HEALTH

Employee health problems are varied—and somewhat inevitable. They can range from minor illnesses such as colds to serious illnesses related to the jobs performed. Some employees have emotional health problems; others have alcohol or drug problems. Some problems are chronic; others are transitory. All may affect organizational operations and individual employee productivity.

There is a small trend to return to the "Company Doctor" model of years ago to help deal with these issues. The HR Perspective discusses the specifics of that model.

LOGGING ON

HealthyCulture.com
For information on services and programs that support healthy organizational cultures, visit this website at www.healthyculture.com.

Employers face a variety of workplace health issues. Previously in this chapter, cumulative trauma injuries and exposure to hazardous chemicals were discussed because OSHA has addressed these concerns through regulations or standards. Other concerns associated with employee health include substance abuse, emotional/mental health, older workers, smoking, and obesity.

Substance Abuse

Use of illicit substances or misuse of controlled substances, alcohol, or other drugs is called **substance abuse**. The millions of substance abusers in the workforce cost global employers billions of dollars annually, although recently there has been a decline in illegal drug use by employees. Most companies have a drug screening policy that focuses on preemployment testing.[25]

A company should have a written policy covering alcohol and drugs and the possession of illegal drugs at work. Such a policy should prohibit employees from coming to work under the influence of alcohol or drugs. The policy should be communicated in writing, and each employee should sign off and understand that failure to take a test can lead to adverse inference.[26]

In the United States, the incidence of substance abuse is greatest among young single men.[27] Also, blue-collar workers are more likely than white-collar

Substance abuse Use of illicit substances or misuse of controlled substances, alcohol, or other drugs.

The "Company Doctor"

Toyota Motor's San Antonio plant is getting rave reviews for its on-site medical center. Louis Aguillon, a line worker who had a nagging back pain, saw the doctor for 20 minutes and paid $5 for the visit. Managed by Take Care Health Systems, which runs clinics, the program is helping Toyota cut costs on big-ticket items including referrals to highly paid specialists, ER visits, and brand-name drugs. Further, employees do not have to leave the plant for treatment.

Company doctors have roots going back to the 1800s, but the tradition began to fade in the 1930s and 1940s on suspicion that the doctors were serving employers' interests. Toyota, Nissan, Harrah's Entertainment, Walt Disney Parks and Resorts, and Walgreens have brought the tradition back. Their efforts offer employees a major break on copays (at Toyota a visit is $5 instead of $15 to see another doctor). Some companies make deposits to employee health savings accounts if they use the in-house services.

At Toyota in San Antonio, the clinic has three doctors, dentists, physical therapists, X-ray capability, and the ability to treat broken bones and handle various emergencies. The prices for these services are about half what others charge. The doctors also screen for long-term problems that might be costly to treat later. At an Ohio plant with a clinic, only 4% of the patients are sent to specialists; most are handled in-house. The percentage of referrals to expensive specialists in the general population is 25%.

The question, of course, is whether health management companies hired to help control costs will act in the patients' best interests. Dr. Johnson at the San Antonio plant responds, "If patients perceive that we place some company's interest over their well-being, they won't come."[28]

workers to abuse substances. Figure 14-9 shows common signs of substance abuse. However, not all signs are present in any one case. A pattern that includes some of these behaviors should be a reason to pay closer attention.[29]

Employers' concerns about substance abuse stem from the ways it alters work behaviors, causing increased tardiness, increased absenteeism, a slower

FIGURE 14-9   **Common Signs of Substance Abuse**

- ◆ Fatigue
- ◆ Slurred speech
- ◆ Flushed cheeks
- ◆ Difficulties walking
- ◆ Inconsistency
- ◆ Difficulty remembering details
- ◆ Argumentative behavior
- ◆ Missed deadlines

- ◆ Many unscheduled absences (especially on Mondays and Fridays)
- ◆ Depression
- ◆ Irritability
- ◆ Emotionalism
- ◆ Overacting
- ◆ Violence
- ◆ Frequently borrowing money

work pace, a higher rate of mistakes, and less time spent at the work station. It can also cause an increase in withdrawal (physical and psychological) and antagonistic behaviors, which may lead to workplace violence.

Alcohol testing and drug testing are used by many employers, especially following an accident or some other reasonable cause. Some employers also use random testing programs. The U.S. Department of Transportation *requires* drug testing for aviation workers, commercial freight carrier employees, railroad workers, mass transit employees, pipeline employees, and commercial vessel operators.

Types of Drug Tests There are several different types of tests for drug use: urinalysis, radioimmunoassay of hair, surface swiping, and fitness-for-duty testing. The innovative fitness-for-duty tests can be used alone or in conjunction with drug testing. These tests can distinguish individuals under the influence of alcohol or prescription drugs to the extent that their abilities to perform their jobs are impaired. Some firms use *fitness-for-duty tests* to detect work performance safety problems before putting a person behind dangerous equipment. As an example, in one firm when a crew of delivery truck drivers comes to work, they are asked to "play" a video game—one that can have serious consequences. Unless the video game machine presents receipts saying they passed the test, they are not allowed to drive their trucks that day. It works like this: the computer has already established a baseline for each employee. Subsequent testing measures the employees against their baselines. Interestingly, most test failures are not drug or alcohol related. Rather, fatigue, illness, and personal problems more frequently render a person unfit to perform a sensitive job.

Handling Substance Abuse Cases The Americans with Disabilities Act (ADA) affects how management can handle substance abuse cases. Current users of *illegal* drugs are specifically excluded from the definition of *disabled* under the act. However, those addicted to *legal* substances (e.g., alcohol and prescription drugs) are considered disabled under the ADA. Also, recovering substance abusers are considered disabled under the ADA.

To encourage employees to seek help for their substance abuse problems, a *firm-choice option* is usually recommended and has been endorsed legally. In this procedure, a supervisor or a manager confronts the employee privately about unsatisfactory work-related behaviors. Then, in keeping with the disciplinary system, the employee is offered a choice between help and discipline. Treatment options and consequences of further unsatisfactory performance are clearly discussed, including what the employer will do. Confidentiality and follow-up are critical when employers use the firm-choice option.

Emotional/Mental Health

Many individuals are facing work, family, and personal life pressures. Although most people manage these pressures successfully, some individuals have difficulty handling the demands. Specific events, such as death of a spouse, divorce, or medical problems, can affect individuals who otherwise have been coping successfully with life pressures. A variety of emotional/mental health issues arise at work that must be addressed by employers. It is important to note that emotional/mental illnesses such as schizophrenia and depression are considered disabilities under the ADA.

Stress that keeps individuals from successfully handling the multiple demands they face is one concern. All people encounter stress; but when "stress overload" hits, work-related consequences can result.[30] Beyond trying to communicate with the employees and relieving some workload pressures, it is generally recommended that supervisors and managers contact the HR staff, who may intervene and then refer affected employees to outside resources through employee assistance programs.

Depression is another common emotional/mental health concern. The effects of depression are seen at all organizational levels, from warehouses and accounting offices to executive suites. Employees who appear to be depressed are guided to employee assistance programs and helped with obtaining medical treatment.

Health and Older Employees

The graying of the workforce has been mentioned previously, but there are implications for health and safety. All signs point to an abundance of older workers, as many are showing signs of working beyond age 65. As noted earlier, there is a diminishing pool of successful younger workers to replace them. Data show that older workers have fewer injuries, but are out of work longer when they do, and these injuries cost more to fix. Musculoskeletal disorders are more severe. Key practices for dealing with older workers are:[31]

- Preventing slips and falls
- Eliminating repetitive stress and heavy lifting
- Using ergonomically sound workspaces
- Emphasizing driver safety
- Providing means for healthy gradual transitions back to work.

Smoking at Work

Arguments and rebuttals characterize the smoking-at-work controversy, and statistics abound.[32] A multitude of state and local laws deal with smoking in the workplace and in public places. In response to health studies, complaints by nonsmokers, and resulting state laws, many employers have instituted no-smoking policies throughout their workplaces. Although employees who smoke tend to complain initially when a smoking ban is instituted, they seem to have little difficulty adjusting within a few weeks. Many quit smoking or reduce the number of cigarettes they inhale and exhale each workday. Some employers also offer smoking cessation workshops as part of health promotion efforts.[33]

Health Promotion

Health promotion
Supportive approach of facilitating and encouraging healthy actions and lifestyles among employees.

Employers concerned about maintaining a healthy workforce must move beyond simply providing healthy working conditions and begin promoting employee health and wellness in other ways. **Health promotion** is a supportive approach of facilitating and encouraging healthy actions and lifestyles among employees. Health promotion efforts can range from providing information and increasing employee awareness of health issues to creating an organizational culture supportive of employee health enhancements, as Figure 14-10 indicates. Going beyond simple compliance with workplace safety and health regulations, organizations engage in health promotion by encouraging employees to make physiological, mental, and social choices that improve their health.

FIGURE 14-10   **Health Promotion Levels**

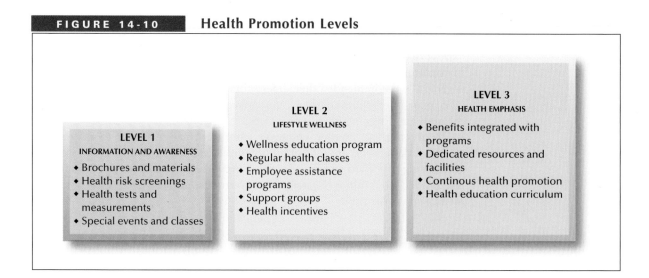

The first level of health promotion (see Figure 14-10) leaves much to individual initiatives for following through and making changes in actions and behaviors. Employers provide information on such topics as weight control, stress management, nutrition, exercise, and smoking cessation. Even though such efforts may be beneficial for some employees, employers who wish to impact employees' health must offer second-level efforts, such as more comprehensive programs and actions that focus on the lifestyle "wellness" of employees. The third level requires a commitment to wellness that is seldom seen in employers.

Obesity Nearly one-third of U.S. adults are obese and another one-third are overweight. Obesity is a fact of modern life and a concern to employers, and a movement to involve employers in employee weight management is apparently gaining momentum. The reason employers are concerned is cost. The economic costs of obesity include doctor visits, diabetes, high blood pressure, higher health care premiums, and lost workdays. To address the increasing problem of obese employees, employers are taking a number of actions. Some firms are offering incentives to workers who are involved in physical fitness programs and lose weight. In one firm with an active program focusing on obese employees, more than 2,000 employees lost over 61,000 pounds as part of the program.

Wellness Programs Employers' desires to improve productivity, decrease absenteeism, and control health care costs have come together in the "wellness" movement.[34] **Wellness programs** are designed to maintain or improve employee health before problems arise by encouraging self-directed lifestyle changes. Early wellness programs were aimed primarily at reducing the cost and risk of disease.[35] Newer programs emphasize healthy lifestyles and environment, including reduced cholesterol and heart disease risks and individualized exercise programs and follow-up. Employer-sponsored support groups have been established for individuals dealing with health issues such as weight loss, nutrition, and smoking cessation. The top-rated topics for wellness programs are stress management, exercise/fitness, screenings/checkups, health insurance education, disease management (heart disease, diabetes, etc.), nutrition and diet, and smoking cessation.[36]

Wellness programs
Programs designed to maintain or improve employee health before problems arise.

Employee assistance program (EAP) Program that provides counseling and other help to employees having emotional, physical, or other personal problems.

Online and Web-based wellness programs have grown in popularity. Ford, Microsoft, Chevron, and Watson Wyatt are just a few of the companies that offer online wellness programs. These programs use information and subtle psychology to motivate people to live healthier lifestyles. They typically focus on exercise, nutrition, sleep, stress, and life balance.

Employee Assistance Programs One method organizations use as a broad-based response to health issues is an **employee assistance program (EAP)**, which provides counseling and other help to employees having emotional, physical, or other personal problems. In such a program, an employer typically contracts with a counseling agency for the service. Employees who have problems may then contact the agency, either voluntarily or by employer referral, for assistance with a broad range of problems. Counseling costs are paid for by the employer, either in total or up to a preestablished limit.[37]

EAPs commonly provide help with troubled employees, problem identification, short-term intervention, and referral services. The most common employee issues dealt with in EAPs are: (1) depression and anxiety, (2) marital and relationship problems, (3) legal difficulties, and (4) family and children concerns. Other areas commonly addressed as part of an EAP include substance abuse, financial counseling, and career advice. EAP participation rates by employees are only 5% to 7%, which is low. This figure indicates that many individuals are not using this health benefit as often as would be expected.[38]

Critical to employee usage of an EAP is preserving confidentiality. For that reason, employers outsource EAPs to trained professionals, who usually report only the numbers of employees and services provided, rather than details on individuals using an EAP. The effectiveness of an EAP depends on how well the employer integrates and supports it in the workplace. Done well, EAPs can help reduce health care and other costs.[39]

MEASURE

Measuring Health Promotion Effects Organizations can assess the effectiveness of their health promotion programs in a number of ways.[40] Looking at participation rates by employees is one means. Although participation rates may not be as high as desired, the programs have resulted in healthier lifestyles for more employees. Cost-benefit analyses by organizations also tend to support the continuation of such programs. The return on investment (ROI) for one firm has been estimated to be $50 million total savings over a 5-year period. This ROI represents a payoff of $3 for every $1 spent on employee wellness efforts.

SECURITY CONCERNS AT WORK

Traditionally, when employers have addressed worker health and safety, they have been concerned about reducing workplace accidents, improving safety practices, and reducing health hazards at work. However, in the past decade, providing security for employees has become important. Notice that virtually all of the areas discussed in the following text have significant HR implications. Heading the list of security concerns is workplace violence.

Workplace Violence

Workplace violence is violent acts directed at someone at work or on duty. For example, physical assault, threats, harassment, intimidation, and bullying all qualify. Workplace violence can occur in four contexts:

- *Criminal*: a crime is committed in conjunction with the violence by a person with no legitimate relationship with the business (e.g., robbery, shoplifting, trespassing).
- *Customer*: a person with a legitimate relationship with the business becomes violent (e.g., patients, students, inmates, customers).
- *Coworker*: a current or past employee attacks or threatens another employee (e.g., contractor, temp).
- *Domestic*: a person who has no legitimate relationship with a business but has a personal relationship with the victim commits some form of violence against an employee (e.g., family member, boyfriend).

LOGGING ON

Center for Aggression Management®

For articles and details on recognizing and handling workplace aggression, visit this website at www .aggressionmanagement.com.

Most workplace homicides were criminal, and only a small number were between coworkers. Work-related homicides have decreased. Nonfatal violence averaged 12.6 incidents per 1,000 workers but was higher for police officers (261/1,000), taxi drivers (128/1,000), bartenders (82/1,000), special education teachers (68/1,000), and junior high teachers (54/1,000).[41] Employees in some of these occupations and others such as nurses routinely receive training on dealing with violent behaviors.[42]

Workplace Violence Warning Signs There are a number of warning signs and characteristics of a potentially violent person at work. Individuals who have committed the most violent acts have had the relatively common profile depicted in Figure 14-11. A person with some of these signs and characteristics may cope for years until a trauma pushes that person over the edge. A profound humiliation or rejection, the end of a marriage, the loss of a lawsuit, termination from a job, or other sources of stress may make a difficult employee turn violent.[43]

Workplace Incivility and Bullying Workplace incivility occurs when rude behavior by ill-mannered coworkers or bosses makes the targets of incivility feel annoyed, frustrated, or offended. Most do not find incivility serious

FIGURE 14-11   Profile of a Potentially Violent Employee

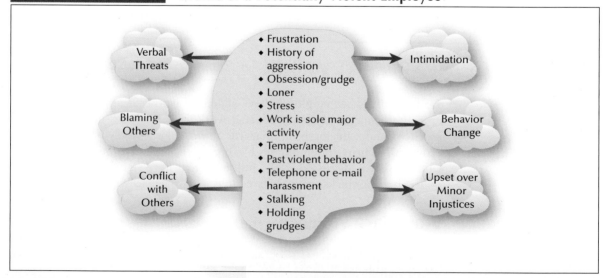

enough for formal action.[44] But incivility can escalate into bullying, which is more likely to require action.[45] Bullying is behavior that the victim perceives as oppressive, humiliating, threatening, or infringing on the victim's human rights. Such behavior must occur over an extended period of time. Bullying, especially by supervisors, can result in damage to the employee and to the organization and turnover.[46]

Perceptions of organizational support moderate the impact on a person's intention to leave an organization due to bullying.[47] This suggests a need for management attention to the problem through training, policies, and codes of conduct.[48]

Domestic Causes of Workplace Violence Too often violence that begins at home with family or "friends" can spill over to the workplace. One in five homicides of women at work is perpetrated by current or former husbands or boyfriends.[49] Also, many abused women report being harassed frequently at work, by telephone or in person, by abusing partners.

A reaction by employers is to ignore obvious signs of domestic violence. In fact, some employers have been sued and found liable for ignoring pleas for help from employees who later were victims of domestic violence in company parking lots or on employer premises.

Dealing with Workplace Violence The increase in workplace violence has led many employers to develop policies and practices for trying to prevent and respond to workplace violence. Policies can identify how workplace violence is to be dealt with in conjunction with disciplinary actions and referrals to EAPs. Training of managers and others is an important part of successful practice.

One application of these policies is a *violence response team*. Composed of security personnel, key managers, HR staff members, and selected employees, this team functions much like a safety committee, but with a different focus. Such a team conducts analyses, responds to and investigates employee threats, and may even help to calm angry, volatile employees.

Employers must be careful because they may face legal action for discrimination if they discharge employees for behaviors that often precede violent acts. For example, in several cases, employees who were terminated or suspended for making threats or even engaging in physical actions against their coworkers then sued their employers by claiming they had mental disabilities covered under the Americans with Disabilities Act.

Post-violence response is another part of managing workplace violence. Whether the violence results in physical injuries or deaths or just intense interpersonal conflicts, it is important that employers have plans to respond afterward. Their response must reassure employees who may be fearful of returning to work or who experience anxiety and sleeplessness, among other reactions. Providing referrals to EAP resources, allowing employees time to meet with HR staff, and arranging for trained counselors on-site are all part of post-violence response efforts.

Security Management

A comprehensive approach to security management is needed to address a wide range of issues, including workplace violence. HR managers may have responsibility for security programs or may work closely with security managers or consultants.

Security Audit In a **security audit**, HR staff conduct a comprehensive review of organizational security. Sometimes called a *vulnerability analysis,* such an audit uses managers inside the organization (e.g., the HR manager and the facilities manager) and outsiders (e.g., security consultants, police officers, fire officials, and computer security experts) to assess security issues.

Typically, a security audit begins with a survey of the area around the facility. Such factors as lighting in parking lots, traffic flow, location of emergency response services, crime in the surrounding neighborhood, and the layout of the buildings and grounds are evaluated. The audit also may include a review of the security available within the firm, including the capabilities of guards. Another part of the security audit reviews disaster plans, which address how to deal with events such as earthquakes, floods, tornadoes, hurricanes, and fires.

Controlled Access A key part of security involves controlling access to the physical facilities of the organization. Many workplace homicides occur during robberies. Therefore, employees who are most vulnerable, such as taxi drivers and convenience store clerks, can be provided bulletproof partitions and restricted access areas.

Many organizations limit access to facilities and work areas by using electronic access or keycard systems. Although not foolproof, these systems can make it more difficult for an unauthorized person, such as an estranged spouse or a disgruntled ex-employee, to enter the premises. Access controls also can be used in elevators and stairwells to prevent unauthorized persons from entering designated areas within a facility.

Controlling computer access may be an important part of securing IT resources. Coordination with information technology resources to change passwords, access codes, and otherwise protect company information may be important.

Violence Training Managers, HR staff members, supervisors, and employees should be trained on how to recognize the signs of a potentially violent employee and what to do when violence occurs.[50] During training at many firms, participants learn the typical profile of potentially violent employees and are trained to notify the HR department and to refer employees to outside counseling professionals. Such training requires observers to notice verbal and nonverbal reactions by individuals that may indicate anger or hostility, and to listen to individuals exhibiting such reactions.

Specific suggestions addressed in training for dealing with potentially violent employees typically include the following:

- Ask questions requiring explanations and longer answers that allow individuals to "vent."
- Respond calmly and nonthreateningly to individuals' emotions, acknowledge concerns, and demonstrate understanding about how the individuals feel.
- Get assistance from others, perhaps a manager not directly affected by the situation being discussed.
- Indicate the need for time to respond to the concerns voiced, and then set up another time for follow-up.
- Notify security personnel and HR staff members whenever employees' behaviors change dramatically or when job disciplinary action may provoke significant reactions by employees.

Security audit
Comprehensive review of organizational security.

Employee Screening and Selection

A key facet of providing security is screening job applicants. HR management is somewhat limited by legal constraints on what can be done, particularly regarding the use of psychological tests and checking of references. However, firms that do not screen employees adequately may be subject to liability if an employee commits crimes later. For instance, an individual with a criminal record for assault was hired by a firm to maintain sound equipment in clients' homes. The employee used a passkey to enter a home and assaulted the owner; consequently, the employer was ruled liable for not doing an adequate background check. Of course, when selecting employees, employers must be careful to use only valid, job-related screening means and to avoid violating federal EEO laws and the Americans with Disabilities Act.

Security Personnel

Providing adequately trained security personnel in sufficient numbers is a critical part of security management. Many employers contract for these personnel with firms specializing in security. If security is handled in-house, security personnel must be selected and trained to handle a variety of workplace security problems, ranging from dealing with violent behavior by an employee to taking charge in natural disasters.

DISASTER PREPARATION AND RECOVERY PLANNING

During the past several years, a number of significant disasters have occurred. Some have been natural disasters, such as hurricanes, major snowstorms, flooding in various states, tornadoes, and forest fires. There also has been concern about terrorism, and some firms have been damaged by fires and explosions. All of these situations have led to HR management having an expanded role in disaster planning.

To prepare for any instance in which organizations and their employees are impacted by such events, crisis management has become important. Yet various surveys have found that about one-third of organizations do not have disaster plans. Of those that do, about half have not tested or revised their plans.[51] For an example of one disaster plan that got tested, see the HR Perspective.

Disaster Planning

For disaster planning to occur properly, three components must be addressed by HR, as shown in Figure 14-12. Imagine that a hurricane destroys the work facility where employees work, as well as many of the employees' homes. Or picture an explosion or terrorist attack that prohibits workers from getting to their workplaces. Such situations illustrate why each of the components in Figure 14-12 has human dimensions to be addressed.

Organizational Assessment Organizational assessment includes establishing a disaster planning team, often composed of representatives from HR, security, information technology, operations, and other areas. The purpose of this team is to conduct an organizational assessment of how various disasters might

Disaster Plan Put to the Test

When the wildfires started in southern California, Los Angeles based TelePacific Communications had it covered. The state's third-largest telecommunications provider had a disaster plan. Further, the plan had been tested through drills earlier in the year. The company was able to respond quickly because it had the plan—but there were problems, as will always be the case. Shutting the offices down was not an option, as customers needed telecommunication capability more than ever.

The fires touched about 45 employees in San Diego and 125 in Irvine. Ten employees had to evacuate their homes, some lost their homes, and smoke permeated the office, making working difficult. What the company did not foresee was voluntary evacuations. Employees in San Diego and Irvine who became concerned about road closures or the smoke-filled offices left work without telling management. The number who did so became a factor in trying to maintain critical business functions.

The disaster plan had been put together by a team who had insights from previous California disasters as well as New York on September 11, 2001. This team effort recognized priorities and critical functions for operations during a disaster. Several things worked well. A GPS system tracked vehicles of employees who were in the field so the company knew where techs were. Two HR professionals oversaw the "War Room," allowing regular updates. Employees suffering direct losses were given pay and other assistance to help, and managers kept contact with most employees and presented a uniform message on what to do.

However, the live test of the plan demonstrated that some changes needed to be made. In the future, e-mail will be used instead of telephones for updates. A vendor put fans and air purifiers in place to fix the office-air problem. Voluntary evacuations have been addressed in the new disaster plan as well.

Ideally, companies should not wait for a disaster to test a plan, but no matter how carefully a plan is done, there will always be deficiencies that surface during a test, as TelePacific Communications found.[52]

affect the organization and its employees. Then a disaster recovery plan is developed to identify how the organization will respond to different situations.

Human Impact Planning A number of areas are part of human impact planning, including items such as having backup databases for numerous company details, along with employee contact information. Who will take

Disaster Planning Components

responsibilities for various duties and how these efforts will be coordinated must be identified. For instance, following Hurricane Katrina, many employers could not reach employees, nor could employees contact their employers. However, firms such as Home Depot and Wal-Mart had databases outside of the Gulf Coast area. Employees could contact any other company location or a national hot line and learn about receiving paychecks, ask benefits questions, and even find out about continuing employment elsewhere. Home Depot allowed evacuees to become employees at any other U.S. location, and these stores had access to employment history and payroll data, making the worker transition easier. Yet estimates are that about a third of employee contact information in employer files is not current.

Disaster Training All of the planning efforts may be wasted if managers and employees are not trained on what to do when disasters occur. This training covers a wide range of topics, including the following:

- First aid/CPR
- Hazardous materials containment
- Disaster escape means
- Employer contact methods
- Organizational restoration efforts

But this training is not sufficient without conducting exercises or simulations for managers and employees to use the training.[53] Much like public schools have tornado evacuation exercises, employers may have site evacuation drills. Regular tests to ensure that information technology and databases are security accessible outside of the main location should occur. Testing responses if a workplace violence attack occurs may identify additional activities needed in an organization. Training must be a continuing consideration, and must reflect updated disaster planning efforts.[54]

Disaster Planning for Disease

A significant worldwide concern is the occurrence of environmental risks. One issue during the past few years has been the spread of various kinds of viruses and flu throughout the world. The global nature of business travel has increased the likelihood of the spread of a deadly virus. Two key issues are whether to evacuate expatriate employees from locations where flu occurs and how to protect local employees if the flu symptoms occur within an area.[55]

The concerns about flu and other pandemic diseases have led OSHA to establish guidelines for employers to use. The guidelines have special sections for firms in the poultry production industry due to their higher vulnerability. Relatively few U.S. employers and other worldwide organizations are prepared for the spread of pandemic flu or any other critical environmental disease. Many of the recommendations for preparations are similar to other types of disaster planning, but specialized policies, programs, and training may be needed. Experts project that there could be a major epidemic disease spread, whether a natural one or one instigated by terrorism. Thus, risk management preparation for this specialized area is part of broader disaster preparation and recovery planning efforts.

SUMMARY

- The four components of risk management are workplace safety and health, employee health/wellness promotion, workplace and worker security, and disaster preparation and recover planning.

- Health is a general state of physical, mental, and emotional well-being. Safety is a condition in which the physical well-being of people is protected. Security is the protection of employees and organizational facilities.

- Global security is of growing importance, and emerging health services, terrorism, and kidnapping are key concerns.

- Workers' compensation coverage is provided by employers to protect employees who suffer job-related injuries and illnesses.

- Both the Family and Medical Leave Act (FMLA) and the Americans with Disabilities Act (ADA) affect employer health and safety policies and practices.

- The Fair Labor Standards Act (FLSA) limits the types of work that younger employees, especially those under the age of 18, can perform.

- The Occupational Safety and Health Act states that employers have a general duty to provide safe and healthy working conditions.

- The Occupational Safety and Health Administration (OSHA) has established enforcement standards to aid in a number of areas, including hazard communication.

- Ergonomics looks at the physical demands of work.

- OSHA addresses employee work assignments, requires employers to keep records on occupational illnesses and injuries, inspects workplaces, and can issue citations for several levels of violations.

- Effective safety management requires integrating three approaches: organizational, engineering, and individual.

- Developing safety policies, disciplining violators, keeping safety records, conducting safety training, communicating on safety issues, establishing safety committees, inspecting work areas for safety concerns, investigating accidents, and evaluating safety efforts are all part of comprehensive safety management.

- Substance abuse, emotional/mental health, workplace air quality, and smoking at work, as common health issues, are growing concerns for organizations and employees.

- Employee health is promoted by employers at several levels to improve organizational operations and individual employee productivity.

- Employers have responded to health problems by establishing and supporting wellness programs and employee assistance programs (EAPs).

- Establishing and maintaining an organizational culture of health continues to pay off for a number of employers.

- Security of workplaces is important, particularly as the frequency of workplace violence increases.

- Employers can enhance security by conducting a security audit, controlling access to workplaces and computer systems, screening employees adequately during the selection process, and providing security personnel.

- Disaster preparation and recovery planning have grown as important HR concerns.

CRITICAL THINKING ACTIVITIES

1. How does one go about controlling workers' compensation costs, and why is that important?

2. What should an employer do when facing an OSHA inspection?

3. As the HR manager of a distribution and warehouse firm with 600 employees, you plan to discuss a company wellness program at an executive staff meeting next week. The topics to cover include what a wellness program is, how it can benefit the company and employees, and the process for establishing it. To aid in developing your presentation to the executives, consult the website www.welcoa.org and other applicable websites you can locate.

4. What should be included in disaster planning for a big employer in New York City that is concerned about terrorism attacks that might shut down the company and part of the city?

HR EXPERIENTIAL PROBLEM SOLVING

Due to an increase in recent employee layoffs because of economic conditions and the increased risk of workplace violence, as well as an increase in domestic restraining orders that several employees have recently obtained against former spouses, company management has decided it is time to take a proactive position and develop a workplace violence action plan. There are many factors to consider, as your company has three locations and more than 500 employees. For information to assist you in identifying workplace violence categories and prevention strategies, visit the website at www.fbi.gov/publications/violence.pdf.

1. Which workplace violence categories are of most concern to your company?

2. What steps and provisions do you need to include in your workplace violence action plan?

CASE

Data Security

Policing the workplace used to mean reminding employees about personal phone calls and making sure that paper clips did not disappear. But with the computer revolution at work that began in the 1990s, checking on employee behavior at work became considerably more technical. The threats to data security, not to mention other threats for potential lawsuits (e.g., sexual harassment), are now more complex as well. New federal laws pertaining to financial and medical records have put increased pressure on companies to protect their data. But auditing user privacy cannot be done without input and buy-in from HR, notes a senior consultant with an IT security firm in Massachusetts.

Whether the concern is in appropriate Internet usage or transferring files outside the company, HR may be the first to learn of a problem. Although the possibility of outside attacks on the computer network is a real problem, the threat of internal security breaches is even greater. The growing insider problem and the sheer volume of electronic messages coming into and out of a company (a large company easily processes one million e-mails per day) present HR with a challenge on data security policy development, implementation, and enforcement.

HR may be asked to "identify personnel at risk" who might require more stringent watching, such as people who are sending out résumés. In many cases, people leaving organizations take advantage of the opportunity to take intellectual property with them. Security software identifying employee behaviors will always require HR involvement. Policy violations, banned sites, and stealing identity data are examples. Companies look very bad when sensitive customer or employee data are stolen or leaked to the public. Employees can easily resent the security measures and see the security as "Big Brother" watching. However, the growth of identity theft and spyware means that more employees have been personally affected by data security and are more likely to recognize the need for their employers' data security efforts.

At Spherion, HR publishes a "computer and telecom resources policy" that specifies appropriate usage and a code of conduct. Employees must read and sign the policy. The company also has an IT Risk Team with members from HR, accounting, internal auditing, and other departments.

There are, of course, attempts at a purely technical solution to the problem. But it is clear that HR must have a role in balancing employee privacy with company risk management. A simple act, such as a bank's loan officer burning credit information to a CD and selling the data to another bank, can undo all the technical protections. The human side—developing a policy, communicating it, helping people understand why it is needed, and applying it fairly—is the big piece for HR.[56]

QUESTIONS

1. How would you communicate a data security policy that required software checking of employees' emails?

2. What elements should a data security policy for a bank include?

3. Employee data theft most frequently occurs with new employees or when an employee has given notice and is leaving. How would you deal with these two very different issues?

SUPPLEMENTAL CASES

What's Happened to Bob?

This case concerns warning signs of possible alcohol use and the consequences at work. (For the case, go to www.cengage.com/management/mathis.)

Communicating Safety and Health Success

This case provides information on the success of safety and health efforts in the workplace. (For the case, go to www.cengage.com/management/mathis.)

NOTES

1. Based on: Howard Pankiratz, "Big Fine in Teen's Death," *The Denver Post*, November 24, 2009, 1A.
2. C. Abrams, et al., "Optimized Enterprise Risk Management," *IBM Systems Journal*, 46, (2007) 219–234.
3. G. Leters, et al., "Towards a Balanced Approach in Risk Identification," *Engineering Management Journal*, Winter 2007, 3–9.
4. "BLS Reports Drop in Nonfatal Injuries, Illnesses," *HR News*, October 28, 2008, www.shrm.org, 1.
5. M. P. McQueen, "Workplace Disabilities on the Rise," *The Wall Street Journal*, May 1, 2007, D1.
6. Tom Starner, "The Dangers of Disability," *Human Resource Executive*, February 2008, 40–46.
7. Rick Jervis, "Hispanic Worker Deaths Up 76%," *USA Today*, July 20, 2009, 1A.
8. Catherine Rampell, "Why 'Falling Back' Is Better than 'Springing Forward,'" *New York Times.com*, November 2, 2009, http://economix.blogs.NYTimes.com, 2.
9. Donna Scimia, "A Common Sense Approach to Reducing Liability in Today's Workplace," *Employee Relations Law Journal*, Autumn 2007, 23–29.
10. Hugh Scullion, et al., "International Human Resource Management in the 21st Century: Emerging Themes and Contemporary Debates," *Human Resource Management Journal*, 17, (2007) 311–312.
11. Michele Campolieti, et al., "Labor Decisions of Disabled Male Workers," *Journal of Labor Research*, 28, (2007) 502–514.
12. David Nevmark, et al., "The Impact of Provider Choice on Worker's Compensation Costs and Outcomes," *Industrial and Labor Relations Review*, 60 (2007), 121–141.

13. "Worker's Comp Costs Decline 4.6 Percent in 2009's First Quarter," www.ioma.com, September 2009, 1.
14. Truls Ostbye, et al., "Obesity and Worker's Compensation," *Arch Intern Med*, 167, April 23, 2007, 766–773.
15. Robert Fisher, "Legal Implications of Mental-Health Issues," *Human Resource Executive Online*, May 2, 2009, www.hreonline.com, 1–3.
16. Bill Leonard, "OSHA Issues Final Rule on Personal Protective Equipment," *HR News*, November 19, 2007, www.shrm.org, 1.
17. "OSHA Unveils New Guidance on Preparing Workplaces for Influenza Pandemic," *Newsline*, February 8, 2007, http://dialog.newsedge.com, 2.
18. *United Autoworkers v. Johnson Controls, Inc.*, 111 S. Ct. 1196 (1991).
19. "OSHA Flags High Injury and Illness Rates," *HR Magazine*, June 2009, 24.
20. Kris Maher, "Injuries Are Under Counted, Studies Say," *The Wall Street Journal*, June 19, 2008, A3.
21. *Marshall v. Barlow's, Inc.*, 98 S. Ct. 1816 (1978).
22. Kris Maher and Robert Matthews, "On the Job Deaths Vex Steel Industry," *The Wall Street Journal*, July 25, 2008, B1.
23. Bruce Horovitz, "Late Shift Proves Deadly to More Fast-Food Workers," *USA Today*, December 13, 2007, B1–B2.
24. Michael Burke, et al., "Relative Effectiveness of Worker Safety and Health Training Methods," *American Journal of Public Health*, 96, (2006) 315–325.
25. Corrie Lykins, "Why Should Employers Just Say Yes to Drug Screening?" *Trendwatcher*, July 31, 2009, 1–3.
26. Nancy Delogv, "Essential Elements of a Drug-Free Workplace Program,"

Professional Safety, November 2007, 48–51.
27. "Drug Free Workplace Policy," *Ceridian Abstracts*, www.hrcompliance.ceridian.com.
28. David Welch, "The Company Doctor Is Back," *BusinessWeek*, August 11, 2008, 48–49.
29. Richard Marcus, "Warning Signs," *Human Resource Executive Online*, May 2, 2009, 1–2, www.hreonline.com.
30. Kathy Gurchiek, "'Mental Health' Days Taken for Family," *HR Magazine*, May 2008, 26.
31. Roy Maurer, "The Future of Work: Safety and Health Issues of an Aging Workforce," July 9, 2009, www.shrm.org, 1–2.
32. Barbara Worthington, "The Butt Stops Here!" *Human Resource Executive*, May 2, 2007, 51–53.
33. Michael O'Brien, "Different Smokes for Different Folks," *Human Resource Executive Online*, October 26, 2009, www.hreonline.com, 1–2.
34. Robert Langreth, "Use Brakes to Stay Health," *Forbes Magazine*, August 24, 2009, 37–39.
35. Anne Moran, "Wellness Programs: What's Permitted?" *Employee Relations Law Journal*, Autumn 2008, 111–116.
36. Dorette Nysewander, "The Business of Wellness," *American Fitness*, 27, (2009) 22–28.
37. Greg Hudson, "Oil and Alcohol: Too Potent a Mix," *Canadian Business*, October 13, 2009, 24.
38. Dave Sharar and Richard Lennox, "A New Measure of EAP Success," September 24, 2009, www.shrm.org.
39. Rabi Bhagat, "International and Cultural Variations in Employee Assistance Programmes," *Journal of Management Studies*, March 2007, 222–242.
40. Ted Miller, "Effectiveness and Benefit/Cost of Beer Based

Workplace Substance Abuse Prevention Coupled with Random Testing," *Accident and Accident Prevention*, 39, (2007) 565–573.

41. John Matchulat, "Separating Fact from Fiction about Workplace Violence," *Employee Relations Law Journal*, Autumn 2007, 14–22.

42. Kari Aquino and Stefan Thau, "Workplace Victimization: Aggression from the Target's Perspective," *Annual Review of Psychology*, 60 (2009) 717–741.

43. Pamela Babcock, "Workplace Stress? Deal with It!" *HR Magazine*, May 2009, 67–70.

44. Lilia Cortina and Vicki Magley, "Patterns and Profiles of Responses to Incivility in the Workplace," *Journal of Occupational Health Psychology*, 14, 2009, 272–288.

45. Brad Estes and Jia Eang, "Integrative Literature Review: Workplace Incivility," *Human Resource Development Review*, 7, (2008) 218–240.

46. Vincent Roscigno, et al., "Supervisory Bullying, Status Inequities, and Organizational Context," *Social Forces*, 87, (2009) 1561–1589.

47. Nikola Djurkovic, et al., "Workplace Bullying and Intention to Leave: The Moderating Effect of Perceived Organizational Support," *Human Resource Management Journal*, 18, (2008) 405–422.

48. Jack Howard, "Employee Awareness of Workplace Violence Policies," *Employee Responsibility and Rights Journal*, 21, 2009, 7–19.

49. Anne O'Leary-Kelly, et al., "Coming into the Light: Intimate Partner Violence and Its Effects at Work," *Academy of Management Perspectives*, May 2008, 57–72.

50. Carol Hymowitz, "Bosses Have to Learn How to Confront Troubled Employees," *The Wall Street Journal*, April 23, 2007, B1.

51. Sonya Premeaux, et al., "Crisis Management of Human Resources," *Human Resource Planning*, 30, No. 3, 39–47.

52. Kathy Gurchiek, "Disaster Plan Put to the Test in California," *HR Magazine*, December 2007, 24.

53. Jason Moats, et al., "Using Scenarios to Develop Crisis Managers," *Advances in Developing Human Resources*, 38, (2008) 1–25.

54. Dian-Yan Liou and Chin-Huang Lin, "Human Resources Planning on Terrorism and Crises in the Asia Pacific Region," *Human Resource Management*, Spring 2008, 49–72.

55. Donald Benson and Katherine Dix, "Pandemic Preparations for the Workplace," *The Colorado Lawyer*, May 2009, 49–56.

56. Based on: Tom Starner, "Watching Out for Big Brother," *Human Resource Executive*, October 16, 2007, 46–52.

15

Employee Rights and Responsibilities

After you have read this chapter, you should be able to:

- Define employment-at-will and discuss how wrongful discharge, just cause, and due process are interrelated.
- Identify employee rights associated with free speech and access to employee records.
- Discuss issues associated with workplace monitoring, employer investigations, and drug testing.
- List elements to consider when developing an employee handbook.
- Describe different kinds of absenteeism and how to measure it.
- Differentiate between the positive approach and the progressive approach to discipline.

Technology Usage and HR Policy Issues

(© Christopher Robbins/Jupiter Images)

Employees use technology for both job-related and personal reasons, on and off the job. For instance, a Florida lumber company lost a $21 million lawsuit caused by an employee having an accident while making cell phone sales calls while driving. To address the various concerns, many employers have established policies regarding technology usage. Such policies generally have the following four elements:

- Voice mail, e-mail, and other electronic files provided by the employer are for business use only.
- Use of these means for personal reasons is restricted and subject to employer review and possible disciplinary action.
- Computer passwords and codes must be available to the employer.
- The employer reserves the right to monitor or search any of the messages and media used for business purposes without notice.

However, court decisions have indicated that reading employee e-mails may violate some privacy rights unless specific security and privacy components are stated properly. As a result, HR professionals and legal advisors have developed employer policies to be identified and distributed online as well as in policy documents. As example, many universities, such as the University of Maryland–Baltimore, use online means to conduct employee and student training on policies involving topics such as sexual harassment, safety, health, and many others. Doing so reflects how the current state of technology is affecting employee/employer rights and responsibilities.[1]

Four interrelated HR issues are considered in this chapter: *employee rights*, *HR policies, absenteeism*, and *discipline*. How are they related? Employees come to work with some rights, but many more are granted or constrained by the HR policies and rules an employer sets. For example, such rules include policies on absenteeism. Further, discipline used against those who fail to follow policies and rules has both employee and employer rights dimensions. The concepts of rights, policies, and discipline change and evolve as laws and societal values change. Indeed, at one time the right of an employer to operate an organization as it might see fit was very strong. However, today that right is offset to varying extents by the increase in employee rights.

EMPLOYER AND EMPLOYEE RIGHTS AND RESPONSIBILITIES

Rights generally do not exist in the abstract. Instead, **rights** are powers, privileges, or interests derived from law, nature, or tradition. Of course, defining a right presents considerable potential for disagreement. For example, does an employee have a right to privacy of communication in personal matters when using the employer's computer on company time? Moreover, *legal rights* may or may not correspond to certain *moral rights*, and the reverse is true as well—a situation that opens "rights" up to controversy and lawsuits.

Statutory rights are the result of specific laws or statutes passed by federal, state, or local governments. Various federal, state, and local laws have granted employees certain rights at work, such as equal employment opportunity, collective bargaining, and workplace safety. These laws and their interpretations also have been the subjects of a considerable number of court cases because employers also have rights.

Rights are offset by **responsibilities**, which are obligations to perform certain tasks and duties. Employment is a reciprocal relationship in that both the employer and the employee have rights and obligations. For example, if an employee has the right to a safe working environment, then the employer must have an obligation to provide a safe workplace. If the employer has a right to expect uninterrupted, high-quality work from the employee, then the worker has the responsibility to be on the job and to meet job performance standards. The reciprocal nature of rights and responsibilities suggests that both parties to an employment relationship should regard the other as having rights and should treat the other with respect.

Rights Powers, privileges, or interests that belong by law, nature, or tradition.

Statutory rights Rights based on laws or statutes passed by federal, state, or local governments.

Responsibilities Obligations to perform certain tasks and duties.

Contractual rights Rights based on a specific contract between an employer and an employee.

Contractual Rights

When individuals become employees, they are likely to encounter both employment rights and responsibilities. Those items can be spelled out formally in written employment contracts or in employer handbooks and policies disseminated to employees. Contracts formalize the employment relationship. For instance, when hiring an independent contractor or a consultant, an employer should use a contract to spell out the work to be performed, expected timelines, parameters, and costs and fees to be incurred.

An employee's **contractual rights** are based on a specific contract with an employer. For instance, a union and an employer may agree on a labor contract that specifies certain terms, conditions, and rights that employees who are

FIGURE 15-1	Provisions in Employment Contracts

EMPLOYMENT CONTRACT

- ◆ Parties to the contract
- ◆ General job duties and expectations
- ◆ Compensation and benefits
- ◆ Terms and conditions of employment
- ◆ Termination/resignation factors
- ◆ Noncompete and nonpiracy agreements
- ◆ Nonsolicitation of current employees
- ◆ Intellectual property and trade secrets

Date:

_____

Employee's signature:

_____

Company representative's signature:

_____

Seal

represented by the union have with the employer. The contract also identifies employers' actions and restrictions.

Employment Contracts Traditionally, employment contracts have been used mostly for executives and senior managers, but the use of employment contracts is filtering down in the organization to include highly specialized professional and technical employees who have scarce skills. An **employment contract** is a formal agreement that outlines the details of employment. Depending on the organization and individuals involved, employment agreements may contain a number of provisions. Figure 15-1 shows common provisions.

Typically, an *identification section* lists the parties to the contract and the general nature of the employee's job duties. The level of compensation and types of benefits are often addressed, including any special compensation, benefits, incentives, or perquisites to be provided by the employer. The employment contract also may note whether the employment relationship is to be for an indeterminate time, or whether it can be renewed automatically after a specified period of time. Finally, the contract may spell out a severance agreement, continuation of benefits, and other factors related to the employee's leaving the employer.

Employment contract
Formal agreement that outlines the details of employment.

Noncompete Agreements Employment contracts may include **noncompete agreements**, which prohibit individuals who leave an organization from working with an employer in the same line of business for a specified period of time. A noncompete agreement may be presented as a separate contract or as a clause in an employment contract. Though primarily used with newly hired employees, some firms have required existing employees to sign noncompete agreements.

Different court decisions have ruled for or against employers that have fired employees who either have refused to sign noncompete agreements or have violated them. For example, an executive at Starbucks accepted a job at Dunkin Donuts. The impact of the case was reviewed and led to legal actions by Starbucks. While this example is still not resolved, it illustrates how noncompete agreement cases can occur. These agreements can be enforced less often in states such as California than in others.[2]

To create an employment contract with a noncompete agreement that is likely to be enforced in most states, it is recommended that the contract have geographical and time limitations (such as 1–2 years). Also, it is recommended that the noncompete agreement be limited to similar jobs and require customer confidentiality.[3] Such contracts may contain *nonpiracy agreements*, which bar former employees from soliciting business from former customers and clients for a specified period of time. Other clauses requiring *nonsolicitation of current employees* can be incorporated into the employment agreement. These clauses are written to prevent a former employee from contacting or encouraging coworkers at the former firm to join a different company, often a competitor.[4]

Intellectual Property An additional area covered in employment contracts is protection of *intellectual property* and *trade secrets*. A 1996 federal law made the theft of trade secrets a federal crime punishable by fines up to $5 million and 15 years in jail. Employer rights in this area include the following:

- The right to keep trade secrets confidential
- The right to have employees bring business opportunities to the employer first before pursuing them elsewhere
- A common-law copyright for works and other documents prepared by employees for their employers

Implied Contracts

The idea that a contract (even an implied or unwritten one) exists between individuals and their employers affects the employment relationship. The rights and responsibilities of the employee may be spelled out in a job description, in an employment contract, in HR policies, or in a handbook, but often they are not. The rights and responsibilities of the employee may exist *only* as unwritten employer expectations about what is acceptable behavior or performance on the part of the employee. Some court decisions have held that if an employer hires someone for an indefinite period or promises job security, the employer has created an implied contract. Such promises establish employee expectations, especially if there has been a long-term business relationship.

Noncompete agreements
Agreements that prohibit individuals who leave an organization from working with an employer in the same line of business for a specified period of time.

Employment Practices Liability Insurance

Workplace litigation has reached epidemic proportions as employees have sued their employers because they believed that their rights were violated. Class-action lawsuits by groups of workers also have expanded, which can be very expensive for employers. For example, some cases have led to claims ranging from less than $1 million to as high as more than $100 million. Although the actual resolution of a case may cost less than the amount of a claim, a case still can be very expensive if the employer is found guilty.

As a result, a significant number of employers have purchased employment practices liability insurance (EPLI) to cover their risks from lawsuits. This insurance covers employer costs for legal fees, settlements, and judgments associated with employment actions when individuals file suits alleging wrongful discharge or discrimination, and for other reasons.[5]

These insurance policies vary depending upon the nature of coverage and the provider. Some exclude payment for certain types of claims by employees and agencies regarding punitive damages caused by employer policies that violate various laws, such as the Fair Labor Standards Act, the Occupational Health and Safety Act, and others.

To determine the level of risk and premiums to be charged to employers wanting EPLI, most insurance carriers review the employers' HR policies and practices. The review may include a detailed look at an employer's HR policy manuals, employee handbooks, employment forms, and other items. It also may involve an examination of the employer's history of employment-related charges and complaints during the past three to five years. In a sense, such a review can be viewed as an audit of the organizational policies and practices regarding employee rights.[6]

LOGGING ON

Human Resources Law Cases®
This website provides information on workplace issues such as employment contracts and other issues. Visit the site at www.hrlawindex.com.

When the employer fails to follow up on the implied promises, the employee may pursue remedies in court. Numerous federal and state court decisions have held that such implied promises, especially when contained in an employee handbook, constitute a contract between an employer and its employees, even without a signed contract document. Many employers acquire special insurance to cover the costs of responding to legal actions on various contracts and employer actions, as the HR Perspective discusses.

RIGHTS AFFECTING THE EMPLOYMENT RELATIONSHIP

As employees have increasingly regarded themselves as free agents in the workplace and as the power of unions has changed in the United States, the struggle between individual employee and employer "rights" has become heightened. Employers frequently do not fare well in court in employee "rights" cases. Not only is the employer liable in many cases, but also individual managers and supervisors have been found liable when hiring or promotion decisions have been based on discriminatory factors or when they have had knowledge of such conduct and have not taken steps to stop it. Several concepts from law and psychology influence the employment relationship: employment-at-will, wrongful or constructive discharge, just cause, due process, and distributive and procedural justice.

Employment-at-Will (EAW)

Employment-at-will (EAW) is a common-law doctrine stating that employers have the right to hire, fire, demote, or promote whomever they choose, unless there is a law or a contract to the contrary. Conversely, employees can quit whenever they want and go to another job under the same terms. An employment-at-will statement in an employee handbook usually contains wording such as the following:

> *This handbook is not a contract, express or implied, guaranteeing employment for any specific duration. Although we hope that your employment relationship with us will be long term, either you or the Employer may terminate this relationship at any time, for any reason, with or without cause or notice.*

National restrictions on EAW include prohibitions against the use of race, age, sex, national origin, religion, and disabilities as bases for termination. Restrictions on other areas vary from state to state. Nearly all states have enacted one or more statutes to limit an employer's right to discharge employees. Also, numerous states allow employees to file breach-of-contract lawsuits because of some provisions in employee handbooks.[7]

EAW and the Courts In general, the courts have recognized three rationales for hearing EAW cases. The key ones are as follows:

- *Public policy exception*: This exception to EAW holds that employees can sue if fired for a reason that violates public policy. For example, if an employee refused to commit perjury and was fired, the employee can sue the employer.
- *Implied contract exception*: This exception to EAW holds that employees should not be fired as long as they perform their jobs. Long service, promises of continued employment, and lack of criticism of job performance imply continuing employment.
- *Good-faith and fair-dealing exception*: This exception to EAW suggests that a covenant of good faith and fair dealing exists between employers and at-will employees. If an employer breaks this covenant by unreasonable behavior, the employee may seek legal recourse.

Over the past several decades many state courts have redefined the employment-at-will and contractual components. Some courts have placed limits on those areas, including when employers exhibit extremely abusive actions. Also, as the nature of workers in their jobs has changed, varying employment contract interpretations have been adapted.[8]

Wrongful Discharge Employers who run afoul of EAW restrictions may be guilty of **wrongful discharge**, which is the termination of an individual's employment for reasons that are illegal or improper. Employers should take several precautions to reduce wrongful-discharge liabilities. Having a well-written employee handbook, training managers, and maintaining adequate documentation are key. Figure 15-2 offers suggestions for preparing a defense against wrongful-discharge lawsuits.

Employment-at-will (EAW) Common-law doctrine stating that employers have the right to hire, fire, demote, or promote whomever they choose, unless there is a law or contract to the contrary.

Wrongful discharge Termination of an individual's employment for reasons that are illegal or improper.

| FIGURE 15-2 | Keys for Preparing a Defense against Wrongful Discharge |

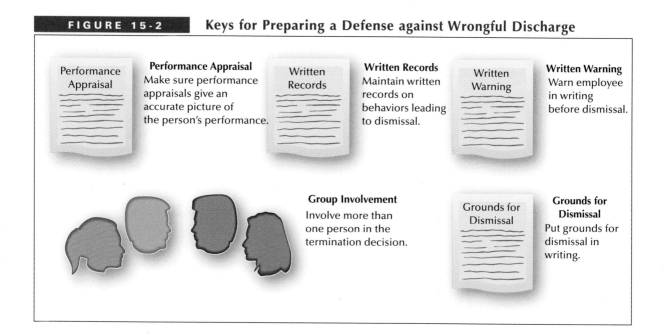

Performance Appraisal
Make sure performance appraisals give an accurate picture of the person's performance.

Written Records
Maintain written records on behaviors leading to dismissal.

Written Warning
Warn employee in writing before dismissal.

Group Involvement
Involve more than one person in the termination decision.

Grounds for Dismissal
Put grounds for dismissal in writing.

A landmark court case in wrongful discharge was *Fortune v. National Cash Register Company*. The case involved the firing of a salesperson (Mr. Fortune) who had been with National Cash Register (NCR) for 25 years.[9] The employee's termination came shortly after he got a large customer order that would have earned him a big commission. Based on the evidence, the court concluded that he was wrongfully discharged because NCR dismissed him to avoid paying the commission, thus violating the covenant of good faith and fair dealing.

Some state courts have recognized certain nonstatutory grounds for wrongful-discharge suits. Additionally, courts generally have held that unionized workers cannot pursue EAW actions as at-will employees because they are covered by the grievance arbitration process. As EAW has changed in interpretations and more wrongful-discharge lawsuits have been brought, employers have become more concerned about legal liability issues.[10]

Constructive Discharge Closely related to wrongful discharge is **constructive discharge**, which is deliberately making conditions intolerable to get an employee to quit. Under normal circumstances, an employee who resigns rather than being dismissed cannot later collect damages for violation of legal rights. An exception to this rule occurs when the courts find that the working conditions were made so intolerable as to *force* a reasonable employee to resign. Then, the resignation is considered a discharge.

Dangerous duties, insulting comments, and not providing reasonable work are examples of actions that can lead to a claim of constructive discharge. For example, two church employees claimed constructive discharge when their benefits and work conditions changed because the church had hired a private detective to investigate the senior pastor. As it turned out, the pastor had been embezzling. Consequently, a settlement was reached with the two employees to eliminate their constructive discharge claim.[11]

Constructive discharge
Process of deliberately making conditions intolerable to get an employee to quit.

Just Cause

Just cause is reasonable justification for taking employment-related action. The need for a "good reason" for disciplinary actions such as dismissal usually can be found in union contracts, but not in at-will situations. The United States has different just-cause rules than do some other countries. Even though definitions of *just cause* vary, the overall concern is fairness. To be viewed by others as *just*, any disciplinary action must be based on facts in the individual case.

One case involving a female employee with three years' experience illustrates how just cause can be interpreted. After taking most of her maternity leave, she was told two weeks before her return that she was being terminated due to a business slowdown. The company said she was among 23 employees fired because of poor performance. Yet the employee had received pay increases and a promotion, had never had any documented performance problems, and then was replaced by a full-time employee. Pointing to these facts, the court ruled that the employee could sue the company.[12]

Due Process

Due process, like just cause, is about fairness. Due process is the requirement that the employer use a fair process to determine if there has been employee wrongdoing and that the employee have an opportunity to explain and defend his or her actions. Organizational justice is a key part of due process.

Organizational Justice Most people have a need to feel the organization is treating employees justly. A wide range of HR activities can affect that perception of justice, including selection processes, job performance activities and evaluations, and disciplinary actions.

Whether employees perceive fairness or justice in their treatment depends on at least three factors that are more psychological than legal in nature.[13] First, people obviously prefer favorable outcomes for themselves. They decide the favorability of their outcomes by comparing them with the outcomes of others, given their relative situations. This decision involves the concept of **distributive justice**, which deals with the question "Were outcomes distributed fairly?" Fairness would not include disciplinary action based on favoritism when some are punished and others are not. Fairness is often dependent on employee perceptions, and is ultimately a subjective determination.

The second factor, procedural justice, focuses on whether the procedures that led to an action were appropriate, clearly understood, and provided an opportunity for employee input. **Procedural justice** deals with the question "Was the decision-making *process* fair?" Due process is a key part of procedural justice when making promotion, pay, discipline, and other HR decisions. If organizations provide procedural justice, employees tend to respond with positive behaviors that benefit the organization in return.

Interactional justice is based on perceived fairness about how a person interacts with others. For example, if a manager is perceived as rude and insults another manager, their relationship may be affected negatively. But if a manager treats the other person with respect and shares information truthfully, then the individuals are more likely to work well together.

Figure 15-3 shows some factors to be considered when combining an evaluation of just cause and due process. How HR managers address these factors determines whether the courts perceive employers' actions as fair.

Just cause Reasonable justification for taking employment-related action.

Due process Requirement that the employer use a fair process to determine employee wrongdoing and that the employee have an opportunity to explain and defend his or her actions.

Distributive justice Perceived fairness in the distribution of outcomes.

Procedural justice Perceived fairness of the processes used to make decisions about employees.

Interactional justice Perceived fairness about how a person interacts with others.

FIGURE 15-3	Criteria for Evaluating Just Cause and Due Process

JUST-CAUSE DETERMINANTS
- Was the employee warned of the consequences of the conduct?
- Was the employer's rule reasonable?
- Did management investigate before disciplining?
- Was the investigation fair and impartial?
- Was there evidence of guilt?
- Were the rules and penalties applied evenhandedly?
- Was the penalty reasonable, given the offense?

DUE PROCESS CONSIDERATIONS
- How have precedents been handled?
- Is a complaint process available?
- Was the complaint process used?
- Was retaliation used against the employee?
- Was the decision based on facts?
- Were the actions and processes viewed as fair by outside entities?

Complaint Procedures and Due Process Complaint procedures are provided by employers to resolve employee complaints or grievances. In most cases, the complaint procedures used to provide due process for unionized employees differ from those for nonunion employees. For unionized employees, due process usually refers to the right to use the formal grievance procedure specified in the union contract. Due process may involve including specific steps in the grievance process, imposing time limits, following arbitration procedures, and providing knowledge of disciplinary penalties. More discussion of the grievance process and procedures in unions can be found in Chapter 16.

Due process procedures for at-will employees are more varied than for union workers and may address a broader range of issues. Many organizations have a variety of means for addressing workplace disputes.[14] Numerous employers, especially smaller ones, use an **"open-door" policy**, which means that anyone with a complaint can talk with a manager, an HR representative, or an executive. However, often the door is not really open, especially if criticisms or conflicts are part of the complaint. For example, despite such a policy, an employee won a judgment against Wal-Mart because of threats from a coworker that were not responded to sufficiently by management.[15] Therefore, nonunion organizations generally benefit from having formal complaint procedures that are used effectively, since they provide due process for employees.

Work-Related Alternative Dispute Resolution (ADR)

Disputes between management and employees over different work issues are normal and inevitable, but how the parties resolve their disputes can become important. Formal grievance procedures and lawsuits provide two resolution methods. However, more and more companies are looking to alternative means of ensuring that due process occurs in cases involving employee rights. Dissatisfaction with the expenses and delays that are common in the court

"Open-door" policy
A policy in which anyone with a complaint can talk with a manager, an HR representative, or an executive.

system when lawsuits are filed explains the growth in alternative dispute resolution (ADR) methods such as arbitration, peer review panels, and ombuds.

Arbitration Disagreements between employers and employees often can result in lawsuits and large legal bills for settlement. Most employees who believe they have experienced unfair discrimination do not get legal counsel, but their discontent and complaints are likely to continue. Consequently, to settle disputes, a number of employers are using arbitration in nonunion situations.

Arbitration is a process that uses a neutral third party to make a decision, thereby eliminating the necessity of using the court system. Arbitration has been a common feature in union contracts. However, it must be set up carefully if employers want to use it in nonunion situations. Because employers often select the arbitrators, and because arbitrators may not be required to issue written decisions and opinions, many see the use of arbitration in employment-related situations as unfair.

Some firms use *compulsory arbitration*, which requires employees to sign a preemployment agreement stating that all disputes will be submitted to arbitration, and that employees waive their rights to pursue legal action until the completion of the arbitration process. Requiring arbitration as a condition of employment is legal, but employers must follow it rather than try to waive its use. Such a problem occurred with Dillard's, in a case where the firm did not participate in its own arbitration agreement.[16] However, in other situations, exceptions have been noted, so a legal check of compulsory arbitration as part of ADR should be done before adopting the practice.

LOGGING ON

American Arbitration Association
Information and resources for arbitration can be found at this association website. Visit the site at www.adr.org.

Peer Review Panels Some employers allow their employees to appeal disciplinary actions to an internal committee of employees. This panel reviews the actions and makes recommendations or decisions. Peer review panels use fellow employees and a few managers to resolve employment disputes. Panel members are specially trained volunteers who sign confidentiality agreements, after which the company empowers them to hear appeals.

These panels have several advantages including fewer lawsuits, provision of due process, lower costs, and management and employee development. Also, peer review panels can serve as the last stage of a formal complaint process for nonunion employees, and their use may identify means that resolve the disputes without court action. Peer review decisions can be made binding to avoid court lawsuits as well.[17] But if an employee does file a lawsuit, the employer presents a stronger case if a group of the employee's peers previously reviewed the employer's decision and found it to be appropriate.

Arbitration Process that uses a neutral third party to make a decision.

Ombuds Individuals outside the normal chain of command who act as problem solvers for both management and employees.

Ombuds Some organizations ensure process fairness through **ombuds**—individuals outside the normal chain of command who act as independent problem solvers for both management and employees. At a number of large and medium-sized firms, ombuds have effectively addressed complaints about unfair treatment, employee/supervisor conflicts, and other workplace behavior issues. Ombuds address employees' complaints and operate with a high degree of confidentiality. Any follow-up to resolve problems is often handled informally, except when situations include unusual or significant illegal actions.

MANAGING INDIVIDUAL EMPLOYEE AND EMPLOYER RIGHTS ISSUES

Employees who join organizations in the United States bring with them certain rights, including *freedom of speech, due process*, and *protection against unreasonable search and seizure*. Although the U.S. Constitution grants these and other rights to citizens, over the years, laws and court decisions have identified limits on them in the workplace. Globally, laws and policies vary, which means more issues for employers with expatriates and local workers in different countries. For example, an employee who voices threats against other employees may face disciplinary action by the employer without the employee's freedom of speech being violated.

Balancing both employers' and employees' rights is a growing HR concern due to more legal and court cases and expanding global workforces. Employers have legitimate rights and needs to ensure that employees are doing their jobs and working in a secure environment, while employees expect their rights, both at work and away from work, to be protected.

The **right to privacy** is defined in legal terms as an individual's freedom from unauthorized and unreasonable intrusion into personal affairs. Although the right to privacy is not specifically identified in the U.S. Constitution, a number of past U.S. Supreme Court cases have established that such a right must be considered. Also, several states have enacted right-to-privacy statutes. A scope of privacy concerns exists in other countries as well.

The dramatic increase in Internet communications, twitters, specialized computers, and telecommunications systems is transforming many workplaces. That is why having an HR culture that incorporates privacy as a key component is important.[18] The use of technology items by employers to monitor employee actions is amplifying concerns that the privacy rights of employees are being threatened.

Privacy Rights and Employee Records

As a result of concerns about protecting individual privacy rights in the United States, the Privacy Act of 1974 was passed. It includes provisions affecting HR recordkeeping systems. This law applies *only* to federal agencies and to organizations supplying services to the federal government. However, similar state laws, somewhat broader in scope, also have been passed. For the most part, state rather than federal law regulates private employers on this issue. In most states, public-sector employees are permitted greater access to their files than are private-sector employees.

LOGGING ON

Privacy, Business and Law
This nonprofit organization is a leading resource for information on new and existing business privacy issues. Visit the website at www.pandab.org.

Employee Medical Records Recordkeeping and retention practices have been affected by the following provision in the Americans with Disabilities Act (ADA):

> *Information from all medical examinations and inquiries must be kept apart from general personnel files as a separate confidential medical record available only under limited conditions specified in the ADA.*

As interpreted by attorneys and HR practitioners, this provision requires that all medical-related information be maintained separately from all other

Right to privacy An individual's freedom from unauthorized and unreasonable intrusion into personal affairs.

FIGURE 15-4 **Employee Record Files**

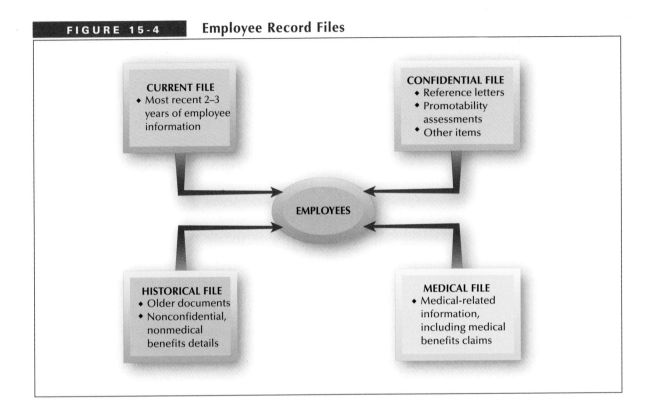

confidential files. The Health Insurance Portability and Accountability Act also contains regulations designed to protect the privacy of employee medical records. Both regular and confidential electronic files must be considered. As a result of all the legal restrictions, many employers have established several separate files on each employee, as illustrated in Figure 15-4.

Security of Employee Records It is important that specific access restrictions and security procedures for employee records be established. These restrictions and procedures are designed to protect the privacy of employees and to protect employers from potential liability for improper disclosure of personal information. For instance, security breaches can occur through employer records regarding an employee's Social Security data, home address, and family details, especially by electronic means.[19]

A legal regulation called the Data Protection Act requires employers to keep personnel records up-to-date and to keep only the details that are needed.[20] The following guidelines are offered regarding employer access and storage of employee records:

- Restrict access to records to a limited number of individuals.
- Use confidential passwords for accessing employee records in various HR databases.
- Set up separate files and restricted databases for especially sensitive employee information.
- Inform employees about which types of data are retained.
- Purge employee records of outdated data.
- Release employee information only with employee consent.

Personnel files and records usually should be maintained for three years. However, different types of records should be maintained for shorter or longer periods of time based on various legal and regulatory standards.

Electronic Records An increasing concern is how electronic records are maintained and secured, given the changes in software, e-mail, and other technology means. Estimates are that more than 200 billion company e-mails are sent daily. Many of these emails may relate to some aspect of electronic records and worker actions. Therefore, employers should establish electronic records policies to ensure legal compliance and to avoid violating individuals' personal rights.[21] Electronic records policies are discussed in more detail later in the chapter.

LOGGING ON

Privacy Rights Clearinghouse
For fact sheets and information on workplace monitoring rights, visit this website at www.privacyrights.org.

Employees' Free Speech Rights

The right of individuals to freedom of speech is protected by the U.S. Constitution. However, that freedom is *not* an unrestricted one in the workplace. Three areas in which employees' freedom of speech has collided with employers' restrictions are controversial views, whistle blowing, and use of the Internet and other technology.

Employee Advocacy of Controversial Views Questions of free speech arise over the right of employees to advocate controversial viewpoints at work. Numerous examples can be cited. For instance, can an employee of a tobacco company join in antismoking demonstrations outside of work? Can a disgruntled employee at a nonunion employer wear a union badge on a cap at work? In one U.S. case, a court decision ruled against a white worker who displayed Confederate flags on his toolbox, which offended some African American employees. The court said that the worker's free speech right was not violated when the employer fired him for refusing to remove the flags.[22] In situations such as these, employers must follow due process procedures and demonstrate that disciplinary actions taken against employees can be justified by job-related reasons.

However, simply because an employer *might be able* to punish public embarrassments, should it do so? Perhaps not—this is the sort of management activity that might be viewed by employees as overreacting by the employer. It may cause other employees to leave, or at least to not respect the employer. The best way to handle these concerns is to make clear the boundaries and expectations through a policy that spells them out and to have a signed nondisclosure privacy agreement.

Whistle Blowing and Sarbanes–Oxley Individuals who report real or perceived wrongs committed by their employers are called **whistle blowers**. The reasons why people report actions that they question vary and often are individual in nature.[23] Many well-known whistle-blowing incidents have occurred in past years at companies such as Enron, Adelphia Communications, and WorldCom. Also, a number of government workers have filed complaints because of actions by their bosses, which then have led to retaliations. An FBI agent filed a whistle-blowing suit after his complaints about wiretapping rules being violated led to his resignation.[24]

Whistle blowers Individuals who report real or perceived wrongs committed by their employers.

However, whistle blowers are less likely to lose their jobs in public employment than in private employment because most civil service systems follow rules protecting whistle blowers. A 2009 U.S. federal amendment said that for private employers to receive federal stimulus funding, they must have the same whistle-blowing regulations as the federal government.[25] However, no comprehensive whistle-blowing law fully protects the right to free speech of both public and private employees.

The culture of the organization often affects the degree to which employees report inappropriate or illegal actions internally or resort to using outside contacts. Employers need to address two key questions in regard to whistle blowing: (1) When do employees have the right to speak out with protection from retribution? (2) When do employees violate the confidentiality of their jobs by speaking out? Even though the answers may be difficult to determine, retaliation against whistle blowers is clearly not allowed. Also, whistle blowing can appear to show a lack of loyalty on the part of an employee, although that may not be a correct interpretation.[26]

The Sarbanes–Oxley Act is intended to remedy company ethical breaches. It adds protection for whistle blowers. But an antiretaliation provision covers *only* complaints made to certain entities, such as a manager/executive and federal regulatory or law enforcement agencies.

Ethical HR Issues on Blogs

"Blogs," or Web logs, provide an easy way for people to post opinions or views on any subject—including work, the boss, the company, company products, and people at work. Blogs also may be created by outsiders, and both positive and negative publicity can be the result. Wal-Mart, McDonalds, and many other firms have experienced this situation.

A major use of blogs for employers is providing information to employees about activities, policies, and practices within the organization. Thus, communication from HR and other departments, as well as from individual employees, can be delivered efficiently and effectively. However, misuse by employees may lead to disciplinary action and even termination.

Because HR policies on blogs may not be established or current, ethical problems can occur in blogs that are personal and not job related, as well as in work-related blogs. For example, an employee may communicate harmless information on friends and family members, as well as on other employees.

Work-related blogs can be either useful or insult managers and coworkers. However, both types can be identified as violating employer policies and lead to firing of employees.

A research study on terminations for either type of blog comments examined how college students and job workers viewed such terminations. The results of the study identified that those surveyed saw firing people for innocuous, harmless blog actions as being inappropriate and creating organizational ethical concerns. However, they viewed terminating persons for work-related negative blog comments as being more appropriate.

Consequently, HR executives and professionals are advised to establish and communicate ethical requirements on blogging. Training of all managers and employees on those HR requirements must be continuous, not just a one-time occurrence. If HR efforts on blogs are done well, employee morale and behaviors can be enhanced.[27]

Technology and Employer/Employee Issues

The extensive growth of technology use by employers and employees is constantly creating new issues to be addressed. Such technology usages as twitters, wikis, social networking, and blogs require attention by employers. For instance, ethical issues surrounding blogs and how they can lead to termination are highlighted in the HR Online.

Monitoring Electronic Communications Employers have a right to monitor what is said and transmitted through their Internet and voicemail systems, despite employees' concerns about free speech. Advances in information and telecommunications technology have become a major employer issue regarding employee and workplace privacy. For example, the use of e-mail increases every day, along with employers' liabilities if they improperly monitor or inspect employees' electronic communications.[28] Many employers have specialized software that can retrieve deleted electronic communications e-mail, and some even record each keystroke made on their computers.

There are recommended actions for employers to take when monitoring technology. Employers should monitor only for business purposes and strictly enforce the policy. For instance, one problem is that most people express themselves more casually in e-mail than they would in formal memos. This tendency can lead to sloppy, racist, sexist, or otherwise defamatory messages. Court cases have been brought over jokes forwarded through e-mails that contained profanity or racist undertones. Another problem is that electronic messages can be sent rapidly to multiple (and sometimes unintended) recipients. Also, the messages can be stored, and often legal cases hinge on retrieval of the messages.[29]

HR Policies on Electronic Communications Given all the time and effort employees spend on technology through both work and personal actions, it is important for HR professionals to provide guidance to executives, managers, and employees. Some areas in which HR policies need to be made can include the following:

- Establishing security and voicemail system
- Communicating that the employer will attempt to monitor security, but it may not be totally guaranteed
- Restricting the use of employee records to a few individuals

As the HR Headline indicates, many employers have developed and disseminated electronic communications policies. Figure 15-5 depicts recommended employer actions, beginning with the development of these policies.

Communicating policies on electronic communications to employees, enforcing them by monitoring employee Internet use, and disciplining offenders are means used by employers to ensure that the Internet is used appropriately. These efforts are necessary because both supervisors and employees can engage in violating electronic monitoring policies and practices.[30]

Employers' efforts also can attempt to guard against some employees' accessing pornographic or other websites that could create problems for the employer. If law enforcement investigations find evidence of such access, the employer could be accused of aiding and abetting illegal behavior. Many employers have purchased software that tracks the websites accessed by employees, and some employers use software programs to block certain websites that are inappropriate for business use.

| FIGURE 15-5 | Recommended Employer Actions Regarding Electronic Communications |

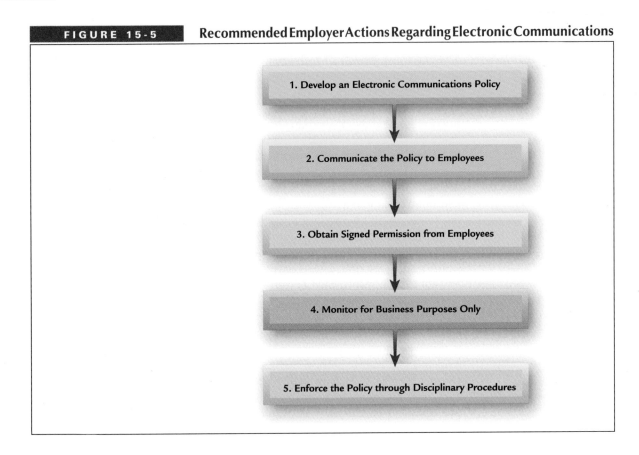

Employee Rights and Personal Behavior Issues

Another area to which employers must give attention is employee personal behavior. Personal behavior on or off the job could be at issue. For example, if an employer investigates off-the-job charges of illegal behavior, an invasion-of-privacy claim might result. On the other hand, failure to do due diligence could jeopardize disciplinary actions that should be taken by employers. Some of the more prevalent concerns in this area are discussed next.

Reviewing Unusual Behavior Employers may decide to review unusual behavior by employees both on and off the job. For instance, if an employee is suddenly wearing many new clothes and spending lavishly, inquiries as to the reasons why and the resources used might be warranted. Another issue is "workforce bullying," which is discussed in the ending case of this chapter.

Organizations and HR also must deal with actions such as employees or managers being inappropriately angry, insulting, or extremely rude to customers, suppliers, or employees at different levels. Even jokes or comments that are inconsiderate can create problems. To respond to such actions, managers and HR professionals should identify what are acceptable and unacceptable behaviors and activities. Meeting privately with persons to discuss concerns and getting feedback is also useful. Documenting such actions in supervisory HR records is recommended.[31]

Dressing and Body Appearance Limitations Employers have put limits on employees' dress and appearance in some situations, including items such as visible tattoos, certain clothing and accessories, and body piercings. Many managers have unwritten dress policies, but legally it is recommended that firms have written dress and appearance policies and codes.[32] The key is to give adequate notice to employees and managers, and to answer their concerns before a dress and appearance code is implemented.

One industry in which dress and appearance codes and policies are important is the retail industry. For instance, a pizza firm in New Mexico prohibits visible tattoos and many kinds of body piercing. However, employers must be careful that the codes do not discriminate against women, racial and ethnic minorities, those with disabilities, or religious individuals. Appearance issues can be the subject of policies that affect employee rights if they are job related.[33]

Off-Duty Behavior An additional employee rights issue concerns personal behavior off the job. Employers encounter special difficulty in establishing "just cause" for disciplining employees for their off-the-job behavior. Most people believe an employer should not control the lives of its employees off the job except in the case of clear job-related consequences. For example, can employees be disciplined for drinking or using tobacco or drugs on their own time away from work? Or, what should an employer do if an employee is an acknowledged transvestite, a member of an activist environmental group, a leader in a racist group, or an exotic dancer on weekends? In some cases, the answer should be "nothing"; in others, action must be taken.

These are just a few examples in which employee rights and personal behaviors can conflict with employer expectations. There really is no law that says an employer cannot discriminate against off-the-job behavior, but society has reservations about employers intruding into personal lives. The litmus test is whether the employee's off-the-job behavior puts the company in legal or financial jeopardy.[34]

BALANCING EMPLOYER SECURITY AND EMPLOYEE RIGHTS

Balancing employer and employee rights is becoming more difficult. On one side, employers have a legitimate need to ensure that employees are performing their jobs properly in a secure environment. On the other side, employees expect the rights that they have both at work and away from work to be protected. The commonplace monitoring of e-mail and voicemail is only one way employers watch the workplace. Technology gives employees who leave an employer the opportunity to take a great deal of valuable company secrets or data with them. For this reason (and others as well), workplace monitoring has increased.

Workplace Monitoring

In the United States, the right of protection from unreasonable search and seizure protects an individual against activities of the government only. Thus, employees of private-sector employers can be monitored, observed, and searched at work by representatives of the employer. Several court decisions have reaffirmed the principle that both private-sector and government employers may search desks, files, lockers, and computer files without search warrants if they believe that work rules have been violated. Also, the terrorist attacks of September 11, 2001, led to passage of the USA Patriot Act, which expanded legislation to allow government investigators to engage in broader monitoring of individuals, including in workplaces, in order to protect national security.

Conducting Video Surveillance at Work Numerous employers have installed video surveillance systems in workplaces. Some employers use these systems to ensure employee security, such as in parking lots, garages, and dimly lit exterior areas. Other employers have installed them on retail sales floors and in production areas, parts and inventory rooms, and lobbies. When video surveillance is extended into employee restrooms, changing rooms, and other more private areas, employer rights and employee privacy collide. It is important that employers develop a video surveillance policy, inform employees about the policy, perform the surveillance only for legitimate business purposes, and strictly limit those who view the surveillance results.

Monitoring Employee Performance Employee activity may be monitored to measure performance, ensure performance quality and customer service, check for theft, or enforce company rules or laws. The common concerns in a monitored workplace usually center not on whether monitoring should be used, but on how it should be conducted, how the information should be used, and how feedback should be communicated to employees.

At a minimum, employers should obtain a signed employee consent form that indicates that performance will be monitored regularly and phone calls will be taped regularly. Also, it is recommended that employers provide employees with feedback on monitoring results to help employees improve their performance and to commend them for good performance. For example, one major hotel reservation center allows employees to listen to their customer service calls and rate their own performance. Then, the employees meet with their supervisors to discuss both positive and negative performance issues.

Employer Investigations

Another area of concern regarding employee rights involves workplace investigations. The U.S. Constitution protects public-sector employees in the areas of due process, search and seizure, and privacy at work, but private-sector employees are not protected. Whether on or off the job, unethical or illegal employee behavior can be a serious problem for organizations. Employee misconduct may include illegal drug use, falsification of documents, misuse of company funds, disclosure of organizational secrets, workplace violence, employee harassment, and theft.

Conducting Work-Related Investigations Workplace investigations can be conducted by internal or external personnel. Often, HR staff and company security personnel lead internal investigations. Until recently, the use of outside investigators—the police, private investigators, attorneys, or others—was restricted by the Fair Credit Reporting Act. However, passage of the Fair and Accurate Credit Transactions (FACT) Act changed the situation. Under FACT, employers can hire outside investigators without first notifying the individuals under investigation or getting their permission.

Workplace investigations are frequently conducted using technology. Such means allow employers to review e-mails, access computer logs, conduct video surveillance, and use other investigative tactics. When using audiotaping, wiretapping, and other electronic methods, care should be taken to avoid violating privacy and legal regulations.

Employee Theft A problem faced by employers is employee theft of property and vital company secrets. White-collar theft through embezzlement, accepting bribes, and stealing company property also is a concern. If the organizational culture encourages or allows questionable behavior, then employees are more likely to see theft as acceptable.

Employee theft and other workplace misconduct can be addressed using a number of methods.[35] Typical methods may include doing an investigation before hiring, using applicant screening, and conducting background investigations. After hire, workplace monitoring can review unusual behaviors, such as those mentioned earlier. Honesty and polygraph tests may be used both before and after a person is hired.

Honesty and Polygraph Tests Pencil-and-paper honesty tests are alternatives to polygraph testing, as mentioned in Chapter 7. These tests are widely used, particularly in the retail industry and others. More than two dozen variations are available. However, their use has been challenged successfully in some court decisions.

For current employees, polygraph testing (performed with lie detectors) is used by some organizations. The Employee Polygraph Protection Act prohibits the use of polygraphs for most preemployment screening and also requires that employees must:

- Be advised of their rights to refuse to take a polygraph exam.
- Be allowed to stop the exam at any time.
- Not be terminated because they refuse to take a polygraph test or solely because of the exam results.

Substance Abuse and Drug Testing

Employee substance abuse and drug testing have received a great deal of attention. Concern about substance abuse at work is appropriate, given that absenteeism, accident/damage rates, and theft/fraud are higher for workers using illegal substances or misusing legal substances such as drugs and alcohol. Estimates by the U.S. Office of National Drug Control Policy are that about 8% of employees are drug abusers, and those persons create significantly more employer medical and workers' compensation claims.[36] Figure 15-6 identifies some of the financial effects of substance abuse. Ways to address substance abuse problems were discussed in Chapter 14. Employee rights concerned with those means are discussed in the following sections.

Drug-Free Workplace Act of 1988 The U.S. Supreme Court has ruled that certain drug-testing plans do not violate the Constitution. Private-employer programs are governed mainly by state laws, which can be a confusing hodgepodge. The Drug-Free Workplace Act of 1988 requires government contractors to take steps to eliminate employee drug use. Failure to do so can lead to contract termination. Tobacco and alcohol do not qualify as controlled substances under the act, and off-the-job drug use is not included. Additionally, the U.S. Department of Transportation requires regular testing

| FIGURE 15-6 | How Substance Abuse Affects Employers Financially |

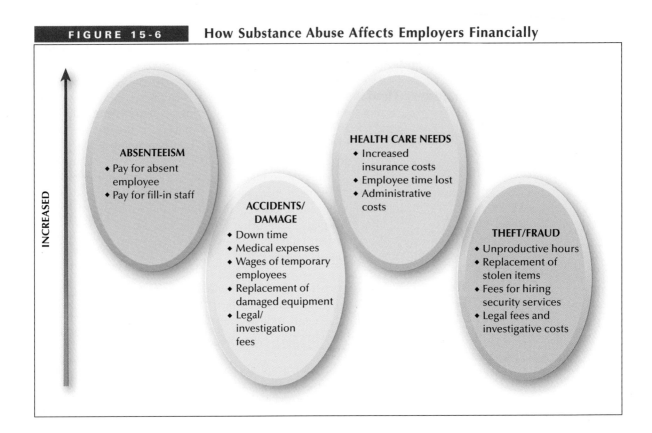

INCREASED

ABSENTEEISM
♦ Pay for absent
  employee
♦ Pay for fill-in staff

**ACCIDENTS/
DAMAGE**
♦ Down time
♦ Medical expenses
♦ Wages of temporary
  employees
♦ Replacement of
  damaged equipment
♦ Legal/
  investigation
  fees

HEALTH CARE NEEDS
♦ Increased
  insurance costs
♦ Employee time lost
♦ Administrative
  costs

THEFT/FRAUD
♦ Unproductive hours
♦ Replacement of
  stolen items
♦ Fees for hiring
  security services
♦ Legal fees and
  investigative costs

of truck and bus drivers, train crews, mass-transit employees, airline pilots and mechanics, pipeline workers, and licensed sailors.

Drug Testing and Employee Rights Unless federal, state, or local law prohibits testing, employers have a right to require applicants or employees to submit to a drug test. Laws on drug testing vary globally, due to different regulations in different countries.[37] Preemployment drug testing is widely used. When employers conduct drug testing of current employees, they generally use one of three policies: (1) random testing of everyone at periodic intervals, (2) testing only in cases of probable cause, or (3) testing after accidents. Means of testing include urinalysis and hair testing, among others.

If testing is done for probable cause, it needs to be based on performance-related behaviors, such as excessive absenteeism or reduced productivity, and not just the substance usage itself. From a policy standpoint, it is most appropriate to test for drugs when the following conditions exist:

• Job-related consequences of the abuse are severe enough that they outweigh privacy concerns.
• Accurate test procedures are available.
• Written consent of the employee is obtained.
• Results are treated confidentially, as are any medical records.
• Employer offers a complete drug program, including an employee assistance program.

Employers win many drug-testing cases in courts, including cases in which a person has been terminated for violating drug policy provisions. For example, a train conductor taking prescription drugs was terminated because he did not give accurate details in a medical screening as part of the employer's drug policy.[38] However, not all employers are enamored with drug testing, and some claim the rate of testing is dropping because it shows no demonstrable return on investment. Also, drug testing for certain employers may restrict the hiring of sufficient numbers of new employees, so employers may reexamine their drug policies.

HR POLICIES, PROCEDURES, AND RULES

HR policies, procedures, and rules greatly affect employee rights (just discussed) and discipline (discussed next). Where there is a choice among actions, **policies** act as general guidelines that help focus those organizational actions. Policies are general in nature, whereas procedures and rules are specific to the situation. The important role of all three requires that they be reviewed regularly.

Procedures provide customary methods of handling activities and are more specific than policies. For example, a policy may state that employees will be given vacations according to years of service, and a procedure establishes a specific method for authorizing vacation time without disrupting work.

Rules are specific guidelines that regulate and restrict the behavior of individuals. They are similar to procedures in that they guide action and typically allow no discretion in their application. Rules reflect a management decision that action be taken—or not taken—in a given situation, and they provide more specific behavioral guidelines than do policies. Certain rules may be violated more than others, and violations may occur more frequently if individual and organizational performance is not what is expected.[39] An example of a rule might be that a vacation day may not be scheduled the day before or after a holiday.

Perhaps more than any other part of the organization, the HR function needs policies, procedures, and rules. People react strongly to differential treatment regarding time off, pay, vacation time, discipline, and other factors. New and smaller employers often start without many of these HR issues well defined. But as they grow, issues become more complex, with policy decisions being made as necessary. Before long the inconsistency and resulting employee complaints bring on the need for clear policies, procedures, and rules that apply to everyone. Therefore, it is important that HR policies be consistent, but also allow some flexibility within the overall policy requirements.[40]

Coordination is necessary between the HR unit and operating managers for HR policies, procedures, and rules to be effective. As Figure 15-7 shows, managers are the main users and enforcers of rules, procedures, and policies, and they should receive some training and explanation in how to carry them out. The HR unit supports managers, reviews policies and disciplinary rules, and trains managers to use them. Often policies, procedures, and rules are provided in employee handbooks.

Policies General guideline that focus organizational actions.

Procedures Customary methods of handling activities.

Rules Specific guidelines that regulate and restrict the behavior of individuals.

Employee Handbooks

An employee handbook can be an essential tool for communicating information about workplace culture, benefits, attendance, pay practices, safety issues, and discipline. The handbooks are sometimes written in a formal legalistic fashion, but

FIGURE 15-7 Typical Division of HR Responsibilities: Policies, Procedures, and Rules

HR UNIT	MANAGERS
• Designs formal mechanisms for coordinating HR policies • Assists in development of organization-wide HR policies, procedures, and rules • Provides information on application of HR policies, procedures, and rules • Trains managers to administer policies, procedures, and rules	• Help in developing HR policies and rules • Review policies and rules with all employees • Apply HR policies, procedures, and rules • Explain rules and policies to all employees • Give feedback on effectiveness of policies and rules

need not be. More common language can make the handbook a positive element. Even small organizations can prepare handbooks relatively easily using available computer software with sample policies. When preparing handbooks, management should consider legal issues, readability, and use. Handbooks may contain many different areas, but some policies commonly covered in them include:

- At-will prerogatives
- Harassment
- Electronic communication
- Pay and benefits
- Discipline
- Hours worked

Legal Review of Language As mentioned earlier, one current trend in the courts is to use employee handbooks against employers in lawsuits by charging a broken "implied" contract. This tendency should not eliminate the use of employee handbooks as a way of communicating policies to employees. In fact, not having an employee handbook with HR policies spelled out understandably can leave an organization open to costly litigation and out-of-court settlements. A sensible approach is to first develop sound HR policies and employee handbooks to communicate them, and then have legal counsel review the language contained in the handbooks. Some legal experts recommend that overuse of legal wording can make handbooks less useful for employees.[41] Several recommendations include the following:

- *Eliminate controversial phrases.* For example, the phrase "permanent employee" may be used to describe a person who has passed a probationary period. This wording can lead to disagreement over what the parties meant by *permanent*. A more appropriate phrase is "regular employee."
- *Use disclaimers.* Courts generally uphold disclaimers, but only if they are prominently shown in the handbook.[42] To ensure that disclaimers are appropriate and create a positive image in the handbook, they should be done carefully. For instance, a disclaimer in the handbook can read as follows:

This employee handbook is not intended to be a contract or any part of a contractual agreement between the employer and the employee. The employer reserves the right to modify, delete, or add to any policies set forth herein without notice and reserves the right to terminate an employee at any time with or without a specific cause.

- *Keep the handbook current.* Many employers simply add new material to handbooks rather than deleting old, inapplicable rules. Those old rules can become the bases for new lawsuits. Consequently, handbooks and HR policies should be reviewed periodically and revised regularly.[43]

To communicate and discuss HR information, a growing number of firms are distributing employee handbooks electronically using an intranet, which enables employees to access policies in employee handbooks at any time. It also allows changes in policies to be made electronically rather than distributed as paper copies.

Communicating HR Information

HR communication focuses on the receipt and dissemination of HR data and information throughout the organization. *Downward communication* flows from top management to the rest of the organization, informing employees about what is and will be happening in the organization, and what the expectations and goals of top management are. *Upward communication* enables managers to learn about the ideas, concerns, and information needs of employees.

Organizations communicate with employees through internal publications and media, including newspapers, company magazines, organizational newsletters, videotapes, Internet postings, and e-mail announcements. Whatever the formal means used, managers should make an honest attempt to communicate information employees need to know. Electronic communications allows for more timely and widespread dissemination of HR policy information.[44] But online usage can present problems because policies may not be viewed appropriately by managers and employees.

EMPLOYEE ABSENTEEISM

One major application of HR policies and practices by employers relates to employees who are absent from their work and job responsibilities. **Absenteeism** is any failure by an employee to report for work as scheduled or to stay at work when scheduled. Being absent from work may seem like a normal matter to an employee. But if a manager needs 12 people in a unit to get the work done, and 4 of the 12 are absent much of the time, the work of the unit will decrease or additional workers will have to be hired to provide results. Estimates are that productivity losses due to absenteeism cost more than $70 billion per year for U.S. employers in total, and one study indicated that employee absenteeism averages about 36% of a company's payroll.[45] Some people have limited concerns about arriving at work late, and tardiness can be closely related to absenteeism, as the HR Perspective describes.

Types of Absenteeism

Absenteeism Any failure by an employee to report for work as scheduled or to stay at work when scheduled.

Employees can be absent from work or tardy for several reasons. Clearly, some absenteeism is inevitable because of illness, death in the family, and other personal reasons. Though absences such as those that are health related are unavoidable and understandable, they can be very costly.[46] Many employers

Effects of Tardiness on Work and Absenteeism

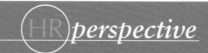

Tardiness, in which persons report late to work, is part of the issue of absenteeism addressed by HR. Whether an employee is a few minutes or a few hours late, tardiness means time away from work, and therefore controlling tardiness is part of controlling absenteeism.[47]

Some tardiness may be less controllable by employees, such as that caused by traffic problems like public transportation delays, road construction, and traffic accidents. However, many employees are late to work for personal, family, or other reasons. For instance, one survey found that about one-fourth of employees were tardy because of lack of sleep the night before. Tardiness also might be related to family issues, such as getting children to school or aiding an elderly or sick relative. Other people may not want to be at an early work meeting.

Regardless of the reasons for it, tardiness amounts to absenteeism and must be addressed by HR. Some ways of addressing it can include the following:

- Establish and consistently communicate policies on lateness as part of absenteeism.
- Remind employees of the consequences of tardiness, especially if it is frequent.
- Have specific discussions with tardy persons on the reasons for their lateness, and then document those reasons as part of HR records.
- If appropriate, consider individual flexible work scheduling, focusing on number of hours worked without having a specific set work time.
- Implement disciplinary actions for persons who are repeatedly or frequently tardy, especially for those who are tardy for reasons that are personal and controllable.

have sick leave policies that allow employees a certain number of paid days each year for those types of *involuntary* absences. However, much absenteeism is avoidable, or *voluntary*. According to a study, about two-thirds of employee absenteeism is due to personal or family reasons.[48]

One problem is that a number of employees see no real concern about being absent or late to work because they feel that they are "entitled" to some absenteeism. In many firms, a relatively small number of individuals are responsible for a large share of the total absenteeism in the organization. Also, individuals' work-related stress and strain can lead to absenteeism.[49]

Regardless of the reason, employers need to know if someone is going to be absent. Various organizations have developed different means for employees to report their absences. Wal-Mart and others have established an automated system in which their employees who will be absent call a special phone number. Others have special electronic notification e-mail accounts.[50] Regardless of the method used, employers need to have a clear policy on how the employee should notify the employer when an absence occurs.

Controlling Absenteeism

Voluntary absenteeism is better controlled if managers understand its causes clearly. Once they do, they can use a variety of approaches to reduce it. Organizational policies on absenteeism should be stated clearly in an employee handbook and emphasized by supervisors and managers. Figure 15-8 shows some common actions that employers use to control absenteeism.

| FIGURE 15-8 | **Employee Absenteeism Control Actions** |

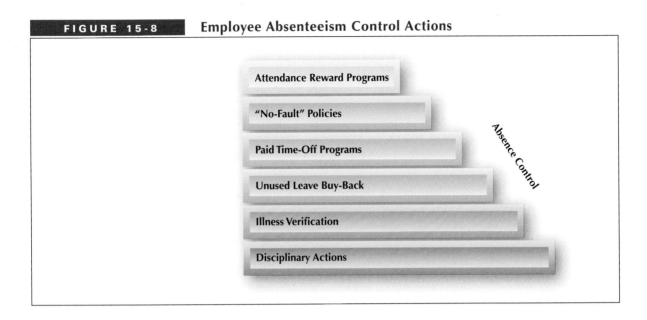

The methods employers use to address absenteeism can be placed into categories. Five of the more prominent ones are as follows:

- *Disciplinary approach*: Many employers use this approach. People who are absent the first time receive an oral warning, and subsequent absences bring written warnings, suspension, and finally dismissal.
- *Positive reinforcement*: Positive reinforcement includes such actions as giving employees cash, recognition, time off, and other rewards for meeting attendance standards. Offering rewards for consistent attendance, giving bonuses for missing fewer than a certain number of days, and "buying back" unused sick leave are all positive methods of reducing absenteeism.
- *Combination approach*: A combination approach ideally rewards desired behaviors and punishes undesired behaviors. This "carrot and stick" approach uses policies and discipline to punish offenders and various programs and rewards to recognize employees with outstanding attendance. For instance, employees with perfect attendance may receive incentives of travel and other rewards.
- *"No-fault" policy*: With a "no-fault" policy, the reasons for absences do not matter, and the employees must manage their own attendance unless they abuse that freedom. Once absenteeism exceeds normal limits, then disciplinary action up to and including termination of employment can occur. The advantages of the no-fault approach are that all employees can be covered by it, and supervisors and HR staff do not have to judge whether absences count as excused or unexcused.
- *Paid-time-off (PTO) programs*: Some employers have paid-time-off programs, in which vacation time, holidays, and sick leave for each employee are combined into a PTO account. Employees use days from their accounts at their discretion for illness, personal time, or vacation. If employees run out of days in their accounts, they are not paid for any additional days missed. PTO programs generally reduce absenteeism, particularly one-day absences, but they often increase overall time away from work because employees use all of "their" time off by taking unused days as vacation days.

MEASURE

HR Metrics: Measuring Absenteeism

A major step in reducing the expense of absenteeism is to decide how the organization is going to record absences and what calculations are necessary to maintain and benchmark their rates. Controlling or reducing absenteeism must begin with continuous monitoring of the absenteeism statistics in work units. Such monitoring helps managers pinpoint employees who are frequently absent and departments that have excessive absenteeism. Various methods of measuring or computing absenteeism exist. One formula suggested by the U.S. Department of Labor is as follows:

$$\frac{\text{Number of person-days lost through job absence during period}}{(\text{Average number of employees}) \times (\text{Number of workdays})} \times 100$$

The absenteeism rate also can be based on number of hours instead of number of days.

One set of metrics that can be calculated is the rate of absenteeism, which can be based on annual, monthly, quarterly, or other periods of time.[51] Other useful measures of absenteeism might include:

- *Incidence rate*: The number of absences per 100 employees each day
- *Inactivity rate*: The percentage of time lost to absenteeism
- *Severity rate*: The average time lost per absent employee during a specified period of time (a month or a year)

Additional information can be gained by separating absenteeism data into long- and short-term categories. Different problems are caused by employees who are absent for one day 10 times during a year, and employees who are absent one time for 10 days. When absenteeism costs are specifically identified, they may include these variables:

- Lost wages and benefits
- Overtime for replacements
- Fees for temporary employees, if incurred
- Supervisor's and manager's times
- Substandard production and performance
- Overstaffing necessary to cover anticipated absences

EMPLOYEE DISCIPLINE

The earlier discussion about employee rights provides an appropriate introduction to the topic of employee discipline, because employee rights often are a key issue in disciplinary cases. **Discipline** is a form of training that enforces organizational rules. Those most often affected by the discipline systems are problem employees. Fortunately, problem employees comprise a small number of employees. If employers fail to deal with problem employees, negative effects for other employees and groups often result.

Common disciplinary issues caused by problem employees include absenteeism, tardiness, productivity deficiencies, alcoholism, and insubordination. Often, discipline occurrences are seen differently by managers and employees. Whereas managers may see discipline as part of changing workers' behaviors, employees often see discipline as unfair because it can affect their jobs and careers.[52]

Discipline Form of training that enforces organizational rules.

Reasons Why Discipline Might Not Be Used

Managers may be reluctant to use discipline for a number of reasons. Some of the main ones include the following:

- *Organizational culture of avoiding discipline:* If the organizational "norm" is to avoid penalizing problem employees, then managers are less likely to use discipline or to dismiss problem employees.
- *Lack of support:* Many managers do not want to use discipline because they fear that their decisions will not be supported by higher management. The degree of support is also a function of the organizational culture.
- *Guilt:* Some managers realize that before they became managers, they committed the same violations as their employees, and therefore they do not discipline others for actions they formerly did.
- *Fear of loss of friendship:* Managers may fear losing friendships or damaging personal relationships if they discipline employees.
- *Avoidance of time loss:* Discipline often requires considerable time and effort. Sometimes it is easier for managers to avoid taking the time required for disciplining, especially if their actions may be overturned on review by higher management.
- *Fear of lawsuits:* Managers are increasingly concerned about being sued for disciplining an employee, particularly in regard to the ultimate disciplinary step of termination.

Effective Discipline

Because of legal concerns, managers must understand discipline and know how to administer it properly. Effective discipline should be aimed at the problem behaviors, not at the employees personally, because the reason for discipline is to improve performance. Distributive and procedural justice suggest that if a manager tolerates unacceptable behavior, other employees may resent the unfairness of that tolerance.

Training of Supervisors Training supervisors and managers on when and how discipline should be used is crucial. Employees see disciplinary action as more fair when given by trained supervisors who base their responses on procedural justice than when discipline is done by untrained supervisors. Training in counseling and communications skills provides supervisors and managers with the tools necessary to deal with employee performance problems, regardless of the disciplinary approaches used.

Approaches to Discipline

The disciplinary system can be viewed as an application of behavior modification to a problem or unproductive employee. The best discipline is clearly self-discipline. Most people can be counted on to do their jobs effectively when they understand what is required at work. But for some people, the prospect of external discipline helps their self-discipline. One approach is positive discipline.

Positive Discipline Approach The positive discipline approach builds on the philosophy that violations are actions that usually can be corrected constructively without penalty. In this approach, managers focus on using fact finding and guidance to encourage desirable behaviors, rather than using penalties to discourage undesirable behaviors. The hope is that employee performance will improve and future disciplinary actions will not be needed.[53] The four steps to positive discipline are as follows:

1. *Counseling:* The goal of this phase is to heighten employee awareness of organizational policies and rules. Often, people simply need to be made aware of rules, and knowledge of possible disciplinary actions may prevent violations.
2. *Written documentation:* If an employee fails to correct behavior, then a second conference becomes necessary. Whereas the first stage took place as a conversation between supervisor and the employee, this stage is documented in written form, and written solutions are identified to prevent further problems from occurring.
3. *Final warning:* If the employee does not follow the written solutions noted in the second step, a final warning conference is held. In that conference, the supervisor emphasizes to the employee the importance of correcting the inappropriate actions. Some firms require the employee to take a day off with pay to develop a specific written action plan to remedy the problem behaviors. The decision day off emphasizes the seriousness of the problem and the manager's determination to see that the behavior is changed.
4. *Discharge:* If the employee fails to follow the action plan that was developed, and further problems exist, then the supervisor can discharge the employee.

The advantage of this positive approach to discipline is that it focuses on problem solving. The greatest difficulty with the positive approach to discipline is the extensive amount of training required for supervisors and managers to become effective counselors, and the need for more supervisory time with this approach than with the progressive discipline approach, which is discussed next.

Progressive Discipline Approach Progressive discipline incorporates steps that become progressively more stringent and are designed to change the employee's inappropriate behavior. Figure 15-9 shows a typical progressive discipline process; most progressive discipline procedures use verbal and written reprimands and suspension before resorting to dismissal. For example, at a manufacturing firm, an employee's failure to call in when being absent from work might lead to a suspension after the third offense in a year. Suspension sends employees a strong message that undesirable job behaviors must change or termination is likely to follow.

Although it appears to be similar to positive discipline, progressive discipline is more administrative and process oriented. Following the progressive sequence ensures that both the nature and the seriousness of the problem are clearly communicated to the employee. Not all steps in progressive discipline are followed in every case. Certain serious offenses are exempted from the progressive procedure and may result in immediate termination. Typical offenses leading to immediate termination include intoxication at work, alcohol or drug use at work, fighting, and theft.

However, if a firm has a progressive discipline policy, it should be followed in every case in which immediate termination is not appropriate. Several court

FIGURE 15-9	Progressive Discipline Process

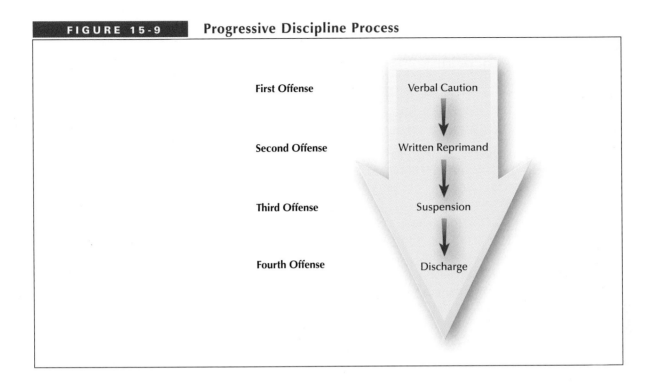

decisions have ruled that failure to follow written policies for progressive discipline can invalidate an employee's dismissal as unlawful retaliation. This type of equal employment claim increased by 18% in one report year.[54]

Discharge: The Final Disciplinary Step

The final stage in the disciplinary process may be called *discharge, firing, dismissal,* or *termination,* among other terms. Regardless of the word used, **discharge** is when an employee is removed from a job at an employer. Both the positive and the progressive approaches to discipline clearly provide employees with warnings about the seriousness of their performance problems before dismissal occurs.

One difficult phase of employee termination is the removal of terminated employees and their personal possessions from company facilities. The standard advice from legal experts is to physically remove the employee as quickly as possible. Often ex-employees are escorted out of the building by security guards. Some firms allow terminated employees to return to their desks, offices, or lockers to retrieve personal items under the observation of security personnel and the department supervisor/manager, but this means the ex-employee may be seen by and may talk with coworkers while still upset or angry. The HR On-the-Job discusses some practices that can make employee termination less difficult.

Termination Considerations Termination happens for a wide range of reasons. One study identified that more than 50% of all employers had terminated employees for inappropriate use and abuse of e-mails. Other causes can be violation of company policies, sexual harassment, off-work criminal behavior, poor performance, and numerous other occurrences.[55]

Discharge When an employee is removed from a job at an employer.

Termination Procedure

Dismissal of an employee can be problematic. The following practices can make it less difficult:

1. *Review evidence.* The disciplining manager, that manager's superior, and an HR representative should review the documentation and make the final determination.

2. *Select a neutral location.* Termination should occur in a neutral location, not in the supervisor/manager's office.

3. *Conduct the termination meeting.* The HR representative and/or the manager informs the employee of the reason for the termination. The manager and the HR representative should remain professional and calm, not be apologetic or demeaning.

4. *Have HR discuss termination benefits.* The HR representative explains the employee's final payroll and benefits. A specific letter can serve as evidence that the employee was notified of the termination decision and details of those rights.

5. *Escort the employee from the building.* This phase is controversial. The goal is to ensure that the employee, who is likely to be upset, is removed from the premises quickly without obvious conflicts or concerns about security.

6. *Notify the department staff.* The manager notifies the department staff that the individual is no longer employed. No details or explanations should be provided.[56]

However, following terminations, HR professionals and managers may be faced with *wrongful termination* claims and lawsuits. These legal challenges can be based on federal, state, and local laws. From a legal standpoint, terminating workers because they do not keep their own promises is likely to appear equitable and defensible in many courts, but nevertheless, it is important for the employer to consistently document reasons for termination and to follow appropriate HR processes discussed earlier. Doing so can increase the possibility that the employer will win termination lawsuits.[57]

Separation Agreements In some termination situations, formal contracts may be used. One type is a **separation agreement**, in which an employee who is being terminated agrees not to sue the employer in exchange for specified benefits, such as additional severance pay or other "considerations."

For such agreements to be legally enforceable, the considerations usually should be additional items that are not part of normal termination benefits. For international employees, different legal requirements may exist in various countries, including certain requirements for severance pay and benefits. When using separation agreements, care must be taken to avoid the appearance of constructive discharge of employees. Use of such agreements should be reviewed by legal counsel.

Separation agreement
Agreement in which a terminated employee agrees not to sue the employer in exchange for specified benefits.

SUMMARY

- The employment relationship is a reciprocal one in which both employers and employees have statutory and contractual rights, as well as responsibilities.
- Contractual rights can be spelled out in an employment contract or be implied as a result of employer promises.
- Employment-at-will gives employers the right to hire and terminate employees with or without notice or cause.
- Courts are changing aspects of employment-at-will relationships through exceptions for violations of public policy, an implied contract, and good faith and fair dealing.
- Wrongful discharge occurs when an employer improperly or illegally terminates an individual's employment.
- Constructive discharge is the process of making conditions intolerable to get an employee to "voluntarily" quit a job.
- Just cause for employment-related activities should exist for taking appropriate employment-related actions.
- Although both due process and organizational justice are not guaranteed for the at-will employees, the courts expect to see evidence of due process in employment-related cases.
- Complaint procedures and due process is important for both unionized and nonunion employees. In nonunion situations, alternative dispute resolution (ADR) means may be used.
- Arbitrations, peer review panels, and ombuds also can be used to address disciplinary actions.

- Balancing employer and employee rights becomes an issue when dealing with privacy rights, access to employee records, free speech, and whistle-blowing situations.
- Employers increasingly are facing privacy, free speech, and other issues in electronic communications, including e-mails, twitters, blogs, wikis, voicemail, and other technology means.
- The rights of employees for personal behavior must be balanced by employers' rights, particularly in regard to individuals' display of behaviors, unique dress or appearance, and questionable off-duty actions.
- Employer investigations protect both employer and employee rights.
- Drug testing provides a useful and legal method for employers to deal with increasing drug problems at work.
- HR policies, procedures, and rules should be in employee handbooks and other communications means. Courts sometimes view employee handbooks as implied contracts.
- Absenteeism is expensive. It can be controlled by discipline, positive reinforcement, use of a no-fault policy, and paid-time-off programs.
- Although employee self-discipline is the goal, positive or progressive discipline is sometimes necessary to encourage self-discipline.
- The final disciplinary phase is discharge of an employee through termination, which might include a separation agreement.

CRITICAL THINKING ACTIVITIES

1. Identify how the issues of due process and just cause are linked to employer disciplinary actions.

2. Discuss the following statement: "Even though efforts to restrict employees' free speech at work may be permissible, such efforts raise troubling questions affecting individual rights."

3. Give some examples of how technology is creating employer/employee rights and policy issues. Then suggest some possible actions that may be needed.

4. Assume that as the HR manager, you have decided to prepare some guidelines for supervisors to use when they have to discipline employees. Gather the information needed, using Internet resources such as www.blr.com and www.workforce.com for sample policies and other details. Then prepare a guide for supervisors on implementing both positive and progressive discipline.

HR EXPERIENTIAL PROBLEM SOLVING

In developing a company workplace violence prevention program, management has become aware of concerns regarding a drug-free workplace. Several employees have recently come to HR requesting a leave of absence to enter a drug rehabilitation program. The managers were not aware of the substance abuse issues relating to these employees. Consequently, management recognizes that a drug-free workplace program will help improve workplace safety and health. These programs also play an important role in fostering safer and drug-free families and communities. To assist HR in developing a drug-free workplace program, visit this website at www.dol.gov/workingpartners.

1. What are the key components that should be included in your company's drug-free workplace program to best meet the needs of both employees and the company?

2. Identify the steps a manager should take if an employee's actions create a suspicion that the employee has reported to work under the influence of substances.

CASE

Dealing with Workplace Bullying

Work-related responsibilities can be challenging for many employees, managers, and executives for numerous reasons. It is not uncommon for all of these people to face challenges in balancing personal and work-life demands, as well as extensive job demands. But the pressure can be increased when "bullying" by bosses or employees is present.

Bullying in workplaces occurs when people are insulted, frightened, pressured strongly by comments, or face numerous other questionable actions by others. The occurrence of bullying is extensive, according to some surveys. For instance, of more than 50 million workers surveyed, about 37% of them said they had been bullied at work. Many of the incidents were by executives, managers, or supervisors who were their bosses. Examples of bullying by bosses included criticizing employees personally with insults or yelling, and making excessive demands. In a smaller study in San Francisco, 45% of 1,000 employees said they had worked for bullying bosses. This illustrates that one important issue of HR policies is how to deal with abusive managers and supervisors.

The differentiation between a demanding, intense boss and one who is a bully is how behavior, comments, and actions are seen by employees. If a manager demands high performance of all workers, rather than just selected ones, this may not be seen as bullying. However, when a boss uses power and aggressiveness to consistently insult and irritate a few people, the boss's actions may be seen as inappropriate. Conduct that can be seen as bullying includes:

• Frequent emotional comments and outbursts
• Use of "power" for self-interest rather than for job- and employer-related issues
• Aggressively demanding tasks and results from subordinates and other managers

A growing HR legal concern is if workforce bullying violates the civil rights of protected class members. Women, racial minorities, older people, individuals with disabilities, and others may be able to file equal employment legal complaints. More than a dozen states have introduced legislation to address bullying through "healthy workplace" requirements. Some lawsuits have been won by workers who have been bullied. For instance, an Indiana hospital employee won an award because of a surgeon who communicated through screaming, cussing, clenched fists, and by other inappropriate means.

However, bullying is not limited to that done by bosses. Employees can be disciplined for how they treat customers, clients, coworkers, and even their managers. Examples include inappropriate or nasty comments, gestures, and other actions.

It is important that employers adopt and reinforce antibullying codes of conduct and policies. Additionally, training all bosses and workers about inappropriate bullying actions can help to reduce incidences of bullying. HR professionals should be proactive and take seriously individuals' complaints of bullying-related actions. Bullying has always occurred in workplaces, but now it has grown into another important HR employer/employee rights and responsibilities issue.[58]

QUESTIONS

1. Based on your work experiences, identify examples of bullying that you have observed by managers, supervisors, and/or coworkers. Discuss what was and was not done, both appropriately and inappropriately, by your employers.

2. If you were an HR professional doing training, what content and policies regarding bullying might you present to employees and managers?

SUPPLEMENTAL CASES

George Faces Challenges

This case describes the problem facing a new department supervisor when HR policies and discipline have been handled poorly in the past. (For the case, go to www.cengage.com/management/mathis.)

Employer Liable for "Appearance Actions"

This case discusses a California court ruling on terminating a female for her personal appearance. (For the case, go to www.cengage.com/management/mathis.)

NOTES

1. Based on Bill Roberts, "Stay Ahead of the Technology Use Curve," *HR Magazine*, October 2008, 57–62; Andrew T. Schlosser, "Putting the Brakes on Driving with Cell Phones," *Business Watch*, Winter/Spring 2007, 1; Dionne Searcey, "Some Courts Raise Bar on Reading Employee Email," *The Wall Street Journal*, November 19, 2009, A17; Donna M. Owens, "Managing Corporate Policies Online," *HR Magazine*, May 2008, 60–72.

2. Joan S. Lublin, "Watch for Legal Traps When You Quit a Job to Work for a Rival," *The Wall Street Journal*, November 6, 2007, B1.

3. Lawrence P. Postol, "Drafting Noncompete Agreements for All 50 States," *Employee Relations Law Journal*, 33 (2007), 65–73.

4. Emily B. York, "Does a Noncompete Agreement Really Offer Any Protection?" *Workforce Management*, October 13, 2009, www.workforce.com.

5. For details on EPLI policies, go to www.epli.com.

6. Based on "Evaluating Employment Practices Liability Insurance," *Baird-Holm Labor & Employment Law Update*, October 2007, 1–3; Eric Krell, "Under the Radar: EPL Insurance," *HR Magazine*, January 1, 2006, www.shrm.org.

7. For details, go to "Contract Disclaimers and Employment-at-Will Policies," *Ceridian Abstracts*, www.hrcompliance.ceridian.com.

8. Katherine V.W. Stone, "Revisiting the At-Will Doctrine . . .," *Industrial Law Journal*, 36 (2007), 84–101.

9. *Fortune v. National Cash Register Co.*, 373 Mass. 96, 36 N.E.2d 1251 (1977).

10. Edward C. Tomlinson and William N. Bockanic, "Avoiding Liability for Wrongful Termination," *Employee Responsibilities and Rights Journal*, 21 (2009), 77–88.

11. Monica Potts, "Bookkeeper and Diocese Settle Lawsuit," *McClatchy-*

Tribune Business News, September 15, 2009.

12. *Batka v. Prime Charter, Ltd.*, No. 2 Civ. 6265 (S.D.N.Y., Feb. 4, 2004), as described in *Workforce Management*, May 2004, 20.

13. For details, see Russell Cropanzano, et al., "The Management of Organizational Justice," *Academy of Management Perspectives*, November 2007, 34–48.

14. Margaret R. Bryant, "Resolving Workplace Disputes Internally," *SHRM Research*, March 1, 2009, www.shrm.org/research.

15. *White v. Wal-Mart* (Ohio Ct. App. 11th Dist., May 2, 2008).

16. "Employer Loses Right to Arbitrate Due to Breach," *Dispute Resolution Journal*, February–April 2006, 5.

17. Tanya M. Marcum and Elizabeth A. Campbell, "Peer Review in Employee Disputes," *Journal of Workplace Rights*, 13 (2008), 41–58.

18. Rita Zeidner, "Out of the Breach . . .," *HR Magazine*, August 2008, 37–41.

19. Jared Shelly, "Hazardous Leaks," *Human Resource Executive*, September 2, 2009, 34–36.

20. For details on the retention of employee records and documents, go to www.hrcompliance.ceridian.com.

21. Michelle V. Rafter, "Electronic Records Management," *Workforce Management Online*, May 2009, www.workforce.com; "Can You Identify the Elements of an Effective Electronic Communications Policy?" *HR Compliance*, July 2009, www.hrcompliance.ceridian.com.

22. *Dixon v. Coburg Dairy Inc.*, No. 02-1266 (4th Cir., May 30, 2003).

23. Marcia P. Miceli, et al., "A Word to the Wise: How Managers and Policy-Makers Can Encourage Employees to Report Wrong-Doing," *Journal of Business Ethics*, 86 (2009), 379–397.

24. Catherine Rampell, "Whistle-Blowers Tell of Cost of Conscience," *Workforce Management*, April 6, 2009, 4.

25. Jessica Marquez, "Firms Getting Stimulus Face Tougher Whistle-Blower Law," *Workforce Management*, April 6, 2009, 4.

26. Jukka Varel, "Is Whistle-Blowing Compatible with Employee Loyalty?" *Journal of Business Ethics*, 85 (2009), 263–275.

27. Based on information from Sean Valentine, et al., "Exploring the Ethicality of Terminating Employees Who Blog," *Human Resource Management*, 20 (2010), 82–108; "The Blog in the Corporate Machine," *The Economist*, February 11, 2006, 55.

28. Barry A. Friedman and Lisa J. Reed, "Workplace Privacy: Employee Relations and Legal Implications of Monitoring E-mail Use," *Employee Responsibilities Rights Journal*, 19 (2007), 75–83.

29. Kristin Byron, "Carrying Too Heavy a Load? The Communication of Miscommunication of Emotion by Email," *Academy of Management Review*, 33 (2008), 309–327.

31. Elaine Herskowitz, "Not Funny," *HR Magazine*, September 2008, 139–142; "Dealing with Anger in the Workforce," *Ceridian Abstracts*, July 1, 2009, www.hrcompliance.ceridian.com; Michael O'Brien, "Managing Rudeness," *Human Resource Executive*, November 2009, 34.

32. Kathleen Koster, "What Not to Wear: Legal, Communication, and Enforcement Tips for Introducing a Dress Code," *Employee Benefit News*, September 1, 2009, 56–57.

33. Steve Taylor, "'Look' Policies Pose Risks," *HR Disciplines*, July 15, 2009, www.shrm.org.

34. Chad Schultz, "The Jury Is Still Out—Way Out," *HR Magazine*, January 2005, 97–100.

35. Keisha-Ann G. Gray, "Searching for Employee Misconduct," *HREOnline*, May 18, 2009, www.hreonline.com.

36. Kathleen Koster, "Drug Tests: Accurate Measures of Impairment or Ineffective Invasions of Privacy?" *Employee Benefit News*, November 2009, 16.

37. Lorna Harris, "Pushing Borders of Drug Testing," *Canadian HR Reporter*, December 1, 2008, 5–6.

38. Amy Onder, "Violation of Drug Policy Grounds for Termination," *HR Magazine*, January 2009, 79.

39. David W. Lehmon and Rangaraj Ramanujam, "Selectivity in Organizational Rule Violations," *Academy of Management Review*, 34 (2009), 643–657.

40. Robert J. Greene, "Effective HR Policies and Practices: Balancing Consistency and Flexibility," *WorldatWork Journal*, Second Quarter 2007, 70–81.

41. John T. Hansen and Radhika Sood, "A Lighter Touch for Handbooks," *HR Magazine*, May 2009, 91–97.

42. *Compton v. Rent-a-Center*, No. 08-6264 (10th Cir., Oct. 20, 2009).

43. Steve Bates, "Employee Handbooks: Every Word Counts," *HR News*, June 26, 2008, www.shrm.org/hrnews.

44. Donna M. Owens, "Managing Corporate Policies Online," *HR Magazine*, May 2008, 69–72.

45. "Shirking Working: The War on Hooky," *BusinessWeek*, November 12, 2007, 73–75; "The Total Financial Impact of Employee Absences," *Mercer Survey*, October 2008, www.kronos.com/absenceanonymous.

46. William Molmen, "Knowing How to Manage Health-Related Absence," *Workspan*, December 2008, 37–41.

47. Michael O'Brien, "Tardiness on the Rise," *HR Executive On-line*, July 22, 2009; "How Can We Best Deal with an Employee Who Is Repeatedly Late for Work?" *HR Compliance*, August 2009, www.hrcompliance.ceridian.com.

48. "CCH Survey Finds Most Employees Call in 'Sick' for Reasons Other than Illness," *CCH 2007 Unscheduled Absence Survey*, www.cch.com

49. W. Darr and G. Johns, "Work Strain, Health, and Absenteeism," *Journal of Occupational Health Psychology* 13 (2008), 292–318.

50. Chris Silva, "Wal-Mart Adopts Automated Absenteeism System," *Employee Benefit News*, February 2007, 12–14.

56. Additional explanations are included in "Managing Employee Attendance," *SHRM Research*, June 15, 2009, www.shrm.org/research.

52. Leanne E. Atwater, et al., "The Delivery of Workplace Discipline: Lessons Learned," *Organizational Dynamics*, 36 (2007), 392–403.

53. Kathy Shaneberger, "When a Staff Member Needs to Improve," *OR Manager*, November 2008, 19–21.

54. Jonathan A. Segal, "A Warning About Warnings," *HR Magazine*, February 2009, 67–70.

55. "More Than Half of Employers Fire Workers for E-Mail, Internet Abuse," *Newsline*, February 29, 2008, www.worldatwork.org.

56. Provided by Nicholas Dayan, SPHR, and Saralee Ryan.

57. For more details, see Deborah Miller, "The Right Things to Do to Avoid Wrongful Termination Claims," *Newsline*, October 2008, www.worldatwork.org; Wendy Bliss and Gene R. Thornton, "Involuntary Termination of Employment in the United States," *SHRM Research*, December 1, 2008, www.shrm.org/research.

58. Based on Stephen M. Paskoff, "Anti-Bullying: A New Era in Workplace Civil Rights?" *Human Resource Executive*, November 19, 2007, 99–102; Nathaniel J. Fast and Serena Chen, "When the Boss Feels Inadequate," *Psychological Science*, 20 (2009), 1–8; Denise Salin, "The Prevention of Workplace Bullying as a Question of Human Resource Management," *Scandinavian Journal of Management*, 24 (2008), 221–231; Teresa A. Daniel, "Tough Boss or Workplace Bully?" *HR Magazine*, June 2009, 83–86; "Tips on Dealing with Workplace Bullying," *Ceridian Abstracts*, May 7, 2009, www.hrcompliance.ceridian.com.

16

Union/Management Relations

After you have read this chapter, you should be able to:

- Describe what a union is and explain why employees join and employers resist unions.
- Identify several reasons for the decline in union membership.
- Explain the nature of each of the major U.S. labor laws.
- Discuss the stages of the unionization process.
- Describe the typical collective bargaining process.
- Define grievance and identify the stages in a grievance procedure.

Business versus Labor—Right to Work Laws

(AP Photo/Paul Sancya)

Edward Sioui had always been able to make a living in Michigan, so he did not worry when he had to move to Arizona to help his mother after she had a heart attack. One year later, frustrated by meager paychecks, he and his wife moved back to Michigan. He blamed the lack of good-paying jobs in Arizona on the "open-shop" or "right-to-work" laws in that state. Under such laws, union membership is not required to get a job and employees can choose not to join the union even if the company is unionized. Clearly such laws have a negative effect on union growth. "You aren't treated with any respect," Sioui says. "You are dispensable and they know it so they treat you that way." He was happy to be back in Michigan even though he was laid off and had no job.

Michigan has been a strong union state, with the percentage of workers represented approaching 1 in 5. Generations of people in Michigan have grown up believing that tough unions would protect jobs and incomes. But during the recession, the unemployment rate in Michigan exceeded 15%—the highest in the nation. Business leaders in Michigan have argued that the strong union tradition is part of the economic problem in that state and that making Michigan a right-to-work state would send a message that they are "open for business." Unions, of course, disagree.

To regain some of its economic strength, Michigan must attract industry. Right-to-work proponents argue that the strong union presence keeps new business away because Michigan is not seen as having a business-friendly environment. That the idea of right-to-work would even be considered in Michigan shows how much power unions have lost in the last decade and a half.[1]

Union Formal association of workers that promotes the interests of its members through collective action.

A **union** is a formal association of workers that promotes the interests of its members through collective action. The very existence of unions depends upon laws and legal action.[2] As a result, politics play a large role in the fortunes of labor unions.[3] Traditionally in the United States, one political party has been more favorable toward labor unions than the other.[4]

An economic look at labor unions reveals "two faces." The "good face" emphasizes the fact that unions give members a "voice" to express dissatisfactions to management that likely would not be expressed otherwise. Some increases in productivity and an increase in earnings for members are typically associated with unionizing. The "bad face" emphasizes the negative effects that union wages have on allocation of resources, decreases in profitability, and productivity decreases when the substantial compensation gains are considered.[5] But unions clearly have a place in the scheme of things, as they provide a balance to the unchallenged decision-making power of management where needed.

Exactly how economic and workforce changes affect employers and unions will be factors in the future of the labor/management relationship. Even though fewer workers have chosen to be union members in recent years than in the past, employers and HR professionals still need to understand the system of laws, regulations, court decisions, and administrative rulings related to the nature of unions. This is important because unions remain a strong alternative for employees in the event of poor HR management.

UNIONS: EMPLOYEE AND MANAGEMENT PERSPECTIVES

Unions did not seem to have a bright future in the 1930s when the National Labor Relations Act (NLRA) was passed, giving unions a legal right to exist. Then they grew to represent about 36% of the workforce in the 1950s, only to see their strength in the private sector drop to less than 8% recently. However, in the public sector, union strength continues to grow.

In the United States, unions follow the goals of increasing compensation, improving working conditions, and influencing workplace rules. When a union is present, working conditions, pay, and work rules are determined through collective bargaining and designated in formal contracts.[6] Part of knowing the current state of unionization in the United States is understanding why employees join unions and why employers resist unionization.

Why Employees Unionize

Whether a union targets a group of employees or the employees request union assistance, the union must win support from the employees to become their legal representative. Over the years employees have joined unions for two general reasons: (1) they are dissatisfied with how they are treated by their employers, and (2) they believe that unions can improve their work situations. If employees do not receive what they perceive as fair treatment from their employers, they may turn to unions for help in obtaining what they believe is equitable.[7] As Figure 16-1 shows, the major factors that can trigger unionization are issues of compensation, working conditions, management style, and employee treatment.

The primary determinant of whether employees want to unionize is management. Reasonably competitive compensation, a good working environment,

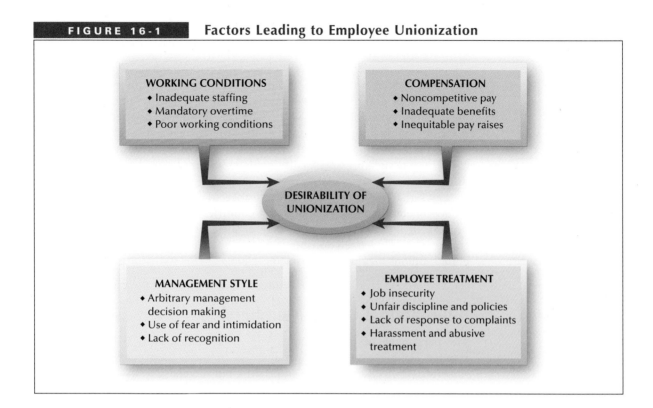

FIGURE 16-1   Factors Leading to Employee Unionization

effective management and supervision, and fair and responsive treatment of workers all act as antidotes to unionization efforts. Unionization results when employees feel disrespected, unsafe, underpaid, and unappreciated, and see a union as a viable option. Once unionization occurs, the ability of the union to foster commitment from members and to remain as their bargaining agent depends on how well the union succeeds in providing the services that its members want.

Why Employers Resist Unions

Employers usually would rather not have to deal with unions because doing so constrains what managers can and cannot do in a number of areas. Generally, union workers receive higher wages and benefits than do non-union workers.[8] In turn, unions sometimes can be associated with higher productivity, although management must find labor-saving ways of doing work to offset the higher labor costs. Some employers pursue a strategy of good relations with unions, while others choose an aggressive, adversarial approach.[9]

HR Responsibilities and Unionization To prevent unionization, as well as to work effectively with unions already representing employees, both HR professionals and operating managers must be attentive and responsive to employees. The pattern of dealing with unionization varies among organizations. In some organizations, operating management handles labor relations and HR has limited involvement. In other organizations, the HR unit takes primary responsibility for resisting unionization or dealing with unionized employees.[10]

UNIONS GLOBALLY

GLOBAL

Globalization, which causes economic competition among workers, companies, and nations around the world, is here to stay. The ability of a country to create jobs and attract investments can be affected by its union bargaining arrangements and labor laws.[11] Changes in information technology have decreased union bargaining power relative to management bargaining power.[12] However, labor unions and labor movements have not been weakened in all cases, despite such pressures. Different laws and traditions have produced very different arrangements in different countries.[13]

Laws that make it easier and cheaper to hire and fire employees may reduce unemployment. But in many countries, such laws cause discomfort because of the great inequality they create in the balance of power in the employer–employee relationship.[14] As the world economy becomes more integrated, unions worldwide are facing changes. The status of global unions is being affected in several ways.

International Union Membership

The percentage of union membership varies significantly from country to country. The highest is in the Scandinavian countries (nearly 50%). Europe has roughly 10% to 30% union membership, but membership in unions is falling in many advanced countries. Collective bargaining is set in law as the way wages are to be determined in Europe. However, in many European countries, artificially high wages and generous benefits have kept the unemployment rate high. The pressures for change are increasing. The range of labor concerns is quite wide and varies from country to country, with child labor an issue in some countries, and changes in participatory employment practices issues in others.

Codetermination Practice whereby union or worker representatives are given positions on a company's board of directors.

In some countries, unions either do not exist at all or are relatively weak. In other countries, unions are closely tied to political parties. For instance, in Italy and France, national strikes occur regularly to protest proposed changes in government policy on retirement, pension programs, and regulations regarding dismissal of employees.

Some countries require that firms have union or worker representatives on their boards of directors. This practice, called **codetermination**, is common in European countries. Differences from country to country in how collective bargaining occurs also are quite noticeable. In the United States, local unions bargain with individual employers to set wages and working conditions. In Australia, unions argue their cases before arbitration tribunals. In Scandinavia, national agreements with associations of employers are the norm. In France and Germany, industrywide or regional agreements are common. In Japan, local unions bargain but combine at some point to determine national wage patterns. Recent labor reform regulations in China are leading to increased union and worker representation in the management of Chinese-owned factories, as discussed in the HR Perspective.

LOGGING ON

Cornell Global Labor Institute
This website provides information and projects on union efforts to strengthen the response to globalization challenges. Visit the site at www.ilr .cornell.edu/globallaborinstitute.

Global Labor Organizations

Global labor relations standards are being addressed by several organizations. The International Labour Organization, based in Switzerland, coordinates the efforts of labor unions worldwide and has issued some principles about rights

Unions in China

In any country, the existence and strength of unions depends on their legal environment. In China the legal environment has recently changed, and the way it has changed is interesting. Uncharacteristically, China first presented a draft labor law and then solicited public comments on the draft. It received more than 200,000 comments from Chinese citizens as well as business groups and international labor groups. Business groups were concerned the new law would raise costs and give them less flexibility to hire and fire as necessary. Labor groups felt there was a need for worker protection and that the business groups were trying to water down the law. A labor lawyer who watched this process (also unusual for China) commented that while the process generated heated debate among law professors, unions, and business, the comments did have an effect on the law that was finally passed.

China wanted the new law to bring more order to the workplace as the private sector continues its rapid expansion. Many workers lack contracts, do not get paid on time, and have little chance for advancement. For instance, Wal-Mart in China has been organized with the help of Andy Stern, the head of the second largest U.S. union.

In China, the All China Federation of Trade Unions has long been criticized by international labor leaders as being more aligned with the communist government than with the workers. However, that "official union" has begun to aggressively unionize multinational companies. Despite the fact the union is not seen as part of a free and independent trade union movement, some international unions are urging support. They note that the success of the new law will depend on how vigilant the government is in enforcing it. As a spokesperson for Adidas suggested, "it all comes down to enforcement."[15]

at work. Such coordination is increasingly occurring as unions deal with multinational firms having operations in multiple countries.

Unions separately and sometimes together push import quotas and other measures to their benefit.[16] Throughout the world unions also are linking up as part of global labor federations. The Union International Network (UIN) is an entity composed of unions from numerous countries. This organization and other international groups are working to establish international policies on child labor, worker safety and health, and training. The UIN is also providing aid and guidance to unions in developing countries, such as those in Africa and Asia. Unions in the United States are very active in these global entities. In some situations, establishing agreements with employers based in the European Union has led to more U.S. union membership in the multinational firms.

U.S. and Global Differences

Union management relations in the United States has taken some approaches different from those in other countries. In the United States, the key focuses have been the following:

- *Economic issues*: In the United States, unions have typically focused on improving the "bread-and-butter" issues for their members—wages, benefits, job security, and working conditions. In some other countries, integration with ruling governmental and political power and activism are equal concerns along with economic issues.

- *Organization by kind of job and employer*: In the United States, carpenters often belong to the carpenters' union, truck drivers to the Teamsters, teachers to the American Federation of Teachers or the National Education Association, and so on. Also, unionization can be done on a company-by-company basis. In other countries, national unions bargain with the government or with employer groups.
- *Collective agreements as "contracts"*: In the United States, collective bargaining contracts usually spell out compensation, work rules, and the conditions of employment for several years. In other countries, the agreements are made with the government and employers, sometimes for only one year because of political and social issues.
- *Competitive relations*: In the United States, management and labor traditionally take the roles of competing adversaries who often "clash" to reach agreement. In many other countries, "tripartite" bargaining occurs between the national government, employers' associations, and national labor federations.

UNION MEMBERSHIP IN THE UNITED STATES

The statistics on union membership tell a disheartening story for organized labor in the United States during the past several decades. As shown in Figure 16-2, unions represented more than 30% of the workforce from 1945 to 1960. But by 2009, unions in the United States represented only 12.4% of all civilian workers and 7.4% of the private-sector workforce. In fact, for the first time, the number of union workers employed by the government outnumbered union members in the private sector. Local, state, and federal union workers made up 51.5% (7.9 million) of all union members while private-sector union members dropped to 7.4 million.[17] The actual number of members has declined in most years even though more people are employed than previously.

But within those averages, some unions have prospered. In the past several years, certain unions have organized thousands of janitors, health care workers, cleaners, and other low-paid workers using publicity, pickets, boycotts, and strikes.

Reasons for U.S. Union Membership Decline

Several general trends have contributed to the decline of U.S. union membership, including deregulation, foreign competition, a larger number of people looking for jobs, and a general perception by firms that dealing with unions is expensive compared with nonunion alternatives. Management at many employers has taken a much more activist stance against unions than during the previous years of union growth, and economic downturns also have had negative impacts.[18]

To some extent, unions may be victims of their own successes. Unions historically have emphasized helping workers obtain higher wages and benefits, shorter working hours, job security, and safe working conditions from their employers. Some believe that one cause for the decline of unions has been their success in getting those important issues passed into law for everyone. Therefore, unions may no longer be seen as necessary for many workers, even

FIGURE 16-2   **Union Membership as a Percentage of the U.S. Civilian Workforce**

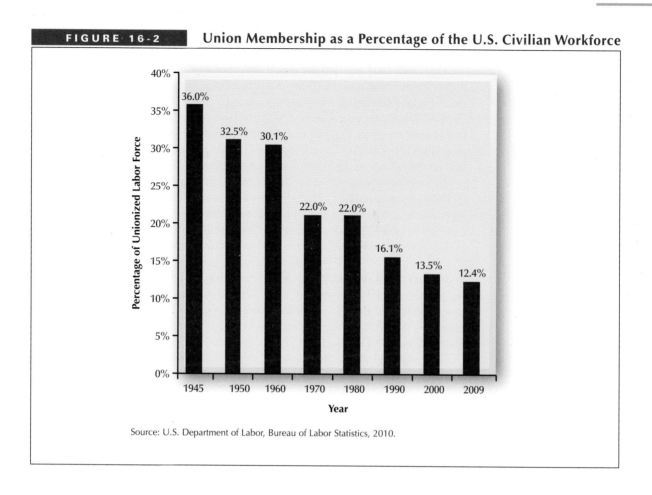

Source: U.S. Department of Labor, Bureau of Labor Statistics, 2010.

though those workers enjoy the results of past union efforts to influence legislation that has been a benefit to them.

Geographic Changes During the past decade, job growth in the United States has been the greatest in states located in the South, the Southwest, and the Rocky Mountains. Most of these states have little tradition of unions, more "employer-friendly" laws, and relatively small percentages of unionized workers.

Another geographic issue involves the movement of many low-skill jobs outside the United States. Primarily to take advantage of cheaper labor, many manufacturers with heavily unionized U.S. workforces have moved a significant number of low-skill jobs to the Philippines, China, Thailand, and Mexico. For instance, the passage of the North American Free Trade Agreement provided a major impetus for moving low-skill, low-wage jobs to Mexico. It removed tariffs and restrictions affecting the flow of goods and services among the United States, Canada, and Mexico. Because of significantly lower wage rates in Mexico, a number of jobs previously susceptible to unionization in the United States have been moved there.

Industrial Changes Much of the decline of union membership can be attributed to the shift in U.S. jobs from industries such as manufacturing, construction, and mining to service industries. There is a small percentage of union members in wholesale/retail industries and financial services, the sectors in which many new jobs have been added, whereas the number of industrial jobs continues to shrink.

One area that has led to union membership decline is the retirement of many union members in older manufacturing firms. Extremely high retiree pensions and health benefits costs have led employers such as Goodyear Tire, Ford Motor Company, General Motors, and others to face demands for cuts in benefits for both current and retired union employees. They also have led to employers reducing the number of current plants and workers, and unions attempting to maintain benefits costs and job security for remaining workers.

In summary, private-sector union membership is primarily concentrated in the shrinking part of the economy, and unions are not making significant inroads into the fastest-growing segments in the U.S. economy. A look at Figure 16-3 reveals that nongovernmental union members are heavily concentrated in transportation, utilities, and other "industrial" jobs.[19]

Workforce Changes Many of the workforce changes discussed in earlier chapters have contributed to the decrease in union representation of the labor force. The decline in many blue-collar jobs in manufacturing has been especially significant. For instance, the United Auto Workers' membership has dropped from 1.5 million in 1980 to about 600,000 currently.

There are growing numbers of white-collar employees such as clerical workers, insurance claims representatives, data input processors, mental health

---

FIGURE 16-3   **Union Membership by Industry**

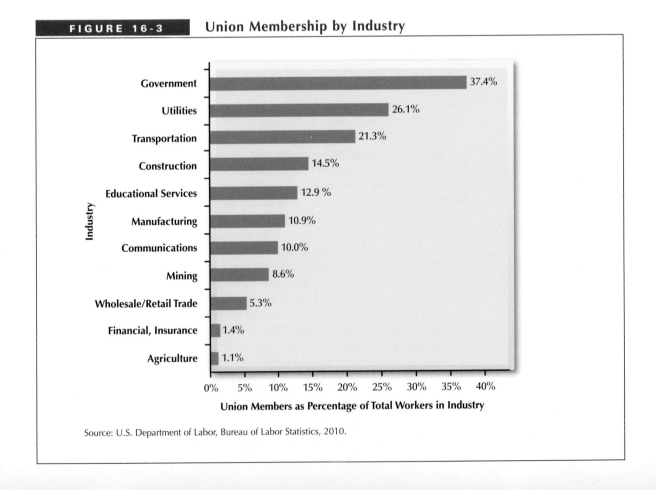

Source: U.S. Department of Labor, Bureau of Labor Statistics, 2010.

aides, computer technicians, loan officers, auditors, and retail sales workers. Unions have increased efforts to organize white-collar workers as advances in technology have boosted their numbers in the workforce. However, unions have faced challenges in organizing these workers.

Many white-collar workers see unions as resistant to change and not in touch with the concerns of the more educated workers in technical and professional jobs. In addition, many white-collar workers exhibit attitudes and preferences quite different from those held by blue-collar union members, and they tend to view unions as primarily blue-collar oriented.

The growing percentage of women in the U.S. workforce presents another challenge to unions. In the past, unions have not been as successful in organizing female workers as they have been in organizing male workers. Some unions are trying to focus more on recruiting female members, and unions have been in the forefront in the push for legislation on such family-related goals as child care, maternity and paternity leave, pay equity, and flexible work arrangements. Women in "pink-collar," low-skill service jobs have been somewhat more likely to join unions than women working in white-collar jobs.

Public-Sector Unionism

Unions have had significant success with public-sector employees. The government sector (federal, state, and local) is the most highly unionized part of the U.S. workforce, with more than 40% of government workers represented by unions. Local government workers have the highest unionization percentage of any group in the U.S. workforce.

Unionization of state and local government employees presents some unique problems and challenges. First, some employees work in critical service areas. It is felt that allowing police officers, firefighters, and sanitation workers to strike endangers public health and safety. Consequently, more than 30 states have laws prohibiting work stoppages by public employees. These laws also identify a variety of ways to resolve negotiation impasses, including arbitration. But government employees seem to believe that unions still give employees in these areas greater security and better ability to influence decisions on wages and benefits than nonunion workers have.

Although unions in the federal government hold the same basic philosophy as unions in the private sector, they do differ somewhat. Previous laws and executive orders have established methods of labor/management relations that consider the special circumstances present in the federal government.

Union Targets for Membership Growth

The continuing losses have led to disagreements among unions about how to fight the decline. Rather than remaining a part of the traditional AFL-CIO labor organization, seven unions split into a new group in 2005. Calling itself Change to Win (CtW), this association has a goal of taking a more aggressive approach to adding union members and affecting U.S. political legislation.

To attempt to counteract the overall decline in membership, unions are focusing on a number of industries and types of workers. One reason why Change to Win split off from the AFL-CIO was to target more effectively the addition of members in the retail, hospitality, home health care, and other service industries.

Professionals Traditionally, professionals in many occupations have been skeptical of the advantages of unionization. However, professionals who have turned to unionization include engineers, physicians, nurses, and teachers.[20] The health care industry has been a specific focus for unionization of professionals such as physicians and physical therapists. Another area of union growth in the past few years has been in nursing. The primary reason health care employees consider union membership is the growth of managed care. A frequent complaint of health care professionals is that they have lost control of patient-care decisions as a result of managed care and the spreading drive to reduce health care costs. This and other complaints have led more health care employees to join unions.

Low-Skilled Workers On the other end of the labor pay scale, unions have targeted low-skilled workers, many of whom have lower-paying, less desirable jobs. Janitors, building cleaners, nursing home aides, and meatpacking workers are examples of groups targeted by unions. For instance, in the health care industry, workers in nursing homes dealing with the elderly are a fast-growing segment of the workforce. Many employees in this industry are relatively dissatisfied. The industry is often noted for its low pay and hard, heavy work, and many employees are women who work as nurses' aides, cooks, and launderers and in other low-wage jobs.

Another group of individuals targeted by unions is immigrant workers in low-skill jobs. Some unions also have been politically active regarding legislation to allow illegal immigrant workers to get work permits and citizenship over time. Although these efforts are not always successful, unions are likely to continue pursuing industries and employers with numerous low-skill jobs and low-skilled workers. The advantages of unionization are especially strong for these employees.

Contingent and Part-Time Workers As many employers have added contingent workers instead of full-time employees, unions have tried to target part-time, temporary, and other employees. A decision by the National Labor Relations Board (NLRB) allows temporary workers to be included in firms to be represented by unions. Time will tell if the efforts to unionize part-time workers and other groups will halt the decline of union membership in the United States. When unions are present, collective bargaining agreements frequently limit the amount of contingent labor that may be used.

UNIONS IN THE UNITED STATES

The union movement in the United States has existed in some form or another for more than two centuries. During that time, the nature of unions has evolved because of legal and political changes.

Historical Evolution of U.S. Unions

The union movement in the United States began with early collective efforts by workers to address job concerns and counteract management power. As early as 1794, shoemakers organized a union, picketed, and conducted strikes. In those days, unions in the United States received very little support from the courts. In 1806, when the shoemakers' union struck for higher wages, a Philadelphia court found union members guilty of engaging in a "criminal conspiracy" to raise wages.

The *American Federation of Labor (AFL)* united a number of independent national unions in 1886. Its aims were to organize skilled craft workers and to emphasize economic issues and working conditions. As industrialization increased in the United States, many factories used semiskilled and unskilled workers. However, it was not until the *Congress of Industrial Organizations (CIO)* was founded in 1938 that a labor union organization focused on semiskilled and unskilled workers. Years later, the AFL and the CIO merged to become the AFL-CIO. That federation is the major organization coordinating union efforts in the United States today despite the split described previously.

LOGGING ON

AFL-CIO
The AFL-CIO home page provides union movement information. Visit the website at www.aflcio.org.

Union Structure

Labor in the United States is represented by many different unions. Regardless of size and geographic scope, two basic types of unions have developed over time. In a **craft union,** members do one type of work, often using specialized skills and training. Examples are the International Association of Bridge, Structural, Ornamental and Reinforcing Iron Workers, and the American Federation of Television and Radio Artists. An **industrial union** includes many persons working in the same industry or company, regardless of jobs held. The United Food and Commercial Workers, the United Auto Workers, and the American Federation of State, County, and Municipal Employees are examples of industrial unions.

AFL-CIO Federation Labor organizations have developed complex organizational structures with multiple levels. The broadest level is the **federation,** which is a group of autonomous unions. A federation allows individual unions to work together and present a more unified front to the public, legislators, and members. The most prominent federation in the United States is the AFL-CIO, which is a confederation of unions currently representing about 10 million workers.

Change to Win The establishment of Change to Win (CtW) in 2005 meant that seven unions with about 6 million members left the AFL-CIO.[21] The primary reason for the split was a division between different unions about how to stop the decline in union membership, as well as some internal organizational leadership and political issues.[22] Prominent unions in the CtW are the Teamsters, the Service Employees International Union, and the United Food and Commercial Workers.

National and International Unions National and international unions are not governed by a federation even if they are affiliated with it. They collect dues and have their own boards, specialized publications, and separate constitutions and bylaws. Such unions as the United Steelworkers of America and the American Federation of State, County, and Municipal Employees determine broad union policy and offer services to local union units. They also help maintain financial records and provide a base from which additional organizing drives may take place. Political infighting and corruption sometimes pose problems for national

Craft union Union whose members do one type of work, often using specialized skills and training.

Industrial union Union that includes many persons working in the same industry or company, regardless of jobs held.

Federation Group of autonomous unions.

unions, as when the federal government stepped in and overturned the results of an officer election held by the Teamsters Union several years ago.

Like companies, unions find strength in size. In the past several years, about 40 mergers of unions have occurred, and a number of other unions have considered merging. For smaller unions, these mergers provide financial and union-organizing resources. Larger unions can add new members to cover managerial and administrative costs without spending funds to organize non-union workers to become members.

Local Unions Local unions may be centered around a particular employer organization or a particular geographic location. The membership of local unions elects officers who are subject to removal if they do not perform satisfactorily. For this reason, local union officers tend to be concerned with how they are perceived by the union members. They often react to situations as politicians do because their positions depend on obtaining votes. The local unions are the focus and the heart of labor/management relations in most U.S. labor organizations.

Local unions typically have business agents and union stewards. A **business agent** is a full-time union official who operates the union office and assists union members. The agent runs the local headquarters, helps negotiate contracts with management, and becomes involved in attempts to unionize employees in other organizations. A **union steward** is an employee who is elected to serve as the first-line representative of unionized workers. Stewards address grievances with supervisors and generally represent employees at the worksite.

> **Business agent** A full-time union official who operates the union office and assists union members.

> **Union steward** Employee elected to serve as the first-line representative of unionized workers.

U.S. LABOR LAWS

The right to organize workers and engage in collective bargaining offers little value if workers cannot freely exercise it. Management has consistently developed practices to prevent workers from organizing employees. Over a period of many years, the federal government has taken action both to hamper unions and to protect them.

Early Labor Legislation

Beginning in the late 1800s, federal and state legislation related to unionization was passed. The two most prominent acts are discussed next.

Railway Labor Act The Railway Labor Act (RLA) of 1926 represented a shift in government regulation of unions. The result of a joint effort between railroad management and unions to reduce transportation strikes, this act gave railroad employees "the right to organize and bargain collectively through representatives of their own choosing." In 1936, airlines and their employees were added to those covered by the RLA. Some experts believe that some of the labor relations problems in the airline industry stem from the provisions of the RLA, and that those problems would be more easily resolved if the airlines fell within the labor laws covering most other industries.

The RLA mandates a complex and cumbersome dispute resolution process. This process allows either the unions or management to use the National Labor Relations Board, a multistage dispute resolution process, and even the power of the President of the United States to appoint an emergency board. The end result of having a prolonged process that is subject to political interference has been that unions often work for two or more years after the expiration of their old contracts because the process takes so long.

Norris-LaGuardia Act The crash of the stock market and the onset of the Great Depression in 1929 led to massive cutbacks by employers. In some industries, the resistance by employees led to strikes and violence. Under laws at that time, employers could go to court and have a federal judge issue injunctions ordering workers to return to work. In 1932, Congress passed the Norris-LaGuardia Act, which guaranteed workers some rights to organize and restricted the issuance of court injunctions in labor disputes.

The Next Stage The economic crises of the early 1930s and the continuing restrictions on workers' ability to organize into unions led to the passage of landmark labor legislation, the Wagner Act, in 1935. Later acts reflected other pressures and issues that required legislative attention. Three acts passed over a period of almost 25 years constitute the U.S. labor law foundation: (1) the Wagner Act, (2) the Taft-Hartley Act, and (3) the Landrum-Griffin Act. Each act was passed to focus on some facet of the relations between unions and management. Figure 16-4 indicates the primary focus of each act. Two other pieces of legislation, the Civil Service Reform Act and the Postal Reorganization Act, also have affected only the governmental aspects of union/management relations.

Wagner Act (National Labor Relations Act)

The National Labor Relations Act, more commonly referred to as the Wagner Act, has been called the Magna Carta of labor and was, by anyone's standards, pro-union. Passed in 1935, the Wagner Act was an outgrowth of the Great Depression. With employers having to close or cut back their operations, workers were left with little job security. Unions stepped in to provide a feeling of solidarity and strength for many workers. The Wagner Act declared, in effect, that the official policy of the U.S. government was to encourage collective bargaining. Specifically, it established the right of workers to organize unhampered by management interference through unfair labor practices.

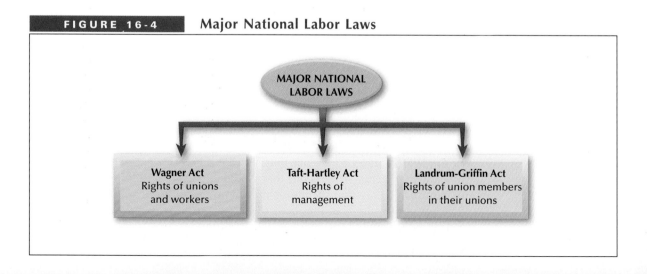

FIGURE 16-4   **Major National Labor Laws**

Unfair Labor Practices To protect union rights, the Wagner Act prohibited employers from using unfair labor practices. Five of those practices were identified as follows:

- Interfering with, restraining, or coercing employees in the exercise of their right to organize or to bargain collectively
- Dominating or interfering with the formation or administration of any labor organization
- Encouraging or discouraging membership in any labor organization by discriminating with regard to hiring, tenure, or conditions of employment
- Discharging or otherwise discriminating against an employee because the employee filed charges or gave testimony under the act
- Refusing to bargain collectively with representatives of the employees

National Labor Relations Board The Wagner Act established the National Labor Relations Board as an independent entity to enforce the provisions of the act. The NLRB administers all provisions of the Wagner Act and of subsequent labor relations acts. The primary functions of the NLRB include conducting unionization elections, investigating complaints by employers or unions through its fact-finding process, issuing opinions on its findings, and prosecuting violations in court. The five members of the NLRB are appointed by the President of the United States and confirmed by the U.S. Senate.

LOGGING ON

National Labor Relations Board
For information on workplace rights and other issues, visit the NLRB website at www.nlrb.gov.

Taft-Hartley Act (Labor Management Relations Act)

The passage in 1947 of the Labor Management Relations Act, better known as the Taft-Hartley Act, was accomplished as a means to offset the pro-union Wagner Act by limiting union actions. It was considered to be pro-management and became the second of the major labor laws.

The new law amended or qualified in some respect all the major provisions of the Wagner Act and established an entirely new code of conduct for unions. The Taft-Hartley Act forbade unions from engaging in a series of unfair labor practices, much like those prohibitions on management behavior. Coercion, discrimination against nonmembers, refusing to bargain, excessive membership fees, and other practices were not allowed by unions. A 1974 amendment extended coverage of the Taft-Hartley Act to private, nonprofit hospitals and nursing homes.

The Taft-Hartley Act also established the Federal Mediation and Conciliation Service (FMCS) as an agency to help management and labor settle labor contract disputes. The act required that the FMCS be notified of disputes over contract renewals or modifications if they were not settled within 30 days after the designated date.

National Emergency Strikes The Taft-Hartley Act allows the President of the United States to declare that a strike presents a national emergency. A national emergency strike is one that would impact an industry or a major part of it in such a way that the national economy would be significantly affected. The act allows the U.S. President to declare an 80-day "cooling off" period during which union and management continue negotiations. Only after that period can a strike occur if settlements have not been reached.

Over the decades, national emergencies have been identified in the railroad, airline, and other industries. For example, the national emergency provisions were involved in a strike of transportation and dock workers throughout the U.S. West Coast states. During the 80-day period, a contract agreement was reached, so a strike was averted.

Right-to-Work Provision One specific provision of the Taft-Hartley Act, section 14(b), deserves special explanation. This section allows states to pass laws that restrict compulsory union membership. Accordingly, several states have passed **right-to-work laws**, which prohibit requiring employees to join unions as a condition of obtaining or continuing employment. The laws were so named because they allow a person the right to work without having to join a union.

Right-to-work laws State laws that prohibit requiring employees to join unions as a condition of obtaining or continuing employment.

Open shop Firm in which workers are not required to join or pay dues to a union.

The states that have enacted these laws are shown in Figure 16-5. In states with right-to-work laws, employers may have an **open shop**, which indicates workers cannot be required to join or pay dues to a union. Thus, even though a union may represent an entire group of employees at a company, individual workers cannot be required or coerced to join the union or pay dues. Consequently, in many of the right-to-work states, individual membership in union groups is significantly lower. For instance, at one Midwestern firm where the employee group is unionized, fewer than 25% of the employees

| FIGURE 16-5 | **Right-to-Work States** |

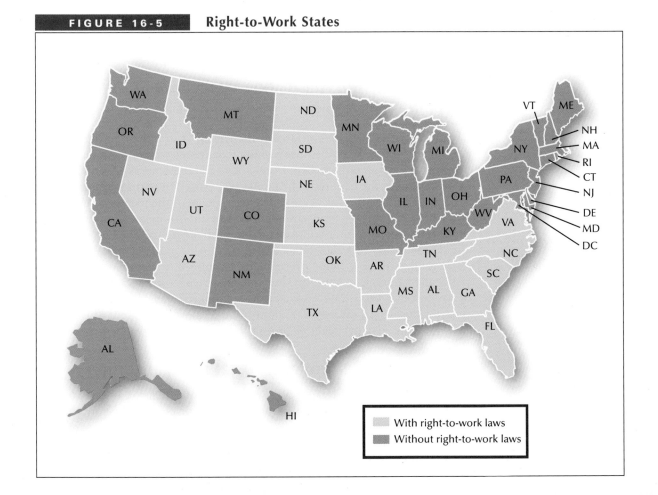

Legend:
- With right-to-work laws
- Without right-to-work laws

actually belong to the union and pay dues. There has been no recent change in which states have right-to-work laws, although people on both sides of this issue continue to argue for change.[23]

The National Right to Work Legal Defense Foundation is an organization that has lobbied for more states to become right-to-work states. Also, that organization has become involved in lawsuits where workers have claimed to have been coerced to join unions.

The nature of union/management relations is affected by the right-to-work provisions of the Taft-Hartley Act. Right-to-work generally prohibits the **closed shop**, which requires individuals to join a union before they can be hired. Because of concerns that a closed shop allows a union to "control" who may be considered for employment and who must be hired by an employer, section 14(b) prohibits the closed shop except in construction-related occupations.

In states that do not have right-to-work laws, different types of arrangements exist. Three of the different types of "shops" are as follows:

- *Union shop*: Requires that individuals join the union, usually 30 to 60 days after being hired
- *Agency shop*: Requires employees who refuse to join the union to pay amounts equal to union dues and fees in return for the representation services of the union[24]
- *Maintenance-of-membership shop*: Requires workers to remain members of the union for the period of the labor contract

The nature of the shop is negotiated between the union and the employer. Often employees who fail to meet the requirements are terminated from their jobs.

Landrum-Griffin Act (Labor Management Reporting and Disclosure Act)

The third of the major labor laws in the United States, the Landrum-Griffin Act, was passed in 1959. Because a union is supposed to be a democratic institution in which union members freely vote on and elect officers and approve labor contracts, the Landrum-Griffin Act was passed in part to ensure that the federal government protects the democratic rights of the members. Under the Landrum-Griffin Act, unions are required to establish bylaws, make financial reports, and provide union members with a bill of rights. The law appointed the U.S. Secretary of Labor to act as a watchdog of union conduct.

In a few instances, union officers have attempted to maintain their jobs by physically harassing or attacking individuals who have tried to oust them from office. In other cases, union officials have "milked" pension fund monies for their own use. Such instances are not typical of most unions, but illustrate the need for legislative oversight to protect individual union members.[25]

Civil Service Reform and Postal Reorganization Acts

Passed as part of the Civil Service Reform Act of 1978, the Federal Service Labor Management Relations statute made major changes in how the federal government deals with unions. The act also identified areas subject to bargaining and established the Federal Labor Relations Authority (FLRA) as an independent agency similar to the NLRB. The FLRA, a three-member body, was given the authority to oversee and administer union/management

Closed shop Firm that requires individuals to join a union before they can be hired.

relations in the federal government and to investigate unfair practices in union organizing efforts.

In a somewhat related area, the Postal Reorganization Act of 1970 established the U.S. Postal Service as an independent entity. Part of the 1970 act prohibited postal workers from striking and established a dispute resolution process for them to follow.

Proposed Legislation

Other laws have been proposed, but at this writing none of them has been passed. One such law would bar companies from replacing workers who go on strike,[26] which means that a union could in effect close a business down because strikers could not be replaced. Replacement workers or "scabs" have allowed companies to defeat union strikes in some cases in the past.

Another proposed law, the "Employee Free Choice Act," would allow unions to sign up workers and become recognized without an election.[27] As a result, the "campaigns" against management that unions dislike would be eliminated, because simply getting 50% of the workers in a unit to sign a card would be sufficient to "vote in" the union.[28] Further, the proposed law would require a contract to be negotiated within a certain time period or one could be imposed by an arbitrator.[29] This approach goes against the U.S. tradition in which negotiated contracts must be agreed to by both parties. The proposed legislation has spawned considerable concern among businesses.[30] Several large employers have resorted to direct actions in opposition to the EFCA.[31]

THE UNIONIZATON PROCESS

The typical union organizing process is outlined in Figure 16-6. The process of unionizing an employer may begin in one of two primary ways: (1) a union targeting an industry or a company, or (2) employees requesting union representation. In the first case, the local or national union identifies a firm or an industry in which it believes unionization can succeed. The logic for targeting is that if the union succeeds in one firm or a portion of the industry, then many other workers in the industry will be more willing to consider unionizing. In the second case, the impetus for union organizing occurs when individual workers at an employer contact a union and express a desire to unionize. The employees themselves—or the union—may then begin to campaign to win support among the other employees.

Organizing Campaign

Like other entities seeking members, a union usually mounts an organized campaign to persuade individuals to join. As would be expected, employers respond to unionization efforts by taking various types of opposing actions.

Employers' Union Prevention Efforts Management representatives may use various tactics to defeat a unionization effort. Such tactics often begin when union publicity appears or during the distribution of authorization cards. Some employers such as Con Agra, Coca-Cola, and Wal-Mart hire consultants who specialize in combating unionization efforts. Using these "union busters," as they are called by unions, appears to enhance employers' chances

FIGURE 16-6   Typical Unionization Process

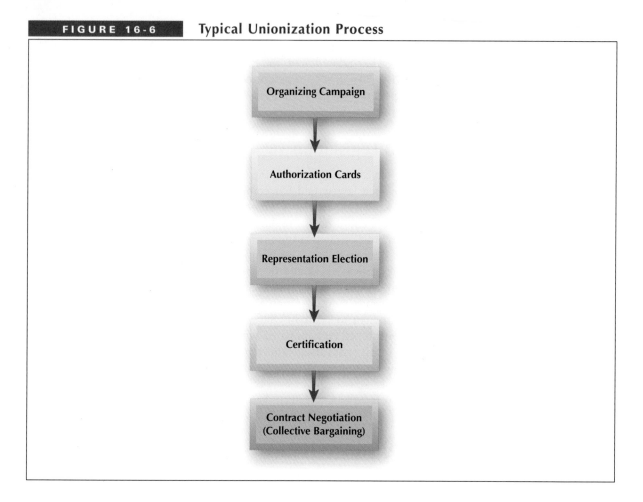

of winning the representation election. Union prevention efforts that may be conducted by consultants or done by management and outside labor attorneys include:[32]

- Holding mandatory employee meetings
- Distributing antiunion leaflets at work and mailing antiunion letters to employees' homes
- Providing and using antiunion videos, e-mails, and other electronic communications

Many employers have created a "no-solicitation" policy to restrict employees and outsiders from distributing literature or soliciting union membership on company premises. Employers without such a policy may be unable to prevent those acts. A policy against solicitation must be a long-term, established approach, not a single action taken to counter a specific and immediate unionization attempt. For example, a Steelworkers union sought certification by the NLRB to be the bargaining agent at an Ohio facility. After the union lost the election by one vote, it protested that the company had interfered with the right to organize when just before the election it adopted a rule prohibiting the posting of pro-union material on an employee bulletin board. The NLRB set aside the first election, and the company lost the second election.

Employers may make strategic decisions and take aggressive steps to remain nonunion. Such a choice is perfectly rational, but may require some specific HR policies and philosophies. For example, "preventive" employee relations may emphasize good morale and loyalty based on concern for employees, competitive wages and benefits, a fair system for dealing with employee complaints, and safe working conditions. Other issues also may play a part in employees' decisions to stay nonunion, but if employers adequately address the points just listed, fewer workers are likely to feel the need for a union to represent them.

Unions' Organizing Efforts The organizing and negotiating successes of unions are tied to the economy and economic trends. For example, see the HR Perspective. The persuasion efforts by unions can take many forms, including personally contacting employees outside work, mailing materials to employees' homes, inviting employees to attend special meetings away from the company, and publicizing the advantages of union membership. Brochures and leaflets can be given to employees as they leave work, mailed to their homes, or even attached to their vehicles, as long as the union complies with the rules established by laws and the NLRB. The purpose of all this publicity is to encourage employees to sign authorization cards.

To encourage individuals to become involved in unionization efforts, unions have adopted electronic means, such as establishing websites where interested workers can read about benefits of unionization. For instance, the Service Employees International Union has websites and chat rooms where nurses at nonunion hospitals can exchange information with unionized nurses. Change to Win and the AFL-CIO both have Web links and blogs available through their websites to provide union information online. These sites explain workers' rights and give examples of the advantages of being union

Good Times, Bad Times   HR *perspective*

Employees join unions when they feel that unions can improve their lots in life. Although union membership has been dropping, the point at which unions might be able to improve more employees' lots in work life may reappear.

The recession weakened employees' bargaining power and that trend is likely to continue. More jobs will be freelance and temporary. As one CEO puts it, "We are all temps now." Employers create "just in time" workforces that can be turned on and off, allowing them to reduce fixed costs. That means the companies have an edge in bargaining power and the risks are pushed to the employees. It is estimated that 26% of the U.S. workforce has "nonstandard" jobs like that held by some workers. Recessions hasten

the trend. Pay for production and nonsupervisory workers (80% of the workforce) is 9% lower now than it was in 1973 when the pay is adjusted for inflation.

Certainly not all workers are pleased with such jobs, but in bad times they have little choice and unions have little opportunity. However, looking into the future, it is possible to see that better times may be coming for labor. In a decade, retirement of the baby boomers could cause labor shortages. A shortage of workers was widely noted before the last recession, and the underlying dynamic has not gone away. The idea of loyalty to an employer has effectively disappeared in many places, and the mechanisms for labor's return remain intact—waiting for better times.[33]

members. Successes in unionizing groups of employees are described. Also, the differences between wages, benefits, and job security are contrasted before and after unionization occurred. However, an employer can prohibit workers from using its e-mail system for union business.[34]

Unions sometimes pay organizers to infiltrate a targeted employer and try to organize workers. In this practice, known as **salting**, the unions hire and pay people to apply for jobs at certain companies; when the people are hired, they begin organizing efforts. The U.S. Supreme Court has ruled that refusing to hire otherwise qualified applicants, solely because they are also paid by a union, violates the Wagner Act. However, employers may refuse to hire "salts" for job-related and nondiscriminatory reasons.[35]

Authorization Cards

A **union authorization card** is signed by employees to designate a union as their collective bargaining agent. At least 30% of the employees in the targeted group must sign authorization cards before an election can be called.

Union advocates have lobbied for changing laws so that elections are not needed if more than 50% of the eligible employees sign authorization cards. As mentioned earlier, the proposed Employee Free Choice Act would eliminate the secret ballot for electing union representation and make it so that the union would automatically represent all workers if more than 50% of the employees signed authorization cards. Some states have enacted such laws for public-sector unionization. Also, some employers have taken a "neutral" approach and agreed to recognize unions if a majority of workers sign authorization cards. Some employers' agreements allow for authorization card checks to be done by a neutral outside party to verify union membership.

However, the fact that an employee signs an authorization card does not necessarily mean that the employee is in favor of a union. It means only that the employee would like the opportunity to vote on having a union. Employees who do not want a union might sign authorization cards because they want management to know they are disgruntled or because they want to avoid upsetting coworkers who are advocating unionization.

Employers and some politicians argue that eliminating elections violates the personal secrecy and democracy rights of employees. The extent of legislative changes will depend on the political composition of the U.S. Congress and presidential reactions to such efforts.

Representation Election

An election to determine if a union will represent the employees is supervised by the NLRB for private-sector organizations and by other legal bodies for public-sector organizations. If two unions are attempting to represent employees, the employees will have three choices: union A, union B, and no union.

Bargaining Unit Before any election, the appropriate bargaining unit must be determined. A **bargaining unit** is composed of all employees eligible to select a single union to represent and bargain collectively for them. If management and the union do not agree on who is and who is not included in the unit, the regional office of the NLRB must make the determination. A major criterion in deciding the composition of a bargaining unit is what the NLRB calls a "community of interest." For example, at a warehouse distribution firm, delivery drivers, accounting clerks, computer programmers, and mechanics would

Salting Practice in which unions hire and pay people to apply for jobs at certain companies to begin organizing efforts.

Union authorization card Card signed by employees to designate a union as their collective bargaining agent.

Bargaining unit Employees eligible to select a single union to represent and bargain collectively for them.

probably not be included in the same bargaining unit; these employees have widely varying jobs, areas of work, physical locations, and other differences that would likely negate a community of interest. Employees who constitute a bargaining unit have mutual interests in the following areas:

- Wages, hours, and working conditions
- Traditional industry groupings for bargaining purposes
- Physical location and amount of interaction and working relationships between employee groups
- Supervision by similar levels of management

Supervisors and Union Ineligibility Provisions of the National Labor Relations Act exclude supervisors from voting for or joining unions. As a result, supervisors cannot be included in bargaining units for unionization purposes, except in industries covered by the Railway Labor Act. But who qualifies as a supervisor is not always clear. The NLRB expanded its definition to identify a supervisor as any individual with authority to hire, transfer, discharge, discipline, and use independent judgment with employees. Numerous NLRB and court decisions have been rendered on the specifics of different situations. A major case decided by the U.S. Supreme Court found that charge nurses with RN degrees were supervisors because they exercised independent judgment. This case and others have provided employers and unions with some guidance about who should be considered supervisors and thus excluded from bargaining units.[36]

Unionization Do's and Don'ts for Managers

HR on-the-job

Employers can take numerous actions to prevent unionization. All managers and supervisors must adhere to NLRB and other requirements to avoid unfair labor practices. Listed below are some common do's and don'ts.

✓ DO (LEGAL)
- Tell employees how current wages and benefits compare with those in other firms.
- Tell employees why the employer opposes unionization.
- Tell employees the disadvantages of having a union (dues, assessments, etc.)
- Show employees articles about unions and relate negative experiences elsewhere.
- Explain the unionization process to employees accurately.
- Forbid distribution of union literature during work hours in work areas.
- Enforce disciplinary policies and rules consistently and appropriately.

✗ DON'T (ILLEGAL)
- Promise employees pay increases or promotions if they vote against the union.
- Threaten to close down or move the company if a union is voted in.
- Spy on or have someone spy on union meetings.
- Make a speech to employees or groups at work within 24 hours of the election. (Before that, it is allowed.)
- Ask employees how they plan to vote or if they have signed authorization cards.
- Encourage employees to persuade others to vote against the union.
- Threaten employees with termination or discipline employees advocating the union.

Election Unfair Labor Practices Employers and unions engage in a number of activities before an election. Both the Wagner Act and the Taft-Hartley Act place restrictions on these activities. Once unionizing efforts begin, all activities must conform to the requirements established by applicable labor laws. Both management and the union must adhere to those requirements, or the results of the effort can be appealed to the NLRB and overturned. The HR On-the-Job highlights some of the legal and illegal actions managers must be aware of during unionization efforts.

Election Process If an election is held, the union needs to receive only a majority of the votes. For example, if a group of 200 employees is the identified bargaining unit, and only 50 people vote, only 26 (50% of those voting plus 1) need to vote yes for the union to be named as the representative of all 200 employees. Typically, the smaller the number of employees in the bargaining unit, the higher the likelihood that the union will win.

If either side believes that the other side used unfair labor practices, the election results can be appealed to the NLRB. If the NLRB finds evidence of unfair practices, it can order a new election. If no unfair practices were used and the union obtains a majority in the election, the union then petitions the NLRB for certification.

Certification and Decertification

Official certification of a union as the legal representative for designated private-sector employees is given by the NLRB, or for public-sector employees by an equivalent body. Once certified, the union attempts to negotiate a contract with the employer. The employer *must* bargain; refusing to bargain with a certified union constitutes an unfair labor practice.

When members no longer wish to be represented by the union, they can use the election process to sever the relationship between themselves and the union. Similar to the unionization process, **decertification** is a process whereby a union is removed as the representative of a group of employees. Employees attempting to oust a union must obtain decertification authorization cards signed by at least 30% of the employees in the bargaining unit before an election may be called. If a majority of those voting in the election want to remove the union, the decertification effort succeeds. Some reasons that employees might decide to vote out a union are that the treatment provided by employers has improved, the union has been unable to address the changing needs of the organizational workforce, or the image of the union has declined. Current regulations prohibit employers from initiating or supporting decertification because it is a matter between employees and unions, and employers must stay out of the process.

Decertification Process whereby a union is removed as the representative of a group of employees.

Collective bargaining Process whereby representatives of management and workers negotiate over wages, hours, and other terms and conditions of employment.

Contract Negotiation (Collective Bargaining)

Collective bargaining, the last step in unionization, is the process whereby representatives of management and workers negotiate over wages, hours, and other terms and conditions of employment. This give-and-take process between representatives of the two organizations attempts to establish conditions beneficial to both. It is also a relationship based on relative power.

Management/union relations in collective bargaining can follow one of several patterns. Figure 16-7 depicts them as a continuum, ranging from conflict to collusion. On the left side of the continuum, management and

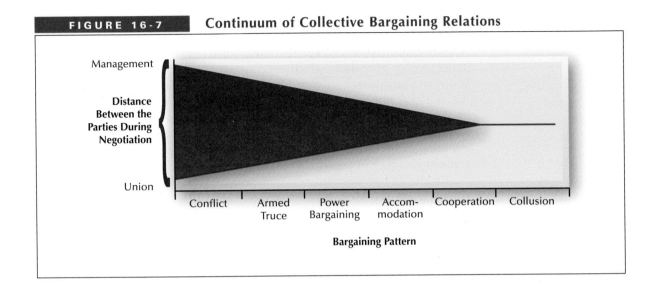

FIGURE 16-7   **Continuum of Collective Bargaining Relations**

Management

Distance
Between the
Parties During
Negotiation

Union

Conflict | Armed Truce | Power Bargaining | Accommodation | Cooperation | Collusion

Bargaining Pattern

the union see each other as enemies. On the right side, the two entities join together in collusion, which is relatively rare in U.S. labor history and is illegal. Most positions fall between these two extremes.

The power relationship in collective bargaining involves conflict, and the threat of conflict seems necessary to maintain the relationship. But perhaps the most significant aspect of collective bargaining is that it is a continuing relationship that does not end immediately after agreement is reached. Instead, it continues for the life of the labor agreement and beyond.[37] Therefore, the more cooperative management is, the less hostility and conflict with unionized employees will be present to carry over to the workplace. However, this cooperation does not mean that the employer agrees to all union demands.

LOGGING ON

LaborNet
This website describes unions, news, legislation, and upcoming union events. Visit the site at www.labornet.org.

COLLECTIVE BARGAINING ISSUES

A number of issues can be addressed during collective bargaining. Although not often listed as such in the contract, management rights and union security are two important issues subject to collective bargaining. These and other issues, common and collective bargaining, are discussed next.

Management Rights

Virtually all labor contracts include **management rights**, which are rights reserved so that the employer can manage, direct, and control its business. By including such a provision, management attempts to preserve its unilateral right to make changes in areas not identified in a labor contract. A typical provision might read as follows:

The employer retains all rights to manage, direct, and control its business in all particulars, except as such rights are expressly and specifically modified by the terms of this or any subsequent agreement.

Management rights Rights reserved so that the employer can manage, direct, and control its business.

Union Security

A major concern of union representatives when bargaining is the negotiation of **union security provisions**, which are contract clauses to help the union obtain and retain members. One type of union security clause in labor contracts is the *no-layoff policy*, or *job security guarantee*. Such a provision is especially important to many union workers because of all the mergers, downsizings, and job reductions taking place in many industrial, textile, and manufacturing firms. However, for these very reasons, management is often unwilling to consider this type of provision.

Union Dues Issues A common union security provision is the *dues checkoff* clause, which provides for the automatic deduction of union dues from the payroll checks of union members. The dues checkoff provision makes it much easier for the union to collect its funds, and without it, the union must collect dues by billing each member separately.

However, federal court cases have been filed that restrict unions from using such checkoff clauses for contributions to political and congressional candidates. A U.S. Supreme Court case supported the constitutionality of state laws that require labor unions to get written consent before using nonmember fees for political purposes. The Court noted that Washington, like many other states, allows public-sector unions to levy fees on nonmember employees, as well as "agency shop" agreements. But it held that under such arrangements, the union must obtain express authorization from the nonmembers to use their agency fees for election-related purposes.[38]

Types of Required Union Membership Another form of union security provision is *requiring union membership* of all employees, subject to state right-to-work laws. As mentioned earlier, a closed shop is illegal except in limited situations within the construction industry. But other types of arrangements can be developed, including union shops, agency shops, and maintenance-of-membership shops, which were discussed earlier.

Classification of Bargaining Issues

The NLRB has defined collective bargaining issues in three ways. The categories it has used are mandatory, permissive, and illegal.

Mandatory Issues Issues identified specifically by labor laws or court decisions as subject to bargaining are **mandatory issues**. If either party demands that issues in this category be subject to bargaining, then that must occur. Generally, mandatory issues relate to wages, benefits, nature of jobs, and other work-related subjects. Mandatory subjects for bargaining include the following:

- Discharge of employees
- Grievances
- Work schedules
- Union security and dues checkoff
- Retirement and pension coverage
- Vacations and time off
- Rest and lunch break rules
- Safety rules
- Profit-sharing plans
- Required physical exam

Permissive Issues Issues that are not mandatory and that relate to certain jobs are **permissive issues**. For example, the following issues can be bargained over if both parties agree: benefits for retired employees, product prices for employees, and performance bonds.

Union security provisions Contract clauses to help the union obtain and retain members.

Mandatory issues Collective bargaining issues identified specifically by labor laws or court decisions as subject to bargaining.

Permissive issues Collective bargaining issues that are not mandatory and that relate to certain jobs.

Illegal Issues A final category, **illegal issues**, includes those issues that would require either party to take illegal action. Examples would be giving preference to union members when hiring employees or demanding a closed-shop provision in the contract. If one side wants to bargain over an illegal issue, the other side can refuse.

COLLECTIVE BARGAINING PROCESS

The collective bargaining process involved in negotiating a contract consists of a number of stages: preparation and initial demands, negotiations, settlement or impasse, and strikes and lockouts. Throughout the process, management and labor deal with the terms of their relationship.

Preparation and Initial Demands

Both labor and management representatives spend considerable time preparing for negotiations.[39] Employer and industry data concerning wages, benefits, working conditions, management and union rights, productivity, and absenteeism are gathered. If the organization argues that it cannot afford to pay what the union is asking, the employer's financial situation and accompanying data become relevant to the process. However, the union must request such information before the employer is obligated to provide it. Typical bargaining includes initial proposals of expectations by both sides. The amount of rancor or calmness exhibited may set the tone for future negotiations between the parties.

Core Bargaining Issues The primary focus of bargaining for both union and management is on the core areas of wages, benefits, and working hours and conditions. The importance of this emphasis is seen in several ways.

Union wages and benefits generally are higher in unionized firms than in nonunionized firms. As shown in Figure 16-8, in a recent year median earnings for union members were $908/week compared with the nonunion amount of $710/week. The additional $198/week represents almost $10,000/year more for union members' wages than nonunion wages. It is common for wages and benefits to be higher in unionized firms.

Continuing Negotiations

After taking initial positions, each side attempts to determine what the other side values highly so that the best bargain can be struck. For example, the union may be asking the employer to pay for dental benefits as part of a package that also includes wage increases and retirement benefits. However, the union may be most interested in the retirement benefits and may be willing to trade the dental payments for better retirement benefits. Management must determine what the union has as a priority and decide exactly what to give up.

Good Faith Provisions in federal law require that both employers and union bargaining representatives negotiate in good faith. In good-faith negotiations, the parties agree to send negotiators who can bargain and make decisions, rather than people who do not have the authority to commit either group to a decision. To be more effective, meetings between the parties should be conducted professionally and address issues, rather than being confrontational. Refusing to bargain,

Illegal issues Collective bargaining issues that would require either party to take illegal action.

FIGURE 16-8   Weekly Earnings of Union and Nonunion Workers

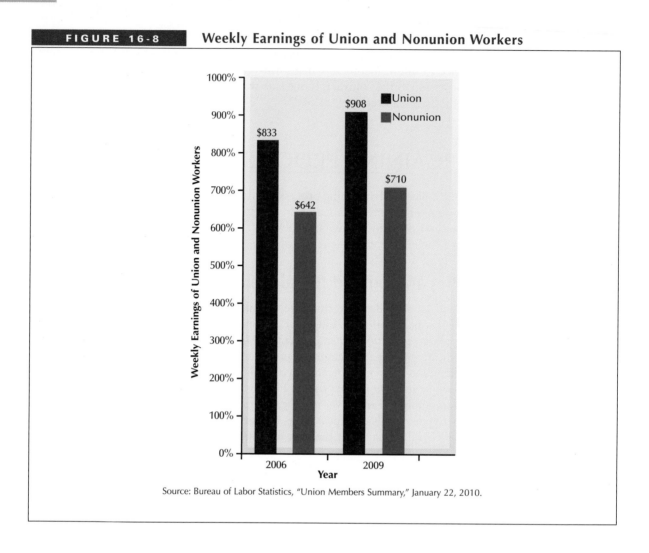

Source: Bureau of Labor Statistics, "Union Members Summary," January 22, 2010.

scheduling meetings at absurdly inconvenient hours, and using other conflicting tactics may lead to employers or unions filing complaints with the NLRB.

Settlement and Contract Agreement

After reaching an initial agreement, the bargaining parties usually return to their respective constituencies to determine if the informal agreement is acceptable. A particularly crucial stage is **ratification** of the labor agreement, which occurs when union members vote to accept the terms of a negotiated labor agreement. Before ratification, the union negotiating team explains the agreement to the union members and presents it for a vote. If the members approve the agreement, it is then formalized into a contract. Figure 16-9 lists the typical items in a labor agreement.

Bargaining Impasse

Ratification Process by which union members vote to accept the terms of a negotiated labor agreement.

Regardless of the structure of the bargaining process, labor and management do not always reach agreement on the issues. If they reach an impasse, then the disputes can be taken to conciliation, mediation, or arbitration.

| FIGURE 16-9 | Typical Items in a Labor Agreement |

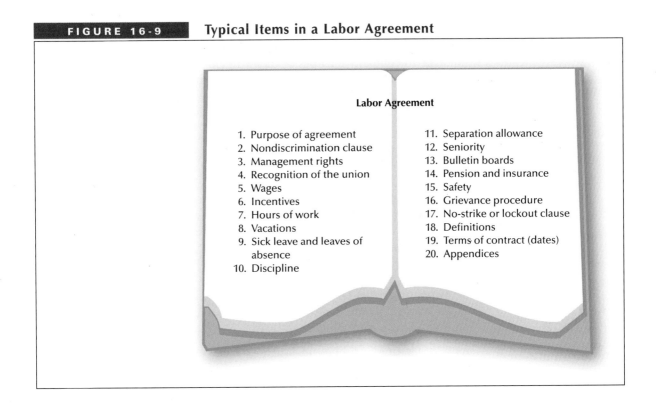

Labor Agreement

1. Purpose of agreement
2. Nondiscrimination clause
3. Management rights
4. Recognition of the union
5. Wages
6. Incentives
7. Hours of work
8. Vacations
9. Sick leave and leaves of absence
10. Discipline
11. Separation allowance
12. Seniority
13. Bulletin boards
14. Pension and insurance
15. Safety
16. Grievance procedure
17. No-strike or lockout clause
18. Definitions
19. Terms of contract (dates)
20. Appendices

Conciliation and Mediation When an impasse occurs, an outside party such as the Federal Mediation and Conciliation Service may help the two deadlocked parties to continue negotiations and arrive at a solution. In **conciliation,** the third party assists union and management negotiators to reach a voluntary settlement, but makes no proposals for solutions. In **mediation,** the third party may suggest ideas for solutions to help the negotiators reach a settlement.

In conciliation and mediation, the third party does not attempt to impose a solution. Sometimes fact finding helps to clarify the issues of disagreement as an intermediate step between mediation and arbitration.

Conciliation Process by which a third party assists union and management negotiators to reach a voluntary settlement.

Mediation Process by which a third party helps the negotiators reach a settlement.

Arbitration Process that uses a neutral third party to make a decision.

Strike Work stoppage in which union members refuse to work in order to put pressure on an employer.

Arbitration In **arbitration,** a neutral third party makes a decision. Arbitration can be conducted by an individual or a panel of individuals. "Interest" arbitration attempts to solve bargaining impasses, primarily in the public sector. This type of arbitration is not frequently used in the private sector because companies generally do not want an outside party making decisions about their rights, wages, benefits, and other issues. However, grievance or "rights" arbitration is used extensively in the private sector. Fortunately, in many situations, agreements are reached through negotiations without the need for arbitration. When disagreements continue, strikes or lockouts may occur.

Strikes and Lockouts

If a deadlock cannot be resolved, an employer may revert to a lockout—or a union may revert to a strike. During a **strike,** union members refuse to work in order to put pressure on an employer. Often, the striking union members picket or demonstrate against the employer outside the place of business by carrying placards and signs.

In a **lockout**, management shuts down company operations to prevent union members from working. This action may avert possible damage or sabotage to company facilities or injury to employees who continue to work. It also gives management leverage in negotiations.

Types of Strikes Five types of strikes can occur:

- *Economic strikes* happen when the parties fail to reach agreement during collective bargaining.
- *Unfair labor practices strikes* occur when union members leave their jobs over what they feel are illegal employer actions, such as refusal to bargain.
- *Wildcat strikes* occur during the life of the collective bargaining agreement without approval of union leadership and violate a no-strike clause in a labor contract. Strikers can be discharged or disciplined.
- *Jurisdictional strikes* exist when members of one union walk out to force the employer to assign work to them instead of to members of another union.
- *Sympathy strikes* take place when one union chooses to express support for another union involved in a dispute, even though the first union has no disagreement with the employer.

As a result of the decline in union power, work stoppages due to strikes and lockouts are relatively rare. In a recent year, only 22 strikes or lockouts occurred nationally, and they were all settled quickly. Many unions are reluctant to go on strike due to the financial losses their members would incur or the fear that a strike would cause the employer to go bankrupt. In addition, management has shown its willingness to hire replacements, and some strikes have ended with union workers losing their jobs.

LOGGING ON

Federal Mediation & Conciliation Service
This service organization provides services and resources to promote stable labor and management relationships. Visit the website at www.fmcs.gov.

Replacement of Workers on Strike Management retains and sometimes uses its ability to simply replace workers who strike. Workers' rights vary depending on the type of strike that occurs. For example, in an economic strike, an employer is free to replace the striking workers. But with an unfair labor practices strike, the workers who want their jobs back at the end of the strike must be reinstated.

UNION/MANAGEMENT COOPERATION

The adversarial relationship that naturally exists between unions and management may lead to strikes and lockouts. However, as noted, such conflicts currently are relatively rare. Even more encouraging is the recognition on the part of some union leaders and employer representatives that cooperation between management and labor unions offers a useful route if organizations are to compete effectively in a global economy.

During the past decade, numerous firms have engaged in organizational and workplace restructuring in response to competitive pressures in their industries. Restructurings have had significant effects, such as lost jobs, changed work rules, and altered job responsibilities. When restructurings occur, unions can take different approaches, ranging from resistance to cooperation. See the HR Perspective for an example of how a union handled a situation at Ford in a cooperative manner.

Lockout Shutdown of company operations undertaken by management to prevent union members from working.

Union Helps Cut Costs at Ford

Jerry Sullivan, head of a United Auto workers local at Ford Motor Company, had fought for job protection, higher pay, and better benefits for his members, but he found himself in a situation in which he agreed to accept the outsourcing of jobs. "Ford is in a desperate situation—if this company goes down I want to be able to look in the mirror and say I did everything I could," said Mr. Sullivan.

Like the other U.S. auto companies, Ford had fallen behind the Asian companies. A key auto manufacturing report showed that it took Ford 36 hours of labor to assemble a car—5 or 6 hours slower than its Asian counterparts. To avoid disaster, Ford asked for help from the union. The company showed the union representatives how big the cost gaps were: $2,400 per vehicle, with labor representing $1,080 to $1,335 of that. The UAW allowed local unions to tear up existing contracts and negotiate new rules.

The talks between the company and union covered many areas, including some sensitive ones such as UAW absenteeism rates. The absenteeism rate at Ford had been about 11%, which was double the rate of Toyota and other companies. Each percentage point cost Ford $20 million a year. Negotiated changes included capping the number of absences per person regardless of the excuse, hiring outside contractors to handle some jobs at one-half the pay, finding outside companies to repair equipment, and moving to four-day, 10-hour workweeks including weekends without overtime.

Further, in some plants, union members agreed to manage operations at work with a raise of only 50 cents per hour. Many more changes occurred as well. About 65% of the employees voted for the changes in Dearborn, Michigan. In other plants, the winning margins were even higher. As a result, when General Motors and Chrysler both had to declare bankruptcy, Ford alone continued on as before.

Mr. Sullivan said, "This is a partnership, right? We are in this together, right?" Apparently he was right.[40]

When unions have been able to obtain information and share that information with their members in order to work constructively with the company management at various levels, then organizational restructurings have been handled more successfully. For example, at General Motors the cost of retiree health care added $1,400 per car at a time when GM *had to* make major cost cuts to stay competitive.[41] Working with the union, the company set up a voluntary employee benefit association. The $35 billion trust allowed GM to get the crushing liabilities for retirees' health care off its books.[42]

Employee Involvement Programs

It seems somewhat illogical to suggest that union/management cooperation or involving employees in making suggestions and decisions could be bad, and yet some decisions by the NLRB appear to have done just that. Some historical perspective is required to understand the issues that surrounded the decisions.

In the 1930s, when the Wagner Act was written, certain employers would form sham "company unions," coercing workers into joining them in order to keep legitimate unions from organizing the employees. As a result, the Wagner Act contained prohibitions against employer-dominated labor organizations.

These prohibitions were enforced, and company unions disappeared. But the use of employee involvement programs in organizations today has raised new concerns along these lines.

Because of the Wagner Act, many employee involvement programs set up in past years may be illegal, according to an NLRB decision dealing with Electromation, an Elkhart, Indiana, firm. Electromation used teams of employees to solicit other employees' views about such issues as wages and working conditions. The NLRB labeled these teams "labor organizations," in line with requirements of the Wagner Act. It further found that the teams were "dominated" by management, which had formed them, set their goals, and decided how they would operate. The results of this and other decisions have forced many employers to rethink and restructure their employee involvement efforts.

Federal court decisions have upheld the NLRB position in some cases and reversed it in others. One key to decisions allowing employee involvement committees and programs seems to be that these entities should not deal directly with traditional collective bargaining issues such as wages, hours, and working conditions. Other keys are that the committees should be composed primarily of workers and that they have broad authority to make operational suggestions and decisions.

Unions and Employee Ownership

Unions in some situations have encouraged workers to become partial or complete owners of the companies that employ them. These efforts were spurred by concerns that firms were preparing to shut down, merge, or be bought out. Such results were likely to cut the number of union jobs and workers.

Unions have been active in helping members put together employee stock ownership plans to purchase all or part of some firms.[43] Such programs have been successful in some situations but have caused problems in others. Some in the labor movement fear that such programs may undermine union support by creating a closer identification with the concerns and goals of employers, instead of "union solidarity."

GRIEVANCE MANAGEMENT

Unions know that employee dissatisfaction is a potential source of trouble for employers, whether it is expressed or not. Hidden dissatisfaction grows and creates reactions that may be completely out of proportion to the original concerns. Therefore, it is important that dissatisfaction be given an outlet. A **complaint**, which is merely an indication of employee dissatisfaction, is one outlet. If an employee is represented by a union, and the employee says, "I should have received the job transfer because I have more seniority, which is what the union contract states," and she submits it in writing, then that complaint becomes a grievance. A **grievance** is a complaint formally stated in writing.

Complaint Indication of employee dissatisfaction.

Grievance Complaint formally stated in writing.

Management should be concerned with both complaints and grievances, because both indicate potential problems within the workforce.[44] Without a grievance procedure, management may be unable to respond to employee concerns because managers are unaware of them. Therefore, a formal grievance procedure provides a valuable communication tool for organizations, whether a union is present or not.

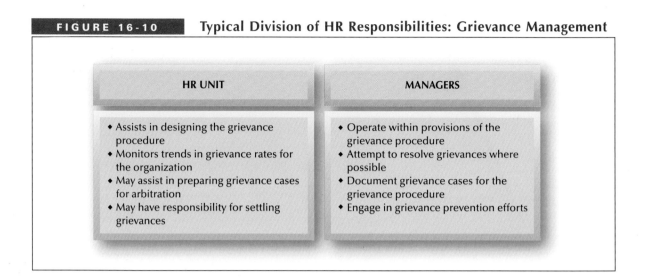

FIGURE 16-10   Typical Division of HR Responsibilities: Grievance Management

HR UNIT	MANAGERS
• Assists in designing the grievance procedure • Monitors trends in grievance rates for the organization • May assist in preparing grievance cases for arbitration • May have responsibility for settling grievances	• Operate within provisions of the grievance procedure • Attempt to resolve grievances where possible • Document grievance cases for the grievance procedure • Engage in grievance prevention efforts

Grievance Responsibilities

The typical division of responsibilities between the HR unit and operating managers for handling grievances is shown in Figure 16-10. These responsibilities vary considerably from one organization to another, even between unionized firms. But the HR unit usually has more general responsibilities. Managers must accept the grievance procedure as a possible constraint on some of their decisions.

Grievance Procedures

Grievance procedures are formal channels of communication designed to resolve grievances as soon as possible after problems arise.[45] First-line supervisors are usually closest to a problem. However, these supervisors are concerned with many other matters besides one employee's grievance, and may even be the subject of an employee's grievance. To receive the appropriate attention, grievances go through a specific process for resolution.[46]

Union Representation in Grievance Procedures A unionized employee generally has a right to union representation if the employee is being questioned by management and if discipline may result. If these so-called *Weingarten rights* (named after the court case that established them) are violated and the employee is dismissed, the employee usually will be reinstated with back pay. Employers are not required to allow nonunion workers to have coworkers present in grievance procedure meetings. However, employers may voluntarily allow such presence.[47]

Steps in a Grievance Procedure

Grievance procedures can vary in the steps included. Figure 16-11 shows a typical grievance procedure, which consists of the following steps:

Grievance procedures
Formal channels of communication used to resolve grievances.

1. The employee discusses the grievance with the union steward (the representative of the union on the job) and the supervisor.
2. The union steward discusses the grievance with the supervisor's manager and/or the HR manager.

| FIGURE 16-11 | **Steps in a Typical Grievance Procedure** |

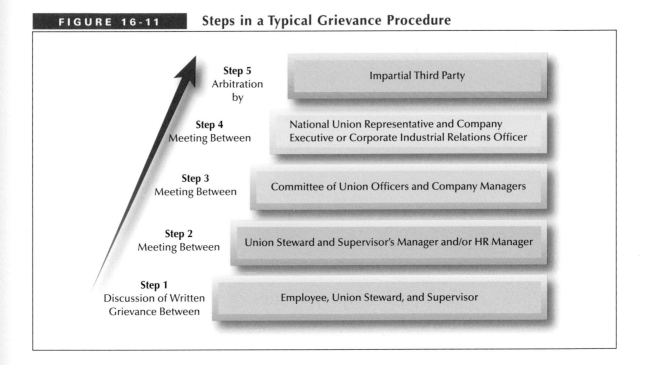

Step 5
Arbitration by — Impartial Third Party

Step 4
Meeting Between — National Union Representative and Company Executive or Corporate Industrial Relations Officer

Step 3
Meeting Between — Committee of Union Officers and Company Managers

Step 2
Meeting Between — Union Steward and Supervisor's Manager and/or HR Manager

Step 1
Discussion of Written Grievance Between — Employee, Union Steward, and Supervisor

3. A committee of union officers discusses the grievance with appropriate company managers.
4. The representative of the national union discusses the grievance with designated company executives or the corporate industrial relations officer.
5. If the grievance is not solved at this stage, it goes to arbitration. An impartial third party may ultimately dispose of the grievance.

Grievance arbitration

Means by which a third party settles disputes arising from different interpretations of a labor contract.

Grievance arbitration is a means by which a third party settles disputes arising from different interpretations of a labor contract.[48] This process should not be confused with contract or issues arbitration, discussed earlier, in which arbitration is used to determine how a contract will be written. The U.S. Supreme Court has ruled that grievance arbitration decisions issued under labor contract provisions are enforceable and generally may not go to court to be changed. Grievance arbitration includes more than 50 topic areas, with discipline and discharge, safety and health, and security issues being most prevalent.[49]

SUMMARY

- A union is a formal association of workers that promotes the interests of its members through collective action.
- Workers join unions primarily because of management's failure to address organizational and job-related concerns.
- Unions are becoming more global as the world economy expands, and global labor federations are expanding, despite differences in approaches.

- The history of unions in the United States indicates that they primarily focus on wages, hours, and working conditions.
- In the United States, current union membership as a percentage of the workforce is down dramatically, being about 12% of the civilian workforce.
- While public-sector unions have grown, unions in general have experienced a decline in mem-

bership due to geographic, industrial, and work-force changes.

- In attempts to grow, unions are targeting professionals, low-skilled workers, and contingent and part-time workers.
- The history of unions in the United States has evolved, and the structural levels of U.S. unions include federations, national and international unions, and local unions.
- The National Labor Code is composed of three laws that provide the legal basis for labor relations today: the Wagner Act, the Taft-Hartley Act, and the Landrum-Griffin Act.
- The Wagner Act was designed to protect unions and workers; the Taft-Hartley Act restored some powers to management; and the Landrum-Griffin Act was passed to protect individual union members.
- Issues addressed by the different acts include unfair labor practices, national emergency strikes, and right-to-work provisions.
- The unionization process includes an organizing campaign, authorization cards, a representation election, certification and decertification, and contract negotiation through collective bargaining.

- Collective bargaining occurs when management negotiates with representatives of workers over wages, hours, and working conditions.
- The issues subject to collective bargaining fall into three categories: mandatory, permissive, and illegal.
- The collective bargaining process includes preparation and initial demands, negotiations, and settlement and contract agreement.
- Once an agreement (contract) is signed between labor and management, it becomes the document governing what each party can and cannot do.
- When an impasse occurs, work stoppages through strikes or lockouts can be used to pressure the other party.
- Union/management cooperation has been beneficial in a number of situations, although care must be taken to avoid violations of NLRB provisions.
- Grievances express workers' written dissatisfactions or differences in contract interpretations.
- A grievance procedure begins with the first-level supervisor and may end—if the grievance is not resolved along the way—with arbitration by a third party.

CRITICAL THINKING ACTIVITIES

1. Discuss the following statement: "If management gets a union, it deserves one."

2. Suppose a coworker just brought you a union leaflet urging employees to sign an authorization card. What may happen from this point on?

3. As the HR manager, you have heard rumors about potential efforts to unionize your warehouse employees. Use the www.genelevine.com website to develop a set of guidelines for

supervisors if they are asked questions by employees about unionization as part of a "union prevention" approach.

4. Public-sector unions now account for more than half of union members, while the private sector accounts for less than half. Why has this change occurred?

HR EXPERIENTIAL PROBLEM SOLVING

There has been some discussion among the employees in your company's manufacturing plant about forming a union. Company management recognizes the discussions may be due to the absence of a formal grievance procedure to assist employees with reporting their concerns and grievances to management. HR has been asked to develop a formal griev-

ance procedure in an effort to develop better labor relations between the employer and the employees and as an avoidance measure to the formation of a union. To assist HR in developing a formal grievance procedure, visit several websites including the ADR/Conflict Resolution link at http://community.linchr.com/employmentguide.

1. Employees in the shipping department have requested the implementation of a "suggestion box" system to help them bring their concerns to the attention of management and to help improve labor relations. Identify the advantages and disadvantages of such a system.

2. If company management determines that the "suggestion box" request will be more cumbersome than helpful, what are some alternative solutions that management can suggest to the employees?

CASE

Teamsters and the Fraternal Order of Police (FOP)

Unions sometimes compete to represent workers, and that has been the case in Colorado with the Denver Sheriff's Department. With budget cuts and tightening discipline, about 125 of the 760 deputies have turned to the Teamsters Union. What they have gotten is Ed Bagwell, Local 17's director of the public service division—a stocky and aggressive person.

Bagwell *is* aggressive. During one meeting, a supervisor looked at his Teamster's shirt and said, "Nice bowling shirt." Bagwell responded by looking at the supervisor's uniform and remarking, "Nice clown suit." After that, the fight was on, and the meeting became so tense that the department ended up closing the meeting and turning the matter over to internal affairs. During another meeting, Bagwell got so mad he invited a supervisor outside. His behavior so offended an assistant city attorney that the attorney wrote to Bagwell's boss about "unnecessarily hostile and inappropriate behavior." At yet another meeting, when Bagwell was asked to tone it down, he roared, "You have no idea how aggressive I can be!"

Such behavior has had the city attorney's office all atwitter, but it seems to resonate with the sheriff's deputies. A group of those deputies want the Teamsters to take over for the Fraternal Order of Police (FOP), which has handled collective bargaining for the deputies since 1993. The momentum is with the Teamsters, which signed up more than 100 deputies in a recent year.

The president of the FOP thinks his union will stave off the Teamsters, who will need votes from more than half of the 700 deputies before the Teamsters can represent them. The Teamsters have insinuated that the existing union is not tough enough, according to the FOP, but the FOP president disagrees. "I think we have in case after case shown that we are willing to fight what we think is a fight," he said.

Two deputies who have recently switched to the Teamsters disagree with the FOP. One deputy who is accused of lying about what he saw in a discipline case involving another deputy has chosen the Teamsters over the FOP to defend him in his disciplinary hearings. The other has switched to the Teamsters because he feels an outside organization will be more likely to challenge the status quo. He says, "It's time for a change."[50]

QUESTIONS

1. Is it good or bad for one union to challenge another to represent these deputies, and why?

2. Discuss whether the aggressive approach of the Teamsters is appropriate and legal under the circumstances.

3. If you were sheriff, which union would you rather deal with? Is there a lesson there?

SUPPLEMENTAL CASES

Wal-Mart and Union Prevention

This case covers Wal-Mart efforts to stay nonunion. (For the case, go to www.cengage.com/management/mathis.)

The Wilson County Hospital

This case deals with labor disputes in a unionized hospital. (For the case, go to www.cengage.com/management/mathis.)

NOTES

1. Sharon Carty, "Unions Try to Hang On as Open-Shop Laws Gain Ground," *USA Today*, July 26, 2007, B1–B2.

2. Melanie Trottman, "Unions Look to Labor Board Picks to Reverse Bush Rulings," *The Wall Street Journal*, June 3, 2009, A2.

3. Moira Herbst, "Big Labor's Big Chance," *BusinessWeek*, September 8, 2008, 026.

4. Bill Leonard, "After Historic Win, Democrats Focus on Workplace Issues," *HR Magazine*, December 2008, 17.

5. Barry Hirsh, "Sluggish Institutions in a Dynamic World: Can Unions and Industrial Competition Coexist?" *Journal of Economic Perspectives*, 22 (2008), 153–176.

6. *Ibid.*, 154–155.

7. Steven Abraham, et al., "The Relationship Among Union Membership, Facets of Satisfaction and Intent to Leave," *Employee Responsibilities and Rights Journal*, 20 (2008), 1–11.

8. John Schmitt, et al., "Unions and Upward Mobility for Low Wage Workers," *Journal of Labor and Society*, 11 (2008), 337–348.

9. Carol Gill, "Union Impact on the Effective Adoption of High Performance Work Practices," *Human Resource Management Review*, 19 (2009), 39–50.

10. Mark Schoeff, "A Step Back," *Workforce Management*, January 19, 2009, 18–22.

11. Mario Bognanno, et al., "Symposium Introduction: Governing the Global Workplace," *Industrial Relations*, 46 (2007), 215.

12. Kenneth Dau-Schmidt and Benjamin Ellis, "The Relative Bargaining Power of Employers and Unions in the Global Information Age," *Working Paper Series*, University of Indiana, 2008, 1–20.

13. Lyle Scruggs and Peter Lange, "Where Have All the Members Gone? Globalization, Institutions and Union Density," *Journal of Politics*, 64 (No. 1), 126–153.

14. S. Dankov and R. Ramalho, "Employment Laws in Developing Countries," *Journal of Comparative Economics*, 37, (2009), 3–13.

15. Based on Andrew Batson, "China Toils over New Labor Law," *The Wall Street Journal*, May 7, 2007, A8; Dexter Roberts, "Rumbles over Labor Reform," *BusinessWeek*, March 12, 2007, 57; Mei Fong and Kris Maher, "U.S. Labor Leaders Aided China's Wal-Mart Coup," *The Wall Street Journal*, June 22, 2007, W1.

16. Kris Maher, "Steelworkers Press the U.S. for Trade Relief," *The Wall Street Journal*, June 3, 2009, B3.

17. "More Union Workers Now in Government," *The Denver Post*, January 23, 2010, 6B.

18. Kris Maher, "Concessions Foreshadow a Tough Year for Unions," *The Wall Street Journal*, January 5, 2009, A3.

19. David Blanchflower, "International Patterns of Union Membership," *British Journal of Industrial Relations*, March 2007, 1–28.

20. Raewyn Connell and June Crawford, "Mapping the Intellectual Labour Process," *Journal of Sociology*, 43 (2007), 187–204.

21. Robert Grossman, "Reorganized Labor," *HR Magazine*, January 2008, 37–41.

22. Gary Chaison, "The AFL-CIO Split: Does It Really Matter?" *Journal of Labor Research*, Spring 2007, 301–311.

23. Len Right, "Amendments: Many Top Executives Fight Right to Work," *The Denver Post*, October 5, 2008, 1K.

24. Joan Biskupic, "Supreme Court Upholds Fee Burden on Unions," *USA Today*, June 15, 2007, 4A.

25. Bill Leonard, "Court Upholds Union Reporting Requirements," *HR Magazine*, July 2008, 24.

26. Jason Riley, "The Election Choice: Unions," *The Wall Street Journal*, October 27, 2008, A19.

27. John Hollon, "A Poor 'Choice,'" *Workforce Management*, January 19, 2009, p. 42.

28. John Matchulat, "The Unions Rejoice Act: An Examination of the Intent and Potential Impact of EFCA," *Employee Relations Law Journal*, Spring 2009, 16–55.

29. Douglas Seaton and Emily Ruhsam, "The Employee Free Choice Act: No Choice for Employer or Employee," *Employer Relations Law Journal*, Spring 2009, 3–15.

30. Melanie Trottman, "Labor Fears Spawn Boom in Workplace Legal Advice," *The Wall Street Journal*, April 8, 2008, B1.

31. Ann Zimmerman and Kris Maher, "Wal-Mart Warns of Democrat Win," *The Wall Street Journal*, August 1, 2008, W1.

32. For example, Jackson Lewis, a law firm with 29 offices nationwide, represents management exclusively; see www.jacksonlewis.com.

33. Kris Maher, "Unions Find the Economy Is No Bargain," *The Wall Street Journal*, April 4, 2008, B4; Peter Coy, et al., "The Disposable Worker," *BusinessWeek*, January 18, 2010, 33–39.

34. Rita Zeidner, "NLRB: Unions Not Guaranteed Use of Company E-Mail," *HR News*, December 28, 2007, www.shrm.org, 1.

35. *Toering Electric Co.*, 351 NLRB No. 18 (Sept. 29, 2009).

36. Leigh Tyson and W. Jonathan Martin, "NLRB Clarifies When an Employee Is a 'Supervisor,'" *Ceridian Abstracts*, www.hrcompliance.ceridian.com.

37. *14 Penn Plaza LLCV v. Pyett*, No. 07-581 (S. Ct. 2009).

38. Joanne Deschenaux, "High Court Upholds Limits on Use of Non Member's Union Fees," *Workplace Law Library—Labor Relations*, June 15, 2007.

39. Eric Krell, "The Rebirth of Labor Relations," *HR Magazine*, February 2009, 57–60.

40. Jeffrey McCracken, "Desperate to Cut Costs Ford Gets Union's Help," *The Wall Street Journal*, March 2, 2007, A1.

41. GM Plans to Address Rising Health-Care Costs with UAW," *Omaha World Herald*, March 15, 2007, 2D.

42. David Welch and Nanette Byrnes, "GM's Health Plan Could Be Contagious," *BusinessWeek*, October 8, 2007, 37.

43. Jacquelyn Yates, "Unions and Employee Ownership: A Road to Economic Recovery," *Industrial Relations*, 45 (2006), 709.

44. Nancy Woodward, "New Guidelines Adopted for U.K. Workplace Grievances," *HR Magazine*, June 2009, 32.

45. Lawrence Nurse and Dwayne Devonish, "Grievance Management and Its Links to Workplace Justice," *Employee Relations*, 29, (2007), 89–109.

46. Annette Cox, et al., "Applying Union Mobilization Theory to Explain Gendered Collective Grievances," *Journal of Industrial Relations*, 49, (2007), 717–738.

47. "Resolving Workplace Disputes Internally," *SHRM*, 2009, www.shrm.org.

48. Matthew Frankiewicz, "How to Win Your Arbitration Case Before It Even Starts," *Labor Law Journal*, 2009, 115–120.

49. Harry Johnson and George Howard Jr., "Creating Workable Arbitration Agreements in the Post Gentry Era," *Employee Relations Law Journal*, Winter 2008, 3–15.

50. Based on: Christopher Osher, "Teamsters Gaining Among Sheriff's Deputies," *The Denver Post*, July 26, 2009, 4B.

Appendix A

HUMAN RESOURCE CERTIFICATION INSTITUTE:
PHR AND SPHR TEST SPECIFICATIONS

The two most utilized levels of certification are the **Professional in Human Resources (PHR)** and the **Senior Professional in Human Resources (SPHR)**. Examination questions for both levels cover a wide range of topics. PHR questions tend to be at an operational/technical level, whereas SPHR questions tend to be more at the strategic and/or policy level. Each question lists *four possible answers,* only one of which is correct.

The test specifications identify six *Functional Areas* plus a *Core Knowledge* section. After each major functional area are the weightings for that area. **The first number in the parentheses is the PHR percentage weighting, and the second number is the SPHR percentage weighting.** Within each area *responsibilities* and *knowledge* topics are specified. Readers of this book can identify specific content information for the PHR and SPHR topics using the www.hrci.org website. Exams can be taken by professionals either online or at designated physical locations.

FUNCTIONAL AREAS:

01 STRATEGIC BUSINESS MANAGEMENT (12%, 29%)

Developing, contributing to, and supporting the organization's mission, vision, values, strategic goals, and objectives; formulating policies; guiding and leading the change process; and evaluating HR's contributions to organizational effectiveness.

Responsibilities:

01 Interpret information related to the organization's operations from internal sources, including financial/accounting, business development, marketing, sales, operations and information technology, in order to contribute to the development of the organization's strategic plan.

02 Interpret information from external sources related to the general business environment, industry practices and developments, technological developments, economic environment, labor pool, and legal and regulatory environment, in order to contribute to the development of the organization's strategic plan.

03 Participate as a contributing partner in the organization's strategic planning process.

04 Establish strategic relationships with key individuals in the organization to influence organizational decision making.

05 Establish relationships/alliances with key individuals and organizations in the community to assist in achieving the organization's strategic goals and objectives.

06 Develop and utilize metrics to evaluate HR's contributions to the achievement of the organization's strategic goals and objectives.

07 Develop and execute strategies for managing organizational change that balance the expectations and needs of the organization, its employees, and all other stakeholders.

08 Develop and align the organization's human capital management plan with its strategic plan.

09 Facilitate the development and communication of the organization's core values and ethical behaviors.

10 Reinforce the organization's core values and behavioral expectations through modeling, communication, and coaching.

11 Develop and manage the HR budget in a manner consistent with the organization's strategic goals, objectives, and values.

12 Provide information for the development and monitoring of the organization's overall budget.

13 Monitor the legislative and regulatory environment for proposed changes and their potential impact to the organization, taking appropriate proactive steps to support, modify, or oppose the proposed changes.

14 Develop policies and procedures to support corporate governance initiatives (for example, board of directors training, whistle-blower protection, code of conduct).

15 Participate in enterprise risk management by examining HR policies to evaluate their potential risks to the organization.

16 Identify and evaluate alternatives and recommend strategies for vendor selection and/or outsourcing (for example, HRIS, benefits, payroll).

17 Participate in strategic decision making and due diligence activities related to organizational structure and design (for example, corporate restructuring, mergers and acquisitions (M&A), offshoring, divestitures). **SPHR ONLY**

18 Determine strategic application of integrated technical tools and systems (for example, HRIS, performance management tools, applicant tracking, compensation tools, employee self-service technologies).

Knowledge of:

01 The organization's mission, vision, values, business goals, objectives, plans, and processes.

02 Legislative and regulatory processes.

03 Strategic planning process and implementation.

04 Management functions, including planning, organizing, directing, and controlling.

05 Techniques to promote creativity and innovation.

06 Corporate governance procedures and compliance (for example, Sarbanes-Oxley Act).

07 Transition techniques for corporate restructuring, M&A, offshoring, and divestitures. **SPHR ONLY**

02 WORKFORCE PLANNING AND EMPLOYMENT (26%, 17%)

Developing, implementing, and evaluating sourcing, recruitment, hiring, orientation, succession planning, retention, and organizational exit programs necessary to ensure the workforce's ability to achieve the organization's goals and objectives.

Responsibilities:

01 Ensure that workforce planning and employment activities are compliant with applicable federal, state, and local laws and regulations.

02 Identify workforce requirements to achieve the organization's short- and long-term goals and objectives (for example, corporate restructuring, M&A activity, workforce expansion or reduction).

03 Conduct job analyses to create job descriptions and identify job competencies.

04 Identify and document essential job functions for positions.

05 Establish hiring criteria based on job descriptions and required competencies.

06 Analyze labor market for trends that impact the ability to meet workforce requirements (for example, SWOT analysis, environmental scan, demographic scan). **SPHR ONLY**

07 Assess skill sets of internal workforce and external labor market to determine the availability of qualified candidates, utilizing third-party vendors or agencies as appropriate.

08 Identify internal and external recruitment sources (for example, employee referrals, online job boards, résumé banks) and implement selected recruitment methods.

09 Evaluate recruitment methods and sources for effectiveness (for example, return on investment (ROI), cost per hire, time to fill).

10 Develop strategies to brand/market the organization to potential qualified applicants.

11 Develop and implement selection procedures, including applicant tracking, interviewing, testing, reference and background checking, and drug screening.

12 Develop and extend employment offers and conduct negotiations as necessary.

13 Administer post-offer employment activities (for example, execute employment agreements, complete I-9 verification forms, coordinate relocations, schedule physical exams).

14 Implement and/or administer the process for non-U.S. citizens to legally work in the United States.

15 Develop, implement, and evaluate orientation processes for new hires, rehires, and transfers.

16 Develop, implement, and evaluate retention strategies and practices.

17 Develop, implement, and evaluate succession planning process.

18 Develop and implement the organizational exit process for both voluntary and involuntary terminations, including planning for reductions in force (RIF).

19 Develop, implement, and evaluate an AAP, as required.

Knowledge of:

08 Federal/state/local employment-related laws and regulations related to workforce planning and employment (for example, Title VII, ADA, ADEA, USERRA, EEOC Uniform Guidelines on Employee Selection Procedures, Immigration Reform and Control Act, Internal Revenue Code).

09 Quantitative analyses required to assess past and future staffing effectiveness (for example, cost-benefit analysis, costs per hire, selection ratios, adverse impact).

10 Recruitment sources (for example, Internet, agencies, employee referral) for targeting passive, semiactive and active candidates.

11 Recruitment strategies.

12 Staffing alternatives (for example, temporary and contract, outsourcing, job sharing, part-time).

13 Planning techniques (for example, succession planning, forecasting).

14 Reliability and validity of selection tests/tools/methods.

15 Use and interpretation of selection tests (for example, psychological/personality, cognitive, motor/physical assessments, performance, assessment center).

16 Interviewing techniques (for example, behavioral, situational, panel).

17 Relocation practices.

18 Impact of total rewards on recruitment and retention.

19 International HR and implications of global workforce for workforce planning and employment. **SPHR ONLY**

20 Voluntary and involuntary terminations, downsizing, restructuring, and outplacement strategies and practices.

21 Internal workforce assessment techniques (for example, skills testing, skills inventory, workforce demographic analysis) and employment policies, practices, and procedures (for example, orientation and retention).

22 Employer marketing and branding techniques.

23 Negotiation skills and techniques.

03 HUMAN RESOURCE DEVELOPMENT (17%, 17%)

Developing, implementing, and evaluating activities and programs that address employee training and development, performance appraisal, talent and performance management, and the unique needs of employees to ensure that the knowledge, skills, abilities, and performance of the workforce meet current and future organizational and individual needs.

Responsibilities:

01 Ensure that human resource development programs are compliant with all applicable federal, state, and local laws and regulations.

02 Conduct a needs assessment to identify and establish priorities regarding human resource development activities. **SPHR ONLY**

03 Develop/select and implement employee training programs (for example, leadership skills, harassment prevention, computer skills) to increase individual and organizational effectiveness. Note that this includes training design and methods for obtaining feedback from training (e.g., surveys, pre- and post-testing).

04 Evaluate effectiveness of employee training programs through the use of metrics (for example, participant surveys, pre- and post-testing). **SPHR ONLY**

05 Develop, implement, and evaluate talent management programs that include assessing talent, developing talent, and placing high-potential employees. **SPHR ONLY**

06 Develop/select and evaluate performance appraisal process (for example, instruments, ranking and rating scales, relationship to compensation, frequency).

07 Implement training programs for performance evaluators. **PHR ONLY**

08 Develop, implement, and evaluate performance management programs and procedures (for example, goal setting, job rotations, promotions).

09 Develop/select, implement, and evaluate programs (for example, flexible work arrangements, diversity initiatives, repatriation) to meet the unique needs of employees. **SPHR ONLY**

Knowledge of:

24 Applicable federal, state, and local laws and regulations related to human resources development activities (for example, Title VII, ADA, ADEA, USERRA, EEOC Uniform Guidelines on Employee Selection Procedures).

25 Career development and leadership development theories and applications.

26 OD theories and applications.

27 Training program development techniques to create general and specialized training programs.

28 Training methods, facilitation techniques, instructional methods, and program delivery mechanisms.

29 Task/process analysis.

30 Performance appraisal methods (for example, instruments, ranking and rating scales).

31 Performance management methods (for example, goal setting, job rotations, promotions).

32 Applicable global issues (for example, international law, culture, local management approaches/practices, societal norms). **SPHR ONLY**

33 Techniques to assess training program effectiveness, including use of applicable metrics (for example, participant surveys, pre- and post-testing).

34 E-learning.

35 Mentoring and executive coaching.

04 TOTAL REWARDS (16%, 12%)

Developing/selecting, implementing/administering, and evaluating compensation and benefits programs for all employee groups that support the organization's strategic goals, objectives, and values.

Responsibilities:

01 Ensure that compensation and benefits programs are compliant with applicable federal, state, and local laws and regulations.

02 Develop, implement, and evaluate compensation policies/programs and pay structures based upon internal equity and external market conditions that support the organization's strategic goals, objectives, and values.

03 Administer payroll functions (for example, new hires, deductions, adjustments, terminations).

04 Conduct benefits programs needs assessments (for example, benchmarking, employee survey).

05 Develop/select, implement/administer, and evaluate benefits programs that support the organization's strategic goals, objectives, and values (for example, health and welfare, retirement, stock purchase, wellness, employee assistance programs (EAP), time-off).

06 Communicate and train the workforce in the compensation and benefits programs and policies (for example, self-service technologies).

07 Develop/select, implement/administer, and evaluate executive compensation programs (for example, stock purchase, stock options, incentive, bonus, supplemental retirement plans). **SPHR ONLY**

08 Develop, implement/administer, and evaluate expatriate and foreign national compensation and benefits programs. **SPHR ONLY**

Knowledge of:

36 Federal, state, and local compensation, benefits, and tax laws (for example, FLSA, ERISA, COBRA, HIPAA, FMLA, FICA).

37 Total rewards strategies (for example, compensation, benefits, wellness, rewards, recognition, employee assistance).

38 Budgeting and accounting practices related to compensation and benefits.

39 Job evaluation methods.

40 Job pricing and pay structures.

41 External labor markets and/or economic factors.

42 Pay programs (for example, incentive, variable, merit).

43 Executive compensation methods. **SPHR ONLY**

44 Non-cash compensation methods (for example, stock options, ESOPs). **SPHR ONLY**

45 Benefits programs (for example, health and welfare, retirement, wellness, EAP, time-off).

46 International compensation laws and practices (for example, expatriate compensation, entitlements, choice of law codes). **SPHR ONLY**

47 Fiduciary responsibility related to total rewards management. **SPHR ONLY**

05 EMPLOYEE AND LABOR RELATIONS (22%, 18%)

Analyzing, developing, implementing/administering, and evaluating the workplace relationship between employer and employee, in order to maintain relationships and working conditions that balance employer and employee needs and rights in support of the organization's strategic goals, objectives, and values.

Responsibilities:

01 Ensure that employee and labor relations activities are compliant with applicable federal, state, and local laws and regulations.

02 Assess organizational climate by obtaining employee input (for example, focus groups, employee surveys, staff meetings).

03 Implement organizational change activities as appropriate in response to employee feedback.

04 Develop employee relations programs (for example, awards, recognition, discounts, special events) that promote a positive organizational culture.

05 Implement employee relations programs that promote a positive organizational culture.

06 Evaluate effectiveness of employee relations programs through the use of metrics (for example, exit interviews, employee surveys).

07 Establish workplace policies and procedures (for example, dress code, attendance, computer use) and monitor their application and enforcement to ensure consistency.

08 Develop, administer, and evaluate grievance/dispute resolution and performance improvement policies and procedures.

09 Resolve employee complaints filed with federal, state, and local agencies involving employment practices, utilizing professional resources as necessary (for example, legal counsel, mediation/arbitration specialists, and investigators).

10 Develop and direct proactive employee relations strategies for remaining union-free in nonorganized locations.

11 Participate in collective bargaining activities, including contract negotiation and administration. **SPHR ONLY**

Knowledge of:

48 Applicable federal, state, and local laws affecting employment in union and nonunion environments, such as antidiscrimination laws, sexual harassment, labor relations, and privacy (for example, WARN Act, Title VII, NLRA).

49 Techniques for facilitating positive employee relations (for example, employee surveys, focus groups, dispute resolution, labor/management cooperative strategies and programs).

50 Employee involvement strategies (for example, employee management committees, self-directed work teams, staff meetings).

51 Individual employment rights issues and practices (for example, employment at will, negligent hiring, defamation, employees' rights to bargain collectively).

52 Workplace behavior issues/practices (for example, absenteeism and performance improvement).

53 Unfair labor practices (for example, employee communication strategies and management training).

54 The collective bargaining process, strategies, and concepts (for example, contract negotiation and administration). **SPHR ONLY**

55 Positive employee relations strategies and nonmonetary rewards.

06 RISK MANAGEMENT (7%, 7%)

Developing, implementing/administering, and evaluating programs, plans, and policies that provide a safe and secure working environment and protect the organization from liability.

Responsibilities:

01 Ensure that workplace health, safety, security, and privacy activities are compliant with applicable federal, state, and local laws and regulations.

02 Identify the organization's safety program needs.

03 Develop/select and implement/administer occupational injury and illness prevention, safety incentives, and training programs. **PHR ONLY**

04 Develop/select, implement, and evaluate plans and policies to protect employees and other individuals, and to minimize the organization's loss and liability (for example, emergency response, evacuation, workplace violence, substance abuse, return-to-work policies).

05 Communicate and train the workforce on the plans and policies to protect employees and other individuals, and to minimize the organization's loss and liability.

06 Develop and monitor business continuity and disaster recovery plans.

07 Communicate and train the workforce on the business continuity and disaster recovery plans.

08 Develop internal and external privacy policies (for example, identity theft, data protection, HIPAA compliance, workplace monitoring).

09 Administer internal and external privacy policies.

Knowledge of:

56 Federal, state, and local workplace health, safety, security, and privacy laws and regulations (for example, OSHA, Drug-Free Workplace Act, ADA, HIPAA, Sarbanes-Oxley Act).

57 Occupational injury and illness compensation and programs.

58 Occupational injury and illness prevention programs.

59 Investigation procedures of workplace safety, health, and security enforcement agencies (for example, OSHA, National Institute for Occupational Safety and Health (NIOSH)).

60 Workplace safety risks.

61 Workplace security risks (for example, theft, corporate espionage, asset and data protection, sabotage).

62 Potential violent behavior and workplace violence conditions.

63 General health and safety practices (for example, evacuation, hazard communication, ergonomic evaluations).

64 Incident and emergency response plans.

65 Internal investigation, monitoring, and surveillance techniques.

66 Issues related to substance abuse and dependency (for example, identification of symptoms, substance-abuse testing, discipline).

67 Business continuity and disaster recovery plans (for example, data storage and backup, alternative work locations and procedures).

68 Data integrity techniques and technology (for example, data sharing, firewalls).

CORE KNOWLEDGE REQUIRED BY HR PROFESSIONALS

69 Needs assessment and analysis.

70 Third-party contract negotiation and management, including development of requests for proposals (RFPs).

71 Communication skills and strategies (for example, presentation, collaboration, influencing, diplomacy, sensitivity).

72 Organizational documentation requirements to meet federal and state requirements.

73 Adult learning processes.

74 Motivation concepts and applications.

75 Training techniques (for example, computer-based, classroom, on-the-job).

76 Leadership concepts and applications.

77 Project management concepts and applications.

78 Diversity concepts and applications.

79 Human relations concepts and applications (for example, interpersonal and organizational behavior).

80 HR ethics and professional standards.

81 Technology to support HR activities (for example, HRIS, employee self-service, e-learning, ATS).

82 Qualitative and quantitative methods and tools for analysis, interpretation and decision-making purposes (for example, metrics and measurements, cost-benefit analysis, financial statement analysis).

83 Change management methods.

84 Job analysis and job description methods.

85 Employee records management (for example, electronic/paper, retention, disposal).

86 The interrelationships among HR activities and programs across functional areas.

87 Types of organizational structures (for example, matrix, hierarchy).

88 Environmental scanning concepts and applications.

89 Methods for assessing employee attitudes, opinions, and satisfaction (for example, opinion surveys, attitude surveys, focus groups/panels).

90 Basic budgeting and accounting concepts.

91 Risk management techniques.

Appendix B

HR MANAGEMENT RESOURCES

Students are expected to be familiar with the professional resources and literature in their fields of study. Five groups of resources are listed in this appendix.

A. Research-Oriented Journals

In HR management, the professional journals are the most immediate and direct communication link between researchers and the practicing managers. These journals contain articles that report on original research. Normally, these journals contain either sophisticated writing and quantitative verifications of the author's findings, or conceptual models and literature reviews of previous research.

Academy of Management Journal
Academy of Management Review
Administrative Science Quarterly
American Behavioral Scientist
American Journal of Health Promotion
American Journal of Psychology
American Journal of Sociology
American Psychological Measurement
American Psychologist
American Sociological Review
Annual Review of Psychology
Applied Psychology: An International Review
British Journal of Industrial Relations
British Journal of Management
Business Ethics
Decision Sciences
Dispute Resolution Quarterly
Employee Responsibilities and Rights Journal
Entrepreneurship Theory and Practice
Ethics and Critical Thinking Journal
Human Organization
Human Relations
Human Resource Development Review
Human Resource Management Journal
Human Resource Management Review
Human Resources Abstracts
Industrial & Labor Relations Review
Industrial Relations

Industrial Relations Journal
Industrial Relations Law Journal
International Journal of Entrepreneurial Behavior and Research
International Journal of Human Resource Management Education
International Journal of Management Reviews
International Journal of Training and Development
International Journal of Selection and Assessment
Journal of Abnormal Psychology
Journal of Applied Behavioral Science
Journal of Applied Business Research
Journal of Applied Psychology
Journal of Business
Journal of Business Communication
Journal of Business and Industrial Marketing
Journal of Business and Psychology
Journal of Business Ethics
Journal of Business Research
Journal of Business Strategy
Journal of Collective Negotiations
Journal of Communication
Journal of Comparative International Management
Journal of Compensation & Benefits
Journal of Counseling Psychology
Journal of Experimental Social Psychology

Journal of Human Resources
Journal of Industrial Relations
Journal of International Business Studies
Journal of International Management
Journal of Knowledge Management
Journal of Labor Economics
Journal of Labor Research
Journal of Leadership and Organizational
    Studies
Journal of Management
Journal of Management Development
Journal of Management Education
Journal of Management Studies
Journal of Managerial Psychology
Journal of Organizational Behavior
Journal of Organizational Change Management
Journal of Organizational Excellence
Journal of Personality and Social Psychology
Journal of Quality & Participation
Journal of Social Issues
Journal of Workplace Learning
Journal of Workplace Rights
New Technology, Work, and Employment
Organization Behavior and Human Decision
    Processes
Personnel Psychology
Personnel Review
Psychological Bulletin
Psychological Review
Public Personnel Management
Quarterly Review of Distance Education
Social Forces
Social Science Research
Work and Occupations

B. Selected Professional/ Managerial Journals

These journals generally cover a wide range of
subjects. Articles in these publications normally
are aimed at HR professionals and managers.
Most articles in these publications are written to
interpret, summarize, or discuss the implications
of research. They also provide operational and
administrative ideas.

Academy of Management Executive
Australian Journal of Management
Benefits and Compensation Solutions
Berkeley Journal of Employment and Labor Law
Business Horizons
Business Journal
Business Week
California Management Review

Columbia Journal of World Business
Compensation and Benefits Review
Corporate Governance
Directors and Boards
Economist
Employee Benefit Plan Review
Employee Benefits News
Employee Relations
Employment Relations Today
Forbes
Fortune
Global HR
Harvard Business Review
Health Resources and Services
    Administration
HR Magazine
Human Capital Management
Human Resource Development International
Human Resource Executive
Human Resource Management
Human Resource Management International
    Digest
IHRIM Link
INC.
Industry Week
International Management
Journal of Network & Systems Management
Labor Law Journal
Long Range Planning
Management Research News
Management Review
Management Today
Managers Magazine
Monthly Labor Review
Nation's Business
Occupational Health & Safety
Occupational Outlook Quarterly
Organizational Dynamics
Pension World
Personnel Management
Psychology Today
Public Administration Review
Public Manager
Public Opinion Quarterly
SAM Advanced Management Journal
Security Management
Sloan Management Review
Training
Training and Development
Workforce Management
Working Woman
Workplace Visions
Workspan
WorldatWork Journal

C. Selected HR Associations/ Organizations

Academy of Management
www.aom.pace.edu
American Arbitration Association
www.adr.org
American Federation of Labor/Congress of Industrial Organizations (AFL-CIO)
www.aflcio.org
American Institute for Managing Diversity
www.aimd.org
American Payroll Association
www.americanpayroll.org
American Psychological Association
www.apa.org
American Society for Industrial Security
www.asisonline.org
American Society for Training and Development
www.astd.org
Australian Human Resource Institute
www.ahri.com.au
Chartered Institute of Personnel and Development (UK)
www.cipd.co.uk
CPR International Institute for Conflict Prevention & Resolution
www.cpradr.org
Employee Benefit Research Institute
www.ebri.org
Foundation for Enterprise Development
www.fed.org
Hong Kong Institute of Human Resource Management
www.hkihrm.org
Human Resource Certification Institute
www.hrci.org
International Association for Human Resource Information Management
www.ihrim.org
International Association of Industrial Accident Boards and Commissions
www.iaiabc.org
International Foundation of Employee Benefit Plans (IFEBP)
www.ifebp.org
International Institute of Human Resource Management
www.iihrm.org
International Personnel Assessment Council
www.ipacweb.org
International Personnel Management Association
www.ipma-hr.org

Labor and Employment Relations Association
www.lera.uiuc.edu
National Center for Employee Ownership
www.nceo.org
National Health Information Resource Center
www.nhirc.org
Social Media Policies
www.socialmediagovernance.com
Society for Human Resource Management
www.shrm.org
Union Resource Network
www.unions.org
World at Work
www.worldatwork.org

D. Selected Government Agencies

Bureau of Labor Statistics
www.stats.bls.gov
Census Bureau
www.census.gov
Department of Labor
www.dol.gov
Employment and Training Administration
www.doleta.gov
Equal Employment Opportunity Commission
www.eeoc.gov
FedStats
www.fedstats.gov
National Institute of Environmental Health Sciences
www.niehs.nih.gov
National Institute for Occupational Safety and Health (NIOSH)
www.cdc.gov/niosh
National Labor Relations Board
www.nlrb.gov
Occupational Safety and Health Administration
www.osha.gov
Office of Personnel Management
www.opm.gov
Pension and Welfare Benefits Administration
www.dol.gov/ebsa
Pension Benefit Guaranty Corporation
www.pbgc.gov
Small Business Administration
www.sba.gov
Social Security Administration
www.ssa.gov
U.S. House of Representatives
www.house.gov
U.S. Senate
www.senate.gov

E. Abstracts, Indices, and Databases

ABI Inform Global
ACM Digital
ArticleFirst
Arts & Humanities Search
Book Review Digest
Books in Print
Business and Company ASAP
ComAbstracts
ContentsFirst
Criminal Justice Abstracts
Dissertation Abstracts
Ebsco Masterfile Premier
Ebsco Online Citations
ECO: Electronic Collections Online
EconLit
Education

ERIC
Essay and General Literature Index
Expanded Academic Index ASAP
Government Periodicals
GPO Monthly Catalog
Health Reference Center
HRAF: Human Relations Area
Human Resource Abstracts
Index to Legal Periodicals and Books
Internet and Personal Computing Abstracts
NCJRS Justice Information Center
NetFirst
Newspaper Source from Ebsco
PAIS: Public Affairs Information Service
PapersFirst
PsycInfo
Readers Guide Abstracts
Sociological Abstracts

Appendix C

MAJOR FEDERAL EQUAL EMPLOYMENT OPPORTUNITY LAWS AND REGULATIONS

Act	Year	Key Provisions
Broad-Based Discrimination		
Title VII, Civil Rights Act of 1964	1964	Prohibits discrimination in employment on basis of race, color, religion, sex, or national origin
Executive Orders 11246 and 11375	1965 1967	Require federal contractors and subcontractors to eliminate employment discrimination and prior discrimination through affirmative action
Executive Order 11478	1969	Prohibits discrimination in the U.S. Postal Service and in the various government agencies on the basis of race, color, religion, sex, national origin, handicap, or age
Vietnam Era Veterans' Readjustment Assistance Act	1974	Prohibits discriminations against Vietnam-era veterans by federal contractors and the U.S. government and requires affirmative action
Civil Rights Act of 1991	1991	Overturns several past Supreme Court decisions and changes damage claims provisions
Congressional Accountability Act	1995	Extends EEO and Civil Rights Act provisions to U.S. congressional staff
Race/National Origin Discrimination		
Immigration Reform and Control Act	1986 1990 1996	Establishes penalties for employers who knowingly hire illegal aliens; prohibits employment discrimination on the basis of national origin or citizenship
Gender/Sex Discrimination		
Equal Pay Act	1963	Requires equal pay for men and women performing substantially the same work
Pregnancy Discrimination Act	1978	Prohibits discrimination against women affected by pregnancy, childbirth, or related medical conditions; requires that they be treated as all other employees for employment-related purposes, including benefits

Act	Year	Key Provisions
Age Discrimination		
Age Discrimination in Employment Act (as amended in 1978 and 1986)	1967	Prohibits discrimination against persons over age 40 and restricts mandatory retirement requirements, except where age is a bona fide occupational qualification
Older Workers Benefit Protection Act of 1990	1990	Prohibits age-based discrimination in early retirement and other benefits plans
Disability Discrimination		
Vocational Rehabilitation Act and Rehabilitation Act of 1974	1973 1974	Prohibit employers with federal contracts over $2,500 from discriminating against individuals with disabilities
Americans with Disabilities Act	1990	Requires employer accommodations for individuals with disabilities

Appendix D

UNIFORM GUIDELINES ON EMPLOYEE SELECTION

The 1978 Uniform Guidelines on Employee Selection Procedures are used by the U.S. EEOC, the U.S. Department of Labor's OFCCP, the U.S. Department of Justice, and the U.S. Office of Personnel Management. These guidelines attempt to explain how an employer should deal with hiring, retention, promotion, transfer, demotion, dismissal, and referral. Under the uniform guidelines, if sued, employers can choose one of two routes to prove they are not illegally discriminating against employees: no disparate impact and job-related validity.

"No Disparate Impact" Approach

Generally, the most important issue regarding discrimination in organizations is the *effect* of employment policies and procedures, regardless of the *intent* of the employer. *Disparate impact* occurs when protected-class members are substantially underrepresented in employment decisions. Under the guidelines, disparate impact is determined with the *4/5ths rule*. If the selection rate for a protected group is less than 80% (4/5ths) of the selection rate for the majority group or less than 80% of the majority group's representation in the relevant labor market, discrimination exists. Thus, the guidelines have attempted to define discrimination in statistical terms. The use of the statistical means has been researched and some methodological issues have been identified. However, the guidelines have continued to be used because disparate impact is checked by employers both internally and externally.

Internal Metrics for Disparate Impact Internal disparate impact metrics compare the results of employer actions received by protected-class members with those received by nonprotected-class members inside the organization. HR activities that can be checked most frequently for internal disparate impact include the following:

- Selection of candidates for interviews from those recruited
- Pass rates for various selection tests
- Performance appraisal ratings as they affect pay increases
- Promotions, demotions, and terminations
- Identification of individuals for layoffs

The calculation that follows computes the internal disparate impact for men and women who were interviewed for jobs at a firm. In this case, the figure indicates that the selection process does have a disparate impact internally. The practical meaning of these calculations is that statistically, women have less chance of being selected for jobs than men do. Thus, illegal discrimination may exist unless the firm can demonstrate that its selection activities are specifically job related.

Internal Disparate Impact Example

Female applicants: 25% were selected for jobs
Male applicants: 45% were selected for jobs

<u>Disparate Impact Determination (4/5 = 80%)</u>

• Male selection rate of 45% × (80%) = 36%
• Female selection rate = 25%

Disparate impact exists because the female selection rate is less than 4/5 of the male selection rate.

External Metrics for Disparate Impact Employers can check for disparate impact externally by comparing the percentage of protected-class members in their workforces with the percentage of protected-class members in the relevant labor markets. The relevant labor markets consist of the areas where the firm recruits workers, not just where those employed live. External comparisons also can consider the percentage of protected-class members who are recruited and who apply for jobs to ensure that the employer has drawn a "representative sample" from the relevant labor markets. Although employers are not required to maintain exact proportionate equality, they must be "close." Courts have applied statistical analyses to determine if any disparities that exist are too high.

The following illustrates external disparate impact metrics using impact analyses for a sample metropolitan area, Valleyville. Assume that a firm in that area, Acme Company, has 500 employees, including 50 African Americans and 75 Latinos/Hispanics. To determine if the company has external disparate impact, it is possible to make the following comparisons:

Protected Class	% of Total Employees at Acme Company	4/5ths of Group in the Population	Disparate Impact?
African American	10% (50/500)	13.6%	Yes (10% < 13.6%)
Latino/Hispanic	15% (75/500)	14.4%	No (15% > 14.4%)

At Acme, external disparate impact exists for African Americans because the company employs fewer of them than the 4/5 threshold of 13.6%. However, because Acme has more Latino/Hispanic employees than the 4/5 threshold of 14.4%, there is no disparate impact for this group.

Statistical comparisons for determining disparate impact may use more complex methods. HR professionals need to know how to do such calculations because external disparate impact must be computed and reported in affirmative action plans that government contractors submit to regulatory agencies.

Racial Distribution in Valleyville (Example)

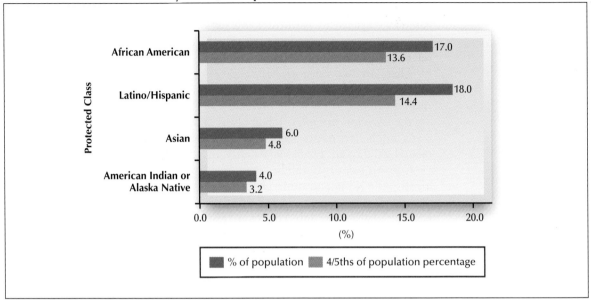

Job-Related Validation Approach

Under the job-related validation approach, virtually every factor used to make employment-related decisions is considered an employment "test." Such activities as recruiting, selection, promotion, termination, discipline, and performance appraisal all must be shown to be job related. Hence, two basic concepts, validity and reliability, affect many of the common means used to make HR decisions.

Validity and Reliability The first concept, *validity,* is simply the extent to which a test actually measures what it says it measures. The concept relates to inferences made from tests. For instance, it may be valid to assume that performance on a mechanical knowledge test may predict performance of a machinist in a manufacturing plant. However, it is probably not valid to assume that the same test scores indicate general intelligence or promotability for a manufacturing sales representative. Another instance would be a general intelligence test; in order for it to be valid, it must actually measure intelligence, and not just a person's vocabulary. Therefore, an employment test that is valid must measure the person's ability to perform the job for which she or he is being hired.

Ideally, employment-related tests will be both valid and reliable. *Reliability* refers to the consistency with which a test measures an item. For a test to be reliable, an individual's score should be about the same every time the individual takes the test (allowing for the effects of practice). Unless a test measures a factor consistently (reliably), it is of little value in predicting job performance.

Validity and Equal Employment

If a charge of discrimination is brought against an employer on the basis of disparate impact, a *prima facie* case must be established. The employer then must be able to demonstrate that its employment procedures are valid and job related. A key element in establishing job relatedness is conducting a *job analysis* to identify the *knowledge, skills, and abilities (KSAs)* and other characteristics needed to perform a job satisfactorily. In one sense, then, current requirements have done management a favor by forcing employers to use job-related employment procedures.

There are two categories of validity in which employment tests attempt to predict how well an individual will perform on the job. In measuring *criterion-related validity,* a test is the *predictor,* and the measures for job performance are the *criterion variables.* Job analysis determines as exactly as possible what KSAs and behaviors are needed for each task in the job. Two types of criterion-related validity are *predictive validity* and *concurrent validity.*

Content validity is validity measured by a logical, nonstatistical method to identify the KSAs and other characteristics necessary to perform a job. Then managers, supervisors, and HR specialists must identify the most important KSAs needed for the job. Finally, a "test" is devised to determine if individuals have the necessary KSAs. The test may be an interview question about previous supervisory experience, or an ability test in which someone types a letter using a word-processing software program, or a knowledge test about consumer credit regulations.

A test has content validity if it reflects an actual sample of the work done on the job in question. For example, an arithmetic test for a retail cashier might contain problems about determining amounts for refunds, purchases, and merchandise exchanges. Content validity is especially useful if the workforce is not large enough to allow other, more statistical approaches.

Many practitioners and specialists see content validity as a commonsense standard for validating staffing and other employment dimensions, and as more realistic than other means. Research and court decisions have shown that content validity is consistent with the Uniform Guidelines also. Consequently, content validity approaches are growing in use.

Appendix E

EEO ENFORCEMENT

Enforcement of EEO laws and regulations in the United States must be seen as a work in progress that is inconsistent and confusing at times. The court system is left to resolve the disputes and interpret the laws. Often the lower courts have issued conflicting rulings and interpretations. The ultimate interpretation often has rested on decisions by the U.S. Supreme Court, although those rulings also have been interpreted differently.

EEO Enforcement Agencies

Government agencies at several levels can investigate illegal discriminatory practices. At the federal level, the two most prominent agencies are the Equal Employment Opportunity Commission (EEOC) and the Office of Federal Contract Compliance Programs (OFCCP).

Equal Employment Opportunity Commission The EEOC has enforcement authority for charges brought under a number of federal laws. Further, the EEOC issues policy guidelines on many topics influencing the EEO. Although the policy statements are not "law," they are "persuasive authority" in most cases.

Office of Federal Contract Compliance Programs While the EEOC is an independent agency, the OFCCP is part of the U.S. Department of Labor and ensures that federal contractors and subcontractors use nondiscriminatory practices. A major thrust of OFCCP efforts is to require that covered employers take affirmative action to counter prior discriminatory practices.

State and Local Agencies In addition to federal laws and orders, many states and municipalities have passed their own laws prohibiting discrimination on a variety of bases, and state and local enforcement bodies have been established. Compared with federal laws, state and local laws sometimes provide greater remedies, require different actions, or prohibit discrimination in more areas.

EEO Compliance

Employers must comply with a variety of EEO regulations and guidelines. To do so, it is crucial that all employers have a written EEO policy statement. They should widely communicate this policy by posting it on bulletin boards, printing it in employee handbooks, reproducing it in organizational newsletters, and reinforcing it in training programs. The contents of the policy should clearly state the organizational commitment to equal employment and incorporate a listing of the appropriate protected classes.

Additionally, employers with 15 or more employees may be required to keep certain records that can be requested by the EEOC, the OFCCP, or numerous other state and local enforcement agencies. Under various laws, employers are also required to post an "officially approved notice" in a prominent place for employees. This notice states that the employer is an equal opportunity employer and does not discriminate.

EEO Records Retention All employment records must be maintained as required by the EEOC. Such records include application forms and documents concerning hiring, promotion, demotion, transfer, layoff, termination, rates of pay or other terms of compensation, and selection for training and apprenticeship. Even application forms or test papers completed by unsuccessful applicants may be requested. The length of time documents must be kept varies, but generally 3 years is recommended as a minimum. Complete records are necessary to enable an employer to respond should a charge of discrimination be made.

EEOC Reporting Forms

Many private-sector employers must file a basic report annually with the EEOC. Slightly different reports must be filed biennially by state/local governments, local unions, and school districts. The following private-sector employers must file the EEO-1 report annually:

- All employers with 100 or more employees, except state and local governments
- Subsidiaries of other companies if the total number of all combined employees equals 100 or more
- Federal contractors with at least 50 employees and contracts of $50,000 or more
- Financial institutions with at least 50 employees, in which government funds are held or saving bonds are issued

Recent changes require that details on employees must be reported by gender, race/ethnic group, and job levels. The most significant change was adding the phrase "two or more races," in order to reflect the multidiverse nature of a growing number of employees.

Applicant-Flow Data

Under EEO laws and regulations, employers may be required to show that they do not discriminate in the recruiting and selection of members of protected classes. Because employers are not allowed to collect such data on application blanks and other preemployment records, the EEOC allows them to do so with a separate applicant-flow form that is not used in the selection process. The *applicant-flow form* is filled out voluntarily by the applicant, and the data must be maintained separately from other selection-related materials. With many applications being made via the Internet, employers must collect this data electronically to comply with regulations on who is an applicant. Analyses of the data collected in applicant-flow forms may help to show whether an employer has underutilized a protected class because of an inadequate flow of applicants from that class, in spite of special efforts to recruit them. Also, these data are reported as part of affirmative action plans that are filed with the OFCCP.

Stages in the Employer's Response to an EEO Complaint

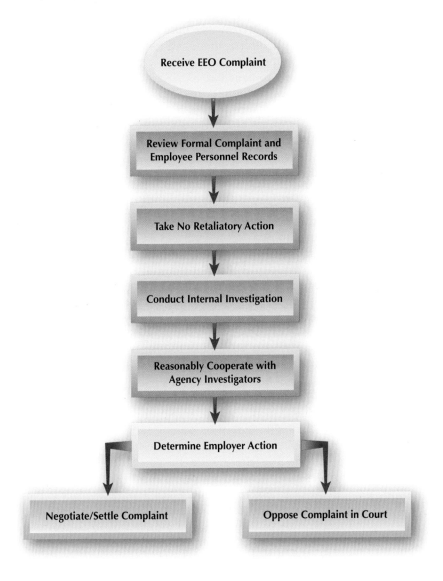

EEOC Compliance Investigation Process

When a discrimination complaint is received by an employer, it must be processed whether it is made internally by a disgruntled employee or by an outside agency. The chart shows the steps required in an employer's response to an EEO complaint.

Notice that the employer should have a formal complaint process in place and should be sure that no retaliatory action occurs. Internal investigations can be conducted by HR staff, but HR staff often utilize outside legal counsel to provide expert guidance in dealing with agency investigations. Internal investigations should occur also when employees make complaints without filing them with outside agencies. Once the employer's investigation is completed, then the decision must be made within to negotiate and settle the complaint or oppose the complaint.

EEOC Complaint Process

To handle a growing number of complaints, the EEOC and other agencies have instituted a system that puts complaints into three categories: *priority*, *needing further investigation*, and *immediate dismissal*. If the EEOC decides to pursue a complaint, it uses the process outlined here, and an employer must determine how to handle it.

In a typical situation, an EEO complaint goes through several stages before the compliance process is completed. First the charges are filed by an individual, a group of individuals, or a representative. A charge must be filed within 180 days of the alleged discriminatory action. Then the EEOC staff reviews the specifics of the charge to determine if it has *jurisdiction*, which means that the agency is authorized to investigate that type of charge. If the EEOC has jurisdiction, it must serve a notice of the charge on the employer within 10 days of the filing; then the employer is asked to respond. Following the charge notification, the major effort of the EEOC turns to investigating the complaint.

During the investigation, the EEOC may interview the complainants, other employees, company managers, and supervisors. Also, it can request additional records and documents from the employer. If sufficient cause is found to support charges that the alleged discrimination occurred, the next stage involves mediation efforts by the agency and the employer. *Mediation* is a dispute resolution process in which a third party helps negotiators reach a settlement. The EEOC has found that use of mediation has reduced its backlog of EEO complaints and has resulted in faster resolution of complaints.

If the employer agrees that discrimination has occurred and accepts the proposed settlement, then the employer posts a notice of relief within the company and takes the agreed-on actions. If the employer objects to the charge and rejects conciliation, the EEOC can file suit or issue a *right-to-sue letter* to the complainant. The letter notifies the complainant that he or she has 90 days to file a personal suit in federal court.

In the court litigation stage, a legal trial takes place in the appropriate state or federal court. At that point, both sides retain lawyers and rely on the court to render a decision. The Civil Rights Act of 1991 provides for jury trials in most EEO cases. If either party disagrees with the court ruling, either can file appeals with a higher court. The U.S. Supreme Court becomes the ultimate adjudication body.

Appendix F

PREEMPLOYMENT INQUIRIES

Given all the protected-category groups, many EEO complaints arise because of inappropriate preemployment inquiries. Questions asked of applicants may be viewed as discriminatory or biased against protected-class applicants. This appendix identifies preemployment inquiries that may or may not be discriminatory. The preemployment inquiries labeled "may be discriminatory" have been so designated because of findings in a variety of court cases. Those labeled "may not be discriminatory" are legal, but only if they reflect a business necessity or are job related. Once an employer tells an applicant he or she is hired (the "point of hire"), inquiries that were prohibited earlier may be made. After hiring, medical examination forms, group insurance cards, and other enrollment cards containing inquiries related directly or indirectly to sex, age, or other bases may be requested.

Guidelines to Lawful and Unlawful Preemployment Inquiries

Subject of Inquiry	It May Not Be Discriminatory to Inquire about . . .	It May Be Discriminatory to Inquire about . . .
1. **Name**	a. Whether applicant has ever worked under a different name	a. The original name of applicant whose name has been legally changed b. The ethnic association of applicant's name
2. **Age**	a. If applicant is over the age of 18 b. If applicant is under the age of 18 or 21 if that information is job related (e.g., for selling liquor in a retail store)	a. Date of birth b. Date of high school graduation
3. **Residence**	a. Applicant's place of residence b. Alternative contact information	a. Previous addresses b. Birthplace of applicant or applicant's parents c. Length lived at current and previous addresses
4. **Race or Color**		a. Applicant's race or color of applicant's skin

(Continued)

Subject of Inquiry	It May Not Be Discriminatory to Inquire about . . .	It May Be Discriminatory to Inquire about . . .
5. National Origin and Ancestry		a. Applicant's lineage, ancestry, national origin, parentage, or nationality b. Nationality of applicant's parents or spouse
6. Sex and Family Composition		a. Sex of applicant b. Marital status of applicant c. Dependents of applicants or child-care arrangements d. Whom to contact in case of emergency
7. Creed or Religion		a. Applicant's religious affiliation b. Applicant's church, parish, mosque, or synagogue c. Holidays observed by applicant
8. Citizenship	a. Whether the applicant is a U.S. citizen or has a current permit/visa to work in the United States	a. Whether applicant is a citizen of a country other than the United States b. Date of citizenship
9. Language	a. Language applicant speaks and/or writes fluently, if job related	a. Applicant's native tongue b. Language used at home
10. References	a. Names of persons willing to provide professional and/or character references for applicant b. Previous work contacts	a. Name of applicant's religious leader b. Political affiliation and contacts
11. Relatives	a. Names of relatives already employed by the employer	a. Name and/or address of any relative of applicant b. Whom to contact in case of emergency
12. Organizations	a. Applicant's membership in any professional, service, or trade organization	a. All clubs or social organizations to which applicant belongs
13. Arrest Record and Convictions	a. Convictions, if related to job performance (disclaimer should accompany)	a. Number and kinds of arrests b. Convictions, unless related to job requirements and performance

(Continued)

14. **Photographs**		a. Photographs with application, with résumé, or before hiring
15. **Height and Weight**		a. Any inquiry into height and weight of applicant, except where a BFOQ exists
16. **Physical Limitations**	a. Whether applicant has the ability to perform job-related functions with or without accommodation	a. The nature or severity of an illness or physical condition b. Whether applicant has ever filed a workers' compensation claim c. Any recent or past operations, treatments, or surgeries and dates
17. **Education**	a. Training applicant has received, if related to the job b. Highest level of education applicant has attained, if validated that having certain educational background (e.g., high school diploma or college degree) is needed to perform the specific job	a. Date of high school graduation
18. **Military**	a. Branch of the military applicant served in and ranks attained b. Type of education or training received in military	a. Military discharge details b. Military service records
19. **Financial Status**		a. Applicant's debts or assets b. Garnishments

SAMPLE HR-RELATED JOB DESCRIPTIONS

Sample Job Description for Human Resource Manager

Identification Section:
Position Title: Human Resource Manager
Department: Human Resources   EEOC Class: O/M
Reports to: President   FLSA Status: Exempt

General Summary: Directs HR activities of the fi rm to ensure compliance with laws and policies, and assists President with overall HR planning

Essential Job Functions:
1. Manages compensation and benefits programs for all employees, resolves compensation and benefits questions from employees, and negotiates with benefits carriers (20%)
2. Ensures compliance with both internal policies and applicable state and federal regulations and laws, including EEO, OSHA, and FLSA (20%)
3. Identifies HR planning issues and suggested approaches to President and other senior managers (15%)
4. Assists managers and supervisors to create, plan, and conduct training and various development programs for new and existing employees (15%)
5. Recruits candidates for employment over telephone and in person. Interviews and selects internal and external candidates for open positions (10%)
6. Reviews and updates job descriptions, assisted by department supervisors, and coordinates performance appraisal process to ensure timely reviews are completed for all employees (10%)
7. Administers various HR policies and procedures and helps managers resolve employee performance and policy issues (10%)
8. Performs other duties as needed and directed by President

Knowledge, Skills, and Abilities:
- Knowledge of HR policies, HR practices, and HR-related laws and regulations
- Knowledge of company products and services and policies and procedures
- Knowledge of management principles and practices
- Skill in operating equipment, such as personal computer, software, and IT systems
- Skill in oral and written communication
- Ability to communicate with employees and various business contacts in a professional and courteous manner
- Ability to organize multiple work assignments and establish priorities
- Ability to negotiate with others and resolve conflicts, particularly in sensitive situations
- Ability to pay close attention to detail and to ensure accuracy of reports and data
- Ability to make sound decisions using available information while maintaining confidentiality
- Ability to create a team environment and sustain employee commitment

Education and Experience: Bachelor's degree in HR management or equivalent, plus 3–5 years' experience

Physical Requirements:	Percentage of Work Time Spent on Activity			
	0%–24%	25%–49%	50%–74%	75%–100%
Seeing Must be able to read computer screen and various reports				X
Hearing Must be able to hear well enough to communicate with employees and others				X
Standing/walking	X			
Climbing/stooping/kneeling	X			
Lifting/pulling/pushing	X			
Fingering/grasping/feeling: Must be able to write, type, and use phone system				X

Working Conditions: Good working conditions with the absence of disagreeable conditions

Note: The statements herein are intended to describe the general nature and level of work performed by employees, but are not a complete list of responsibilities, duties, and skills required of personnel so classified. Furthermore, they do not establish a contract for employment and are subject to change at the discretion of the employer.

Sample Job Description for Compensation Manager

Job Title: Compensation Manager	**JOB CODE:** _____
Supervisor's Title: Vice President of Human Resources	**GRADE:** _____
Department: Human Resources	**FLSA STATUS:** <u>Exempt</u>
	EEOC CLASS: <u>O/M</u>

General Summary: Responsible for the design and administration of all cash compensation programs, ensures proper consideration of the relationship of compensation to performance of each employee, and provides consultation on compensation administration to managers and supervisors

Essential Duties and Responsibilities:

1. Prepares and maintains job descriptions for all jobs and periodically reviews and updates them. Responds to questions from employees and supervisors regarding job descriptions (25%)
2. Ensures that Company compensation rates are in line with pay structures. Obtains or conducts pay surveys as necessary and presents recommendations on pay structures on an annual basis (20%)
3. Develops and administers the performance appraisal program and monitors the use of the performance appraisal instruments to ensure the integrity of the system and its proper use (20%)
4. Directs the job evaluation process by coordinating committee activities and resolves disputes over job values Conducts initial evaluation of new jobs prior to hiring and assigns jobs to pay ranges (15%)
5. Researches and provides recommendations on executive compensation issues. Assists in the development and oversees the administration of all annual bonus payments for senior managers and executives (15%)
6. Coordinates the development of an integrated HR information system and interfaces with the Management Information Systems Department to achieve departmental goals for information needs (5%)
7. Performs related duties as assigned or as the situation dictates

Required Knowledge, Skills, and Abilities:

1. Knowledge of compensation and HR management practices and approaches
2. Knowledge of effective job analysis methods and survey development and interpretation practices and principles
3. Knowledge of performance management program design and administration
4. Knowledge of federal and state wage and hour regulations
5. Skill in writing job descriptions, memorandums, letters, and proposals
6. Skill in use of word processing, spreadsheet, and database software
7. Ability to make presentations to groups on compensation policies and practices
8. Ability to plan and prioritize work

Education and Experience: Equivalent of a college degree in Business Administration, Psychology, or related field plus 3–5 years experience in HR management, 2–3 of which should include compensation administration experience. An advanced degree in Industrial Psychology, Business Administration, or HR Management preferred, but not required.

Physical Requirements:	Rarely (0%–12%)	Occasionally (12%–33%)	Frequently (34%–66%)	Regularly (67%–100%)
Seeing: Must be able to read reports and use computer				X
Hearing: Must be able to hear well enough to communicate with coworkers				X
Standing/walking	X			
Climbing/stooping/kneeling	X			
Lifting/pulling/pushing	X			
Fingering/grasping/feeling: Must be able to write, type, and use phone system				X

Working Conditions: Normal office working conditions with the absence of disagreeable elements

e: The statements herein are intended to describe the general nature and level of work being performed by employees, and are not to be construed as an exhaustive responsibilities, duties, and skills required of personnel so classified. Furthermore, they do not establish a contract for employment and are subject to change at cretion of the employer.

Glossary

A

Absenteeism Any failure by an employee to report for work as scheduled or to stay at work when scheduled.

Acceptance rate Percent of applicants hired divided by total number of applicants offered jobs.

Active practice Performance of job-related tasks and duties by trainees during training.

Adult learning Ways in which adults learn differently than younger people.

Adverse selection Situation in which *only* higher-risk employees select and use certain benefits.

Affirmative action Employers are urged to hire groups of people based on their race, age, gender, or national origin to make up for historical discrimination.

Affirmative action plan (AAP) A document reporting on the composition of an employer's workforce, required for federal contractors.

Alternate work arrangements Nontraditional schedules that provide flexibility to employees.

Applicant pool All persons who are actually evaluated for selection.

Applicant population A subset of the labor force population that is available for selection using a particular recruiting approach.

Arbitration Process that uses a neutral third party to make a decision.

Assessment centers Collections of instruments and exercises designed to diagnose individuals' development needs.

Attitude survey A survey that focuses on employees' feelings and beliefs about their jobs and the organization.

Autonomy Extent of individual freedom and discretion in the work and its scheduling.

Availability analysis Identifies the number of protected-class members available to work in the appropriate labor markets for given jobs.

B

Balanced scorecard A framework used to report a diverse set of performance measures.

Balance-sheet approach Compensation plan that equalizes cost differences between the international assignment and the same assignment in the home country.

Base pay Basic compensation that an employee receives, usually as a wage or salary.

Behavior modeling Copying someone else's behavior.

Behavioral interview Interview in which applicants give specific examples of how they have performed a certain task or handled a problem in the past.

Benchmark jobs Jobs found in many organizations that can be used for the purposes of comparison.

Benchmarking Comparing the business results to industry standards.

Benefit An indirect reward given to an employee or group of employees as part of membership in the organization.

Blended learning Learning approach that combines methods, such as short, fast-paced, interactive computer-based lessons and teleconferencing with traditional classroom instruction and simulation.

Blind to differences Differences among people should be ignored and everyone should be treated equally.

Bona fide occupational qualification (BFOQ) Characteristic providing a legitimate reason why an employer can exclude persons on otherwise illegal bases of consideration.

Bonus One-time payment that does not become part of the employee's base pay.

Broadbanding Practice of using fewer pay grades with much broader ranges than in traditional compensation systems.

Burden of proof What individuals who file suit against employers must prove in order to establish that illegal discrimination has occurred.

Business agent A full-time union official who operates the union office and assists union members.

Business necessity A practice necessary for safe and efficient organizational operations.

Business process reengineering (BPR) Measures for improving such activities as product development, customer service, and service delivery.

C

Career Series of work-related positions a person occupies throughout life.

Career paths Represent employees' movements through opportunities over time.

Cash balance plan Retirement program in which benefits are based on an accumulation of annual company contributions plus interest credited each year.

Central tendency error Occurs when a rater gives all employees a score within a narrow range in the middle of the scale.

Churn Hiring new workers while laying off others.

Closed shop Firm that requires individuals to join a union before they can be hired.

Codetermination Practice whereby union or worker representatives are given positions on a company's board of directors.

Cognitive ability tests Tests that measure an individual's thinking, memory, reasoning, verbal, and mathematical abilities.

Collective bargaining Process whereby representatives of management and workers negotiate over wages, hours, and other terms and conditions of employment.

Commission Compensation computed as a percentage of sales in units or dollars.

Compa-ratio Pay level divided by the midpoint of the pay range.

Compensable factor Job value commonly present throughout a group of jobs within an organization.

Compensation committee Subgroup of the board of directors that is composed of directors who are not officers of the firm.

Competencies Individual capabilities that can be linked to enhanced performance by individuals or teams.

Competency-based pay Rewards individuals for the capabilities they demonstrate and acquire.

Complaint Indication of employee dissatisfaction.

Compressed workweek A workweek in which a full week's work is accomplished in fewer than five 8-hour days.

Conciliation Process by which a third party assists union and management negotiators to reach a voluntary settlement.

Concurrent validity Measured when an employer tests current employees and correlates the scores with their performance ratings.

Constructive discharge Process of deliberately making conditions intolerable to get an employee to quit.

Consumer-driven health (CDH) plan Health plan that provides employer financial contributions to employees to help cover their own health-related expenses.

Contingent worker Someone who is not an employee, but a temporary or part-time worker for a specific period of time and type of work.

Contractual rights Rights based on a specific contract between an employer and an employee.

Contrast error Tendency to rate people relative to others rather than against performance standards.

Contributory plan Pension plan in which the money for pension benefits is paid by both employees and the employer.

Copayment Strategy of requiring employees to pay a portion of the cost of insurance premiums, medical care, and prescription drugs.

Core competency A unique capability that creates high value and differentiates an organization from its competition.

Correlation coefficient Index number that gives the relationship between a predictor variable and a criterion variable.

Cost-benefit analysis Comparison of costs and benefits associated with training.

Craft union Union whose members do one type of work, often using specialized skills and training.

Cross training Training people to do more than one job.

Cumulative trauma disorders (CTDs) Muscle and skeletal injuries that occur when workers repetitively use the same muscles to perform tasks.

D

Decertification Process whereby a union is removed as the representative of a group of employees.

Defined-benefit plan Retirement program in which employees are promised a pension amount based on age and service.

Defined-contribution plan Retirement program in which the employer makes an annual payment to an employee's pension account.

Development Efforts to improve employees' abilities to handle a variety of assignments and to cultivate employees' capabilities beyond those required by the current job.

Disabled person Someone who has a physical or mental impairment that substantially limits life activities, who has a record of such an impairment, or who is regarded as having such an impairment.

Discharge When an employee is removed from a job at an employer.

Discipline Form of training that enforces organizational rules.

Disparate impact Occurs when members of a protected category are substantially underrepresented as a result of employment decisions that work to their disadvantage.

Disparate treatment Occurs when members of a group are treated differently from others.

Distributive justice Perceived fairness in the distribution of outcomes.

Diversity Differences in human characteristics and composition in an organization.

Draw Amount advanced against, and repaid from, future commissions earned by the employee.

Dual-career ladder System that allows a person to advance up either a management or a technical/professional ladder.

Due diligence A comprehensive assessment of all aspects of the business being acquired.

Due process Requirement that the employer use a fair process to determine employee wrongdoing and that the employee have an opportunity to explain and defend his or her actions.

Duty Work segment composed of several tasks that are performed by an individual.

E

Effectiveness The ability to produce a specific desired effect or result that can be measured.

Efficiency The degree to which operations are done in an economical manner.

Electronic human resource management systems (e-HRM) The planning, implementation, and application of information technology to perform HR activities.

Employee assistance program (EAP) Program that provides counseling and other help to employees having emotional, physical, or other personal problems.

Employee engagement The extent to which individuals feel linked to organizational success and how the organization performs positively.

Employee stock ownership plan (ESOP) Plan designed to give employees significant stock ownership in their employers.

Employment-at-will (EAW) Common-law doctrine stating that employers have the right to hire, fire, demote, or promote whomever they choose, unless there is a law or contract to the contrary.

Employment contract Formal agreement that outlines the details of employment.

Entitlement philosophy Assumes that individuals who have worked another year are entitled to pay increases, with little regard for performance differences.

Environmental scanning The assessment of internal and external environmental conditions that affect the organization.

Equal employment Employment that is not affected by illegal discrimination.

Equity Perceived fairness between what a person does and what the person receives.

Ergonomics Study and design of the work environment to address physical demands placed on individuals.

Essential job functions Fundamental job duties.

Exempt employees Employees who are not paid overtime.

Exit interview An interview in which individuals who are leaving an organization are asked to give their reasons.

Expatriate A citizen of one country who is working in a second country and employed by an organization headquartered in the first country.

F

Federation Group of autonomous unions.

Feedback Amount of information employees receive about how well or how poorly they have performed.

Flexible benefits plan Program that allows employees to select the benefits they prefer from groups of benefits established by the employer.

Flexible spending accounts Benefits plans that allow employees to contribute pretax dollars to fund certain additional benefits.

Flextime Scheduling arrangement in which employees work a set number of hours a day but vary starting and ending times.

Forced distribution Performance appraisal method in which ratings of employees' performance levels are distributed along a bell-shaped curve.

Forecasting Using information from the past and the present to identify expected future conditions.

401(k) plan Agreement in which a percentage of an employee's pay is withheld and invested in a tax-deferred account.

G

Gainsharing System of sharing with employees greater-than-expected gains in profits and/or productivity.

Garnishment A court order that directs an employer to set aside a portion of an employee's wages to pay a debt owed a creditor.

Glass ceiling Discriminatory practices that have prevented women and other protected-class members from advancing to executive-level jobs.

Global market approach Compensation plan that attempts to be more comprehensive in providing base pay, incentives, benefits, and relocation expenses regardless of the country to which the employee is assigned.

Graphic rating scale Scale that allows the rater to mark an employee's performance on a continuum.

Green-circled employee Incumbent who is paid below the range set for a job.

Grievance Complaint formally stated in writing.

Grievance arbitration Means by which a third party settles disputes arising from different interpretations of a labor contract.

Grievance procedures Formal channels of communication used to resolve grievances.

H

Halo effect Occurs when a rater scores an employee high on all job criteria because of performance in one area.

Health General state of physical, mental, and emotional well-being.

Health maintenance organization (HMO) Plan that provides services for a fixed period on a prepaid basis.

Health promotion Supportive approach of facilitating and encouraging healthy actions and lifestyles among employees.

Health reimbursement arrangement (HRA) Health plan in which the employer sets aside money in a health reimbursement account to help employees pay for qualified medical expenses.

Health savings accounts (HSAs) High-deductible health plans with federal tax advantages.

Host-country national A citizen of one country who is working in that country and employed by an organization headquartered in a second country.

Hostile environment Sexual harassment in which an individual's work performance or psychological well-being is unreasonably affected by intimidating or offensive working conditions.

HR audit A formal research effort to assess the current state of HR practices.

HR generalist A person who has responsibility for performing a variety of HR activities.

HR metrics Specific measures tied to HR performance indicators.

HR specialist A person who has in-depth knowledge and expertise in a limited area of HR.

Human capital The collective value of the capabilities, knowledge, skills, life experiences, and motivation of an organizational workforce.

Human capital return on investment (HCROI) Directly shows the operating profit derived from investments in human capital.

Human capital value added (HCVA) Calculated by subtracting all operating expenses *except* for labor expenses from revenue and dividing by the total full-time head count.

Human economic value added (HEVA) Wealth created per employee.

Human resource (HR) management Designing management systems to ensure that human talent is used effectively and efficiently to accomplish organizational goals.

Human resource planning Process of analyzing and identifying the need for and availability of human resources so that the organization can meet its objectives.

I

Illegal issues Collective bargaining issues that would require either party to take illegal action.

Immediate confirmation Based on the idea that people learn best if reinforcement and feedback are given as soon as possible after training.

Individual-centered career planning Career planning that focuses on an individual's responsibility for a career rather than on organizational needs.

Industrial union Union that includes many persons working in the same industry or company, regardless of jobs held.

Informal training Training that occurs through interactions and feedback among employees.

Interactional justice Perceived fairness about how a person interacts with others.

J

Job Grouping of tasks, duties, and responsibilities that constitutes the total work assignment for an employee.

Job analysis Systematic way of gathering and analyzing information about the content, context, and human requirements of jobs.

Job description Identification of the tasks, duties, and responsibilities of a job.

Job design Organizing tasks, duties, responsibilities, and other elements into a productive unit of work.

Job duties Important elements in a given job.

Job enlargement Broadening the scope of a job by expanding the number of different tasks to be performed.

Job enrichment Increasing the depth of a job by adding responsibility for planning, organizing, controlling, or evaluating the job.

Job evaluation Formal, systematic means to identify the relative worth of jobs within an organization.

Job family Group of jobs having common organizational characteristics.

Job posting System in which the employer provides notices of job openings and employees respond by applying for specific openings.

Job rotation Process of shifting a person from job to job.

Job satisfaction A positive emotional state resulting from evaluating one's job experiences.

Job sharing Scheduling arrangement in which two employees perform the work of one full-time job.

Job specifications The knowledge, skills, and abilities (KSAs) an individual needs to perform a job satisfactorily.

Just cause Reasonable justification for taking employment-related action.

K

Knowledge management The way an organization identifies and leverages knowledge in order to be competitive.

L

Labor force population All individuals who are available for selection if all possible recruitment strategies are used.

Labor markets External supply pool from which organizations attract employees.

Leniency error Occurs when ratings of all employees fall at the high end of the scale.

Living wage Earnings that are supposed to meet the basic needs of an individual working for an organization.

Lockout Shutdown of company operations undertaken by management to prevent union members from working.

Lump-sum increase (LSI) One-time payment of all or part of a yearly pay increase.

M

Managed care Approaches that monitor and reduce medical costs through restrictions and market system alternatives.

Management by objectives (MBO) Performance appraisal method that specifies the performance goals that an individual and manager identify together.

Management mentoring Relationship in which experienced managers aid individuals in the earlier stages of their careers.

Management rights Rights reserved so that the employer can manage, direct, and control its business.

Mandatory issues Collective bargaining issues identified specifically by labor laws or court decisions as subject to bargaining.

Marginal job functions Duties that are part of a job but are incidental or ancillary to the purpose and nature of the job.

Market banding Grouping jobs into pay grades based on similar market survey amounts.

Market line Graph line that shows the relationship between job value as determined by job evaluation points and job value as determined by pay survey rates.

Market pricing Use of market pay data to identify the relative value of jobs based on what other employers pay for similar jobs.

Massed practice Practice performed all at once.

Mediation Process by which a third party helps the negotiators reach a settlement.

Motivation The desire within a person causing that person to act.

Multinational corporation (MNC) A corporation that has facilities and other assets in at least one country other than its home country.

N

Negligent hiring Occurs when an employer fails to check an employee's background and the employee injures someone on the job.

Negligent retention Occurs when an employer becomes aware that an employee may be unfit for work but continues to employ the person, and the person injures someone.

Nepotism Practice of allowing relatives to work for the same employer.

Noncompete agreements Agreements that prohibit individuals who leave an organization from working with an employer in the same line of business for a specified period of time.

Noncontributory plan Pension plan in which all the funds for pension benefits are provided by the employer.

Nondirective interview Interview that uses questions developed from the answers to previous questions.

Nonexempt employees Employees who must be paid overtime.

O

Offshoring The relocation by a company of a business process or operation from one country to another.

Ombuds Individuals outside the normal chain of command who act as problem solvers for both management and employees.

"Open-door" policy A policy in which anyone with a complaint can talk with a manager, an HR representative, or an executive.

Open shop Firm in which workers are not required to join or pay dues to a union.

Organizational commitment The degree to which employees believe in and accept organizational goals and desire to remain with the organization.

Organizational culture The shared values and beliefs in an organization.

Organizational mission The core reason for the existence of the organization and what makes it unique.

Organization-centered career planning Career planning that focuses on identifying career paths that provide for the logical progression of people between jobs in an organization.

Orientation Planned introduction of new employees to their jobs, coworkers, and the organization.

Outsourcing Transferring the management and performance of a business function to an external service provider.

P

Paid-time-off (PTO) plan Plan that combines all sick leave, vacation time, and holidays into a total number of hours or days that employees can take off with pay.

Panel interview Interview in which several interviewers meet with candidate at the same time.

Pay compression Occurs when the pay differences among individuals with different levels of experience and performance become small.

Pay equity The concept that the pay for all jobs requiring comparable knowledge, skills, and abilities should be the same even if actual job duties and market rates differ significantly.

Pay grades Groupings of individual jobs having approximately the same job worth.

Pay survey Collection of data on compensation rates for workers performing similar jobs in other organizations.

Pay-for-performance philosophy Requires that compensation changes reflect performance differences.

Pension plan Retirement program established and funded by the employer and employees.

Performance appraisal Process of determining how well employees do their jobs relative to a standard and communicating that information to them.

Performance consulting Process in which a trainer and an organization work together to decide how to improve organizational and individual results.

Performance management Series of activities designed to ensure that the organization gets the performance it needs from its employees.

Performance standards Indicators of what the job accomplishes and how performance is measured in key areas of the job description.

Permissive issues Collective bargaining issues that are not mandatory and that relate to certain jobs.

Perquisites (perks) Special benefits—usually noncash items—for executives.

Person/job fit Matching the KSAs of individuals with the characteristics of jobs.

Person/organization fit The congruence between individuals and organizational factors.

Phased retirement Approach in which employees gradually reduce their workloads and pay levels.

Physical ability tests Tests that measure an individual's abilities such as strength, endurance, and muscular movement.

Placement Fitting a person to the right job.

Policies General guidelines that focus organizational actions.

Portability A pension plan feature that allows employees to move their pension benefits from one employer to another.

Predictive validity Measured when test results of applicants are compared with subsequent job performance.

Predictors of selection criteria Measurable or visible indicators of selection criteria.

Preferred provider organization (PPO) A health care provider that contracts with an employer or an employer group to supply health care services to employees at a competitive rate.

Primacy effect Occurs when a rater gives greater weight to information received first when appraising an individual's performance.

Procedural justice Perceived fairness of the processes used to make decisions about employees.

Procedures Customary methods of handling activities.

Productivity Measure of the quantity and quality of work done, considering the cost of the resources used.

Profit sharing System to distribute a portion of the profits of an organization to employees.

Protected category A group identified for protection under EEO laws and regulations.

Psychological contract The unwritten expectations employees and employers have about the nature of their work relationships.

Psychomotor tests Tests that measure dexterity, hand—eye coordination, arm—hand steadiness, and other factors.

Q

Quid pro quo Sexual harassment in which employment outcomes are linked to the individual granting sexual favors.

R

Ranking Performance appraisal method in which all employees are listed from highest to lowest in performance.

Rater bias Occurs when a rater's values or prejudices distort the rating.

Ratification Process by which union members vote to accept the terms of a negotiated labor agreement.

Realistic job preview Process through which a job applicant receives an accurate picture of a job.

Reasonable accommodation A modification to a job or work environment that gives a qualified individual an equal employment opportunity to perform.

Recency effect Occurs when a rater gives greater weight to recent events when appraising an individual's performance.

Recruiting Process of generating a pool of qualified applicants for organizational jobs.

Red-circled employee Incumbent who is paid above the range set for a job.

Reinforcement Based on the idea that people tend to repeat responses that give them some type of positive reward and avoid actions associated with negative consequences.

Repatriation Planning, training, and reassignment of global employees to their home countries.

Responsibilities Obligations to perform certain tasks and duties.

Retaliation Punitive actions taken by employers against individuals who exercise their legal rights.

Return on investment (ROI) Calculation showing the value of an investment.

Right to privacy An individual's freedom from unauthorized and unreasonable intrusion into personal affairs.

Rights Powers, privileges, or interests that belong to a person by law, nature, or tradition.

Right-to-work laws State laws that prohibit requiring employees to join unions as a condition of obtaining or continuing employment.

Risk management Involves responsibilities to consider physical, human, and financial factors to protect organizational and individual interests.

Rules Specific guidelines that regulate and restrict the behavior of individuals.

S

Sabbatical Time off the job to develop and rejuvenate oneself.

Safety Condition in which the physical well-being of people is protected.

Salaries Consistent payments made each period regardless of the number of hours worked.

Salting Practice in which unions hire and pay people to apply for jobs at certain companies to begin organizing efforts.

Security Protection of employees and organizational facilities.

Security audit Comprehensive review of organizational security.

Selection The process of choosing individuals with the correct qualifications needed to fill jobs in an organization.

Selection criterion Characteristic that a person must possess to successfully perform work.

Selection rate Percentage hired from a given group of candidates.

Self-directed team Organizational team composed of individuals who are assigned a cluster of tasks, duties, and responsibilities to be accomplished.

Self-efficacy People's belief that they can successfully learn the training program content.

Seniority Time spent in an organization or on a particular job.

Separation agreement Agreement in which a terminated employee agrees not to sue the employer in exchange for specified benefits.

Serious health condition Health condition requiring in-patient, hospital, hospice, or residential medical care or continuing physician care.

Severance benefits Temporary payments made to laid-off employees to ease the financial burden of unemployment.

Severance pay Security benefit voluntarily offered by employers to individuals whose jobs are eliminated or who leave by mutual agreement with their employers.

Sexual harassment Actions that are sexually directed, are unwanted, and subject the worker to adverse employment conditions or create a hostile work environment.

Situational interview Structured interview that contains questions about how applicants might handle specific job situations.

Situational judgment tests Tests that measure a person's judgment in work settings.

Skill variety Extent to which the work requires several different activities for successful completion.

Spaced practice Practice performed in several sessions spaced over a period of hours or days.

Special-purpose team Organizational team formed to address specific problems, improve work processes, and enhance the overall quality of products and services.

Statutory rights Rights based on laws or statutes passed by federal, state, or local governments.

Stock option plan Plan that gives employees the right to purchase a fixed number of shares of company stock at a specified price for a limited period of time.

Stock purchase plan Plan in which the employer provides matching funds equal to the amount invested by the employee for the purchase of stock in the company.

Straight piece-rate system Pay system in which wages are determined by multiplying the number of units produced by the piece rate for one unit.

Strategic HR management Use of employees to gain or keep a competitive advantage.

Strategic planning The process of defining organizational strategy and allocating resources toward its achievement.

Strategy An organization's proposition for how to compete successfully and thereby survive and grow.

Stress interview Interview designed to create anxiety and put pressure on applicants to see how they respond.

Strictness error Occurs when ratings of all employees fall at the low end of the scale.

Strike Work stoppage in which union members refuse to work in order to put pressure on an employer.

Structured interview Interview that uses a set of standardized questions asked of all applicants.

Substance abuse Use of illicit substances or misuse of controlled substances, alcohol, or other drugs.

Succession planning The process of identifying a plan for the orderly replacement of key employees.

Sustainabilty Being able to continue to operate, survive, and adjust to significant changes.

T

Task Distinct, identifiable work activity composed of motions.

Task identity Extent to which the job includes a "whole" identifiable unit of work that is carried out from start to finish and that results in a visible outcome.

Task significance Impact the job has on other people.

Tax equalization plan Compensation plan used to protect expatriates from negative tax consequences.

Team interview Interview in which applicants are interviewed by the team members with whom they will work.

Telework Employees work with technology via electronic, telecommunications, and Internet means.

Third-country national A citizen of one country who is working in a second country and employed by an organization headquartered in a third country.

Total rewards Monetary and nonmonetary rewards provided by companies to attract, motivate, and retain employees.

Training Process whereby people acquire capabilities to perform jobs.

Turnover The process in which employees leave an organization and have to be replaced.

U

Undue hardship Significant difficulty or expense imposed on an employer in making an accommodation for individuals with disabilities.

Union Formal association of workers that promotes the interests of its members through collective action.

Union authorization card Card signed by employees to designate a union as their collective bargaining agent.

Union security provisions Contract clauses to help the union obtain and retain members.

Union steward Employee elected to serve as the first-line representative of unionized workers.

Unit labor cost Computed by dividing the average cost of workers by their average levels of output.

Utilization analysis Identifies the number of protected-class members employed in the organization and the types of jobs they hold.

Utilization review Audit of services and costs billed by health care providers.

V

Variable pay Compensation linked to individual, group/team, and/or organizational performance.

Vesting Right of employees to receive certain benefits from their pension plans.

Virtual team Organizational team composed of individuals who are separated geographically but linked by communications technology.

W

Wages Payments calculated directly from the amount of time worked by employees.

Well pay Extra pay for not taking sick leave.

Wellness programs Programs designed to maintain or improve employee health before problems arise.

Whistle blowers Individuals who report real or perceived wrongs committed by their employers.

Work Effort directed toward accomplishing results.

Work flow analysis Study of the way work (inputs, activities, and outputs) moves through an organization.

Work sample tests Tests that require an applicant to perform a simulated task that is a specified part of the target job.

Workers' compensation Security benefits provided to persons injured on the job.

Wrongful discharge Termination of an individual's employment for reasons that are illegal or improper.

Y

Yield ratio Comparisons of the number of applicants at one stage of the recruiting process with the number at the next stage.

Author Index

Subject Index